READINGS

Publisher: Joseph Opiela
Development Manager: Janet Lanphier
Development Editor: Adam Beroud
Senior Supplements Editor: Donna Campion
Media Supplements Editor: Jenna Egan
Executive Marketing Manager: Megan Galvin-Fak
Production Manager: Douglas Bell
Project Coordination, Text Design, and Electronic Page Makeup: Elm Street
    Publishing Services, Inc.
Cover Design Manager: John Callahan
Cover Designer: Laura Shaw
Cover Illustration: *Le Cabinet de Curiosties,* 1997, by Susanne Schuenke (20th
    century / German). Courtesy of SuperStock, Inc.
Photo Research: Photosearch, Inc.
Senior Manufacturing Buyer: Dennis J. Para
Printer and Binder: R. R. Donnelley and Sons Company–Crawfordsville
Cover Printer: Coral Graphics, Inc.

Library of Congress Cataloging-in-Publication Data
Ballenger, Bruce P.
    The Curious Writer / Bruce Ballenger.
        p.cm.
Includes Index.
    ISBN 0-321-27705-8
        1. English language—Rhetoric—Manuals, etc. 2. Interdisciplinary approach
    in education—Manuals, etc. 3. Academic writing—Manuals, etc. I. Title.
    PE1408.B37 2005
    808'.042—dc22   2004020879

Please visit our website at http://www.ablongman.com/ballenger.

ISBN 0-321-27705-8

4 5 6 7 8 9 10—DOC—07 06

THE CURIOUS WRITER

Bruce Ballenger
Boise State University

PEARSON

Longman

New York   San Francisco   Boston
London   Toronto   Sydney   Tokyo   Singapore   Madrid
Mexico City   Munich   Paris   Cape Town   Hong Kong   Mon

THE CURIOUS WRITER

Bruce Ballenger

Boise State University

PEARSON

Longman

New York   San Francisco   Boston
London   Toronto   Sydney   Tokyo   Singapore   Madrid
Mexico City   Munich   Paris   Cape Town   Hong Kong   Montreal

Publisher: Joseph Opiela
Development Manager: Janet Lanphier
Development Editor: Adam Beroud
Senior Supplements Editor: Donna Campion
Media Supplements Editor: Jenna Egan
Executive Marketing Manager: Megan Galvin-Fak
Production Manager: Douglas Bell
Project Coordination, Text Design, and Electronic Page Makeup: Elm Street
    Publishing Services, Inc.
Cover Design Manager: John Callahan
Cover Designer: Laura Shaw
Cover Illustration: *Le Cabinet de Curiosties,* 1997, by Susanne Schuenke (20th
    century / German). Courtesy of SuperStock, Inc.
Photo Research: Photosearch, Inc.
Senior Manufacturing Buyer: Dennis J. Para
Printer and Binder: R. R. Donnelley and Sons Company–Crawfordsville
Cover Printer: Coral Graphics, Inc.

For permission to use copyrighted material, grateful acknowledgment is made
to the copyright holders on pp. CR-1 and CR-2, which are hereby made part of
this copyright page.

Library of Congress Cataloging-in-Publication Data
Ballenger, Bruce P.
    The Curious Writer / Bruce Ballenger.
        p.cm.
Includes Index.
    ISBN 0-321-27705-8
        1. English language—Rhetoric—Manuals, etc. 2. Interdisciplinary approach
in education—Manuals, etc. 3. Academic writing—Manuals, etc. I. Title.
PE1408.B37 2005
808'.042—dc22   2004020879

Please visit our website at http://www.ablongman.com/ballenger.

ISBN 0-321-27705-8

 4 5 6 7 8 9 10—DOC—07 06

BRIEF CONTENTS

Part One
THE SPIRIT OF INQUIRY

Part Two
INQUIRY PROJECTS

Part Three
INQUIRING DEEPER

Part Four
REINQUIRING

DETAILED CONTENTS

Chapter 2
Reading as Inquiry   37

Chapter 5
Writing a Profile   147

Chapter 6
Writing a Review   195

Chapter 8
Writing an Argument   283

Chapter 9
Writing a Critical Essay   329

Chapter 9
Writing a Critical Essay   329

Chapter 10
Writing an Ethnographic Essay   389

Part Three
INQUIRING DEEPER

Chapter 11
Writing a Research Essay   439

Chapter 13
Using and Citing Sources   549

Part Four
REINQUIRING

Chapter 14
Revision Strategies   617

Chapter 15
The Writer's Workshop   669

INSTRUCTOR PREFACE

The first time I mention that my composition course is "inquiry based," it doesn't register with the students. They have no idea what I mean, but they're pretty sure that I'm going to tell them, and maybe even lecture at length about the topic. After all, they're used to being talked at. Within minutes, however, we're all *experiencing* the process of inquiry when I pass a bottle of spring water around the class inviting each student to raise a question about it. In ten minutes, the list of questions tops forty and the bottle is still going around, from hand to hand. "Why is it put in plastic bottles?" "How did they decide to use a label with these colors?" "Who decides what 'spring water' is, anyway?" "How does this compare to tap water?"

As we tire of generating questions, I ask the students to imagine that they are editors for *Discovery Magazine*.

"You've decided that you'd like to commission a piece on bottled water, but you'd like to give the freelance writer an idea about the question he or she might begin with," I say. "Which of the questions that we generated might be good opening questions for an investigation of the topic? In other words, which of these questions are 'researchable?'"

A few years ago, the Carnegie Foundation asked a group of leading scholars, teachers, and intellectuals to investigate the current state of undergraduate education at America's research universities. The Boyer Commission report was unequivocal about the problems: "The experience of most undergraduates at most research universities is that of receiving what is served out to them. In one course after another they listen, transcribe, absorb, and repeat, essentially as undergraduates have done for centuries." The investigators called for a "new model" of undergraduate education that would "turn the prevailing undergraduate culture of receivers into a culture of inquirers, a culture in which faculty, graduate students, and undergraduates share an adventure of discovery . . ." In particular, they added, "The first year of university experience needs to provide new stimulation for intellectual growth and a firm grounding in inquiry-based learning."

The "adventure of discovery" is what many of us love about writing. Our students often enter our composition classrooms with little experience using language as a tool of learning. Then we help them to understand that writing can be a means for finding out what they didn't know they knew, and that the process of revision can lead to a fresh way of seeing things; pretty soon even some resistant writers welcome the invitation to sit down and write. They've discovered that they can write to learn.

Most of us *already* teach inquiry, although not all may realize it. For instance, our writing classes invite students to be active participants in making knowledge in the classroom through peer review workshops. When we ask students to fastwrite or brainstorm we encourage them to suspend judgment and openly explore their feelings or ideas. And when we ask students to see a draft as a first look at a topic, and revision as a means of discovering what they may not have noticed, we teach a process that makes discovery its purpose. Indeed, most composition classrooms create a "culture of inquirers" rather than passive recipients of what their teachers know.

That's why the Boyer Commission's call for an inquiry-based freshman year resonated with me and so many others. Initially, I saw its relevance to one of the most common writing assignments in the composition course—the research paper—and this led me to write my book *The Curious Researcher*. But an inquiry-based approach can and should permeate every assignment in the entire sequence of freshman writing courses. I also thought that while much of what we already do involves inquiry-based learning, we should explicitly make the spirit of inquiry—its practices, methods, and purposes—the focus of the writing course, generating ideas that students can apply not only in our classrooms but in their work in other disciplines.

INQUIRY IN THE WRITING CLASSROOM

Historically, composition teachers have struggled to decide what besides reading and writing skills students could export to their other classes and, later, into their lives. Often, we vaguely refer to "critical thinking" skills. *The Curious Writer* offers a comprehensive approach for teaching *inquiry*. This idea also may seem vague until you consider the following.

First, think about what is required to create a culture of inquirers in the composition course. How do we create the learning environment that will foster such a culture? I believe there are at least five key features of an inquiry-based classroom on nearly any subject.

1. *Create an atmosphere of mutual inquiry.* Students are used to seeing their teachers as experts who know everything students need to learn. But in an inquiry-based classroom instructors are learners, too. They ask questions not because they already know the answers but because there might be answers they haven't considered.

2. *Emphasize questions before answers.* The idea that student writers begin with an inflexible thesis or a firm position on a topic *before* they engage in the process of writing and thinking is anathema to inquiry-based learning. Questions, not preconceived answers, lead to new discoveries.

3. *Encourage a willingness to suspend judgment.* Student culture at most schools works against this. Papers get written at the last minute, multiple deadlines in multiple classes compete for students'

time, and multiple-choice tests or lecture courses imply that there is one true answer and the teacher knows it. To suspend judgment demands that we trust the process that will lead us to new insights. This requires both faith in the process and the time to engage in it. The composition course, with its emphasis on process, is uniquely suited to nurture such faith.

4. *Introduce a strategy of inquiry.* It's not enough to simply announce that we're teaching an inquiry-based class. We have to introduce students to the *strategy of inquiry* we'll be using. In the sciences, the experimental method provides a foundation for investigations. What guidance will we give our students in the composition course? *The Curious Writer* features a strategy that is genuinely multidisciplinary, borrowing from science, social science, and the humanities.

5. *Present inquiry in a rhetorical context.* An essay, a research project, an experiment, any kind of investigation is always pursued with particular purposes and audiences in mind. In an inquiry-based class, the *situation* in which the inquiry project is taking place is always considered.

You'll find all of these elements of inquiry-based learning integrated in *The Curious Writer*. For example, each assignment in Part Two, "Inquiry Projects," leads students toward writing subjects that offer the most potential for learning. Rather than write about what they already know, students are always encouraged to choose a topic because they want to find out more about it. In addition, the discussion questions that follow the student and professional essays are crafted to do more than simply test their comprehension of the piece or reduce it to a single theme. In many cases, questions are open ended and can lead students in many directions as they analyze a reading. *The Curious Writer* maintains a voice and persona throughout the book that suggests that I am working along with the students as a writer and a thinker, which is exactly the experience of mutual inquiry I try to create in my classes. Finally, *The Curious Writer* is organized around a strategy of inquiry that is present in every assignment and nearly every exercise. Introduced in Part One, "The Spirit of Inquiry," I call on the model often in every subsequent chapter. The inquiry strategy is the thematic core of the book.

THE INQUIRY STRATEGY OF *THE CURIOUS WRITER*

A strategy of inquiry is simply a process of discovery. In the sciences, this process is systematic and often quite formal. The model I use in this book borrows from science in some ways through its insistence on continually looking closely at the "data" (sensory details, facts, evidence, textual passages, and so on) and using it to shape or test the writer's ideas about a subject. But the heart of the model is the alternating movement between

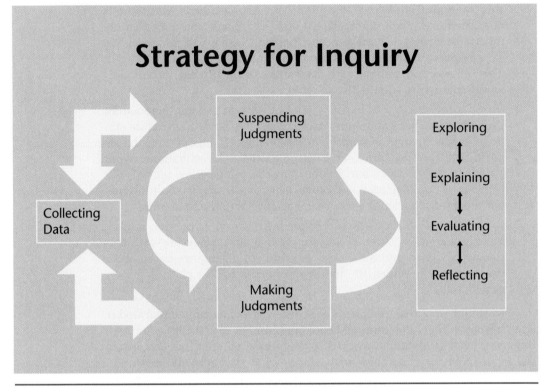

Strategy for Inquiry

Suspending Judgments

Collecting Data

Making Judgments

Exploring

↕

Explaining

↕

Evaluating

↕

Reflecting

FIGURE A In nearly every assignment in *The Curious Writer*, students will use this strategy of inquiry.

two modes of thinking—creative and critical—in a dialectical process. One way of describing this is shifting back and forth between suspending judgment and making judgments (see Figure A).

To help students see how questions can help them to see their writing subjects in new ways, I offer four categories of questions—those that explore, explain, evaluate, and reflect—and return to these frequently, particularly in the early stages of the inquiry process. These will be most evident in the follow-up questions to the many readings throughout *The Curious Writer*. A strategy of inquiry is useful only if it makes sense to students; I've tried very hard, particularly in the first section of the book, to make the model comprehensible.

OTHER FEATURES

Because the inquiry-based approach is so central to *The Curious Writer*, it's crucial for students to work through the first three chapters in Part One, "The Spirit of Inquiry." Part Two—the largest—focuses on "inquiry projects." The range of assignments in this part should satisfy the needs of most composition instructors. If your university is lucky enough to have a two-semester sequence, *The Curious Writer* includes assignments suitable for both courses, including personal, argument, and research essays. Also included is the ethnographic essay, a form that engages students in field research; *The Curious Writer* is the first major text to include ethnography.

The book's focus on genres of writing also makes it appealing for advanced composition courses. For example, assignments such as the profile, review, and proposal help students see how to apply what they've learned to distinct rhetorical situations and help them to understand how those situations shape the genres.

In recent years, I've become interested in reading strategies, a topic that I never mentioned as a novice teacher. There was simply so much to say about the writing process that I didn't think reading was a topic that should get much airtime. Yet like writing, students bring many prior beliefs and assumptions about reading into our classrooms, and since reading is always an important part of teaching writing, I've come around to talking more about it. *The Curious Writer* reflects this. Chapter 2, "Reading as Inquiry," is devoted to the topic. The best thing about this is that the inquiry model I promote for writing applies just as easily to reading. I've also expanded the discussion to reading images. This emphasis on visual rhetoric echoes the latest developments in composition in response to the growth of the Web and the growing visual literacy of our students.

Finally, the approach of *The Curious Writer* grows in part from my own scholarship on research writing, particularly the criticism that research is an activity that is too often isolated in the writing course. Students understandably get the idea that research is reserved only for the research paper if they're asked to do it only when they're assigned a research project. This book makes research a part of every assignment, from the personal essay to the proposal, emphasizing that it is a useful source of information, not a separate genre.

This is the third textbook I've written with the "curious" moniker. Since all are inquiry-based, the word is a natural choice. And while I'm very interested in encouraging my students to be curious researchers, readers, and writers, I also hope to remind my colleagues who use the books that we should be curious, too. We should model for our students our own passion for inquiring into the world. We should also celebrate what we can learn from our students, and not just about writing, or the many topics they might choose to write about. I'm curious every time I walk into the writing classroom what my students will teach me about myself. That's a lifetime inquiry project for all of us, as teachers and as people.

APPROACHES TO TEACHING WITH THE BOOK

The Instructor's Manual, written by my colleague Michelle Payne, will give you detailed suggestions about ways to teach *The Curious Writer*. Here are a few additional suggestions drawn with a much broader stroke.

I organized the book to span, if necessary, a two semester composition course, though it can easily be adapted to one semester. Typically, in a two semester sequence the first course focuses on writing process, exposition, critical analysis, writing to learn, and so on. The second semester often focuses on argument and research. A single semester composition course tries to combine them all. Fortunately, *The Curious Writer* is extremely flexible, with ample material to keep students busy for one or two semesters.

Sequence

Whether you use this book for one course or two, it's wise to introduce *The Curious Writer* to students by first working through Part One, "The Spirit of Inquiry," since this section lays the foundation for all that follows. The many exercises in these chapters will help students experience firsthand what we mean by inquiry. Part Two, "Inquiry Projects," is the heart of the book. I've organized chapters in an order that roughly follows typical composition courses, beginning with genres that draw heavily on students' personal experiences and observations and then moving them outward towards other sources of information and encounters with other people's experiences and ideas. In a one semester course, for example, you might begin with the personal essay, and then move to the profile, followed by the review, and then the argument or research essay. This builds nicely by challenging students to work with more sources of information and leads to a more sophisticated understanding of persuasion and rhetoric. A two-semester course has the luxury of more assignments, of course, allowing you to potentially use most of Inquiry Projects in Part Two.

Certain assignments clump together. For example, while arguably all writing is persuasive, the following genres are most explicitly so: proposal, review, argument, critical essay, and often the research essay. A course that focuses on argument might emphasize these assignments. A research-oriented course might exploit the wealth of material with a strong emphasis on outside sources, including the proposal, review, argument, research essay, and ethnography. A single semester composition course that attempts coverage of critical thinking and writing as well as research and argument might move from personal essay to profile, and then provide coverage of argument through the review or critical essay, move on to the argument, and finish with the ethnographic and research essays.

Integrating the Research and Revision Sections

An unusual feature of the book is its treatment of research skills and revision. Research is an element of every assignment but it receives special attention in Part Three, "Inquiring Deeper," where students are introduced not only to the research essay but to research strategies and skills. Hopefully, you will find that this section, particularly Chapter 12, "Research Techniques," is immediately relevant since students will be encouraged to consider research angles in every assignment they tackle. Consider assigning this chapter early in your course, particularly the sections on developing a working and deep knowledge of a subject.

Similarly, revision is an element of every assignment. That's hardly a novel idea but what is unusual is that *The Curious Writer* devotes an entire section of the book, Part Four, "Reinquiring," to revision. Like the section on research, the chapters on revision are relevant to students from their very first assignment. The first half of Chapter 14, "Revision Strategies," is a useful introduction to what it means to revise, and this might be material that you assign early on in your course. The chapter also features specific revision strategies that your students will use in every assignment.

Chapter 15, "The Writing Workshop," can also be assigned at any time and in sections. Consider having your students read the first half of that chapter—an introduction to peer review—before the first class workshops. The second half of the chapter focuses on "Methods of Responding," specific workshop formats that are most helpful for drafts at different stages in the writing process. Ask students who are responsible for presenting their work to read about the method of response they'll use in their workshop as preparation for it.

Using the Exercises

Learning follows experience, and the exercises in *The Curious Writer* are intended to help students make sense of the ideas in the text. I often plan the exercises as an in-class activity, and then assign the relevant reading to follow up that experience. Sometimes the discussion following these in-class exercises is so rich that some of the assigned reading becomes unnecessary. The students get it without having to hear it again from the author. More often, though, the reading helps students to deepen their understanding of what they've done and how they can apply it to their own work.

However, assigning all of the exercises isn't necessary. Don't mistake their abundance in the book as an indication that you must march your students lock step through every activity or they won't learn what they need to. *The Curious Writer* is more flexible than that. Use the exercises and activities that seem to emphasize key points that *you* think are important. Skip those you don't have time for or that don't seem necessary. If you're like me, you also have a few rabbits of your own in your hat, exercises and activities that may work better with the text than the ones I suggest.

FOR INSTRUCTORS

The following instructor resources are free to qualified adopters of Longman English textbooks.

The Instructor's Resource Manual
ISBN 0-321-18759-8
This manual includes several sample syllabi, as well as a helpful introduction that will offer general teaching strategies and ideas for teaching writing as a form of inquiry. It also gives a detailed overview of each chapter and its goals, ideas for discussion starters, handouts and overheads, and a large number of additional writing activities that teachers can use in their classrooms to supplement the textbook.

The Longman Instructor's Planner
ISBN 0-321-09247-3
This planner includes weekly and monthly calendars, student attendance and grading rosters, space for contact information, Web references, an almanac, and blank pages for notes.

The Allyn & Bacon Sourcebook for College Writing Teachers, Second Edition
ISBN 0-205-31603-4
This collection of writings on important theories and pedagogies in composition studies includes selections written by some of today's foremost scholars and teachers. Articles range from discussing how to integrate critical thinking and reading into writing instruction to methods for responding to and evaluating student writing to dealing with grammar and editing.

An Introduction to Teaching Composition in an Electronic Environment
ISBN 0-205-29715-3
This text is designed for instructors who have an "average" knowledge of computers overall and very little training or experience on how they can be used beneficially in the composition classroom.

Comp Tales
ISBN 0-321-05088-6
This collection of stories by college writing teachers is organized around current topics of debate in composition studies and on key issues for new writing teachers.

In Our Own Voice: Graduate Students Teach Writing
ISBN 0-205-30696-9
This selection of articles about teaching first year writing by graduate students gives will help other graduate student teachers become better prepared for the composition classroom.

The Longman Guide to Community Service-Learning
in the English Classroom and Beyond
ISBN 0-321-12749-8
Provides a definition and history of service-learning, as well as an overview of how service-learning can be integrated effectively into the college classroom.

Using Portfolios
ISBN 0-321-08412-8
This essential guide addresses the pedagogical and evaluative uses of portfolios, and offers practical suggestions for implementing a portfolio evaluation system in a writing class.

Teaching in Progress: Theories, Practices, and Scenarios, **Third Edition**
ISBN 0-321-08564-7
Ideal for training new instructors, this popular guide presents a variety of composition theories and teaching approaches and includes brief cases and scenarios illustrating theoretical issues in real-world settings. An anthology of articles on teaching writing is also featured.

The Longman Guide to Classroom Management
ISBN 0-321-09246-5
Includes helpful strategies for dealing with disruptive students in the classroom and the "do's and don'ts" of discipline.

FOR STUDENTS

Technology and Media

NEW! MyCompLab 2.0 Website
www.mycomplab.com
MyCompLab 2.0 offers all the strengths of 1.0, but adds exciting new features that makes this market-leading site even more useful for composition students and instructors.

Writing
- ***Exchange:*** Pearson's online peer and instructor writing review program. Use Exchange to comment on student papers at the word, sentence, paragraph, or paper level—or have students review each other's work.
- ***Process:*** Guided assistance through the stages of the writing process, with interactive worksheets and in-depth exercises for each stage.
- ***Activities:*** Provides 100 different writing activities in which students respond to videos, images, websites, and writing prompts.

- *Model Documents Gallery:* An extensive collection of 50 sample papers, reports, and documents from across the curriculum.
- *Web Links:* Presents a wealth of online resources to help students improve their writing.
- *Student Bookshelf:* An online reference library of e-books.

Grammar

- *Diagnostics:* Two new research-based 50-question diagnostic tests comprehensively assess student skills in basic grammar, sentence grammar, mechanics, punctuation, and style. Results pages provide overall proficiency scores in these categories as well as question-by-question feedback. Based on their results, students are linked to handbook explanations and to appropriate practice exercises.
- *ExerciseZone:* Over 3,000 NEW self-grading practice items cover all major topics of grammar, style, and usage with questions reflecting college-appropriate level and content. Feedback links students to more practice and to handbook explanations. NEW! Sentence and paragraph editing exercises.
- *ELL ExerciseZone:* Over 1,000 self-grading practice tests for students whose first language is not English.
- *MyCompLab Handbook:* Explanations of the most common errors in grammar, mechanics, and usage.
- *Web Links:* Presents a wealth of online resources to help students improve their grammar.

Research

- *ResearchNavigator:* Access to credible, reliable sources, including EBSCO's ContentSelect database and The New York Times Search-by-Subject archive, plus hundreds of pages of material on the research process itself.
- *Avoiding Plagiarism:* A self-guided exploration of the issue of plagiarism, these tutorials teaches students to recognize plagiarism and avoid its practice in both MLA and APA formats.

Tutor Center. Students using MyCompLab receive complimentary access to Longman's English Tutor Center. Our live, qualified college instructors help students use resources in MyCompLab effectively and will review student papers for organization and consistent grammar errors.

MyDropBox. Instructors who have ordered a MyCompLab Value Pack for their course can receive complimentary access to MyDropBox, a leading plagiarism detection service.

MyCompLab 2.0 is also available in WebCT, Blackboard, and Course-Compass online course management platforms.

Take Note! **Version 2.0**
ISBN 0-321-13608-X
Take Note! is a complete information-management tool for students working on research papers or other projects that require the use of outside sources. This cross-platform CD-ROM integrates note taking, outlining, and bibliography management into one easy-to-use package. Now includes even more templates for citing electronic sources and updated to correspond to the latest APA Guidelines.

Research Navigator Guide for English, 2004
ISBN 0-321-20277-5
Written by Eric Branscomb and Doug Gotthoffer, this guide includes a 12-month access code to ResearchNavigator and all the tips and instructions a student needs to effectively use this powerful online resource.

PRINT SUPPLEMENTS FOR STUDENTS

NEW! Longman Grammar and Documentation Study Card
ISBN 0-321-29203-0
Packed with useful information, this colorful study card is an 8-page guide to key grammar, punctuation, and documentation skills. Laminated for durability, this Study Card will provide students with a useful reference for years to come.

NEW! The Longman Writer's Portfolio and Student Planner
ISBN 0-321-29609-5
This unique portfolio/planner includes an assessing/organizing area (including a grammar diagnostic test, a spelling quiz, and project planning worksheets), a before and during writing area (including peer review sheets, editing checklists, writing self-evaluations, and a personal editing profile), and an after-writing area (including a progress chart, a final table of contents, and a final assessment).

10 Practices of Highly Successful Students
ISBN 0-205-30769-8
Murphy's popular supplement helps students learn crucial study skills, offering concise tips for a successful career in college. Topics include time management, test-taking, reading critically, stress, and motivation.

The Longman Writer's Journal
ISBN 0-321-08639-2
Written by Mimi Markus, this journal contains helpful journal writing strategies, sample journal entries by other students, and many writing prompts and topics to get students writing.

The Longman Researcher's Journal
ISBN 0-321-09530-8

Designed to help students work through the steps involved in writing a research paper, each section contains record-keeping strategies, checklists, graphic organizers, and pages for taking notes from sources.

The Longman Editing Exercises
ISBN 0-205-31792-8

This print supplement allows students to practice correct English in context with dozens of paragraph editing exercises in various topic areas of grammar, style and punctuation.

ESL Worksheets, Third Edition
ISBN 0-321-07765-2

These worksheets provide ESL students with extra practice in areas they find the most troublesome. Diagnostic tests, suggested writing topics, and an answer key are included.

Peer Evaluation Manual, Seventh Edition
ISBN 0-321-01948-2

Offers students forms for peer critiques, general guidelines, and specific forms for different stages in the writing process and for various types of papers.

Literacy Library Series
- *Workplace Literacy,* Second Edition (ISBN 0-321-12737-4)
- *Academic Literacy* (ISBN 0-321-06501-8)

This series offers informed, detailed guidelines for writing in academic, public, and workplace communities.

Analyzing Literature: A Guide for Students, Second Edition
ISBN 0-321-09338-0

This supplement provides critical reading strategies, writing advice, and sample student papers to help students interpret and discuss literary works from a variety of genres.

Newsweek Offer
The perfect supplement to any text, this award-winning publication gets students reading, writing, and thinking about what's going on in the world around them. Students can have *Newsweek* delivered directly to their front door for only .59 cents an issue each week for 12 weeks ($7.08), which will be added to the cost of the book. Instructors who assign *Newsweek* receive weekly lesson plans, quizzes, and work-sheets. Longman will also provide a free interactive workbook for students.

The Penguin-Putnam Discount Program
Offered in conjunction with Penguin-Putnam, this program allows a variety of Penguin titles to be packaged with any Longman textbook at a 60% discount. Visit www.ablongman.com/penquin for more details.

Dictionaries and Thesauruses

The New American Webster Handy College Dictionary, Third Edition
ISBN 0-451-18166-2
This superior paperback reference text contains more than 100,000 entries, including clear and concise definitions, selected etymologies, current phrases, slang, abbreviations, and scientific terms. **Free** when ordered packaged with most Longman textbooks.

The Oxford American Desk Dictionary and Thesaurus, Second Edition
ISBN 0-425-18068-9
This one-of-a-kind reference book combines both of the essential language tools—a dictionary and a thesaurus—in a single, integrated A-to-Z volume. The 1,024 page book offers more than 150,000 entries, definitions, and synonyms so you can find the right word every time, as well as appendices of valuable quick-reference information.

The Oxford Essential Thesaurus
ISBN 0-425-16421-7
This concise, easy-to-use thesaurus includes 175,000 synonyms in a simple A-to-Z format, more than 10,000 entries, extensive word choices, example sentences and phrases, and guidance on usage, punctuation.

Merriam-Webster's Collegiate® Dictionary, Tenth Edition
ISBN 0-321-10494-3
Celebrating over 150 years of excellence, this high quality, best-selling hardcover reference includes thousands of definitions, spellings, pronunciations, and etymologies. With more than 160,000 entries, and over 250,000 definitions, this dictionary is "The Voice of Authority."

ACKNOWLEDGMENTS

Years ago, when I was writing my dissertation, my daughter Rebecca, then five, asked her mother what would happen when I finally finished writing the thing. "When Daddy is done," she wondered, "will he still be my Daddy?" She's older now, and asks different questions that have mostly to do with how I feel about certain celebrities and what might be my favorite movie of all time. Becca's earlier question still amuses me, but it haunts me, too. It's a reminder that writing a book is a very self-centered way to live. To write books is to risk your relationships with the other people you love unless they are very patient and very forgiving, or you are able to somehow free yourself from the clutches of an unfinished chapter that will not leave you alone.

In the three years it took to write this book, I haven't managed my writing time and family time as well as I could have. Fortunately, my wife and kids were very patient and very forgiving, and I'm grateful for that, even more so because I don't deserve it. Thank you Karen, Rebecca, and

Julia. Now that I've finally returned, I'll try to never let another book keep me away from you for so long.

The development editor for this project, Adam Beroud, diligently saw it through while having a baby and moving across the country. While authors enjoy all of the credit for books like these, a good editor is often the difference between a mediocre book and a good one. Many times, Adam saved me from mediocrity. With grace, graciousness, and great saavy, he guided me through a wilderness of manuscript pages numbering in the thousands to safely arrive at publication. *The Curious Writer* is the product of Adam's imagination as well as mine.

My friends sustained me personally and professionally while at work on *The Curious Writer,* and one in particular, Michelle Payne, a colleague at Boise State, constantly reassured me that my vision for this book was sound and that it would make a difference for writing teachers and their students. Even more important, she reminded me to walk away from this project from time to time and reenter the world of my friends and family, people with whom I had often failed to be fully present. I co-authored *The Curious Reader* with Michelle, and when she agreed to write the Instructor's Manual, Appendixes, and Companion Website of *The Curious Writer,* I was delighted. I knew it would be far better than any instructor's manual I could write. I am deeply grateful for her friendship.

I'm fortunate to have other colleagues who have contributed to this book. Devan Cook, also at Boise State, is relentless in her praise of the *Curious* series and modest about her contributions to the thinking that shaped the books, especially this one. Devan has influenced my understanding of revision and style, and contributed directly to the chapter on argument. Brock Dethier, at Utah State University, is an unwitting collaborator on all of my textbooks. Our conversations usually occur while I'm tagging along behind him while we hike several thousand vertical feet; I listen and learn while trying to catch my breath.

Bonnie Sunstein and Elizabeth Chiseri-Strater's pioneering work on ethnography in composition inspired my own attempts at teaching the ethnographic essay, and the chapter on that form in this book is my modest attempt to do what Elizabeth and Bonnie do so well. I relied heavily on Richard Fulkerson's work on argumentative writing for Chapter 8, and borrowed William Badke's definition of "working knowledge" for the chapter on research strategies. Ann Berthoff's "dialogue journal" is the inspiration for what I'm calling here the "double-entry journal." Her work is the foundation for much of this book. Donald Murray, my friend and first professional mentor, was the first to teach me to write "badly," and for that I'm forever grateful.

A former graduate student of mine, Susan Kirtley, who is now a promising young professor, contributed significantly to my thinking about computers and writing. Her work in that area is going to have an impact on the field.

Boise State colleagues who have contributed directly or indirectly to this book include Marcy Newman, Jill Heney, Paul Spencer, Julie Ewing, Jeff Wilhelm, Nancy McGowan, Mike Markel, Teresa Dewey, Marlys Hersey, Bud Pederson, Karen Uehling, Tom Peele, Mike Mattison, Chuck Guilford, Richard Leahy, Katie Quick, and Gail Shuck.

Many students of these helpful colleagues contributed their writing to *The Curious Writer*. A few students did even more, and I'd like to thank four of them—Margaret Parker, Jon Butterfield, Lana Kuchta, and Amy Garrett—who spent a semester working with me to develop the book. They tried the exercises and assignments, and contributed much of the student writing that adds life to *The Curious Writer*. Among the other student contributors were Jeremy Johnson, Julie Bird, Micaela Fisher, Mike Peterson, and Kelly Sundberg. In nearly twenty-five years of teaching, I've had thousands of students, and I've been a student—as well as an instructor—to many of them. They've taught me more than they will ever know about how writers learn to write well, and they've taught me how to teach writing.

Reviewers of books like these can be crucial to their development. I was lucky enough to have some of the best reviewers I've ever had, including the following: Jeffrey T. Andelora, Mesa Community College; Ken Autrey, Francis Marion University; Sandra Barnhill, South Plains College; Patrick Bizzaro, East Carolina University; Sara M. Blake, El Camino College; Pamela S. Bledsoe, Surry Community College; Libby Bradford Roeger, Shawnee Community College; Sharon Buzzard, Quincy College; Maria A. Clayton, Middle Tennessee State University; Dr. Keith Coplin, Colby Community College; Rachelle Darabi, Indiana University/Purdue University–Fort Wayne; Virginia B. Earnest, Holmes Community College–Ridgeland; Terry Engebretsen, Idaho State University; Shari Hammond, Southwest Virginia Community College; Anneliese Homan, State Fair Community College; David C. Judkins, University of Houston; Robert Lamm, Arkansas State University; James C. McDonald, University of Louisiana–Lafeyette; Rhonda McDonnell, Arizona State University; Bryan Moore, Arkansas State University; John D. Moore, Eastern Illinois University; Margaret P. Morgan, University of North Carolina–Charlotte; Dr. Peter E. Morgan, University of West Georgia; Brigid Murphy, Pima Community College; Robin L. Murray, Eastern Illinois University; Dorothy J. Patterson, Oakwood College; Steven R. Price, Mississippi College; Mark Reynolds, Jefferson Davis Community College; David H. Roberts, Samford University; Elaine J. Roberts, Judson College; Robert A. Schwegler, University of Rhode Island; Dr. Bonita Selting, University of Central Arkansas; Vicki Stieha, Northern Kentucky University; Elizabeth A. Stolarek, Ferris State University; Lisa Tyler, Sinclair Community College; Marjorie Van Cleef, Housatonic Community College; Worth H. Weller, Indiana University Purdue University–Fort Wayne; Ann R. Wolven, Lincoln Trail College; and Richard T. Young, Blackburn College.

Finally, I'd like to thank Joseph Opiela, senior vice president and publisher at Longman Publishers. He's seen me through three *Curious* books, never wavering in his faith that each would work. More than ten years ago, Joe took a gamble on an untested textbook author when he published an unusual book on how to write research papers. He's still gambling on me, and for that I'm grateful.

BRUCE BALLENGER

STUDENT PREFACE

In a way, a textbook on writing just doesn't make sense. You don't learn to write by reading about it. You learn by doing it. So you'll be doing a lot of writing using *The Curious Writer,* work ranging from private journal writing to carefully researched and cited research essays. And when you run into problems, or have questions, or wonder what someone else might have done with the same assignment, what you read in this book will have more meaning. In other words, this book is designed around a very simple idea: learning follows experience. Throughout *The Curious Writer,* I'll invite you to try journal exercises or assignments, and then provide you with information to help reflect on what you did. How could you have done it differently? What might make it better? How does this apply to other writing situations?

I also know that you've been writing for years, and not just in school. You write e-mails to friends, maybe keep a journal, or have even authored a Web page. On any subject about which we have a great deal of prior experience, we form beliefs that are very hard to change. Writing is one of those subjects. Therefore one of the goals of *The Curious Writer* is to challenge you to reexamine those beliefs about how writing gets done. They're not all wrong, of course, but a big part of learning is "unlearning" assumptions or beliefs that get in the way of doing your best work.

INQUIRY AS A FOCUS

As you read this book, "inquiry" is a word you'll hear a lot. I use that word—and that idea—often in *The Curious Writer,* not to be trendy or annoying, but because it is so central to why I wrote this book. This book is part of a larger movement to encourage undergraduates to participate in the experience of discovery that is the heart of the university. Rather than simply becoming passive recipients of knowledge, inquiry-based learning invites you to ask questions rather than settle for easy answers, encourages you to find problems and explore solutions, and makes the act of finding out as important as the effort to prove.

Writing is an important part of the process of discovery, not only because it is a tool for reporting what you find out, but because writing itself is a means of discovering what you didn't know you knew. Using techniques such as fastwriting and brainstorming, I've tried to create the conditions that will help you be surprised by what you think and say. You may find this hard to believe; I know I did. After years of writing research papers, lab reports, note cards, and carefully crafted holiday letters to family and friends, I understood writing as a tool for reporting only what I already thought. Then one day I had a graduate class with Donald Murray, one of the pioneers of modern writing instruction. Don taught me to write "badly," and it changed my writing forever.

I want you to write badly, too, because it will help you to write well.

USING A JOURNAL

Something that will help you write well is a journal. You may have had prior experiences with a journal—maybe good, maybe bad—but throughout this book I'll ask you to use one. A journal is a great place to write openly and honestly and, yes, badly, by letting the words run out ahead of you instead of hammering each one into place. If it's working, your journal will serve up a feast of surprises: topics that you wouldn't have discovered unless you wrote your way to them, information that you never imagined you could collect, and insights into what you think and feel about what you've observed, what you've read, or what you've discussed.

You could keep a diary, but that's not the kind of journal I have in mind. In fact, when working with *The Curious Writer* you might simply use the notebook you bought for the class as your journal. This is where you'll take notes, indulge in fastwriting to find a topic, make a cluster of a topic you've found, brainstorm a list, draft an outline, and explore your response to an assigned reading. If you keep it up and take it seriously, I think you'll find this kind of journal will not only help you generate ideas but also think them through.

Although the writing in your journal often won't be very good (it may be unfocused, at times incoherent, and mechanically flawed), this writing *counts*. It will help you write your papers and it will help you think more deeply. The many discoveries and surprises that a journal can yield will also keep you writing, wondering what will happen next.

ORGANIZATION OF THE BOOK

The Curious Writer is divided into four parts. Part One, "The Spirit of Inquiry," lays the groundwork for your writing and reading in later sections. The three chapters that constitute Part One explore what I mean when I talk about "inquiry." In particular, you'll be introduced to a "strategy of inquiry" that you'll use throughout the book. I'll also show you how the acts of reading and writing involve many of the same process.

Chapter 1, "Writing as Inquiry," helps you to clarify your existing beliefs about writing and reading. It begins the "unlearning" process. Chapter 2, "Reading as Inquiry," emphasizes reading as a process much like writing. Both demand very similar things of you: trying to make sense of sometimes contradictory or ambiguous information and then trying to discover what you think about it. You'll also learn that we "read" pictures in much the same way we read texts. This is a nice metaphor for talking about reading written materials, but in our increasingly image-laden world, "visual literacy"—knowing how to analyze the purposes and persuasiveness of pictures—is an important skill, and one that you'll be able to hone throughout *The Curious Writer*.

Chapter 3, "Ways of Inquiring," is built on the idea that in inquiry the opening questions you ask about your subject affect the way you see it. Asking questions is like the process of taking multiple photographs of a subject, but varying the distance, the angle, or the time of day with each shot. I'll introduce four basic "angles" for seeing: exploring, explaining, evaluating, and reflecting. You'll use these as ways of inquiring into your own experiences, into things that you read, and into things you observe throughout the book.

Part Two introduces seven inquiry projects that will give you a chance to apply Part One's strategy of inquiry to actual writing situations. Several genres are covered and you'll explore new ways of approaching them. For instance, while a personal essay and an argument—two forms you'll encounter in Part Two—might seem polar opposites, you'll find that the essential acts of mind that each type of essay demands are pretty much the same.

If writing an essay is like building a house, then Part Three, "Inquiring Deeper," is the hardware store, a place you'll visit regularly throughout the process to find tools and collect useful information. Part Three also features an extended research essay assignment that will provide practice using research strategies. Chapter 12, "Research Techniques," introduces practical research strategies to help you net the best information from the Web, the library, or the instructor down the hall. Chapter 13, "Using and Citing Sources," shows how to correctly use and cite sources, with a special emphasis on strategies for avoiding plagiarism. The MLA and APA documentation guidelines also are discussed. Usually chapters like these are attached like barnacles to the research paper assignment, as if research were something writers only did when assigned to write "The Research Paper." But research is a source of information that can inform any kind of writing, and you may turn to these chapters even when you're writing a personal essay or review.

Part Four, "Reinquiring," focuses on revision and writer's workshops. Revision is often a process too frequently overlooked by young writers. I'm convinced, though, that writers who begin to master the revision process—writers who can recognize the problems in their drafts and come up with ideas to solve them—are the most accomplished writers.

Appendixes don't usually get much attention, but the appendixes in *The Curious Writer,* written by my colleague Dr. Michelle Payne, are full of tips on how to deal with practical writing situations, including taking an essay exam, writing a literary review, or compiling an annotated bibliography. There's also a wealth of information about using portfolios, something your instructor might require in this class.

Additionally, *The Curious Writer's* Companion website, also prepared by Michelle Payne, provides valuable information on the book, including an overview of its objectives, sample student essays; useful Internet links; and writing exercises that will help you assess what you're learning. You can find the website at: www.ablongman.com/ballenger.

GETTING AN "A"

"How can I get an 'A' in this course?" I can't tell you how many times I've been asked this question, and since I'm not teaching your class I can't really tell you. But because your instructor chose to use *The Curious Writer,* I think I can tell you how to make the most of this book.

- *Keep up with the reading.* You might be tempted to blow off the reading and just skip to the assigned exercise or writing project. But I've tried to surround each activity with information that will help you understand what you're trying to do and how you might do it better, so doing the reading will be worthwhile.

- *Do the journal work.* One of the biggest problems I see in students' writing is that they don't have enough information—they work from scarcity rather than abundance. Much of the journal work in *The Curious Writer* is designed to address this problem. Even if your instructor doesn't read your journal, the writing you do there will make an enormous difference in the quality of your work.

- *Understand exactly what the assignments are asking you to do.* You'll learn a lot about analyzing rhetorical situations in this book, and a key part of that is assessing audience and purpose. Each assignment in Part Two carefully describes its goals and features. Keep these in mind as you work, and ask your instructor about any additional things you should consider with each assignment.

- *Seize research opportunities.* One of the principles behind this book is that research isn't just for research papers. Virtually any writing assignment, including the personal essay, can benefit from collecting information from reading and interviews. Each assignment chapter includes a range of suggestions for research angles. Use these whenever you can because they'll make your writing more informative and more interesting.

- *Welcome uncertainty and ambiguity.* This goes completely against instinct. Confusion and uncertainty typically are to be avoided at all costs because they get in the way of finishing the job. But ambiguity is a natural part of the process of inquiry. If you're uncertain what you think, then you're much more likely to experience the pleasures of surprise and discovery.

- *See revision as an opportunity for new learning.* This book, perhaps more than any other, challenges writers to truly embrace the process of revision as "reseeing." Fixing sentences and catching grammatical errors is a small, though important, part of this; reexamining your initial ideas, taking a new look at the evidence, collecting more information, analyzing the structure of your thinking, or even shifting to a new topic—these are all the kinds of "deep" revision that reward the writer with new learning.

Part One
THE SPIRIT OF INQUIRY

Chapter 1
Writing as Inquiry

Chapter 2
Reading as Inquiry

Chapter 3
Ways of Inquiring

A researcher writes field notes on the black rhino of the Nambian desert. Writing as inquiry stems from the desire to know more about ourselves and the world we live in.

Writing as Inquiry

Just the other night I was writing a card to my old friend Linda, someone I went to college with and haven't seen in twenty-five years. As I wrote, my words scribbled in a heavy black pen, she began to appear before me again. I saw her in geology class, a few rows up, wearing a black raincoat and rubber boots, carefully putting her straight black hair behind an ear so she could see her notes. I hadn't seen her so clearly in years, and the writing brought her back. Most of us have had this experience—the power of words to summon images, memories, and feelings—which is why we sometimes indulge, often with pleasure, in writing letters, cards, and e-mails to friends and family.

Yet a great many of us admit that we really don't like to write, particularly when forced to do it, or we express a clear preference for certain kinds of writing and dislike for others: "I just like to write funny stories" or "I like writing for myself, and not for other people" or "I hate writing research papers." I can understand this, because for years I felt much the same way. I saw virtually no similarities between my note to Linda and the paper I wrote for my philosophy class in college. Words that had power in one context seemed flimsy and vacant in another. One kind of writing was fairly easy, the other was sweating blood. How could my experience as a writer be so fundamentally different? In other words, what's the secret of writing well in a range of contexts *and* enjoying it more? Here's what I had to learn:

1. All writing can offer the joy of discovery, the opportunity to speak and be heard, and the satisfaction of earned insight.
2. A key to writing well is understanding the *process* of doing it.

I'm not really sure they are particularly novel, but both ideas were a revelation to me when I finally figured them out late in my academic career, and they changed the way I wrote for good. These two insights—that the pleasures of writing can span genres and situations, and that thinking about *how* we write matters—are guiding

What You'll Learn in This Chapter

- Why it pays to spend time thinking about your writing process.
- Why learning to write well often involves *unlearning* things you already believe.
- How an understanding of rhetoric will help you analyze writing situations.
- What it means to be a writer who is motivated by a spirit of inquiry.
- How to harness both creative and critical ways of thinking to come up with new ideas.

3

principles of this book. After reading *The Curious Writer,* I won't guarantee that haters of writing will come to love it, or that lovers of writing won't find writing to be hard work. But I do hope that by the end of the book you'll experience some of the same pleasures I found writing to my friend Linda in most writing situations, and that you'll be able to adapt your own writing process to meet the demands of whatever situation you encounter.

The process of becoming a more flexible and insightful writer must begin by exploring what you already believe it means to write well and learning a bit about how we can talk about writing as a process. In this chapter, I'll also introduce you to an idea that will be at the heart of every activity and assignment in *The Curious Writer:* the habits of mind and practices that will encourage you to adopt the "spirit of inquiry" as a motive for writing. This may sound a bit lofty and abstract. But by chapter's end I hope you'll recognize some very practical implications of this approach that will help you with any writing assignment. One of these implications—dialectical thinking—sounds like the kind of phrase you may associate with dull bearded men. I think you'll find, however, that it's a way of thinking that simply makes sense. By the end of this chapter, I hope you'll also see that "bad" writing makes sense, too, and that you'll use it again and again to write your best stuff.

MOTIVES FOR WRITING

Why write? You could probably build a long list of reasons in a minute or two, perhaps beginning facetiously: "Because I *have* to!" But as you consider the many situations that call for writing and the purposes for doing it, I suspect that most will fall under a broad and obvious category: to say something to someone else. I'm less confident that you will see another broad motive for writing, partly because it gets less attention: we write to *discover* what we want to say.

These two motives for writing—to *share* ideas with others and to *discover* what the writer thinks and feels—are equally important.

But both these two motives may arise from a still deeper spring: a sense of wonder and curiosity or even confusion and doubt, a desire to touch other people, or an urge to solve a problem. These feelings can inspire what I call the *spirit of inquiry,* a kind of perspective toward the world that invites questions, accepts uncertainty, and makes each of us feel some responsibility for what we say. This inquiring spirit should be familiar to you. It's the feeling you had when you discovered that the sun and a simple magnifying glass could be used to burn a hole in an oak leaf. It's wondering what a teacher meant when he said that the Second World War was a "good" war and Vietnam was a "bad" war. It's the questions that haunted you yesterday as you listened to a good friend describe her struggles with anorexia. The inquiring spirit even drives your quest to find the best DVD player, an effort that inspires you to read about the technology and visit *Consumer Reports Online.*

BELIEFS ABOUT WRITING

Most of us have been taught about writing since the first grade. We usually enter college with beliefs about how best to write a paper, which rules govern school writing, and even how to improve at composing. As I mentioned earlier, I've learned a lot about writing since my first years in college, and a big part of that learning involved unraveling some of my prior beliefs about writing. In fact, initially, I'd say that my development as a writer had more to do with *unlearning* some of what I already knew than it did with discovering new ways to write. Actually, that's one of the central findings of learning theorists: When learners have considerable prior knowledge of a subject, they often need to reexamine their beliefs to determine if those beliefs are accurate or helpful. Until they do this, any new learning in the subject can be limited. In keeping with this philosophy, we need to evaluate what you already believe about writing. Only after you articulate your beliefs can you begin an ongoing examination of whether those beliefs are obstacles or aids to new learning about writing.

EXERCISE 1.1

What Do You Believe?

STEP ONE: From the list below, identify *the one belief* about writing that you agree with most strongly, and *one* that you're convinced isn't true.

1. Writing proficiency begins with learning the basics and then building on them, working from words to sentences to paragraphs to compositions.

2. The best way to develop as a writer is to imitate the writing of the people you want to write like.

3. People are born writers. Either you can or you can't do it.

4. The best way to develop as a writer is to develop good reading skills.

5. Practice is the key to a writer's development. The more a writer writes, the more she will improve.

6. Developing writers need to learn the modes of writing (argument, exposition, description, narration) and the genres (essays, research papers, position papers, and so on).

7. Developing writers should start with simple writing tasks, for instance, telling stories, and move to harder writing tasks, such as writing a research paper.

8. The most important thing that influences a writer's growth is her belief that she can learn to write well.

9. The key to becoming a better writer is finding your voice.

STEP TWO: Spend five minutes writing in your notebook or journal about *why* you agree with the one belief and disagree with the other. This is an open-ended "fastwrite." You should write fast and without stopping, letting your thoughts flow in whatever direction they go. Try not to think about what you want to say before you write it, and don't worry about whether you're writing well or making sense (see *One Student's Response* below for an example).

Journal Prompts

- *When* did you first start agreeing or disagreeing with the belief? Can you remember a particular moment or experience as a student learning to write that drove this home?

- *What* do you mean, exactly, when you say you agree or disagree with the belief? Can you explain more fully why you think the belief is true or false?

- *Who* was most influential in convincing you of the truth or falsity of the belief?

Rules for Fastwriting

1. There are no rules.
2. Don't try to write badly, but give yourself permission to.
3. To the extent you can, think *through* writing rather than before it.
4. Keep your pen moving.
5. If you run out of things to say, write about how weird it is to run out of things to say until new thoughts arrive.
6. Silence your internal critic.
7. Don't censor yourself.

ONE STUDENT'S RESPONSE

JON'S JOURNAL

EXERCISE 1.1

STEP TWO

I agree that writing is a natural human activity that we are all capable of. Anyone capable of thinking understands language. That's truly all that one needs to begin. The only problem that arises is that writing for one's self contains limitations. He is the rare person that can be satisfied with his own praise. There is something within the human spirit that understands that other people may know more than we do. This drives us on for a response from others. This requires a set standard for communication. This, in turn, requires rules. These are things that a successful writer must learn.

I don't agree with the next statement about imitation. Mr. Studabacher is a good man and a good writer and he pushes this theory a little bit. He says that we should learn to borrow without plagiarism. Imitation can only be a beginning—a starting block for the creation of our own voice and ideas . . .

INQUIRING INTO THE DETAILS

JOURNALS

Throughout *The Curious Writer,* I invite you to write in a journal. Some people have an abiding fear of journals: so-called journalphobia. These are usually students who were forced to keep a journal in some class and found it a chore, or who tried to keep a journal at home and had little to show from the experience but blank pages. If you suffer from this condition, use a notebook instead of a journal. The two terms are synonymous. It's not what you call it that counts—it's what you do inside of it!

Why do I want you to use a journal? One reason is that it is easier to write freely in this medium than it is when confronting the first page of a rough draft. Also, it's okay to write badly in journals and, as you will see later in this chapter, that's a good thing.

What kind of journal should you use? That's up to you. The writer Natalie Goldberg advises that a journal with a cartoon character on the cover will help you take yourself and your writing less seriously, which will help loosen up your writing. Some students just use the ubiquitous spiral notebook, which works just fine. For a variety of reasons, others find the digital journal best. They may be able to write faster and with more ease using a keyboard instead of pen; keeping a journal on the computer might even be required if you're taking your class in a computer lab.

Unlearning Unhelpful Beliefs

You shouldn't be surprised when I say that I have a lot of theories about writing development; after all, I'm supposedly the expert. But we are *all* writing theorists, with beliefs that grow out of our successes and failures as students who write. Because you don't think much about them, these beliefs often shape your response to writing instruction without you even knowing it. For example, I've had a number of students who believe that people are born writers. As far as I can tell, they mean that there is some kind of writing gene that some folks have and some don't. This belief, of course, would make any kind of writing course a waste of time because writing ability would be a genetic problem.

A much more common belief is that learning to write is a process of building on basics, beginning with words, then working up to sentences, paragraphs, and perhaps whole compositions. This belief was very common when I was taught writing. I remember slogging my way through Warriner's *English Grammar and Composition* in the seventh and eighth grade, dutifully working through chapter after chapter, beginning with parts of speech, parts of sentences, sentences, and then paragraphs. It wasn't until page 377 of *English Grammar and Composition* that I was urged to write a whole composition, a topic whose section was the smallest in the book.

Along with a lot of experts on writing instruction, I don't think that this foundational approach to writing development is very effective. I know it didn't help me become a better writer, and while I can still diagram a sentence, that's never a skill I call on when I'm composing. As a matter of fact, fifty years of research confirms that teaching formal grammar separately from writing essays is largely a waste of time. Despite this, formal grammar instruction persists, testimony to the subversive power of common sense. (Isn't it common sense that we should always learn the basics first?)

Unlearning involves rejecting common sense *if* it conflicts with what actually works. Throughout this book, I hope you'll constantly test your beliefs about writing against the experiences you're having with it. Pay attention to what seems to work for you and what doesn't; mostly, I'd like you at least initially to play what one writing instructor calls the believing game. Ask yourself, *What do I have to gain as a writer if I try believing this is true?*

The Beliefs of This Book

One of the metaphors I very much like about writing development is one offered by writing theorist Anne Berthoff. She said learning to write was like learning to ride a bike. You don't start by practicing handlebar skills, move on to pedaling practice, and then finally learn balancing techniques. You get on the bike and fall off, get up and try again, doing all of those separate things all at once. At some point, you don't fall and you pedal off down the street. Berthoff said writing is a process that involves *allatonceness* (all-at-once-ness), and it's simply not helpful to try to practice the subskills separately. This is one belief about writing development shared by this book. Obviously, then, *The Curious Writer* is nothing like Warriner's *English Grammar and Composition,* but what other beliefs *does* it embrace?

Any number of beliefs—the importance of critical thinking, the connection between reading and writing, the power of voice and fluency, and the need to listen to voices other than your own—all guide the structure of this book. There is one belief, though, that under girds them all: *The most important thing that influences a writer's growth is the conviction that he or she can learn to write well.* Faith in your ability to become a better writer is key. From it grows the motivation to learn how to write well.

Faith isn't easy to come by. I didn't have it as a writer through most of my school career because I assumed that being placed in the English class for underachievers meant that writing was simply another thing, like track, that I was mediocre at. For a long time, I was a captive to this attitude. But then, as a college freshman, I wrote a paper I cared about and the writing started to matter, not because I wanted to impress my instructor but because I discovered something I really wanted to say, and say well. I didn't settle for mediocrity after that.

As someone who wasn't too keen on writing for a very long time, I know how difficult it is to develop compelling reasons to write, particularly when the writing is required. I had to learn, among other things, that my teacher wasn't responsible for supplying the motivation (though I acknowledge that deadlines can help). I had to find a way to approach a writing assignment that made it seem like an opportunity to learn something.

It turns out that the way you *initially* see a writing assignment—any assignment, really—influences your attitude toward it. To illustrate this point, consider the questions below. Which one of the two responses *best* describes your own feelings when confronted with a writing assignment?

Which opening question are you most likely to ask yourself?

❑ How can I be successful   ❑ What can I learn?
   at this?

How do you feel when problems arise as you're writing?

❑ I don't have the   ❑ I expect challenges.
   necessary skills.

How do you view your instructor?

❏ Someone who should tell me exactly what he or she wants.

❏ Someone who can help me solve my writing problems.

What do you consider your main goal?

❏ I want to show I'm a decent writer.

❏ I want to develop my writing skills.

It may have been hard to limit yourself to just these responses because our attitudes are much more complex than this. You may also have found yourself checking the responses in both columns. But if your choices tended toward the left column, it's likely that your attitude toward writing is driven by *performance* goals. In other words, you want to perform well on a writing assignment for your instructor, for your peers, for your friends, for yourself. If you found yourself agreeing with the items in the right column, *learning goals* seem to dominate how you feel about writing assignments; that is, you are less interested in how well you perform than you are in developing your writing abilities. You see the challenge of a writing assignment as a learning opportunity.

There is nothing wrong with your attitude if it leans more towards performance than learning. Each type of goal has its place. Just remember this about performance-oriented writing: Along with the desire for success inevitably comes anxiety about failure. Fearfulness is not a very comfortable place from which to write or to learn. If you're willing to consider making learning rather than performance goals a priority as you work through *The Curious Writer,* you're much more likely to develop your writing abilities. And you might even find that you can use writing in ways you never thought possible. Consider, then, beginning your study of college writing with the opening question, *What can I learn?*

Ⓠ INQUIRING INTO THE DETAILS

PORTFOLIOS

One method for evaluating your development as a writer is by using a *portfolio,* which is a collection of work you assemble throughout a semester and submit to your instructor at the end of the course. If your instructor uses portfolios, she may grade some of your work as you go along, but the main way your writing abilities will be assessed is often the total body of work in your portfolio. This means that until you hand in your final drafts, everything is pretty much a work-in-progress, and for much of the course you can focus on learning goals—say, finding new methods to begin and end your essays, or improving your editing skills. Performance goals, such as getting a decent grade, only become a priority at the end of the course. I'll have much more to say about portfolios later (see Appendix A).

WRITING SITUATIONS AND RHETORICAL CHOICES

When I was in high school, I took my girlfriend Jan Dawe to downtown Chicago to see a concert. I was a new driver, unused to navigating the tight spaces in the city's underground parking garages. Driving my parents' car, I managed to clip a cement barrier and put a long dent in the side of the vehicle. I was mortified, of course—first, because I felt like such an idiot in front of my high school girlfriend, and second, because I was pretty sure my parents would get mad. If you were in a similar situation and decided to write a letter to your parents explaining the incident, what might you consider as you ponder the following questions about how to compose it?

- How should I come across to my parents? What's the appropriate tone for the letter?
- What would be the best way to begin?
- How important is reason and logic in the letter? How important is emotion and feeling?

Now imagine that you're going to write a letter to your best friend describing the same incident. Would your answers to these questions be any different?

One way of analyzing this writing situation, or indeed any other, is by using something called *the rhetorical triangle,* which reveals the dynamic relationships among a writer, his subject, and his audience (see Figure 1.1).

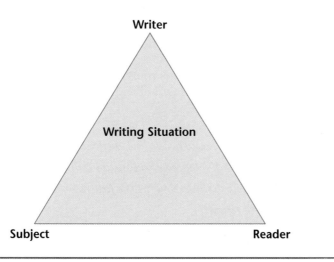

FIGURE 1.1 **The rhetorical triangle.**

What the triangle implies is pretty straightforward—to write effectively, you must simultaneously address three main factors: your own perspective as the writer, the topic you are writing about, and the people you are writing for. The word "rhetorical," of course, comes from "rhetoric," the classical term for the study and practice of written and verbal communication. In fact, the rhetorical triangle has its origins in ancient Greece and the thinking of Aristotle, who first set down the principles of effective communication more than 2,000 years ago.

The three legs of the rhetorical triangle come together to shape the writing situation. The particularities of each leg—the writer, the subject, and the audience—determine the context of the writing situation. Consider again the dinged car dilemma. In that scenario, one thing is clear: both of the proposed letters has a distinct—and different—*audience*. One letter addressed the writer's parents, who own the car, and the other addressed the writer's friend, who has a different interest in the problem. While the writer and the subject would seem to be the same for both letters, given the different audiences, it's very possible that the writer's perspective could shift from one letter to the other. After all, preparing an admission of fault to one's parents could very well compel a writer to look at himself differently than he would while composing a comparable admission to a friend. Similarly, while the accident would remain an important topic in both letters, in the letter to the friend it might be presented as but one example of a broader subject, such as the problems the writer has confronted in dating (or driving). The permutations for this and any other writing situation are almost endless, but they all rest on the three legs of the rhetorical triangle.

I've always believed that my writing students are far more rhetorically sophisticated than they let on. When I pose the car episode as a writing situation, most instinctively know that each letter should present the subject differently, and that those differences have everything to do with the two different audiences. But what also is evident is the range of choices the situation presents to the writer, even if he were writing to only one of the audiences. For example, the letter to the parents might adopt an apologetic tone—the writer presents himself as contrite—but also might begin with a more firm, even aggressive statement of responsibility:

Dear Mom and Dad,

I've made a mistake, and I want to tell you about it. While driving Jan to the concert last night, I badly dented the Ford while making a turn in the parking garage. First, you should know I take full responsibility for this, and insist on paying for the repairs...

Or the letter might make an appeal to emotion, working the sympathy angle.

Dear Mom and Dad,

Well, you've always said that parking downtown is hell. I discovered that firsthand last night when I followed your advice and parked in the underground garage off Michigan Avenue. That experience left its mark on me, and, I'm sorry to say, your car as well...

Each approach seems plausible, and it's hard to know which would be most effective without knowing more about the particular situation—for instance, what the parents are like and the writer's history of car accidents. But as you can see, analyzing the situation presents the writer with a range of choices.

Writing involves evaluating situations and making choices like these. *The Curious Writer* offers you tools to help analyze various writing situations and explores a range of choices that might be appropriate in each, choices that speak to the form your writing might take, the processes you might use to generate information, and the revision strategies you should consider. Ultimately, you will have to make your own rhetorical choices about how best to respond to any one writing situation.

HABITS OF MIND

When I first started teaching writing, I noticed a strange thing in my classes. What students learned about writing through the early assignments in the class didn't seem to transfer to later assignments, particularly research papers. What was I doing wrong, I wondered? Among other things, what I failed to make clear to my students was how certain "essential acts of mind" were present in every assignment, from the very first to the very last. What bound the writing course together was the idea of academic inquiry and the habits of mind—or *dispositions* as one writer describes them—that lead students to see how writing can be a process of discovery.

Start with Questions, Not Answers

A lot of people think that writing is about recording what you already know, which accounts for those who choose familiar topics to write on when given the choice. "I think I'll write about _____," the thinking goes, "because I know that topic really well and already have an idea what I can say." Unfortunately, the result of writing about what you already know is too often an uninspired draft full of generalizations and clichés.

What do you do about this problem? *Make the familiar strange.* This means finding ways to see what you've seen before in ways you haven't yet seen it. For years, I've asked some of my writing students to take photographs of any subject they want. Predictably, most students choose to take pictures of familiar things—their rooms or apartments, the trees outside the window, campus buildings, local landscapes—and they almost always take one picture of each subject. The result is that these photographs are rarely surprising. They see these familiar subjects in very familiar ways. But when I ask them to return to a single subject and take multiple pictures of it there are almost always surprises, and fresh ways of seeing the subject.

It's apparent that there are multiple ways of seeing the same thing, and of course this is one of the things that we often admire about good writing—it offers a perspective on something familiar that we hadn't considered before. One of the ways writers accomplish this is by using questions. Questions shift a writer's perspective on a subject much like distance, angle, and light alter a photographer's ways of seeing a tree or a building.

Therefore, in an inquiry-based approach to writing, you'll choose a writing topic that raises questions about how you think or feel over one that you have all figured out. Almost any topic can raise interesting questions. *There are no boring topics, only uninteresting questions.* The key is to approach any topic with a sense of wonder and curiosity: *Why are houseflies so hard to kill? What distinguishes the cultures of skaters and snowboarders? When do most marriages fail and what can be done about it? Why do young people join gangs?*

Suspend Judgment

What's one of the most common problems I see in student writers? Poor grammar? Lack of organization? A missing thesis? Nope. *It's the tendency to judge too soon and too harshly.* A great majority of my students, including really smart, capable writers, have powerful internal critics, or as the novelist Gail Godwin once called them, "Watchers at the Gates." This is the voice you may hear when you're starting to write a paper, the one that has you crossing out that first sentence or that first paragraph over and over until you "get it perfect." As you'll see later, this voice isn't demonic; you need it. "Watchers at the Gates" are, as Godwin said, "excellent critics after inspiration has been captured" and "dependable, sharp-eyed readers of things already set down." The problem, of course, is that many of us allow our Watchers to keep us from setting down much of anything. The blank page or screen offers nothing for our internal critics to scrutinize except the glaring failure to get words on the page or screen in the first place.

I've seen "bad" writing transform students who once hated writing into people who see writing as a useful tool for thinking, and even a source of pleasure.

The only way to overcome this problem is to suspend judgment. In doing so, you essentially tell your Watchers this: *It's okay to write badly.*

I never try to write badly, of course, but whenever I'm stuck in the middle of something, or can't figure out what to say or where to begin, or

WRITING WITH COMPUTERS

KEEPING AN ELECTRONIC JOURNAL

If you decide to do most of your journal writing on a computer, you should get in the habit of periodically backing up your work on a separate drive, diskette, or comparable storage device. You should also print out hard copies of your work (even if they contain errors—remember you are permitted to write "badly") and keep them in a three-ring binder. Computers can crash, taking all of your files with them. Also, when it comes time to read back over your own writing, the printed page is usually easier on the eyes than a computer screen. Keep in mind, too, that writing on a computer can feel more formal than writing by hand, a feeling that could potentially disrupt the uninterrupted flow of your fastwriting. To eliminate potential distractions, you might consider blacking out your computer screen or, if you have trouble typing without seeing your words, at least turning off the automatic spell and grammar check functions of your word processor. Finally, even though computers can be a useful tool for the journal writer, it is still wise to keep a small, paper journal with you at all times so that you can record your thoughts whenever you feel the need to do so, not just when you are sitting in front of a computer.

even when I don't have a clue about my subject, I simply start writing. Sometimes it's absolutely horrible. But just as often, there's a glint of an idea, or direction, or topic, and away I go, trying to keep up with the vein of thought branching in all directions. The British novelist E. M. Forster once said, "How do I know what I think until I see what I say?" I've come to have a lot of faith in this idea. Rather than using my journal the way I used to—to try to write beautiful, eloquent prose—I use the journal simply to think things through; that the prose stinks sometimes doesn't bother me anymore.

We know how powerful our internal critics can be, insisting that every word be spelled right, and every thought sharp. Our Watchers can't abide bad writing. One of the conditions that makes bad writing possible for me is that my Watchers are not voices I honor in my journal, at least not when I want to use my journal to think something through.

Now, I know it must seem odd that a book on writing would talk about the virtues of writing badly, but it can be a useful tool for solving all kinds of writing problems. It's an approach I encourage you to use throughout *The Curious Writer*. I've seen bad writing turn slow writers into faster ones, procrastinators into initiators. I've seen bad writing help students who always wrote short papers begin to generate longer, more thoughtful essays. Best of all, I've seen bad writing transform students who once hated writing into people who see writing as useful tool for thinking, and even a source of pleasure.

Conditions That Make "Bad" Writing Possible

1. Willingness to suspend judgment.
2. Ability to write fast enough to outrun your internal critic.
3. Belief that confusion, uncertainty, and ambiguity help thought rather than hinder it.
4. Interest in writing about "risky" subjects, or those that you don't know what you want to say about until you say it.

Search for Surprise

One of the key benefits of writing badly is *surprise*. This was a revelation for me when I first discovered the virtues of bad writing in graduate school. I was convinced that you never pick up the pen unless you know what you want to say, which may account for my struggles with journal writing. Suddenly, I stumbled on a new way to use writing—not to *record* what I already knew about a subject, but to *discover* what I actually thought. This way of writing promised a feast of surprises that made me hunger to put words on the page.

E X E R C I S E   1 . 2

A Roomful of Details

STEP ONE: Spend ten minutes brainstorming a list of details based on the prompt below. Write down whatever comes into your mind, no matter how silly. Be specific and don't censor yourself.

> Try to remember a room you spent a lot of time in as a child. It may be your bedroom in the back of the house at the edge of the field, or the kitchen where your grandmother kneaded bread or made thick red pasta sauce. Put yourself back in that room. Now look around you. What do you see? What do you hear? What do you smell?

STEP TWO: Examine your list. If things went well, you will have a fairly long list of details. As you review the list, identify one detail that

Brainstorming

- Anything goes.
- Don't censor yourself.
- Write everything down.
- Be playful but stay focused.

surprises you the most, a detail that seems somehow to carry an unexpected charge. This might be a detail that seems connected to a feeling or story. You might be drawn to a detail that confuses you a little. Whatever its particular appeal, circle the detail.

STEP THREE: Use the circled detail as a prompt for a seven-minute fastwrite. Begin by focusing on the detail: What does it make you think of? And then what? And then? Alternatively, begin by simply describing the detail more fully: What does it look like? Where did it come from? What stories are attached to it? How does it make you feel? Avoid writing in generalities. Write about specifics, that is, particular times and places, moments and people. Write fast, and chase after the words to see where they want to go. Give yourself permission to write badly.

ONE STUDENT'S RESPONSE

MARGARET'S JOURNAL

EXERCISE 1.2

STEP THREE

Detail: Pillows that spelled our names

The pillows that spelled our names sat on our beds against the wall. I slept on the top bunk, I think. Mostly I think I wanted the bunk that she got—if she was on the bottom then I wanted it. If she wanted the top then that was inevitably the coolest bunk. My pillows spelled out "Margy" in red, green fabric, with white lace tracing the edges. They were ugly, Christmassy shades, antiquish. Freckly. Our mom made them just for us girls, not the three boys. I didn't get my whole name spelled out because it is eight letters long, but Chelsea got all seven of hers. Her colors were blue-yellow, a color scheme that to this day I find elegant and beautiful. Her colors were fresh and alive and mine seemed dusty, old, plain, like my old-lady name . . . But they were fun, they made bed-making an exercise in identity, these are my colors—red, green, brown like my hair and eyes and freckles and hers were gold like her almost white blond hair and bright blue eyes. This is us. . .

"Did anything surprise you?" That's one of the first questions I ask my students after an open-ended fastwriting exercise. With any exercise, some students answer, "No, nothing surprised me." But there are almost always an equal number of students who nod, or who simply ignore the question because they haven't stopped writing even after the time is up. This is the experience I most want my students to have, particularly early in a writing course, because they discover, often for the first time, that they can write to learn more about something.

There are at least three kinds of surprise you may experience after completing a fastwriting exercise like the one above:

1. Surprise about *how much* writing you did: "I never thought I had that much to say about that." Even if the writing doesn't lead to an essay or provide material for an assignment, this discovery is crucial. Remember, the fastwriting was prompted by just one detail. "Who would have guessed that I could write three pages about a broken old chair!"

2. Surprise about discovering an *unexpected topic.* The poet Richard Hugo wrote that there were two kinds of these—triggering topics and generated topics. Writers often begin with one idea about their subject, but the writing leads them to another, better idea, one they wouldn't have discovered without following the trail of words.

3. Surprise about discovering a *new way of understanding a topic.* Consider Margaret's response to Exercise 1.2 in *One Student's Response* above. Margaret writes about embroidered pillows she and her sister received from their mother, a seemingly innocuous detail until her writing suddenly takes a reflective turn: *They made bed-making an exercise in identity* . . . Quite unexpectedly, Margaret has discovered new way of understanding her childhood bed pillows.

The kind of surprises you encounter doing this sort of writing may not always be profound. They may not even provide you with obvious essay topics. With any luck, though, by hunting for surprises in your own work you will begin to experience the pleasure of writing *to learn.* That's no small thing, particularly if you've always believed writers should have it all figured out before they pick up the pen.

Finally, remember that *the more you look the more you see.* Memories, texts, objects, data, experiences, art, whatever, are all much more likely to yield surprise if we prolong our gaze, resisting the temptation to rush to easy conclusions.

INQUIRING INTO THE DETAILS

INVENTION STRATEGIES

Perhaps without knowing it, you have already practiced some writing techniques designed to help you generate material. These *invention strategies* include fastwriting, listing, brainstorming, questioning, and even conversation. You can use these techniques in any writing situation when you need to gather more information, find a topic, or explore what you think. We call on these strategies often in the exercises and assignments that follow.

At first, spending time doing all this writing and thinking before you actually begin a draft may seem like waste of time. After all, your goal is to finish the assignment. But if you want to find a focused topic that means something to you and write it with enough information, then invention strategies such as fastwriting will prove invaluable. They produce the raw material that can be shaped, like clay on a potter's wheel, into something with form and meaning. But really the best thing about invention strategies is that they often generate material that is ripe with surprise.

Invention Strategies

- **Fastwriting:** The emphasis is on speed, not correctness. Don't compose, don't think about what you want to say before you say it. Instead, let the writing lead, helping you to discover what you think.

- **Listing:** Fast lists can help you generate lots of information quickly. They will often be in code, with words and phrases that have meaning only for you. Let your lists grow in waves—think of two or three items and then pause until the next few items rush in.

- **Clustering:** This nonlinear method of generating information, also called mapping, relies on webs and often free association of ideas or information. Begin with a core word, phrase, or concept at the center of a page, and build branches off it. Follow each branch until it dies out, return to the core and build another. (See page 126.)

- **Questioning:** Questions are to ideas what knives are to onions. They help you to cut through to the less obvious insights and perspectives, revealing layers of possible meanings, interpretations, and ways of understanding. Asking questions complicates things but rewards you with new discoveries.

- **Conversing:** Fastwriting with the mouth. When we talk, especially to someone we trust, we work out what we think and feel about things. We listen to what we say, but we also invite a response, which leads us to new insights.

- **Researching:** This is a kind of conversation, too. We listen and respond to other voices who have said something or will say something if asked about topics that interest us. Reading and interviewing are not simply things you do when you write a research paper but activities to use whenever you have questions you can't answer on your own.

- **Observing:** When we look closely at anything we see what we didn't notice at first. Careful observation of people, objects, experiments, images, and so on generates specific information that leads to informed judgment.

WRITING AS A PROCESS

Hunting is not those heads on the wall. This is the title of an essay by Amiri Baraka, a writer and intellectual, who argues that it is the *process* of bringing art into being that is the essential element of a creative act, not the end product. In other words, it's the *act* of painting, not the painting itself that matters most. I wouldn't go quite that far when describing writing—the process and the final product are inseparable—but generally students pay far too little attention to the writing process in their rush to get the writing done. The result is that rich possibilities, including new ideas and perspectives, are short-circuited before they have a chance to be explored. The key to writing well is to understand the writing process. That way we get more control over it.

Recognizing the Challenges

There are no writers who don't have challenges of some kind: *There are no writers, including those who publish, who don't face difficulties in their writing.* The difference between an experienced writer and a less experienced one is that the experienced writer recognizes the challenges and has figured out ways to solve them.

Consider, for example, the process of John McPhee, a writer of creative nonfiction articles and books on topics ranging from birch bark canoes to oranges. Pulitzer Prize winner McPhee is of the "stone-kicking school" of journalism; its philosophy is that if you want to discover the story you want to tell, you must spend a lot of time just hanging around with the people who know something about your subject. McPhee does this, spending as much as a year interviewing and observing people and things, as well as reading up on his subject. The result of this kind of investigation is pages and pages of notes, a mother lode of information, and this is McPhee's writing challenge: how to organize all that information and find the story he wants to tell. Over the years, McPhee has worked this out. When his notes get lengthy, he organizes them by topic in three ring binders, and then he transfers the topics to index cards, which he posts on a bulletin board above his desk. McPhee constantly plays with the order of the cards, experimenting with different beginnings, middles, and ends, constantly on the hunt for a structure that will bring all the information to life. When he finds it, he begins writing the piece, following the trail he worked out on the bulletin board in front of him.

John McPhee established this process through trial and error. He stuck with the strategies that seemed to improve the results and abandoned the strategies that didn't. I offer you this story not because McPhee's process is one I recommend. It's an approach that's peculiar to this one writer in a particular situation, a writer who must figure out how to orga-

The writer John McPhee, winner of
the Pulitzer Prize.

nize a tremendous amount of information in a meaningful way. What I
want to suggest is that if you recognize your writing challenges as solvable
issues that are often related to *how* you approach a particular writing task,
then you will become a more versatile and more skilled writer. Seeing the
link between writing challenges and the writing process means that most
writers can improve if they become more aware of *how* they approach a
particular writing situation that creates the challenges for them.

EXERCISE 1.3

What Is Your Process?

Take a moment and analyze your own writing challenges. The following
questions might help you develop a profile of your writing process in certain situations, and help you identify problems you might want to address
by altering your process.

STEP ONE: Complete the Self-Evaluation Survey.

Self-Evaluation Survey

1. When you're given a school writing assignment, do you wait until the last minute to get it done?

    Always——Often——Sometimes——Rarely——Never

2. How often have you had the experience of learning something you didn't expect through writing about it?

    Very often——Fairly often——Sometimes——Rarely——Never

3. Do you generally plan out what you're going to write before you write it?

    Always——Often——Sometimes——Rarely——Never

4. "Prewriting" is used to describe activities that some writers engage in before they begin a first draft. They might include freewriting or fast-writing, making lists, brainstorming or mapping, collecting informa-tion, talking to someone about the essay topic, reading up on it, or jot-ting down ideas in a notebook or journal. How much prewriting do you tend to do for the following types of assignments? Circle the ap-propriate answer.

    *   A personal essay:

        A great deal——Some——Very little——None——Haven't written one
    *   A critical essay about a short story, novel, or poem:

        A great deal——Some——Very little——None——Haven't written one
    *   A research paper:

        A great deal——Some——Very little——None——Haven't written one
    *   An essay exam:

        A great deal——Some——Very little——None——Haven't written one

5. At what point in writing an academic paper do you usually get stuck? Check all that apply.

    ❑ Getting started

    ❑ In the middle

    ❑ Finishing

    ❑ I never get stuck (go on to Question 9)

    ❑ Other _____

6. If you usually have problems getting started on an academic paper or essay, which of the following do you often find hardest to do? Check

all that apply. (If you don't have trouble getting started, go on to Question 7.)

❑ Deciding on a topic

❑ Writing an introduction

❑ Finding a good place to write

❑ Figuring out exactly what you're supposed to do for the assignment

❑ Finding a purpose or focus for the paper

❑ Finding the right tone

❑ Other _____

7. If you usually get stuck in the middle of a paper, which of the following causes the most problems? (If writing in the middle of a paper isn't a problem for you, go on to Question 8.)

❑ Keeping focused on the topic

❑ Finding enough information to meet page length requirements

❑ Following my plan for how I wanted to write the paper

❑ Bringing in other research or points of view

❑ Organizing all my information

❑ Trying to avoid plagiarism

❑ Worrying about whether the paper meets the requirements of the assignment

❑ Worrying that the paper just isn't any good

❑ Messing with citations

❑ Other _____

8. If you have difficulty finishing an essay or paper, which of the following difficulties are typical for you? Check all that apply.

❑ Composing a last paragraph or conclusion

❑ Worrying that the paper doesn't meet the requirements of the assignment

❑ Worrying that the paper just isn't any good

❑ Trying to keep focused on the main idea or thesis

❑ Trying to avoid repeating yourself

❑ Realizing you don't have enough information

❑ Dealing with the bibliography or citations

❑ Other _____

9. Rank the following descriptions or approaches to revision so that it reflects the strategies you use *most often to least often* when rewriting academic papers. Rank the items 1–6, with the strategy you use most often as a 1 and least often as a 6.

_____ I usually just tidy things up—editing sentences, checking spelling, looking for grammatical errors and other proofreading activities.

_____ I mostly look for ways to reorganize existing information in the draft to make it more effective.

_____ I generally try to fill holes by adding more information.

_____ I do more research.

_____ I often completely change the focus or even the main idea in the revision, rewriting sections, adding or removing information, and rearranging the order of things.

_____ I rarely do any rewriting at all.

_____ Other (please describe) _____

10. Finally, do you tend to impose a lot of conditions on when, where, or how you think you write most effectively? For example, do you need a certain pen, do you always have to write on a computer, must it be quiet or noisy, or do you often write best under pressure? Are there certain kinds of places you need to be to write effectively? Or can you write under a range of circumstances, with few or no conditions? Circle one.

Lots of conditions——Some——A few——No conditions

If you do impose conditions on when, where, or how you write, create a list below of what some of those conditions are:

1.

2.

3.

4.

STEP TWO: In small groups, discuss the results of the survey. Begin by picking someone who will be in charge of tallying the answers to each question. Post these on the board or a piece of newsprint so they can be added to the class totals. Analyze the results for your group. In particular, discuss the following questions:

- Are there patterns in the responses? Do most group members seem to answer certain questions in similar or different ways? Are there interesting contradictions?
- Based on these results, what "typical" habits or challenges do writers in your class seem to share?
- What struck you most?

Thinking About Your Process

We are creatures of habit. This applies to writing, too. Even experienced writers have deeply ingrained habits, some of them quite sensible, some quirky. Donald Murray always works in the morning and always in his basement office with a view of the river. Novelist Mitch Wieland always writes with a No. 2 pencil and a yellow legal pad; only later does he compose on the computer. Some writers must smoke, chew gum, or drink. Some must write in bed. Rachel, a former student, would always come to class on the day a draft was due with dark circles under her eyes; she insisted that the only way she could write good papers was to pull an all-nighter before the assignment was due.

When we do something more than a few times we often develop habits like these. Sometimes we don't even think about them. But we develop other habits with some awareness—waiting until the last minute to write a draft seemed to work for Rachel the first time she tried it, an accidental strategy she first used when she forgot a paper was due and was forced to crank it out at the last minute. Likewise, Mitch Wieland's fondness for pencils and legal pads to draft a short story or novel is a practice he developed early on without much deliberation. He likes the way he thinks with a pencil in his hand, and perhaps the feel and sound of the lead scratching on paper.

The habits we consciously develop become less conscious as time goes on, and pretty soon it isn't even a question whether television and school work mix well together, or if last-minute drafts are the only way to compose. When these habits *are* scrutinized, we often immediately assume that they are part of the best—if not the *only*—way to proceed with a task. "It's always worked for me," Rachel said every time.

However, reflecting on *how* we go about doing something is as central to intellectual activities as it is to athletic ones. Coaches often help a tennis player deconstruct and then revise a backhand, or a swimmer refine a flip turn, but consider how infrequently we do this kind of reflection on how we do academic tasks. *Metacognitive thinking,* or thinking about thinking, is a fairly sophisticated intellectual activity but it's an essential one for this simple reason: *The more we think about a process the more control we get over it.*

Reading and writing are two processes that are central to life—including academic life—and the time you spend reflecting on how you engage in both activities is time well spent. That's why the composition course emphasizes discussion and analysis of the writing process, and will include many moments like the one I had with Rachel after she told me that she wrote her best stuff at the last minute.

"Are you sure?" I asked.

"I think so," she said. "But I never really thought about it much."

The survey you completed is the beginning of reflection on your own writing process. This kind of reflection will be done again and again throughout this book so that by the end you will have written a narrative of thought that tells the story of your reading and writing processes, and how you change those processes to produce better writing more efficiently. The reflective letter in your portfolio (see Appendix A), might be where you finally tell that story in full, perhaps beginning with what the survey revealed about your own habits, rituals, and challenges as you began this book.

Linear versus Recursive Models

There is no single writing process—a kind of recipe every writer can follow—that will reliably produce "good" writing. But there are certain elements of the writing process that are fairly common to all writers. What distinguishes one writer's process from another's is *when* they invoke an element and in what situations. Timing is crucial in the writing process, as it is in any process from making fudge to space shuttles. But what are these elements of the writing process? Many experts have proposed models to describe it. You may be familiar with some of the models. For example, one of the simplest models for the writing process is depicted in Figure 1.2, which shows a linear model that moves, step by step, from prewriting to writing to rewriting. Typically, prewriting represents things a writer does to generate information and clarify intention. The term from classical rhetoric that roughly equates with prewriting is *invention.* As we discussed earlier, prewriting can include a range of activities from brainstorming

FIGURE 1.2   **A linear model of the writing process.**

and fastwriting to note taking, conversation, and formal research. Writing is the process of producing the draft. Rewriting, of course, is revision and all that it entails, from tidying up sentences to entirely changing a paper's focus or even its topic.

The only problem with the linear model is that it moves in one direction, and most writing theorists agree that the writing process just doesn't work that way. Instead, movement within the process proceeds in a *recursive* fashion, that is, it moves back and forth from one stage to the next. Writers do not simply march forward, step-by-step, completing one stage of the writing process and then moving on to a subsequent stage. Writing, like life, is more complicated than that. For example, I initially drafted this chapter fairly quickly, relying on what I already knew about writing process models. Only later did I consult the books on my shelf and collect more information about the writing process—double-checking what I had said and adding information I may not have thought of at the time of my initial draft. When I have some background knowledge about my subject my approach often is to draft *and then* prewrite *and then* rewrite.

In other words, writers don't always begin at the "beginning" of the writing process and they may return to a step they've already attempted. Sometimes they'll leap over a step or return to it later. A better description of the writing process, then, looks like Figure 1.3.

Remember the rhetorical triangle we discussed earlier? How you approached the writing process depends on each of the three elements in the triangle: yourself, your audience, and your subject. The genre—or the form you are writing in—also makes a difference. For example, you won't use the same writing process to compose an essay exam that you would to write a journal entry.

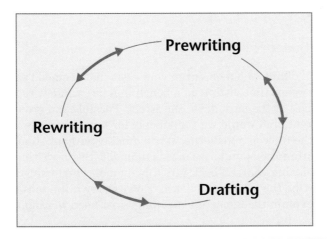

FIGURE 1.3   **A recursive model of the writing process.**

Dialectical Thinking

The recursive model of the writing process focuses on the back and forth movement between the different stages of process. The sort of thinking writers do as they move through the process also is done in a back and forth manner, but instead of moving between the different stages of the process, *dialectical thinking* shifts between two contrasting modes of thought, one creative and the other critical in nature.

The word *dialectical* has several meanings, many of which focus on the relationship between opposing ideas or forces. In dialectical thinking, it is the relationship between creative and critical modes of thought that is important. Why? Because the interplay between the creative and the critical can foster new and deeper ways of understanding.

Dialectical thinking is not something that comes naturally to most people and, while you might think otherwise, the critical mode of thought isn't the problem. I mentioned earlier that most writers have strong internal critics—the "Watchers at the Gates" who are quick to criticize and judge. "That's a stupid sentence," they hiss. "You really don't know what you're trying to say, do you?" The critical self is all too present for most of us. What we tend to be less aware of is our creative self. This side may surface in a fastwrite that uncovers an unexpected subject, or in the pleasure of making lists of places you remember from childhood. Much like children, our creative selves are playful, open to surprise and discovery.

One of the key benefits of writing badly is surprise.

Unfortunately, for many writing students these two selves are often at war with each other. This is a pity. Imagine the results if you could get the creative and the critical to collaborate. As a writer, you could be both playful *and* judgmental, open things up *and* narrow them down. That's the key to dialectical thinking when it's applied to the writing process.

EXERCISE 1.4

Practicing Dialectical Thinking

STEP ONE: Think of a moment in your past that seemed typical for you. Perhaps you spent time sitting on a bench in a bay window reading or playing football at the park down the street. Possibly you grew up with an alcoholic parent, and would wait anxiously for him to come home. Use this moment as the topic of a *fastwrite*. Write quickly without stopping but try to remain within the boundaries of this moment. Begin writing in the present tense, putting yourself back into this moment, and using all of your senses. Describe the moment in detail. Don't worry if the tense shifts, and don't try to explain the moment's meaning. Just keep writing.

STEP TWO: After your fastwrite, skip a few lines in your journal, and compose a response to one or more of the following questions about your writing experience.

- What difference would it make in how you approached the fastwrite if you knew that you would read the results aloud to others?
- Did you imagine an audience other than yourself?
- What, if anything, surprised you?
- What problems arose during the fastwrite, if any, and how did you resolve them?
- Was there anything different about the ways you approached the writing from the ways you usually do?

STEP THREE: Reread your initial fastwrite, underlining words, lines, or passages that seem significant in some way. Now compose a short paragraph that begins with the following words:

As I look back on the moment, I now realize that. . .

STEP FOUR: Make another entry in your notebook that reflects on your experience with the preceding step. Compare and contrast your experience composing the paragraph in Step Three with that of the fastwrite in Step One. The following questions might help you think about this.

- What distinguishes the writing in Step Three from Step One? For example, did you feel more emotionally involved with one or the other?
- Which was harder to write? Why?
- Which seemed to yield the most surprises?
- Which step required the most thought? What kind of thinking did it seem to demand?
- What problems arose, if any, in Step Three that didn't arise in Step One? Or were the problems similar? How did you resolve them?

ONE STUDENT'S RESPONSE

JON'S JOURNAL

EXERCISE 1.4

STEP ONE

Birds chirp overhead as the squirrels quickly dash through the branches like schoolchildren would burst through the door at recess. Directly behind me, Aunty Val is hanging her laundry out to dry. Directly in front of me lies the sort of structure that all children would dream of having. It's as tall as my house! A rope dangles from the top down to the ground. I have never climbed this to the top and I don't think that I ever will. If I ever got to the top of this structure, I would climb the wooden ladder built on the side. Or maybe take the few steps up to the monkey bars, swing to the end, and try to climb up from there. But I rarely paid any attention to this structure at all. Today is no exception. I am sitting in the sandbox with my springer spaniel and the dismembered corpses of hundreds of GI Joes that felt the heat of battle and now lay in shallow, unmarked sand graves . . . I can hear my brothers and the neighbor kid fight over who shot first, why he didn't die, and whether or not he was wearing Kevlar. That was the beauty of the GI Joes, they didn't whine, or cheat. When it was their time they simply snapped and died. Then, they were satisfied with mass burials. . .

STEP THREE
As I look back on this moment, I realize that as a child, I was extremely self-contained. I could keep myself entertained as easily, if not better than I could be entertained by others. I wonder what changed between now and then? Now, I hate being alone. . .

STEP FOUR
In step one, I created a meaningless scene. In step three, I learned something from the scene. I felt emotionally tied to this paragraph. It made me look at something that I hadn't before, I used to be an introvert. . .

Calling the two opposed modes of thought creative and critical is a helpful shorthand for the different *types* of thought. But "seeing" what I mean might be helpful.

In Figure 1.4, creative thinking is represented by the Sea and critical thinking by the Mountain. Exercise 1.2 provided a recent experience of swimming in the Sea—during the fastwriting you swam like mad, immersing yourself in details you remembered about a childhood moment.

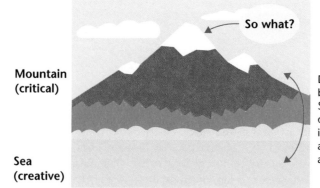

Mountain (critical)

So what?

Dialectical movement back and forth from Sea to Mountain: observations of and ideas about believing and doubting, specifics and generalities.

Sea (creative)

FIGURE 1.4   Dialectical thinking: the Mountain and the Sea.

You may have found yourself encountering specifics you did not know you knew, collecting information about the moment that wasn't easily recovered any other way. This was the work of creative thinking. In the Sea, we often swim fast and even recklessly, hoping to bump into something interesting. You are swimming in the Sea whenever you suspend judgment and generate raw material through fastwriting, brainstorming, mapping, listing and other open-ended writing techniques. The Sea is often a pleasant place to be: Our internal critics are at ease; we are usually writing only for our own eyes; and there is often a certain playfulness to our work that encourages surprise and discovery, which is what creative thinking is all about.

The Mountain, on the other hand, provides a convenient vantage point for seeing where it is we've swum. It is on the Mountain that we begin to notice patterns of meaning in the Sea. Note in the excerpt from Jon's journal above how a seemingly meaningless scene describing play with toy soldiers acquires substance when Jon is forced to place the experience in perspective. Jon is essentially looking down from the Mountain onto the Sea below. Exercise 1.4 showed you what it's like to climb the Mountain. In Step Three, I encouraged you to reread your initial fastwrite critically, and compose a brief reflective passage that began *As I look back on this, I now realize that. . .* I was attempting to force you from the creative mode of thinking—the Sea—to a critical mode—the Mountain.

On the Mountain you ask questions like these:

- What seems important here?
- What do I understand now that I didn't understand then?
- Are there any patterns in the information I've collected or the story I've told?
- What details seem significant? Why?

Many students tell me that climbing the Mountain forces them to have more emotional distance from their material, to begin to consider their audience, to ask questions such as, "What sense might someone else make of this material?" But there is one question that should keep popping into your head while you are looking down from the Mountain onto the Sea. It is a question that ultimately every piece of writing must answer:

So what?

So what? can be a pretty harsh question, and I find some students tend to ask it too soon in the writing process, before they've fully explored their topic or collected enough information. That may have been your experience when you suddenly found yourself high and dry, forced to reflect on possible meanings of a moment you've only written about for eight minutes. When you can't come up with an answer to *So what?,* it's time to climb down off the Mountain and return to the Sea, where you will seek more details, more information, and more evidence.

There's another danger, too. Some writers insist on climbing too high on the Mountain in their enthusiasm to find the idea, the concept, the thesis, or even the lesson that seems to account for what they've found in the sea. At high altitudes, abstractions abound. For example, Thomas started writing about his experience of returning to his neighborhood after being away at school. It seemed strange. Everything seemed different, and Thomas found it especially awkward spending time with a few of his old friends. When he jumped into the Sea, Thomas found himself writing about an argument he had with his best friend one night. When prompted to reflect on this moment, he concluded that "true friends are hard to find" (see Figure 1.5). Such an idea is so big, so abstract, and so familiar that it doesn't really say much. Thomas answered the *So what?* question, but climbed too high to find the answer.

It is on the beach, not on the summit of the Mountain, where writers should spend most of their time. The beach is close to the Sea and what it offers—the details, the memories, the evidence—is the information that

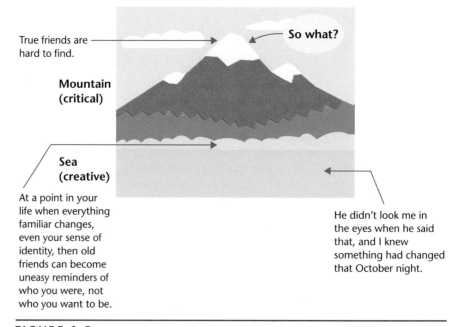

FIGURE 1.5   **Dialectical thinking: the Mountain and the Sea, Thomas' example.**

needs to be refined, shaped, and qualified by critical thinking. On the beach, Thomas discovers a more specific, more surprising way of understanding his experience: "At a point in your life when everything familiar changes, even your sense of identity, then old friends can become an uneasy reminder of who you were, not who you want to be."

Remember, too, this process is *dialectical;* it consists of a back and forth conversation between two opposing modes of thought. The writing process is always more productive if the writer alternates between the Sea and the Mountain—from creative thinking to critical thinking. Generate information and then reflect on its meaning and then generate some more. As you start to develop a thesis on the Mountain, plunge back into the Sea to test it against the evidence, then emerge from the water and refine the thesis some more.

What I'm describing through this metaphor is an action that many writers do instinctively. As they're composing, they're constantly shifting between contrasting modes of thought, from collecting to focusing, from generating to criticizing, from showing to telling, from exploring to reflecting, from believing to doubting, from playing to judging (see Figure 1.6).

Certain activities—such as fastwriting and composing—encourage these contrary ways of thinking. Learning to balance these opposing forces is what dialectical thinking is all about. In practice, however, many begin-

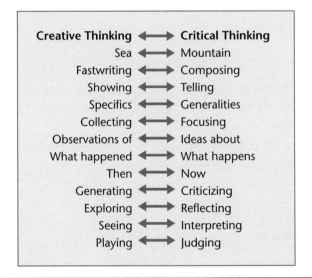

Creative Thinking	⟷	Critical Thinking
Sea	⟷	Mountain
Fastwriting	⟷	Composing
Showing	⟷	Telling
Specifics	⟷	Generalities
Collecting	⟷	Focusing
Observations of	⟷	Ideas about
What happened	⟷	What happens
Then	⟷	Now
Generating	⟷	Criticizing
Exploring	⟷	Reflecting
Seeing	⟷	Interpreting
Playing	⟷	Judging

FIGURE 1.6 When writers use dialectical thinking, they move back and forth between two opposing modes of thought—the creative and the critical. One seems playful and the other judgmental; one feels open-ended and the other more closed. Certain activities such as fastwriting or brainstorming promote one mode of thought, and careful composing or reflection promotes another.

ning writers give too much emphasis to either one mode of thinking or the other, a tendency that accounts for many of the challenges these writers face within their own writing processes.

Spend too much time locked in the critical mode of thinking and your internal critic takes over. This voice pinches off the flow of material generated by creative thinking. The writing then comes slowly and painfully, and it rarely yields surprise. Topics are abandoned before the writer fully has explored their potential. Working from scarcity, the writer is compelled to use all the material they have at hand, often resulting in writing that feels forced, incomplete, or obvious.

On the other hand, give too much free reign to creative thinking and the artist runs wild. The problem here isn't scarcity but rather overabundance. It's a poverty of riches, for without a critical eye to provide shape and direction, the writer is unable to present all of his material in a coherent and meaningful fashion.

Other challenges result when writers fail to move back and forth between creative and critical modes. One excursion into creative thinking followed by a second into critical thinking is rarely enough to produce good writing. Writers need to move back and forth between the two modes until they come to see their topics in interesting ways that differ from what they might have creatively or critically thought about the topic when they started the writing process.

EXERCISE 1.5

Overcome Your Own Challenges

STEP ONE: Consult again the Self-Evaluation Survey you completed in Exercise 1.3. Based on what you've learned so far, answer the two bulleted questions below.

- What are the biggest challenges to your writing process?
- How can you overcome these challenges?

USING WHAT YOU HAVE LEARNED

When I was in college I used to say this to anyone who asked how I felt about writing: *I don't like writing but I love having written.* What I meant, of course, is that I often felt satisfaction with the product of writing—the paper or essay—but didn't like the work that it took to produce it. This belief didn't help me improve as a writer because it prevented me from finding things about the process that could actually be okay, and even pleasurable, things like finding out what I didn't know I knew. I never imagined surprise was possible. I hope this chapter initiated a reexamination of your own beliefs about writing. I hardly expect a revolution in your thinking, but maybe one or two things you once thought were true of writing may at least be in doubt, particularly if you think those beliefs get in the way of your progress. Carry that openness to revise your thinking into every assignment in this book and you may be surprised at what you can do.

You now know more about your writing process. You've identified what seems to go well and when you get into trouble. The habit of reflecting on your process will be invaluable as you face each new writing situation because each one presents different problems and choices. Understanding the basic rhetorical principles—considering how to present yourself to particular audiences on particular subjects—will help. You already know more than you think about rhetoric.

You'll also have the chance to try out dialectical thinking, a process that may seem a little dizzying. In a way, it should, because both the writing process and dialectical thinking involve a great deal of back and forth movement, the sort of mental gymnastics you perform with the pen in your hand or your fingers on the keyboard. I've pushed you into the Sea and forced you to climb the Mountain, shifting your thinking back and forth between creative and critical modes.

Does it feel natural? Probably not. At least not yet. But I hope you'll find that your understanding of the writing process becomes more intuitive as you read further in the book. You may modify your writing process, add a step here or skip one there, prolong the process or cut it short, depending on the writing situation and your rhetorical concerns. Whatever you do, though, you need to make choices based on an understanding of how they will influence your process. This is the key to making you a productive, confident writer.

If the popularity of the *Harry Potter* books is any indication, kids are still reading despite the competition for their free time from TV, films, and computer games. Indeed, the *Harry Potter* phenomenon is worldwide. The girl above, from Kuala Lumpur, Malaysia, waits in line to purchase a copy of *Harry Potter and the Order of the Phoenix*.

Reading as Inquiry

The day the fifth *Harry Potter* book came out, ticket sales tanked for the summer blockbuster *The Incredible Hulk.* J. K. Rowling's book's sales also easily eclipsed box office receipts for the movie's opening day, leading one observer to conclude that the "post-Napster generation" is not, as many believe, so wedded to MTV-inspired fast cuts and special effects that a long narrative can't sustain their attention. *Harry Potter and the Order of the Phoenix* is 870 pages.

Clearly, young people are still reading. Yet, while the dire predictions some people made warning about the impending end of literacy have been overblown, there is no denying that the written word is running up against some stiff competition. Images *are* powerful methods of communicating in contemporary American culture. Images, moving or otherwise, demand our attention and we give it willingly. We are image consumers, hungry for the latest Brad and Jennifer shots in *People,* live streaming video of rumbling Humvees in the Iraqi desert, digital pictures of a sister's new baby, and supposedly candid video from TV reality shows. Visual literacy—the ability to comprehend and interpret these images—is more important than ever.

By the time we get to college, of course, we tend to take literacy—both textual and visual—for granted. Sure, we may find an individual essay, story, image, or film to be moving, offensive, or difficult, but we rarely think very long about the effect that image or essay was designed to have on us, or how our own process of "reading" an image or essay might help us see this design.

My students fret about writing. But they don't seem to get very worked up about the challenges of reading. It doesn't seem nearly as complicated. But reading is complex, and in this chapter I'll show you how the writing process involves some of the same mental activities and even similar rhetorical choices used in reading. I'll also show you how writing can help you read better. And while how we "read" pictures is a great way to talk about the reading process generally, it's

What You'll Learn in This Chapter

- How your existing beliefs about reading might be obstacles to reading rhetorically.

- What connections exist between the writing and reading process.

- How to use the double-entry journal to encourage dialectical thinking.

- How to apply some of the same strategies to reading pictures that you do to reading texts.

- How to understand the unique grammar of images.

Americans have an insatiable appetite for celebrity photos, "reading" them carefully for a variety of meanings.

also a useful topic in its own right, since texts and images so often work together these days.

MOTIVES FOR READING

Why read? The reason for the *Harry Potter* phenomenon seems pretty clear: J. K. Rowling writes entertaining books. But pleasure is not a motive that seems to apply to most academic reading—it's just something you have to do to study for the test or write the paper. However, reading to inquire, while not always a source of pleasure, can offer the satisfaction of surprise and discovery, just as writing to inquire can. Think about why you typically read in academic situations:

- You read to comprehend information that may be on the test.
- You read to collect information that will help you write your paper.
- You read to analyze an issue or an argument that is relevant to the subject of a course.

• You read to describe the choices a writer made about how to say things.

All of these motives are relevant to reading for inquiry but they are always pursued in the context of your own investigation. In other words, you read because it will help answer questions that you have about a topic. This is, in part, an open-ended process in which you set out to discover what you think, and along the way welcome confusion and ambiguity as a natural condition of the search.

What does this mean? It means that you never read just to collect information, but you read to have a conversation with it. You go back and forth between what an author says and what you think about what he or she says. *Does this help answer a question I've posed? Does it inspire me to see things differently? Does it complicate what I already believe?*

Reading with the spirit of inquiry turns books, essays and articles into one side of a dialogue that you're having with yourself and an author. The meaning of a text (or an image) isn't fixed forever—engraved in stone tablets like a message from above—but worked out between the two of you, the author and the reader. This turns reading into a much more complicated intellectual activity, but it also makes reading more interesting because you create the conditions for surprise, for learning, and for discovery.

BELIEFS ABOUT READING

Most of us aren't very aware of our reading strategies and habits. Why should we be? After all, isn't reading just reading? How many ways can you do it? The way we go about learning how to read, however, is similar to the way we learn how to write. We start at an early age, perhaps even before we get to school. Along with the learning, we acquire beliefs that inform our response to *how* we read. These beliefs, though, can help or hinder our progress as readers. Once again, then, we need to assess our beliefs. Only by understanding *how* we read in certain situations can we acquire more control over what we get out of the reading experience.

EXERCISE 2.1

What Do You Believe?

STEP ONE: From the list below, choose *two* qualities that you believe best characterize a "good" reader.

1. Only has to read things once to understand what an author is saying.

2. Can find the hidden meanings in the text.

3. Takes notes while reading.

4. Reads slowly and carefully, and doesn't proceed unless she understands what she has read.

5. Pays attention to his feelings about what he is reading.

6. Tries to find support for what she already believes.

7. Understands that all sources and all authors are biased.

8. Tries to find the author's theme or thesis.

9. Focuses mostly on the important parts of the text, things such as the beginning, ending, and titles.

10. Pays most attention to details, facts, statistics.

11. Avoids reading things that don't interest him.

12. Reads with certain questions or goals in mind.

STEP TWO: Describe through fastwriting a moment or person you associate with reading. For example, fastwrite about sitting on the couch with your father, your head resting on his chest, feeling the vibrations of his chest as he read *Stuart Little*.

STEP THREE: Answer the following questions in your journal.

• Do you think you're a good reader? Why or why not?

• How would you describe your own reading habits and methods?

STEP FOUR: Share the results of the previous three steps in a class discussion and then consider the following questions:

• Did you find that your beliefs were widely shared by others in the class?

• Did you find that others generally considered themselves competent readers?

• Did all competent readers have similar beliefs and reading habits?

• How important were your early reading experiences in shaping your beliefs about reading?

Most reading instruction seems to focus on comprehension—you know, the SAT- or ACT-inspired kind of situation in which you are asked to read something and then explain what it means. This often becomes an exercise in recall and vocabulary, an analytical challenge in only the most general way. Essentially, you train yourself to distinguish between specifics and generalities, and loosely follow the author's reasoning. In English classes, sometimes we are asked to perform a similar exercise with stories or poems—what is the theme or what does it mean?

Questions such as these send students off on what is essentially an archeological expedition where they must dig for hidden meaning. The "right" answers to the questions are in the text, like a buried bone; you just have to find them. Sometimes the expedition is successful, sometimes not. The trouble with this type of exercise has less to with its success rate than it does with the belief that it tends to foster, which is that *all meaning resides in the text and the reader's job is merely to find it*. This belief limits the reader's interaction with the text. If meaning is fixed within the text, embedded like a bone in antediluvian mud, then all the reader has to do is dig to find that meaning. Digging isn't a bad thing, but reading can be so much more than laboring at the shovel and sifting through dirt.

Only by understanding how we read in certain situations can we acquire more control over what we get out of the reading experience.

Our many experiences with reading inside and outside of school inevitably lead us to develop assumptions about what reading demands. That's why it's so crucial to draw those beliefs into the open where you can examine them in the light.

READING SITUATIONS AND RHETORICAL CHOICES

It's impossible to make choices about how you should read without knowing the reading situation. *What are you reading? Why are you reading it?* Only by knowing the answers to these questions, can you make informed choices about *how* you should read. In this sense, reading situations demand the same sort of rhetorical choices that writing situations do. What's surprising, though, is that we rarely talk about choices when we discuss reading.

As a matter of fact, we rarely talk much about reading at all except to practice the reading skills that might help students do well on the reading comprehension section of the SAT or ACT. This is probably a good thing because those are high-stakes tests for college-bound students. But the Saturday morning computerized placement test is only one very specific rhetorical situation. Recall the rhetorical triangle—it also applies to reading situations.

In the reader's rhetorical triangle, the reader moves to the apex of the triangle and the writer moves down to one of the lower legs (see Figure 2.1). The reader's portion of the triangle includes the reader's purpose for reading the text and the particular habits and strategies he brings to his reading. The subject includes not only the main topic of the reading but the form or genre in which it is presented. The author's purpose shapes the third portion of the triangle. Combined, the three work to determine the context of each reading situation. The verbal SAT exam, for instance, in part involves reading short passages and answering multiple-choice comprehension questions. Speed is important. The significance of the test and

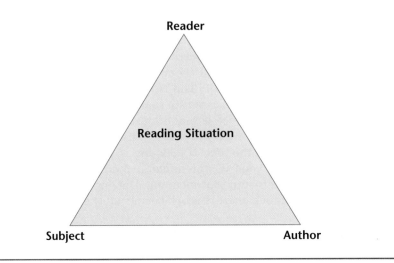

FIGURE 2.1 **The reader's rhetorical triangle.**

the speed required to complete it will influence the reader's portion of the triangle. So too will the subject, which is presented in the form of multiple-choice questions. The author's intent in composing the questions—to test comprehension—also plays its part in shaping the reading situation.

A test situation differs greatly from one in which the same person is asked to read a Ralph Ellison short story and write a critical essay about it for her English class. Here the author's perspective may be harder to interpret. The subject, presented in short story form, is also likely to be more ambiguous in its message than multiple choice questions. The reader also will bring different reading habits to the text, reading slowly and perhaps repeatedly, to tease out the meaning.

Each reading situation, then, requires its own rhetorical choices. But how do you know which rhetorical choices to make? A recent study of reading strategies used by college undergraduates found that what distinguished academically successful readers from those who were less successful was agreement with the following statement: *I evaluate whether what I am reading is relevant to my reading goals.*[1] Students with lower GPAs generally didn't consider goals when they were reading and rarely varied their reading strategies. The less successful readers made the same rhetorical choices regardless of the reading situation. The more successful readers, on the other hand, tailored their rhetorical choices to address the needs of the reading situation.

[1]Taraban, Roman, Kimberly Rynearson, and Marcell Kerr. "College Students' Academic Performance and Self-Reports of Comprehension Strategy Use." *Reading Psychology* 21 (2000): 283–308.

READING AS A PROCESS

Rhetorical reading begins with understanding reading as a process. As with the writing process, the more we know about our own reading process the more control we have over it and the more we are likely to get out of our reading. There's nothing difficult about understanding reading as a process, but doing so may challenge some of your existing beliefs about how reading works.

Linear versus Recursive Models

In the last chapter, I discussed two models for understanding the writing process. The first model moved in one direction from prewriting to writing to rewriting. The second model moved back and forth among these three stages. The two models of the reading process that I want you to consider here operate in a similar fashion. The conventional model is linear—information flows in one direction from the text to the readers (see Figure 2.2). Here, while the readers may have to actively dig within the text for information, the manner in which they receive the information is relatively passive. Meaning resides squarely within the text.

The second model is recursive. It suggests that our understanding of what a text means exists as a two-way *transaction* between the reader and author, the product of a back and forth dialogue between what the author is saying and what the reader thinks the author is saying (see Figure 2.3). In this model, the reader interprets, analyzes, reflects on, and thoroughly questions the information in the text; the meaning that emerges doesn't reside on the pages, but somewhere in between the reader and the text. As you will see, the recursive model of the reading process often involves writing *while* you read. You will also learn that the back and forth movement represented by this model is guided by the reading situation and the rhetorical choices that the reader makes in response to the situation.

FIGURE 2.2   A linear model of the reading process.

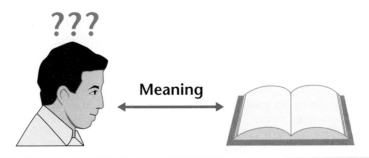

FIGURE 2.3   **A recursive model of the reading process.**

EXERCISE 2.2

Reading Strategies

STEP ONE: Read the following short excerpt from an article titled "Dinosaur Dreams: Reading the Bones of America's Psychic Mascot."

DINOSAUR DREAMS
Reading the Bones of America's Psychic Mascot
Jack Hitt

1   Sixty-five million years ago, conservatively speaking, the last dinosaurs lay down and died—on the ground, beside rivers, in tar pits. Then, about a hundred years ago, they got back up and have been pretty busy ever since. Hardly a week goes by that they don't make the news, because of a new theory about either how they lived or how they died. There might be word of a new prime-time TV deal, another revelry (Dinofest V is planned for next year), a new exhibit, the goings-on of paleontological hunk Paul Sereno, a Spielberg script, a hot toy, a legal dispute about some bones, an egg.

2   In America, where dinosaurs do most of their work (and always have), they periodically disappear from view and then resurface, like John Travolta or Democrats, capturing and losing our cycling interest. Dinosaurs are distinctly American, not only because our scholars have so often been at the forefront of fossil discoveries and paleontological theory but because the popular dinosaur is a wholly owned projection of the nationalist psyche of the United States. Their periodic rebirth in pop culture neatly signals deep tectonic shifts in our sense of ourself as a country.

Even glancing appearances can be telling. After Newt Gingrich rampaged through the House of Representatives and seized power in 1994, he placed a skull of T. rex in his office. When [President Bill Clinton] got a new dog, he called him, strangely, "Barney"—a name most closely associated with a phony dinosaur who masks his cheerful dimness with sticky compassion. ■

STEP TWO: Compose a summary of the passage in your journal. Make sure you express your understanding of the passage's main idea *in your own words*.

STEP THREE: Review the list of reading perspectives in the "Inquiring into the Details" box on page 46. Which perspectives did you use to complete the exercise? Also, make a list of the reading behaviors you used, if any, to complete the previous two steps. Reading behaviors include underlining, highlighting, note-taking, writing in the margin, listing, rereading, skimming, exploratory writing, conversation with others about the text, taking a break, or copying passages (see list below). When you are done, answer the following questions:

- Did you note any pattern to the way you used the behaviors (when, how much, which ones)? Were the perspectives you adopted pretty typical for you?
- Would you have used different behaviors or perspectives if your purpose had not been to summarize the passage but instead had been to write a one-page argument against the author's claims in the passage?

Types of Reading Behaviors

What do you actually *do*, if anything, when you read for school?
- Underline
- Highlight
- Make marginal notes
- Write in your journal
- Converse with someone about the text
- Reread
- Skim
- Take lots of breaks
- Copy down important passages or facts

A good first step to using the recursive model of the reading process is to find ways that you can *actively* interact with the text so that you're having a conversation with the material. Simple strategies such as underlining, highlighting, note-taking, writing in the margins, listing, or rereading help begin this conversation. Doing nothing—the default mode for many readers—is the intellectual equivalent of being a couch potato. Conversations also work best when *both* participants are listening and responding to each other, and like any conversation how you listen and respond depends on the stance or perspective you take toward what you're hearing.

The behaviors and perspectives that you use when reading depend on the rhetorical situation. For example, you'll likely mark up a poem in *The Longman Anthology of World Literature* differently than an article in *Sociology Quarterly*. If your motive is simply to summarize an article on Canada's drug laws, you'll ask yourself different questions than if you're analyzing the claims of an editorial on the ethics of downloading free music. But there are certain "essential acts of mind" that occur in almost all reading situations, and you'll find them mighty familiar.

INQUIRING INTO THE DETAILS

READING PERSPECTIVES

When we read, we always adopt certain perspectives toward a text, usually unconsciously. But one of the best ways to read strategically is to consciously *shift* our perspective while we read. Like changing lenses on a camera or changing the angle, distance, or time of day to photograph something, this shift in reading perspective illuminates different aspects of a text. Here are some of the perspectives you might take:

- **Believing:** What the author says is probably true. Which ideas can I relate to? What information should I use? What seems especially sound about the argument?

- **Doubting:** What are the text's weaknesses? What ideas don't jibe with my own experience? What are the gaps in the information or the argument? What isn't believable about this?

- **Updating:** What does this add to what I already know about the subject?

- **Hunting and Gathering:** What can I collect from the text that I might be able to use?

- **Interpreting:** What might be the meaning of this?

- **Pleasure Seeking:** I just want to enjoy the text and be entertained by it.

- **Connecting:** How does this information relate to my own experiences? What is its relationship to other things I've read? Does it verify, extend, or contradict what other authors have said?
- **Reflecting:** How was this written? What makes it particularly effective or ineffective?
- **Resisting:** This doesn't interest me. Why do I have to read it? Isn't "Survivor" on television right now?

Dialectical Thinking

The sort of thinking we do while engaged in the reading process is comparable to the thinking we do when involved in the writing process. We move back and forth between creative and critical modes of thought, shifting between specifics and generalities, collecting and focusing, narrating and criticizing, generating and reflecting. Again, this is dialectical thinking and the Mountain and Sea metaphor still applies (see Chapter 1). Many of the questions we asked for writing are the same for reading: *What does this mean? Why might this fact or detail be significant? How does this connect with what I already know? What do I understand from reading this that I didn't understand when I began? Is this believable and convincing?*

Like writers, readers sometimes climb the Mountain before they swim in the Sea. For example, one reader might begin with a particular purpose: He just bought a hand-held computer and must read the instructions to find out how it works. In this writing situation, there's very little need to swim, or use creative thinking. Instead, the reader climbs the Mountain, using critical thinking to decipher the instructions and apply them to the task at hand. But many texts we read in college are either much less explicit or much more challenging to understand than the instructions to a hand-held computer. Nor is the sense of purpose so obviously clear. How do we make sense of texts like these? Move back and forth between the two contrary modes of thought, trying to answer the same essential question that nags us as writers: *So what?*

I'll show you how this works. Consider the following fact from the October 2003 "Harper's Index," the magazine's monthly listing of information about nearly everything:

> Percentage of Palestinians in refugee camps who say that given a choice they would live nowhere but Israel: 10

What's the significance of this fragment of information? Does it seem important? In other words, *so what* if very few Palestinians in refugee camps would choose to live in Israel if given the chance? It's only possible to attach meaning to such a fact if you can bring your own knowledge to reading it. You have to supply the context. In this case, you need to know something about the Palestinian and Israeli conflict. Now, read the following two additional facts from the same issue of "Harper's Index."

> Percentage (of Palestinians in refugee camps) who say they would accept compensation and homes in a Palestinian state: 54

> Percentage of Jewish settlers in the West Bank and Gaza who say they would relocate if compensated: 83

What do all three facts add up to? Collectively, what do they imply about the conflict in the Middle East?

When you read this information, your initial encounter is with the facts themselves—you are merely collecting, open to a range of possible meanings. But to understand their significance you have to ascend the mountain where you can provide the outside knowledge you bring to your reading of almost anything: *Okay, I know that Jewish settlements on disputed lands are in the way of peace, and that some Palestinian leaders insist on claiming parts of the existing Israeli state. But these facts seem to suggest that both Jewish settlers and Palestinian refugees might be open to compromise.* Up on the Mountain, the patterns in what you read become apparent, preparing you for more encounters with information in the Sea as you read on.

It is this back and forth between Sea and Mountain, between collecting and interpreting, between generating and judging, that give rise to meaning and understanding when you read. There are some very practical ways to encourage this kind of thinking when you read, including something called the *double-entry* or *dialogue journal*, which is introduced later in the chapter.

Believing and Doubting

Another way to engage dialectical thinking is to move back and forth between believing and doubting the author's claims as we read. The *believing game* and the *doubting game* are two terms that writing teacher Peter Elbow introduced to describe how we might look at texts or experiences.[2] Elbow argues that our tendency to doubt or be critical of what we hear or read is only half of what we need to be able to reason and inquire well. He suggests we also need to play the believing game, to "try on" accepting the truth of another's arguments, claims, or experiences, and to search for "virtues or strengths we otherwise might miss," even if we disagree.

Believing and doubting are opposed stances, obviously, and adopting both of them when reading a book or an article isn't always easy, particularly when you have strong feelings about a topic or an author. But I think you'll be amazed at the how the shift between the two sparks new ways of thinking.

There are other stances, too, and some of them are described in the earlier "Inquiring into the Details: Reading Perspectives" box. These may come into play depending on what you're reading and why. But believing and doubting can be particularly useful, especially in academic situations.

[2]Elbow, Peter. "Methodological Believing and Doubting: Contraries in Inquiry." In *Embracing Contraries*. New York: Oxford Press, 1986.

EXERCISE 2.3

Practicing Dialectical Thinking

STEP ONE: Read the essay that follows.

THE IMPORTANCE OF WRITING BADLY
Bruce Ballenger

I was grading papers in the waiting room of my doctor's office the other day, and he said, "It must be pretty eye-opening reading that stuff. Can you believe those students had four years of high school and still can't write?"   1

I've heard that before. I hear it almost every time I tell a stranger that I teach writing at a university.   2

I also hear it from colleagues brandishing red pens who hover over their students' papers like Huey helicopters waiting to flush the enemy from the tall grass, waiting for a comma splice or a vague pronoun reference or a misspelled word to break cover.   3

And I heard it this morning from the commentator on my public radio station who publishes snickering books about how students abuse the sacred language.   4

I have another problem: getting my students to write badly.   5

Most of us have lurking in our past some high priest of good grammar whose angry scribbling occupied the margins of our papers. Mine was Mrs. O'Neill, an eighth-grade teacher with a good heart but no patience for the bad sentence. Her favorite comment on my writing was "awk," which now sounds to me like the grunt of a large bird, but back then meant "awkward." She didn't think much of my sentences.   6

I find some people who reminisce fondly about their own Mrs. O'Neill, usually an English teacher who terrorized them into worshipping the error-free sentence. In some cases that terror paid off when it was finally transformed into an appreciation for the music a well-made sentence can make.   7

But it didn't work that way with me. I was driven into silence, losing faith that I could ever pick up the pen without breaking the rules or drawing another "awk" from a doubting reader. For years I wrote only when forced to, and when I did it was never good enough.   8

Many of my students come to me similarly voiceless, dreading the first writing assignment because they mistakenly believe that how they say it matters more than discovering what they have to say.   9

10   The night before the essay is due they pace their rooms like expectant fathers, waiting to deliver the perfect beginning. They wait and they wait and they wait. It's no wonder the waiting often turns to hating what they have written when they finally get it down. Many pledge to steer clear of English classes, or any class that demands much writing.

11   My doctor would say my students' failure to make words march down the page with military precision is another example of a failed education system. The criticism sometimes takes on political overtones. On my campus, for example, the right-wing student newspaper demanded an entire semester of Freshman English be devoted to teaching students the rules of punctuation.

12   There is, I think, a hint of elitism among those who are so quick to decry the sorry state of the sentence in the hands of student writers. A colleague of mine, an Ivy League graduate, is among the self-appointed grammar police, complaining often about the dumb mistakes his students make in their papers. I don't remember him ever talking about what his students are trying to say in those papers. I have a feeling he's really not that interested.

13   Concise, clear writing matters, of course, and I have a responsibility to demand it from students. But first I am far more interested in encouraging thinking than error-free sentences. That's where bad writing comes in.

14   When I give my students permission to write badly, to suspend their compulsive need to find the "perfect way of saying it," often something miraculous happens: Words that used to trickle forth come gushing to the page. The students quickly find their voices again, and even more important, they are surprised by what they have to say. They can worry later about fixing awkward sentences. First, they need to make a mess.

15   It's harder to write badly than you might think. Haunted by their Mrs. O'Neill, some students can't overlook the sloppiness of their sentences or their lack of eloquence, and quickly stall out and stop writing. When the writing stops, so does the thinking.

16   The greatest reward in allowing students to write badly is that they learn that language can lead them to meaning, that words can be a means for finding out what they didn't know they knew. It usually happens when the words rush to the page, however, awkwardly.

17   I don't mean to excuse bad grammar. But I cringe at conservative educational reformers who believe writing instruction should return to primarily teaching how to punctuate a sentence and use *Roget's Thesaurus*. If policing student papers for mistakes means alienating young writers from the language we expect them to master, then the exercise is self-defeating.

It is more important to allow students to first experience how lan-   18
guage can be a vehicle for discovering how they see the world. And what
matters in this journey—at least initially—is not what kind of car you're
driving, but where you end up. ▪

STEP TWO: Carefully copy lines or passages from the essay that you
found interesting, puzzling, provocative, or central to its argument, as you
understand it. Copy these passages onto a blank page on the left side of
your notebook or journal.

STEP THREE: PLAY THE BELIEVING GAME. To start with, assume the truth of the author's claims. *What evidence from your own experience or knowledge, or from the text itself, might lead you to believe some
of the things said in the essay?* Explore this in a fastwrite on the right
page of your journal, opposite the page on which you copied the passage. If
the writing stalls, look left and find something to respond to in one of the
quoted passages you collected.

STEP FOUR: PLAY THE DOUBTING GAME. Skip a few lines, and
shift your stance to one that is critical of the essay's claims. What do you
suspect might be the weakness of the argument? What do you know from
your own experience and knowledge that contradicts the claims? What
does the essay fail to consider? Do this in a fastwrite just below the one
you completed from Step One. Again, if your pen slows, look on the left for
quotations from the excerpt that will get you going again.

STEP FIVE: MAKE A CLAIM OF YOUR OWN. Based on what
you've learned from these two contrary perspectives—believing and doubting—compose a paragraph that states what you believe about the idea
that "bad" writing is important.

STEP SIX: REFLECT ON THE PROCESS. Reflect on your experience
with this exercise. Make an entry in your journal that explores some of
the following questions:

- What, if anything, do you understand about your reading habits or
  perspectives now that you didn't fully understand before this exercise?
- Which came more easily—doubting or believing? What perspectives
  on the topic might not have emerged if you hadn't been forced to shift
  stances?
- Can you see any similarities between your writing and reading
  processes? Differences?

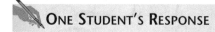 ONE STUDENT'S RESPONSE

TODD'S JOURNAL

EXERCISE 2.3

COLLECTING	FOCUSING

STEP TWO: Writing Down Quotations

"I find some people who reminisce fondly about their own Mrs. O'Neill, usually an English teacher who terrorized them into worshipping the error-free sentence. In some cases that error paid off when it was finally transformed into an appreciation for the music a well-made sentence can make."

"There is, I think, a hint of elitism among those who are so quick to decry the sorry state of the sentence in the hands of student writers."

"If policing student papers for mistakes means alienating young writers from the language we expect them to master, then the exercise is self-defeating."

"It is more important to allow students to first experience how language can be a vehicle for discovering how they see the world. And what matters in this journey—at least initially—is not what kind of car you're driving, but where you end up."

STEP THREE: The Doubting Game

I know enough people who have had a strong grammar background to believe that this happens more often than the author implies. Some people really like to study grammar and mechanics, and isn't it common sense that you should learn the basics before you learn how to put them all together? I also wonder what the writer means about "elitism." What is elitist about helping students to write correctly, something that will help a lot of students get better jobs. After all, even if teaching grammar doesn't help some people write better, the world expects correctness. And writers quickly get into trouble if they can't punctuate, spell, or dangle their modifiers. . .

STEP FOUR: The Believing Game

On the other hand, making people afraid to write doesn't seem like a good idea either. In a way it can be elitist if grammar is taught as rules, handed down by the grammar god (someone invented by these "defenders" of the language). You get the impression that if you dangle a modifier you're a bad person. There's something moral about the whole thing that bothers me. I really like the idea that "policing" essays can be "alienating for your writers" because I've felt that way at times. I hand in a paper to

COLLECTING	FOCUSING
	a professor and I don't feel he or she has paid any attention to my ideas. . .
	STEP FIVE: Making a Claim
	So-called "bad" writing can be useful for some writers who struggle with perfection. But students who lack basic grammar skills will be punished for it in school and in the workplace. Therefore, teachers have an obligation to teach it.
	STEP SIX: Reflecting on the Exercise
	It was weird to shift stances. I really wanted to spend more time playing the "believing game" because I basically agreed with the article. This suggests that when I read something I agree with, I automatically read it looking for confirmation of what I already believe. The "doubting game" shook me out of that, and. . .

INQUIRING INTO THE DETAILS

THE DOUBLE-ENTRY JOURNAL

A double-entry journal is essentially a written dialogue between a reader and a text. As a reader you ask questions, make connections, and note memories and associations.

Here's how it works: You can either draw a line down the middle of a page to make two columns, or you can use the spine of your notebook for the line and use two opposing pages.

What the Text Says	What I Think
In the left column, write out the passages from the reading that confuse you, surprise you, make you think of other ideas, seem key to your understanding of what it says, and so on.	Then in the right column, write out your response to those passages. Sometimes you'll do a fastwrite, other times you may simply jot down quick thoughts.

What the Text Says	What I Think
• Jot down direct quotes, paraphrases, summaries, facts, claims. • Note page numbers next to each passage or summary/paraphrase. Put them in the far right margin next to the borrowed material or ideas.	Play the doubting game, questioning the source; play the believing game, trying to find its virtues, even if you disagree. • Shift to other reading perspectives. • Tell the story of your thinking about what you're reading: *My initial reaction to this is . . . but now I think . . . and now I think . . .* • List questions you have about the source's ideas; your emotional responses; other ideas or readings it connects to.

Continue this process for the entire reading, moving back and forth across the columns. Remember that you want to explore your response to a text, make connections to other works and your own writing, and analyze the writer's choices in terms of language, style, detail, and so forth. *Be sure to note all the bibliographic information from the source at the top of the page.*

Adapting to Unfamiliar Reading Situations

Studies on reading are unambiguous about one thing: What most affects readers' comprehension of a text is their prior knowledge of its topic. Texts on familiar subjects are clearly easier to read and respond to, but generally the reading you're required to do in college demands that you confront books and articles about things you may know little about. Frequently, these texts adopt the *discourse,* or language and conventions, of the field for which they were written, a field with which you may have little experience. Other times you'll be asked to read primary sources—the original writings of important thinkers—which may be written in the style and structure of another time or place. Reading situations such as these require us to modify our reading process.

Of course, it's quite common when reading in such situations to feel little connection to the author or his ideas, at least initially. *What is this person talking about? What does this mean to me? How boring!* In adapting our reading process to these rhetorical situations, then, the challenge is to use dialectical thinking to actively seek out the connections between your own experiences and knowledge and the author's text. The key is to use *writing* to help you to work out what you think about what you've read, focusing especially on what you find confusing, puzzling, or significant.

I realize that getting you to write as you read is a tough sell. You're pressed for time, and you just want to get the reading done. But I'm confident that if you take a little time to use writing to hold up your end of the conversation with a text, you'll discover the pleasures of seeing the story of your own thinking unfold before you, and if you have to write about what you read, you're essentially beginning a draft. In other words, not only will you come up with better ideas, you may also work more efficiently.

EXERCISE 2.4

Further Practice: An Adaptive Response

Frequently you'll be asked to read some pretty difficult texts in your college classes, books or articles that are a thicket of ideas that may be hard to see through. Try using the dialectical thinking method to analyze the following passage, one that is typical of the kind of texts you'll encounter.

STEP ONE: COLLECT. As you read the excerpt below from David F. Noble's book, use the double-entry journal technique to collect lines or passages that you find significant, interesting, or puzzling. Carefully copy these on the left page of your journal. Consider reading the excerpt through at least once *without* taking notes and then begin collecting in your journal during the second or third reading.

from THE FORCES OF PRODUCTION
A Social History of Industrial Automation
David W. Noble

It is a staple of current thinking about technological change that such   1
a "successful" technology, having become dominant, must have evolved in
some "necessary" way. Implicit in the modern ideology of technological
progress is the belief that the process of technological development is
analogous to that of natural selection. It is thus assumed that all technological alternatives are always considered, that they are disinterestedly
evaluated on their technical merits, and that they are then judged according to the cold calculus of accumulation. Any successful technology,
therefore—one which becomes the dominant and ultimately the only
solutions to a given problem—must, by definition, be the best, for it
alone has survived the rigors of engineering experimentation and the trials of the competitive marketplace. And, as the best, it has become the
latest, and necessary, step along the unilinear path of progress.

2   This dominant "Darwinian" view of technological development rests upon a simple faith in objective science, economic rationality, and the market. It assumes that the flow of creative inventions passes progressively through three successive filters, each of which further guarantees that only the "best" alternatives survive. The first, the objective technical filter, selects the most scientifically sound solutions to a given problem. The second, the pecuniary rationality of the hard-nosed businessman, screens out more fanciful technical solutions and accepts only those which are practical and economically viable. The third, the self-correcting mechanism of the market, dooms the less savvy businessman and thus insures that only the best innovations survive.

3   But this facile faith assumes too much, and explains too little. It portrays technological development as an autonomous and neutral technical process, on the one hand, and a coldly rational and self-regulating economic process, on the other, neither of which accounts for people, power, institutions, competing values, or different dreams. Thus it begs and explains away all important historical questions: The best technology? Best for whom? Best for what? Best according to what criteria, what visions, according to whose criteria, whose visions? ■

STEP TWO: EXPLORE. When you feel satisfied you've collected enough, use the lines or passages you've gathered on the left page as prompts for fastwriting on the right. When the writing stalls, skip a line, look to the left, and find something else to jumpstart your writing. *When you can, write about your own observations and experiences with technology that might help you think about what Noble is trying to say. Tell stories.* Remember, questions, not answers, should direct your fastwriting. Keep writing until you feel you have a grip on some of what Noble seems to be saying about technology and your own response to his ideas.

STEP THREE: FOCUS. Adopt a critical mode of thinking for a moment. Use the writing and information you've collected so far, and compose a paragraph response that summarizes, in your own words, Noble's argument and offers your own response to it. This response should complete the following sentence: *Based on your understanding, the most significant thing Noble has to say is. . .*

STEP FOUR: REFLECT. Finally, make an entry in your journal that reflects your experience with this exercise. Some questions that might prompt your thinking include the following:

- Did your reading process in this exercise differ significantly from the process you used when you read "The Importance of Writing Badly" in Exercise 2.3?

- What did you find most helpful about the double-entry journal method? What was least helpful?

- Can you connect any moments of insight or discovery in your journal with particular moves you made, perhaps asking a certain question or shifting the focus of your writing?

- How did you struggle with this reading? How did it come easily? What might you do differently when you encounter texts like these?

My ten-year-old daughter Julia is working on a research paper on James I, the British king who presided over America's first colony, Jamestown. She's shared with me some of the facts she's collected, including the report that the king had an incredibly long tongue. Julia has taken a lot of notes, and I'm tempted to tell her to think dialectically as she reads, but I'm pretty sure she would roll her eyes. It is a pretty fancy term. But the process I describe in this text isn't really complicated at all. Whether you are reading or writing, thinking dialectically simply involves harnessing impulses that you already possess—the desire to be open-minded and surprised by what you see and the tendency to be critical, to narrow things down and make some sense of the mess. These impulses, when used strategically, will make writing and reading a genuine exercise in inquiry, one that will lead to the kind of learning you expected when you signed on for college.

Reading with the spirit of inquiry turns books, essays and articles into one side of a dialogue that you're having with yourself and an author.

WRITING WITH COMPUTERS

READING ONLINE DOCUMENTS

When you read an online document with multiple pages and links to other sites, you may want to use the bookmark or favorites function of your Web browser to mark important pages so you can easily return to them later. Another way to manage your online reading is to take notes while you read. There are many ways you can do this. You can print out a hard copy of the document and annotate it. Alternately, you can write notes into a separate word processing document, switching between windows as you read and write notes. If you are not working on your own computer, you can put your notes into an e-mail to yourself. The advantage of writing your notes with a word processor is that you can cut and paste material from the online document and insert it into your notes as you read. You can then use the highlight function of the word processor to mark key passages and use colored text or the comment function to insert annotations directly into the material.

"READING" IMAGES

Images abound, of course, and not just on TV, your cell phone, or the Web. More and more of my students are using images in their papers, and I find myself using them more than ever in my teaching. You simply can't talk about effective persuasion without considering the rhetoric of images, which is one reason why there are so many images throughout *The Curious Writer* and why I decided to end this chapter by briefly introducing you to visual literacy. To read well, then, is to develop some skills at understanding both what we read and what we see.

It's pretty obvious that images and texts have a lot in common. For example, a good picture is *composed*—the visual elements are arranged a certain way with a certain idea in mind. Images also have their own *grammar,* but rather than using words and syntax, images use color, lines, shape, and texture, all of which combine for a certain effect. The rhetorical reading triangle (Figure 2.3) applies to images as it applies to any other text because these elements—composition and grammar—are combined for a certain purpose and for a certain audience. And, just like writing, visual images take a range of forms, from advertisements to oil paintings, and each of these genres ask to be "read" differently (see Exercise 2.5).

Finally, the meaning of an image isn't fixed. Earlier in the chapter, I mentioned that we work out the meaning of what we read by having a conversation with it, one that is always conducted in a particular context. Each reader brings certain experiences and knowledge to a reading, and this will influence what that reader thinks the text means. The same is true of reading images. For example, your reading of the 1950s advertisement for Wildroot Cream-Oil that follows will be quite different from the reading its designers intended.

For all of these reasons, the recursive process and dialectical thinking both apply as well to analyzing pictures as they do to reading and writing.

Some Strategies for Reading Images

You can analyze images and written texts in many of the same ways, but since each has a different "language"—one works with words and the other with visual elements—the actual practices of analysis differ a bit. Here are some things to keep in mind:

- **Look closely.** Pictures, naturally, appeal to sight. Your skills of close observation, consequently, are probably as important when reading images as rereading is when analyzing a written text.

- **Find the subject.** Like a piece of writing, an image is usually focused on a particular visual subject that can be seen in the context of other elements of the picture. We intuitively look first at the very center of an image for the main subject, but some images may be designed to draw our eyes in other directions. Why would they do this? What might be the motive?

An ad for Wildroot Cream-Oil Hair Tonic from the 1950s.

- **Understand the context.** It helps to know when and where a photograph was taken. This knowledge helps shape our response and helps us understand the photographer's motives for taking the pictures. Knowing which magazine a particular advertisement appeared in also can provide valuable clues about purpose and audience. But the context of an image also includes the experiences and knowledge *the viewer* brings to the image, too. How might your interpretation of an image be influenced by your own history and historical vantage point?

- **Understand the genre.** You are already an expert on the many forms that images take. You intuitively know that you should "read" an advertisement differently from an oil painting, a movie differently from a documentary photograph. Like written forms, visual genres give readers clues about how they should be read, and we typically know the purposes behind different forms. It's not hard, for example, to recognize the persuasive purpose of a car ad, but the purposes of other genres may be more ambiguous. For instance, what is the purpose of a painting by Van Gogh?

- **What's the story?** Images can tell stories, too. For example, the 1950s ad for Wildroot Cream-Oil on page 59 has a strong narrative element that isn't too hard to figure out: If you've got a really swell gal, she'll send you Wildroot instead of a letter because it's your hair she really cares about. Happy users of the product will also enjoy that "successful look," which has everything to do with sex appeal. Sometimes discovering the story in an image is a good starting point for analyzing its message: is this story one that is designed to appeal to a certain audience; does it reflect certain cultural values; is the story current?

- **Analyze the interaction of words and pictures.** Web pages typically combine words and pictures. Some pictures have captions or are positioned carefully near certain text. Words and images are intended to work together—to *reinforce* each other. Notice how text and image elaborate on and extend a particular message. Also notice which element exploits emotions and which emphasizes reason.

EXERCISE 2.5

Reading Images

If an image is a kind of text that can be read like writing can, then the recursive reading model and dialectical thinking should help you analyze pictures, paintings, and ads, too. Try to apply those methods to the images the follow.

STEP ONE: Closely examine each of the five images that follow. Choose one you want to work with.

STEP TWO: Begin your "reading" of the image as you would a printed text, using the dialectical approach. Open your journal to two blank opposing pages. Begin on the left page and jump into the sea. Fastwrite about the image, letting the writing wander wherever it leads you. But begin with the following prompt: *When I first look at this picture, I think or feel _____. And then I think _____. And then . . . And then. . . .* Whenever the writing stalls, repeat the phrase "and then." Write for five minutes without stopping.

STEP THREE: Now work on the right page with your more critical mind. Reread your fastwrite, and then try to focus your thinking about the picture by answering the question: *What story or stories does the image seem to be*

Edward Hopper, *Nighthawks, 1942.* (Oil on canvas, 84.1 X 152.4 cm. Friends of American Art Collection, 1942.51. Reproduction, The Art Institute of Chicago.)

Couple holding hands outside of cemetery.

C. R. Miller, *America's Strength, All of Us Pulling Together*, c. 1950.

Johnnie & Zeek from the Lower West Side series by Milton Rogovin. Photo courtesy of the Rogovin Collection (MiltonRogovin.com). Copyright 1952–2002 Milton Rogovin. All Rights Reserved.

Tourists on toes of Buddha Colossus in Leshan, China.

telling? Remember that what makes a picture powerful is that it tells stories that transcend the moment the image captures, trying to say something larger about its subject, about our lives, or about a product.

STEP FOUR: Now return to the image, looking at it again closely. On the left page of your journal, collect information—specific details—from the picture or ad that seems to provide support for the story or stories you believe the image inspires. Here's where it helps to know a little about the grammar of images.

- As you look at the pictures, pay attention to color. How does that contribute to feeling?
- What is the main visual subject? Where do you find your eyes are drawn, and how is that accomplished?
- Are there clues about context, things like *when* or *where* the image was created?
- Are there rhetorical clues? What do you see in the image (or text) that suggests it targeted a particular audience? Does it include text or visual details that suggest a certain story, theme, or message?

STEP FIVE: On the right page of your notebook, compose a 250-word response that explains, using supporting evidence from the picture you chose, your interpretation of its meaning.

USING WHAT YOU HAVE LEARNED

Inquiry-based writing and reading begins with an open-eyed sense of wonder. Instead of initially asking, "What should I say?" you ask, "What do I think?" You begin the process trying to find the questions that interest you, knowing that there isn't necessarily a single right answer. At the same time, you know that just as you open up possible meanings, at some point you need to narrow them. You are both creative *and* critical. I've used the metaphor of the Sea and the Mountain to describe this back and forth between collecting and focusing, exploring and evaluating, narrating and reflecting.

As you continue in *The Curious Writer,* I'll encourage you to apply this process to nearly every assignment. Before long, it will become second nature to you; you'll find yourself naturally shifting back and forth between the creative and the critical. Techniques such as fastwriting and listing, the double-entry journal, and generating questions will help this along as will what you discover in Chapter 3, when you are introduced to opening questions that can shift your gaze from the Mountain and lead you to new ways of seeing nearly any topic.

Dorthea Lange's famous Great Depression-era photograph, *Migrant Mother*.

Ways of Inquiring

3

In March 1936, while the Great Depression still gripped the nation, documentary photographer Dorthea Lange was driving along a quiet California road when she passed a sign that said, "Pea Picker's Camp." Lange already had finished a project for the federal Resettlement Administration that focused on migrant families devastated by the depression, but twenty miles after passing the sign she turned her car around to get just a few more photos. At the camp, Lange was "drawn like a magnet" to a mother and her children. Lange later remembered that she did "not remember how I explained my presence or my camera to her,"

> . . . but I do remember she asked me no questions. I made five exposures, working closer and closer from the same direction. I did not ask her name or her history. She told me her age, that she was thirty-two. She said that they had been living on frozen vegetables from the surrounding fields, and birds that the children killed. She had just sold the tires from her car to buy food. There she sat in that lean-to tent with her children huddled around her, and seemed to know that my pictures might help her, and so she helped me. There was a sort of equality about it.

Lange's last-minute decision to return to take a few more pictures proved opportune. Her image, "Migrant Mother," is perhaps the most famous twentieth century American documentary photograph, and it remains among the most requested picture in the Library of Congress archive.

In the last chapter, we discussed the correlation between textual and visual literacy. A photograph, like an essay, involves composition and visual grammar. In Lange's photograph of the migrant mother, for example, she consciously arranged certain visual elements to create an emotional effect. Like writing, a good photograph is full of information, too. There are exactly three children in this picture surrounding Florence Thompson, and they are wearing similar rough

What You'll Learn in This Chapter

- How questions create fresh perspective on any subject.

- How you can use certain categories of questions—those that explore, explain, evaluate, and reflect—to think more deeply about any subject.

- How you can combine question asking with dialectical thinking to discover what you want to say.

fabric clothing. None faces the camera. Florence's gaze seems fixed on some distant place, her mouth is set, and her brow seems furrowed. All of these details work together to say more than they say individually, to tell a story not just about the impact of the Great Depression but about motherhood and family.

You can develop your own interpretation of "Migrant Mother" using dialectical thinking, perhaps beginning by openly exploring how the picture connects with your own experiences and observations. This might lead you to focus on a "reading" of the photograph that emphasizes the anxieties of mothering or the shame of poverty in America. But there are ways to make the inquiry process a bit more methodological, ways that you can deliberately shift your perspective to see a subject freshly. How? Ask the right questions.

Years ago, I spent an afternoon taking photographs of an old wagon on a rolling New Hampshire hill. I got up early on a September morning hoping to take advantage of the slanting light and the shreds of mist that hung on the hayfield. I resolved to take an entire roll of the wagon, and I literally circled it, taking shot after shot. By the fourth of fifth shot, I started to see the wagon in ways I'd never seen it. I saw how the beads of dew covered the bleached wood of the wagon's wheel. I saw how the ironwork of the driver's bench created a shadow on the grass that was a tangle of geometric shapes.

What I'm describing is the process of revision. But the anecdote also comes to mind now because it illustrates how different questions will shift your gaze on a topic. They help you circle the wagon, changing your angle and revealing certain aspects of the subject and not others. Behind each question is a different perspective.

In this chapter, I'll suggest four ways of seeing, each prompted by a different opening question. Combined with dialectical thinking, these stances—*exploring, explaining, evaluating,* and *reflecting*—are a foundation of inquiry-based learning that will help you with every assignment in this book, and in any situation in which you want to figure out what you think. We'll apply these ways of seeing to a range of texts, both written and visual, and I hope you'll find yourself circling the wagon in much the same way I did years ago.

OPENING QUESTIONS FOR INQUIRY

All inquiry begins with questions. Indeed, the *opening questions* we ask largely determine our response to a subject. These questions shape the stance we take toward both the writing process and the reading process. These opening questions are situational. For example, in writing they depend on our particular subject, on who we're writing for, and our purposes at any given moment in the process. Recall the rhetorical triangle from

Chapter 1: The rhetorical choices we make are informed by the questions we ask in response to the writing situation. While opening questions will vary from one writing situation to the next, we can group them into categories that conform to four different ways of inquiring into a subject, which are:

1. **Exploration:** This way of inquiring is suited to the personal investigation of a subject. When we explore we are receptive to a subject much like a child is to new experiences. We are curious and open to new ways of seeing; in fact, when we explore we expect to learn and discover things about ourselves and the subject. Questions for exploration include:

   - What does this mean to me, or how do I think or feel about it?

   - What do I notice first? And then what? And then?

   - What interests me most about this? What additional questions does it raise?

   - How do my own personal knowledge and experiences affect the way I feel and what I see?

2. **Explanation:** This way of inquiring is designed to help describe, define, or classify a subject. We explain as an effort to clarify things, perhaps first for ourselves and then for others. If exploration opens things up, explanation helps nail things down so we can start to make sense of them. Questions for explanation include:

   - How does this work? Why does it work? How does this clarify things?

   - What does it look like?

   - How does it compare to something else?

   - What do I understand this to be saying?

3. **Evaluation:** This way of inquiring seeks to make and support an argument, a claim, or a position about a subject. Evaluation always involves a judgment of some sort—this is good or bad, useful or useless, relevant or irrelevant, or somewhere in between. It also encourages an examination of the evidence, sometimes to help form a judgment or to make a judgment convincing. Questions for evaluation include:

   - What's my take on this?

   - Do I see this the way most other people do?

   - All things considered, what's most convincing here? What's least convincing?

   - What do I see that supports what I believe? What do I see that complicates or contradicts what I believe?

4. Reflection: This way of inquiring is focused not on the subject, but rather on the writer/reader and the process through which she engages her subject. Reflection demands a kind of self-awareness most of us aren't used to because it focuses on our *methods of thought* as well as our actions. Questions for reflection include:

- What do I notice about how I think about or do this?
- How do I compare how I approach this task with how I approach another one?
- What are the patterns of thinking or doing that I usually follow when I do this? Did those patterns change at all?
- How do I feel about my performance?

All inquiry begins with questions. Indeed, the opening questions we ask largely determine our response to a subject.

Each of these four ways of inquiring compels writers to take a different stance toward a subject, be it a text, a memory, an observation, a conversation, a photograph, or another process. Each shapes how writers see a subject (or themselves), much like taking a series of different photographs of the wagon on the hill that was mentioned earlier. Imagine, for example, that you're writing an essay on a proposed student tuition hike at your school. If you begin the inquiry process by asking, "What do I think about a tuition hike?" (exploration) then you'll read the university's proposal much differently than if you start by asking, "What's least convincing?" (evaluation) about the university's proposal. The questions you ask fundamentally shift your ways of seeing.

EXPLORATION

When we ask questions of exploration our engagement with subject is personal: *How do I feel about this? What does it mean to me? What do I think?* Through these questions, the writer can openly investigate her feelings and thoughts and find a personal point of attachment to the subject. This way of inquiring is particularly useful when you're writing on something about which you're uncertain. It can help you suspend judgment even when doing so runs counter to your instincts. You think, for example, that an assigned reading is boring. Maybe so, but by asking questions of exploration you might break through this initial reaction and discover something surprising about the reading that holds your interest.

This way of inquiring isn't just for fastwriting or journal work. Exploration can also inform much more publicly oriented inquiry into a subject. Historically, the personal essay is a genre that relies heavily on exploration (see Chapter 4, "Writing a Personal Essay"). Writers of personal essays constantly take measure of their emotional relationship with their subjects, much the way we do when we're writing for ourselves in our journals. This public performance of the inquiring *I* has an interesting effect on readers—we feel a sense of intimacy with the writer that is often absent in other writing genres. Ironically, questions that would seem to free us from concern for our audience can also wind up making our writing more accessible to that audience.

When should you try exploration as a way of inquiring? This is not easy to sum up because writing situations vary so greatly, but it helps to think rhetorically. We've already mentioned one element of the rhetorical triangle—*the writer*—that is very important. The other two elements of the triangle, *audience* and the *subject* or *text* will also shape our decision. In many ways, our *purpose* in pursuing an investigation into a subject is the most decisive factor of all. There are other less obvious factors to consider, too, including how much *time* the writer has for the task, the amount of *expertise* or knowledge required to write well on the subject, and the form—or *genre*—in which the writer must express himself. Taken together, all of the above factors will shape our decision about if and to what extent we use this way of inquiring. Let's look closer at how this works.

1. **The Writer:**

   - Whenever we write, we decide who we want to be. I know this sounds odd, because aren't you always the same person when you write? Not really. Often unconsciously, we create a persona in writing, a certain self that we hope will be perceived a certain way by readers. More than any other way of inquiring, exploration can free you from worrying about how you will be perceived, which often leads to refreshing honesty about what you think and feel.

2. **Audience:**

   - Exploration is often most productive when writers write for themselves, with no one looking over their shoulders.

   - On the other hand, when exploration is made public it is a way of inquiring that is genuinely conversational—writers and readers collaborate, in a way, in the experience of figuring something out. In situations where the writer craves this kind of intimacy with real or imagined readers, exploration can be attractive.

3. **Purpose:**

   - Exploration can be most useful when you don't know your purpose in writing about something, but would like to discover it. It's a way of inquiring that most welcomes the disruption of questions, beginning with *What do I think and feel about this?* And *Is this really true?*

4. **Time:**

   - This way of inquiring takes time; in fact, some writers might consider it an incredibly inefficient way to write, considering all the time spent figuring things out in a journal or on the page. But all of this exploration can pay off in a big way: you can discover a topic you might not have found if you had not written your way to it. Even more important, you might discover what you didn't know you knew.

- Exploration is not of way of inquiring that you will use very much if tight deadlines are involved. You wouldn't use it, for instance, when confronted with a thirty-minute essay exam because there wouldn't be much time to discover what you want to say.

5. **Expertise:**

- Exploring can yield the most surprises when you don't know what you think or feel about your topic. Because it is an open-ended way of inquiring, there's plenty of room to circle a subject and see it from many perspectives. This may give you a richer under-standing of your topic than when, for example, you quickly choose a claim to argue or a thesis to explain.

- Even topics that you think you know a lot about can yield more through exploration, if this way of inquiring helps you find the right questions to ask.

6. **Genre:**

- This way of inquiring can be used to write in any genre, but it is most encouraged—and expected—in the personal essay. It can also be useful in the research essay.

- Invention strategies like fastwriting always involve exploration. This way of inquiring also informs sketches and early drafts.

E X E R C I S E   3 . 1

Exploring "Migrant Mother"

STEP ONE: Study Dorthea Lange's photograph at the front of this chap-ter. Pay attention to how it makes you feel, but try to avoid rushing to judgment about how you might interpret the image; that is, hold off decid-

---

Exploration

The Writer: Writes most honestly

Audience: Concern is usually low

Purpose: To discover

Time: Relatively time-consuming

Expertise: Not necessarily required

Genre: Personal essays, sometimes research essays, journal writing, sketches, and early discovery drafts

---

ing what seems to be the *dominant feeling* it evokes in you, or what the photograph *says* to you.

STEP TWO: In your journal, *explore* your reactions to this photograph through a fastwrite. Your writing should be open-ended—but avoid making up a story about the woman and her children. For now, at least, focus your fastwrite on what you see, feel, and think about the image.

Journal Prompts

If you need a prompt, choose one of the options below:

- **Narrative of thought:** *When I first look at the picture, I feel or think _____. And then _____. And then _____. And then . . . and then . . . And now?*

- **Telling details:** Quickly make a list of at least five details from the image that strike you. Choose one to begin with and write quickly about why that detail seems to stand out, what it makes you think and feel, and how it might hint about the meaning of the whole photograph for you. Whenever that writing stalls, choose another detail from your list and use it as a prompt in a similar way.

STEP THREE: After fastwriting, reread what you've written. Underline sentences or passages in your writing that say or imply what you think or feel Lange's photograph is about. Where do you come closest to naming the dominant impression it creates, or what it seems to say to you? In other words, where did you shift from creative to critical thinking? Discuss what you discovered in class. If you were to write a one or two sentence caption for the photograph, what would you write?

ONE STUDENT'S RESPONSE

LANA'S JOURNAL

EXERCISE 3.1

STEP ONE
Narrative of thought: When I first look at the picture I feel or think that I know this person—that I am sometimes this person. I can feel the pressure of having children depending upon you to provide them with the basic needs of life. I find it hard to imagine that this woman is 32. I feel that she is beautiful—there is a dignity that surrounds her rather than despair over her situation. . . .

Telling details:

1. the neck of the little girl on the right
2. the way the woman's hand is pulling on her face

3. the children are looking away
4. the monochromatic color of the clothes
5. the woman isn't looking at the camera

The most telling detail for me is the little girl on the right . . . the back of her neck and messed up hair remind me of the way Lucy looks when she first wakes up in the morning. I like how the children are looking away as if the mother is shielding them from the camera or maybe even the concrete reality of their lives. Overall, all of my feelings towards this photo relate to my own experiences as a mom and the feelings I have towards my life and my children. I get the feeling that this woman is strong and independent and proud of her efforts to provide . . .

STEP TWO
The main feeling communicated by Lange's photograph "Migrant Mother" is the mother's desire to protect her children and preserve her dignity and self-respect in spite of her physical situation. The position of her children in the photograph—looking away from the camera, bodies positioned to fit like puzzle pieces with the mother's body—demonstrate the mother's desire to protect her children from the harsh realities of their life . . .

EXPLANATION

We explain things all the time. This is something parents are acutely aware of, especially if they have a kid like my daughter Julia.

"Who are the Israelis?" she asks as we listen to National Public Radio on the way to school, "and why are they always talking about them?"

"Who is talking about them?"

"The people on the radio," she says. "They are always talking about the Israelis and the Palestinians."

How do I begin to explain a conflict that has its roots in several thousand years of history, one complicated by religious differences and political alliances that seem to defy resolution? What Julia knows seems much simpler: a Palestinian family in Gaza was killed by Israeli soldiers who were retaliating for a suicide attack in Jerusalem that killed thirteen. Do I begin by explaining Moses' exodus from Egypt and the Jews' historic claims to the Holy Land or the Muslim's conquest of the region in the seventh century? Or do I explain the creation of the Israeli state following World War II and the demise of Palestine? What I realize, as Julia impatiently waits for me to say something, is that I know much less than I thought I knew about the history of this conflict.

As this example suggests, we tend to use explanation with an audience in mind. But by explaining things to ourselves we can learn a lot, too, because this way of inquiring exposes gaps in our knowledge. Clearly, in attempting to explain the conflict between the Israelis and the Palestinians to my daughter I was forced to confront the limits of my own knowledge on the subject.

A common technique in psychotherapy is something called "say back." In couples counseling, for example, one partner may be required to listen carefully to his or her spouse talk, and then say back what he or she heard. The method is great for helping couples really listen to and understand each other, something that is ordinarily difficult to do amid life's daily distractions. The explanatory power of say back is much like power of summarizing or paraphrasing something you've read or experienced. By challenging writers to use their own words, summarizing and paraphrasing allow writers to take possession of the information, to make it their own by articulating their understanding of the information in their own words. Summarizing and paraphrasing can also expose the gaps in our knowledge. You thought you understood a subject, but upon reading over your summary or paraphrase of the subject, you now aren't so sure that's the case. Is there another way to understand the subject so you can explain it better? Have you missed something you need to know in order to understand the subject?

This way of inquiring involves much more than simply reporting information. It's a way of clarifying thought, enhancing understanding, making useful comparisons, and exposing gaps. For me, trying to explain the Middle East conflict to Julia and writing this book were two experiences that involved discoveries that made them much more than mere recitations of fact and detail.

Practical factors that can influence our decision to use this way of inquiring include the following:

1. **The Writer:**
   - How well do you really understand a subject you're reading or writing about? Explaining things to yourself, or to an audience, will expose gaps in your knowledge.
   - Writers who take care to clarify their subjects—making useful comparisons, offering succinct summaries and definitions, and so on—earn the gratitude of their readers. These writers create a persona in the work that is more persuasive because they seem to really want their readers to understand their topic.

2. **Audience:**
   - Explanation is usually directed at an audience, the real or imagined readers with whom writers want to share their understanding of a subject. To effectively communicate their understanding to an audience, writers need to be able to see their subject from the audience's perspective.

- Writers can, however, also be an audience for their own explanations. We explain things to ourselves to get a better grasp of information.

3. **Purpose:**
   - The aim of explanation is to inform and thus it drives all attempts to describe, define, compare, and classify subjects.
   - Explanation can be used to find gaps in the writer's knowledge or to increase his understanding.
   - Explanation can also provide a useful context for understanding the writer's questions, concerns, or ideas.

4. **Time:**
   - Explanation requires time. Describing a situation completely is not an activity that can be rushed.
   - Explanation tends to proceed more rapidly when conducted for the sake of the writer alone and not an audience.

5. **Expertise:**
   - Explanation requires knowledge about a subject. The writer must know the subject well enough or must conduct research to gain sufficient knowledge to explain the subject. Since prior knowledge is rarely complete, research is often necessary to fill gaps in the writer's knowledge.
   - Explanation also can help a writer test her understanding of something new.

6. **Genres:**
   - Explanation is an element in all genres of writing.
   - Explanation plays a prominent role in argument, as any effort to support a claim requires the explanation of evidence.
   - Two common note-taking techniques, summarizing and paraphrasing, embody this way of inquiring.

Explanation

The Writer: Cares that the reader understands

Audience: Usually (but not always) a major concern

Purpose: To inform and provide context

Time: Usually time-consuming

Expertise: Required

Genres: Applies to all genres

E X E R C I S E 3 . 2

Explaining a Marketing Strategy

For obvious reasons, advertisers are some of the most rhetorically savvy people around. They have something to sell, and in order to do it they carefully tailor their messages to certain audiences. But even before they figure out what to say, they decide on the medium in which to say it. For example, if an advertiser is after men between the ages of twenty-one and forty, then *Esquire* magazine might be the choice. If an advertiser is after women in a similar age group, then *Cosmopolitan* might be a good choice.

The two ads that follow on pages 76 and 77 promote quite different products. Try to use explaining as a way of inquiring to clarify the marketing strategy in each ad.

STEP ONE: Open your journal to blank opposing pages. On the left page, make a fast list that describes, in order, the details your eyes take in as you look at each advertisement: What do you notice first? Then what? Then what? And then? Be as specific as possible; that is, rather than saying "the man's arm," note "the sculpted biceps in the man's left arm."

STEP TWO: Based on what your eyes are drawn to in each ad, what *story* does each ad seem to be telling to its intended audience? On the right page of your journal, tell those stories in your own words, and then explain why you think the story the ad seems to be telling would (or would not) succeed in selling its product to its intended audience.

STEP THREE: In small groups, compare the two ads and discuss which of the two ads you think is the more effective and why.

ONE STUDENT'S RESPONSE

DAVID'S JOURNAL
EXERCISE 3.2

STEP ONE:	STEP TWO:
A list of things I notice in the Guess ad: <ul><li>Man's unbuttoned white shirt</li><li>Black tie is unkempt</li><li>Man's hair like Jeff Bridges</li><li>White boots with pointed tips</li><li>Both women extremely skinny</li></ul>	If you're a man and wear Guess clothes, then you'll feel young and sexy, and won't feel the need to get dressed up. It's the casual style that will attract women— even more than one at the same time! - and they won't mind being much better dressed than you. Let it all hang out! She won't mind, and either will she!

Guess advertisement

STEP ONE:	**STEP TWO:**
• Kissing woman on left, woman on right unbothered, smiling • Dirty street • Emerging from restaurant? • Hairless chest	

ENYCE advertisement

EVALUATION

To evaluate something is to judge it or to form an opinion about it. Evaluating things—restaurants, the quality of play in the NBA, the religious motives of terrorists such as Osama Bin Laden—is something we all do naturally. These evaluations tend to lead us to do and say certain things to support our opinions or to make our claims convincing, first to ourselves and then to others. Indeed, evaluation is really the driving force behind argument.

As a way of inquiring, evaluation shares much with exploration. Both hinge on the writer's emotional response to a subject. Exploration, however, is much more open-ended in its approach, more receptive to doubt and uncertainty about the subject. Evaluation, on the other hand, is focused exclusively on making and supporting a judgment about the subject. In sum, you use exploration when your purpose is *to discover* and you use evaluation when your purpose is *to prove,* although both ways of inquiring can be used together to great effect.

While we constantly evaluate things for ourselves, we usually reserve written evaluation for an audience. Our concern, then, is to convince others to feel the same way we do about the subject. To do so, we usually have to clarify and to elaborate on our thinking.

Indeed, since all evaluation stems from what are essentially subjective value judgments, a tension always exists between our *desire* to prove our point and our *need or willingness* to learn more about the subject. Most, if not all issues worth arguing about are complex. In learning more about them, we can actually make it harder to prove our point. We might even be compelled to change our minds about the subject. This may be a good thing in terms of fostering a deeper understanding of the world, but it's bound to slow down the writing process. You may not have the time required to fully explore the complexities of a subject. Charged with evaluating the impact of the war in Afghanistan on the U.S. relationship with Uzbekistan or the meaning of the water imagery in Kate Chopin's story "The Awakening," you might feel compelled to come up with an assertion you can prove right away. Will you ignore evidence that doesn't support your claim? Will you allow the evidence to shape your understanding? Will you use it only to confirm your claim?

When used as a way of inquiring, evaluation should never be used merely to support a claim. Evaluation involves making judgments *and* testing them against the evidence. The discoveries that result should shape the claims you make. Evaluation, then, is essentially a form of dialectical thinking.

What factors will inform our decision to use this way of inquiring?

1. **The Writer:**
   - When someone makes a judgment we disagree with—"Today's college students are more interested in being entertained than in learning"—we immediately evaluate the speaker. Is this someone who seems reasonable or fair-minded? Someone we can trust? Someone who knows what she's talking about? Writers who make judgments are keenly aware of their audience, and present a persona in their writing that is most likely to have a positive impact.

2. **Audience:**
   - Evaluation usually is directed at an audience, although the work of arriving at a judgment may be done backstage, in a journal, or early discovery draft.

- An important way to analyze an audience is to ask yourself, "Is this audience already inclined to agree with my judgment or disagree with it? Might they have no opinion?" How you answer these questions will influence what you say and how you say it.

3. Purpose:

- The aim of evaluation is *to prove*. Use this way of inquiring to make and support claims.

- Asking yourself evaluation questions is also a great way to shift from creative to critical thinking at any point in the process when you need to decide what you're trying to say about something.

4. Time:

- The time required for evaluation is entirely a function of the subject in question and the depth of inquiry. If the subject is simple and the depth relatively shallow, then evaluation can be quick. If the subject is complex and the scrutiny deep, then evaluation can take some time. Of course, the deeper the inquiry, the richer and more insightful the evaluation will be.

- Combining exploration and evaluation is a potent way to discover what you think, but can be time-consuming.

5. Expertise:

- Evidence, either from prior knowledge or research, is needed to support one's claim. The stronger the evidence, the stronger the judgment. The weaker the evidence, the weaker the judgment.

- Again, the amount of information needed will be a function of the subject and the depth of the inquiry.

- In some cases, you may begin with little expertise, only a desire to discover what you think. Combine open-ended inquiry such as exploration and move to more focused evaluation questions, from creative to critical.

6. Genre:

- Evaluation is required in most genres, particularly academic genres. Indeed, most of your writing in college will involve evaluation of some kind or another.

- You will use evaluation in an argument, a proposal, a review, a critical essay, and a research essay, which are discussed in later chapters. While you must use evaluation in these genres, you will also employ other ways of inquiring in them, too.

- Evaluation is a prerequisite to argumentative writing.

Evaluation

The Writer: A calculated presence

Audience: Concern for is high

Purpose: To prove

Time: Function of subject and depth of inquiry

Expertise: Generally, the higher the better

Genres: Most academic genres

EXERCISE 3.3

Evaluating "Generation X Goes to College"

Evaluate the excerpt below from Peter Sacks's book, *Generation X Goes to College*. Sacks, a journalism teacher at an unnamed college, narrates his experiences as a first-time instructor and comes to some sobering conclusions about college students. Although his focus is on Generation X, a group that has since passed on to the job market, I hear exactly the same complaints about this generation of college students. They want to be entertained. They are lazy. They can "dish it out" but "can't take it." How would you judge Sacks's claims?

STEP ONE: Carefully read the excerpt, and on the left page of your notebook jot down quotations that you find provocative, puzzling, truthful, or doubtful. Write down at least three quotations.

STEP TWO: On the opposing page of your notebook, respond in a fast-write to one or more of the quotations you collected. In this step, however, first play the believing game; that is, try to see things the way Sacks sees them for five minutes. What do you agree with? What would you concede might be true? What seems his strongest argument, or his most believable evidence? How does what he say connect with your own experiences and observations?

STEP THREE: Now play the doubting game. On the right page of your journal, continue your fastwriting on the excerpts you selected, but this time take a critical stance. What does Sacks fail to understand? What does he fail to consider? How do your own experiences and observations challenge his judgments?

STEP FOUR: Reread the excerpt and your journal work. Craft a 200-word response to Sacks's views of college students. What is your own take on students and what is your evaluation of his claims?

from GENERATION X GOES TO COLLEGE
Peter Sacks

I would encounter this look and The Attitude often. It was a look of ut-   1
ter disengagement. At first, I was confused and bewildered by it and
thought there must be something terribly wrong with me and the way I
taught. But even after I began to strategically adapt to my situation, I would
continue to get Those Looks accompanied by The Attitude. And I eventually would conclude that I was a good teacher, that it wasn't me who was
the problem but a culture of young people who were born and bred to sit
back and enjoy the spectacle that engulfed them. They seemed to resent
that I obviously couldn't measure up to the standards for amusement that
they learned on *Sesame Street* in their formative years, standards later reinforced by *Beverly Hills 90210, Cosmopolitan,* Nirvana, and Pearl Jam. What's
more, they were conditioned by an overly nurturing, hand-holding educational system not to take responsibility for their own actions. But until I
began to accurately assess my new environment, I often reacted with a visible irritation to such scenes as bored guys with backwards baseball caps. I
would learn that this was a classic case of people who could dish it out, but
who couldn't take it; and the trouble for me was that these young people
collectively held a great deal of power in this place, a rather key point that I
didn't fully comprehend at first. Until I understood this, my relationship
with some of my classes developed at times into all out war. ∎

✒ ONE STUDENT'S RESPONSE

MARGARET'S JOURNAL

EXERCISE 3.3

STEP ONE: The Believing Game

Remember that movie "The Burbs," starring Corey Feldman, among others? His
character was particularly amusing, and significant for this discussion, because
rather than watching cable, he found his neighborhood drama so fascinating that
he invited friends over to watch the spectacle. I remember my dad saying something like, "The TV generation—everything is entertainment to them!" At one
point in the film, when all mayhem is breaking loose, the police are showing up,
and Tom Hanks and his pals have burned down their serial killer neighbor's home,
Feldman erupts with glee and shouts, "The Pizza Dude is here!" I thought of him
while reading this essay, because my generation is pretty entertainment oriented.
Maybe video games and unlimited TV have turned us all into passive morons . . .

STEP TWO: Doubting Game

Okay, give me a break . . . this man is convinced that he is a fabulous teacher, yet many of his classes have evolved into an "all out war?" One has to wonder what his definition of a good teacher is, then. He comes off like a whiny, overly sensitive person who after discovering that he is an ineffective teacher chooses to blame it on his students rather than consider that he might be a crucial part of the problem. He never discussed how he tried to reach his students or whether he altered his teaching methods, besides compromising his high standards. I have had plenty of demanding teachers in college, and while many students bitch and moan about the workload and the difficulty, I have found that a majority of students thrive on high expectations . . . For this reason I seriously doubt his claim that he is a good teacher.

REFLECTION

Some of you may remember the television program *The Wonder Years*. Set in the turbulent 1960s, the show offered a glimpse of a boy and his middle-class family navigating the cultural upheavals of the time as well as the ordinary challenges of growing up. What was interesting about the show, though, was its narration. While viewers watched the boy Kevin deal with his family and friends in a changing society, the voice of a much older Kevin reflected on the meaning of those relationships and events, providing perspective that was unavailable to the boy while he was actually experiencing them.

As a way of inquiring, reflection is a lot like playing the part of the adult Kevin. Through reflection it is possible to increase the learning and self-knowledge we get from writing by looking back on the experience of writing. This means finding the right distance from which to see what's not necessarily apparent in the moments of engagement. It also means learning to ask the questions that help us to see not just what we've written or what it means, but *how* we've done the writing and how we might be able to do it better. You've already had a fair amount of practice with this in *The Curious Writer* as you've reflected on the processes you used to complete the exercises and assignments. Indeed, one of the book's central claims is that only by reflecting on your process can you control it.

This way of inquiring may not yet come naturally to you. Reflection, in some ways, seems quite different from exploration, explanation, and evaluation. The object of reflection is not *what* you're writing or reading about, but *how* you are writing and reading about the subject. This way of inquiring requires us *to witness and report on ourselves*. Reflection is a form of self-assessment. By employing it, we can learn to identify and overcome our writing challenges. *What problems do you have in this writing situation? What might be some of the ways you could solve them? What's working? What's not? What's typical about your process? What's unique about your process in this situation?*

All of these questions force you backward, away from the immediate demands of the writing task, and encourage you to see *how* you write and think. Remember writing *is* thinking. The payoff for reflecting is much more than figuring out when to resort to fastwriting or how to revise. It's discovering your patterns of thought and how they can be extended or changed to let you write with more insight.

Factors that influence this way of inquiring include:

1. The Writer:

- The writer looks in the mirror when she reflects. It's sometimes a bit odd because who you might see is a stranger to you: a self at work, thinking, writing, and reading. This is a familiar self, but not one that you watch very often, at least from the outside. For this reason, reflection is a way of inquiring that is hard to get used to, but it is increasingly effective as you become more and more familiar with the writer and reader in the mirror.

2. Audience:

- This way of inquiring can be composed for others, usually your instructor or peers, but can be valuable if written solely for you.
- If your audience is your instructor, she will be interested in how clearly you see yourself and how well you can use the language of the writing and reading process to describe your challenges and your strengths.

3. Purpose:

- Reflection helps you get control over your processes, such as writing and reading, so that you're more efficient and adaptable at both.
- Reflection is also a good way of solving problems when you get stuck in the middle of a process, or if you want to learn as much as you can about future applications of a process after you've tried it.

4. Time:

- Reflection takes time, of course, but it also takes *timing*. There are certain stages in the writing and reading processes that are particularly ripe for reflective thinking, such as when you're stuck, when you've finished a sketch or a draft, before revision, and after you've revised. Reflection can be useful anytime you've reached a point in the process when stepping back from the task and considering the process would be helpful.

5. Expertise:

- Knowledge of your subject is not necessary; knowledge of yourself and how you engage in your process is. Expertise here entails a willingness to look openly at how you do things and how you think in certain situations.
- A working knowledge of the writing and reading processes is helpful, as well as some familiarity with the language we use to talk about those processes.

6. Genre:

- Current genres that involve reflection include portfolios (see Appendix A), cover letters with assignments, and other forms of self-evaluation.

- As inquiry-based teaching and learning theories become more widespread, forms of reflective writing will be assigned more frequently in classes.

Reflection

The Writer: *You* are the subject

Audience: Concern can be low or high

Purpose: To gain control over a process

Time: Takes time and *timing*

Expertise: You're already an expert on yourself

Genres: Journal writing, reflective letters, self-assessments, portfolio

---

EXERCISE 3.4

Reflecting on Your Process

Reflect on the process of completing any of this chapter's preceding exercises (Exercises 3.1 through 3.3).

STEP ONE: Take a few minutes and review all the journal work you generated from the exercises. As you do, make two lists:

1. Things I usually do when writing.
2. Things that are new to me.

In the first column, jot down activities, processes, ways of seeing or thinking, or techniques that you *often* use when writing for school that you used when doing the exercises. In the second column, list activities, processes, ways of seeing or thinking, or techniques that you *rarely* use or have *never* used when writing for school.

STEP TWO: In small groups, discuss your lists.

- How do your experiences with the exercises compare to others in your group?
- What part of the process in the exercises seemed most familiar? Least familiar?
- What did you find most useful in the exercises? Least useful?
- What do you notice about what members of your group were taught about the writing process in earlier school experiences?

- Which ways of inquiring were the richest ways of seeing for you? Which presented difficulty?

✒ ONE STUDENT'S RESPONSE

MARLA'S JOURNAL

EXERCISE 3.4

STEP ONE

1. Things I usually do when writing
   - Wait until the last minute
   - Just get started on the draft
   - Try to get it right in the first draft so I don't have to revise
   - Figure out what I want to say first
   - Try to write the perfect first sentence

2. Things that are new to me
   - That it's okay to write "bad"
   - You can change your mind about what you think
   - It's important to collect a lot of information before you start
   - The journal can help
   - I like exploring but don't much like explaining

SYMPHONIC INQUIRY

When we write, we rarely make exclusive use of just one of the four ways of inquiring. Instead, we explore, explain, evaluate, and reflect in concert, unconsciously shifting from one to the other. Even in a fastwrite, the seeming refuge of exploration, writers often make use of explanation, evaluation, and reflection as they circle a subject and discover their feelings and motives.

When you bring all four ways of inquiring together you achieve symphonic inquiry. But how do you do that? Learning the opening questions to ask yourself helps a lot. Soon, asking these questions becomes second nature. Taking time to reflect on how you're approaching a task also helps, particularly for an apprentice to inquiry-based learning. For instance, perhaps your essays come up a bit short on information and your instructor complains that your ideas are fairly obvious. Reflecting on this, you realize that you tend to short-circuit exploration in a rush to judgment. Next time, you try doing more open-ended writing in your journal before you try to come up with a thesis.

You also can incorporate some practical techniques into your reading and writing processes that promote symphonic inquiry. The double-entry journal, or some variation of it, can really help you to shift back and forth between creative and critical thinking. You also might establish the habit of writing summaries or other explanations of the things you're reading in your notebook or in the margins of the article you're reading. Shifting from one way of inquiring to another is like shifting from one instrument to another. You're both a composer and the conductor of this orchestra, and your task is to create the music of surprise and discovery.

You're both a composer and the conductor of this orchestra, and your task is to create the music of surprise and discovery.

EXERCISE 3.5

Creating Music with "A Voice for the Lonely," by Stephen Corey

STEP ONE: COLLECT. Read Stephen Corey's "A Voice for the Lonely" using a double-entry journal to collect notes as you read. On the left page of your journal, jot down passages that seem important to your understanding of the piece, facts, important details, and so on. Collect any fragments from the essay that you'd like to think more about, perhaps because you find them puzzling, powerful, or potentially significant.

A VOICE FOR THE LONELY
Stephen Corey

1   The right silence can be a savior, especially in these days of motorcycles, leaf blowers, and malls that thrum with a thousand voices and dozens of sundry machines. Five or six days a week, I get up pretty early—generally around 4 A.M.—and one of the things I like most about those last hours of darkness is their stillness. The house is quiet, the streets are quiet, and (except on weekends, when some of the serious drunks are hanging on) the all-night restaurants are quiet. Reading and writing and thinking come more easily when you know you won't be interrupted, and over the past twenty years I've never found a better mental bodyguard than the hours before dawn.

2   I got my first serious training as an early riser when I acquired a newspaper delivery route in seventh grade: three miles of widely scattered houses on the edge of Jamestown, New York, and beyond—just me, the moon, darkness, and the various faces of silence. I recall stop-

ping my brisk walk sometimes, especially in winter when every step squeaked and crunched on the snow that nearly always covered the ground, and marveling at how there were no sounds except those of my own making. But just as often, that quiet made me nervous, even though my hometown was awfully safe in those days. I learned to offset the urge to look over my shoulder by carrying a pocket-sized transistor radio.

3   The music helped me to cope with more than just the empty morning streets—I was, as I said, in seventh (and then eighth, and finally ninth) grade during those lone marches. In short, I was just learning something of what much of that music was about: love—lost, found, hoped for, and despaired of.

4   Most habits die hard, and old ones can seem immortal. Last week, I was up as usual at 4 A.M., and I headed out in the car toward the nearest newspaper box. As always during these quick runs, I flipped on the radio for some wake-up rhythms to jolt my system for the solitary work time soon to come back at the house.

5   Instead of music, I caught the voice of the all-night deejay just as she was saying, "We have tragic news in over the wire: singer Roy Orbison is dead . . ." She gave a quick flurry of details (heart attack, Hendersonville, North Carolina, hospital), repeated the central fact—"Roy Orbison, dead at 52"—and then (my heart applauds her still for this) said not a word but cut straight into "Only the Lonely."

6   There I was, cruising down the abandoned city street with the radio now up as loud as I could stand it, mouthing the rising and falling words, rocking side to side as I held the wheel, and riding Orbison's waiting, nearly-cracking voice back twenty-four years to the passenger seat of Jon Cresanti's Volkswagen beetle.

7   We're told these days that the hottest and fastest wire into memory is our sense of smell, but music must run a close second. Some songs carry us into a certain mood, some to a general region of our past lives, and some to a very particular moment and situation in time. Jon and I were brought together by chance and loneliness for a couple of months during our sophomore year in high school. The alphabetical seating in our homeroom put us next to each other in the back row, and Jon was a talker. We hadn't known each other before: we came from different parts of town, had different friends, and moved through different sequences of classes. But for a while we found a bond: my girlfriend had recently dropped me after more than a year of going steady, and Jon had eyes for a girl who had none for him.

8 I had time—all the time I was no longer spending with my girl. John had a car and was old enough to drive it, having failed a grade and thereby become a crucial year older than the typical sophomore. I signed on board, and we cruised day after day, weekend after weekend, killing time and eating at the wondrous new "fast food restaurant" that had just opened. We sat in his car eating 15-cent hamburgers and 12-cent french fries near the real golden arches, the kind that curved up and over the entire little structure (no inside seating, no bathrooms)—and, naturally, listening to the radio. The Four Seasons were with us, as were The Beach Boys, Nat King Cole, The Supremes.

9 But in those two desperate months of shotgunning for Jon, there was only one song that really mattered, one song we waited for, hoped for, and even called the radio station and asked for: Roy Orbison's "Pretty Woman."

10 That opening handful of heavy guitar notes (a lovesick teenager's equivalent of Beethoven's Fifth) carried us into a world of possibility, a world where a moment's fancy could generate love, where losers could be winners just by wishing for success. The pretty woman walks on by, and another failure has occurred—but suddenly, the downward sweep of the wheel is reversed as the woman turns to walk back, and there is nothing in the world but fulfillment of one's dreams.

11 Pop songs are full of such stuff, of course, and have been for as long as the phonograph record and the radio have been with us; we get all kinds of talk about the importance of television in modern life, but I think we need more examination of the ways we have been encompassed by music. I'm not talking about ranting "discussions" of the immorality of certain strains of pop music, but some real studies of the much wider and deeper implications of growing up in a world awash with radio waves.

12 Needless to say, I wasn't concerned about such matters there in the McDonald's parking lot. I wouldn't even have thought about what it was in Orbison's singing that made him so important to me. I took the words of the song's story for their relevance to my own emotional state, and I floated with those words inside a musical accompaniment that both soothed and roused my fifteen-year-old body.

13 When I heard of Orbison's death, I found myself wanting to figure out just what it was in that strange voice that might have been so compelling for me and others across the years. I think it might be in the way the voice itself often seems about to fail: in Orbison's strange and constant modulations, from gravelly bass-like sounds to strong tenor-like passages to piercing falsetto cries, there is the feeling for the listener that the singer is always about to lose control, about to break down under the

weight of what he is trying to sing. Never mind that this is not true, that Orbison's style was one carefully achieved; what we are talking about here is emotional effect, the true stuff of pop and country music.

If Roy could make it, we could make it. And if Roy could stand fail-   14
ing, so could we.

This feeling of camaraderie with the faraway record star increased   15
for me, I think, the first time I saw him. He was so ordinary looking—
no, he was so *homely,* so very contrary to what one expects romantic musical heroes to look like. He was *us.*

The right singer, the right sadness, the right silence. The way I heard   16
the story of the death of Orbison's wife in 1966 (and the way I'll keep
believing it) was that the two of them were out motorcycling when an
errant car or truck hit them from an angle. She was riding just a few feet
to the side of and behind him, so the other vehicle clipped the back of his
cycle but caught hers full force. I've never gotten over this chilling illustration of the forces of circumstance and the fate of inches, so much so
that over the years I have regularly found the story called to mind for
retelling in classrooms or at parties.

I graduated from high school the year of the accident, and Orbison   17
disappeared from the national music scene. (It wasn't until recently that I
heard how the death of two sons by fire in 1967 compounded Orbison's
private tragedies.) Oddly, there is a way in which the disappearance or
the death of a singer these days doesn't really matter to his or her listeners, since that person is still present in exactly the same way as before.
All the songs take on a slightly new cast, but the singer still lives in a way
that one's own deceased relatives and friends cannot.

When my girl wanted me back, I dropped Jon's friendship and never   18
tried to regain it—a not-very-commendable way to be. But we were
glued for a while by those banging Orbison notes and those erratic vo-
cals, and maybe that was enough, or at least all that one could hope for.

Music can block out silence, on dark scary roads and in moments of   19
loneliness. But there's also a sense or two in which a song can create silence: when we're "lost in a song" the rest of the world around us makes,
for all practical purposes, no sound. And in an even more strange way, a
song we love goes silent as we "listen" to it, leaving us in that rather primitive place where all the sounds are interior ones—sounds which can't be
distinguished from feelings, from pulsings and shiverings, from that gut
need to make life stronger than death for at least a few moments.

When "Only the Lonely" faded, that wonderful deejay still knew   20
enough not to say a word. She threw us straight forward, 4:15 A.M., into
"Pretty Woman." ▪

STEP TWO: EXPLORE. On the opposing right page of your journal, begin an open-ended fastwrite that explores your reaction to the facts and details of the story that you have written on the left hand page. Answer the following questions: *What does the essay mean to you? In what ways does it connect to your own experience? What does it make you think or feel? What might the passages or other fragments you collected mean, and how might they contribute to the themes of the essay?*

STEP THREE: FOCUS. Shift to a critical mode of thinking, and analyze what you have written and collected so far. In no more than three sentences, state what you currently believe to be the main concept or idea behind Corey's essay. This is your thesis statement. Do this in the right column, underneath your fastwriting from the previous step.

STEP FOUR: EXPLAIN. Immediately below your thesis statement, explain to yourself how the passages or fragments you collected from the essay in the left column (and others you may yet gather) contribute to your interpretation of "A Voice for the Lonely."

STEP FIVE: COLLECT. Reread the essay, and collect evidence—quotes, passages, details—that seem to support or extend your thesis. Add these to the notes you've already collected on the left page of your notebook.

STEP SIX: FOCUS. Revise your thesis statement to reflect your latest thinking about Corey's essay. Do this on the right page.

STEP SEVEN: EVALUATE. Reread your journal, and jot down in the right column at least four reasons you think your interpretation of the essay is correct. These are "because" statements that might naturally follow your thesis. For example, "I think Corey's essay is about _____ because _____."

STEP EIGHT: DRAFT. Using the writing and thinking you've generated so far, draft a 300- to 500-word response to the essay. It should declare and support your thesis statement. If you can, begin your piece with a passage from "A Voice for the Lonely" that is important to your understanding of the essay.

STEP NINE: REFLECT. After completing your response, write a cover letter for it addressed to your instructor. You letter should address the following questions:

- As you were using your writing to think through your response to Corey's essay did you find that your ideas about it evolved or did they stay pretty much the same? Did anything surprise you?
- Which step in the exercise seemed most productive for you? Why?
- Can you imagine how you might use a process like this to write your own essays?

WRITING WITH COMPUTERS

USING THE COMMENTS FUNCTION

The comments function of your word processor can be a particularly useful tool for reflecting on your own writing. This function allows you to reflect at length on any word or passage within your draft without actually inserting any words into the text. To add comments to a word processor document, just highlight a word or passage and select the comment function under the *Insert* menu. A window will then appear in which you can compose your comments. When you complete your comments, the word or passage in question will remain highlighted in the main text but your comments will only appear if you move and hold the cursor over the highlighted text. While you can easily go back and delete your comments individually, if you are going to make extensive comments throughout the draft, it is advisable to save a copy of the original draft and make your comments to the copy.

- What comparisons would you make between your experience in this exercise and the other four exercises in this chapter? What questions do you have about the four ways of inquiring?

USING WHAT YOU HAVE LEARNED

Section Two: Inquiry Projects, which follows, will introduce a range of genres and writing assignments. While each has different features and purposes, I believe you'll find that the *process* of composing these essays draws heavily on what you've learned about writing in these first three chapters. Whether you're writing a personal essay or a research paper, some of the same things will guide you:

- The spirit of inquiry will guide your writing.
- You will use the power of questions to help you to see what isn't immediately obvious.
- You will employ constructive habits of mind, such as making the familiar strange, suspending judgment, and searching for surprise.
- You will make rhetorical choices based on the needs of the writing or reading situation.
- You will use dialectical thinking to guide your writing and reading processes, moving back and forth between the creative and the critical.
- You will use exploration, explanation, evaluation, and reflection to get the most out of your inquiry projects.
- You will experience the pleasure of using writing to not only say what you already know but to discover what you didn't know you knew.

Part Two
INQUIRY PROJECTS

Writing a personal essay is often like seeing an old picture of yourself. It thrusts you back into a particular time and place, but at the same time you see yourself from a certain distance, bringing knowledge and understanding to past events that you didn't have when they occurred. This publicity photograph of my mother, brother, and me in the 1950s returns me to that world and at the same time I see what I couldn't have seen then: a time when fathers were often missing from the picture while working mothers, like mine, had to move gracefully from family to job, proving themselves at both.

Writing a Personal Essay

4

WRITING ABOUT EXPERIENCE

Certain subjects demand to be "essayed." Some years ago, for example, I was invited to serve on a panel at a national conference of writing teachers that would look at what it might mean to be men teaching men. At question was whether we, as male teachers, had noticed anything about the kind of topics male composition students chose when invited to write about their personal experiences and how we reacted to those topics. At first, I was flattered by the invitation. My fellow panelists were among the top scholars in the field and I was just finishing my doctorate. Then I panicked. This was a potentially explosive subject that I had a range of feelings about, some of which I thought might insult some of my former male students. The worst thing, however, was that I really didn't know what I wanted to say, and I was very reluctant to make an argument—the usual way of forming an academic paper—that I wasn't sure I believed. Fortunately, I had recently embraced a form of inquiry that seemed to accommodate my confusion and conflicted feelings: the personal essay.

As a form, the *personal* essay places the writer at center stage. This doesn't mean that once there the writer's responsibility is to pour out her secrets, share her pain, or confess her sins. Some essays do have these confessional qualities, but more often they do not. Yet a personal essayist, no matter what the subject of his or her essay, is still *exposed*. There is no hiding behind the pronoun "one," as in "one might think" or "one often feels," no lurking in the shadows of the passive voice: "This paper will argue. . . ." The personal essay is first person territory.

In this sense, the personal essay is much like a photographic self-portrait. Like a picture, a good personal essay tells the truth, or it

What You'll Learn in This Chapter

- How personal essays can help you with academic writing.

- What distinguishes a personal essay from other forms.

- How to write a sketch.

- Why a confusing topic may be better than one you have all figured out.

- Questions for revising personal essays.

tells *a* truth about the writer/subject, and it often captures the writer at a particular moment of time. Therefore, the experience of taking a self-portrait, or confronting an old picture of oneself taken by someone else, can create the feeling of exposure that writing a personal essay often does.

But it does more. When we gaze at ourselves in a photograph we often see it as yanked from a larger story about ourselves, stories that thread their way through our lives and give us ideas about who we were and who we are. This is what the personal essay demands of us: We must somehow present ourselves truthfully and measure our past against the present. In other words, when we hold a photograph of ourselves we know more than the person we see there knew, and as writers of the personal essay, we must share that knowledge and understanding with readers.

MOTIVES FOR WRITING A PERSONAL ESSAY

The *essai* was a term first coined by the sixteenth century French nobleman Michel de Montaigne, a man who had lived through occurrences of the plague, the bloody civil war between French Catholics and Protestants, and his own ill health. These were tumultuous and uncertain times when old social orders and intellectual traditions were under assault, and it proved to be ideal ferment for the essay. The French verb "essaier" means *to attempt* or *to try,* and the essay became an opportunity for Montaigne to work out his thoughts about war, the education of children, the evils of doctors, and the importance of pleasure. The personal essay tradition inspired by Montaigne is probably unlike the essays you are familiar with in school. The school essay is often formulaic—a five paragraph theme, or thesis-example paper—while the personal essay is an open-ended form that allows for uncertainty and inconclusiveness. It is more about the process of coming to know than presenting *what* you know. The personal essay attempts *to find out* rather than *to prove.*

It is an ideal form of inquiry if your purpose is exploratory rather than argumentative, and if you're particularly interested in working out the possible relationships between your subject and yourself. Because the personal essay is openly subjective, the writer can't hide. The intruding *I* confronts the writer with the same questions, over and over again: Why does this matter to me? What do I make of it? How does this change the way I think of myself and the way I see the world? Because of this, one of the principal dangers of the personal essay is that it becomes narcissistic; it goes on and on about what the writer thinks and feels, and the reader is left with that nagging question—*So what?* The personal essayist must always find some way to hitch the particulars of her experience to something larger—an idea, a theme, or even a feeling that readers might share.

On the other hand, one of the prime rhetorical advantages of the personal essay is its subjectivity. Because it is written with openness and honesty, the essay is often a very intimate form, inviting the reader to share in the writer's often-concealed world. In the personal essay, we often get to see the face sweating under the mask. Honesty is one of the essay's primary virtues, and because the form allows for uncertainty and confusion, the writer doesn't need to pretend that she has *the* answer, or that he knows more than he lets on about his subject.

PERSONAL ESSAYS AND ACADEMIC WRITING

In some ways, the personal essay might seem like a dramatic departure from the kind of academic writing you've done in other classes. Openly subjective and sometimes tentative in its conclusions, the personal essay is a relatively open form that is not predictably structured like much academic writing. Additionally, the tone of the personal essay is conversational, even intimate, rather than impersonal and removed. If your sociology or economics professor will never ask for a personal essay, why bother to write one in your composition class?

It's a fair question. While the pleasures of personal essay writing can be significant, and reason alone to write essays, there are other important reasons to practice the form. The most obvious is that the essay, more than any other form, gives you an opportunity to use exploring as a method of inquiry, and to practice those habits of mind that are so important to academic inquiry: suspending judgment, tolerating ambiguity, and using questions to challenge easy assumptions.

But the purpose of writing personal essays in your composition class goes beyond this. For one thing, the essay emphasizes the *process* of coming to know about yourself and your subject, exposing your reasoning and the ways you use knowledge to get at the truth of things. Reflecting on these things in a personal essay can tell you a lot about how you think. The *dialectical thinking* required by the personal essay—the movement back and forth between critical and creative thinking—should also prove to be a useful mental exercise for a range of academic situations. Finally, much of what you are asked to write in college depends on your willingness to step forward and express a belief, make an assertion, or pose a relevant question. The personal essay is a form that puts the writer in the spotlight. You can't hide in the wings, concealed in the shadow of other people's opinions or someone else's findings. What *you* think is what the essay is all about.

> *The* dialectical thinking *required by the personal essay—the movement back and forth between critical and creative thinking—is a useful mental exercise for a range of academic situations.*

FEATURES OF THE FORM

There are many different kinds of personal essays, of course, but there are certain conventions that are present in most of them. Keep these in mind as you read the professional essays that follow. Which of the conventions below seem present? Can you detect any others?

- *Personal essays are usually written in the first person.* There is no pretense of scientific objectivity in personal essays. What makes them work is the tension between the subject and the writer as the writer reaches for new understandings.

- *The subject of the essay is often commonplace.* Although essayists sometimes write about dramatic things, they most often are interested in the drama of everyday life. Fine essays have been published, for example, about hats, houseflies, and summer lakes. The essayist's thoughts about such things may catapult her beyond the ordinary, but the topic is often humble.

- *Narrative is often the primary method of development.* Personal essays often tell two kinds of stories—they relate narratives of the writer's experiences and observations, and they tell the story of the writer's thinking about what those experiences and observations might mean.

- *The thesis can be implicit, and it frequently emerges late, rather than at the beginning, of the essay.* In some ways, the personal essay is the most literary of the academic forms—it tells stories, relies heavily on details, it shows *and* tells. As a result, the meaning of an essay can be implied rather than stated directly, and because essays are often used to describe *the process* of coming to know something, insight is usually earned later rather than at the beginning of the telling.

- *Of the four sources of information, the personal essay relies on memory and observation most of all.* Because of the subjectivity of the essay, the writer often reports *what has happened* to her as a means to account for *what happens.* However, interview and research can enrich a personal essay by challenging the writer to consider other voices and other information (see Chapter 11, "Writing a Research Essay").

- *The essay often mimics the dialectical process that helped the writer compose it, shifting back and forth from the then and now, what happened to what happens, and showing and telling.* Because the essay, more than any other form of inquiry, often focuses on the process of coming to know, essays themselves often capture this process in action. See if you can see evidence of this movement in the essays that follow.

PERSONAL ESSAY

Most of us know the work of George Orwell (born Eric Blair) from his novels, particularly *Animal Farm* and *Nineteen Eighty-Four,* but he also was a prolific journalist and essayist. Many of his best-known essays recount his experiences as a member of the Indian Imperial Police for the British colonial government in Burma; he wrote the essay that follows retrospectively about that time in his life.

Orwell is an interesting personal essayist because he had strong feelings about two things: writing style and politics. These concerns come together in his famous essay, "Politics and the English Language" (1946), in which Orwell rails against the pretentiousness and lack of precision of modern prose, and particularly the poisoning of the language by political jargon. Orwell wrote that "political language—and with variations this is true of all political parties, from Conservatives to Anarchists—is designed to make lies sound truthful and murder respectable, and to give an appearance of solidity to pure wind."

Orwell's prescription for good writing, which is exemplified in "A Hanging," turns on the virtues of simplicity: Never use a long word when a short one will do, if it is possible to cut a word always cut it, and avoid stale language and overused metaphors. He also urged writers to avoid meaningless abstractions and to focus on "pictures and sensations" that bring those abstractions to life. Lurking behind the narrative you're about to read, one that is rich with such pictures and sensations, Orwell makes a point that certainly might have been explained more generally. But would it have been as effective that way? (Actually, "A Hanging" could easily be classified as an argumentative essay, highlighting how difficult it is to neatly place a piece of writing in a specific genre.)

Personal essays are often structured to mimic the thinking process that led to their creation, the back and forth from the mountain of reflection to the sea of experience, from telling to showing, from what happens to what happened. That movement is quite obvious in "A Hanging." Can you see it?

A HANGING
George Orwell

It was in Burma, a sodden morning of the rains. A sickly light, like yellow tinfoil, was slanting over the high walls into the jail yard. We were waiting outside the condemned cells, a row of sheds fronted with double bars, like small animal cages. Each cell measured about ten feet by ten and was quite bare within except for a plank bed and a pot for drinking water. In some of them brown silent men were squatting at the inner bars, with their blankets draped round them. These were the condemned men, due to be hanged within the next week or two.

One prisoner had been brought out of his cell. He was a Hindu, a puny wisp of a man, with a shaven head and vague liquid eyes. He had a thick, sprouting moustache, absurdly too big for his body, rather like the moustache of a comic man on the films. Six tall Indian warders were guarding him and getting him ready for the gallows. Two of them stood by with rifles and fixed bayonets, while the others handcuffed him, passed a chain through his handcuffs and fixed it to their belts, and lashed his arms tight to his sides. They crowded very close about him, with their hands always on him in a careful, caressing grip, as though all the while feeling him to make sure he was there. It was like men handling a fish which is still alive and may jump back into the water. But he stood quite unresisting, yielding his arms limply to the ropes, as though he hardly noticed what was happening.

3   Eight o'clock struck and a bugle call, desolately thin in the wet air, floated from the distant barracks. The superintendent of the jail, who was standing apart from the rest of us, moodily prodding the gravel with his stick, raised his head at the sound. He was an army doctor, with a gray toothbrush moustache and a gruff voice. "For God's sake hurry up, Francis," he said irritably. "The man ought to have been dead by this time. Aren't you ready yet?"

4   Francis, the head jailer, a fat Dravidian in a white drill suit and gold spectacles, waved his black hand. "Yes sir, yes sir," he bubbled. "All iss satisfactorily prepared. The hangman iss waiting. We shall proceed."

5   "Well, quick march, then. The prisoners can't get their breakfast till this job's over."

6   We set out for the gallows. Two warders marched on either side of the prisoner, with their rifles at the slope; two others marched close against him, gripping him by arm and shoulder, as though at once pushing and supporting him. The rest of us, magistrates and the like, followed behind. Suddenly, when we had gone ten yards, the procession stopped short without any order or warning. A dreadful thing had happened—a dog, come goodness knows whence, had appeared in the yard. It came bounding among us with a loud volley of barks, and leapt round us wagging its whole body, wild with glee at finding so many human beings together. It was a large woolly dog, half Airedale, half pariah. For a moment it pranced round us, and then, before anyone could stop it, it had made a dash for the prisoner and, jumping up, tried to lick his face. Everyone stood aghast, too taken aback even to grab at the dog.

7   "Who let that bloody brute in here?" said the superintendent angrily. "Catch it, someone!"

8   A warder, detached from the escort, charged clumsily after the dog, but it danced and gamboled just out of his reach, taking everything as part of the game. A young Eurasian jailer picked up a handful of gravel and tried to stone the dog away, but it dodged the stones and came after us again. Its yaps echoed from the jail walls. The prisoner, in the grasp of the two warders, looked on incuriously, as though this was another formality of the hanging. It was several minutes before someone managed to catch the dog. Then we put my handkerchief through its collar and moved off once more, with the dog still straining and whimpering.

9   It was about forty yards to the gallows. I watched the bare brown back of the prisoner marching in front of me. He walked clumsily with his bound

arms, but quite steadily, with that bobbing gait of the Indian who never straightens his knees. At each step his muscles slid neatly into place, the lock of hair on his scalp danced up and down, his feet printed themselves on the wet gravel. And once, in spite of the men who gripped him by each shoulder, he stepped slightly aside to avoid a puddle on the path.

It is curious, but till that moment I had never realized what it means to de- 10 stroy a healthy, conscious man. When I saw the prisoner step aside to avoid the puddle I saw the mystery, the unspeakable wrongness, of cutting a life short when it is in full tide. This man was not dying, he was alive just as we are alive. All the organs of his body were working—bowels digesting food, skin renew- ing itself, nails growing, tissues forming—all toiling away in solemn foolery. His nails would still be growing when he stood on the drop, when he was falling through the air with a tenth of a second to live. His eyes saw the yellow gravel and the gray walls, and his brain still remembered, foresaw, reasoned— reasoned even about puddles. He and we were a party of men walking to- gether, seeing, hearing, feeling, understanding the same world; and in two minutes, with a sudden snap, one of us would be gone—one mind less, one world less.

The gallows stood in a small yard, separate from the main grounds of the 11 prison, and overgrown with tall prickly weeds. It was a brick erection like three sides of a shed, with planking on top, and above that two beams and a crossbar with the rope dangling. The hangman, a gray-haired convict in the white uniform of the prison, was waiting beside his machine. He greeted us with a servile crouch as we entered. At a word from Francis the two warders, gripping the prisoner more closely than ever, half led half pushed him to the gallows and helped him clumsily up the ladder. Then the hangman climbed up and fixed the rope round the prisoner's neck.

We stood waiting, five yards away. The warders had formed in a rough cir- 12 cle round the gallows. And then, when the noose was fixed, the prisoner began crying out to his god. It was a high, reiterated cry of "Ram! Ram! Ram! Ram!" not urgent and fearful like a prayer or cry for help, but steady, rhythmical, al- most like the tolling of a bell. The dog answered the sound with a whine. The hangman, still standing on the gallows, produced a small cotton bag like a flour bag and drew it down over the prisoner's face. But the sound, muffled by the cloth, still persisted, over and over again: "Ram! Ram! Ram! Ram! Ram!"

The hangman climbed down and stood ready, holding the lever. Minutes 13 seemed to pass. The steady, muffled crying from the prisoner went on and on, "Ram! Ram! Ram!" never faltering for an instant. The superintendent, his head on his chest, was slowly poking the ground with his stick; perhaps he was counting the cries, allowing the prisoner a fixed number—fifty, perhaps, or a hundred. Everyone had changed color. The Indians had gone gray like bad coffee, and one or two of the bayonets were wavering. We looked at the lashed, hooded man on the drop, and listened to his cries—each cry another second of life; the same thought was in all our minds: oh, kill him quickly, get it over, stop that abominable noise!

14   Suddenly the superintendent made up his mind. Throwing up his head he made a swift motion with his stick. "Chalo!" he shouted almost fiercely.

15   There was a clanking noise, and then dead silence. The prisoner had vanished, and the rope was twisting on itself. I let go of the dog, and it galloped immediately to the back of the gallows; but when it got there it stopped short, barked, and then retreated into a corner of the yard, where it stood among the weeds, looking timorously out at us. We went round the gallows to inspect the prisoner's body. He was dangling with his toes pointed straight downward, very slowly revolving, as dead as a stone.

16   The superintendent reached out with his stick and poked the bare brown body; it oscillated slightly. "*He's* all right," said the superintendent. He backed out from under the gallows, and blew out a deep breath. The moody look had gone out of his face quite suddenly. He glanced at his wrist watch. "Eight minutes past eight. Well, that's all for this morning, thank God."

17   The warders unfixed bayonets and marched away. The dog, sobered and conscious of having misbehaved itself, slipped after them. We walked out of the gallows yard, past the condemned cells with their waiting prisoners, into the big central yard of the prison. The convicts, under the command of warders armed with lathis, were already receiving their breakfast. They squatted in long rows, each man holding a tin pannikin, while two warders with buckets marched round ladling out rice; it seemed quite a homely, jolly scene, after the hanging. An enormous relief had come upon us now that the job was done. One felt an impulse to sing, to break into a run, to snigger. All at once everyone began chattering gaily.

18   The Eurasian boy walking beside me nodded toward the way we had come, with a knowing smile: "Do you know, sir, our friend [he meant the dead man] when he heard his appeal had been dismissed, he pissed on the floor of his cell. From fright. Kindly take one of my cigarettes, sir. Do you not admire my new silver case, sir? From the boxwalah, two rupees eight annas, Classy European style."

19   Several people laughed—at what, nobody seemed certain.

20   Francis was walking by the superintendent, talking garrulously: "Well, sir, all hass passed off with the utmost satisfactoriness. It was all finished—flick! like that. It iss not always so—oah, no! I have known cases where the doctor wass obliged to go beneath the gallows and pull the prissoner's legs to ensure decease. Most disagreeable!"

21   "Wriggling about, eh? That's bad," said the superintendent.

"Ach, sir, it iss worse when they become refractory! One man, I recall, 22
clung to the bars of hiss cage when we went to take him out. You will scarcely
credit, sir, that it took six warders to dislodge him, three pulling at each leg.
We reasoned with him. 'My dear fellow,' we said, 'think of all the pain and
trouble you are causing to us!' But no, he would not listen! Ach, he was very
troublesome."

I found that I was laughing quite loudly. Everyone was laughing. Even the 23
superintendent grinned in a tolerant way. "You'd better all come out and have
a drink," he said quite genially. "I've got a bottle of whisky in the car. We could
do with it."

We went through the big double gates of the prison into the road. "Pulling 24
at his legs!" exclaimed a Burmese magistrate suddenly, and burst into a loud
chuckling. We all began laughing again. At that moment Francis' anecdote
seemed extraordinarily funny. We all had a drink together, native and European
alike, quite amicably. The dead man was a hundred yards away.   [1931]

Inquiring into the Essay

Throughout *The Curious Writer,* I'll invite you to respond to readings such
as Orwell's "A Hanging," using questions based on the four methods of inquiry discussed in Chapter 3. The questions below, therefore, encourage
you to explore, explain, evaluate, and reflect to discover and shape what
you think about the reading. If you're using a double-entry journal, use
these questions to prompt writing on the right page of your notebook. Use
the opposing left page to collect passages, details, and quotations from the
reading that you think might be important.

1. Begin by openly exploring your reaction to "A Hanging." Fastwrite for
   five minutes but begin by focusing on a particular line or passage from
   the essay that you found puzzling, significant, or potentially important. Ask yourself questions to keep your pen and your mind moving.

2. Choose a line or passage from the essay (perhaps the one you began
   with in the previous question) that you think gets to the heart of
   Orwell's purpose in the essay. Compose an explanation of why you
   think this passage is significant.

3. Orwell is making an evaluation in "A Hanging," although the essay
   initially just seems like an interesting story. What is his claim? Is it
   convincing? What reasons and evidence does he provide to support
   it? Is Orwell's approach in this essay more effective in making his
   point than a more conventional argument might have been? Why?

4. Reflect on how "A Hanging" seems to conform to the features of
   the personal essay described earlier. In what ways does it depart
   from them?

PERSONAL ESSAY

It is impossible to avoid the tentacles of fashion. As much as I spurn what's trendy, my decision to wear an old pair of topsiders rather than the intricate leather Italian-made sandals my wife bought me *is* a decision. I act *against* fashion in the deliberate ways that some people act to keep up with it. It is not, by the way, a character flaw to want to be fashionable; it just takes more effort than I'm willing to give.

But there is a time in nearly everyone's life—usually when we are children or adolescents—when we simply must have something because everyone else does. For Barbara Kingsolver, it was white go-go boots. Remembering this desire becomes an occasion for Kingsolver to reflect on her own entanglements with fashion, and particularly how she might respond when her own daughter wants the 1990s equivalent of go-go boots. Like most personal essays, this one tells stories but it never strays from larger questions about conformity, identity, and parenting.

LIFE WITHOUT GO-GO BOOTS
Barbara Kingsolver

1   Fashion nearly wrecked my life. I grew up beyond its pale, convinced that this would stunt me in some irreparable way. I don't think it has, but for a long time it was touch and go.

2   We lived in the country, in the middle of an alfalfa field; we had no immediate access to Bobbie Brooks sweaters. I went to school in the hand-me-downs of a cousin three years older. She had excellent fashion sense, but during the three-year lag her every sleek outfit turned to a pumpkin. In fifth grade, when girls were wearing straight shifts with buttons down the front, I wore pastel shirtwaists with cap sleeves and a multitude of built-in petticoats. My black lace-up oxfords, which my parents perceived to have orthopedic value, carried their own weight in the spectacle. I suspected people noticed, and I knew it for sure on the day Billy Stamps announced to the lunch line: "Make way for the Bride of Frankenstein."

3   I suffered quietly, casting an ever-hopeful eye on my eighth-grade cousin whose button-front shifts someday would be mine. But by the time I was an eighth grader, everyone with an iota of social position wore polka-dot shirts and miniskirts. For Christmas, I begged for go-go boots. The rest of my life would be endurable if I had a pair of those white, calf-high confections with the little black heels. My mother, though always inscrutable near Christmas,

seemed sympathetic; there was hope. Never mind that those little black heels are like skate blades in inclement weather. I would walk on air.

On Christmas morning I received white rubber boots with treads like a pair of Michelins. My mother loved me, but had missed the point.   4

In high school I took matters into my own hands. I learned to sew. I contrived to make an apple-green polyester jumpsuit that was supremely fashionable for about two months. Since it took me forty days and forty nights to make the thing, my moment of glory was brief. I learned what my mother had been trying to tell me all along: high fashion has the shelf life of potato salad. And when past its prime, it is similarly deadly.   5

Once I left home and went to college I was on my own, fashion-wise, having bypassed my cousin in stature and capped the arrangement off by moving to another state. But I found I still had to reckon with life's limited choices. After classes I worked variously as a house cleaner, typesetter, and artists' model. I could spend my wages on trendy apparel (which would be useless to me in any of my jobs, particularly the latter), or on the lesser gratifications of food and textbooks. It was a tough call, but I opted for education. This was Indiana and it was cold; when it wasn't cold, it was rainy. I bought an army surplus overcoat, with zip-out lining, that reached my ankles, and I found in my parents' attic a green pith helmet. I became a known figure on campus. Fortunately, this was the era in which army boots were a fashion option for co-eds. And besides, who knew? Maybe under all that all-weather olive drab was a Bobbie Brooks sweater. My social life picked right up.   6

As an adult, I made two hugely fortuitous choices in the women's-wear department: first, I moved out West, where the buffalo roam and hardly anyone is ever arrested for being unstylish. Second, I became a novelist. Artists (also mathematicians and geniuses) are greatly indulged by society when it comes to matters of grooming. If we happen to look like an unmade bed, it's presumed we're preoccupied with plot devices or unifying theories or things of that ilk.   7

Even so, when I was invited to attend an important author event on the East Coast, a friend took me in hand.   8

"Writers are *supposed* to be eccentric," I wailed.   9

My friend, one of the people who loves me best in the world, replied: "Barbara, you're not eccentric, you're an anachronism," and marched me down to an exclusive clothing shop.   10

It was a very small store; I nearly hyperventilated. "You could liquidate the stock here and feed an African nation for a year," I whispered. But under pressure I bought a suit, and wore it to the important author function. For three hours of my life I was precisely in vogue.   11

12   Since then it has reigned over my closet from its dry-cleaner bag, feeling unhappy and out of place, I am sure, a silk ambassador assigned to a flannel republic. Even if I go to a chichi restaurant, the suit stays home. I'm always afraid I'll spill something on it; I'd be too nervous to enjoy myself. It turns out I would rather converse than make a statement.

13   Now, there is fashion, and there is *style*. The latter, I've found, will serve, and costs less. Style is mostly a matter of acting as if you know very well what you look like, thanks, and are just delighted about it. It also requires consistency. A friend of mine wears buckskin moccasins every day of her life. She has daytime and evening moccasins. This works fine in Arizona, but when my friend fell in love with a Tasmanian geologist and prepared to move to a rain forest, I worried. Moccasins instantaneously decompose in wet weather. But I should have known, my friend has sense. She bought clear plastic galoshes to button over her moccasins, and writes me that she's happy.

14   I favor cowboy boots. I don't do high heels, because you never know when you might actually have to get somewhere, and most other entries in the ladies-shoes category look to me like Ol' Dixie and Ol' Dobbin trying to sneak into the Derby, trailing their plow. Cowboy boots aren't trying. They say, "I'm no pump, and furthermore, so what?" That characterizes my whole uniform, in fact: oversized flannel shirts, jeans or cotton leggings, and cowboy boots when weather permits. In summer I lean toward dresses that make contact with the body (if at all) only on the shiatsu acupressure points; maybe also a Panama hat; and sneakers. I am happy.

15   I'm also a parent, which of course calls into question every decision one ever believes one has made for the last time. Can I raise my daughter as a raiment renegade? At present she couldn't care less. Maybe obsessions skip a generation. She was blessed with two older cousins whose sturdy hand-me-downs she has worn from birth, with relish. If she wasn't entirely a fashion plate, she also escaped being typecast. For her first two years she had no appreciable hair, to which parents can clamp those plastic barrettes that are gender dead giveaways. So when I took her to the park in cousin Ashley's dresses, strangers commented on her blue eyes and lovely complexion; when she wore Andrew's playsuits emblazoned with trucks and airplanes (why is it we only decorate our boys with modes of transportation?), people always commented on how strong and alert my child was—and what's his name?

16   This interests me. I also know it can't last. She's in school now, and I'm very quickly remembering what school is about: two parts ABCs to fifty parts Where Do I Stand in the Great Pecking Order of Humankind? She still rejects stereotypes, with extraordinary good humor. She has a dress-up collection to

die for, gleaned from Goodwill and her grandparents' world travels, and likely as not will show up to dinner wearing harem pants, bunny ears, a glitter-bra over her T-shirt, wooden shoes, and a fez. But underneath it all, she's only human. I have a feeling the day might come when my daughter will beg to be a slave of conventional fashion.

I'm inclined to resist, if it happens. To press on her the larger truths I finally absorbed from my own wise parents: that she can find her own path. That she will be more valued for inward individuality than outward conformity. That a world plagued by poverty can ill afford the planned obsolescence of *haute couture.*   17

But a small corner of my heart still harbors the Bride of Frankenstein, eleven years of age, haunting me in her brogues and petticoats. Always and forever, the ghosts of past anguish compel us to live through our children. If my daughter ever asks for the nineties equivalent of go-go boots, I'll cave in.   18

Maybe I'll also buy her some of those clear plastic galoshes to button over them on inclement days.   19

Inquiring into the Essay

Explore, explain, evaluate, and reflect on Kingsolver's "Life Without Go-Go Boots."

1. Explore your own experiences with fashion. Perhaps begin, as Kingsolver did in her essay, by fastwriting about the first fashionable piece of clothing you longed to have. Or focus on your own memories of the fashion trends that swept around and through you when you were younger. Write for seven minutes.

2. Explain where in "Life Without Go-Go Boots" ascends the mountain of reflection, and collectively what do these ideas say about conformity, identity, fashion, or parenting? In other words, what does Kingsolver seem to be saying in this essay?

3. Some view fashion consciousness as a sign of superficiality. Using evidence from Kingsolver's essay and other sources including your own observations, make an evaluation of the role of fashion in your life and, in a larger sense, American culture.

4. Did you like reading this essay? Why? What *specifically* were some of the qualities of "Life Without Go-Go Boots" that you found compelling or interesting? What does this say about your own tastes as a reader? Did you dislike the piece? Can you be specific about why and what it says about your reading tastes? Since we are required to read many kinds of texts, particularly in college, is it possible to change your tastes in reading? How?

PERSONAL ESSAY

The essay that follows shows what Bailey White, a Georgia elementary school teacher and commentator on National Public Radio, does with the personal essay. She writes with charm and grace about little things often linked to her southern life and heritage. Don't be fooled, however; there is a fierce intelligence behind what seem to be simple essays. "Forbidden Things" is a piece that ponders White's reaction to the ubiquitous signs of warning often encountered in public places. Who might be responsible for them, she wonders, and what is he like?

As you read "Forbidden Things," consider which of the features of the personal essay listed earlier seem present in Bailey's work. In particular, is there an implicit theme in this essay, and if so, what might it be? What is Bailey trying to say here about warning signs?

FORBIDDEN THINGS
Bailey White

1   I was leaning over the little railing, looking down into the Devil's Millhopper, an interesting geological formation and the focal point of a Florida state park. Waterfalls plunge 120 feet down into a bowl-shaped sinkhole; maidenhair ferns and moss grow in little crevices along the steep, sloping sides of the gorge; and a beautiful mist rises up.

2   I stood there, gazing down, and feeling a reverence for these spectacles of the natural world. I felt the slow sweep of geologic time. I felt the remnants of the spiritual significance this place had had for the Indians who lived here for thousands of years. I felt the wonder and awe of the first European explorers of Florida looking down into this chasm for the first time.

3   Then another feeling crept over me, a deep, almost atavistic longing. It was the urge to throw something down into the Devil's Millhopper. I looked around. A stone or a stick would do, but what I really wanted was a piece of food, the nibbled end of a hotdog bun or a wedge of chocolate cake without the icing. Then I noticed the sign, one of those tastefully unobtrusive state park signs:

DO NOT THROW FOOD OR TRASH IN GORGE

4   It was 4:00 A.M. I was at the Los Angeles, California, bus station, my next-to-last stop on a dreary transcontinental bus trip—three days and three nights on a Greyhound bus. My back ached, my knees ached, my head ached. Ever

since El Paso, Texas, my seatmate had been an old man who chain-smoked Marlboro cigarettes and sucked and slobbered over a perpetual ham sandwich that kept oozing out of a greasy crumple of waxed paper.

I longed for a bath in my own bathtub, and then a deep sleep in my own   5
bed, stretched out full-length between clean sheets. But, I thought, pushing open the door of the bus station bathroom, if I just wash my feet and my hair I will be all right. I lined up my soap, my washrag, and my little bottle of shampoo on the back of the sink and took off my shoes and socks. Ahh, I thought. Then I saw the sign on the mirror:

DO NOT WASH HAIR OR FEET IN SINK

A few weeks ago I went into our little downtown restaurant and saw that   6
it had replaced its tired old salad bar with a gorgeous saltwater aquarium with sea anemones, chunks of living coral, and big slow-moving colorful fish with faces I could almost recognize. I spent my whole lunchtime staring into that tank, mesmerized by the fish as they gracefully looped and glided, sending the tentacles of the sea anemones into slow twirls and fanning out the tall grasses.

When I finished my sandwich I noticed that there were a couple of crumbs   7
left on my plate, just the size to pinch between thumb and finger. Oh, I thought, to pinch up those crumbs and dip my fingers down into the water, breaking through the smooth surface into the coolness and silence of that peaceful world. One of the fish would make a looping turn, his odd exophrhalmic eyes would rotate slowly in their sockets and fix upon the crumbs in my fingers. Then he would angle up, and I would feel for just one exquisite instant those thorny fish lips rasping across my fingertips. With rising delight and anticipation, I pinched up a crumb, two crumbs. I scrabbled across the plastic top of the tank, found the little door, lifted it open—and then I saw the sign:

DO NOT FEED THE FISH

*   *   *   *   *   *   *   *   *   *

WE PROHIBIT CLIMBING IN ANY MANNER
FROM OR ALONG THE CANYON RIM

DO NOT PICK FLOWERS

NO SMOKING EATING OR DRINKING

NO SWINGING FROM VINES IN TREES

NO PEDESTRIAN TRAFFIC IN WOODS

NO FISHING

NO SWIMMING

NO TRESPASSING

8   Don't get me wrong; I approve of these prohibitions. Imagine the nasty mess in the bottom of the Devil's Millhopper if every self-indulgent tourist threw a piece of food into the sinkhole. Imagine the puddles on the floor and the plumbing complications in the Los Angeles bus station if every weary trans-continental washed her hair and feet in the sink. Imagine the deadly scum of grease on the surface of that saltwater aquarium if every fish-dazed diner fed the catalufa his last mayonnaise-coated crumbs.

9   But sometimes I wonder: Who makes up these necessary and useful rules, and how does he know so well the deep and touching urges of human beings to pick flowers, walk in the woods, climb canyon walls, swing from vines, and feed already well-nourished animals? I imagine with distaste a mean, sour, silent little man skulking around in public places, watching us furtively with squinny eyes while scribbling on his pad with a gnawed pencil. In national parks he disguises himself as a tourist in reflective sunglasses and plaid Bermuda shorts. "Bryce Canyon," he notes with a smirk, "Urinating on hoodoos and off cliffs." In zoos he wears khaki and lurks in the shadows, hiding behind a bag of peanuts. 'Touching giraffe's tongue through fence wire. . . . Feeling camel's hump," he scribbles.

10   At night he goes home, and in his stark white workshop, illuminated with fluorescent lights, he makes those signs. Rounded letters routed out of boards for the parks: "We Prohibit. . . ., No . . ., and No. . ." Spiky green on white zoos: "Do Not, Not Allowed, . . . Is." And-we-mean-it black and white for commercial establishments: "Absolutely NO . . ., Are Required, We Forbid. . ."

11   I imagine, one night, as he works late stacking and bundling signs for the next day's delivery, the tendril of a grapevine creeps in at his window. When his back is turned, its pale noose will gently nudge around him.

12   "No Touching!" he will admonish.

13   But with a clutch and a snatch the vine will retract, and he will find himself yanked through the night sky above a central Florida state park.

14   "Do Not, Swing from Vines!" he will shriek.

15   And with that, the vine will untwine and drop him into the vortex of a limpid spring.

16   "No Swimming!" he will sputter as the dark, icy water closes over his head. As he sinks, strange, pale-colored fish will swim up and cock their eyes at him.

17   "Do Not Feed the Fish," he will squeak. But, slowly and precisely, the fish will angle up, move in, and then, all over, he will feel the pick pick pick of those prickly lips.

INQUIRING INTO THE ESSAY

Use the four methods of inquiry—exploring, explaining, evaluating, and reflecting—to think through writing about White's essay and to analyze her approach.

1. An appeal of the personal essay is its focus on experiences or feelings the reader and writer share. We all, for example, have feelings about rules. In your notebook, begin a fastwrite that explores your own experiences and observations about "forbidden things." Begin by remembering a time when you consciously broke the rules. Describe what happened in detail. Skip a line, and write about another moment of dutifully following the rules, and maybe having complicated feelings about it. As you look back on these, how do you feel about them?

2. Remember the aphorism to "show, and don't tell" that is often given to fiction writers? Essays, unlike some short stories, generally show *and* tell, moving from the sea to the mountain and back again. Can you detect that movement in this essay? Where? Explain what you noticed about when and where the essay shifts from narration to reflection.

3. Is everything, even a story like this one, an evaluation? Is Bailey White attempting to convince the reader of something? If so, what? What is her central claim and what evidence does she offer to support it?

4. Create a graph of your interest in this essay, as shown in Figure 4.1. Put the paragraph numbers on the horizontal axis and your level of interest, scored from 1 to 5 (with 5 being highest interest and 1 lowest

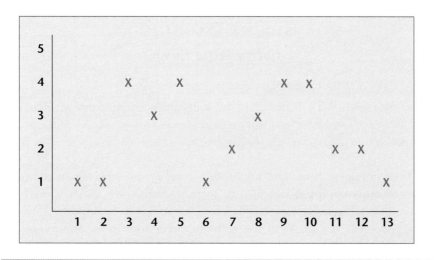

FIGURE 4.1 An example of a graph of reader interest. The horizontal axis lists paragraph numbers and the vertical axis lists the level of interest.

interest), on the vertical axis. Plot the graph and compare your graph with others in the class. Discuss which paragraphs seemed to generate the highest and lowest levels of reader interest. What are the particular qualities of each? Reflect on what your own graph says about you as a reader.

PERSONAL ESSAY

America is a nation of immigrants, and their stories often haunt their children. Judith Ortiz Cofer moved from Puerto Rico as a child with her family in the mid-1950s to a barrio in Paterson, New Jersey. There she became both part of and witness to a familiar narrative, that of the outsider who finds herself wedged between two worlds, two cultures, and two longings: the desire to return "home" and the desire to feel at home in the new place. While this is a story most immigrants know well, it is also a deeply personal one, shaded by particular places, prejudices, and patterns.

Cofer tells her story in an unusual way—it weaves together two separate narratives, each told simultaneously, and divides the essay into sections. Contemporary personal essays frequently use a collage or segmented structure, and they do it for many reasons. In "Silent Dancing," for example, Cofer exploits the juxtaposition of her story of living in Paterson as a child with an account of a home movie where the silent revelers—all relatives and friends—pose for the camera. Told together, the two stories create a tension that is brittle with meaning. Which world do the people in the home movie inhabit—the old one or the new one? How does Cofer's own story compare with the one that is implied in the film? Do both narratives imply the same idea about cultural conflict and assimilation?

SILENT DANCING
Judith Ortiz Cofer

1   *We have a home movie of this party. Several times my mother and I have watched it together, and I have asked questions about the silent revelers coming in and out of focus. It is grainy and of short duration, but it's a great visual aid to my memory of life at that time. And it is in color—the only complete scene in color I can recall from those years.*

2   We lived in Puerto Rico until my brother was born in 1954. Soon after, because of economic pressures on our growing family, my father joined the United States Navy. He was assigned to duty on a ship in Brooklyn Yard—a place of cement and steel that was to be his home base in the States until his retirement more than twenty years later. He left the Island first, alone, going to New York City and tracking down his uncle who lived with his family across

the Hudson River in Paterson, New Jersey. There my father found a tiny apartment in a huge tenement that had once housed Jewish families but was just being taken over and transformed by Puerto Ricans, overflowing from New York City. In 1955 he sent for us. My mother was only twenty years old, I was not quite three, and my brother was a toddler when we arrived at El Building, as the place had been christened by its newest residents.

My memories of life in Paterson during those first few years are all in shades of gray. Maybe I was too young to absorb vivid colors and details, or to discriminate between the slate blue of the winter sky and the darker hues of the snow-bearing clouds, but that single color washes over the whole period. The building we lived in was gray, as were the streets, filled with slush the first few months of my life there. The coat my father had bought for me was similar in color and too big; it sat heavily on my thin frame.   3

I do remember the way the heater pipes banged and rattled, startling all of us out of sleep until we got so used to the sound that we automatically shut it out or raised our voices above the racket. The hiss from the valve punctuated my sleep (which has always been fitful) like a nonhuman presence in the room—a dragon sleeping at the entrance of my childhood. But the pipes were also a connection to all the other lives being lived around us. Having come from a house designed for a single family back in Puerto Rico—my mother's extended-family home—it was curious to know that strangers lived under our floor and above our heads, and that the heater pipe went through everyone's apartment. (My first spanking in Paterson came as a result of playing tunes on the pipes in my room to see if there would be an answer.) My mother was as new to this concept of beehive life as I was, but she had been given strict orders by my father to keep the doors locked, the noise down, ourselves to ourselves.   4

It seems that Father had learned some painful lessons about prejudice while searching for an apartment in Paterson. Not until years later did I hear how much resistance he had encountered with landlords who were panicking at the influx of Latinos into a neighborhood that had been Jewish for a couple of generations. It made no difference that it was the American phenomenon of ethnic turnover which was changing the urban core of Paterson, and that the human flood could not be held back with an accusing finger.   5

"You Cuban?" one man had asked my father, pointing at his name tag on the navy uniform—even though my father had the fair skin and light brown hair of his northern Spanish background, and the name Ortiz is as common in Puerto Rico as Johnson is in the United States.   6

"No," my father had answered, looking past the finger into his adversary's angry eyes. "I'm Puerto Rican."   7

"Same shit." And the door closed.   8

9   My father could have passed as European, but we couldn't. My brother and I both have our mother's black hair and olive skin, and so we lived in El Building and visited our great-uncle and his fair children on the next block. It was their private joke that they were the German branch of the family. Not many years later that area too would be mainly Puerto Rican. It was as if the heart of the city map were being gradually colored brown—*café con leche* brown. Our color.

10   *The movie opens with a sweep of the living room. It is "typical" immigrant Puerto Rican decor for the time: the sofa and chairs are square and hard-looking, upholstered in bright colors (blue and yellow in this instance) and covered with the transparent plastic that furniture salesmen then were so adept at convincing women to buy. The linoleum on the floor is light blue; where it had been subjected to spike heels, as it was in most places, there were dime-size indentations all over it that cannot be seen in this movie. The room is full of people dressed up: dark suits for the men, red dresses for the women. When I have asked my mother why most of the women are in red that night, she has shrugged and said, "I don't remember. Just a coincidence." She doesn't have my obsession for assigning symbolism to everything.*

11   *The three women in red sitting on the couch are my mother, my eighteen-year-old cousin, and her brother's girlfriend. The* novia *is just up from the Island, which is apparent in her body language. She sits up formally, her dress pulled over her knees. She is a pretty girl, but her posture makes her look insecure, lost in her full-skirted dress, which she has carefully tucked around her to make room for my gorgeous cousin, her future sister-in-law. My cousin has grown up in Paterson and is in her last year of high school. She doesn't have a trace of what Puerto Ricans call* la mancha *(literally, the stain: the mark of the new immigrant—something about the posture, the voice, or the humble demeanor that makes it obvious to everyone the person has just arrived on the mainland). My cousin is wearing a tight, sequined, cocktail dress. Her brown hair has been lightened with peroxide around the bangs, and she is holding a cigarette expertly between her fingers, bringing it up to her mouth in a sensuous arc of her arm as she talks animatedly. My mother, who has come up to sit between the two women, both only a few years younger than herself, is somewhere between the poles they represent in our culture.*

12   It became my father's obsession to get out of the barrio, and thus we were never permitted to form bonds with the place or with the people who lived there. Yet El Building was a comfort to my mother, who never got over yearning for *la isla*. She felt surrounded by her language: the walls were thin, and voices speaking and arguing in Spanish could be heard all day. *Salsas* blasted out of radios, turned on early in the morning and left on for company. Women seemed to cook rice and beans perpetually—the strong aroma of boiling red kidney beans permeated the hallways.

Though Father preferred that we do our grocery shopping at the super-   13
market when he came home on weekend leaves, my mother insisted that she
could cook only with products whose labels she could read. Consequently,
during the week I accompanied her and my little brother to La Bodega—a
hole-in-the-wall grocery store across the street from El Building. There we
squeezed down three narrow aisles jammed with various products. Goya and
Libby's—those were the trademarks that were trusted by her *mamá,* so my
mother bought many cans of Goya beans, soups, and condiments, as well as little cans of Libby's fruit juices for us. And she also bought Colgate toothpaste
and Palmolive soap. (The final *e* is pronounced in both these products in
Spanish, so for many years I believed that they were manufactured on the
Island. I remember my surprise at first hearing a commercial on television in
which "Colgate" rhymed with "ate.") We always lingered at La Bodega, for it
was there that Mother breathed best, taking in the familiar aromas of the foods
she knew from Mamá's kitchen. It was also there that she got to speak to the
other women of El Building without violating outright Father's dictates against
fraternizing with our neighbors.

Yet Father did his best to make our "assimilation" painless. I can still see   14
him carrying a real Christmas tree up several flights of stairs to our apartment,
leaving a trail of aromatic pine. He carried it formally, as if it were a flag in a
parade. We were the only ones in El Building that I knew of who got presents
on both Christmas and *día de Reyes,* the day when the Three Kings brought gifts
to Christ and to Hispanic children.

Our supreme luxury in El Building was having our own television set. It   15
must have been a result of Father's guilt feelings over the isolation he had im-
posed on us, but we were among the first in the barrio to have one. My
brother quickly became an avid watcher of Captain Kangaroo and Jungle Jim,
while I loved all the series showing families. By the time I started first grade, I
could have drawn a map of Middle America as exemplified by the lives of characters in *Father Knows Best, The Donna Reed Show, Leave It to Beaver, My Three Sons,*
and (my favorite) *Bachelor Father,* where John Forsythe treated his adopted
teenage daughter like a princess because he was rich and had a Chinese house-
boy to do everything for him. In truth, compared to our neighbors in El
Building, *we* were rich. My father's navy check provided us with financial security and a standard of living that the factory workers envied. The only thing his
money could not buy us was a place to live away from the barrio—his greatest
wish, Mother's greatest fear.

In the home movie the men are shown next, sitting around a card table set up in one cor-   16
ner of the living room, playing dominoes. The clack of the ivory pieces was a familiar

sound. I heard it in many houses on the Island and in many apartments in Paterson. In Leave It to Beaver, the Cleavers played bridge in every other episode; in my childhood, the men started every social occasion with a hotly debated round of dominoes. The women would sit around and watch, but they never participated in the games.

17　　*Here and there you can see a small child. Children were always brought to parties and, whenever they got sleepy, were put to bed in the host's bedroom. Babysitting was a concept unrecognized by the Puerto Rican women I knew: a responsible mother did not leave her children with any stranger. And in a culture where children are not considered intrusive, there was no need to leave the children at home. We went where our mother went.*

18　　Of my preschool years I have only impressions: the sharp bite of the wind in December as we walked with our parents toward the brightly lit stores downtown; how I felt like a stuffed doll in my heavy coat, boots, and mittens; how good it was to walk into the five-and-dime and sit at the counter drinking hot chocolate. On Saturdays our whole family would walk downtown to shop at the big department stores on Broadway. Mother bought all our clothes at Penney's and Sears, and she liked to buy her dresses at the women's specialty shops like Lerner's and Diana's. At some point we'd go into Woolworth's and sit at the soda fountain to eat.

19　　We never ran into other Latinos at these stores or when eating out, and it became clear to me only years later that the women from El Building shopped mainly in other places—stores owned by other Puerto Ricans or by Jewish merchants who had philosophically accepted our presence in the city and decided to make us their good customers, if not real neighbors and friends. These establishments were located not downtown but in the blocks around our street, and they were referred to generically as La Tienda, El Bazar, La Bodega, La Botánica. Everyone knew what was meant. These were the stores where your face did not turn a clerk to stone, where your money was as green as anyone else's.

20　　One New Year's Eve we were dressed up like child models in the Sears catalogue: my brother in a miniature man's suit and bow tie, and I in black patent-leather shoes and a frilly dress with several layers of crinoline underneath. My mother wore a bright red dress that night, I remember, and spike heels; her long black hair hung to her waist. Father, who usually wore his navy uniform during his short visits home, had put on a dark civilian suit for the occasion: we had been invited to his uncle's house for a big celebration. Everyone was excited because my mother's brother Hernan—a bachelor who could indulge himself with luxuries—had bought a home movie camera, which he would be trying out that night.

21　　Even the home movie cannot fill in the sensory details such a gathering left imprinted in a child's brain. The thick sweetness of women's perfumes mixing with the ever-present smells of food cooking in the kitchen: meat and plantain *pasteles,* as well as the ubiquitous rice dish made special with pigeon peas—*gandules*—and seasoned with precious *sofrito* sent up from the Island by somebody's mother or smuggled in by a recent traveler. *Sofrito* was one of the items that women hoarded, since it was hardly ever in stock at La Bodega. It was the flavor of Puerto Rico.

The men drank Palo Viejo rum, and some of the younger ones got weepy. The first time I saw a grown man cry was at a New Year's Eve party: he had been reminded of his mother by the smells in the kitchen. But what I remember most were the boiled *pasteles,* plantain or yucca rectangles stuffed with corned beef or other meats, olives, and many other savory ingredients, all wrapped in banana leaves. Everybody had to fish one out with a fork. There was always a "trick" *pastel*—one without stuffing—and whoever got that one was the "New Year's Fool."

There was also the music. Long-playing albums were treated like precious china in these homes. Mexican recordings were popular, but the songs that brought tears to my mother's eyes were sung by the melancholy Daniel Santos, whose life as a drug addict was the stuff of legend. Felipe Rodríguez was a particular favorite of couples, since he sang about faithless women and broken-hearted men. There is a snatch of one lyric that has stuck in my mind like a needle on a worn groove: *De piedra ha de ser mi cama, de piedra la cabezera . . . la mujer que a mi me quiera . . . ha de quererme de veras. Ay, Ay, Ay, corazón, porque no amas . . .* I must have heard it a thousand times since the idea of a bed made of stone, and its connection to love, first troubled me with its disturbing images.

The five-minute home movie ends with people dancing in a circle—the creative filmmaker must have set it up, so that all of them could file past him. It is both comical and sad to watch silent dancing. Since there is no justification for the absurd movements that music provides for some of us, people appear frantic, their faces embarrassingly intense. It's as if you were watching sex. Yet for years, I've had dreams in the form of this home movie. In a recurring scene, familiar faces push themselves forward into my mind's eye, plastering their features into distorted close-ups. And I'm asking them: "Who is *she?* Who is the old woman I don't recognize? Is she an aunt? Somebody's wife? Tell me who she is."

"See the beauty mark on her cheek as big as a hill on the lunar landscape of her face—well, that runs in the family. The women on your father's side of the family wrinkle early; it's the price they pay for that fair skin. The young girl with the green stain on her wedding dress is *la novia*—just up from the Island. See, she lowers her eyes when she approaches the camera, as she's supposed to. Decent girls never look at you directly in the face. *Humilde,* humble, a girl should express humility in all her actions. She will make a good wife for your cousin. He should consider himself lucky to have met her only weeks after she arrived here. If he marries her quickly, she will make him a good Puerto Rican–style wife; but if he waits too long, she will be corrupted by the city, just like your cousin there."

26   "She means me. I do what I want. This is not some primitive island I live on. Do they expect me to wear a black mantilla on my head and go to mass every day? Not me. I'm an American woman, and I will do as I please. I can type faster than anyone in my senior class at Central High, and I'm going to be a secretary to a lawyer when I graduate. I can pass for an American girl anywhere—I've tried it. At least for Italian, anyway—I never speak Spanish in public. I hate these parties, but I wanted the dress. I look better than any of these *humildes* here. *My* life is going to be different. I have an American boyfriend. He is older and has a car. My parents don't know it, but I sneak out of the house late at night sometimes to be with him. If I marry him, even my name will be American. I hate rice and beans—that's what makes these women fat."

27   "Your *prima* is pregnant by that man she's been sneaking around with. Would I lie to you? I'm your *tiá política,* your great-uncle's common-law wife—the one he abandoned on the Island to go marry your cousin's mother. *I* was not invited to this party, of course, but I came anyway. I came to tell you that story about your cousin that you've always wanted to hear. Do you remember the comment your mother made to a neighbor that has always haunted you? The only thing you heard was your cousin's name, and then you saw your mother pick up your doll from the couch and say: 'It was as big as this doll when they flushed it down the toilet.' This image has bothered you for years, hasn't it? You had nightmares about babies being flushed down the toilet, and you wondered why anyone would do such a horrible thing. You didn't dare ask your mother about it. She would only tell you that you had not heard her right, and yell at you for listening to adult conversations. But later, when you were old enough to know about abortions, you suspected.

28   "I am here to tell you that you were right. Your cousin was growing an *americanito* in her belly when this movie was made. Soon after, she put something long and pointy into her pretty self, thinking maybe she could get rid of the problem before breakfast and still make it to her first class at the high school. Well, *niña,* her screams could be heard downtown. Your aunt, her *mamá,* who had been a midwife on the Island, managed to pull the little thing out. Yes, they probably flushed it down the toilet. What else could they do with it—give it a Christian burial in a little white casket with blue bows and ribbons? Nobody wanted that baby—least of all the father, a teacher at her school with a house in West Paterson that he was filling with real children, and a wife who was a natural blonde.

29   "Girl, the scandal sent your uncle back to the bottle. And guess where your cousin ended up? Irony of ironies. She was sent to a village in Puerto Rico to live with a relative on her mother's side: a place so far away from civilization that you have to ride a mule to reach it. A real change in scenery. She found a man

there—women like that cannot live without male company—but believe me, the men in Puerto Rico know how to put a saddle on a woman like her. *La gringa,* they call her. Ha, ha, ha. *La gringa* is what she always wanted to be . . ."

The old woman's mouth becomes a cavernous black hole I fall into. And as I fall, I can feel the reverberations of her laughter. I hear the echoes of her last mocking words: *la gringa, la gringa!* And the conga line keeps moving silently past me. There is no music in my dream for the dancers.   30

When Odysseus visits Hades to see the spirit of his mother, he makes an offering of sacrificial blood, but since all the souls crave an audience with the living, he has to listen to many of them before he can ask questions. I, too, have to hear the dead and the forgotten speak in my dream. Those who are still part of my life remain silent, going around and around in their dance. The others keep pressing their faces forward to say things about the past.   31

My father's uncle is last in line. He is dying of alcoholism, shrunken and shriveled like a monkey, his face a mass of wrinkles and broken arteries. As he comes closer I realize that in his features I can see my whole family. If you were to stretch that rubbery flesh, you could find my father's face, and deep within *that* face—my own. I don't want to look into those eyes ringed in purple. In a few years he will retreat into silence, and take a long, long time to die. *Move back, Tío,* I tell him. *I don't want to hear what you have to say. Give the dancers room to move. Soon it will be midnight. Who is the New Year's Fool this time?*   32

INQUIRING INTO THE ESSAY

Explore, explain, evaluate, and reflect on Cofer's "Silent Dancing."

1. In the 1950s and 1960s, many saw America as a "melting pot." The idea then was that although we may have many different immigrant backgrounds, we should strive towards some common "Americanism." For some, this is still a powerful idea, but for others the melting pot is a metaphor for cultural hegemony or even racial prejudice, a demand that difference be ignored and erased rather than celebrated. In your journal, write about your own feelings on this controversy. Tell the story of a friend, a relative, a neighbor who was an outsider. Tell about your own experience. What did it mean to assimilate, and at what cost?

2. Because essays often have a delayed thesis, or have greater weight toward the end, the final paragraphs often have particular significance. Explain the possible meanings of the last paragraph—and particularly the last few lines—of "Silent Dancing."

3. Does this essay make an evaluation, and if so, what is it asserting about cultural assimilation in America during the 1950s and 1960s? Is Cofers' evaluation still relevant?

4. One of the most common reasons students cite for liking a story is that "they could relate to it." Does that criterion apply here? Reflect on whether it's a standard you often use as a reader to judge the value of something. What exactly does it mean to "relate to" a text?

 SEEING THE FORM

SELF-PORTRAIT BY FRANCES BENJAMIN JOHNSTON

In the striking self-portrait that follows, American photographer Frances Benjamin Johnston represents herself in ways in which most nineteenth

Frances Benjamin Johnston, *Self-Portrait* (1896)

century woman wouldn't dare. Her skirts are hiked up to her knees, she holds a burning cigarette between her fingers, and clutches a beer mug on her lap. Johnston carefully composed the picture to offer a very particular version of herself. Photographic self-portraits like this one are similar to personal essays in a number of respects. They often tell a story, and the photographer, like the essayist, is a subject of the work, sometimes *the* subject. We also consider a photograph to be "authentic." We assume, for instance, that this is the real Frances Benjamin Johnston, not someone else's impression or interpretation of her. When we read a personal essay, a work of nonfiction, we also assume that the *I* of the essay is the author of the piece, not some character or other invention.

As writers of personal essays, don't we attempt to represent ourselves as authentically and honestly as we can? Aren't we basically trying to present verbal pictures of ourselves and our experiences? But how accurate are these self-representations? And if the comparison between a self-portrait such as Johnston's picture and the personal essay is an accurate one, what does it imply about how we might write our own essays, but also how we might read the personal essays of other people?

EXERCISE 4.1

Photographic Autobiography

STEP ONE: Find a picture of yourself, preferably from the past, or use a camera and compose a self-portrait. The self-portrait shouldn't be a random shot of your face, but a photograph that is composed to say something about who you are. Choose an appropriate location or setting. Consider what you'll be doing in the picture. Decide whether the picture will be a close-up or a long shot, including all or just part of you.

STEP TWO: Once you have a picture, set it before you and begin fast-writing using the following prompt: *As I look at this picture, it makes me think about _____. And then I think about _____. And then . . . And then . . .*

Feel free to digress and tell a story about yourself, or about the moment captured in the photograph, or perhaps about that time in your life. If you're writing about a self-portrait, explain to yourself what you notice in the photograph, and especially what it seems to be saying that you might not have expected when you took the picture.

Stop and look at the image whenever you feel the urge to inspire more writing.

STEP THREE: Now skip a few lines in your journal. Take a critical stance for a moment and answer one of the following questions:

- What do I understand now about myself that I didn't fully understand when this picture was taken?

- What does this self-portrait say about me that I didn't expect it to say?

DISCUSSION QUESTIONS: Your instructor may ask you to share your photographs or some of the writing that emerged from this exercise. In a full class or small groups consider the following questions:

- Did you feel exposed sharing your pictures or your writing? Did this make it harder to be honest about yourself?

- What surprised you most about the process of doing the exercise?

- Finding some reflective distance—moving away from the story you're telling to consider what it might mean—is an important part of writing a personal essay. Did looking at the picture give you some new perspective on who you were or who you are? Was this distance easy to find?

▪ THE WRITING PROCESS ▪

INQUIRY PROJECT: Writing a Personal Essay

You'll write a 1,000-word personal essay that explores some aspect of your experience. Your instructor may provide additional details. Choose your topic carefully. Because of the essay's exploratory methods, the best topics are those that you want to write about *not* because you know what you think, but because you want to *discover* what you think. The essay should have the following qualities:

- It must do more than tell a story; there must be a *purpose* behind telling the story that speaks in some way to someone else.

- It should, ultimately, answer the *So what?* question.

- Your essay should include some reflection to explain or speculate about what you understand *now* about something that you didn't understand *then*.

- It should be richly detailed. Seize opportunities to *show* what you mean, rather than simply explain it.

Thinking About Subjects

When you are assigned a personal essay, it's essential to embrace uncertainty and be willing to suspend judgment. This form of inquiry, more than any other, seems most useful when the writer has chosen a subject *because* he doesn't know what he wants to say about it. This is risky. Obviously, one of the risks when you start out with uncertainty is that you might end up that way, too; your draft may just seem to go nowhere. This *is* a problem, but it's something that often can be addressed in revision. The key to writing strong personal essays is accepting that first drafts might be real stinkers. But there's a payoff to this risk—the personal essay frequently yields surprise and discovery. You may well find out what you didn't know you knew, and that is among the greatest pleasures of a writer.

As you play with the prompts that follow, then, be particularly vigilant about pursuing subject matter that is confusing to you, that raises the hair on the back of your neck, or just makes you say to yourself, "I'm not sure what I think or feel about that."

Generating Ideas

Begin exploring possible subjects by generating material in your notebook. This should be an open-ended process, a chance to use your creative side by jumping into the sea and swiming around without worrying too much about making sense or trying to prejudge the value of the writing or the subjects you generate. In a sense, this is an invitation to play around.

✎ ONE STUDENT'S RESPONSE

MARGARET'S JOURNAL: LISTING QUESTIONS

Is my cat extremely unusual or can any cat be taught to walk and be as needy and attached as her?

Does testosterone really make one more confident? Is there a correlation between high T and aggressiveness?

How did I once find Dr. Laura so compelling?

Why are women seldom loyal to each other? How are female friendships different from male ones? Can women and men be friends without an underlying sexual tension?

Listing Prompts. Lists can be rich sources of triggering topics. Let them grow freely, and when you're ready, use an item as the focus of another list or an episode of fastwriting. The following prompts should get you started.

1. Make a fast list of experiences you've had that you can't forget. Reach into all parts and times of your life.

2. Make a list of questions that have always nagged you about the following: school, men or women, fast food, television, public restrooms, shoes, and sports.

Fastwriting Prompts. In the early stages of generating possible topics for an essay, fastwriting can be invaluable, *if* you allow yourself to write "badly." Initially, don't worry about staying focused; sometimes you find the best triggering topics by ranging freely. Once you've tentatively settled on something, use a more focused fastwrite, trying to generate information and ideas within the loose boundaries of your chosen topic. Here are some fastwriting prompts that might yield useful discoveries for a personal essay:

1. Choose an item from any of the lists above as a prompt. Just start fastwriting about the item; perhaps start with a story, a scene, a situation, a description. Just follow the writing to see where it leads.

2. Most of us quietly harbor dreams—we hope to be a professional dancer, a good father, an activist, an Olympic luger, or a novelist. Begin a fastwrite in which you explore your dreams. When the writing stalls, ask yourself questions: *Where did this dream come from? Do I still believe in it? What moments did it seem within reach? What moments did it fade?* Plunge into those moments.

3. What was the most confusing time in your life? Choose a moment or scene that stands out in your memory from that time, and writing in the present tense, describe what you see, hear, and do. After five minutes, skip a line and choose another moment. Then another. Make a collage.

Visual Prompts. Sometimes the best way to generate material is to see what we think in something other than sentences. Boxes, lines, and arrows, charts, or even sketches can help us to see more of the landscape of a subject, especially connections between fragments of information that aren't as obvious in prose. The clustering or mapping method is useful to many writers early in the writing process as they try to discover a topic. (See the "Inquiring into the Details" box that follows for more details on how to create a cluster.) Figure 4.2 shows my cluster from the first prompt below.

1. What objects would you most regret losing in a house fire? The answer would likely reveal something about your passions, your longings, even your regrets. Choose a most-treasured object as the core for a cluster. Build a web of associations from it, returning back to the detail in the core whenever a strand dies out. One of the wonderful complexities of being human is that we are sometimes deeply conflicted (I'm not suggesting this is always fun). Pair two opposed feelings that you consider typical of yourself. For example,

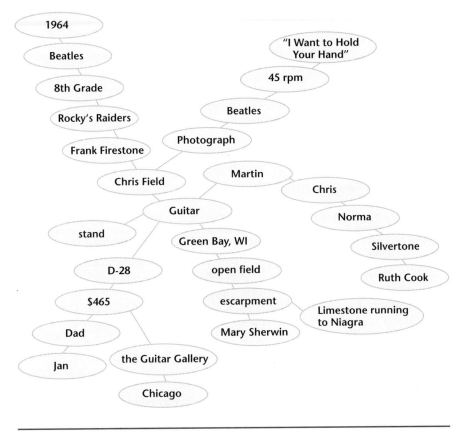

FIGURE 4.2 A cluster built around the one object I would most regret losing in a house fire: my Martin guitar.

ambivalence/commitment, fear/risk taking, loneliness/sociable, beautiful/ugly, composed/flaky, and so on. Use these paired words as a core for a cluster.

2. Draw a long line on a piece of paper in your journal. This is your life. Divide the line into segments that seem to describe what feels like distinct times in your life. These may not necessarily correspond to familiar age categories like adolescence or childhood. More likely, the periods in your life will be associated with a place, a relationship, a dilemma, a job, a personal challenge, and so on, but since this is a timeline, these periods will be chronological. Examine your timeline, and as a fastwrite prompt, put two of these periods in your life together. Explore what they had in common, particularly how the earlier period might have shaped the later one. See Figure 4.3 for a sample timeline.

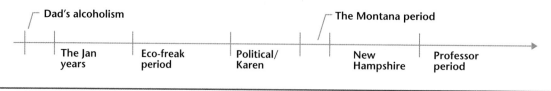

FIGURE 4.3 A sample timeline from my own life.

INQUIRING INTO THE DETAILS

CLUSTERING OR MAPPING

One of the virtues of clustering as a method of generating information is that it defies the more linear nature of writing, putting one sentence after another in a chain of thought. When you make a cluster, there are multiple chains, each growing from a core word, phrase, or idea. In Figure 4.2, I clustered the word "guitar." I'm not just thinking of any guitar, of course, but my 1969 Martin D-28 with Brazilian rosewood and the ding on the front. This is the one object I'd rescue from a fire.

Clusters are in code; each item in the web says more than it says, at least to me, because I'm familiar with its meaning. You don't have that kind of knowledge, obviously, so my cluster wouldn't say much to you. Each strand suggests a story, an idea, or a feeling that I might explore.

Typically, clustering is most useful at the beginning of the writing process as you test a possible subject and want to see its landscape of possibilities. I can see, for example, possible essays about not only the significance of this guitar, but essays on the eighth grade, my old friend Chris Field, and the natural history of limestone. The best clusters are richly suggestive that way, but they're only starting places for more writing. How do you cluster?

1. Begin with a blank page in your journal. Choose a core word, phrase, name, idea, detail, or question, write it in the middle of the page and circle it.

2. Relax and focus on the core word or phrase, and when you feel moved to do so, build a strand of associations from the core, circling and connecting each item. Write other details, names, dates, place names, phrases, and so on—whatever comes to mind.

3. When a strand dies out, return to the core and begin another. Keep clustering until the page looks like a web of associations. Doodle, darkening lines and circles, if that helps you to relax and focus.

> 4. When you feel the urge to write, stop clustering and use one of the strands as a prompt for journal work.

Research Prompts. Things we hear, see, or read can be powerful prompts for personal essays. Bailey White's essay, for instance, was inspired by an encounter with a sign at a Florida state park. It's tempting to believe that personal essays are always about the past, but just as often essayists are firmly rooted in the present, commenting and pondering on the confusions of contemporary life. In that sense, personal essayists are researchers, always on the lookout for material. Train your eye with one or more of the following prompts.

1. Return to the list of questions you made in the earlier "Listing Prompts" section. Choose one nagging question about any of the subjects you were asked to consider and set aside time to explore it by carefully *observing* them. Write down exactly what you see . . . and what you think about it. (The double-entry notebook method is particularly useful for this).

2. Newspaper "filler"—short stories often about odd or unusual things—can be a wonderful source of inspiration for personal essays. Read your local paper for a few days, clipping these brief articles. Paste them in your journal and use them as prompts for fastwriting.

3. Although the Internet offers infinite opportunities for procrastination, with some focus it can also be a great source for jump-starting ideas. What happened to your best friend from kindergarten? Type her name into the Google search engine and find out. (Be sure to put quotation marks around the person's name for a faster search.) Think about your favorite vacation—a search for "The Grand Canyon" might help jog your memory. Or perhaps checking out the "News of the Weird" on Yahoo! might remind you of your own childhood antics.

Judging What You Have

Generating may produce messy, incoherent writing that would earn you bad grades in most classes. Its virtue, however, should be obvious by now: "bad" writing gives a writer material to work with, and it's always better to work from abundance than scarcity. But if this material is going to go anywhere, it must be judged, shaped, and evaluated; the writer must emerge from the sea of experience and use the vantage point that the mountain of reflection offers to see the patterns on the waves.

The initial challenge in producing a first draft is clarifying your topic: What are you really writing about? Later, you'll confront the *So what?* question: What are you trying to *say* about that topic? Don't reject material too soon. Suspend judgment for a bit and work through the following questions as you scrutinize the material you've collected so far in your journal.

What's Promising Material and What Isn't? A good topic for a personal essay need not be dramatic or profound; in fact, some of the most compelling essays are about quite ordinary things. But as you examine your journal writing so far, consider the following:

- **Abundance.** What subject generated the most writing? Do you sense there is much more to write about?

- **Surprise.** What material did you find most confusing in interesting ways? *Was there something that surprised you*—perhaps a feeling you didn't expect to feel, or a memory that seems charged, or an observation that challenged your preconceptions?

- **Confusion.** What subject raises questions you're not sure you can answer easily? The personal essay is a mode of inquiry that permits uncertainty, and even some inconclusiveness, so it lends itself to material that makes you wonder.

- **Honesty.** What subjects are you willing to write honestly about? The personal nature of the personal essay often leads us to material that may be uncomfortable or even private. However, you should not write essays that make you feel overly vulnerable or unsafe; that stuff should probably stay in your journal. Pursue subjects that you're willing to share.

Questions About Purpose and Audience. Writing should be seen in a particular situation, addressing certain subjects, and serving certain purposes for certain audiences. Knowledge about this rhetorical situation is really the only way a writer can determine what makes a piece good. With open-ended forms like the essay, however, worrying too much about purpose and audience too soon in the writing process can intrude on the development of promising subjects. The essay, unlike other genres, directly challenges the writer to work out her relationship with a subject, a process that takes place in the open, with the reader as witness. At times, it's a little like dancing nearly naked on a table in a crowded restaurant. *But initially, the essayist is the essay's most important audience.* The writer's motive is straightforward: *What do I want to understand about this that I don't fully understand now?*

The personnal essay, unlike other genres, directly challenges the writer to work out her relationship with the subject, a process that takes place out in the open, with the reader as witness.

This personal motive will guide you in choosing a topic for your draft, but before long, the rhetorical questions become more urgent. As you evaluate your journal writing and begin to draft your essay, consider these additional questions:

- Did your instructor provide guidelines for the personal essay assignment that might influence your treatment of the material? For example, did she specify a certain audience for this draft or a certain structure or approach for the essay? If so, will the material fit those guidelines?

- Who is your audience? If your draft will be peer-reviewed how can this subject be compelling to others in the class? Is it something they would find interesting or relevant?

- Is there a particular question that drives your exploration of this subject? Can you make the question explicit as a way of focusing your draft? For example, *Why was I relieved when my father died?* Or *Why is it true that men never ask directions, consult maps, or read instruction manuals?*

Questions for Reflection. After you've generated enough material on your topic, seize opportunities to get out of the sea of experience and up on the mountain of reflection. You may do this as you're writing in your journal, thinking about your topic in the shower, or talking about it with friends. Remember that this move to reflect is an essential part of the dialectical thinking that helps writers make sense of things, going back and forth between *what happened* and *what happens,* between *showing* and *telling,* and *observations of* and *ideas about.* In the personal essay, this movement is not just something that occurs in a writer's journal but often appears in the finished essay; in some cases, a reader can clearly see in an essay this movement between sea and mountain. If you need help getting out of the water, questions are the best way to do it. Use one or more of the following questions as prompts for thinking or writing in your journal.

- What do you understand now about this topic that you didn't fully understand when you began writing about it?

- What has surprised you most? Why?

- What seems to be the most important thing you're trying to say so far?

- Focus on how your thinking has changed about your topic. Finish this seed sentence as many times as you can in your notebook: *Once I thought _____, and now I think _____.*

- Quickly write a narrative of thought about your topic: *When I began writing about my father's alcoholism, I thought I felt relieved when he died. Then I decided that when he died some part of me died with him, and then I realized that the real truth is . . . .*

- Finish this sentence in your journal: *As I look back on this, I realize that . . .* Follow that sentence with another, and another until you feel there's nothing more to say.

Writing the Sketch

It's hard to say when it's time to begin composing the draft, particularly with open-ended forms such as the personal essay. Because the essay invites

> ### ✐ WRITING WITH COMPUTERS
>
> #### CUTTING VERSUS DELETING
>
> In revising your draft, your first reflex may be to delete the sentences and paragraphs you want to replace. This is a perfectly acceptable strategy, but for certain key passages, it may be to your advantage to use your word processor's cut and paste function to preserve the text you are replacing. You can cut the material to be revised and paste it either at the end of your draft or in a separate document created expressly to store such passages. The benefit of doing this is that as you move forward with your draft you may eventually want to reintroduce some of the material that you replaced earlier. If you delete material outright, your options for recovering the material at a later point are restricted to consulting a copy of the previous draft (which you should always save as a separate file) or relying on your memory.

writers to tackle itchy, confusing subjects, and its mode of inquiry is largely exploratory, it may seem as if you could stay in the shelter of your journal for a long time. On the other hand, you might be uncomfortable with all the time you're spending with "bad" writing and rush to the draft too soon, before you have enough material. Working from abundance is particularly important when you're using writing to discover, the essayist's main motive.

Before you write a full draft, you'll compose a *sketch* or two of what seems to be the most promising material. A sketch is a brief treatment—probably no more than 300 words—that is composed with a sense of audience but not necessarily a clear sense of a thesis, theme, or controlling idea (see Chapter 1). One of the ways you want to use the sketch is to try out a topic, attempting to clarify your purpose in writing about it. Later, you'll revise a sketch into a draft personal essay.

Your instructor may ask you to write several sketches using the most promising material you've developed from the prompts. *The following apply to all sketches.*

- *The sketch should have a tentative title*. This is crucial because a title can hint at a possible focus for the revision.
- *The sketch should be approximately 300 to 500 words*. The sketch is a brief look at a topic that may later be developed into a longer essay.
- *The sketch should be a relatively fast draft*. Avoid the temptation to spend a lot of time crafting your sketch. Fast drafts are easier to revise.
- *The sketch may not have a clear purpose or theme*. That's what you hope to discover by writing the sketch.
- *The sketch should have a sense of audience*. You're writing your sketch to be read by someone other than you. That means you need to explain what may not be apparent to someone who doesn't know you or hasn't had your experiences.

- *The sketch should be richly detailed.* Personal essays, especially, rely on detail to help the writer, and later, the reader, to see the possible meanings of events or observations. Essayists are inductive, working from particulars to ideas, starting in the sea and then moving to the mountain and then back to the sea again. In early drafts especially, it's important to get down the details by drawing on all your senses: what exactly was the color of the wallpaper, how exactly did the beach smell at low tide, how exactly did the old man's hand feel in yours, what exactly did the immigration officer say?

STUDENT SKETCH

A hundred years ago, death was relatively commonplace in most American communities. The infant mortality rate was high, and people—especially men—typically did not live into their seventies. In fact, the mortality rate from 1920 to 1973 for those twenty-five or younger in America declined an incredible 83 percent. Some call ours a death-free society because we are so insulated from its realities. Someone else cares for the bodies prior to cremation and burial, and when we do see the dead, they are made to look as if they are alive.

All of this may help explain why we struggle so when death does visit us, as it inevitably will. The difficulty of sorting through our feelings about the loss of a family member or a friend makes it an excellent topic for a personal essay. The form encourages writers to explore ambiguities and attempt to work out mysteries. In the student sketch that follows, Lana Kuchta does just that, trying to think through the wisdom of the advice many of us have received when faced with dying relatives: to remember them as they were, avoid seeing them as they are. Like most sketches, this one doesn't arrive at an answer to the writer's questions. There is no theme or thesis yet. But it does tease out a great deal of specific information that Lana can work with later.

THE WAY I REMEMBER
Lana Kuchta

In the past months three people I knew fairly well have died. All of these deaths were expected to some degree because the people had terminal illnesses. This whole thing is really hard for me to grasp right now—the sheer volume of death surrounding me confuses me about how I feel about death and these friends and how I should remember them. Invariably when we talk about someone who is terminally ill, we say that we hope the person goes quickly for their sake as well as the sake of their family. After all, no one wants to have memories of a prolonged death. We want to remember the person as they were before they got sick.

2   I haven't always felt this way. For a long time after my grandpa died, I was angry that my family wouldn't let me see him in the days before his death. They had good reason for not wanting me to venture into that hospital room where death hung like pea-soup fog over his bed. I was eight months pregnant with my second son, Elliot. I was already dilated to 3.5 cm and Nora, the midwife, wanted me to wait a little longer before I had him. She felt that the stress of my grandpa's condition would send me into full-blown labor.

3   I saw my Grandpa for the last time on a Monday. He was in a lot of pain, but the doctors hadn't increased the pain medication yet. He was still himself that day. We talked briefly about my job and the baby and Austin, my other son who wasn't quite a year old yet. It was hard for me to see him this way and as we sat silently searching for things to say I counted contractions. I know he is going to die soon; I can feel it, I hope that he will live long enough to meet the baby I am carrying. He was tired and when a nurse came to do something, I left and said I would see him in a couple of days. I didn't mean to lie about this; I really did expect that I would see him again. His condition worsened and no one would let me into his room. They told me it was better for me to remember him the way he was.

4   And they were right, but even if they weren't I don't think the images that would come to mind when I thought of my grandpa would be the last image I have of him in the hospital. The last image of him I like to remember is just a month or so before he went into the hospital. I am at his house for a visit. It is July in Redding, California and every day that month was over 110 degrees. My grandpa and grandma have air conditioning and it is just what my bloated pregnant body needed. We sat in their living room with the big picture window that overlooked the Sacramento River. My grandpa plays with Austin on the floor. Austin is crawling around, exploring, and pulling himself up on the furniture. Grandpa tickles him and they both laugh. Watching them play on the floor is nice, but I know that grandpa is sick again. The cancer is back and I know it even though none of us know this yet. But I am happy to be sitting in the air-conditioned house, watching grandpa play with my son.

5   I need to believe that it was better that I didn't get to see him one last time because it is all I have to hold onto now. Anything else is obviously too painful, and I realize this as I write through blurry tears that threaten to roll down my face and smear the inside of my glasses. I know my grandpa would hate this public display of emotion. He was a no bullshit kind of guy and had a very low tolerance for crying. I try to think about other things like the way he was always moving. His hands were always jingling the change in his pocket or he was drumming his fingers on some piece of furniture. He was loud and opinionated, but it was a good thing.

He showed that he had a passion for life and he wasn't afraid to speak up   6
for what he believed in.

He was generous, but he expected you to work hard for what you had. He   7
wouldn't just hand money over to you, but he would give you a low interest
loan with easy payback terms.

Just as I am now glad that I didn't see him just before he died. There are   8
things about my life since he died that I'm glad he didn't have to see. I'm glad
he didn't know that my first marriage ended in a messy divorce.

It has been fourteen years since he died and four since my grandma died.   9
My uncle now lives in their house on the Sacramento River. I went back to
that house this summer for the first time since my grandma died. I was nervous about this. I didn't know what to expect, what I would feel, what I would
say. The house was different, yet the same in so many ways. When the kids and
I got into the car, Austin said that it was weird being there because the house
still smells the same after four years.

In the end though I am glad to have the memories of change rattling in a   10
pocket, dirty jokes, Neapolitan ice cream, the river, the smell of cut lumber,
and all the other things that remind me of him.

Moving from Sketch to Draft

A sketch is often sketchy. It's generally underdeveloped, sometimes giving
the writer just the barest outline of his or her subject. But as an early
draft, a sketch can be invaluable. It might hint at what the real subject is,
or what questions seem to be behind your inquiry into the subject. A sketch
might suggest a focus for the next draft, or simply a better lead. Learning
to read your sketches for such clues takes practice.

Evaluating Your Own Sketch. Initially, you're the most important reader
of your own sketches. It's likely that you're in the best position to sense the
material's promise because you understand the context from which it
sprang better than any reader can. What are the clues you should look for
in a sketch?

1. What surprised you? Might this discovery be the focus of the draft?
   Chances are, if it surprised you, it will surprise your readers.

2. What is the most important line in the sketch? What makes it important? Might this line be a beginning for more fastwriting? Might
   it be the theme or controlling idea of the draft?

3. What scene, moment, or situation is key to the story you're telling?
   Could this be the lead in the draft?

Methods for Peer Review of Sketches

1. Choose a partner, exchange sketches, read, and comment both in writing and through conversation.
2. Create a pile of sketches in the middle of the classroom. Everyone takes one (not your own, obviously), provides written comments, returns it the pile, and takes another. Repeat this until you've read and commented on at least four sketches.
3. Share sketches online on the class Web site.

---

4. What's your favorite part of the sketch? What would happen if you cut it?

Questions for Peer Review. If you'll be sharing your sketch with one or more of your classmates, you'll likely need most help with clarifying your purpose and focus for a draft. It's less helpful in these early stages to receive editorial comments about sentences, especially questions about grammar and mechanics. Here are some useful questions that might guide peer responses to your personal essay sketches.

- What does the writer seem to want to say but doesn't quite say in the sketch?
- What line appears most important to the meaning of the sketch, as you understand it?
- What was most surprising about what the writer said or showed?
- What part of the story seems most important? What part might need to be told and isn't?

Reflecting on What You've Learned. Before you begin working on the draft of your personal essay, take a few minutes in your journal to think about your thinking. Finish the following sentence, and follow it in a fast-write for at least five minutes. *The thing that struck me most about writing and sharing my sketch on _____, was. . . .* When you finish, quickly complete the following sentences:

1. The *real* story I seem to be trying to tell is _____.
2. So what? I'd answer that question by saying _____.
3. The main thing I'm planning to do in the draft is _____.

Research and Other Strategies: Gathering More Information

You may be itching to move on with the draft. That's understandable. If everything has gone well so far, then your sketch has already given you a sense of direction and some ideas about how to develop your topic. But remember the importance of that dialectical movement between sea and mountain, or collecting and composing. Now that you have a topic and a tentative sense of purpose for your personal essay, journal work can be even more valuable because it can be *more focused*. Before you begin composing the draft—or during that process—consider using the following prompts to generate more information in your notebook:

- *Explode a moment.* Choose a scene or moment in the story or stories you're telling that seems particularly important to the meaning of the essay. Re-enter that moment and fastwrite for a full seven minutes, using all your senses and as much detail as you can muster.
- *Make lists.* Brainstorm a list of details, facts, or specifics about a moment, or scene, or observation. Make a list of other experiences that seem connected to this one (see *"Cluster"* below).
- *Research.* Do some quick-and-dirty research that might bring in other voices or more information that will deepen your consideration of the topic. For example, find out exactly how long that solar eclipse was back in 1983, and whether it was in July as you seem to remember. Interview a local expert on your topic. (For more information on where to look for information, see Chapter 12, "Research Techniques".) Do some background reading.
- *Cluster.* In your journal, try to move beyond narrating a single experience and discover other experiences, moments, or scenes that might help you see important patterns. Use the list above of related experiences or observations, and fastwrite about those, or develop a cluster that uses a key word, phrase, or theme as its core, and build a web of associations. For example, let's say your sketch is about your experience working with the poor in Chile. Have you had other encounters with extreme wealth or extreme poverty? Can you describe them? What do they reveal about your feelings or attitudes about poverty or your reactions to what happened in Chile? See Figure 4.4.

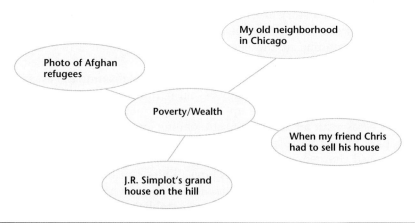

FIGURE 4.4 **The start of a cluster built around Poverty/Wealth.**

Composing the Draft

Some of my students get annoyed at all the "stuff" I encourage them to do before they begin a first draft of a personal essay. In some cases, all the journal work isn't necessary; the writer very quickly gets a strong sense of direction and feels ready to begin composing. But from the beginning I've encouraged you to gravitate toward topics that you find confusing, and with that kind of material exploratory writing is time well spent. Remember, too, that journal writing counts as writing. It not only offers the pleasures of surprise, but it can ultimately make the drafting process more efficient by generating material that you won't have to conjure up during those long, painful periods of staring at the computer screen wondering what to say next. This front-end work may also help abbreviate the end of the writing process—essentially, all this mountain and sea work in your journal and sketches is revision (see Chapter 14 for more on prewriting as a method of revision).

As you begin drafting, keep in mind what you've learned from your writing so far. For example,

- What is the question(s) that is behind your exploration of this topic?
- What do you understand now that you didn't understand fully when you started writing about it?
- How can you show *and* explain how you came to this understanding?

Methods of Development. How might you use some of the typical forms of development to develop your subject?

Narrative. The backbone of the personal essay is often, but not always, narrative. Remember, however, that narrative can work in an essay in at least three ways: (1) you tell an extended story of what happened, (2) you tell one or more anecdotes or brief stories, or (3) you tell the story of your thinking as you've come to understand something you didn't understand before. Often a single essay uses all three types of narrative.

When we tell a story of what happened, we naturally begin at the beginning: "I awoke startled by the unearthly buzz of the alarm clock." But sometimes beginning at the beginning is the worst place to begin. (See Chapter 14 for more about "leads.") You should explicitly or implicitly establish your focus in the first few paragraphs, and opening the essay with the first thing that happened may reveal nothing about your purpose. It just establishes that you woke up. For example, note how Bailey White began her essay with an anecdote about leaning over the railing at a Florida state park gazing with "awe and wonder" at Devil's Millhopper, a gorge that seemed charged with "spiritual significance" and a sense of timelessness. In contrast, a few paragraphs later, White reveals a less uplifting desire—she has the urge to throw "the nibbled end of a hotdog bun" down the gorge. Within a few paragraphs, Bailey establishes the tension that will drive the piece: the conflict between what's obviously responsible behavior and our secret desires to do a little wrong.

Consider beginning your draft with an anecdote (like White's) or the part of the story you want to tell that best establishes your purpose in the essay. If you're writing about the needless destruction of a childhood haunt by developers, then consider opening with the way the place looked *after* the bulldozers were done with it.

Judith Ortiz Cofer's essay illustrates how a personal essay can stitch together not just one narrative but several stories, all of which are connected by the essay's theme or question. Notice as well how the stories defy chronology. Time in writing is nothing like real time. You can write pages about something that happened in seven minutes, as George Orwell did in "The Hanging," or cover twenty years in a paragraph. You can ignore chronology, as Bailey White did, if it serves your purpose, too. They key is to tell your story or stories in ways that emphasize what's important. Ask yourself, *What does the reader most need to know to understand my thinking and feelings about this topic? What should I show about what happened that gives a reader a clear sense of what* happens?

Using Evidence. How do you make your essay convincing, and even moving to an audience? It's in the details. This is a form that thrives, like most literary genres, on particularity: what exactly did it look like, what exactly did she say, what exactly did it sound and smell like at that moment? Evidence that gives a personal essay authority are details that make a reader believe the writer can be trusted to observe keenly and to remember accurately.

Remember the middle of Orwell's essay, "The Hanging," when he witnesses a young man on the way to the gallows? In typical fashion, Orwell relies on understated details to dramatize his realization that he'd never fully considered "what it means to destroy a healthy, conscious man."

> It was about forty yards to the gallows. I watched the bare brown back of the prisoner marching in front of me. He walked clumsily with his bound arms, but quite steadily, with that bobbing gait of the Indian who never straightens his knees. At each step his muscles slid neatly into place, the lock of hair on his scalp danced up and down, his feet printed themselves on the wet gravel. And once, in spite of the men who gripped him by each shoulder, he stepped slightly aside to avoid a puddle.

After *seeing* a condemned man avoid a puddle, we're prepared for Orwell's declaration that "cutting a life short when it is in full tide" is "unspeakably wrong." Without that memorable observation, we're more likely to dismiss Orwell's statement about capital punishment as merely opinion; details *involve* the reader in ways the mere explanation of feelings or ideas often doesn't. We feel along with the writer, we are implicated in his experience.

As you draft your essay, remember the subtle power of details. Tell, but always show, too.

Workshopping the Draft

If your draft is subject to peer review (see Chapter 15 for details on how to organize workshop groups), think carefully about the kind of responses you need from readers at this point in the process. In general, you should encourage comments that make you want to write again.

Reflecting on the Draft. To prepare for workshop, make an entry in your journal that explores your feelings about the draft:

- What do you think worked?
- What do you think needs work?

Following the workshop session, do a follow-up entry in your notebook that summarizes what you heard, what made sense and what didn't, and how you plan to approach the next draft. Your instructor may ask you to share this information in a cover letter submitted with the revision.

Questions for Readers. There are many ways for a writer to structure responses to a draft. Some of them are discussed in detail in Chapter 15, "The Writer's Workshop." The key is to find a way to get what you need *at this stage in the writing process* that will be most helpful as you revise.

There are a few questions, however, that you might pose to your group that are particularly relevant to the personal essay:

1. Is there a story I'm telling that I need to develop more? Is there a story I'm not telling that I should?
2. What do you think is the *real* story? In other words, what idea or theme is lurking beneath the accounts of my experiences and observations?
3. What seems the most important detail, the one that seems to say more than it says, that *reveals* some important feeling, attitude, or idea? What detail seems less important, less revealing?
4. Do I move too high on the mountain of reflection, saying what seems obvious or overly abstract and general? If so, what questions do you have about what I say that might get me to come down closer to the sea, where I'm more likely to have better insights?
5. Do I explain things that are unnecessary to explain, that are better told through *showing* rather than *telling*?

Revising the Draft

I think revision is one of the most misunderstood aspects of writing. I recently surveyed about sixty advanced placement high school students and most thought that revision mostly involved tinkering—maybe "fixing" a sentence, running spellcheck, or adding a detail. Think about the word—"re-vision"—which implies *re-seeing*. This is much more than tinkering; it is an effort to discover new ways of understanding your topic, your questions, your thesis, and your own understandings. Another common misconception is that revision is something that only comes at the end of the writing process. In doing all the journal work you've already done a lot of revision. You've circled your subject trying to discover a topic and what you might say about it.

Personal essay drafts typically have some of the following problems:

- They don't answer the *So what?* question. Are you telling a story but don't help your readers understand *why* you're telling it?

- There is too much sea and not enough mountain. In other words, do you *reflect* sufficiently in the draft, contributing your new understandings of what happened?

- There isn't enough detail. Since personal essays often rely heavily on narrative, they should show as well as tell. That is, help readers not only understand the significance of your experiences but in some small way experience those significant moments themselves.

GUIDE TO REVISION STRATEGIES		
PROBLEMS IN THE DRAFT (CHAPTER 14)	**PART**	**PAGE NUMBER**
Unclear purpose ■ Not sure what the essay is about? Fails to answer the *So what* question?	1	633
Unclear thesis, theme, or main idea ■ Not sure what you're trying to say?	2	639
Lack of information or development ■ Needs more details; more showing and less telling?	3	646
Disorganized ■ Doesn't move logically or smoothly from paragraph to paragraph?	4	650
Unclear or awkward at the level of sentences and paragraphs ■ Does draft seem choppy or hard to follow at the level of sentences or paragraphs?	5	656

Refer to Chapter 14, "Revision Strategies," for ideas addressing the problems outlined in the preceding table and how to revise your draft following your workshop. Remember that a draft may present problems in more than one category.

Polishing the Draft

After you've dealt with the more global issues in your draft—is it sufficiently focused, does it answer the *So what?* question, is it organized, and so on—you must deal with the local issues. You've carved the stone into an appealing figure but now you need to polish it. Are your paragraphs coherent? How do you manage transitions? Are your sentences fluent and concise? Are there any errors in spelling or syntax? Section 5 of Chapter 14 can help you focus on these issues.

Before you finish your draft, make certain that you've worked through the following checklist:

- ❏ Every paragraph is about one thing.
- ❏ The transitions between paragraphs aren't abrupt.
- ❏ The length of sentences varies in each paragraph.
- ❏ Each sentence is concise. There are no unnecessary words or phrases.
- ❏ You've checked grammar, particularly for verb agreement, run-on sentences, unclear pronouns, and misused words (*there/their, where/were,* and so on). (See the handbook for help with these grammar issues.)
- ❏ You've run your spellchecker and proofed your paper for misspelled words.

STUDENT ESSAY

The personal essay that follows impressed me not only because it was eloquently written and honest, but because of the way it worked through a question and an idea. Too often we forget that it is some idea we want to mull over or question we want to explore that is the backbone of the personal essay. Telling a story, or several stories, is often a part of a personal essay but those stories always are about something larger.

As you read "Holy Jealousy," notice how dramatically former student Micaela Fisher shifts from narration to exposition, from showing to telling, from the sea to the mountain. Like George Orwell's essay earlier in this chapter, these movements are pretty obvious. One risk is telling too much and narrating too little; good narration often keeps a piece moving, while exposition tends to slow it down. Consider what happens here.

HOLY JEALOUSY
Micaela Fisher

"Micaela, I want you to cultivate your friendship with him," she assured   1
skeptical me, yet again. "I am not jealous of the relationship the two of you
share—I know it's clean, and I support it. Please don't hesitate in your friendship with him because of me."

Why did it bother me that my friend so willingly sanctioned my new   2
friendship with her boyfriend? Why did it take me so long until I accepted that
she truly wasn't jealous of the extensive time I spent with him? That she was
okay with our sharing racquetball, chess, music, theology, hugs, even while
she was away at school?

I wanted her to be jealous. Not because my relationship with him wasn't   3
clean, but because theirs was a relationship I believed in. And I knew jealousy
needed to protect it.

Jealousy is not categorically evil. Envy is evil, and when we equate jeal-   4
ousy with envy, then it is quite wrong. But "jealousy" doesn't really mean
"envy." Envy is craving what belongs to someone else; jealousy is craving what
belongs to oneself. Envy is toxic, a destroyer of good things. Jealousy is a protector of the sacred. As my friend earnestly reiterated her lack of concern over
my intensifying friendship with her boyfriend, my instincts chorused their
own concerns: "Where is the jealousy, the guardian of this relationship? Who
will keep it sacred?" Jealousy in its proper place is born out of loving protection, and it is both an instinctive (emotional) mechanism for guarding the relationship and a deliberate act of aggression toward what would threaten it. The
jealousy reflex is intended to lead to removal of the threat. When it does so, it
is a good thing.

Jealousy *can* stem from insecurity, though when it does it is more accu-   5
rately called envy, because it demands from another more than it rightfully
owns. Insecure jealousy is jealousy gone wrong, a corruption of a useful appa-
ratus and a poison to a relationship. Insecurity always robs from others.

The marriage of my high school friend and her thirty-year-old husband is   6
a frightening example to me of insecure jealousy. William "protects" his wife
by requiring her to stay home all day every day with their two little boys. In
truth, it is his enormous insecurity that drives him to keep her sequestered
away from even women friends lest she discover companionship outside of
him. Perhaps I'm being too hard on him; yet it does make me shudder when a
twenty-one-year-old girl is so incredibly isolated that she becomes an unper-
son apart from her husband. William crosses the line. There is nothing healthy
or good about his "jealousy." There is not anything good about a jealousy that
forces a person to be less than who she is.

7   On the other extreme, a nominal commitment with no territorial patrolling whatsoever is not healthy either. A relationship in which each partner is at liberty to roam without any sense of inhibition is a lifeless relationship, or a strained one since one of the partners is probably suffering without using his or her mechanism for jealousy. A relationship is by nature exclusive—"I like you" means "I choose you from among all others"—and jealousy is a keeper of the relationship.

8   I think my parents model a healthy amount of jealousy in their marriage. My dad is sensitive and manly in a way that often thaws women, so he ends up interacting with a lot of women, and my mom can be spunky in a way that catches the eyes of some men. While neither of them seems to impose regimentation on the other, they are honest to each other about concerns that come up in their interactions with the opposite sex. My dad told me about a time when Mom was much younger and couldn't see that a certain man had a sexual interest in her and Dad told her he strongly preferred that she avoid the man. He mentioned times she's asked him not to spend much energy with certain women. The way they use jealousy seems to me the way its supposed to be used—as a protector of the marriage, as a very loving thing, as a signal that this person they love, the part of this person they own, is being stolen by someone other and they won't just quietly allow it. That's jealousy.

9   Jealousy was missing in the relationship of my two friends. It seemed to me a lack of honesty on their parts, and that bothered me. But in a dating relationship rather than a marriage, jealousy is a more complex machine—the boundary lines are more difficult to define. There isn't absolute commitment as with the vows of marriage; there's something that seems worthy of protection, but nothing justly inviolable. My friend did not own her boyfriend and could not rationally restrict his interactions with me. Yet, theirs was not a cavalier relationship; they'd been dating seriously for more than two years. It was a relationship worthy of protection, I thought, and it wasn't being properly defended.

10   The guy was my best friend at school. We debated theology and argued philosophy and competed in everything from guitar performances to racquetball games. Our views on much of what we discussed were dissonant, but we both loved to engage our minds in intellectual aerobics. We deserved each other's pedantry. He widened my world and I widened his, and we were very close friends for a whole year.

11   The girl was gone to school; she and I exchanged letters and poetry, both of us preferring old-fashioned correspondence to email and phone. There was less tension in this friendship, but enough difference between us

for us to sharpen each other. She told me my friendship with him was good for both of us and that it was something for which she was thankful. So I trusted her on that; and she trusted me with him. They were two people that I loved fiercely.

But people can sustain only so much intimacy. While the two of them   12
were trying to deepen their relationship, I was subtracting time and energy from them both, I subconsciously listened for her to say, "Hey, Micaela, you're taking time from him that should belong to me. We need to draw some bound- ary lines here—my relationship with him is suffering and needs defending." She was reluctant to do so because jealousy seemed to her all insecure reac- tion. But I wanted to feel jealousy from her so that I could be sure theirs was a protected relationship.

And eventually, it happened: jealousy kicked in. The exclusivity of their re-   13
lationship was being violated by the energy invested in my friendship with him, she felt, and boundaries were needed. I agreed. I lost my racquetball and chess partner and my best school friend. That continues to pain me, but I know it was a loving judgment that caused her to ask for exclusive space, and I was glad to honor her request. I respect her jealousy and hope it extends to anyone who might come close enough to threaten their allegiance to each other—without it, their relationship is in continual danger of being diluted or undermined. I am encouraged to watch the boundary lines of this relationship become distinct, guarded, as my friends prepare for marriage. Jealousy has done its work.

Far from being categorically destructive, jealousy is a healthy response to   14
threats. The mechanism of jealousy should not be ignored. It is only through jealousy, jealousy rooted in love, that the sacred remains holy.

EVALUATING THE ESSAY

Discuss or write about your response to Micaela Fisher's essay using some or all of the following questions.

1. What is the essay's greatest strength? Is this something you've no- ticed in your own work, or the drafts of classmates?

2. Is the balance between exposition and narration, showing and telling, handled well in "Holy Jealousy?" Does it read fairly quickly or does it drag at points?

3. The essay uses line breaks between sections. What do you think of this technique? What are its advantages and disadvantages?

4. What would you recommend to Fisher if she were to revise "Holy Jealousy?"

USING WHAT YOU HAVE LEARNED

My students often love writing personal essays. At its best, the genre is a rare opportunity to reexamine our lives and better understand our experiences. The insights we earn are often reward enough, but what have you learned in this assignment that you might apply in other writing situations?

1. The personal essay you wrote relies heavily on narrative and personal experience. How might an ability to tell a good story, using your experiences or the experiences of others, be a useful academic skill? How might you use it to write a paper for another class?

2. The personal essay is a deeply subjective form which would seem to put it at odds with formal academic writing which seems to strive for "objectivity." Are they at odds?

3. Based on your experience writing a personal essay, what do you think are its most important qualities? If you were to write more personal essays, what would you strive to do next time?

Maine lobstermen heading out to sea.

Writing a Profile

5

WRITING ABOUT PEOPLE

Some years ago, when I was writing a book on the culture of the New England lobster fishing industry, I wandered into the lighthouse keeper's house in Pemaquid Point, Maine. The lighthouse, built in 1827, was automated—like all but one lighthouse on the East coast—but the empty keeper's house had been turned into a tiny fishing museum. I found my way there one late spring day, stepped inside, and was greeted by Abby Boynton, sitting on a folding chair working on needlepoint. I had come to look at historical objects related to lobster fishing, but instead I encountered Abby, an elderly widow whose husband, a local lobsterman, had died of cancer several years before.

We struck up a conversation, and within minutes she was leading me to the back of the museum to show me a picture book, now out of print, that documented a few days of her husband's work at the traps offshore from New Harbor, Maine. She told me the story of the New York photographer who asked her husband if he wouldn't mind company fishing that day. "He was always taking people out," she said, "so my husband said 'sure.'" That trip with the photographer led to other trips and the book that followed, *Fred Boynton, Lobsterman.* The museum copy was well thumbed and the binding was broken, but Mrs. Boynton assured me that there were still a few copies around. "I've got two copies at home," she said, "but I can't part with those. They'll be nice for the kids and the grandchildren."

Abby Boynton showed me a picture of the New Harbor house she lived in with Fred all the years they were married. She moved three years ago because it was "too much house." As I was leaving she directed me to a model of her husband's boat, the *Dwayne B,* in a back room of the museum. It was named after their youngest son. A brass plaque on the boat model said, "In memory by his friends and fellow fishermen."

What You'll Learn in This Chapter

- How the profile and the academic case study are related.

- What distinguishes the profile from other forms.

- Interview techniques.

- Ways to find a profile subject who is representative of a certain group of people.

- Questions for revising a profile.

What was it like being a lobster fisherman's wife? I asked, heading towards the sunshine. "Spent most of my time trying to keep his dinner warm," said Mrs. Boynton, resuming her post in the folding chair by the door. I glanced at the needlepoint in her lap, but couldn't read the stitched letters, which had not yet formed a word. After my fifteen minutes with Abby Boynton that seemed fitting; what didn't need a plaque or a label in this museum was the most powerful thing I found there. It occurred to me later that Abby Boynton was as bound to her husband's memory as she was to life. Only now she keeps more than his dinner warm as she waits.

This accidental interview with the fisherman's wife reveals much more than I could explain about one aspect of community in Maine's fishing villages—the partnership between spouses who have chosen such a hard life. I can't imagine a better way to dramatize the level of devotion these marriages can demand than Abby Boynton's shrine to the memory of her husband—a worn book, a dusty model of his boat, and picture of the New Harbor home they shared. You can hear it in her voice, too, and how quickly she directs a stranger to these relics. But all of this probably doesn't need explaining; you can sense it from the vignette.

This is a piece that could have easily continued, perhaps including information from the book *Fred Boynton, Lobsterman,* or interviews about Abby and Fred from others in New Harbor who knew them. It might have included statistics about the divorce rate among Maine fishing families, or information about the economic pressures on families during a bad fishing season—all the factors that might easily make it hard for a marriage to survive. Most of all, I might have spent more time with Abby Boynton. The result would have been a profile, not a vignette, that would put a face on the idea that lobster fishing is difficult, but for many, a good life.

MOTIVES FOR WRITING A PROFILE

E. B. White, author of the children's classics *Charlotte's Web* and *Stuart Little* and many essays for the *The New Yorker* magazine, once offered this advice: "If you want to write about mankind, write about a man." You already know the importance of anchoring specifics to generalities, showing to telling, and observations of things with ideas about them. The profile is a form that accomplishes this by giving a general idea or feeling a face. Through Abby Boynton we presumably can see something about other fishermen's wives and families. In that sense, the profile is like the personal essay—the experiences and particulars about a living subject creates, as Scott Russell Sanders once said, "a door through which [readers] might have passed." In a profile, however, the obvious subject is usually not the writer but the person she writes about.

There may be no better way of dramatizing the impact of a problem, the importance of a question, or the significance of an idea than showing how it presents itself in the life of one person.

The profile is a familiar form in the popular magazine. We can't seem to know enough about other peoples' lives. The celebrity profile is ubiquitous, but some of the best profiles are of ordinary people like Abby Boynton who are typical in some way of the people touched by the subject a writer is interested in. There may be no better way of dramatizing the impact of a problem, the importance of a question, or the significance of an idea than showing how it presents itself in the life of one person.

THE PROFILE AND ACADEMIC WRITING

While the profile may not be a common academic form, the case study is, and in a sense a profile is a form of extended case study. Almost any topic affects people's lives (if it doesn't, is it really that significant or interesting?). The profile or case study attempts to document these impacts. For example, suppose you're interested in examining the success of your university's commitment to ethnic and racial diversity—a principle the administration has publicly embraced. One way to approach the topic is to profile one international student. What has been her experience on campus? Which campus programs have proved useful? What programs are needed? The voice of your profile subject and the details of her experience would help to dramatize an otherwise abstract policy debate, and the story she tells could offer a foundation from which to explore the issue.

You can write a profile in the service of an argument or as a way of exploring the personal impact of an event. The profile may be part of a larger project that examines some aspect of a local culture, cultural trend, or place (see "Writing an Ethnographic Essay," Chapter 10). It can, like good fiction, provide insight into the complexities of the human mind and soul.

More than any other form of inquiry, the profile relies on interview for information—the voice of the writer's subject should come though—as well as observation, particularly those revealing details that say something about the character or feelings of the person profiled. In some cases, these details are merely descriptive—what the subject looks like, for instance. However, telling details can often be indirect evidence of a person's character. For example, in "Turning Point," the profile of Phillip Petit that appears later in this chapter, the writer briefly describes where Petit "hangs out" as a tiny room up a spiral staircase in the rafters of a New York cathedral, one of the world's largest. This so-called office contains, appropriately, the things that are essential to Petit's profession of tightrope walking, including ropes and rigging all "stowed as neatly as a yacht's navigational gear." The location of Petit's hangout and its careful order both suggest the man's love of both altitude and grace, which he combines in the beauty of a walk on a high wire.

Writers who want to practice interview skills—a key method of collecting information in communications and the social sciences—will find the profile a useful challenge.

FEATURES OF THE FORM

Some typical characteristics of the form include the following:

- *A profile usually provides a detailed look at one person.* The key is to decide who that person should be. The kind of profiles you'll likely write won't be of celebrities, who are inherently interesting subjects because of their fame. Instead, you'll profile someone much more ordinary, but possibly *typical* or representative of a culture, place, situation, or topic.

- *Alone, a profile may not provide enough substantiation for an argument.* While the writer may choose a profile to dramatize a problem or provide support for a claim, it's always dangerous to generalize from a single case, particularly if the typicality of the subject is in doubt.

- *A profile uses narrative as a method of organization.* Like in the personal essay, storytelling is frequently the backbone of the profile. This may take the form of a series of anecdotes about the writer's subject, or the subject's account of an experience. Frequently, the story of the interview itself, told chronologically, is the organizing tool for the profile (see, for example, Lauren Slater's "Dr. Daedalus" later in the chapter).

- *The profile is usually written from one of two points of view—either the writer narrates in the first person or the subject is portrayed in the third person, and the writer stays out of the way.* Point of view is a crucial decision in the profile because, unlike many other forms, there are choices to make. A profile told in the first person can give an added dimension of the writer's own feelings and reactions, but risks distracting the reader from the real subject, the person being profiled. Portraying the subject in the third person loses the drama of the interaction between the writer and the person profiled, but keeps the focus on the subject.

- *Profiles go beyond mere description of subjects and reveal information about character much the way a short story does, through telling details and the subject's own voice.* Like most nonfiction forms, the profile shows *and* tells. But the profile writer is more likely to use literary techniques such as telling details, dialogue, and even scenes to communicate some dominant impression or idea about the subject. Letting the subject speak for herself is particularly important, but to do this well makes special demands on the writer. (See "Inquiring into the Details: Tape Recorders" later in the chapter.)

- *A strong beginning is essential, particularly when the subject of a profile isn't famous.* We read a celebrity profile because of the fame of its subject. But when writing about ordinary people, we need to quickly give readers a reason to be interested. What is it about Bert, for example, that makes him an interesting focus for a piece on Florida State's reputation as a party school? Within a paragraph or two, the writer tells us that Bert's a 24-year-old undergraduate who mixes a drink at 10 A.M. on a Tuesday, and "seemed to be vying for the honor of being the top partyer at the nation's top party school." Both pieces of information are hook enough for most readers; notice also, though, that the writer makes the case immediately that Bert, while not typical, may be representative of the extremes some students go to in order to be party animals at Florida State.

- *Scene and setting often provide useful information in a profile.* We know characters not just by what they say but what they do and where they do it. A profile often allows the reader to glimpse a subject in action in settings or situations that are revealing. For a profile of a biology professor, that might be knee-deep in a stream, sampling stoneflies.

- *The more time writers can spend with their subjects, the more revealing the profile.* The reason is obvious. You'll get to know your subject far better if you can conduct more than a single interview. It's also easier to write a profile—to write anything—when you're working from abundance rather than scarcity. The more information you have about your subject, the easier it is to focus the piece, and the more likely you are to get to the truth of things about your subject.

PROFILE

One of the most memorable segments on the TV show *Seinfeld* was about the "soup Nazi," a character inspired by the following profile. Published in *The New Yorker* by one of the staff writers, "Soup" profiles soup chef Albert Yeganeh, the tough-talking, impatient, demanding owner of a small restaurant on West Fifty-fifth Street. The force of Yeganeh's personality comes through brilliantly in this piece especially because the writer steps aside and lets the man speak for himself through extensive—and sometimes lengthy—quotations. It's hard to overstate how important it is to allow readers to hear the voices of profile subjects.

But this essay is also a great example of how important close and careful observation is to a profile. We can know people by the contexts in which they live and work, something that we could simply explain—"Yeganeh owns a soup restaurant on West Fifty-fifth Street in New York"—or describe—"The first thing you notice about it is the awning, which proclaims 'Homemade Hot, Cold, Diet Soups.' These more specific observations bring the man's tiny world to life around him and contribute powerfully to our understanding of who he is.

SOUP

Anonymous, The New Yorker

1   When Albert Yeganeh says "Soup is my lifeblood," he means it. And when he says "I am extremely hard to please," he means that, too. Working like a demon alchemist in a tiny storefront kitchen at 259-A West Fifty-fifth Street, Mr. Yeganeh creates anywhere from eight to seventeen soups every weekday. His concoctions are so popular that a wait of half an hour at the lunchtime peak is not uncommon, although there are strict rules for conduct in line. But more on that later.

2   "I am psychologically kind of a health freak," Mr. Yeganeh said the other day, in a lisping staccato of Armenian origin. "And I know that soup is the greatest meal in the world. It's very good for your digestive system. And I use only the best, the freshest ingredients. I am a perfectionist. When I make a clam soup, I use three different kinds of clams. Every other place uses canned clams. I'm called crazy. I am not crazy. People don't realize why I get so upset. It's because if the soup is not perfect and I'm still selling it, it's a torture. It's *my* soup, and that's why I'm so upset. First you clean and then you cook. I don't believe that ninety-nine per cent of the restaurants in New York know how to clean a tomato. I tell my crew to wash the parsley *eight* times. If they wash it five or six times, I scare them. I tell them they'll go to jail if there is sand in the parsley. One time, I found a mushroom on the floor, and I fired that guy who left it there." He spread his arms, and added, "This place is the only one like it in . . . in . . . the whole earth! One day, I hope to learn something from the other places, but so far I haven't. For example, the other day I went to a very fancy restaurant and had borscht. I had to send it back. It was *junk.* I could see all the chemicals in it. I never use chemicals. Last weekend, I had lobster bisque in Brooklyn, a very well-known place. It was *junk.* When I make a lobster bisque, I use a whole lobster. You know, I never advertise. I don't have to. All the big-shot chefs and the kings of the hotels come here to see what *I'm* doing."

3   As you approach Mr. Yeganeh's Soup Kitchen International from a distance, the first thing you notice about it is the awning, which proclaims "Homemade Hot, Cold, Diet Soups." The second thing you notice is an aroma so delicious that it makes you want to take a bite out of the air. The third thing you notice, in front of the kitchen, is an electric signboard that flashes, saying, "Today's Soups . . . Chicken Vegetable . . . Mexican Beef Chili . . . Cream of Watercress . . . Italian Sausage . . . Clam Bisque . . . Beef Barley . . . Due to Cold Weather . . . For Most Efficient and Fastest Service the Line Must . . . Be Kept Moving . . . Please . . . Have Your Money . . . Ready . . . Pick the Soup of Your Choice . . . Move to Your Extreme . . . Left After Ordering."

"I am not prejudiced against color or religion," Mr. Yeganeh told us, and he   4
jabbed an index finger at the flashing sign. "Whoever follows that I treat very
well. My regular customers don't say anything. They are very intelligent and
well educated. They know I'm just trying to move the line. The New York cop
is very smart—he sees everything but says nothing. But the young girl who
wants to stop and tell you how nice you look and hold everyone up—*yah!*" He
made a guillotining motion with his hand. "I tell you, I hate to work with the
public. They treat me like a slave. My philosophy is: The customer is always
wrong and I'm always right. I raised my prices to try to get rid of some of
these people, but it didn't work."

The other day, Mr. Yeganeh was dressed in chef's whites with orange   5
smears across his chest, which may have been some of the carrot soup cooking
in a huge pot on a little stove in one corner. A three-foot-long handheld mixer
from France sat on the sink, looking like an overgrown gardening tool. Mr.
Yeganeh spoke to two young helpers in a twisted Armenian-Spanish barrage,
then said to us, "I have no overhead, no trained waitresses, and I have the
cashier here." He pointed to himself theatrically. Beside the doorway, a glass
case with fresh green celery, red and yellow peppers, and purple eggplant was
topped by five big gray soup urns. According to a piece of cardboard taped to
the door, you can buy Mr. Yeganeh's soups in three sizes, costing from four to
fifteen dollars. The order of any well-behaved customer is accompanied by little waxpaper packets of bread, fresh vegetables (such as scallions and
radishes), fresh fruit (such as cherries or an orange), a chocolate mint, and a
plastic spoon. No coffee, tea, or other drinks are served.

"I get my recipes from books and theories and my own taste," Mr. Yeganeh   6
said. "At home, I have several hundreds of books. When I do research, I find
that I don't know anything. Like cabbage is a cancer fighter, and some fish is
good for your heart but some is bad. Every day, I should have one sweet, one
spicy, one cream, one vegetable soup—and they *must* change, they should always taste a little different." He added that he wasn't sure how extensive his
repertoire was, but that it probably includes at least eighty soups, among them
African peanut butter, Greek moussaka, hamburger, Reuben, B.L.T., aspara-
gus and caviar, Japanese shrimp miso, chicken chili, Irish corned beef and cabbage, Swiss chocolate, French calf's brain, Korean beef ball, Italian shrimp and
eggplant Parmesan, buffalo, ham and egg, short rib, Russian beef Stroganoff,
turkey cacciatore, and Indian mulligatawny. "The chicken and the seafood are
an addiction, and when I have French garlic soup I let people have only one
small container each," he said. "The doctors and nurses love that one."

A lunch line of thirty people stretched down the block from Mr. Yeganeh's   7
doorway. Behind a construction worker was a man in expensive leather, who

was in front of a woman in a fur hat. Few people spoke. Most had their money out and their orders ready.

8   At the front of the line, a woman in a brown coat couldn't decide which soup to get and started to complain about the prices.

9   "You talk too much, dear," Mr. Yeganeh said, and motioned her to move to the left. "Next!"

10   "Just don't talk. Do what he says," a man huddled in a blue parka warned.

11   "He's downright rude," said a blond woman in a blue coat. "Even abusive. But you can't deny it, his soup is the best."

INQUIRING INTO THE ESSAY

Use the four methods of inquiry—exploring, explaining, evaluating, and reflecting—to generate a response to "Soup."

1. Use a "narrative of thought" response to explore your initial reactions to "Soup." Immediately after reading the piece, open your notebook and begin a five-minute fastwrite, starting with the following phrase: *The first thing that comes to mind after reading this essay is _____. And then . . . And then . . .* Whenever the writing stalls, seize on the phrase "and then" to get you going. Feel free, however, to digress on some aspect of the profile you want to think about through writing. After five minutes, stop and finish the following sentence: *Now that I look back on what I've said, the thing that strikes me the most about this essay is . . . .*

2. Summarize the main idea of each of the eleven numbered paragraphs in the essay. Explain what you notice about the structure of the essay. Does it have a logical order? Would you argue for a different one?

3. Review the essay and any writing you've done on the essay. Make a quick list of words that best describe Yeganeh. Choose one of them, and using evidence from the essay, find specific information that supports the choice. What is the strongest evidence you found that best explains the aptness of the word you chose to describe him? Evaluate the qualities of good evidence in a profile essay.

4. Go ahead and admit it. You like reading *People* occasionally (or maybe often). It's the first magazine I pick up in the doctor's waiting room. Reflect for a moment on what you find so appealing about reading profiles of celebrities. Now consider how you felt about reading "Soup." Were your motives and responses the same? How would you distinguish between a *People* piece on Nicole Kidman and the *The New Yorker* profile of Albert Yeganeh?

PROFILE

It's good to remember that plastic surgeons do more than nose jobs and face lifts. They can rebuild our bodies after accidents, restoring severely damaged fingers and faces, saving us from the loss of the familiar. Perhaps more than any other physicians, plastic surgeons are guided by cultural standards that dictate what looks "right." This may be why the plastic surgeon profiled in Lauren Slater's "Dr. Daedalus" is so disturbing; he dares to imagine breaking the rules. Dr. Rosen is less interested in what looks good than what might work better. Why settle for "normal" ears when they can be "beefed up" so we can have the "range of an owl?" And why not wings? Might we learn to fly like angels?

The profile you are about to read is excerpted from a longer piece that appeared in *Harper's* in 2001. It's a good contrast to the previous essay, "Soup," because the writer chooses to be part of this essay, referring to her own feelings and reactions to her subject and what he says. Slater uses the story of getting to know Dr. Rosen as the narrative backbone of the piece. The choice to do this has its advantages, and principal among them is that telling the story of meeting and getting to know your profile subject is an easy way to organize the material. But there are risks, too. Does the writer get in the way because she makes herself a subject of the profile, too?

DR. DAEDALUS
Lauren Slater

PART I: BEAUTIFUL PEOPLE

Joe Rosen, plastic surgeon at the renowned Dartmouth-Hitchcock Medical Center, and by any account an odd man, has a cold. But then again, he isn't sure it's a cold. "It could be anthrax," he says as he hurries to the car, beeper beeping, sleet sleeting, for it's a freezing New England midwinter day when all the world is white. Joe Rosen's nose is running, his throat is raw, and he's being called into the ER because some guy made meat out of his forefinger and a beautiful teenager split her fine forehead open on the windshield of her SUV. It seems unfair, he says, all these calls coming in on a Sunday, especially because he's sick and he isn't sure whether it's the flu or the first subtle signs of a biological attack. "Are you serious?" I say to him. Joe Rosen is smart. He graduated cum laude from Cornell and got a medical degree from Stanford in 1978. And we're in his car now, speeding toward the hospital where he reconstructs faces, appends limbs, puffs and preens the female form. "You really wonder," I say, "if your cold is a sign of a terrorist attack?"

Joe Rosen, a respected and controversial plastic surgeon, wonders a lot of things, some of them directly related to his field, others not. Joe Rosen wonders, for instance, whether Osama bin Laden introduced the West Nile virus to this country. Joe Rosen wonders how much bandwidth it would take to make virtual-reality contact lenses available for all. Joe Rosen wonders why both his ex-wife and his current wife are artists, and what that says about his deeper interests. Joe Rosen also wonders why we insist on the kinds of conservative medical restraints that prevent him from deploying some of his most creative visions: wings for human beings; cochlear implants to enhance hearing, beefing up our boring ears and giving us the range of an owl; super-duper delicate rods to jazz up our vision—binocular, beautiful—so that we could see for many miles and into depths as well. Joe Rosen has ideas: implants for this, implants for that, gadgets, gears, discs, buttons, sculpting soft cartilage that would enable us, as humans, to cross the frontiers of our own flesh and emerge as something altogether . . . what? Something other.

3   And we're in the car now, speeding on slick roads toward the hospital, beeper beeping, sleet sleeting, passing cute country houses with gingerbread trim, dollops of smoke hanging above bright brick chimneys; his New Hampshire town looks so sweet. We pull into the medical center. Even this has a slight country flair to it, with gingham curtains hanging in the rows of windows. We skid. Rosen says, "One time I was in my Ford Explorer with my daughter, Sam. We rolled, and the next thing I knew we were on the side of the highway, hanging upside down like bats." He laughs.

4   We go in. I am excited, nervous, running by his bulky side with my tape recorder to his mouth. A resident in paper boots comes up to us. He eyes the tape recorder, and Rosen beams. Rosen is a man who enjoys attention, credentials. A few days ago he boasted to me. "You shouldn't have any trouble with the PR people in this hospital. I've had three documentaries made of me here already."

5   "Can I see them?" I asked.

6   "I don't know," Rosen answered, suddenly scratching his nose very fast. "I guess I'm not sure where I put them," and something about his voice, or his nose, made me wonder whether the documentaries were just a tall tale.

7   Now the resident rushes up to us, peers at the tape recorder, peers at me. "They're doing a story on me," Rosen says. "For *Harper's.*"

8   "Joe is a crazy man, a nutcase," the resident announces, but there's affection in his voice.

9   "Why the beeps?" Rosen asks.

10   "This guy, he was working in his shop, got his finger caught in an electric planer . . . . The finger's hamburger," the resident says. "It's just hamburger."

11   We go to the carpenter's cubicle. He's a man with a burly beard and sawdust-caked boots. He lies too big for the ER bed, his dripping finger held high in the air and splinted. It does look like hamburger.

I watch Rosen approach the bed, the wound. Rosen is a largish man, with   12
a curly head of hair, wearing a Nordstrom wool coat and a cashmere scarf. As a
plastic surgeon, he thinks grand thoughts but traffics mostly in the mundane.
He has had over thirty papers published, most of them with titles like
"Reconstructive Flap Surgery" or "Rhinoplasty for the Adolescent." He is
known among his colleagues only secondarily for his epic ideas; his respect in
the field is rooted largely in his impeccable surgical skill with all the toughest
cases: shotgunned faces, smashed hands.

"How ya doin'?" Rosen says now to the carpenter. The carpenter doesn't   13
answer. He just stares at his mashed finger, held high in the splint.

Rosen speaks softly, gently. He puts his hand on the woodworker's dusty   14
shoulder. "Looks bad," he says, and he says this with a kind of simplicity—or is
it empathy?—that makes me listen. The patient nods. "I need my finger," he
says, and his voice sounds tight with tears. "I need it for the work I do."

Rosen nods. His tipsiness, his grandiosity, seem to just go away. He stands   15
close to the man. "Look," he says, "I'm not going to do anything fancy right
now, okay? I'll just have my guys sew it up, and we'll try to let nature take its
course. I think that's the best thing, right now. To let nature take its course."

The carpenter nods. Rosen has said nothing really reassuring, but his tone   16
is soothing, his voice rhythmic, a series of stitches that promises to knit the
broken together.

We leave the carpenter. Down the hall, the teenage beauty lies in still   17
more serious condition, the rent in her forehead so deep we can see, it seems,
the barest haze of her brain.

"God," whispers Rosen as we enter the room. "I dislike foreheads. They get   18
infected so easily."

He touches the girl. "You'll be fine" he says. "We're not going to do any-   19
thing fancy here. Just sew you up and let nature take its course."

I think these are odd, certainly unexpected words coming from a man   20
who seems so relentlessly anti-nature, so visionary and futuristic in his interests. But then again, Rosen himself is odd, a series of swerves, a topsy-turvy,
upside-down, smoke-and-mirrors sort of surgeon, hanging in his curious cave,
a black bat.

"I like this hospital," Rosen announces to me as we leave the girl's room. "I   21
like its MRI machines." He pauses.

"I should show you a real marvel," he suddenly says. He looks around him.   22
A nurse rushes by, little dots of blood on her snowy smock. "Come," Rosen
says.

We ride the elevator up. The doors whisper open. Outside, the sleet has   23
turned to snow, falling fast and furious. The floor we're on is ominously quiet,
as though there are no patients here, or as though we're in a morgue. Rosen is

ghoulish and I am suddenly scared. I don't know him really. I met him at a medical-ethics convention at which he discussed teaching *Frankenstein* to his residents and elaborated, with a little light in his eye, on the inherent beauty in hybrids and chimeras, if only we could learn to see them that way. "Why do we only value the average?" he'd asked the audience. "Why are plastic surgeons dedicated only to restoring our current notions of the conventional, as opposed to letting people explore, if they want, what the possibilities are?"

24   Rosen went on to explain other things at that conference. It was hard for me to follow his train of thought. He vacillates between speaking clearly, almost epically, to mumbling and zigzagging and scratching his nose. At this conference he kangaroo-leapt from subject to subject: the army, biowarfare, chefs with motorized fingers that could whip eggs, noses that doubled as flashlights, soldiers with sonar, the ocean, the monsters, the marvels. He is a man of breadth but not necessarily depth. "According to medieval man," Rosen said to the convention, finally coming clear, "a monster is someone born with congenital deformities. A marvel," he explained, "is a person with animal parts—say, a tail or wings." He went on to show us pictures, a turn-of-the-century newborn hand with syphilitic sores all over it, the fingers webbed in a way that might have been beautiful but not to me, the pearly skin stretched to nylon netting in the crotch of each crooked digit.

25   And the floor we're on now is ominously quiet, except for a hiss somewhere, maybe some snake somewhere, with a human head. We walk for what seems a long time. My tape recorder sucks up the silence.

26   Rosen turns, suddenly, and with a flourish parts the curtains of a cubicle. Before me, standing as though he were waiting for our arrival, is a man, a real man, with a face beyond description. "Sweeny," Rosen says, gesturing toward the man, "has cancer of the face. It ate through his sinus cavities, so I scraped off his face, took off his tummy fat, and made a kind of, well, a new face for him out of the stomach. Sweeny, you look good!" Rosen says.

27   Sweeny, his new face, or his old stomach, oozing and swollen from this recent, radical surgery, nods. He looks miserable. The belly-face sags, the lips wizened and puckered like an anus, the eyes in their hills of fat darting fast and frightened.

28   "What about my nose." Sweeny says, and then I notice: Sweeny has no nose. The cancer ate that along with the cheeks, etc. This is just awful. "That comes next. We'll use what's left of your forehead." A minute later, Rosen turns to me and observes that pretty soon women will be able to use their buttocks for breast implants. "Where there's fat," Rosen says, "there are possibilities."

INQUIRING INTO THE ESSAY

Use the four methods of inquiry to think about "Dr. Daedalus."

1. Profiles aren't just about a person. The writer deliberately selects a person because he or she stands in for certain ideas, questions, or problems. In "Dr. Daedalus," Lauren Slater writes that Joe Rosen "wonders why we insist on the kinds of conservative medical restraints that prevent him from deploying his most creative visions: wings for human beings; cochlear implants to enhance hearing . . . super-duper delicate rods to jazz up our vision . . . " He asks later in the essay, "Why do we value the average?" What do you think of these medical restraints? Are they wise? Is what Rosen proposing daring and imaginative or somehow immoral or unethical? Fastwrite openly for five minutes exploring your own thoughts about these questions.

2. If you've ever seen the movie *Elephant Man,* then the closing anecdote about Sweeney is especially painful. How are we to respond to Sweeney—with pity or disgust? Explain how you felt Slater handled her own response to Sweeney. How does his story influence your thinking about the questions the profile raises about the possibilities of plastic surgery?

3. Does this essay make an evaluation about the questions Rosen raises? What is Slater's argument?

4. Profiles tell true stories about someone. Short stories that focus on a single character are fiction. Does that make a difference in how you read them?

PROFILE

Phillip Petit is an important part of the lore of the fallen World Trade Center towers. One day in August 1974, while the towers were still being finished, Petit and a few friends made their way to the top of both buildings with the rigging that would allow Petit to erect a wire more than 1,300 feet above the ground. What followed captured New Yorkers' imaginations. Petit spent 45 minutes walking the wire between the two towers, enjoying the applause and the honking of car horns below until he literally ran into the waiting arms of police.

This wasn't Petit's first stunt, nor would it be his last. In the profile that follows, first published in *Smithsonian Magazine,* writer Rudolph Chelminski tries to understand why Petit might say, "When I see three oranges I juggle, and when I see two towers I walk." What could motivate a man to take such risks?

TURNING POINT
Rudolph Chelminski

What turned the tide of public regard [for the World Trade Center] was not the bigness of the place but the way it could be momentarily captured by fanciful gestures on a human scale. It was the French high-wire artist Philippe Petit crossing between the towers on a tightrope in 1974 . . .

—*New York Times,* September 13, 2001

1   WAS IT ONLY twenty-seven years ago? It seems a lifetime, or two, has passed since that August morning in 1974 when Philippe Petit, a slim, young Frenchman, upstaged Richard Nixon by performing one of the few acts more sensational—in those faraway times—than resigning the presidency of the United States.

2   A week before his twenty-sixth birthday, the nimble Petit clandestinely strung a cable between the not-yet-completed Twin Towers, already dominating lower Manhattan's skyline, and for the better part of an hour walked back and forth over the void, demonstrating his astonishing obsession to one hundred thousand or so wide-eyed gawkers gathered so far below.

3   I missed that performance, but last summer, just two weeks before the 1,360-foot-tall towers would come to symbolize a ghastly new reality, I persuaded Petit to accompany me to the top and show me how he did it and, perhaps, explain why. I was driven by a long-standing curiosity. Ever since reading about his exploit in New York, I had felt a kind of familiarity with this remarkable fellow. Years before, I had watched him at close range and much lower altitude, in another city on the other side of the pond.

4   In the 1960s, the Montparnasse area of Paris was animated by a colorful fauna of celebrities, eccentrics, and artistic characters. On any given day, you might run into Giacometti walking bent forward like one of his skinny statues, Raymond Duncan (Isadora's brother) in his goofy sandals and Roman toga, or Jean-Paul Sartre morosely seeking the decline of capitalism in the Communist daily, *L'Humanité*. And after nightfall, if you hung around long enough, you were almost certain to see Philippe Petit.

5   When he might appear was anyone's guess, but his hangouts were pretty well known: the corner of Rue de Buci and Boulevard St. Germain; the sidewalk outside Les Deux Magots, or directly under the terrace windows of La Coupole. Silent and mysterious, this skinny, pasty-faced kid dressed in black would materialize unannounced on his unicycle, a shock of pale blond hair escaping from under a battered top hat. He would draw a circle of white chalk on the sidewalk, string a rope between two trees, hop up onto it, and, impas-

sive and mute as a carp, go into an improvised show that combined mime, juggling, prestidigitation, and the precarious balancing act of loose-rope walking. After an hour or so he would pass the hat and, as wordlessly as he had arrived, disappear into the night.

Then, on a drizzly morning in June 1971, the kid in black suddenly showed up dancing on a barely perceptible wire between the massive towers of Notre Dame Cathedral. For nearly three hours, he walked back and forth, mugged, saluted, and juggled Indian clubs while angry gendarmes waited for him to come down. When he finally did, they arrested him for disturbing the peace.   6

Disturbing the peace was a good part of what it was all about, of course, because Petit was out to prove something. Notre Dame was his first great coup, the sensational stunt that was to become his trademark. It was also his first declaration of status: he was not a mere street entertainer but a performer, an artiste. Ever since that June morning, he has dedicated himself to demonstrating his passionate belief that the high wire—his approach to the high wire, that is—transcends the cheap hype of circus "daredevil" routines to become a creative statement of true theater, as valid as ballet or modern dance.   7

Getting that point across has never been easy. After gratifying Petit with a few front-page pictures, the French establishment gave a Gallic shrug, dismissed him as a youthful crank, and returned to more serious matters—like having lunch and talking politics. There was a very interesting story to be told about this young loner who had learned the art of the *funambule* (literally, "rope walker") all by himself as a teenager, but the Parisian press ignored it. Within a couple of days, his Notre Dame stunt was largely forgotten.   8

Stung, Petit resolved to take his art elsewhere and began a long vagabondage around the world, returning to Paris for brief spells before setting off again. Traveling as light as a medieval minstrel and living hand to mouth, he carried his mute personage from city to city, juggling for his supper. None of his onlookers could know that back in his tiny Parisian studio—a rented broom closet he had somehow converted into a dwelling—he had a folder marked "projects."   9

Two years after the Notre Dame caper, the skinny figure in black appeared with his balancing pole between the gigantic northern pylons of the Sydney Harbour Bridge in Australia. Petit had strung his cable there just as furtively as he had done at Notre Dame, but this time the police reacted with brainless if predictable fury, attempting to force him down by cutting one of his cavalettis, the lateral guy ropes that hold a sky walker's cable steady. Flung a foot up in the air when the cavaletti sprang free, Petit managed to land square on the cable and keep his balance. He came in and was manacled, led to court, and found guilty of the usual crimes. The owner of a Sydney circus offered to pay his $250 fine in return for a tightrope walk two days later over the lions' cage.   10

11   And then came the World Trade Center. Petit had been planning it ever since he was nineteen when, in a dentist's waiting room, he saw an article with an artist's rendering of the gigantic towers planned for New York's financial district. ("When I see three oranges I juggle," he once said, "and when I see two towers I walk.") He ripped the article from the magazine and slipped it into his projects file.

12   The World Trade Center would be the ultimate test of Petit's fanatically meticulous planning. For Notre Dame and Sydney, he had copied keys to open certain locks, picked others, and hacksawed his way through still others in order to sneak his heavy material up into place for the sky walk. But New York presented a much more complicated challenge. The World Trade Center buildings were fearfully higher than anything he had ever tackled, making it impossible to set up conventional cavalettis. And how to get a cable across the 140-foot gap between the South and North Towers, anyway, in the face of omnipresent security crews?

13   There was one factor in Petit's favor: the buildings were still in the final stages of construction, and trucks were regularly delivering all sorts of material to the basement docks, to be transferred to a freight elevator and brought up to the floors by workers of all descriptions. Wearing hard hats, Petit and an accomplice hauled his gear to the top of the South Tower (his walking cable passed off as antenna equipment) while two other friends similarly made their way to the roof of the North Tower, armed with a bow and arrow and a spool of stout fishing line. Come nightfall, they shot the arrow and line across the 140-foot gap between the towers. Petit retrieved the line, pulled it over until he was in possession of the stronger nylon cord attached to it, then tied on the heavy rope that would be used to carry his steel walking cable over to the other side.

14   As Petit paid out the rope and then the cable, gravity took over. The cable ran wild, shooting uncontrollably through his hands and snaking down the side of the giant building before coming up short with a titanic *thwonk!* at the steel beam to which Petit had anchored it. On the North Tower, holding fast to the other end of the heavy rope, his friends were pulled perilously close to the roof's edge. Gradually, the four regained control and spent the rest of the night hours pulling the cable up, double-cinching the anchor points, getting it nearly level, tensioning it to three tons with a ratchet, and finally attaching a set of nearly horizontal cavalettis to the buildings. At a few minutes past seven A.M., August 7, 1974, just as the first construction workers were arriving on the rooftop, Petit seized his balancing pole and stepped out over the void.

15   The conditions weren't exactly ideal. Petit had not slept for forty-eight hours, and now he saw that the hurry-up rigging job he had carried out in the dark had resulted in a cable that zigzagged where the improvised cavalettis

joined it. Sensitive to wind, temperature, and any sway of the buildings, it was also alive—swooping, rolling, and twisting. At slightly more than twenty-six feet, his balancing pole was longer and heavier—fifty-five pounds—than any he had ever used before. Greater weight meant greater stability, but such a heavy load is hard enough to tote around on terra firma, let alone on a thin wire in midair at an insane altitude. It would require an uncommon debauch of nervous energy, but energy was the one thing Petit had plenty of.

With his eyes riveted to the edge of the far tower—wire walkers aren't sup- 16
posed to look down—Petit glided his buffalo-hide slippers along the cable, feeling his way until he was halfway across. He knelt, put his weight on one knee, and swung his right arm free. This was his "salute," the signature gesture of the high-wire artist. Each has his own, and each is an individual trademark creation. Arising, he continued to the North Tower, hopped off the wire, double-checked the cable's anchoring points, made a few adjustments, and hopped back on.

By now traffic had 17
stopped in the environs of Wall Street, and Petit could already hear the first police and ambulance sirens as he nimbly set forth again. Off he went, humming and mumbling to himself, puffing grunts of concentration at tricky moments. Halfway across, he steadied, halted, then knelt again. And then, God in heaven, he lay down, placing his spine directly atop the cable and resting the balancing pole on his stomach. Breathless, in Zen-like calm, he lay there for a long moment, contemplating the red-eyed seabird hovering motionless above him.

Time to get up. But how do you do it, I asked Petit as we stood to- 18
gether on the roof of the South Tower, when the only thing between you

and certain death is a cable under your body and fifty-five extra pounds lying on your belly?

19   "All the weight on the right foot," he replied with a shrug. "I draw my right foot back along the cable and move the balancing bar lower down below my belt. I get a little lift from the wire, because it is moving up and down. Then I do a sit-up and rise to a standing position, with all the weight on my right foot. It takes some practice."

20   He got up. Unable to resist the pleasure of seeing New York at his feet, he caressed the side of the building with a glance and slowly panned his eyes all the way down to the gridlocked traffic below. Then he flowed back to the South Tower. "I could hear the horns of cars below me," he recalled, relishing the memory. "I could hear the applause too. The *rumeur* [clamor] of the crowd rose up to me from four hundred meters below. No other show person has ever heard a sound like that."

21   Now, as he glided along north to south, a clutch of police officers, rescue crews, and security men hovered with arms outstretched to pull him in. But Petit hadn't finished. Inches from their grasp, he did a wire walker's turn-around, slipping his feet 180 degrees and swinging his balancing bar around to face in the other direction. He did his elegant "torero's" walk and his "prome-nader's" walk; he knelt; he did another salute; he sat in casual repose, lord of his domain; he stood and balanced on one foot.

22   After seven crossings and forty-five minutes of air dancing, it began to rain. For his finale he ran along the cable to give himself up. "Running, ah! ah!" he had written in one of his early books. "That's the laughter of the wire walker." Then he ran into the arms of waiting police.

23   Petit's astonishing star turn created a sensation the likes of which few New Yorkers had ever seen. Years later, the art critic Calvin Tompkins was still so impressed by what Petit had done that he wrote in *The New Yorker:* "He achieved the almost unimaginable feat of investing the World Trade Center . . . with a thrilling and terrible beauty."

24   Ever resourceful, Petit worked out a deal with the Manhattan district attorney. In lieu of punishment or fine, and as penance for his artistic crime, he agreed to give a free performance in Central Park. The following week he strung a 600-foot wire across Turtle Pond, from a tree on one side to Belvedere Castle on the other. And this time he nearly fell. He was wearing the same walking slippers and using the same balancing pole, but security was relaxed among the fifteen thousand people who had come to watch him perform, and kids began climbing and jumping on his cavalettis. The wire twitched, and suddenly he felt himself going beyond the point of return.

But he didn't go all the way down. Instinctively squirming as he dropped,   25
he hooked a leg over the wire. Somehow, he managed to swing himself back
up, get vertical, and carry on with the performance. The crowd applauded
warmly, assuming it was all part of the act, but Petit doesn't enjoy the memory. Falling is the wire walker's shame, he says, and due only to a lack of concentration.

In the years since his World Trade Center triumph, Petit has disdainfully   26
turned away all offers to profit from it. "I could have become a millionaire," he
told me. "Everyone was after me to endorse their products, but I was not going to walk a wire dressed in a hamburger suit, and I was not going to say I
succeeded because I was wearing such and such a shirt." Continuing to operate
as a stubbornly independent freelance artist, he has organized and starred in
more than seventy performances around the world, all without safety nets.
They have included choreographed strolls across the Louisiana Superdome in
New Orleans, between the towers of the Laon Cathedral in France, and a
"Peace Walk" between the Jewish and Arab quarters of Jerusalem. In 1989, on
the bicentennial of the French Revolution, he took center stage in Paris—
legally and officially this time—by walking the 2,300-foot gap between the
Trocadéro esplanade on the Right Bank, over the Seine, and up to the second
tier of the Eiffel Tower.

Today, at fifty-two, Petit is somewhat heavier than in his busking days in   27
Paris, and his hair has turned a reddish blond, but neither his energy nor his
overpowering self-confidence has waned in the least. He shares a pleasantly
rustic farmhouse at the edge of the Catskills near Woodstock, New York, with
his longtime companion, Kathy O'Donnell, daughter of a former Manhattan
publishing executive. She handles the planning, producing, problem-solving,
and money-raising aspects of Petit's enterprises while they both think up new
high-wire projects and he painstakingly prepares them. Petit supplements his
income from performances with, among other things, book royalties and fees
from giving lectures and workshops.

His preferred place of study is his New York City office. Knowing what   28
an artiste he is, you would not expect to find him in an ordinary building,
and you would be right. Petit hangs out at the Cathedral of St. John the
Divine, the world's biggest Gothic cathedral, at Amsterdam Avenue and
112th Street. His office is a balustraded aerie in the cathedral's triforium,
the narrow gallery high above the vast nave. Behind a locked entryway, up a
suitably medieval spiral staircase and then down a stone passageway, the rare
visitor to his domain comes upon a sturdy door bearing a small framed sign:
Philippe Petit, Artist in Residence. Behind that door, stowed as neatly as a yacht's
navigational gear, lie his treasures: thousands of feet of rope coiled just so,

all manner of rigging and tensioning equipment, floor-to-ceiling archives, maps and models of past and future walk projects, and shelves upon shelves of technical and reference books.

29   It was another of his coups that got him there. In 1980 he offered to walk the length of the nave to raise funds for the cathedral's building program. He was sure he had the perfect occasion for it: Ascension Day. The cathedral's then dean, the ebullient James Parks Morton, famous for his support of the arts, was enthusiastic, but his board of trustees vetoed the idea as too dangerous. Petit sneaked a cable crosswise over the nave and did his walk anyway. Once again the police came to arrest him, but Morton spoiled their day by announcing that Petit was artist in residence and the cathedral was his workplace. And so he came to be.

30   Over the years, taking his title seriously, Petit reciprocated by carrying out a dozen wire walks inside and outside the cathedral. He figures that by now he has raised half a million dollars for the still uncompleted cathedral's building program, and enjoys pointing out the small stone carving of a wire walker niched in among the saints in the main portal. "It is high art," Morton says of Petit's work. "There is a documented history of wire walkers in cathedrals and churches. It's not a new idea, but his walk here was his first in an American cathedral."

31   Sometimes after six P.M., when the lights go out, the big front door slams shut, and the cathedral closes down for the night, Petit is left alone in the mineral gloom of St. John with his writing, sketches, calculations, chess problems, poetry, and reveries. The comparison to Quasimodo is immediate and obvious, of course, but unlike Notre Dame's famous hunchback, Petit wants nothing more than to be seen, in the ever greater, more ambitious, and spectacular shows that fill his dreams. One night after he took me up to his cathedral office, he gazed longingly at a print of the Brooklyn Bridge—what a walk that could be! But there is, he assured me, plenty more in his projects file. A walk on Easter Island, from the famous carved heads to the volcano. Or the half-mile stretch over open water between the Sydney Harbour Bridge and the celebrated Opera House.

32   Even more than all these, though, there is one walk—*the* walk, the ultimate, the masterpiece—that has filled his dreams for more than a decade. It's the Grand Canyon. Prospecting in the heart of the Navajo nation by air in 1988, Petit discovered the ideal spot for crowning his career: a ruggedly beautiful landscape off the road from Flagstaff to Grand Canyon Village, where a noble mesa soars at the far end of a 1,200-foot gap from the canyon's edge. The gap is deeper than it is wide, 1,600 feet straight down to the Little Colorado River.

Petit's eyes glowed as he went through the mass of blueprints, maps,   33
drawings, and models he has produced over all the years of planning the
Canyon Walk. Only one thing is missing: money. Twice now, the money people
have backed out at the last minute.

But none of that seemed to matter when I spoke to Petit a few days after   34
the September 11 catastrophe struck. He could scarcely find words for his sorrow at the loss of so many lives, among them people he knew well—elevator
operators, tour guides, maintenance workers. "I feel my house has been destroyed," he said. "Very often I would take family and friends there. It was my
pride as a poet and a lover of beautiful things to show as many people as possible the audacity of those impossible monoliths."

Haunted, as we all are, by the images of the towers in their final moments,   35
Petit told me it was his hope that they would be remembered not as they appeared then but as they were on that magical August day more than a generation ago, when he danced between them on a wire and made an entire city
look up in awe. "In a very small way I helped frame them with glory," he said,
"and I want to remember them in their glory."

Inquiring into the Essay

Once again, use the four methods of inquiry to investigate your thoughts
and feelings about Chelminski's profile of Phillipe Petit.

1. To walk a high wire some 1,300 feet above the ground requires,
   among other things, that the walker manage his fear. Is that an extraordinary skill? In your notebook, explore a moment when you
   were required to manage your fear, probably in a less dramatic way.
   First plunge into the Sea of Critical Thinking and write about a moment, scene, or situation in which you in a sense were a high wire
   walker. At the end of the fastwrite, compose a paragraph about how
   your experience helps you to understand Petit, at least a little.

2. If one of Chelminski's motives was to discover what might motivate
   a man to walk on a wire between the World Trade Center towers,
   explain how the writer seems to answer that question in the profile.
   Refer to particular passages.

3. The fact is, Petit broke the law. Make an argument for or against
   the renegade in American culture, using Petit as a central example.

4. Reflect on what it might be like if you were the subject of a profile.
   What would be your fears? What might motivate you to agree to be
   profiled?

SEEING THE FORM

CONSUELO CLOOS BY JUDY DATER

The photographer and the painter who are after a truthful portrait of someone confront the same problem as the writer: How can you possibly capture the complexity of a human being in a single image or on a few pages? The answer, of course, is that you can't. The best you can do is reveal some aspect of who they are, some particular impression. Look closely at Judy Dater's photograph of Consuelo Cloos. What is your strongest im-

Judy Dater, *Consuelo Cloos,* 1980. Gelatin silver print, 13/12 X 10 1/4".
Collection Fred Jones Jr. Museum of Art, the University of Oklahoma, Norman;
Purchase, 1982. Reproduced with the permission of Judy Dater.

pression of this woman? And what exactly do you see in the photograph that contributes to that impression?

Just as profile writers' purposes lead them to select some information on their subjects and leave out other information, a photographer like Dater selects a certain visual setting and angle for seeing her subject. Dater also waits for a moment in which certain gestures might give us a glimpse into her subject's psychology. We can't really know *Consuelo Cloos* through this one picture. But Dater helps us to see some part of her. What do you see?

If you were to choose a word or phrase that best describes your dominant impression of Consuelo Cloos, what would it be? If you were trying to help someone else see the picture that way what details would you point to in the image? What does this suggest about an important element of profile writing?

▪ THE WRITING PROCESS ▪

INQUIRY PROJECT: Representative Profile

Write a 1000- to 1,200-word profile of someone who strikes you as representative, in some ways, of a larger group. For example, write a profile of your neighbor, the Harley Davidson aficionado, because he seems typical, in some ways, of bikers. Profile a nurse because that's a profession you're interested in. Write about an African American student on your predominantly white campus to discover what of his or her experience might represent the experience of other minority students there. Your instructor may give you additional instructions.

Work toward a profile that has the following qualities:

- It is ultimately organized around ways your profile seems representative or typical of the larger group to which your subject belongs.
- The profile includes at least three anecdotes, or little stories, that help reveal this theme.
- You bring in the voice of your subject through selective quotations.
- The end of the essay circles back to the beginning.

Thinking About Subjects

Sometimes you don't choose the subject; he or she chooses you. That was frequently my experience when I researched my book on lobsters—as I traveled and talked to people about the subject I was researching, I found fascinating people whose experience, like Abby Boynton's, would powerfully reveal some aspect of lobstering that seemed important. One way to find suitable profile subjects, therefore, is simply to look for them in the course of doing your research. Who have you read or heard about or perhaps met who might provide a useful focus for a subject in which you're interested?

On the other hand, you might have an idea of who you'd like to profile now, someone you know or would like to know. But if you'd like to play around with some ideas, the following prompts should help. As always, keep generating ideas until you feel you have some potentially promising material.

Generating Ideas

Play with possible subjects, withholding judgment for the moment about what might be a good one. Again, as in the previous chapter, don't let your critical side stifle your creative side. At this point in the process, you can let yourself swim freely.

Listing Prompts. To select a topic within which you'd like to find someone to profile, try the following:

1. Make a quick list of issues or controversies in the local community that people talk about or that have gotten your attention.
2. Make a quick list of issues or controversies that have garnered attention on your college campus.

✍ ONE STUDENT'S RESPONSE

BRUCE'S JOURNAL

LIST OF LOCAL ISSUES

Foothills preservation
Water rights
Mayor recall campaign
Downtown parking
Guns in the home
Governor's anti-terrorism measures
Preservation of Owhyee's as wilderness
Preservation of White Clouds
Minimum wage for migrant workers
State street traffic

Choose one of the controversies that interests you, and try the first two steps in the "Research Prompts" section that follows.

You can also begin with an interview subject and discover what issues or ideas might be relevant, or simply choose a subject because you find the person interesting and you're not sure why. Try this listing prompt:

- Who have you known whom you can't forget? Make a fast list, examining all times and parts of your life.

Fastwriting Prompts. Fastwriting is a great way to loosen up your creative side and at the same time generate raw material. Below are a few prompts to get you writing:

1. Choose a name from the list you generated above—who have you known whom you can't forget? Choose someone you find interesting for some reason. Perhaps it's a grandfather who tells stories about the war, or an old friend who now works at the Museum of Sex in New York City (yes, there really is one). Maybe your friend's mother is a writer who is on the verge of publishing her first book of poems and you wonder what it feels like. Write the person's name at the top of a journal page. Begin a fastwrite in which you describe in detail the scene or situation in which you last saw and talked to your subject. Follow the writing from there.

2. Think of one word that best describes the character or personality of a subject you might profile. Arrogant? Generous? Selfless? Narcissistic? Put that word at the top of a journal page and create two scenes that *show* that word. For a challenge, don't mention the word at all in your scenes.

Visual Prompts. Maps, clusters, lines and arrows, charts, or even sketches can help us piece together subjects in ways that writing sometimes cannot. Consider the following options:

1. Put the name of a possible profile subject in the center of a cluster. Build a web of associations for five minutes, and then begin fastwriting when you feel the urge.

2. Go through old photographs for ideas about profile subjects; this might be especially useful for reminding yourself of family and friends who might be good subjects.

Research Prompts. It is impossible to write a profile without conducting research of some sort, if not in the library or online, then in the field with one's subject. Doing some research up front, then, can be a useful way to find a subject to write about.

✎ **ONE STUDENT'S RESPONSE**

BRUCE'S JOURNAL

RESEARCH ON LIST OF ISSUES

ISSUE	INTERVIEW SUBJECTS
Recall	Margaret the storekeeper, Mayor Coles
Owyhee's wilderness	Congressperson Simpson, Pat Ford
Migrant workers	Miguel Gomez, Rep. Bieter
Foothills preservation	Jack Coulter, Mayor, Nancy Maynard.

1. Return to the list you generated earlier in "Listing Prompts." Choose a controversy in the community or on campus as the focus for your profile. Check the community and campus newspapers to discover who has been active as advocates on the issue, or who has been impacted by it. Is any one person suitable for a profile?

2. Discuss your topic with your friends or people in your class. Who do they know that would be good as a profile subject?

3. On the Internet, search the archives of the local newspaper to find the names of potential profile subjects on an issue or controversy in which you're interested.

4. If you have a career interest, a profile of a working member of the profession can be compelling. Call the state professional association for suggestions about how to find an interview subject, or ask friends and family for suggestions.

Judging What You Have

You should have a considerable body of material to work with now. It may not be coherent at this point, but again it's always better to work from abundance rather than from scarcity. It's your job now to use your critical side to judge, shape, and evaluate this material.

What's Promising Material and What Isn't? Let's look critically at the material you've generated. How will you choose the best profile subject? Consider the criteria below:

- *Accessibility*. You're interested in the experience of death row inmates at the super-maximum prison in the next county. An obvious choice of a subject is the guy recently convicted of a local rape and murder who was sentenced last week to the death penalty. Can you get to talk to him? Probably not. His attorneys may be preparing an appeal, or your request for an interview might be one of many, most of which come from news organizations. If you could talk to him, would there be sufficient time for the interview? The greatest subject in the world is no good to you if he or she's inaccessible.

- *Background.* Lacking time to spend with an interview subject, writers often look for information that may already exist; perhaps an article or two, a diary, a cigar box full of old pictures. This background information can provide extremely useful material to supplement what the writer gets in a face-to-face interview. Might there be such information on a possible subject?

- *Typicality.* Is the subject representative in some way of an aspect of a topic you'd like to investigate? Every human being is unique, obviously, but we all occupy certain categories of human experience. I've been interviewed, for example, as an English professor, a book author, and an expert on the methods of dispatching lobsters. Am I typical of each category? Gee, I don't like to think so, but some of my experiences are typical.

- *Extremity.* On the other hand, what you may look for is a subject who doesn't represent the norm in a category of experience but an extreme. Bert, a Florida State undergraduate, was a great subject for a piece on the nation's top party school not because he represented the norm of male party animals but because he was so radically committed to that lifestyle. Bert isn't typical, in that sense, but rather a dramatic example of how out of hand things can become.

- *Spontaneity.* Profiles of politicians or celebrities are particularly challenging because they have learned to "manage" an interview. That is, they've developed the skills to control the course of an interview, ensuring that what they plan to say gets said and little more. Less experienced subjects, the kind you are most likely to profile, often have appeal because they *aren't* practiced at talking about themselves. There's freshness and even naiveté sometimes about what they say and how they say it that makes profiles particularly compelling.

- *Quotability.* This doesn't necessarily mean articulateness. I remember a devastating profile some years ago of the New York socialite Cornelia Guest. Her remarkable inarticulateness at expressing her personal values and commitments to charities were quotable *because* they were so goofy. The reader's dominant impression of Guest from the piece was that she was a complete airhead. On the other hand, the people you may least expect to be articulate about their experiences can just blow you away. Sometimes you simply can't know how quotable a subject might be until the interview. But if you do know beforehand that someone speaks in an interesting way, you may have a great profile subject.

- *Willingness.* I put this last for a reason. Most of us assume that people are resistant to the kind of interviews a profile demands. A few profile subjects may, at first, be resistant to the *idea* of being interviewed, but in reality people simply love to talk about themselves. An interview gives a subject a willing listener; how often do we enjoy the undivided attention of someone who is vitally interested in what we have to say about ourselves? A profile subject may have concerns—perhaps discomfort with what they might reveal about themselves, or initial distrust of the interviewer who may be a stranger—but by and large it's hard to find an unwilling subject.

Questions About Audience and Purpose. As always, profile writing begins with a personal motivation. Is there something you think you can learn from your subject, perhaps something about an aspect of the world you are interested in, or something about the human spirit? By interviewing someone else is it possible to even learn something about yourself? You might also begin with a simpler, less grand, but no less important motive: Is there something this subject knows or feels that should be documented and preserved? This is one reason we interview and profile family members and friends, but personal motive is not enough reason to write a profile—the piece must hold interest for readers who may not immediately share your fascination in Uncle Leopold's account of his marriage to Aunt Edna. As always, the *So what?* question lurks in the background.

The profile can, like good fiction, provide insight into the complexities of the human mind and soul.

As you evaluate the material you've generated, consider some of the following purposes that transcend your personal ones.

- *Which possible profile subject best fits the details of the assignment?* Your instructor may have provided guidance on how to approach the profile, including suggestions about choices of a profile subject or things to consider about audience. Which subject seems to best fit these guidelines?

- *Does this profile subject help illuminate an idea, issue, or controversy that might interest some of your readers?* Remember the "Migrant Mother?" That portrait pointed to larger social issues. One of the appeals of Chelminski's profile of Philipe Petit is that, after September 11, 2001, the account of Petit's tight roping between the Twin Towers years earlier becomes a poignant reminder of not only courage, but loss, danger, and cowardice. Lauren Slater's profile of Dr. Rosen in "Dr. Daedalus" is not just about the plastic surgeon but also the ethics of tampering with the human form.

- *Does a profile subject provide a focus on an interesting bit of history?* One of the ways to write a focused treatment of a larger historical event or story is to find someone who lived it. If you want to write, for example, about the internment of the Japanese during World War II, the particulars of Kaz Kasamoto's experience as a child in one of the camps will give readers a dramatic glimpse at this sad piece of American history.

- *Does a profile subject represent a "type" of person that might interest readers?* Perhaps you're interested in the culture of sorority life on your campus and you have a willing subject who has belonged to Kappa Kappa Gamma for the last three years. Or perhaps you want to become a registered labor and delivery nurse. A profile of a working obstretric nurse will not only teach you something about your career choice but convince others that such a job is interesting, demanding, or not for them.

- *Is the profile subject an interesting character?* Don't be fooled. Even so-called ordinary people can be fascinating if you can get them to let their masks slip a little. But what makes a subject inherently interesting even if, for example, the person isn't a "type," didn't experience a bit of history, or can't represent an issue or idea? In a word, *surprise.* What often makes profile subjects interesting is that they shatter our assumptions about people and how they are in the world—a 90-year-old man who still hikes 14,000 foot peaks, a 14-year-old college student, a therapist with marital problems, a lesbian activist in rural Mississippi, the president of an antifraternity fraternity. We are all composed of contradictions like these, but some are more surprising than others.

- *Who is your audience?* A key factor in any writing situation is audience. Who are you writing for in this assignment and which possible profile subjects would that audience find most compelling?

Interviewing

His interview subjects sometimes see John McPhee, one of the great profile writers, as "thick-witted". At times, McPhee seems to ask the same questions over and over, and he frequently seems to possess only the most basic information about his subjects. According to William Howarth, when McPhee "conducts an interview he tries to be as blank as his notebook pages, totally devoid of preconceptions." It's his theory that unless his interview subjects "feel superior or equal to their interviewer" they won't talk as freely or at length. McPhee never uses a tape recorder, but jots down spare notes in a notebook—these are the telling details and facts that reveal his subject's character.

McPhee is what some have called an immersion journalist, someone who spends substantial time with his subjects, getting to know them more intimately. This is the best basis for writing a profile because it generates enough information to get closer to the truth about the subject. But it's also a difficult approach for student writers who rarely have that time to spend; that's why the availability of background information on the person you hope to profile can be so useful. Still, this general principle still stands: *The more time you can spend talking with your interview subject, the better the profile will be.* If at all possible, then, plan on requesting more than a single time to talk, or at least an extended time—perhaps an hour or more—if only one meeting is possible.

You can find more information about interviewing techniques in Chapter 12, "Research Techniques," but the following tips should help you get started developing a plan for your interviews.

Making Contact. I'm a fairly shy guy. In fact, when I began writing nonfiction articles many years ago the worst part of the work was calling people to ask for their time to do an interview. These conversations almost always ended well for a simple reason—people love to talk about themselves. That's hardly surprising. After all, how often do we enjoy for more than a few minutes the undivided attention of someone who appears fascinated by everything we say, and even writes some of it down? E-mail has made the process of contacting an interview subject less intimidating, although it's not a totally satisfactory substitute for a phone conversation.

Asking a family member or friend to be an interview subject is easy, but how do you ask a stranger? You start by introducing yourself and straightforwardly describing the profile assignment, including your feeling that the subject would be a great focus for your piece. You must be prepared to answer the almost inevitable follow-up question: "Well, gee, I'm flattered. But what is it about me that you find interesting?" Here's where McPhee's elementary knowledge is crucial: Although you need to know only a very little about your interview subject, you must know enough to say, for instance, that you're aware of his role in a bit of history, are aware of his involvement in a local issue, or recognize him as being knowledgeable about a topic you find of interest.

What you want from this initial contact is time. The conventional interview—when you sit across from your informant asking questions and writing down answers—can be very useful, but it may be more productive if you can spend time *doing* something with your profile subject that relates to the reason you've chosen him. For example, if you are profiling an environmental activist, spend a few hours walking the trail through a threatened piece of prairie that the activist cares about or is trying to defend. Your interview with a homeless woman could take place during lunch at the local shelter. *Seeing* your subject in a meaningful situation can generate far more information than the conventional interview. Imagine what those situations might be.

What do you do if your subject doesn't want to be interviewed? In that unlikely event, you're permitted to ask why. If your reassurances aren't sufficient to change the person's mind, then you need to find another subject.

Conducting the Interview. You've arranged a time and place for an initial conversation. Should you prepare questions? Sure, but be prepared to ignore them. Interviews rarely go as planned, and if they do, they are often disappointing. An interview is a *conversation,* and these are best when they head in unexpected directions. Go with the flow in the initial interview; if there are informational questions you have to ask, you can save them for the next time.

There are certain generic questions that can reveal things about a subject's character. These are more *open-ended questions* that often lead in surprising and interesting directions. Some of these open-ended questions include:

- In all your experience with _____, what has most surprised you?
- What has been the most difficult aspect of your work?
- If you had the chance to change something about how you approached _____, what would it be?
- Can you remember a significant moment in your work on _____? Is there an experience with _____ that stands out in your mind?
- What do you think is the most common misconception about _____? Why?
- What are significant trends in _____?
- Who or what has most influenced you? Who are your heroes?
- If you had to summarize the most important thing you've learned about _____, what would you say? What is the most important thing that people should know or understand?

Note taking during an interview is a challenge. A popular method is to use a tape recorder (see "Inquiring into the Details: Tape Recorders"), but even if you do it's essential to take handwritten notes as well. While the tape recorder will capture the voice of your subject, it will not collect the essential details of the scene. You have to do that. Jot down any facts, details, phrases, mannerisms, or even personal reactions you have during the interview. This is crucial. Don't worry if these notes are fragmentary. Immediately after you conclude the interview you can write out a fuller account, using the fragments as prompts.

INQUIRING INTO THE DETAILS

TAPE RECORDERS

There are advantages and disadvantages to using a tape recorder to record your interview. If you do record you will have a complete account of your conversation, which can free you up to take notes on your subject's mannerisms, environment, and such. When recording you might also feel more able to participate in the conversation if you aren't obsessed with transcribing your subject's words. However, many people are unsettled by the recorders, feeling unable to speak freely or to open up with a machine recording their every "um" or pause. Ultimately you'll decide which approach you think is best, but should you use a tape recorder, here are some tips:

- Practice at home first. Set up the tape recorder and make sure you have fresh batteries as well as an extension cord. Be sure to have extra tapes. Label your tape with the name of the subject and date of your interview. Then turn on the machine and record a few minutes of testing. When you finally meet with your subject your machine should be absolutely ready to go, with a minimum of fiddling.

- Ask your interview subject if you can use the recorder. If the answer is no, don't record.

- If possible, place the recorder somewhere unobtrusive (but not too far away—you still want it to pick up the conversation).

- No matter what, take notes as if the recorder isn't on. The tape recorder should be your backup, not your primary source of information. (In my experience, technology often fails when it is most needed. Therefore the recorder may record your test conversation perfectly but fail when you are in the actual interview.)

- Once you get home, transcribing your conversation may reveal ideas, themes, and quotes you don't remember. Transcribing is incredibly time-consuming, but can be well worth the effort.

While my students have used the double-entry journal effectively as a note taking format for profiles, putting the observed information and quotations on the left page and personal responses on the right, I'm keen on those pocket-sized memo books. They're incredibly unobtrusive, easy to carry, and force you to be spare. I especially like the ease with which I can take the memo pad out and put it away, at times using it to signal to my subject that I'm more—or less—interested in something he's saying.

Listening and Watching. The art of interviewing relies, more than anything else, on the craft of listening. Few of us are good listeners, which is why profile writing can be so hard. First you must control your anxiety about getting things down, asking the next question, and making your subject relaxed. It is only then that you can give your interview subject your full attention. Novice interviewers should remember that the quality of the conversation matters more than anything else, including careful note taking and asking clever questions. You can always call back to check your facts or prompt your subject to repeat something memorable. E-mail can be a useful follow-up method for such things.

What makes a good conversation? When it generates the kind of information that will help you write the profile, including:

- *Stories.* Interesting stories and anecdotes that will help you build a narrative backbone to your essay.
- *Memorable quotations.* A typical interview produces only a handful of these so don't desperately write down everything a subject says. Wait until you hear something that is nicely put or distinctive, particularly quotes that reveal something about your subject's character.
- *Background information.* This can be in the form of stories, but might also be basic but essential information such as your subject's age, place of birth, and history of involvement in relevant jobs or issues.
- *Feeling.* A good conversation is an honest one in which the subject is willing to let the mask slip to reveal the face sweating underneath. Be alert to those moments of feeling when your subject seems to be revealing herself—what *really* matters to her, what might be hard, where she finds joy.

Moments of honesty are often signaled by body language. I once interviewed a New Hampshire lobsterman, and after a long day of setting traps with him I offhandedly asked whether he hoped his sons and daughters would go into the business. He had spent most of the day talking about how much he loved the independent lifestyle, and so when he didn't reply immediately to my question I paid attention. I noticed him looking at his hands, roughened by saltwater and toughened by the thick plastic line he roped to the traps. "Too much work for what they get out of it," he said suddenly. The response surprised me, and I think I would have missed it if I hadn't noticed him looking at his hands. Mannerisms can be revealing, but so can the things a profile subject surrounds herself with—the books in the bookshelf, the type of car she drives, or the style of her house. Collect these observations as you would any other kind of evidence—scrupulously and with care.

INTERVIEW NOTES

Below are interview notes that Margaret Parker took in preparation for writing the powerful profile, "Medical Student," which appears at the end of this chapter. As you read her notes, imagine the kinds of questions she had to ask to produce this kind of specific information about her subject, JD. Note the care Parker takes to get the facts straight, as well as her work to create a story through scenes and characterizations.

Your interview notes are the main source of information for your profile. If they're skimpy—brief or vague—you can't possibly write a profile that brings your subject to life.

SELECTED INTERVIEW NOTES
"MEDICAL STUDENT"
Margaret Parker

"Oh my God JD you look so . . . together!"

Day begins at 3:30 AM and ends at 8:30. Every fifth day "On-Call," goes to bed around nine in the student call room, divided by a sheet, sleeps in scrubs and sweatshirt and thick socks because it's freezing, around midnight a trauma comes in and have to do surgery. Then back to work the next day at 5:00 AM, start with rounds and quizzed at 6:30 by residents.

110 hr/week is average . . . 120 hrs one week because she had call three times.

Operating Room (OR) environment—everything is sterile, only see eyes of people, must keep hands between waist and shoulders at all times, if not, the OR nurses scream at you and you have go leave and rescrub, shames, OR nurses like Nazis, her first week she was screamed at constantly, you just don't realize how hard it is to keep hands in place and the terror of getting yelled at. Just trying to please and doing really menial tasks like holding retractors or skin and muscle back so that the surgeon can do his thing, back spasms, very exhausting for five or eight hours, terrified to move. Med students are everybody's peon, the OR nurses are the worst . . .

The Worst Day

Supposed to be there at 5:00 for rounds, and meet with residents at 6:30 for the residents, her alarms didn't go off and the clock read 5:45. It takes forty-five minutes to drive from her apartment to Olympia Fields hospital, arrives at 6:27, "peeing my pants," Kelley—a short mall rat junior high looking girl, starts screaming at all of them, she asks JD a question and she doesn't know it, she walks away and the team is angry with JD. She scrubs in for the surgery, a cholesectomy of a 16 yr. old girl, expected to last two hours, hands drop below the waist slightly and the OR nurse screams "I don't believe this crap, Student, you better go rescrub", the attending with open contempt in his eyes, the resident satisfied smirk barely detectable below the mask, holds the camera in the stomach for hours, the surgery starts to go badly, it is apparent it will take much longer than two hours, drags into its fourth hour, struggle to keep still, back spasms, "Wrong Godamn direction!", everybody in shock, the camera is still in the girl's stomach, nobody moves to do anything, then he gets a hold of himself and resumes, it goes on, terrified, trying not to shake, part of her wants to walk out, screw him, she didn't sign up for this, paying 30,000 grand a year to be shaken and terrorized by psychopaths, but she stays, five

Notice how careful the writer is to collect specific details —exact times, descriptions, and so on.

In her notes, the writer integrates quotations within the overall narrative. She organizes her notes by roughly following the the story she wants to tell. This often isn't possible because you don't yet know the story when you interview.

hours the surgery is over, "God walks out", Kelly comes up and says, "Oh my God JD, don't worry about it, he's a jerk", and for a second these words are gratefully received, felt like an abused woman wanted to get in a car wreck so she wouldn't have to go, cried the whole way home, calculating the hours till she has to go back

The Team

Ryan—top of his class, wanted to do surgery but after the first week decided on Family UP practice or ER, counseled each other every day, go and hid and bitch

Keith "Special K"—disorder, you name it he's got it, OCD, super book smart but no social skills, disappears for hours, she tried to follow him but he lost her, then her friend Bernie called and swore that he saw him on campus, a good 45 minutes away, "Where the f—k is Keith," SD had to take over his surgeries because certain nurses wouldn't work with him, he touched his head and was generally unresponsive to their abuse, yet they wouldn't tell him, "SD tell him to put on his scrubs, tell him to go away", every night nightmares

Kelly—"so bipolar", seems like your chatty mall rat friend but then she turns into a demon

Trauma was better, the people were nicer, she was more valued, did useful things like chest compressions, took patient histories so they read her notes, Wendy Marshall the head honcho—British, teacher in every aspect, 'Pump-firing away of questions…'

"I have always wanted to be a doctor, and I couldn't really explain why. It was kind of a joke during my medical school interviews, because they always ask you, why do you want to be a doctor? And I'd reply with the generic, I wanna help people. But I guess now I think that I really like talking to people, and maybe in medicine I can help them. I think talking is the most important way to help sick people, not the real medicine that they teach you in school. People have such absolute faith in their doctor, and I love that feeling, that people confide in me."

Here the writer breaks with the narrative to get down descriptions of other characters.

An extended quotation. These help the reader really hear your subject's voice, and they can be quite revealing. They're also hard to get without a tape recorder or excellent note-taking skills.

Writing the Sketch

When you think you've collected enough information about your profile subject from interviews, observations, and background research, compose a 500-word typewritten sketch. The sketch is a brief treatment of a promising subject that may lack a clear sense of purpose but does not lack specific information. For your profile sketch, try to incorporate the following elements:

- At least two potentially revealing anecdotes or brief stories about your profile subject.
- At least two strong quotations from your subject.
- A title.
- A paragraph of background information, including your informant's age, a physical description, and perhaps relevant job or personal history.
- A strong lead (perhaps one of the anecdotes) and an ending that somehow returns to the beginning.

Moving from Sketch to Draft

A sketch is generally underdeveloped, sometimes giving the writer just the barest outline of his subject. But as an early draft, a sketch can be invaluable. It might hint at what the "real" subject is, or what questions seem to be behind your inquiry into the subject. A sketch might suggest a focus for the next draft, or simply a better lead. Here are some tips for finding clues in your sketch about directions you might go in the next draft.

Evaluating Your Own Sketch. It might seem like an impossible task to capture in a couple pages the complexity of the person you interviewed the other day. You must begin evaluating your sketch with more reasonable ambitions. It *is* impossible to capture the whole person, but what you are working toward in your profile is to capture an *aspect* of that person, some particular quality that stands out. That quality may be an impression you're trying to create—for example, this is an incredibly selfless individual—or it might be the particular contribution your subject is making to a controversy, an argument or an idea. Read your sketch, then, paying attention to one or both of those purposes:

1. *Dominant impression.* What feeling or personality trait do I want to communicate about my profile subject? Can I name it? Is there evidence in the sketch that points to this?
2. *Role.* What exactly am I trying to show—or might I show in the next draft—about my subject's participation in an idea, an issue, or an event?

Questions for Peer Review. Peer review of sketches can help writers clarify purpose. You've already done some thinking about that, now ask readers for help. You might pose the following questions:

- If you were to use one word to describe your main impression of the person I profiled, what would it be?
- What evidence would you point to in the sketch that contributes to that impression?

- Did you find my portrait sympathetic or critical?
- In a sentence, what seems to be my subject's main point of view, attitude, or belief?
- What one detail—a fact, an observation, description, or quotation—struck you as most revealing? What did it reveal?
- What would you like to know more about it the next draft?

Methods for Peer Review of Sketches

1. Choose a partner, exchange sketches, read and comment both in writing and through conversation.
2. Create a pile of sketches in the middle of the classroom. Everyone takes one (not your own, obviously), provides written comments, returns it the pile, and takes another. Repeat this until you've read and commented on at least four sketches
3. Share sketches online on the class Web site.

Reflecting on What You've Learned. Before you begin composing the next draft, make a journal entry that explores your thinking about the sketch and everything you heard. Begin an entry with the prompt, *Based on what I've learned so far about my profile subject, the main thing I seem to be trying to show is _____.*

Follow this prompt, continuing to reflect on what your intentions might be in the next draft. When the writing stalls, skip a line, a make a quick list: *The three things I heard during peer review that I want to remember include:* 1) _____; 2) _____; and 3) _____.

Research and Other Strategies: Gathering More Information

If you emerged from the experience of writing and sharing your sketch with a stronger sense of purpose, then you're close to being ready to draft. If you didn't, return to your notes or share your sketch with a few more readers. In either case, you'll probably need to collect more information before you begin the draft. Most important, plan another interview with your subject. This one will likely be quite different; now that you have a clearer purpose for your profile, your questions will be directed at getting the information you need to more fully develop your piece. For example, suppose you were profiling a student activist who is working on behalf of local migrant farm workers. Peer review of your sketch helped clarify your intentions—you'd like to show how instrumental student leaders like your profile subject were in the struggle last year to guarantee a minimum wage for migrant workers. In a follow-up interview, you'd likely ask that question directly: How important *were* student activists in that legislative battle? Your questions also might inspire your subject to tell stories about key moments in that struggle, particularly if they highlight the effectiveness of young activists. Can you see how useful a follow-up interview can be once you've determined your purpose? It's likely to generate invaluable information that could well be key to the success of the profile.

There are other sources of information you might consider as well:

- Interview people who know your profile subject.
- If your subject is a public figure, do library or Web research for background.

The quotes and information you gather can be used in your profile, usually with attribution. Research the idea, issue, or event, if any, that provides the context for your profile.

Composing the Draft

If you haven't collected enough information, you'll run aground pretty quickly in the draft. One of the signs of not enough information include using everything you've gathered about your profile subject, including information that may not be relevant to your purpose. Alternatively, you might simply write short, failing to meet the page length requirement. If you encounter these obstacles, return to the generating exercises earlier in the chapter or the tips listed above.

WRITING WITH COMPUTERS

TIPS FOR REVISION

From a practical standpoint, revising your drafts on a computer can be easier than doing so on paper. You can copy, paste, delete, and insert new text into the draft on a computer with a mouse click or a few simple keystrokes. As you work through multiple drafts, though, you should save each draft as a separate file. For ease in identification, number or insert the date of composition into each file name (for example, "draft3.doc" or "draft07.14.doc"). Saving copies of each draft will allow you (and potentially others, including your instructor) to evaluate your progress from one draft to the next. It will also give you the option of picking up again from an earlier draft if you find that your later drafts have moved in a direction that ultimately proves unrewarding. You should also print out and keep hard copies of each draft. Why? Your computer may seem completely reliable, but it only takes one bad experience to prove this isn't the case. Hard copies can be scanned or retyped, potentially saving you from having to start over. Also, when it comes time to read back over your drafts, the printed page is usually easier on the eyes than a computer screen.

If you're confident that you're working from abundance, consider beginning the drafting process by writing multiple leads. For example, work toward three one-paragraph beginnings—perhaps each focused on a different anecdote—and decide which one seems to point the draft in the direction you want it to go and might be most likely to capture your readers. Once you've chosen a lead, follow it. You'll likely find that the leads you didn't use will find a place for themselves somewhere else in the draft.

Methods of Development. There are various strategies you can pursue to develop your profile.

Narrative. The profile is a form that often relies on narrative. It can do this in several ways; perhaps the most familiar is that the piece tells the story of the writer's encounter with his subject. For example, "Turning Point," Rudloph Chelminski's profile of the high-wire artist Philipe Petit, not only recounts stories from Petit's past but includes several anecdotes in which the author follows Petit into his world and describes what happened: a return visit to the World Trade Center years after Petit walked the towers, and a visit to Petit's office just below the vaulted ceilings of a New York church. Profile writers are often drawn to the first-person account—my day with my subject—which is obviously a convenient structure if that matches the experience of the interviewer. My profile of the lobsterman's wife used this method of development. However, consider whether a first-person point of view interrupts the narrative too much and interferes with the reader's view of the profile subject.

Known to Unknown. If your profile subject is a public figure, and your motive is to reveal a less well-known aspect of your subject's life or work, beginning the essay with information that first seems to confirm public perceptions but then promises to challenge them—in other words, moving from what's known to what's less known—can be an effective way to structure the profile. This is a quite common method of development in the celebrity profile.

Using Evidence. The most authoritative information in a profile is the voice of your subject. It is also the information that will be most heavily scrutinized by the subject herself: "Did I really say that?" Readers of the profile often believe that the subject's voice is the most authentic information because it is less mediated by the writer, an assumption that isn't always accurate. After all, unless quotations come directly from the tape recorder, the interviewers have to rely on their note taking skill. Even with a recorded transcription, it's common practice for writers to tidy up bad grammar and remove irrelevant utterances such as "uh" and "um."

Profile writers must also establish their authority by giving readers a sense that the writers are keen and careful observers, and this is created through careful use of not just quotation but detail, description, and research. Consider how the author of "Soup" did this when profiling restaurant owner Albert Yeganeh.

Workshopping the Draft

If your draft is subject to peer review (see Chapter 15 for details on how to organize workshop groups), think carefully about the kind of responses you need from readers at this point in the process. The following questions might help you prepare.

Reflecting on the Draft. As you prepare your draft for peer review, think about what you most need in a response. Are you reasonably confident that the purpose and focus of your profile is clear? Or are you feeling anxious about how well you managed to pull it all together? Your initial feelings about the draft will be a factor in the kind of response you request from your group.

- Make a journal entry in which you reflect in a five-minute fastwrite about how you feel about the draft. What worked? What needs work?
- If the writing stalls, consider this question: *If I could change the process of writing this draft, from initially generating a subject to write about to this first draft, what would I change?* Follow this with a fastwrite until you have nothing more to say.

Questions for Readers. As you prepare for peer review, there are also certain questions that are particularly useful to consider when drafting profiles. Pose any of these to your group that seem relevant to your draft or possible plans for revision.

1. What dominant impression did the draft create of its subject? What words would you use to describe that impression?
2. In a sentence or two, what does the draft seem to be *saying* about its subject?
3. Does the end strain to return to the beginning, or does it give the profile a sense of wholeness or unity?
4. What is the strongest/weakest quote? What is the strongest/weakest anecdote?
5. What do you want to know about the profile subject that the draft doesn't say?
6. Did you find this person interesting? Why or why not?

Revising the Draft

In a sense, you've been revising all along. All the prewriting you did in your journal to find a subject, the questions you asked yourself to discover possible angles, and the interviewing to find the stories you might tell, not to mention drafting a sketch and reviewing it in workshop—all of these ac- tivities challenge you to constantly "re-see" your subject and your purpose in writing about the person; but there are more opportunities to discover what you might want to say and how best to say it. (Chapter 4, "Revision Strategies," will help you understand more fully what it means to "re-see" a draft or sketch and how that can lead to fresh discoveries at nearly any point in the writing process.)

Profiles typically have some of the following problems, most of which can be addressed by selecting appropriate revision strategies, or by repeat- ing some of the earlier steps in this chapter.

- The draft lacks a single coherent theme, or dominant impression. Is your profile organized from beginning to end around one main thing you're trying to say about your subject?

- The theme or dominant impression is obvious but isn't developed with enough specific information. Do you need to do another interview?

- You find your subject interesting, but you haven't given your readers enough reason to agree. Does your lead make a strong enough case? Is there another story you should tell?

Refer to Chapter 14, "Revision Strategies," for ideas on how to revise your draft following your workshop. Use the following table as a guide to the appropriate revision strategies for your draft, and remember that a draft may present problems in more than one category.

GUIDE TO REVISION STRATEGIES		
PROBLEMS IN THE DRAFT (CHAPTER 14)	**PART**	**PAGE NUMBER**
Unclear purpose ▪ Not sure what the essay is about? Fails to answer the *So what* question?	1	633
Unclear thesis, theme, or main idea ▪ Not sure what you're trying to say?	2	639
Lack of information or development ▪ Needs more details; more showing and less telling?	3	646
Disorganized ▪ Doesn't move logically or smoothly from paragraph to paragraph?	4	650
Unclear or awkward at the level of sentences and paragraphs ▪ Does draft seem choppy or hard to follow at the level of sentences or paragraphs?	5	656

Polishing the Draft. After you've dealt with the big issues in your draft—is it sufficiently focused, does it answer the *So what?* question, is it well organized, and so on—you must deal with the smaller problems. You've created an appealing figure but now you need to polish it. Are your paragraphs coherent? How do you manage transitions? Are your sentences fluent and concise? Are there any errors in spelling or syntax? Section 5 of Chapter 14 can help you focus on these issues.

Before you finish your draft, make certain that you've worked through the following checklist:

- ❏ Every paragraph is about one thing.
- ❏ The transitions between paragraphs aren't abrupt.
- ❏ The length of sentences varies in each paragraph.
- ❏ Each sentence is concise. There are no unnecessary words or phrases.
- ❏ You've checked grammar, particularly verb agreement, run-on sentences, unclear pronouns, and misused words (*there/their, where/were,* and so on). (See the handbook at the end of the book for help on all of these grammar issues.)
- ❏ You've run your spell checker and proofed your paper for misspelled words.

STUDENT ESSAY

What impresses me most about the following profile is the way that Margaret Parker managed to write in a style that captures the intensity of her subject's experience during a single day as a medical student. The piece has a breathless, panicked quality that wonderfully matches the writer's purpose in the profile. The essay is also richly detailed, keeping our attention riveted on the subject throughout. An amazing thing about this is that Parker didn't actually witness the story she writes about; all of the material was gathered from her interviews (see "Selected Interview Notes: 'Medical Student' by Margaret Parker," earlier in the chapter). Can you imagine what questions she must have asked to be able to write these scenes?

MEDICAL STUDENT
Margaret Parker

The Worst Day

Something is terribly wrong. For starters, she feels almost rested. The deep 1
black pitch of the room has begun to soften into the gray light of dawn. JD's
stomach plummets as she sees the glaring red numbers on her alarm clock.

5:45 a.m. Ohmygodohmygodohmygod . . . 2

She swears she set the alarm for 3:30 the night before, but it didn't go off. 3
Rounds start at 6:30, but she's supposed to arrive at Olympia Fields Hospital
by 5:00 a.m. to examine all her patients and prepare for the resident's inquisi-
tion at 6:30. There's no time to brush her teeth, eat, drink, think; she throws
on some clothes, dives into her car and screams obscenities in the air throughout the frantic forty-five minute drive. By some miracle she makes it to the
hospital by 6:27. Ryan and Keith, the other third-year medical students on her
surgery rotation team, cast disapproving glances tinged with terror in her direction.

Chief Resident Kelly saunters up to the students; even at this ungodly 4
hour she is bright-eyed and menacing, ready for the kill. She assesses each of
them with a consciously intimidating drawn-out glare, and once again displaying an uncanny instinct for sensing weakness in her prey, zones her attention
on JD.

"Hey Student, tell me about Mrs. Gomez's labs." 5

The collective fear of the group is palpable. JD bites the bullet and replies 6
the unthinkable, "I don't know."

Rage and disgust wash over Kelly's face. "You're all so pathetic," she says, 7
and then turns and walks away. Rounds end early this morning; they have all
failed.

Ryan won't even look at her he's so furious and even Keith snorts angrily 8
and stomps off. If Keith thinks you're a loser, you know it must be true. The
residents call him "Special K" because he suffers from obsessive-compulsive
disorder and just about every other mental illness you can imagine. He hasn't
been able to adapt to the turbo-intense lifestyle of the general surgery rotation. He'll show up to his scheduled surgery without his scrubs, ask the same
question repeatedly, or simply disappear for hours at a time. On any other day
the "team screw-up" award would invariably go to him, but on this hellish
morning, JD has emerged the winner.

But there's no time to dwell. She has to go to the pre-op room and scrub 9
in for surgery. This morning she will assist Dr. Donnelly, Chief Attending
Surgeon, Kelly, and an OR nurse in the cholesectomy of a sixteen-year-old

girl. Donnelly isn't too worried about it; he told the girl's parents it would take two hours, max.

10   All scrubbed-in and donning a surgical mask, cap, and scrubs, JD marches into the OR room where the others are already waiting for her. For just a split second, her hands fall below her waist, and she immediately corrects her stance and looks around to make sure no one has seen her slip. The OR nurse is fuming in her direction. It amazes JD how much emotion a person can express when half of her face is covered with a mask.

11   "Student get the hell outta here and rescrub! Jesus!" she booms throughout the room. Donnelly and Kelly roll their eyes and share a moment of mutual disgust.

12   JD can't believe she did this again, and on this morning of all mornings. Her first week of surgery was pure torture as she was constantly being thrown out of the OR for allowing her hands to drift out of the sacred "waist to shoulders" zone, but she's a sharp girl, and their scare tactics had effectively beat it into her. But her tardiness this morning has frazzled her nerves, and she's not herself.

13   She sucks in a deep breath, closes her eyes, and reenters the OR to begin the surgery. Donnelly has her position a long probe with a tiny camera attached to it into the patient's stomach so he can view what he is doing on a TV monitor. She must hold this position in complete stillness for the entire surgery.

14   The two-hour mark passes, and it becomes clear to all that the procedure is not going well. Donnelly starts swearing and muttering under his mask, and the tension in the room rises. Three and a half hours. Donnelly is seething; he just can't seem to get it right. He snaps at JD to turn the camera at a different angle; she does this. He barks at her to turn it again, just slightly to the right, and she complies.

15   Then he snaps.

16   "Student you've got it the wrong goddamn way!" he snarls at her, grabbing her arm and painfully bearing his fingers into her. He loses it, starts shaking her violently in spite of the instrument she is still holding inside the patient's stomach. Kelly and the nurse stare dumbly at them both.

17   Donnelly stops shaking her, composes himself and turns his focus back on the patient. The others emerge from their stupor and do the same. JD is dumbfounded. Should she leave, walk out? If she had an ounce of self-respect left she would. Who does this guy think he is? But she knows if she leaves, he'll fail her, and she's worked way too hard to fail now.

18   After five hours, the surgery is a success. Donnelly closes the patient up, and with the air of a god, swaggers out of the OR. Once he's outside and well out of earshot, Kelly whispers to JD conspiratorially: "Oh my God JD, don't worry about it . . . he's such a jerk."

For a split second, JD's eyes water over and she is touched by this rare display of kindness from the girl she calls "the demon." But it doesn't last. It dawns on her that Kelly hadn't said a word to Donnelly; she'd let him take it all out on the medical student to save her own ass.   19

Thank God for Ryan. He doesn't hold a grudge from this morning; he can't afford to. JD and Ryan barely knew each other before this rotation began, but war has a way of bonding soldiers together. They spend the hours between surgery and rounds seeking out hiding places in the hospital where they spew out all the crap they've had to deal with that day. As they whisper in a janitor's closet, a voice sounds over the hospital intercom: "Surgery extern report to OR-3, surgery extern, report to OR-3."   20

"Why do they call us 'externs'? That makes it sound like we get to go home," she laughs.   21

"Doesn't 'Special K' have surgery in 3 today?" Ryan asks.   22

"Oh crap," JD says. She knows what this means. There's a certain OR nurse who refuses to work with Keith. He simply lacks the Pavlovian response mechanism that allows creatures to learn from negative feedback; no matter how much she screams at him, he continues to touch his head in the OR and let his arms droop to his sides. But no one will tell Keith that he's been banned. Instead they page JD to fill in for him and leave Keith clueless.   23

JD jogs over to OR-3 where Keith is purposefully scrubbing in. As usual, no one has told him. The OR nurse approaches JD. "Student, tell him he can't scrub in."   24

"Uh, Keith," she says, "why don't you go check on your patients' labs or something."   25

Keith looks crushed as the situation sinks in. He knows he is failing, and every day he seems more and more unstable. He mutters some obscenity and storms off. JD scrubs in for another five-hour procedure.   26

It's 8:00, almost time to go home. She's had nothing to eat or drink all day. Surgeons severely limit their intake of liquids because they cannot under any circumstances leave the OR to use the bathroom. Her urine is bloody from dehydration. After evening rounds are over, she slugs into the locker room to change back into her normal clothes. Keith is standing there, perfectly still, wearing ridiculously skin-tight scrubs.   27

"JD," he says in a faraway voice without looking at her, "do you have any trauma scissors?"   28

"Sure," she says. "Why?"   29

"These scrubs are so tight," he says. "I don't know how I ever got into them. Could you cut them off of me?"   30

JD ponders this for a moment, wondering if he has finally lost it completely.   31

32   "Sure, Keith." She starts at his feet and cuts a sliver all the way up to his neckline. He peels them off like skin and stands before her in his boxers. An eerie, uncomfortable silence lingers between them. She gathers her things and leaves.

33   JD climbs into her car and starts the drive home. She starts crying, and soon her whole body is heaving with sobs. As she drives on the busy Chicago streets, the thought that's been pestering her mind like a virus since she began the surgery rotation returns to her. She fantasizes about swerving off the road—oh, not to die, really, just to be injured enough to not have to go back to that hellhole tomorrow. She doesn't want to be a doctor anymore, not if this is what it is really like. If she weren't $75,000 in debt, she would drop out right now and never look back. It's almost 9:00. In six and a half hours it will all begin again.

EVALUATING THE ESSAY

1. How does Margaret Parker craft the essay to give it the panicked, breathless feeling that contributes so much to her overall profile of JD? What does she do at the sentence and paragraph level that gives it those qualities?

2. "Medical Student" focuses on a single day. In what other ways might you use time to help you organize and focus a profile?

3. Like many profiles, "Medical Student" focuses on a single person as part of an effort to give the reader a glimpse at a category of people (med students) or experiences (internships at hospitals). Is there a danger of overgeneralizing from a specific case? How do writers avoid that?

4. If the essay were to continue, what else would you want to know or see about JD and the life she leads?

USING WHAT YOU HAVE LEARNED

You've read published profiles and one written by a student. You've also had the chance to write your own. What have you learned about the profile genre of writing and how might you use this in other writing situations?

1. What are the ethical obligations of writers to their profile subjects? For example, do you think it should be a standard practice for subjects to approve profiles before they're published? What is reasonable for a profile subject to expect from a writer?

2. While a profile isn't an academic form, can you imagine how you might use some of the methods and approaches you tried here in papers for other classes?

3. A profile of one person who is representative of a larger social group is decidedly unscientific. It just isn't possible to make scientifically reliable generalizations about the group from a single case. Then what good is a profile?

French movie poster for *Amelie*.

Writing a Review

WRITING THAT EVALUATES

One of the occasions when I feel fairly stupid is after watching a movie with my wife, Karen. She always wants to know what I think. I don't have much of a problem arriving at a gut reaction—I loved the movie *Amelie,* for example, but I have a hard time saying why. Beyond statements such as, "It was pretty good," or "It was pure Hollywood," a comment I mean to be critical, the conversation scares me a little because Karen is wonderfully analytical and articulate when describing her feelings about a film. In comparison, I stutter and stammer and do my best to go beyond a simple judgment.

Essentially, Karen is asking me to evaluate a film, to make a judgment about its quality. This is something we do all the time. Buying a pair of jeans involves evaluating the reputation of the manufacturer, the quality of the denim and its particular design, and especially aesthetic judgments about how the jeans look on us when we wear them. I think most of us like to think these decisions are quite rational. On the contrary, many of our evaluations are more emotional than logical. We *really* do buy that pair of jeans because an ad suggests that we'll look sexy or attractive in them. Or consider this: How would you evaluate the quality of your mother or father's parenting? Will this be a rational judgment? It's unlikely. Even though we're qualified to make such a judgment—after all, who is a better authority on the parenting skills of parents than their children—often our views toward our parents are always awash in feelings.

You remember evaluation as one of the four ways of inquiring, and you've already practiced it in Chapter 3 and responses to the readings in other chapters. You know, then, that part of the challenge of evaluating something is keeping an open mind, sometimes *despite* our initial feelings about it. Since all evaluation stems from what are essentially subjective value judgments, a tension always exists be-

What You'll Learn in This Chapter

- The role of evaluation in a review.

- How feelings and reason can form the basis of evaluation.

- What distinguishes the review from other forms.

- Questions that will help you revise a review.

tween our *desire* to prove our point and our *need or willingness* to learn more about the subject.

That emotion figures into our judgments of things isn't a bad thing. It's a human thing. But one of the reasons it's useful to consciously consider *how* we make such judgments is that we're more likely to introduce logical considerations in mostly emotional evaluations, or emotional considerations in mostly logical ones. This awareness also helps us suspend judgment long enough to get a more balanced look at something.

Evaluation involves three things:

1. *Judgment.* Something is good or bad, useful or not useful, relevant or not relevant, convincing or not convincing, worth doing or not worth doing, or perhaps shades in between.

2. *Criteria.* This forms the basis by which we judge whether something is good or bad, useful or not useful, and so on. If we were to evaluate a car, for example, our criteria might be performance or appearance or cost or any combination of the three. Often our criteria are implicit; that is, we aren't even consciously aware of the criteria that inform judgments. The more familiar we are with the thing—say, cars, movies, or mystery novels—the more elaborate and sophisticated the criteria become.

3. *Evidence.* Criteria provide the principles for making a judgment but evidence—specific details, observations, or facts about the thing itself—is what makes an evaluation persuasive. That's why simply saying, "This assigned reading is boring" produces blank stares from your instructor. What exactly makes it dull? Is the language of the article filled with jargon, and which passage exactly illustrates this well?

If this sounds a lot like making an argument, you're right, because evaluation is the basis of argument. But I suspect that emotion, at least initially, figures more in our judgments of things than our reasoned arguments about them. In fact, evaluation can be a way of seeding the field of argument because it helps you identify the things about which you have strong opinions.

MOTIVES FOR WRITING A REVIEW

I rarely write reviews. But evaluative writing is one of the most common kinds of writing I do, from commenting on student papers, to writing reference letters for former students, to writing a memo to my colleagues about a proposed departmental policy. Evaluative writing is an enormously practical form, relevant in all sorts of situations in and out of school. Quite simply, we turn to it when we are asked to make a judgment of value, and then develop that judgment into something that goes beyond a gut reaction and unstated assumptions.

Beginning in Chapter 3, you were introduced to some of the opening questions that might guide your thinking and seeing: *What's my take on this? Do I see this the way most other people do? All things considered, what's most convincing here? What's least convincing? What do I see that supports what I believe? What do I see that complicates or contradicts what I believe?*

All of these questions imply that evaluation is a pretty logical process, but more often it begins with a feeling—which, again, is not a bad thing—and evaluative writing helps you work from that feeling outward into reason, which will make your judgment persuasive to others *and* help shape your future judgments about other, similar things. That's why my conversations with Karen about movies, once I stop feeling stupid, can be so helpful because she challenges me to find reasons for what I feel, reasons that I am slowly learning to apply to my judgments of other films.

> *If you feel strongly about something, turn to evaluative writing and thinking as a way of helping you and others to understand why.*

If you feel strongly about something, turn to evaluative writing and thinking as a way of helping you and others to understand why.

THE REVIEW AND ACADEMIC WRITING

We don't usually think of the review as an academic form, although you may be asked to review a film you're shown in an English class or perhaps a performance in a theater class. But evaluative writing, a process you'll practice when writing a review, is among the most common types of writing in all kinds of college classrooms. Here are just a few examples:

- In a literature class, you may be asked to evaluate the effectiveness of a story or a character.
- In a theater class, you may write a review of a dramatic performance.
- In a science class, you may need to evaluate the methodology of an experiment.
- In a composition class, you're often asked to evaluate the writing of peers.
- Philosophy frequently involves the evaluation of arguments.
- Business writing may require evaluation of a marketing strategy, a product, or a business plan.

Once you start thinking about evaluative writing, you'll find it everywhere—the book reviews in the Sunday *Times,* the music reviews in *Spin,* the analysis of Web sites on websitesthatsuck.com. It's probably the most common form of workplace writing, too, from assessing the performance of an employee to evaluating a plan to preserve historic buildings.

FEATURES OF THE FORM

Like all forms of writing, evaluation genres vary widely. Perhaps the least likely form is one in which the writer formally announces a judgment, lists criteria, and then offers evidence using the criteria. That is, at least, an approach that you'll have a hard time finding outside of school. Much evaluative writing is more subtle than that—and much more interesting—because the writer blends judgments, criteria, and evidence seamlessly throughout. If you've ever read a review of a band, a computer, or a book, you probably never noticed its structure because if the review is well-written the structure isn't noticeable. But there are features that most reviews share, and many of them are a part of all kinds of evaluative writing.

- *A review is usually clear about categories.* Of course, the effectiveness of all writing depends on responding to a certain situation, but evaluative writing is particularly sensitive to the *category* of thing you're writing about. For example, the inverted pyramid in Figure 6.1 shows the narrowing of categories of film, working toward a more limited category—say, feature films about space travel. It's easier to come up with convincing criteria to judge a narrower category than a broad,

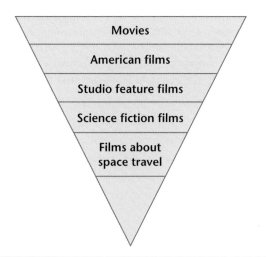

FIGURE 6.1 Narrowing the category of evaluation. One of the keys for developing useful and relevant criteria for judging something is making sure that you're focusing on the neighborhood, not the globe. In this example, it's much more helpful to talk about what makes a good Hollywood science fiction film about space travel than attempt to describe the qualities of the much broader category, all movies. After all, what makes a foreign art film effective is probably different from what makes a romantic comedy effective.

general one. Reviewers are often very careful to state clearly the kind of thing they're reviewing.

- *Reviews usually describe the thing they evaluate.* How much you describe depends on your readers' knowledge of what you're evaluating. If they haven't seen the performance, don't know the actor, haven't read the book, or don't know the type of product you're reviewing, then readers need the necessary background to understand what exactly you're talking about. Summaries can be vital. For example, a review of Ani DiFranco's latest CD might explain that her music seems to straddle folk and rock, and that she's known for her intricate lyrics and political convictions. Some of this description may also be part of the evidence you offer.

- *Evaluation criteria are matched to purpose, category, and audience.* Obviously, a writer has reasons for making a judgment about something. Always in the back of the writer's mind is the purpose of the evaluation: what exactly he or she is writing about (and *not* about). If your aim is to help businesses understand which Web sites are likely to sell the most T-shirts your criteria will be different from that used to evaluate the Web sites nonprofit groups might use to educate people about world hunger. Like all persuasive writing, the review is shaped by its audience. This can affect your approach in several ways. If you're writing a review for an audience that hasn't read Elise Blackwell's novel, *Hunger,* you'll need to spend more time providing background on the book than you would if you were writing for an audience—perhaps your instructor—who was familiar with it. In addition, always analyze whether your readers might already have opinions—positive or negative—toward the thing you're reviewing. If you're praising the virtues of Microsoft's new operating system to an audience of Mac users, your pitch—the amount and quality of evidence you offer, and so on—needs to be much stronger than if you are writing for Windows lovers.

- *In reviews, feelings often lead judgment but they are never enough.* Although evaluation is a form of argument, reason doesn't always lead judgment. Frequently, we first *feel* something—the Web site turns us off, or the new music video is captivating, or the reading assignment puts us to sleep. These feelings often lead us to an initial judgment—something we might acknowledge to readers—but they are never enough. The challenge of persuasive evaluation is to introduce reason into the process.

- *Judgments range from an overall assessment (e.g. it was good or bad, helpful or useless, and so on) to more specific commentary on particular evidence or aspects of the thing.* Music critic Neal Pollack (see his review later in this chapter) doesn't merely argue that the Rolling Stones, recent tours are boring, but that the band is also culturally irrelevant, a "Vegas headliner show, not a rock outfit." These judgments don't reside in one place in some kind of grand thesis, but are scattered throughout Pollack's essay, working toward a more complicated assessment of the band.

- *Reviews frequently attempt to offer a balanced assessment.* Hey, it can't be *all* bad. (Okay, sometimes it is.) The most persuasive negative evaluations tend to include some positive judgments, and positive evaluations frequently make some concessions about a thing's flaws. This isn't just a rhetorical ploy, but recognition that things are never that simple.

- *Criteria may be stated or unstated.* You'll rarely find a piece of evaluative writing that neatly lists all the criteria used to judge the thing; in fact, some criteria may be implicit. Why? A common reason is that the writer and audience *share* certain assumptions about how to judge the value of a thing. It goes without saying, for example, that a writer for the conservative magazine *National Review* would be critical of a proposal for national health care that advocates a new federal government program. Generally speaking, conservatives oppose the growth of federal government, so why state it as a criterion for rejecting the proposal?

- *Relevant comparisons may form the backbone of a review.* Our fascination with winners and losers is reflected in one of the most ubiquitous evaluations in American culture: rankings. We rank cars, movies, music videos, celebrities' tastes in fashion, colleges, cameras, diets, and Web sites. All of these kinds of evaluations fundamentally depend on identifying a certain class of things—a particular car type, or kind of music—and comparing things that belong to that class. The key, of course, is making sure that the things you're comparing do indeed belong in the same class, that you're comparing apples to apples and not apples to oranges.

REVIEW

Teen slasher movies have been around a long time, and while they are condemned for excessive violence, sexual exploitation, and banality, such films continue to thrive. Moviegoers have flocked to *Scream, Nightmare on Elm Street, Friday the 13th,* and their many sequels. The slasher movie, a subgenre of the horror film, is so well established and formulaic that it is ripe for parody, something that director Wes Craven does in the film *Scary Movie.*

In the movie review that follows, *Slate* critic Bryan Curtis evaluates the 2003 remake of the 1974 film *The Texas Chainsaw Massacre* and uses his familiarity with this category of horror movie to suggest that the new film offers a little bit more than blood, gore, and innocence betrayed. Notice especially how Curtis's review has a number of the features typical of the form that were discussed earlier in the chapter. What are they?

THE BEST LITTLE CHOPHOUSE IN TOWN
The Allure of the *Texas Chainsaw Massacre*
Bryan Curtis

The appeal of *The Texas Chainsaw Massacre* (1974) was best explained by its   1
director, Tobe Hooper, who declared, "This film is about meat." In one sense, most horror pictures are about meat—they linger on teenage legs, breasts, and thighs. *Chainsaw,* on the other hand, wants to show us the preparation and consumption of human flesh. When Leatherface, the film's butcher, drags a victim into his abattoir, you half expect to see the words "Paid for by the American Beef Council" at the bottom of the frame.

Chainsaw spawned three sequels, and this week it stands exhumed for a re-   2
make, directed by Marcus Nispel. But the new film is a cynical exercise in fright and disgust, where the original had a deep resonance to it. In fact, it was one of the most relentless scare pictures ever made.

The grist is this: The Sawyer family, a clan of wayward cannibals, lives a   3
quiet life of rural isolation in the Texas Panhandle. Their farmhouse is trimmed with cattle skulls and chicken feathers, not unlike a half-dozen gifts shops in downtown Austin. The Sawyers feast on day-tripping tourists and hawk the leftover victuals at a barbecue shack down the road. The family mascot is Leatherface—nee Bubba Sawyer Jr.—who serves as chief cook and executioner. Leatherface wears an opaque mask, black cowboy boots, and, most wonderfully, a ring of fat around the waist—he's the only cinematic demon who could stand to lose 20 pounds. When he's in full-on Julia Child mode, whipping up a batch of sweetbreads, he adds lipstick and a woman's wig and morphs into the family's matriarch.

The Texas Panhandle is the turf of novelist Larry McMurtry, whose cow-   4
boy protagonists have none of the hillbilly giddiness of the Sawyers. But McMurtry's work and *Chainsaw* share a deep connection. McMurtry believes the underpopulated Texas landscape exerts a violent influence on its inhabitants; the Sawyers, in a sense, are the manifestation of that violence. The family includes an old man (Jim Siedow), a grave-digging hitchhiker (Edwin Neal), and wizened Grandfather Sawyer (John Dugan), a clone of the mummified mother in *Psycho* (1960). Their prey in *Chainsaw* is five nubile hippies, who have piled into a van to search for an abandoned mansion. The teens stumble into

the Sawyer home, where Leatherface offs them one by one. The weapons he uses—in descending order of utility—are a sledgehammer, chainsaw, and meat hook.

5   Thirty years later, nothing about the setup seems particularly ingenious— nothing, at least, to justify four additional films. The lasting appeal of *Chainsaw,* I think, has more to do with the organic way that Hooper and his co-writer, Kim Henkel, approach the material. Most horror films place a demon in an idyllic world; order is restored simply by throwing the demon out. *Chainsaw* makes it seem like the Sawyers have risen up from the Texas soil, that they're as much a part of the landscape as cottonwood trees. When a lone teen survivor, Sally (Marilyn Burns), escapes at the end of the film, you don't feel the relief you feel in more conventional scare pictures. You feel the Sawyers will remain there unmolested for 100 years (or 100 sequels), feeding at their leisure.

6   The film's final shot lingers on Leatherface, spinning in the sunlight as his chainsaw whirs. It's one of four or five images of great beauty here—you respond to it despite the high level of gore. Hooper shot the film in grainy 16mm, which gives the picture the look of a homemade travelogue. (Later, when given millions to make Hollywood fare like *Poltergeist* [1982], he lost his touch.) Much of the dialogue was composed on the fly, and the troupe of lightly trained actors was asked to improvise the rest. It's the documentary-like quality that allowed the filmmakers—for both the original and this week's remake—to fib in the promotional material that *Chainsaw* is based on "true" events. In fact, it's based only slightly on the serial killer Ed Gein, who inspired *Psycho* and Thomas Harris' *The Silence of the Lambs.*

7   *Chainsaw* gave birth to the multipart horror franchises that have filled multiplexes for the last two decades and may have convinced Hollywood that good money lay in bloodwork. (It has likely grossed over $100 million since its release.) In 1974, the critics were particularly unkind. Roger Ebert wrote, "It's without apparent purpose, unless the creation of fright and disgust is a purpose." Hooper has repeatedly shirked the charge, claiming that he made *Chainsaw* as a reaction to—get ready—Watergate and Vietnam.

8   I'd bet he had something simpler in mind, like scaring people out of their pajamas. If that was his mission, then he has nothing to be ashamed of. *Chainsaw* is a whirling dervish of a movie, but it takes every one of its killings seriously. It's a counterweight to films like *Scream* (1996), which use horrific violence as fuel for laughs and genre deconstruction, while at the same time wallowing in gore. Since when does screen violence, if handled with skill, disqualify a film from being art? Some nights, we crave the violence. We're hungry for it.

INQUIRING INTO THE ESSAY

Explore, explain, evaluate and reflect on *The Best Little Chophouse in Town.*

1. The essay ends with these two provocative sentences: "Some nights, we crave the violence. We're hungry for it." Does the success of films such as *Jason vs. Freddy* or *The Texas Chain Saw Massacre* depend on this craving for violence? Do you watch horror movies because you *like* to be scared? What's behind this desire? Fastwrite for seven minutes in your journal, exploring your reaction to the last two lines in Curtis's essay and your own feelings and attitudes toward slasher movies. Write as well about the idea that people pay money to be scared out their wits. Why?

2. Analyze the ways that *The Best Little Chophouse in Town* reflects the "Features of the Form" listed earlier in the chapter. Explain exactly where in Curtis's essay he seems to incorporate those features.

3. Reread the last two paragraphs of the essay. Consider the claim that Curtis is making there, that "screen violence, if handled with skill" may elevate a film like *The Texas Chainsaw Massacre* to the status of "art." Do you agree with that claim? Based on your own moviegoing experience, what would be your argument on the question?

4. One way to get better as a writer who persuades readers is to pay attention to how *you* respond to written arguments. Tell the story of your thoughts and feelings as you read Curtis's review. Reread the essay, pausing after the first paragraph to write for two minutes in your journal about what you're feeling about Curtis, what he's saying, and how he's saying it. Do the same thing halfway through the piece, and then finally at the end. What story do these three episodes of writing tell about your experience of the essay?

REVIEW

Published reviews of books, films, and music are among the most common forms of evaluative writing. Neal Pollack, whose piece on a recent Rolling Stones tour follows, is an unusual practitioner of the form. He calls his recent book, *Neal Pollack's Anthology of American Literature,* a work of satire, "the greatest book ever written by an American." But believe this: Pollack does not like the Rolling Stones. His review of the band's recent American tour is certainly funny, but it's also a serious critique of the Stones' continuing efforts to remain an active part of the rock scene. Is the piece successful?

Pollack's voice in this essay has an edge of satire, and he adopts a very conversational style; you never forget who the author is. One of the challenges of much writing, especially argumentative writing, is that the writer needs to establish his authority. In other words, readers should be inclined to believe or trust what the writer has to say because they find the writer credible. The rhetorical term for this is *ethos,* and it can be established in a number of ways: by choosing a particular voice or tone, by appearing reasonable and balanced, and by creating an appropriate relationship between reader and writer. For a writer like Pollack, ethos can really matter. How does Pollack come across to you? Do you trust the honesty of his judgment about the Stones, even if you don't agree with it?

ROCK ON? YEAH, IN CHAIRS
Neal Pollack

1   In late fall of 1989, my friend Marc and I took the least rock 'n' roll road trip imaginable. We drove from our dorm, in the suburbs of Chicago, to his parents' house in Indianapolis, because we had tickets to see the Rolling Stones. The drive was flat, ugly and uneventful. We didn't smoke a joint, drink a beer or crank up the stereo. We were more like a couple of retirees going to the reservation casino to play slots than two 19-year-olds on a rock pilgrimage.

2   The show was in a nondescript indoor sports arena. We'd spent 25 bucks each on pretty good seats, something like 10th row, just to the right of the stage. Man, were we excited! We were about to see the legendary Rolling Stones, the greatest rock band of all time. The lights went out. We heard the distinct hiss of smoke pots, and then a pop. Fire spurted on either side of the stage. The lights blew on in full glare, and there he was. Mick Jagger! In spangled pants! Singing! Look, there was Keith Richards, playing guitar! And the other guys! For two minutes, I found myself thoroughly entertained. For 10 minutes, I was at least amused. But my heart gradually chilled as I realized what I had really paid for—a two-hour set of golden oldies, accompanied by flaccid pyrotechnics. The Stones trudged mechanically through the horrible songs from their horrible "Steel Wheels" album. They played their greatest hits, just like on the radio, only with worse backup singers. I stopped cheering. Then I stopped applauding. I didn't say it that night, but I knew the hard truth. The Stones were boring. By the time the show was over, I wasn't a Rolling Stones fan anymore.

3   Now, as the Stones launch yet another culturally irrelevant North American tour on Tuesday at the Fleet Center in Boston, which, like their

previous five tours, is certain to be their last, I still want to smack myself for having been so lame. In the late 80's, Public Enemy, Sonic Youth, R.E.M., the Replacements, Husker Du and many other more obscure bands were going full strength. Guns 'n' Roses, the true Rolling Stones of their era in terms of attitude and showy stage presence, released "Appetite for Destruction." Indie music in cities like Seattle, Minneapolis, Chicago and Los Angeles still meant something more than a fashion pose. It was right there for me, if I'd only paid attention. So how could I have possibly thought that seeing the Rolling Stones in Indianapolis would have anything to do with rock 'n' roll?

Well, I'd been marketed to successfully. I grew up in the suburbs of   4
Phoenix, the least rock 'n' roll place on earth, during the rise of "classic rock" radio, which poisoned my mind for almost a decade. There, in the desert, literal and cultural, I was the willing tool of every sleazy corporate programming executive told by the record megaliths to push Pink Floyd and Led Zeppelin, to play "Carry on My Wayward Son" and "Hot Blooded" during morning drive time. I heard so much bad music, but almost never got exposed to the actually good rock music that came out of the classic rock era—the Stooges, the Modern Lovers, the Velvet Underground, Big Star and, to use K-Tel parlance, many more. I'd been so thoroughly brainwashed that I thought Huey Lewis and the News had a hot sound. I bought the single of "Addicted to Love" and the Billy Joel live in the Soviet Union album. My taste in music was, frankly, pathetic. My only exposure to the Rolling Stones came when "Start Me Up" was played at junior-high dances.

The first great album I heard was the Stones' "Let It Bleed," which had   5
miraculously found its way into my parents' collection alongside the Beach Boys' "Surfin' U.S.A." and cast recordings of Broadway shows starring Carol Burnett. There was even a mint-condition poster of the band inside the jacket, which means my parents had rarely if ever listened to the record. But I did, often. The pops and skips of vinyl gave "Midnight Rambler" an extra layer of menace. "Love in Vain" sounded as if it'd been recorded by the devil under a bridge somewhere. The album was, and is, authentically weird. I'd never heard anything like it and didn't again until a friend made a tape of the Velvet Underground's 1968 "White Light/White Heat" for me a few years later. I spent the subsequent years listening to both volumes of "Hot Rocks," a Stones greatest-hits collection, more than any other album in my wimpy little collection.

AFTER that Indy show in 1989, I listened to "Hot Rocks" a lot less often,   6
and then not at all. I started working at the college radio station, albeit as a newscaster, and discovered rock records made by people who were actually younger than my parents. By 22, I was only modestly less of a music idiot (I

skipped a small-venue Nirvana show because I had a paper due), but at least I'd seen the Pogues fronted by Shane McGowan and the Pixies before they broke up. I sold all my Stones albums to a used-record store for credit. They were worth nothing to me, because they'd outlived their usefulness.

7   To someone my age who's seen or heard hundreds of more vital bands, the Stones are, or should be, distant popular history. They are a Vegas headliner show, not a rock outfit. In his book "Rock Til You Drop" (Verso Books, 2001), the definitive word on the senescent Stones, John Strausbaugh calls them "The Historical Reenactment of the Once-Great Rolling Stones." I would no sooner buy tickets to a community-theater production of "The Unsinkable Molly Brown," or an Andy Williams concert, than see the Stones again. Every time the Stones tour, someone publishes an essay begging them to stop, calling them on their dull new songs, mocking Sir Mick's withering frame and grotesque dance moves, but to what end? It's like accusing Ringling Brothers clowns of going through the motions.

8   My very important opinion on this topic is not just generational animus. I'm no fan, particularly, of Bruce Springsteen or Bob Dylan, but at least their current music acknowledges and reflects the fact that they're not so young anymore. In the last five years, I've seen many musical acts of the Stones' generation or even older, including Johnny Cash, James Brown, Merle Haggard, George Jones, Willie Nelson, Solomon Burke and Aretha Franklin. Some of the performers seemed tired, while others put on inspirational shows that I'll always talk about. But I never left any of those concerts feeling empty or ripped off as I did when I saw the Stones. Earlier this year, I went to an Iggy Pop show in Philadelphia. Even though Iggy filled half the time with mediocre material off his new album, he still threw together one of the best rock concerts I've ever seen. He made Mick Jagger look like an animatronic dancing bear. And much of his audience was under 40. Iggy meant something to them, because he still rocks.

9   Teenagers now, because of countless technological advances, have many opportunities to discover great music, both from the present and the past. But the Stones are going to get all kinds of corporate radio play with this latest "Licks" tour to promote the October release of "Forty Licks," a retrospective double album that includes a whopping four new songs. The tour will extend well into next year if you include the Asian and Australian dates. The air will be full of three-song Rolling Stones "rock blocks," and some stupid 15-year-old boy in some culturally cosseted upper-middle-class suburb somewhere will hear "Mother's Little Helper" for the first time and think the Stones are cool. He may even spend the 85 bucks or more they're asking for tickets. At those prices, with this musical product, the kid will get over the Rolling Stones, and fast.

INQUIRING INTO THE ESSAY

Use the four ways of inquiring—exploring, explaining, evaluating, and reflecting—to consider your response to Pollack's review.

1. Brainstorm a short list of music or musicians that influenced your life in some way. Choose one work or musician or band and fastwrite in your journal about that time in your life, and how the music or musician influenced you. At some point, explore how you feel about that work or musician today. What would be your judgment of its quality?

2. Explain the criteria Pollack seemed to use as the basis for his judgments about the current relevance and quality of the Rolling Stones and their music. Which seem reasonable? Which don't?

3. In your own words, summarize the basic argument in Pollack's essay that would justify his judgment that the Rolling Stones will get more attention than they deserve.

4. Evaluate one of the claims Pollack makes in his essay. First play the "believing game" and then the "doubting game." For example, are the Rolling Stones or bands like it "culturally irrelevant"? Does corporate marketing influence fans' responses to musicians as much as Pollack suggests?

5. At the heart of this topic is a simple question: What makes music and musical acts endure over time and between generations? It's not hard to think of a number of rock bands like the Beatles, for example, that have managed to find fans spanning three generations. The work of Beethoven and Bach would not be considered culturally irrelevant after 250 years. What would you argue are some of the key factors that make music endure?

6. Pollack seems to be a guy who has no problem arriving at and expressing an opinion. What about you? Do you have a difficult time judging things—from movies to people—or are you pretty opinionated? Reflect on your personal experiences with making judgments. Were you encouraged to express your opinion at home or at school? When have your judgments gotten you into trouble, and can you imagine ways you could have avoided it? What bothers you about others who are judgmental? Whose judgments do your respect? Why? Fastwrite about these questions in your journal.

REVIEW

Dog food companies sell dog food to people, not to dogs, and so it isn't too surprising that one company might boast that its dog food is a "Premium Oven Baked Lamb Recipe," or that another will tantalize dogs with "rich, beefy gravy." Pet food is an $11-billion-dollar industry in the United States, and apparently the competitive edge goes to those companies that can convince pet owners that Buster or Tabitha will dine at least as well as the rest of the family.

The fine print, of course, tells a different story. Most dog foods have "by-products," or all the remains of chickens and/or cows that aren't thought fit for human consumption—intestines, gizzards, bones, lungs, and ligaments. Rendered restaurant grease gives some dog foods that delightful scent.

Ann Hodgman decided she would take the advertising claims of several pet food companies at face value. If Gravy Train dog food creates a really "rich, beefy gravy," then shouldn't it taste good to the pet owner as well as the pet? In the essay that follows, "No Wonder They Call Me a Bitch," Hodgman reports on her experiences taste-testing some of the more popular brands. Her review makes us all regret ever sampling that dog bone from the bag when we were too young to know better.

Before you start reading the essay, consider following the procedure described in the first question in "Inquiring into the Essay" at the end of the piece.

NO WONDER THEY CALL ME A BITCH
Ann Hodgman

1　　I've always wondered about dog food. Is a Gaines-burger really like a hamburger? Can you fry it? Does dog food "cheese" taste like real cheese? Does Gravy Train actually make gravy in the dog's bowl, or is that brown liquid just dissolved crumbs? And exactly what *are* by-products?

2　　Having spent the better part of a week eating dog food, I'm sorry to say that I now know the answers to these questions. While my dachshund, Shortie, watched in agonies of yearning, I gagged my way through can after can of stinky, white-flecked mush and bag after bag of stinky, fat-drenched nuggets. And now I understand exactly why Shortie's breath is so bad.

3　　Of course, Gaines-burgers are neither mush nor nuggets. They are, rather, a miracle of beauty and packaging—or at least that's what I thought when I was little. I used to beg my mother to get them for our dogs, but she always said they were too expensive. When I finally bought a box of cheese-flavored Gaines-burgers—after 20 years of longing—I felt deliciously wicked.

4　　"Dogs love real beef," the back of the box proclaimed proudly. "That's why Gaines-burgers is the only beef burger for dogs with real beef and no meat by-products!" The copy was accurate: meat by-products did not appear in the list of ingredients. Poultry by-products did, though—right there next to preserved animal fat.

One Purina spokesman told me that poultry by-products consist of necks, intestines, undeveloped eggs and other "carcass remnants," but not feathers, heads or feet. When I told him I'd been eating dog food, he said, "Oh, you're kidding! Oh no!" (I came to share his alarm when, weeks later, a second Purina spokesman said that Gaines-burgers *do* contain poultry heads and feet—but *not* undeveloped eggs.)

Up close my Gaines-burger didn't much resemble chopped beef. Rather, it looked—and felt—like a single long, extruded piece of redness that had been chopped into segments and formed into a patty. You could make one at home if you had a Play-Doh Fun Factory.

I turned on the skillet. While I waited for it to heat up I pulled out a shred of cheese-colored material and palpated it. Again, like Play-Doh, it was quite malleable. I made a little cheese bird out of it; then I counted to three and ate the bird.

There was a horrifying rush of cheddar taste, followed immediately by the dull tang of soybean flour—the main ingredient in Gaines-burgers. Next I tried a piece of red extrusion. The main difference between the meat-flavored and cheese-flavored extrusions is one of texture. The "cheese" chews like fresh Play-Doh, whereas the "meat" chews like Play-Doh that's been sitting out on a rug for a couple of hours.

Frying only turned the Gaines-burger black. There was no melting, no sizzling, no warm meat smells. A cherished childhood illusion was gone. I flipped the patty into the sink, where it immediately began leaking rivulets of red dye.

As alarming as the Gaines-burgers were, their soy meal began to seem like an old friend when the time came to try some *canned* dog foods. I decided to try the Cycle foods first. When I opened them, I thought about how rarely I use can openers these days, and I was suddenly visited by a long-forgotten sensation of can-opener distaste. *This* is the kind of unsavory place can openers spend their time when you're not watching! Every time you open a can of, say, Italian plum tomatoes, you infect them with invisible particles of by-product.

I had been expecting to see the usual homogeneous scrapple inside, but each can of Cycle was packed with smooth, round, oily nuggets. As if someone at Gaines had been tipped off that a human would be tasting the stuff, the four Cycles really were different from one another. Cycle-1, for puppies, is wet and soyish. Cycle-2, for adults, glistens nastily with fat, but it's passably edible—a lot like some canned Swedish meatballs I once got in a care package at college. Cycle-3, the "lite" one, for fatties, had no specific flavor; it just tasted like dog food. But at least it didn't make me fat.

Cycle-4, for senior dogs, had the smallest nuggets. Maybe old dogs can't open their mouths as wide. This kind was far sweeter than the other three

5

6

7

8

9

10

11

12

Cycles—almost like baked beans. It was also the only one to contain "dried beef digest," a mysterious substance that the Purina spokesman defined as "enzymes" and my dictionary defined as "the products of digestion."

13   Next on the menu was a can of Kal-Kan Pedigree with Chunky Chicken. Chunky chicken? There were chunks in the can, certainly—big, purplish-brown chunks. I forked one chunk out (by now I was becoming more callous) and found that while it had no discernible chicken flavor, it wasn't bad except for its texture—like meat loaf with ground-up chicken bones.

14   In the world of canned dog food, a smooth consistency is a sign of low quality—lots of cereal. A lumpy, frightening, bloody, stringy horror is a sign of high quality—lots of meat. Nowhere in the world of wet dog foods was this demonstrated better than in the fanciest I tried—Kal Kan's Pedigree Select Dinners. These came not in a can but in a tiny foil packet with a picture of an imperious Yorkie. When I pulled open the container, juice spurted all over my hand, and the first chunk I speared was trailing a long gray vein. I shrieked and went instead for a plain chunk, which I was able to swallow only after taking a break to read some suddenly fascinating office equipment catalogs. Once again, though, it tasted no more alarming than, say, canned hash.

15   Still, how pleasant it was to turn to *dry* dog food! Gravy Train was the first I tried, and I'm happy to report that it really does make a "thick, rich, real beef gravy" when you mix it with water. Thick and rich, anyway. Except for a lingering rancid-fat flavor, the gravy wasn't beefy, but since it tasted primarily like tap water, it wasn't nauseating either.

16   My poor dachshund just gets plain old Purina Dog Chow, but Purina also makes a dry food called Butcher's Blend that comes in Beef, Bacon, and Chicken flavor. Here we see dog food's arcane semiotics at its best: a red triangle with a *T* stamped into it is supposed to suggest beef; a tan curl, chicken; and a brown *S*, a piece of bacon. Only dogs understand these messages. But Butcher's Blend does have an endearing slogan: "Great Meaty Tastes—without bothering the Butcher!" *You know, I wanted to buy some meat, but I just couldn't bring myself to bother the butcher . . . .*

17   Purina O.N.E. ("Optimum Nutritional Effectiveness") is targeted at people who are unlikely ever to worry about bothering a tradesperson. "We chose chicken as a primary ingredient in Purina O.N.E. for several reasonings," the long, long essay on the back of the bag announces. Chief among these reasonings, I'd guess, is the fact that chicken appeals to people who are—you know—*like us.* Although our dogs do nothing but spend 18-hour days alone in the apartment, we still want them to be *premium* dogs. We want them to cut down on red meat, too. We also want dog food that comes in a bag with an attractive design, a subtle typeface and no kitschy pictures of slobbering golden retrievers.

Besides that, we want a list of the Nutritional Benefits of our dog food— 18
and we get it on O.N.E. One thing I especially like about this list is its constant
references to a dog's "hair coat," as in "Beef tallow is good for the dog's skin
and hair coat." (On the other hand, beef tallow merely provides palatability,
while the dried beef digest in Cycle provides palatability *enhancement*.)

I hate to say it, but O.N.E. was pretty palatable. Maybe that's because it 19
has about 100 percent more fat than, say, Butcher's Blend. Or maybe I'd been
duped by the packaging; that's been known to happen before.

As with people food, dog snacks taste much better than dog meals. 20
They're better-looking too. Take Milk-Bone Flavor Snacks. The loving-hands-
at-home prose describing each flavor is colorful; the writers practically choke
on their own exuberance. Of bacon they say, "It's so good, your dog will think
it's hot off the frying pan." Of liver: "The only taste your dog wants more than
liver—is even more liver!" Of poultry: "All those farm fresh flavors deliciously
mixed in one biscuit. Your dog will bark with delight!" And of vegetable:
"Gardens of taste! Specially blended to give your dog that vegetable flavor he
wants—but can rarely get!"

Well, I may be a sucker, but advertising *this* emphatic just doesn't convince 21
me. I lined up all seven flavors of Milk-Bone Flavor Snacks on the floor. Unless
my dog's palate is a lot more sensitive than mine—and considering that she
steals dirty diapers out of the trash and eats them, I'm loath to think it is—she
doesn't detect any more difference in the seven flavors than I did when I tried
them.

I much preferred Bonz, the hard-baked, bone-shaped snack stuffed with 22
simulated marrow. I liked the bone part, that is; it tasted almost exactly like
the cornmeal it was made of. The mock-marrow inside was a bit more problematic: in addition to looking like the sludge that collects in the treads of my
running shoes, it was bursting with tiny hairs.

I'm sure you have a few dog food questions of your own. To save us time, 23
I've answered them in advance.

Q. *Are those little cans of Mighty Dog actually branded with the sizzling word*
BEEF, *the way they show in the commercials?*

A. You should know by now that that kind of thing never happens.

Q. *Does chicken-flavored dog food taste like chicken-flavored cat food?* 24

A. To my surprise, chicken cat food was actually a little better—more
chickeny. It tasted like inferior canned pâté.

Q. *Was there any dog food that you just couldn't bring yourself to try?*

A. Alas, it was a can of Mighty Dog called Prime Entree with Bone
Marrow. The meat was dark, dark brown, and it was surrounded by gelatin
that was almost black. I knew I would die if I tasted it, so I put it outside for
the raccoons.

INQUIRING INTO THE ESSAY

Use the four ways of inquiring to develop your responses to "No Wonder They Call Me a Bitch."

1. Explore your reaction to Hodgman's essay by reading and responding to it in three separate fastwrites.

   a. First, read the first or lead paragraph and then go to your notebook and spend three minutes exploring your first thoughts: How does the author come across? What do you expect will come next? What questions does the beginning raise?

   b. Stop halfway through the article, after you finish the paragraph that begins, "In the world of canned dog food . . . " Fastwrite for another three minutes, telling the story of your thinking about the piece up to this point: How has your thinking changed since the beginning? Do you have a clearer sense of what the writer is trying to say? Where do you expect the essay will go from here?

   c. Finally, fastwrite for another three to five minutes after you finish the essay. Now what do you think? What seems to be Hodgman's point? Were your expectations met and your questions answered?

2. How effective is the ending of Hodgman's essay? Why might she choose such an unconventional ending?

3. This is an interesting review because Hodgman uses the pet food companies' own advertising claims as criteria for judging their products. Do you think her approach is balanced and fair? Is it persuasive?

4. It's nearly impossible to resist the pun that the title, "No Wonder They Call Me a Bitch" is in bad taste. All right, it is impossible. Does Hodgman overdo it? Under what circumstances can description of disgusting things be effective in writing, and under what circumstances does it become ineffective?

5. If you responded episodically to the essay, following the directions in Question 1, what did you notice about how your expectations shaped your response to Hodgman's essay? Is the writer entirely responsible for shaping your expectations as a reader? What do you contribute?

👓 SEEING THE FORM

CHOOSING THE BEST PICTURE

Most image editing software these days relies heavily on the photographer's judgment. For example, consider the multiple reviews of the digital

photograph above, a picture of my daughter. Which do you think is the strongest image? Is it the picture in the center—the software program's default choice—or perhaps one of the alternative images that surround it?

Most of us have very little photographic experience, so suddenly this decision becomes befuddling. We have multiple reviews of the same image, each slightly different. On what basis will we decide? By now you know that the best judgments arise from criteria that we're applying to the particular situation. But since very few of us who use these software programs have much expertise in photography, do we know enough to develop helpful criteria? How would you solve this problem? Which of the images would you choose and on what basis would you make that decision? What does this suggest to you about the challenge of developing criteria for evaluation?

EXERCISE 6.1

What Makes a Good Movie?

In a culture weaned on cinema, one of the most common judgments we make is whether we liked or disliked the movie we just saw. Consider what it is exactly that makes a movie good or bad.

STEP ONE: First, into the sea and indulge in some creative thinking. Draw a line down the middle of a blank page in your journal, and on the left side spend thirty seconds brainstorming a list of your favorite movies. These could be current films or those you saw some time ago.

STEP TWO: In the right column, jot down the name of the worst movie you ever saw. If you can think of more than one, write those down, too.

STEP THREE: Now, onto the mountain, and apply some critical thinking to what you've done to this point. Look at your lists. Do the films you like have anything in common? Are they a similar genre? Do they involve similar stories or themes? Similar directors or actors? Similar methods of storytelling? Similar periods of filmmaking? Might they have moved you in some similar ways? Next, consider how the films you disliked might *differ* from those you liked. Might they have been a different genre, or involve different methods of storytelling, and so on? Share your lists and your thoughts about this in a small group.

STEP FOUR: Follow up this conversation by focusing your discussion on the question we started with: *What makes a good movie?* What criteria might you use to make such a judgment? In your group, generate a list of these on a piece of newsprint on the wall. You might begin by narrowing the question a bit. Perhaps you want to generate a list of the ways to evaluate certain *kinds* of movies: Hollywood films, art films, or certain genres, such as romantic comedies or action films. After twenty minutes, share these lists with the rest of the class.

STEP FIVE: Out of class, do some research. Search the Web for what other people think about this question. Type the phrase "What makes a good movie" (remember the quotation marks) into the search window of Google and browse some of the documents it produces. You'll find a range of things, from quirky Web logs and online essays from individuals, to articles by film experts. Print out any articles you find interesting, perhaps those that offer criteria you hadn't considered or that challenge your views about judging movies.

STEP SIX: OPTION 1: Drawing on the insights about how to evaluate film you developed from your writing, class discussion, and research, present a five-minute evaluation of your favorite—or least favorite—film to the rest of your class. Make sure this presentation includes all three of the features of evaluation mentioned earlier: judgment, criteria, and evidence.

STEP SIX: OPTION 2: Write a 400-word sketch that evaluates the qualities of a film you love or despise. Workshop these in class.

For whichever option selected, evaluate these presentations or sketches using the following criteria:

1. Did the writer or speaker's judgment seem fair and reasonable?

2. Were the criteria for judgment clear and relevant to the thing being judged and were they reasonably applied?

3. What was the most convincing evidence offered? What was the least convincing?

4. Was the evaluation interesting? Did it help you not only see the movie differently, but movie watching differently?

ONE STUDENT'S RESPONSE

MARGARET'S JOURNAL

EXERCISE 6.1

STEP FOUR: WHAT MAKES A GOOD MOVIE?

A good movie (not comedies) should have characters with which the audience may identify. Whether they are likable or not doesn't seem that relevant. There should be a purpose, but this needn't be a moral, and it needn't be a singular purpose. There should just be something that the movie says to the audience. The character needs to undergo a change.

■ THE WRITING PROCESS ■

INQUIRY PROJECT: Writing a Review

Write a 1,000- to 1,200-word review. You choose the subject—a performance, a book, a Web site, a consumer product, a film, whatever. Just make sure your review has the following qualities:

■ You're able to put your subject in a manageable category for more useful comparisons; for example, rather than evaluating a Web site against all others, you're going to focus on Web sites for classroom use.

■ The essay has all three elements of evaluation: judgment, criteria, and evidence.

> - The criteria are reasonable and appropriate for what you're evaluating; they aren't overly idealistic or general.
> - The evaluation seems balanced and fair.

Thinking About Subjects

Evaluation can be a way of seeding the field of argument because it helps you identify the things about which you have strong opinions.

Possible subjects for a review abound. What will you choose? Perhaps you're a sports fan who regularly seeks information on the Web. Which sites strike you as the most informative? Which would you recommend? Or maybe you are interested in photography, but really don't have any idea how to evaluate the landscape shots you took during a recent trip to Maine. Are they any good? The best inquiry projects begin with a question, not an answer, so try to choose a topic because you want to discover what you think instead of one about which you already have a strong opinion. You'll learn more and probably write a stronger, more balanced, more interesting essay.

Generating Ideas

Begin exploring possible subjects for a review by generating material in your notebook. This should be an open-ended process, a chance to use your creative side by jumping into the sea and swimming around without worrying too much about making sense or trying to prejudge the value of the writing or the subjects you generate. In a sense, this is an invitation to play around.

Listing Prompts. Lists can be rich sources of triggering topics. Let them grow freely, and when you're ready, use an item as the focus of another list or an episode of fastwriting. The following prompts should get you started.

1. Take a piece a paper and fold it into four equal columns. You'll be making four different brainstormed lists. In the first column, write "Things I Want." Spend two minutes making a quick list of everything you wish you had but don't—a new computer, a classical guitar, a decent boyfriend, and so on. In the next column, write "The Jury is Still Out." In this column, make a fast list of things in your life that so far are hard to judge—the quality of the school you attend, this textbook, your opinion about the films you saw last month, how well Susie cuts your hair, and so on. In the third column, write "My Media." Devote a fast list to particular films, TV shows, books, Web sites, or musicians you like or dislike—jot down whatever you watch, listen to, or read regularly. Finally, make a list of "Things of Questionable Quality." Try to be specific. Don't worry if any of these lists contain some of the same items; there are plenty of overlaps between them.

Fastwriting Prompts. Remember, fastwriting is a great way stimulate creative thinking. Turn off your critical side and let yourself write "badly."

1. Choose an item from any of the four lists above as a prompt for a seven-minute fastwrite. Explore your experience with the subject, or how your opinions about it have evolved.

2. Begin with the following prompt, and follow it for five minutes in a fastwrite: *Among the things I have a hard time judging is* _____. . . If the writing stalls, shift subjects by writing, *And another thing I can't judge is* _____ . . .

Visual Prompts. Sometimes the best way to generate material is to see what we think represented in something other than sentences. Boxes, lines, webs, clusters, arrows, charts, or even sketches can help us to see more of the landscape of a subject, especially connections between fragments of information that aren't as obvious in prose.

1. On a blank page in your journal, cluster the name of an artist, musician, film, book, author, performance, band, building, academic course or major, restaurant, university bookstore, PDA, computer, food store, or pizza joint. Cluster the name of anything about which you have some sort of feeling, positive or negative. Build a web of associations: feelings, details, observations, names, moments, facts, opinions, and so on. Look for a single strand in your essay that might be the beginning of a review.

2. Draw a sketch of what you think is an *ideal version* of something you need or use often: a computer, a classroom, a telephone, a wallet or handbag and so on. If you could design such a thing, what would it look like? Use this as a way of evaluating what is currently available and how it might be improved.

Research Prompts. The depth of a review depends on the writer's knowledge of the criteria and evidence through which she judges her subject. Unless she is already an expert on her subject, then, research of some form will be a necessity. At this stage in the writing process, a little advance research can help you find a subject.

1. Do an Internet or library search for reviews on one of your favorite films, books, sports teams, artists, and so on. Do you agree with the evaluations? If not, consider writing a review of your own that challenges the critics.

2. Take a walk. Look for things to evaluate that you see as you wander on and off campus—downtown architecture, the quality of local parks, paintings in the art museum, neighborhoods, coffee shops. You'll be amazed at how much is begging for a thoughtful judgment.

WRITING WITH COMPUTERS

SPELLING, GRAMMAR, AND STYLE CHECKERS

The spelling, grammar, and style checkers on today's word processors can offer you considerable help in polishing a draft, but you should never become too reliant on them; each has limitations. While spell checkers can quickly identify typos and show you the correct spellings for misspelled words, they can only help you with words that appear in their dictionaries, which tend to cover far fewer words than the best unabridged dictionaries you can find in print (this may change in the future). Spell checkers also cannot locate commonly confused words that you might have written into your draft, words such as *your* and *you're* or *it's* and *its.* Grammar checkers must be used very carefully as they are much less reliable than spell checkers. Although they can help you identify a structural problem in a sentence, the suggestions grammar checkers offer for correcting the problem are often just a likely to be wrong as they are right. Writers tend to use style checkers much less frequently than either spelling checkers or grammar checkers, which is unfortunate because they can help you identify problematic tendencies in your writing. You may have a habit of using the passive voice, the verb *to be,* or repeating words or phrases. Perhaps you write in an uninterrupted series of long or short sentences. Style checkers can point these tendencies out, but their limitation is that they cannot offer you quick and easy solutions for correcting these problems.

3. Here's an entertaining generating activity: Plan a weekend of movie watching with a few friends. Ask each of them to contribute two or three titles of their favorite films, then rent a slew of them, and when you're thoroughly spent watching movies, discuss which might be most interesting to review.

Judging What You Have

Generating may produce the messy, incoherent writing that would earn you bad grades in most classes. Its virtue, however, should be obvious by now: "bad" writing gives a writer material to work with. Remember it's always better to work from abundance than scarcity. But if this material is going to go anywhere, it must be judged, shaped, and evaluated.

What's Promising Material and What Isn't?   My favorite coffee shop in my hometown of Boise, Idaho, is a place called the Flying M. It's a funky place with an odd assortment of furniture, overstuffed couches, worn armchairs, and wobbly tables. On the walls, there's work from local artists, mostly unknowns with talent and unusual taste. There are other coffee places in town, including the ubiquitous Starbucks, and another more local chain called Moxie Java. I don't find much difference in the coffee at any of these places, and they're all rather pleasant. What makes me prefer the Flying M?

I've never really thought about it. That's one of the reasons I liked the idea of reviewing my favorite local coffee house when the Flying M appeared on one of my lists. The best inquiry-based projects begin when you're not quite sure what you think and want to explore a topic to find out.

- *Is there anything in your lists and fastwrites that you might have an initial judgment about but really haven't considered fully?* For example, you really dislike the sixties architecture that dominates your campus but you're not quite sure what it is about it that leaves you cold.

- *As you consider possible subjects for your review, are there some that clearly offer the possibility of comparison with other, similar things in that category?* Often judgment is based on such comparisons (remember Ann Hodgman's "No Wonder They Call Me a Bitch"?), although we may not really think about it much. Comparison isn't always essential, however, but it can be helpful. For instance, while I can't really distinguish the coffee served at Starbucks, Moxie Java, or Flying M—it's all good—I'm pretty sure that my preferences have more to do with the atmosphere. If there were only one place to get a latte in town then this wouldn't be an issue, but because there are many, I have the luxury of comparison. The pleasant but orderly and efficient atmosphere of Starbucks is strikingly different from the mildly chaotic, nearly Bohemian feel of Flying M, and it's through the contrast that I'm aware of my preferences.

- *Do any of your possible subjects offer the possibility of primary research, or research that might involve direct observation?* Can you listen to the music, attend the performance, read the novel, examine the building, visit the Web site, look at the painting? If I were doing this assignment, I'd choose a review of local cafes over other possible topics because it would give me an excuse to drink coffee and hang out in some of my favorite haunts. This is called research. Seriously.

Questions About Audience and Purpose   If I write a review of Boise's coffee house scene, I can immediately think of where I could publish it. *The Boise Weekly* is a local alternative magazine that frequently features food reviews and has an audience that certainly includes a high percentage of gourmet coffee drinkers. Many readers of the *Weekly* have direct experience with the coffeehouses I'd review and may even have judgments of their own about which are best. I'm reasonably confident that they might care about what I have to say on the topic.

Although you likely won't publish your review, consider which topics might be relevant to your intended audience, which in this case might be others in your composition class. Might they already have some kind of *stake* in considering your judgments about it? Since gourmet coffee drinkers abound these days, my topic seems to meet this criterion. But don't necessarily reject a topic because your readers aren't already interested in it. In some cases, your review can persuade readers that they *do* have a stake in the thing you're evaluating, though they may not know it. For example, your review of a local garage band may argue, among other things, that their music is potentially influential far beyond their limited local fans, and all lovers of rock should take note. However, certain more arcane topics, such as your judgment about the best motherboard for a gaming computer, may have a very limited audience, no matter what you say.

EXERCISE 6.2

From Jury to Judgment

Writing an evaluation of a thing requires that you become something of an expert about it. As you complete the following steps of the exercise, you'll generate material to work with that will make writing the draft much easier.

STEP ONE: Begin with a focused fastwrite that explores your initial feelings and experiences, if any, about your subject. In your notebook, use one of the following prompts to launch an exploration of your personal experiences with your topic. If the writing stalls, try another prompt to keep you going for five to seven minutes.

- *Write about your first experience with your subject.* This might be, for example, the first time you remember visiting the restaurant, or hearing the performer, or seeing the photographs. Focus on scenes, moments, situations, and people.

- *Write about what you think might be important qualities of your subject.* Ideally, this would be what the thing should be able to do well or what effects it should have on people who use it or see it. Say you're evaluating laptop computers for college students—under which conditions would a laptop be most useful? What have you noticed about the way you use one? In which common situations do student laptops prove vulnerable to damage? What have you heard other people say they like or dislike about their machines?

- *Write about how the thing makes you feel.* So much of our evaluation of a thing begins with our emotional responses to it. You love the photography of Edward Weston, or the music of Ani DiFranco, or you really dislike Hitchcock movies. Explore not just your initial good, bad, or mixed feelings about your subject but from where those feelings arise. For instance, when you listen to DiFranco's lyrics, do they move you in some way, are they emotionally suggestive, do they trigger certain feelings and memories and associations?

- *Compare the thing you're evaluating with something else that's similar.* I appreciate the Flying M café largely because it's so different from Starbucks. Focus your fastwrite on a relevant comparison, teasing out the differences and similarities and thinking about how you feel about them.

STEP TWO: Research your subject on the Web, gathering as much relevant background information as you can.

- *Search for information on product Web sites or Web pages devoted specifically to your subject.* If your review is on Ford's new electric car, visit the company's Web site to find out what you can about the vehicle. Find the Rolling Stones's home page or fan site for your review of the band's new CD.

- *Search for existing reviews or other evaluations on your subject.* One way to do this is to use a search engine such as Google, using the keyword "review or reviews" (or "how to evaluate") along with your subject. For example, "laptop reviews" will produce dozens of sites that rank and evaluate the machines. Similarly, there are countless reviews on the Web of specific performers, performances, CDs, consumer products, and so on.

STEP THREE: If possible, interview people about what they think. You may do this formally, by developing a survey (see "One Student's Response: Amy's Journal: A Survey of Hiking Trails"), or informally by simply asking people what they like or dislike about the thing you're evaluating. Also consider whether you might interview someone who's an expert on your subject. For example, if you're evaluating a Web site, ask people in the technical communications program what they think about it, or what criteria they might use if they were reviewing something similar.

STEP FOUR: This may be the most important step of all: *Experience* your subject. Visit the coffee houses, examine the Web site, listen to the music, attend the performance, read the book, view the painting, visit the building, look at the architecture, watch the movie. As you do this, gather your impressions and collect information. The best way to do this methodically is to collect field notes, and the double-entry journal is a good note-taking system for this purpose. Put your observations on the left page and explore your impressions and ideas on the opposing right page of your notebook.

ONE STUDENT'S RESPONSE

AMY'S JOURNAL

A SURVEY OF HIKING TRAILS

A student who was reviewing the quality of hiking trails in her community left a survey pinned to a post in a plastic pouch at each trailhead. Among the questions she asked were the following:

What do you like best about this trail?

What do you like least?

How would you rank this trail against others in town?

The survey provided the student with both statistical information on the popularity of certain trails and comments that she could use in her essay.

By now, you have some background information on your subject and have gathered observations and impressions that should shape your judgment about it. Maybe you've decided the film is a stinker, the CD is the best one you've heard, or the student union isn't meeting students' needs. After comparing Starbucks and the Flying M—and visiting both places—I'm even more convinced about which one I prefer. But why? This is a key stage in process of evaluation—on what basis do you make the judgment? In other words, what *criteria* are you using?

Thinking About Criteria

Professional reviewers—say consultants who evaluate marketing plans or people who write film reviews—may not sit down and make a list of their criteria. They're so familiar with their subjects that they've often internalized the criteria they're using, and their clients and readers may not insist on knowing on what they base their judgments. But it can be enormously helpful at this stage in the process to try to articulate your criteria, at least as a way of thinking more thoroughly about your subject. Okay, so you think your university's student union fails to meet students' needs, but why? One way to think about criteria is to try to establish the qualities of something *good* in the category you're reviewing. For example, what does a good university student union—in other words, one that does meet students' needs—look like? What are some of its features?

Criteria might be quite personal. There are certain things that *you* think are important about a coffee house, student union, modern dance performance, fusion jazz CD, and so on. These opinions are what make the review yours, and not somebody else's. But they should be reasonable to others. Your criteria for judgment shouldn't set an unrealistic standard or seem nitpicky or irrelevant.

INQUIRING INTO THE DETAILS

COLLABORATING ON CRITERIA

Need help determining the criteria for your evaluation? Asking others for their opinions can help. Consider the following strategy:

1. Write the category of the thing you're reviewing—a modern dance performance, coffee houses, a rap CD, a science fiction novel, and so on—on the top of a piece of newsprint.
2. Post your newsprint on the wall of your classroom.
3. For twenty minutes, everyone in class rotates around the room to each newsprint, trying to answer the following question about the category listed there: *In your judgment, what makes a particularly good _____?* (e.g. rap song, science fiction story, coffee house, etc).
4. Briefly list your criteria for judging each category on the newsprint, or elaborate on a criteria that is already there. In other words, in your mind what makes a good _____?
5. If you don't know that much about the category, make a reasonable guess about a basis for judging it.

I asked my daughter Rebecca, a dancer, what criteria she would use to judge a modern performance (see the accompanying box). I don't completely understand all of the criteria she listed since I know little about dance, but her list seems sensible and I can imagine how it might guide her in evaluating the next performance of the Balance Dance Company. What I don't understand, she can explain to me.

As you write your sketch, keep your criteria in mind. You may not mention all of them, or even any of them in your draft, but they'll help direct you to the evidence you need to make your judgment seem persuasive to others.

Becca's Criteria

A good modern dance performance has . . .

1. Interesting features—props, comedy or music?
2. Something improvised
3. Visible expressions of the dancers' enjoyment
4. Interesting variation
5. Good balance in choreography between repetition and randomness
6. Beginning, middle, and end, seamlessly joined

Writing the Sketch

As with the other inquiry projects, begin with a sketch of your review. This should be about 500 to 600 words (two to three double-spaced pages) and include the following:

- A tentative title
- An effort to help readers understand why they might have a stake in the thing you're evaluating. What's significant about this particular CD, book, performance, place, or product?
- Specific evidence from the thing itself to help explain and support your judgment of it.

STUDENT SKETCH

One of the things I like about Mike Peterson's sketch in praise of the Russell Crowe film *Gladiator* is how clearly he explains his criteria for a good movie. He's clearly done some thinking about it, and that helps me to believe that he isn't just shooting from the hip; Peterson applies reason to his judgment of the movie. This is also a good sketch because it suggests areas for more development in the next draft. I like his criteria, for example, but I'd like him to say a little bit more about each of them, and talk in more specific ways about how they apply to *Gladiator.*

If you were workshopping this sketch, what would you recommend to Mike about the next draft? What do you think needs more development?

GLADIATOR: GOOD HOLLYWOOD
Mike Peterson

1   I recently watched a one-hour special on the History channel called "*Gladiator:* History or Hollywood?" that focused on all the historical discrepancies in the film. They concluded that while they used some historically known names and got a few facts correct, the movie had veered too far from the truth to be believable and was given the final judgment of being just Hollywood. I began watching the documentary with a lot of interest, since I had seen the movie at least ten times, but by the end I was rolling my eyes and ready to change the channel. They were right, *Gladiator* was pure Hollywood. My only rebuttal: "Who cares? It was a great movie."

Like other epic movies involving historical figures, *Gladiator* takes some   2
liberty with the historical facts to present a movie that is relatively short and
captivating. Like the films *Brave Heart* and *The Patriot,* certain characters and
plots had to be added to give the movie audience-pleasing flair: love scenes,
deceit, and personal conflicts.

I have a small list of criteria I use to judge a movie. First, it has to speak to   3
me; give me a reason to want to watch it. Sometimes movies are based around
some cool special effects or a couple of one-liners that someone thought
would be great on the big screen. Those movies can be fun, especially when
watched with friends.

But the movies that become classics and are watched over and over again   4
are those that speak to people. They face a difficult moral question, or deal
with real problems of life, and somehow make us want to be better people.
Gladiator does just that as we watch the imprisoned Maximus deal with the loss
of his family and freedom. We also see Commodus's struggle with greed, frustration, and ignorance. Another theme is the question of where your loyalty
lies, do you follow your heart or your sworn leader?

My second criterion for a good movie is that the movie and characters   5
have to be believable; we have to be able to relate to them. Maximus in
Gladiator is believable. He not only possesses the good traits that people want,
but has his own personal struggles that show his humanity. The movie takes
great care to show his home and family back in Spain, and after serving several

years with the Roman army all he wants to do is get back to them. I think most people can appreciate that feeling. Not many people would sympathize with him had he been a blood-hungry general who would rather rule Rome than be with his family. The main characters in good movies don't have to be heroes or larger than life. We simply have to recognize them as human like ourselves.

6   Finally, I judge a movie by its ending. The most important two things about a movie are the first fifteen minutes, and the last fifteen minutes. Nothing is worse than sitting through a great two hour movie only to have a weak ending. Sometimes it feels like the movie makers couldn't find a good conclusion so they either thaw it out or just end it abruptly. Endings that are loose, unbelievable, or that aren't true to the rest of the movie are instant killers. Endings don't have to be happy either. Even inconclusive endings can be good, as long as they leave you thinking about the movie, and as long as the movie gave you enough material to come to your own conclusion.

7   The ending of *Gladiator* is true to the story. Maximus is true to himself and those around him, he defeats the Emperor while saving his honor, and you feel happy for him that he is finally in a better place with his family that he missed so much (which goes back to the importance of being able to relate to the characters).

8   The first time I saw *Gladiator* I left the movie theater a little disgruntled about the ending. Why did Maximus have to die, and why would the emperor himself get into the arena? But the more I thought about it the more I realized how solid the ending was. Which led me to watch it again.

9   History or Hollywood? Who cares. It takes more than just getting your history right to make a good movie.

Moving from Sketch to Draft

A sketch usually gives the writer just the barest outline of his or her subject. But as an early draft, a sketch can be invaluable. It might hint at what the real subject is, or what questions seem to be behind your inquiry into the subject. A sketch might suggest a focus for the next draft, or simply a better lead. Learning to read your sketches for such clues takes practice. The following suggestions should help.

Evaluating Your Own Sketch   A sketch is an early draft, it should help expose gaps that you can fill in revision. Begin evaluating your sketch by looking for the following possible omissions:

1. Do you provide enough background about what you're reviewing so that readers unfamiliar with the subject know enough to believe and understand your claims?

2. Did you feel that your treatment of the topic was balanced? For example, did you include perspectives that differ from yours?

3. Do you use any helpful comparisons?

4. Are your judgments supported by specific evidence? Is there enough of it?

5. After having written the sketch, has your judgment changed at all? Should you strengthen, qualify, or elaborate on it? Do you feel as if it would be more honest to change it altogether?

Questions for Peer Review. Since a review is a form of persuasive writing, comments from other readers are crucial. In your workshop session, get your peers to comment on how persuasive they find your sketch by asking some of the following questions:

- After reading the sketch, what one thing do you remember most?

- Do you agree with my review of _____? If so, what did you find *least* convincing? If you disagreed, what did you find *most* convincing?

- What criterion seemed key to my judgment? Are there others that you thought I might mention but didn't?

- How do I come across in the sketch? Do I seem to know what I'm talking about? Or does it seem like a rant?

Reflecting on What You've Learned. Following your workshop session, write for five to seven minutes in your journal, beginning with a fastwrite in which you try to remember everything that you heard. Do this double-entry style, on the left-facing page of your notebook. It will help you remember if you tell the story of your workshop session: *The workshop began when . . . And then, . . . And then, ...* When you're done trying to recall everything you can about what group members said to you, shift to the opposing right page and fastwrite about your reactions to what they said. What made sense? What didn't? How might you try one or more of the suggestions you like in the next draft?

Research and Other Strategies: Gathering More Information

If your workshop went well, you might feel ready to start the next draft. But remember this: It is always best to work from an abundance of information. It almost always pays off to resist the temptation to rush the draft and spend a little more time collecting information that will help you write it. Consider the following:

Re-experience. Probably the single most useful thing you can do to prepare for the next draft is to collect more observations of your subject. That might be impossible if you're reviewing a one-time event like a concert. But if you can collect more information at the coffee house, or find more Web sites to compare, or watch the video of the film again, you're likely to learn a lot that will help you write the draft. Why? You're much more focused now on what you think, what criteria most influence that judgment, and what particular evidence you were lacking in the sketch that will make your review more convincing.

Interview. If you opted not to spend much time talking to people, you should strongly consider collecting the comments, opinions, and observations of others about the subject of your review. If you reviewed a concert or other event, find others who attended to interview. If you reviewed a film, get a small group of friends to watch the movie with you and jot down their reactions afterward. If it would be helpful to collect data on how people feel, consider designing a brief survey,

Also consider interviewing someone who is an expert on the thing you're reviewing. Talk to the architect who designed the student union building you find so student-unfriendly. Interview Web designers about the do's and don'ts of informational Web sites; ask them what they think of the sports site you admire so much. Talk to a professional musician or salesperson who loves the acoustic guitar you reviewed.

Read. Go to the library and search for information about your subject. That will make you more of an expert. Look for books and articles in the following categories:

- *Information about how it's made or designed.* You love Martin's newest classical guitar but you really don't know much about the rosewood used in it. Search for books and articles on the qualities of wood guitar makers value most.
- *Other reviews.* Search the Web and the library for other reviews of your subject. If you're reviewing a consumer product or some aspect of popular culture, check a database of general interest periodicals such as *The General Reference Center* or *Reader's Guide Abstracts*. Also check newspaper databases. Has anyone else written about your topic?
- *Background information on relevant people, companies, traditions, local developments, and so on.* For example, if you're reviewing Bob Dylan's new CD, it would be helpful to know more about the evolution of his music. Check the electronic book index for a Dylan biography. Reviewing a modern dance performance? Find out more about the American tradition in the genre by checking the *Encyclopedia of Dance and Ballet* in the library's reference room.

Composing the Draft

One of my favorite writers is essayist E. B. White, author of the familiar children's books *Stuart Little* and *Charlotte's Web*. In a less famous work, an essay that reviewed the work of Don Marquis, White focuses on a book of poetry written by a cockroach, *archy and mehitabel*. This cockroach (Marquis's creation, of course) spent the nighttime hours banging on the keys of a typewriter composing poems and conversing with a cat who was Cleopatra in another life. Because he couldn't reach the shift key, the cockroach wrote everything in lower case. You probably don't know this book or this author, but after reading this lead don't you want to know more about both?

> Among books of humor by American authors, there are only a handful that rest solidly on the bookshelf. This book about Archy and Mehitabel, hammered out at such awful cost by the bug hurling himself at the keys, is one of those books. It is funny, it is wise; it goes right on selling, year after year. The sales do not astound me; only the author astounds me, for I know (or think I do) at what cost Don Marquis produced these gaudy and irreverent tales.

Like all good leads, White's begins by raising questions. A book produced at "awful cost" about *a bug* "hurling himself at the keys?" Certainly we can see how this is costly labor for the insect, but why for its human author? In just a few sentences, White has given us a reason to want to know more about a book we've probably never heard of. One of the challenges of writing a good review is exactly this one: How can you quickly establish two things—that the thing you're evaluating is a significant subject, and that you can be trusted to review it thoughtfully and fairly?

White does this by raising interesting questions and by implying he has inside knowledge about his subject, Don Marquis, that he promises to share. There are many ways to begin an essay that create reader interest in your subject and establishes your credibility as an evaluator. For example, Neal Pollack, in the essay on the Rolling Stones you read earlier, takes a risk by hoping that his brash, frank persona will interest you in his review. He doesn't bother to sell his subject, assuming that readers know the Rolling Stones and their significance as an early rock band.

Here are some other approaches to a strong lead for a review:

- Begin with a common misconception about your subject and promise to challenge it.

- Begin with an anecdote that reveals what you like or dislike.

- Help readers realize the relevance of your subject by showing how it's used, what it says, or why it's needed in a familiar situation.

- Provide interesting background that you readers may not know.

Methods of Development. What are some ways to organize your review?

Narrative. You only have to remember Neal Pollack's earlier review of a Rolling Stones concert to see how you might use narrative in a review.

If you're reviewing a performance or any other kind of experience that has a discrete beginning and end, then telling a story about what you saw, felt, and thought is a natural move. Another way to use narrative is to tell the story of your thinking about your subject, an approach that lends itself to a delayed thesis essay where your judgment of final claim comes late rather than early. For example, you began the book admiring Stephen King's storytelling skill but that admiration shifted as you read it. Your review, then, essentially becomes the story of that change in perspective and what exactly influenced it.

Comparison/Contrast. You already know that comparison of other items in the same category you're evaluating—say, other science fiction films, or other electric cars, or laptops—can be a useful approach to writing an evaluation. If comparison is an important element, you might structure your essay around it, looking first at a comparable item and then contrasting it with another. For example, one way to write my review of Boise coffee houses is to compare Starbucks and the Flying M. Since Starbucks is the corporate version of the American coffee franchise, I could begin my essay by establishing Starbucks as the standard against which I evaluate my locally owned coffee place. If it is useful, I could keep drawing on that contrast throughout the essay, or establish it just at the beginning, focusing more on Flying M's qualities.

Question to Answer. One of the most straightforward methods of structuring a review is to simply begin by raising the question we explored earlier: *What makes _____ good?* This way, you make your criteria for evaluation explicit. From there, the next move is obvious—how well does the thing you're evaluating measure up? If the question is what makes a modern dance performance memorable, the answer for Rebecca is the five or six things she listed—spontaneity, variation, interesting scene or costume changes, seamless shifts between the beginning, middle, and end. Now she can apply these criteria to what she saw at the Balance Dance Company's performance last night.

Using Evidence. The most important evidence in an evaluation is your observations of the thing itself. These should be specific. Who was the best performer, or who was the worst? When did that become obvious during the show? What did he or she say or do? What exactly do I mean by the "nearly Bohemian" atmosphere of Flying M? What does "nearly Bohemian" look like? Which lyrics suggest the Britney Spears is a poor writer? This evidence will most likely be gathered by you through what is called *primary research*. You'll attend the concert, listen to the CD, or visit the coffee house. It's possible that you may also use evidence from secondary sources; for example, what did another critic say or observe? But in general, the most authoritative evidence in an evaluation comes from direct observation.

Workshopping the Draft

If your draft is subject to peer review, see Chapter 15 for details on how to organize workshop groups and decide on how your group can help you, something that depends on how you feel about the work so far and the quality of your draft. The following journal activities and questions should help you make the most of your opportunity to get peer feedback on your work-in-progress.

Reflecting on the Draft. Prepare for peer review of your draft by spending three minutes fastwriting in your journal from the following prompt: *The thing that I liked most about this draft was* . . . Now fastwrite for three more minutes beginning with the following prompt: *The thing that bothered me most about this draft was* . . .

Finally, choose one part of your draft that you are *least* sure of; perhaps you think it's unconvincing or cheesy or unclear. Present this passage to your workshop group and ask what they think without initially voicing your concerns about it.

Questions for Readers. Since evaluative writing is meant to be persuasive, pose some questions for your workshop group that help you gauge how convincing your draft is.

1. At what point in the draft did you think my argument was most effective?
2. When was it least effective?
3. Did you care about what I was evaluating? If not, how might I make you care more?
4. How do I come across as a speaker in this essay? What descriptive words would you use to describe me (e.g., fair, critical, serious, nitpicky, etc.)?
5. Is there a relevant comparison I might have made here but didn't?

Option for Review Essay Workshop

1. Divide each workshop group into two teams—believers and doubters.
2. Believers are responsible for presenting to doubters why the writer's review is convincing and fair.
3. Doubters challenge the writer's judgments and respond to the believer's claims.
4. The writer observes this conversation without participating.
5. After five minutes, believers and doubters drop their roles and discuss with writer suggestions for revision.

Revising the Draft

"Rewriting is the essence of writing," the old saying goes. But too often rewriting is limited to changing a word here and there, maybe adding or cutting a sentence or two, or checking for run-on sentences. These activities are certainly an element of revision—and an important one—but as the word implies, it's important to "re-see" both what you are trying to say as well as how you try to say it. Chapter 14, "Revision Strategies," is a useful introduction to the revision process for any essay, including the review. It emphasizes ways writers can break the bonds that limit their ability to find new ways of seeing the draft.

Review drafts also have some fairly typical problems, most of which can be addressed by repeating some of the steps in this chapter or selecting appropriate revision strategies in Chapter 14.

- Do you provide enough background on your subject for readers who aren't as familiar with it as you?

- Is the draft's *ethos* effective? In other words, does the writer come across as both judgmental yet fair, authoritative yet cautious? Is the tone or voice of the draft persuasive to its audience?

- Is there enough evidence? Does the draft offer enough specific information about its subject so that the reader can understand exactly why the writer makes a particular judgment about it?

- Does the draft stay focused on its thesis? Is the writer's judgment clear and is the draft organized around it?

GUIDE TO REVISION STRATEGIES		
PROBLEMS IN THE DRAFT (CHAPTER 14)	**PART**	**PAGE NUMBER**
Unclear purpose ▪ Not sure what the essay is about? Fails to answer the *So what* question?	1	633
Unclear thesis, theme, or main idea ▪ Not sure what you're trying to say? Judgment isn't clear?	2	639
Lack of information or development ▪ Needs more details; more evidence from the review subject. ▪ Criteria need work?	3	646
Disorganized ▪ Doesn't move logically or smoothly from paragraph to paragraph?	4	650
Unclear or awkward at the level of sentences and paragraphs ▪ Does draft seem choppy or hard to follow at the level of sentences or paragraphs?	5	656

Use the preceding table as a guide to the appropriate revision strate-gies. Remember that a draft may present problems in more than one cat-egory.

Polishing the Draft

After you've dealt with the big issues in your draft—is it sufficiently fo-cused, does it answer the *So what?* question, is it well organized, and so on—you must deal with the smaller problems. You've carved the stone into an appealing figure but now you need to polish it. Are your paragraphs co-herent? How do you manage transitions? Are your sentences fluent and concise? Are there any errors in spelling or syntax? Section 5 of Chapter 14 can help you focus on these issues.

Before you finish your draft, make certain that you've worked through the following checklist:

- ❑ Every paragraph is about one thing.
- ❑ The transitions between paragraphs aren't abrupt or awkward.
- ❑ The length of sentences varies in each paragraph.
- ❑ Each sentence is concise. There are no unnecessary words or phrases.
- ❑ You've checked grammar, particularly verb agreement, run-on sen-tences, unclear pronouns, and misused words (*there/their, where/were,* and so on). (See the handbook at the end of the book for help on all of these grammar issues.)
- ❑ You've run your spell checker and proofed your paper for misspelled words.

STUDENT ESSAY

The student who wrote the sketch on *The Gladiator* earlier in this chapter in revi-sion became more interested in thinking about what he thinks are the criteria of a good movie than in writing specifically about *The Gladiator.* Sketches can work like that. They get us more interested in exploring an idea than the particular subject that gave rise to it.

In his second draft, Mike Peterson decided to focus on thrillers and the im-portance of their endings. This lead him to consider an entirely different film—Cameron Crowe's *Vanilla Sky.* This is a great draft for several reasons. First, Peterson does a great job using research to beef up his review. He draws on other reviews of the film to support his judgments about it. He also does a nice job connecting this film to others. Does it matter that his readers may not have seen these other films? If you haven't seen *Vanilla Sky,* does this review make sense to you?

That's one of the major challenges of writing a good review—providing enough background to readers who aren't familiar with what you're writing about. Does the author pull this off? How?

OPEN YOUR EYES, CAMERON CROWE
Mike Peterson

1   Is a good twist the ultimate goal of a good thriller? Over the past few years it would seem the answer is yes. Recently, starting with M. Knight Shyamalan's *The Sixth Sense,* moviegoers have been in love with the idea that the great movie they are watching is about to blow their mind with an unexpected change at the end, leaving moviemakers to hear the trophy words they crave, "I didn't see that one coming!"

2   When Cameron Crowe's *Vanilla Sky* hit the theaters, moviegoers once again raced to pay their eight fifty in promise of a great movie with a great twist. Our imaginations were sparked by the haunting sound of Penelope Cruz's voice whispering, "open your eyes," in the captivating trailer. Unfortunately for most viewers, "open your eyes" were the words coming from our date, telling us to wake up in time to watch the last five minutes of the movie. The big "twist" we were promised ended up just being a last-minute improbable explanation of the hundred and thirty minutes of fizzled plot.

3   Cameron Crowe understands the importance of a good cast. Like his movies *Fast Times at Ridgemont High,* and the almost-good *Almost Famous,* Crowe aims to deliver a promising movie by including a cast of talented actors who have chemistry together. He is able to achieve this only at times in *Vanilla Sky.* The main character David Aames is played by Tom Cruise. He is a millionaire playboy with too much free time who plays up the yuppie life with best friend Brian Shelby, played by the always-likeable David Lee.

4   Aames is faced with a burning unhappiness and low-self esteem masked by his good looks and toothy smile. It is hard to sympathize with somebody with the looks of Cruise who is faced with the awful dilemma of having to choose between having sex with beautiful Julie Gianni (Cameron Diaz), or the multitude of other beautiful women within his reach. What makes him even less appealing is that he ends up stealing Brian's girlfriend, Sofia Serrano, played by Penelope Cruz. The one we end up feeling sorry for is Brian.

5   There is no denying the chemistry between Diaz and Cruise in the film. Julie is Aames's "sex buddy." But as Aames decides to spend the night with Sofia, he learns the hard way that Julie's promises of non-committal sex are just words. Aames gets in her car as she is waiting for him outside. She speeds

through the streets of Manhattan with a maniacal look on her face as she reminds Aames that, "when you have sex with a person, your body makes a promise, whether you recognize it or not."

Beyond its vulgar and disturbing aspects, the conversation raises the question of what makes us happy, which becomes a central theme through the rest of the movie. Diaz's performance is Oscar worthy. While creating a believable character she also provides a raunchy chemistry between her and the equally raunchy Aames. Her performance also helps us to understand Aames' sex dilemma. While Julie is beautiful and available, her underlying tone is scary and obsessive. I felt that from the beginning of the movie until the devastating moment when she drives off of a bridge, killing herself and horribly disfiguring Aames' face.

The rest of the movie focuses on Aames dealing with his disfigurement and his relationship with Sofia. Theirs was the relationship in the movie that needed the most chemistry. Like in *Captain Corelli's Mandolin,* we are reminded in *Vanilla Sky* that Penelope Cruz is a wonderfully sweet woman with a great smile who just can't act. Her character spends most of the movie looking down, and we are left to wonder if it is because she is portraying someone with low self-esteem or if it is because she can't remember her lines. The reality of the chemistry is that like in Stanley Kubrick's *Eyes Wide Shut,* audiences were left with a creepy voyeuristic feeling as they watched the real life couple pound it out on the screen.

Aside from having the chemistry in the wrong place, and the viewer sympathizing with the wrong characters, Crowe goes wrong in his attempt to deliver a thought provoking plot that leads up to the big finish. A key ingredient in a psychologically based movie is to provide enough clues along the way to keep us guessing, and if nothing else, to keep us interested.

Crowe is afraid of a smart audience and his obsession with a fantastic twist at the end leaves us with a story line that seems to promise nothing until the last moments. He is so afraid of us figuring it out ahead of time that he avoids anything that gives the story weight and meaning. We are left with a polished presentation but no content.

The result was a lot of confusion with the last couple of minutes explaining everything we had just spent two hours watching. It's like hearing someone spending five minutes building up a joke, stuttering on the punch line, then spending another minute having to explain why the joke was funny. One review I read described the ending well, comparing it to listening to a great song on your stereo then as you're about to be swept away in the finale your speakers blow, and all that you get is a shallow tone, mimicking the song but providing no depth or resonance.

11   *Vanilla Sky* is an adaptation of Alejandro Amenabar's 1997 import *Abre Los Ojos.* Penelope Cruz starred in both. This original Chilean version was very popular in Latin America, and when compared with *Vanilla Sky* is easier to follow and not so abrupt at the end. The earthy ambience of Amenabar's story is replaced by Hollywood sleekness, which detracts from the central question of what makes us happy. *Vanilla Sky's* attempt to answer the question gets lost in superficial markers of success and happiness.

12   Crowe could have easily fixed some of his mistakes. First and foremost, audiences would have appreciated a shorter film. Longwindedness does moviemakers no favors. If having a long movie were important to him, Crowe could have at least given us something to chew on. In Shyamalan's *The Sixth Sense,* we are given a story line that would have left us satisfied even without the twist. *Vanilla Sky,* on the other hand, depends entirely on its twist at the expense of the movie.

13   The level of creepiness could have been toned down as well. Tom Cruise looking like playboy phantom of the opera with a form-fitting latex mask was eerie. It didn't invoke feelings of empathy but simply reminded us of Cruise's vanity. *Entertainment Weekly* posed the question of, "What do you get when you take away Tom Cruise's face? The answer, not very much."

14   *Vanilla Sky* successfully turned me off to movies promising a great twist at the end. Like most viewers, I just want to see a good movie that isn't dependent on the last five minutes to make sense. Tom Cruise in an interview with Oprah said that *Vanilla Sky* is like a roller coaster as the plot unfolds. For the rest of the world who didn't know the plot ahead of time, it was merely a roller coaster that didn't seem to end. But Cruise was right in a sense, most of us did feel dizzy and ready to vomit when it was all over.

EVALUATING THE ESSAY

1. Peterson argues in "Open Your Eyes" that audiences expect thrillers to have a great "twist" at the end. Do you understand from reading the essay what makes a great twist and what makes one fail?

2. If you haven't seen *Vanilla Sky,* did you find the review relevant and interesting? Why or why not?

3. Is the last line of the essay too strongly stated?

4. Peterson writes that "Crowe is afraid of a smart audience." Does the essay convince you of that?

USING WHAT YOU HAVE LEARNED

1. A review is a form of argument. Spend sixty seconds making a focused list of everything you learned about how to write persuasively from this assignment.

2. Judgments aren't always rational; in fact, we often have gut reactions that guide our evaluations of people and things. What have you learned in this chapter about how you might approach judgments in ways that combine both feelings and reason?

3. Suppose you had to evaluate the methodology of a biology experiment, or the effectiveness of a business plan. What are the first three things you would do?

A woman in Zimbabwe waiting for food aid. Famine in southern Africa, particularly Zimbabwe, continued into 2004. Finding a solution to this problem remains a pressing need for both the region and the world at large.

Writing a Proposal

WRITING ABOUT PROBLEMS AND SOLUTIONS

A small group of students sits around the round table in my office. Two are college sophomores, one is a junior, and the other is about to graduate. We're talking about problems each of us would love to solve. "I've got a short story due at three this afternoon and I've only written three pages," says Lana. Everyone nods sympathetically. "I'd really like to feel better about work," confides Amy, who works as a chef at a local restaurant. "Most days I just don't want to go." Margaret, who sits across the table from me, is a history major, familiar with the making and unmaking of nations and other grand narratives of colonialism, war, and social change. Her problem, however, is a bit more local. "I can't get my boyfriend to clean up the apartment," she says.

What about you, they ask me?

"The problem I most want to solve today is how to avoid getting scalded in the shower when someone in my house flushes the toilet," I say, getting into the spirit of things.

This conversation had not gone quite the way I expected. I know these students are socially engaged, politically aware, and academically gifted people. When I asked about problems that need solutions I expected that they might mention local issues such as housing developments that threaten the local foothills, or perhaps the difficulty of nontraditional students adjusting to the university, or possibly budget cuts that threaten the availability of courses next semester. If they had been thinking on a larger scale, say nationally or even internationally, perhaps the conversation would have turned to the spiraling federal deficit or the famine in Zimbabwe. Of course, I hadn't asked them to suggest social or economic problems. I had simply asked them what problems most vexed them at the moment.

I should not have been surprised that these would be boredom with work, too little time, and a messy boyfriend. These problems are quite real, and they demand attention, now. One was easy to solve.

What You'll Learn in This Chapter

- How to define a problem so that your readers have a stake in the solution.

- Some of the features of the proposal form.

- What makes a proposal persuasive.

- Questions that will help you revise a proposal.

Lana would carve out extra time in the afternoon to finish her story—"I already know what I need to do," she says. But the other two problems—disenchantment with work and a boyfriend who's a slob—well, both Amy and Margaret saw these not so much as problems but realities they had to live with. In fact, all the students admitted that they rarely look at the world from the perspective of problem solving.

"What if you did?" I ask.

"Then I guess I'd ask myself if there was an opportunity to learn something," says Amy.

Problems of Consequence

While not all problems are equally solvable, the process of seeking and proposing solutions can be rewarding if you see, as Amy did, the opportunity to learn. There's another motivation, too: if the problem is shared by others, whatever you discover may interest them. Part of the challenge is recognizing problems *of consequence*. What makes a problem consequential?

1. It potentially affects a number of people.
2. The solution may not be simple.
3. There may be multiple solutions and people disagree about which is best.

My problem with getting scalded in the shower if somebody flushes a toilet is certainly a problem of consequence for me. It's painful. And I know that more than a few people have this problem. But the solution isn't complicated; all I need to do is go to Ace Hardware and buy a device for the showerhead that senses dramatic temperature change. Problem solved. But what about Margaret's problem with her boyfriend? Is that a problem of consequence? Undoubtedly, there are lots of people with messy mates, the solution is not at all obvious (just ask Margaret), and there are likely multiple ways of dealing with the problem. But has anyone else said anything about the topic? Like many other forms of inquiry, problem solving usually requires some research. After all, if we already knew the solution we wouldn't have the problem. A final consideration, then, is whether anyone else has said something about the problem that might help you think about the best ways to solve it.

A quick search of the Web and several of the university library's databases of articles produced an article on the psychological need of some women for tidiness, a Web page with advice on "Living with a Messy Man," and several scholarly articles on orderliness in the workplace and perceptions of messiness. That's not a bad beginning for background on an essay that looks at the problem and proposes some possible solutions. While Margaret may not succeed in her effort to get her boyfriend to pick up his socks, she will probably learn a few things about how to deal with the problem.

Problems of Scale

While our personal problems are very real, and they can be problems of consequence, the challenges of world hunger, war, environmental destruction, economic development, and human rights matter to far more people on the planet. These are also among the most complex problems to solve. I'm always delighted when writers in my classes are passionate about these issues, and they certainly can be great topics for writing. But as always, narrowing the topic to something manageable—with a limited focus that allows you to decide what *not* consider—is a crucial first step. Obviously, you're not going to have anything meaningful to say about solving the world's hunger problems in a five-page essay (see Figure 7.1). But it might be possible to write a focused essay about the troubles over food production in Zimbabwe, once one of Africa's most productive agricultural nations. Even better, narrow the topic further and investigate the particular U.S. aid policies that are failing to help feed hungry Zimbabwe children. Your interest in hunger can also easily lead to topics with a local an-

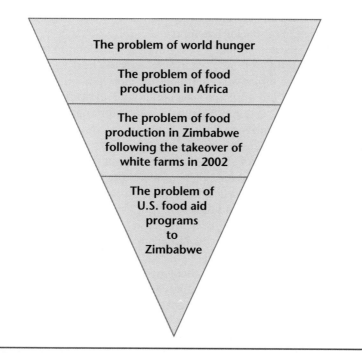

FIGURE 7.1   Narrowing the focus of the problem. Most of us want to find solutions to the big problems of the world, but big problems such as world hunger are complicated and do not readily yield to simple solutions. Unless you are writing a book length proposal, then, it is better to narrow the focus of the problem to which you will propose solutions.

gle—say, the reluctance of some hungry families in your community to use food stamps because of a local supermarket's policies. By focusing on the narrower problem you can often reveal aspects of the larger problem much more powerfully.

The *scale* of the problems that you choose to explore, and their potential consequence, are two initial considerations when writing to solve problems. But why would you want to write about a problem in the first place?

MOTIVES FOR WRITING PROPOSALS

The most obvious motive for using this form of inquiry is because *you care about something*—perhaps avoiding procrastination, having a more obedient dog, reducing air pollution in the valley, helping non-native speakers transition more successfully to the university, or investigating hunger in southern Africa. There might be something in your personal life, your community, or world that you'd like to change. One of the great things about seeing through the framework of problem solving is that it can transform what once seemed like an intractable, frustrating difficulty into something that you can fix, resolve, or change for the better. It's a way of finding hope, as well as an opportunity for learning.

Since presenting a problem and offering solutions is another form of persuasion—after all, you may want to convince others that your solutions are reasonable and effective—then another motive for using problem/solution forms is to change people's behavior and attitudes. In most cases, you're writing about a topic because it's a real problem, and if so, then there's usually an audience for the solution. In that sense, writing that solves problems is a very practical form of inquiry, as well as fairly common one. The explosion of "how to" and "self-help" books and articles is evidence of the popularity of writing that attempts to solve problems. People often write proposals, another form of writing that solves problems, to companies, to foundations, or to governments. The writer's motives in these and similar works are often to persuade readers to do something differently, to encourage particular consumer, political, or social behaviors.

One of the great things about seeing through the framework of problem solving is that it can transform what once seemed like an intractable, frustrating difficulty into something that you can fix, resolve, or change for the better.

A final motive for choosing to focus on problems and solutions is to explore. Perhaps you're concerned with the retention rate of fellow Latino students at your university following their freshman year. You're aware the dropout rate is high. You also know that the solutions to this problem are complicated, and at this stage of learning about the problem you're most interested in discovering what other universities have done. In some cases, you might be as interested in the problem as you are in its solutions, particularly if it's a problem you don't fully understand or weren't even aware of.

Whatever your motive—to explore, persuade, or learn—writing about problems and solutions is a way of making a difference in things as personal as procrastination or as worldly as African famine. It can be a way to take control over problems that seemed distant or intractable or simply inevitable, and hope is always a good thing.

THE PROPOSAL AND ACADEMIC WRITING

There are also numerous academic situations that involve writing to solve problems. The case study approach, popular in business, medicine, and some social sciences, is essentially the presentation of a real-world problem for you to solve. Related to this is the growing popularity of problem-based learning, particularly in the sciences. Problem-based learning is an approach to inquiry that begins with a messy problem, rather than a question, and involves learners in coming up with tentative solutions. In these cases, writers' intentions may be less to persuade readers that certain solutions are best, but to suggest a range of possibilities to consider.

In some classes, you'll be asked to write proposals. For example, political science courses may include an assignment to write a policy proposal, or an essay that looks at a specific public policy problem—say, the organization of the city government, or the state's role in wolf management (a big issue here in Idaho)—and suggest some possible solutions. In a marketing class, you might be asked to draft a proposal for dealing with a particular management problem. How do you motivate workers in a period when wages and benefits are flat? Research proposals are very common in the natural and physical sciences. These identify a particular problem—air pollution inversions in the valley, energy inefficiencies in buildings, declining populations of bull trout—and then propose a certain research program to study it. All of these forms of the proposal differ in the details but they share many features and certainly an overall purpose: to get people to do something differently.

FEATURES OF THE FORM

The proposal is an academic form but it's even more common in everyday settings and situations. You can find writing that solves problems in the brochure at your doctor's office that suggests ways to deal with depression; you'll find it in your local newspaper in editorials that back a tax to create more parks; you'll find it in the case studies on marketing a new toy in your business textbook; you'll find it in the countless magazine articles and books that focus on "how to" and "self-help," on topics from anorexia to removing water marks on antique furniture.

The proposal is one of the most common forms of writing about problems and solutions. Here are some of its features:

- *Proposals usually deal with* both *problems and solutions.* What's interesting is seeing how the emphasis on each varies (see the next two points).

- *Proposals that emphasize solutions usually work from the premise that there is agreement on the problem.* That brochure in the doctor's office on depression may devote a single panel describing the various ways the illness presents itself, and the rest of the brochure on what those who suffer from depression can do about it. Everybody agrees that depression is a problem, so it isn't necessary to persuade readers of the fact, therefore the emphasis is on solutions.

- *Proposals that emphasize the problem usually work from the premise that the problem isn't well known or well understood.* I recently read an article in *The New York Times* that described, at length, the problem that teen stars like Britney Spears have in holding their audience as they get older. Apparently, it's a problem shared by virtually all people who become celebrities as children, and "the majority don't get to the next level." Much of the article explored the nature of this problem because it isn't widely understood. The discussion of solutions was relatively brief, and of course featured an analysis of Madonna's many successful transformations.

- *The writer usually includes outside perspectives on the problem or its solutions.* If you're writing about a problem of consequence, then other people have said something about it or will have something to say if you ask them. Occasionally, the writer might be an expert on the topic and won't think it's necessary to do much research. But more often, we learn about the problem as we seek to solve it and actively seek outside perspectives and ideas.

- *Proposals that advocate certain solutions often use visual rhetoric.* If a main motive is to persuade people to buy something, support something, fund something, vote for something, or otherwise change their behavior, then writers may focus on the many visual ways they might get their point across. Some proposals use graphic devices like bulleted lists or boldfaced headlines and other techniques for emphasis, drawing readers' attention to elements of the proposal that make it easier to read, more convincing, or give the impression that the writer is professional.

- *Proposals justify their solutions.* You know, of course, that any claim is more convincing with supporting evidence, and solutions are a kind of argumentative claim. Typically, proposals that offer certain solutions over others offer evidence—or justifications—for why. A proposal that calls for a memorial statue that pays tribute to Vietnam veterans rather than creating a rose garden in their name might feature evidence from interviews with local vets or information about the success of similar monuments in other communities. Successful grant proposals depend on a convincing justification that would persuade a foundation or agency to fund one solution over competing ones.

PROPOSAL

Procrastination is one of the biggest problems on campus. At least that's what most of my students believe. Some see it as an inevitable, or even preferred, way of working, typified by the familiar comment that "I work best under pressure." Others lament the habit but can't work their way out of it. In fact, there are remedies for procrastination—and even a wealth of academic research on its psychology.

Maia Szalavitz's essay on procrastination does a great job of bringing some of that research to bear on the procrastination problem. She argues that one key to overcoming the problem is to understand how your own beliefs might contribute to it. One of the things I like about this piece is that it demonstrates that a proposal can be really interesting reading. "Stand and Deliver," which appeared in *Psychology Today* magazine, opens with an anecdote or case study, and makes good use of subtitles. Do you find it convincing?

STAND AND DELIVER
Maia Szalavitz

At the age of 37, Jared, a would-be professor in New York state, should be on tenure track at a university, perhaps publishing his second or third book. Instead, he's working on a dissertation in sociology that he'd planned to complete a decade ago. He's blown two "drop-dead" deadlines and is worried about missing a third. His girlfriend is losing patience. No one can understand why a guy they consider brilliant doesn't "just do it." Nor, for that matter, can Jared: "If I could change it, believe me, I would," he swears.

Jared is among the one in five people who chronically procrastinate, jeopardizing careers and jettisoning peace of mind, all the while repeating the mantra: "I should be doing something else right now."

Procrastination is not just an issue of time management or laziness. It's about feeling paralyzed and guilty as you channel surf, knowing you should be cracking the books or reconfiguring your investment strategy. Why the gap between incentive and action? Psychologists now believe it is a combination of anxiety and false beliefs about productivity.

4   Tim Pychyl, Ph.D., associate professor of psychology at Carleton University in Ottawa, Canada, tracked students with procrastination problems in the final week before a project was due. Students first reported anxiety and guilt because they had not started their projects. "They were telling themselves 'I work better under pressure' or 'this isn't important,'" says Pychyl. But once they began to work, they reported more positive emotions; they no longer lamented wasted time, nor claimed that pressure helped. The results of this study will be presented at the Third International Conference on Counseling the Procrastinator in Academic Settings in August. Psychologists have focused on procrastination among students because the problem is rampant in academic settings; some 70 percent of college students report problems with overdue papers and delayed studying, according to Joseph Ferrari, associate professor of psychology at Chicago's DePaul University.

5   Pychyl also found that procrastination is detrimental to physical health. College students who procrastinate have higher levels of drinking, smoking, insomnia, stomach problems, colds and flu.

6   So why can't people just buckle down and get the job done?

False Beliefs

7   Many procrastinators are convinced that they work better under pressure, or they'll feel better about tackling the work later. But tomorrow never comes and last-minute work is often low quality. In spite of what they may believe, "Procrastinators generally don't do well under pressure," says Ferrari. The idea that time pressure improves performance is perhaps the most common myth among procrastinators.

Fear of Failure

8   "The main reason people procrastinate is fear," says Neil Fiore, Ph.D., author of *The Now Habit*. Procrastinators fear they'll fall short because they don't have the requisite talent or skills. "They get overwhelmed and they're afraid they'll look stupid." According to Ferrari, "Procrastinators would rather be seen as lacking in effort than lacking in ability." If you flunk a calculus exam, better to loudly blame it on the half-hour study blitz, than admit to yourself that you could have used a tutor the entire semester.

Perfectionism

9   Procrastinators tend to be perfectionists—and they're in overdrive because they're insecure. People who do their best because they want to win don't procrastinate; but those who feel they must be perfect to please others often put

things off. These people fret that "No one will love me if everything I do isn't utter genius." Such perfectionism is at the heart of many an unfinished novel.

Self-Control

Impulsivity may seem diametrically opposed to procrastination, but both can be part of a larger problem: self-control. People who are impulsive may not be able to prioritize intentions, says Pychyl. So, while writing a term paper you break for a snack and see a spill in the refrigerator, which leads to cleaning the entire kitchen. 10

Punitive Parenting

Children of authoritarian parents are prone to procrastinate. Pychyl speculates that children with such parents postpone choices because their decisions are so frequently criticized—or made for them. Alternatively, the child may procrastinate as a form of rebellion. Refusing to study can be an angry—if self-defeating—message to Mom and Dad. 11

Thrill-Seeking

Some procrastinators enjoy the adrenaline "rush." These people find perverse satisfaction when they finish their taxes minutes before midnight on April 15 and dash to the post office just before it closes. 12

Task-Related Anxieties

Procrastination can be associated with specific situations. "Humans avoid the difficult and boring," says Fiore. Even the least procrastination-prone individuals put off taxes and visits to the dentist. 13

Unclear Expectations

Ambiguous directions and vague priorities increase procrastination. The boss who asserts that everything is high priority and due yesterday is more likely to be kept waiting. Supervisors who insist on "prioritizing the Jones project and using the Smith plan as a model" see greater productivity. 14

Depression

The blues can lead to or exacerbate procrastination—and vice versa. Several symptoms of depression feed procrastination. Decision making is another problem. Because depressed people can't feel much pleasure, all options seem equally bleak, which makes getting started difficult and pointless. 15

INQUIRING INTO THE ESSAY

Explore, explain, evaluate, and reflect on "Stand and Deliver."

1. According to Szalavitz's article, about 70 percent of college students say they have problems with procrastination. Do you? Fastwrite for five minutes about your own procrastination habits. Under what circumstances do you find yourself putting things off? What do you say to yourself when you do? What does Szalavitz say in her article that seems to apply to your experience? Tell the story of a memorable procrastination experience, or your most recent one.

2. Without rereading the essay, in your journal make a list of the points you remember from "Stand and Deliver." Then explain why these ideas, claims or facts seem to stand out in your mind. Did it have something to do with how they were presented in the essay or with your own knowledge of the topic?

3. This essay seems pretty convincing. Play the "doubting game" in your journal for five minutes and see if you can find gaps, unanswered questions, or unconvincing assertions in the piece. If you were to do some follow-up research on the topic, what would you look into?

4. The odds are very high that you have a fair amount of personal knowledge about procrastination. In other words, you can probably "really relate to this topic." Reflect on how familiarity with something influences how you read and how you think about it. One way to consider this is to compare your reading and thinking processes on a topic that you know very little about, or can't "relate to."

PROPOSAL

The debate over what to do with the site where New York's World Trade Center towers once stood is a deeply emotional topic. This is both understandable and appropriate. But it also makes the resolution enormously difficult. How can we both honor the site as sacred ground and at the same time build something that reflects the resilience of the city and the nation? Some see reconstruction as a way to send a message to terrorists, other see it as a way to memorialize the dead. Proposals abound. Among the most common is the idea that developers should simply rebuild the twin towers pretty much the way they were.

Into this debate wade James Kunstler and Nikos A. Salingaros, two experts on urban design, who argue in the article that follows that "the age of skyscrapers is at an end." While the two don't have specific ideas about what should be done with the World Trade Center site, they argue here that rebuilding the towers isn't the solution. Instead, they believe in something called "new urbanism" that would emphasize a ten-story limit on buildings and dispersion of office space into neighborhoods. The whole idea that "no new megatowers will be built" and many of those remaining will be "dismantled" is obviously controversial. The article, when published on the Web, generated scores of critical and supportive messages. What do you think about the solution Kunstler and Salingaros propose? Do you find their argument convincing?

The End of Tall Buildings

James Howard Kunstler and Nikos A. Salingaros

Our world has changed dramatically.

Watching video of the burning twin towers of the World Trade Center in the few minutes before they both collapsed, we were struck by what appeared to be the whole history of the skyscraper captured in vignette. In the blocks east and south of the World Trade Center stood the earlier skyscrapers of the 20th century, including some of the most notable prototypes of that epoch. Virtually all of these pre-1930 ultra-tall buildings thrust skyward with towers, turrets, and needles, each singular in its design, as though reaching up to some great spiritual goal as yet unattained. And there, in contrast stood the two flaming towers of the World Trade Center, with their flat roofs signifying the exhaustion of that century-long aspiration to reach into the heavens, their failure made even more emphatic in the redundancy of their banal twin-ness. Then they and everything inside them imploded into vapor and dust, including several thousand New Yorkers whose bodies will likely never be found. 1

The United States was attacked by terrorists on September 11, 2001. With the recent tragedies comes a sobering reassessment of America's (and the World's) infatuation with skyscrapers. We feel very strongly that the disaster should not only be blamed on the terrorist action, but that this horrible event exposes an underlying malaise with the built environment. 2

We are convinced that the age of skyscrapers is at an end. It must now be considered an experimental building typology that has failed. Who will ever again feel safe and comfortable working 110 storeys above the ground? Or sixty storeys? Or even twenty-seven? We predict that no new megatowers will be built, and existing ones are destined to be dismantled. This will lead to a radical transformation of city centers—which, however, would be an immensely positive step towards improving the quality of urban life. The only megatowers left standing a century hence may be in those third-world coun- 3 tries who so avidly imported the bric-a-brac of the industrialized world without realizing the damage they were inflicting on their cities. This essay looks at criticisms of tall buildings, while offering some practical solutions.

Tall buildings generate urban pathologies.

4   In a paper entitled "*Theory of the Urban Web*" published in the *Journal of Urban Design* (Volume 3, 1998, pages 53–71), Salingaros outlined structural principles for urban form. The processes that generate the urban web involve nodes, connections, and the principles of hierarchy. Among the theoretical results derived were multiple connectivity—in which a city needs to have alternative connections in order to stay healthy—and the avoidance of over concentration of nodes. When the second pathology occurs, such as in segregated use zoning, and in monofunctional megatowers, it kills the city by creating a mathematical singularity (where one or more quantities become extremely large or infinite). Many pathologies of contemporary cities are traced to ideas of early modernist planning that appeared in a totally unrealistic context in the 1920s. We quote from that paper (page 62):

> Without a sufficient density and variety of nodes, functional paths (as opposed to unused ones that are purely decorative) can never form. Here we come up against the segregation and concentration of functions that has destroyed the urban web in our times. There are simply not enough different types of nodes in any homogeneous urban region to form a web. Even where possibilities exist, the connections are usually blocked off by misguided zoning laws. Distinct types of elements, such as residential, commercial and natural, must intertwine to catalyze the connective process. Dysfunctional cities concentrate nodes of the same type, whereas functional cities concentrate coupled pairs of contrasting nodes.

5   In all cases and to some degree, high-rise buildings deform the quality, the function, and the long-term health of urbanism in general by overloading the infrastructure and the public realm of the streets that contain them. Leon Krier has referred to this as "urban hypertrophy," making the additional point that overloading any given urban center tends to prevent the organic development of new healthy, mixed urban fabric anywhere beyond the center. (Leon Krier, *Houses, Palaces, Cities,* St. Martin's Press, 1984.) Bear in mind, too, that some of the sturdiest and even aesthetically pleasing tall buildings of the early 20th century are only now approaching the end of their so-called "design life." What is their destiny?

6   The worst offender in this urban destruction is the monofunctional megatower. Paradoxically, it has become an icon of modernity and progress—how can images from the 1920s be considered modern? Indoctrination at its most

subversive has successfully identified the glass and steel boxes of Ludwig Mies van der Rohe with a phony "efficiency." Voices raised against the skyscraper include that of the architect and urbanist Constantine Doxiades (documented by Peter Blake in *Form Follow Fiasco,* 1974, page 82):

> My greatest crime was the construction of high-rise buildings. The most successful cities of the past were those where people and buildings were in a certain balance with nature. But high-rise buildings work against nature, or, in modern terms, against the environment. High-rise buildings work against man himself, because they isolate him from others, and this isolation is an important factor in the rising crime rate. Children suffer even more because they lose their direct contacts with nature, and with other children. High-rise buildings work against society because they prevent the units of social importance—the family . . . the neighborhood, etc.—from functioning as naturally and as normally as before. High-rise buildings work against networks of transportation, communication, and of utilities, since they lead to higher densities, to overloaded roads, to more extensive water supply systems—and, more importantly, because they form vertical networks which create many additional problems— crime being just one of them.

Peter Blake condemned megatowers in *Form Follows Fiasco* on several points. One was the disastrous wind shear that their surfaces created; the other was fires that had burned out of control in two skyscrapers in Latin America. He warned the world that (page 150):   7

> The first alternative to Modern Dogma should obviously be a moratorium on high-rise construction. It is outrageous that towers more than a hundred stories high are being built at a time when no honest engineer and no honest architect, anywhere on earth, can say *for certain* what these structures will do to the environment—in terms of monumental congestion of services (including roads and mass-transit lines), in terms of wind currents at sidewalk level, in terms of surrounding water tables, in terms of fire hazards, in terms of various sorts of interior traumata, in terms of despoiling the neighborhoods, in terms of visually polluting the skylines of our cities, and in terms of endangering the lives of those within or without, through conceivable structural and related failures.

We just saw two of the tallest buildings in the world burn and implode so   8
that all their construction material (and contents—furniture plus people) was particulated and the residue compressed into the space of the underground parking garage. All of this happened on the order of minutes. Did noone read Blake's warnings? Certainly many people did, but the persuasive force of the modernist architectural image of slick, shiny towers going all the way back to Le Corbusier's first drawings in the 1920s was more seductive than practical realities and risks.

9   As of September 11, 2001, we cannot afford to be so complacent—or so easily entranced by the totems of "modernity." Every would-be terrorist who is now a child will grow up and be instructed by those surreal, riveting images of the two airplanes crashing into the World Trade Towers.

A new urban life, and alternatives to megatowers.

10   The New Urbanism has some (though by no means all) solutions that could reintroduce life into formerly dead urban environments. These ideas go back to several authors, including Christopher Alexander. In his book *A Pattern Language* (1977) Alexander proposed with his co-authors 253 "patterns" that describe how to satisfy human needs in the built environment, from the scale of a city, down to the scale of detailed construction in a room. Two of those patterns are relevant to our discussion:

> Pattern 21: FOUR-STORY LIMIT. There is abundant evidence to show that high buildings make people crazy. Therefore, in any urban area, no matter how dense, keep the majority of buildings four stories high or less. It is possible that certain buildings should exceed this limit, but they should never be buildings for human habitation.

> Pattern 62: HIGH PLACES. The instinct to climb up to some high place, from which you can look down and survey your world, seems to be a fundamental human instinct. Therefore, build occasional high places as landmarks throughout the city. They can be a natural part of the topography, or towers, or part of the roofs of the highest local building—but, in any case, they should include a physical climb.

11   We agree that the first of these "patterns" might appear utopian and irrelevant to the industrialized world. However, our purpose is to reexamine the most basic aspects of urbanism, and in particular to look at those factors that have been destroyed by the megalomania of architects and the speculative greed of builders.

12   A city requires high buildings, but not all of them should be high, and they should certainly be of mixed use.

13   It is not possible to state with any certainty exactly what the optimum height of buildings ought to be, since buildings greater than ten storeys are an experimental product of industrial technology—itself an experiment for which the results are not yet in. We do know that the center cities of Paris, London and Rome achieved excellent density and variety at under ten storeys, and have continued to thrive without succumbing to the extreme hypertrophy characteristic in American urbanism.

14   Within the upper limits of proven traditional type, it might be prudent to confine future constructions to, perhaps, ten-story office buildings, whose four

bottom storeys are strictly residential. Coexisting with the first type might be five-storey residential buildings with a commercial ground floor devoted to retail and restaurants. Both of these are a good compromise between traditional typologies, the ideal solutions proposed by Alexander, and the unfortunate, inhuman, alienating extant urbanisms that have been produced by modernist planning.

One of the most pressing commercial questions after the terrorist devastation of lower Manhattan is: where is the financial world going to find several million square feet of office space? The answer is right in front of our noses. Move into and renovate the numerous depressed areas just a few subway stops away. With the proper mixed zoning legislation that needs to protect residents and guarantee a thriving street life, this could mark the rejuvenation of parts of the city that for years have had the same bombed-out appearance as "ground zero" of the Twin Towers has now (except that the slums are not shown on the evening news).   15

President Bill Clinton has set a shining example by moving his offices into Harlem.   16

Should the Twin Towers be rebuilt as a symbol of the defiance of the American people, as some sentimentalists have proposed in the aftermath of their collapse? We think not. If nothing else, it would be a disservice to humanity to rebuild proven deathtraps. Obsessively returning to the models of yesterday's tomorrow would refute mankind's past architectural achievements—and, curiously, would be a frightening parallel to the dogmatism that led the terrorists to do their mission.   17

It's the fault of the architects.

Why are the above solutions, all available for decades now, not implemented to regenerate our cities? Several factors, including zoning, commercial speculation, and the tax structure created a favorable situation for erecting megatowers. That era is now over. We conclude with a broad indictment of the architectural and building professions as responsible for destroying our cities, and for putting people at risk in firetraps from which they can never be evacuated in time. From Bernard Rudofsky in *Streets for People* (1969), page 339:   18

> Unlike physicians, today's architects are not concerned with the general welfare; they are untroubled by scruples about strangling the cities and the misery that this entails. Architects never felt the urge to establish ethical precepts for the performance of their profession, as did the medical fraternity. No equivalent of the Hippocratic oath exists for them. Hippocrates' promise that "the regiment I adopt shall be for the benefit of my patients according to my ability and judgement, and not for their hurt or for any wrong" has no counterpart in their book. Criticism within the profession—the only conceivable way to spread a sense of

responsibility among its members—is tabooed by their own codified standards of practice. To bolster their ego, architects hold their own beauty contests, award each other prizes, decorate each other with gold medals, and make light of the damning fact that they do not amount to any moral force in this country.

19   Charles, the Prince of Wales spoke out courageously against megatowers, and was consequently accused by architects and the media as being "against progress." The reaction was so severe that for a while his succession to the throne was in question. It is worth recalling his remarks, which, through his choice of words, now seem eerily prophetic. In criticizing the then-unbuilt Canary Wharf tower in London, Charles said (*A Vision of Britain,* 1989, page 55):

> What hope for London now? Cesar Pelli's tower may become the tomb of modernistic dogma. The tragedy is that it will cast its shadow over generations of Londoners who have suffered enough from towers of architectural arrogance.

20   Charles's remarks were only one decade too early.

INQUIRING INTO THE ESSAY

Explore, explain, evaluate, and reflect on "The End of Tall Buildings" in your notebook or in class discussion using some of the following questions.

1. Explore your own reaction to tall buildings. Can you recall the last time you were in one or looked up at a skyscraper from street level? What affect did it have on you? Was this positive or negative? Have your feelings about being in or around tall buildings changed since September 11? Fastwrite for seven minutes about your experiences with urban landscapes.

2. Explain what the authors mean by "urban hypertrophy," at least as you understand it.

3. Do an Internet search on "skyscrapers," perhaps investigating background on how they're built, by whom, and why. What were the motives of the architects of skyscrapers in other American cities? Explain how these either confirm or challenge the charge in "The End of Tall Buildings" that it is architects' "megalomania" or the developer's "greed" that accounts for the construction of tall buildings in the United States.

4. Evaluate the claim in the reading that "the age of skyscrapers is at an end," which is probably the central argument of the essay. Do you find this claim persuasive? What evidence is provided to support it? What evidence did you expect and not find in the essay?

5. As readers, we pick up cues in a piece of writing that tell us we're reading an argument of some sort. Consider for a moment reading a personal essay like those in Chapter 4 or a work of short fiction. These aren't forms we usually consider persuasive. What cues do you pick up on in an essay such as "The End of Tall Buildings" that suggest you're reading an argument that you don't notice in those other forms? Reflect on how you therefore read them differently. What makes you feel comfortable or receptive to an argument? Is that different from what makes you believe a personal essay or short story?

PROPOSAL

I'm nostalgic about my last year in high school, the only one that I didn't feel like an outsider. But was it academically relevant? To be honest, I can't even remember what classes I took my senior year, but then again I can't remember too many of the classes I took the other three years, either. In the popular imagination, "senioritis" takes over during the final year of high school and students supposedly pretty much do nothing but take easy classes when they show up for classes at all.

The article that follows briefly examines this problem, and one solution that has been offered by some legislators: eliminate the senior year altogether. "Is it Time to Ditch Senior Year?" isn't a fully developed proposal by any means. But it does identify a familiar problem and suggest one solution. What was your senior year like, and does it make sense to you to eliminate it altogether? What would you propose to make it more meaningful?

IS IT TIME TO DITCH SENIOR YEAR?
Caroline Hsu

If it's fifth period, it must be time for Hacky Sack for high school senior   1
Jess Rojas. Second period the Boulder, Colorado, student spends staring into space at the library, and the rest of his day isn't much more challenging: The 17-year-old claims he can get A's or B's with little or no effort. Rojas's problem? He's got senioritis, a condition that has afflicted him since he was accepted into the University of Colorado-Boulder last month. "I'm not taking

any classes that I need to graduate," says Rojas, who finished his requirements by the end of junior year, "I'm ready for college now."

2   Rojas just may get his wish. Last month, in an effort to stem rising budget problems, members of the powerful joint budget committee of the Colorado legislature proposed eliminating the 12th grade and rolling the $271 million saved into a universal prekindergarten program. "In my opinion, not a lot of 12th graders are learning much," says Colorado state Sen. Dave Owen, a member of the budget committee. "Maybe we need to put more money at the lower end of the scale rather than the higher end."

3   Senior year, and what to do with it, have become the subject of an ongoing national debate. In June, before Colorado's proposed radical amputation, Florida passed legislation that permits students to graduate from high school with 18 credits instead of 24, effectively allowing students to graduate after their junior year. At the heart of both states' attempted solutions is a fundamental question: What is senior year for? In many schools today, it's a nebulous time when collegebound students with acceptance letters in hand often lose their motivation to learn, while other students, having fulfilled minimal high school graduation requirements, report to school for just a few classes. "Nobody claims the senior year," says Michael W. Kirst, a professor of education at Stanford who studies the subject. "The high schools don't know what to do with it; the colleges won't say what should be done with it, and the students are acting rationally by getting the signal that none of it matters." Indeed, Kirst believes that problems inherent in the misspent senior year won't be solved until policymakers take a "K–16" approach toward education—one that integrates all school levels seamlessly.

4   The disconnect between the K–12 curriculum and higher education is underscored in Colorado. A month before Senator Owen suggested eliminating the senior year, the Colorado Commission on Higher Education published new requirements for public university entrance that included four years of English and four years of math for the class of 2010—a schedule that would seem to require four years of high school.

5   **Catch-up.** One look at college remediation rates might suggest that more, not less, intensive learning in high school is what's needed. In fall 2000, 76 percent of postsecondary institutions offered high-school-level remedial reading, writing, or mathematics courses, and 28 percent of freshmen enrolled in at least one of them. Colorado says college remediation at its state colleges costs anywhere from $15 million to $21 million a year. In Virginia, Gov. Mark Warner developed a plan to combat similar losses by beefing up senior year with online Advanced Placement courses and a vocational pro-

gram that would provide tech-minded students one semester of free community college classes.

But while policymakers debate whether 12th grade should be an intense college-prep year or a vocational program, or cut completely, some students think the senior year should be left just the way it is. Katie Miller, a senior at Boulder High School, has finished her core math, English, and science requirements and is spending the year taking almost all art and photography classes. Some might see her schedule as typical senior slacking, but Miller, who hopes to attend art school in Seattle, is feeling more focused than ever as she prepares her application portfolio. "Instead of getting school over with, I'm actually enjoying it."

6

INQUIRING INTO THE ESSAY

Use the four ways of inquiring to think through your response to Caroline Hsu's essay.

1. What do you remember from your senior year in high school? Brainstorm a quick list of moments that stand out. Are they similar in any way? Choose one for a focused fastwrite. Put yourself back into that moment and describe what you're doing, using all of your senses. Write for five minutes. Choose another moment from your list, and do the same thing.

2. Reread your fastwrites from the preceding question. Finish this sentence: *As I look back on these moments now, I realize that . . . .* Finish that same sentence at least two more times. In your journal, explain what your writing so far suggests to you about the relevance and significance of your senior year in high school. What does this imply about where you stand on the proposal to eliminate the senior year?

3. Research the issue on the Web. Try Googling the words *eliminate senior year high school.* Then evaluate the proposal that the senior year should be eliminated to save money and avoid wasting students' time.

4. As you know, a proposal is a form of argument, and when it comes to controversies like the one discussed here, most of us begin with a certain view. Reflect on your own views for a moment. Was that true as you thought about the idea of eliminating the senior year in high school? Were you resistant to changing your mind as you thought more deeply about the issue? How hard is it for you to suspend judgment when you begin with one, even if it's tentative? What are some strategies for overcoming this resistance to changing your mind?

 SEEING THE FORM

STOP TORTURING CHICKS?

Interest group ads like the one below are proposals. They identify a problem and then propose a solution. What's interesting about this advertisement for the organization People for the Ethical Treatment of Animals (PETA) is that it has to do a fair amount of work convincing its audience that there is a problem in the first place, and it's pretty subtle about the solution. Does this make the ad ineffective?

What this proposal doesn't do is show us how Kentucky Fried Chicken (KFC) "tortures" chickens. It simply makes a bold statement that it does. Then at the bottom of the sign, half concealed by a chick, is PETA's name. What is the ad's purpose? What solution does it offer and is that solution justified or explained in any way? What does the success of this ad depend on? What does a written proposal have to do that a visual proposal like this one can avoid? Finally, do you think the ad is effective?

☞ ONE STUDENT'S RESPONSE

ROSITTA'S JOURNAL

THINKING ABOUT THE PETA AD

This ad seems to have all sorts of mixed messages. Certainly, it seems to assume that the viewer agrees that torturing "chicks" is a problem, but then there is the human "chick" who is delivering the claim. What are we to make of her? She doesn't look particularly tortured, unless the ad is supposed to imply that she's been tortured by the torture. Hmmm . . . I think that the only way this ad works as a proposal is if the view agrees that there is a problem, which makes me think that the audience for this proposal are people who already might be inclined to think so. The solution is pretty unclear. Adopt a chick? My boyfriend would certainly be willing to adopt this one. I wonder why the PETA logo is covered up. This makes me think even more that this is an ad for people who already agree on the problem, and already might accept the solution. But what is it? Give to PETA?

■ THE WRITING PROCESS ■

INQUIRY PROJECT: Writing a Proposal

There's a problem that needs to be solved and you have an idea how to do it. That's the general purpose of this assignment. Ultimately, you'll write a 1,000- to 1,500-word draft that has the following features:

- It addresses a problem of consequence, and is written to an audience that might be interested in solutions.
- It is a problem of local concern. In other words, the scale of the problem is limited to those that in some way affect your community.
- You justify the solutions you propose.
- The form of your proposal is linked to your purpose and audience.

Thinking About Subjects

The process of seeking and proposing solutions can be rewarding if you see the opportunities to learn.

Amy, Lana, and Margaret, the three students with whom I talked about problems at the start of this chapter, didn't have much trouble coming up with them: Amy hates her work, Lana procrastinates, and Margaret has a messy boyfriend. Initially, each problem seemed a relatively private matter, hardly a suitable topic for a proposal. But it became apparent later that at least one of them—Margaret's problem with her boyfriend—was actually something that was both shared by other women and a topic about which something had been said.

Perhaps you already have a topic in mind for your proposal. But if you don't, or you want to explore some other possibilities, begin by generating a list of problems you'd like to solve without worrying about whether they're problems of consequence. Also don't worry too much yet whether you have solutions to the problems you're generating. You can come up with those later. Try some of the generating exercises below.

Generating Ideas

Play with some ideas about subjects for the proposal assignment. Remember not to prejudge the material at this stage.

Listing Prompts. Lists can be rich sources of triggering topics. Let them grow freely, and when you're ready, use an item as the focus of another list or an episode of fastwriting. The following prompts should get you started.

1. In your journal, spend three minutes brainstorming a list of problems in your personal life that you'd like to solve. Let the ideas come in waves.

2. Spend three minutes brainstorming a list of problems *on your campus,* at *your workplace,* or *in the local community* that affect you in some way, or that you feel something about. Don't worry about repeating items from the list you made in listing prompt 1.

3. Explore some possible causes of the problem by finishing the following sentence as many times as you can: *This is a problem because* _____.

Fastwriting Prompts. In the early stages of generating possible topics for an essay, fastwriting can be invaluable, *if* you allow yourself to write badly. Initially, don't worry about staying focused; sometimes you find the best triggering topics by ranging freely. Once you've tentatively settled on something, use a more focused fastwrite to try to generate information and ideas within the loose boundaries of your chosen topic.

✒ ONE STUDENT'S RESPONSE

CAESAR'S JOURNAL

LISTING PROMPTS
Problems in my life

Procrastination

Can't stick to a budget

Credit card debt

Hate the winter

Failing calculus

Girlfriend prefers Hector

Balancing studying and social life

Can't afford to travel

Work too much

Problems on campus

No sense of community

Drying up of work-study funds

Not enough diversity

Lines at the registrar

Recent tuition hike

Legislature underfunds higher
  education

Lousy food at the SUB

Textbooks are too expensive

Waiting list for childcare center

Problems in community

Over-development of foothills

Litter and degradation of Boise River

Too few child-care options

Hate crimes

Concert venues inadequate

Traffic

Air pollution in Valley

Smell from sugar beet factory

Range fires

1. Pick any of the items from the lists above as a launching place for a five minute fastwrite. Explore some of the following questions:

   • When did I first notice this was a problem?

   • What's the worst part about it?

   • What might be some of its causes?

   • What moment, situation, or scene is most typical of this problem? Describe it as if you're experiencing it by writing in the present tense.

   • How does this problem make me feel?

   • What people do I associate with it?

2. Depending on how familiar you are with a problem that interests you, do a five-minute focused fastwrite that explores solutions, beginning with the sentence, *I think one of the ways to deal with _____ is _____.* Follow that sentence as long as you can. When the writing stalls, use the following prompt, *Another possible solution to the problem of _____ might be _____.* Repeat these prompts as often as you can for ten minutes.

⌕ INQUIRING INTO THE DETAILS

CAUSATION

One of my favorite clichés is "this is a solution in search of a problem." Obviously, there's no point in proposing a solution if you can't win agreement that there's a problem in the first place. But once you do establish that there is a problem the next thing is to examine what *causes* the problem. Controlling some of the causes may be the beginning of finding the solution. This exercise might help you discover those possibilities in the problem you've chosen to explore.

Begin with some journal work to flesh out your initial understandings and feelings about the problem.

1. At the top of a journal page, write *Causes*. Brainstorm a quick list of things that you believe contribute to or cause the problem. These might be composed as "because" statements. For example, if the problem is the lack of diversity on your campus, make a fast list of possible reasons by beginning with *There is a lack of diversity on the Boise State campus* because. . .

   - Idaho is sometimes perceived as a state with racial problems
   - There are too few scholarships targeted to minorities
   - The history of African Americans and Latinos in Idaho isn't widely known among whites
   - Campus organizations don't do enough to promote diversity
   - There are too few courses in the curriculum that would appeal to minority students
   - And so on.

   Remember that at this point you're brainstorming a fast list of *possible* causes. You may or may not know enough about the causes of the problem to be very certain about what you're saying here.

2. Choose *one* of the causes on your list that seems most plausible to you as contributing significantly to the problem, *or* that you find most interesting. Use this as a prompt for a five-minute fastwrite. Explore some of the following questions:

   - Do you have any personal experience with this particular cause?
   - In what ways, exactly, might it contribute to the problem?
   - Does this possible cause of the problem suggest anything about a possible solution?

- When you compare it with other possible causes, what makes this one unique or significant?

If the writing stalls, choose another cause from your list in Step 1, and explore it through writing using the questions above, if they're helpful.

One of the things this exercise might do is help you to use cause/effect as a mode of inquiry that exposes relationships, and not just the connections between the problem and some of the reasons it exists, but also the problem and its possible solutions. Remember, your goal is to write a proposal; it's not enough to simply dramatize the problem. For example, if one possible cause of the lack of diversity on campus is a curriculum that has little appeal to minorities, then one solution might be to create more courses in things like African American literature. It's easy to imagine that an entire proposal might focus on this particular solution, suggesting a range of courses across the disciplines that might be added to recruit minority students.

Visual Prompts. Cluster a problem that concerns you. Build associations that help you to think about people you associate with the problem, situations when it's most obvious, how it makes you feel, things that might cause the problem, and even possible solutions.

Research Prompts. Research—reading, observing, and talking to people—can be enormously generative at any stage in the inquiry process, including the beginning. It's one of the best ways to discover a topic, and almost always generates information you can use later in your essay once you've chosen a topic. Try some of the following research prompts to help you along.

1. Interview your classmates about what they think are the biggest problems facing them as students. Interview student or faculty leaders or administrators about what they think are the biggest problems facing the university community. Do the same with community leaders.

2. Design an informal survey targeted to a particular group that you're interested in—students, student-athletes, local businesspeople, sports fans, migrant workers, and so on. This group may or may not be one to which you belong. Discover what they believe are the most serious problems they face.

3. Become a student of a local newspaper. In particular, pay attention to the letters to the editor and the local community pages. What seems to be a recurrent problem that gets people's attention? Clip articles, letters, or editorials that address the problem.

Judging What You Have

Feeling a little overwhelmed? See problems everywhere? It can be wearing to focus on what's wrong with your life, your university, and your community. But remember your ultimate goal is to write a proposal that suggests ways these problems might be resolved. You may have already explored some of these solutions, but if you haven't, don't worry; you'll get the chance later. Begin by scrutinizing the material you generated for possible topics.

What's Promising Material and What Isn't?   We've talked about some initial judgments you can make. Now look at the material you generated in the fastwrites, lists, research, or clusters and ask yourself which of the problems listed *do you care about the most,* or which *are you most interested in?* Once you've selected some tentative topics for your proposal, narrow them down using the following questions:

- *Is it a problem of consequence?* Remember that you want to develop a proposal that addresses a problem that isn't merely a private matter but one that others care about, too. To be sure, private problems can be problems of consequence; for example, more than a few women have boyfriends who are slobs if the number of pages on the Web that address the problem is any indication. But campus and community problems are much more likely to be problems of consequence. How do you know whether your topic qualifies? Ask yourself this question: Are there more than a few people who recognize the problem and take it seriously?

- *Is there an identifiable audience for proposals about how to solve the problem?* A key part of the assignment is writing your proposal with a particular audience in mind. Can you readily identify who that audience might be? An audience for a proposal about addressing tuition hikes might be the administration of your school, or even the president of the university. You might also write to fellow students, or more narrowly, the student governing body.

- *If you're not already an expert on the problem, or have few ideas about solutions, have others said something on the subject?* One reason to choose a particular problem is that you're an expert on it. Say you know a lot about the problems of being a nontraditional student on your campus because you just happen to be one. You may also have ideas about how to address the problems you care about. But sometimes, even if you know a lot about the problem, you may be pretty clueless about solutions. That's when research comes in. Quickly search the Web and relevant library databases to see if others have written about the problem, directly or indirectly. Also consider whether there might be experts to interview about the problem and its solutions.

- *Which subject offers you the most opportunity for learning?* Amy saw problem solving as an opportunity to learn. This is most likely to occur if you choose to write about something that you may not fully understand. These are almost always the best topics for an inquiry-based project.

Questions About Audience and Purpose. This assignment asks that you identify an audience for your proposal. When you do, consider what exactly might be your purpose with respect to that audience. Do you want to:

- *Inform* them about the problem and explore possible solutions?
- *Advocate* certain solutions as the best ways to solve the problem?
- *Inform and advocate,* dramatizing the problem because your audience may not fully appreciate and understand it, and then persuade them to support the solutions you favor?

Depending on which of the preceding purposes describe your intentions, your approach to writing the proposal may differ. For instance, if your purpose is to advocate certain solutions then you may assume that your readers are already familiar with the problem. The emphasis of your draft, therefore, will be to provide clear explanations and justifications for the solutions you propose. You might also exploit visual rhetoric—photographs of the problem—to better make your points. In an advocacy proposal, the key question to ask first is: *Who has the power to implement the solutions I advocate?* That's the audience you want to address.

On other hand, your audience may simply need to better understand the true nature of the problem you're writing about. You'll likely still address the audience in a position to do something about the problem, but you might lavish more attention on informing them about the problem before you propose solutions. The essay on procrastination you read earlier is a good example of a proposal like this. While we all might assume that we understand the problem of procrastination, the writer's research suggested that it was more complicated than most people thought.

If your purpose is to inform readers about the problem and explore possible solutions, then your treatment of the topic may vary. Not only might you spend time helping readers appreciate the problem, your proposal might also emphasize a whole range of possible solutions. The tone of the piece might also be more tentative.

Questions of Form. Although it might be premature to decide *the form* your proposal will take, sometimes an awareness of purpose and audience will suggest an approach. For example, if Cheryl's purpose is to advocate for a new nontraditional student center on campus, and her audience is school administrators, then she'll need to consider how best to get her message across. She might, for example, write her proposal in the form of a letter to the university's president. Gerald's proposal on how to deal with Internet plagiarism on campus might be written as a Web page that could be used as a link on the writing program or writing center's site.

Research Considerations. Research provides crucial support for most proposals and it is not too soon to do a little even at this early stage in the process. For example, say your topic is diversity on your campus. What have other universities done to create a curriculum that is "friendly" to minorities? What kinds of course offerings do successfully diverse campuses feature? A quick search on Google produced a whole range of relevant documents, including a description of a new degree program that emphasizes diversity, a profile of about fifty colleges and their efforts to promote it, and useful definitions of diversity and multiculturalism, including how these might be stated as goals of a college curriculum.

While it's useful to do some quick and dirty research on your topic (for which the Web is ideal), avoid the temptation to while away the hours doing it. Collect just enough information to get you thinking and to give you relevant material you might incorporate in the sketch.

Writing the Sketch

Begin by drafting a sketch of your proposal. It should:

- Be at least 500 to 600 words
- Have a tentative title
- Be written with the appropriate audience in mind
- Not only dramatize the problem, but advocate or explore solution(s).

You might also develop this sketch in a form that you think might be particularly effective given your purpose and audience. Perhaps your sketch will be a letter, for example, or the text of a brochure, or an ad, or an essay.

STUDENT SKETCH

Can you imagine a fast food restaurant that exclusively serves vegetarian food? Amy Garrett suggests that the food would be "deceptively vegetarian," exploiting all the recent advances in soy-based hamburgers and hot dogs so that consumers could satisfy their cravings for fast food without the fat. One of the best things she discovered in the sketch was a name for the franchise: the "Happy Cow."

If you were advising Amy in a workshop about how to revise this piece into a longer draft, what would you suggest? Where should she add more information, for example? Does she sufficiently establish the problem she's trying to solve, and does the solution seem convincing? How could it be more convincing in a next draft? What might lure you to the "Happy Cow" for a veggie burger?

THE HAPPY COW
Amy Garrett

Tom and I were talking about how I can never find good food in restaurants. We were sitting in Elmer's eating breakfast and I was so impressed that they have this page in the menu called "The Exercise Room" which offers low-fat and healthy food. I thought someone should open up a Weight Watcher's restaurant, not call it the Weight Watcher's Restaurant, but something catchy, and serve good healthy food, with their point values listed and all of the women and men who attend meetings would find out about the restaurant and they would take their families and friends. It wouldn't necessarily be obvious that the restaurant was affiliated with Weight Watchers. The food would be good, so no one would mind, they'd be better off for it really and the members of Weight Watchers would be comfortable and happy.

Then, I remembered Tom and I had talked about opening a healthy, vegetarian fast food restaurant. Not some hippy shack, but McDonald's and Burger King for vegetarians. A real fast food restaurant, same thing, only healthy and "deceptively vegetarian." I love garden burgers and smartground, the fake ground beef, because it tastes exactly like ground beef and I can have tacos and stuffed bell peppers. Everything from Morningstar Farms is wonderful, especially the breaded chicken patties, which are only 3 points for Weight Watchers and taste exactly, EXACTLY like a breaded chicken patty with the nasty processed chicken, only it isn't nasty processed chicken pulp, it's tofu and vegetable protein and good stuff.

We thought, what a great idea! We just need a financial backer. My little sister has a great head for business; she was a business major and now she's a leadership major, but she is still very smart with money. Oh, and we'd be sure to be kind to the Earth, everything would be recycled. It's cheaper anyway. Like 90% of our trash is recyclable, we're just too lazy. Working as a cook for 8 years I've seen every single restaurant I worked at throw all of their trash away, even break down all of the cardboard and not stack it to take to the recycling plant, but throw it away too. It's infuriating. Even in the National Parks!

4   Yep. It made me mad too, but they said that it was too expensive. Someone needs to put some corporate money into these changes. There is no way that it is really too expensive to save the Earth. It's too expensive to let it go to waste one can and one box at a time. But obviously we don't care, we don't even take care of our own bodies, why would we take care of the Earth? See, that's why it's such a great idea. People are lazy, they need someone to do it for them. Most people know that they need to eat better and be more conscientious, but they just don't do it. Too busy, too lazy, too stuck in their routine. So, we'll make it super, fast food easy. And then, when the slow changes start to happen, people will feel better and then start taking a stand. It's proactive. Instead of complaining and waiting for everyone to change all at once, we'll give them a little push and hope for some realizations to dawn.

5   We'd call it The Happy Cow because we wouldn't destroy the Earth, our bodies or sweet, innocent cows, who have a lot of good karma coming for the way they've been treated the last 100 years or more! In fact we could use a cow as the mascot; McDonald's uses a happy clown, why not a happy cow?

Moving from Sketch to Draft

Prepare your sketch for revision by assessing it yourself and inviting comments from peers in workshop.

Evaluating Your Own Sketch. Before your proposal is subject to peer review, answer the following questions. Your instructor may ask you to hand in your responses with your sketch or simply make an entry in your notebook.

1. Assume that you're a reader who might be critical of your proposals. What do you say in the sketch that such a reader might disagree with? What might those objections be? Have you adequately responded to them or addressed them in the sketch?

2. Are there parts of the problem you're addressing here that you don't understand yet? Are there things about the solutions you propose that you need to know more about? What are they?

3. Have you changed your mind about anything on this topic after writing the sketch? If so, what?

Questions for Peer Review. Since the assignment asks you to draft your proposal with a particular audience in mind, your workshop discussions may require a bit more imagination than usual. As when you evaluated your own sketch, you may have to ask your peer reviewers to imagine themselves as the readers you want them to be. For example, suppose your

![] WRITING WITH COMPUTERS

TRACKING CHANGES TO A DRAFT

The track changes function of today's word processors offers you a fast and efficient way to record additions and deletions made to a draft. You can usually find this function under the tools menu. After being initiated, it will show changes, on screen, on a printed page, or both, by inserting a vertical line in the left margin and by using a stylistic treatment to indicate the deletions and additions. In the example below, the changed text is presented in blue, the deleted text is struck out, and the added text is underlined.

> ~~My name is shmael~~. <u>Call me Ishmael.</u> Some years ago—never mind how long precisely—having little or no money in my purse, and nothing of particular to interest me on shore, I thought I would sail about a little and see the watery part of the world.

After you finish revising the draft, you can accept or reject any or all of the changes that you have made. When you accept a change, the deleted text disappears and the added text is reformatted to look like the original. When you reject a change, the text automatically goes back to the original. With some word processors you can even use the track changes function to identify the differences between separate drafts.

Use the track changes function if you need to show someone else, perhaps an instructor or a co-author, your specific revisions to a draft. Also, if you struggle to write a first draft and then find yourself reluctant to make changes when it comes time for revision, you may find this tool liberating. After all, why worry about changing the first draft when you can see the deleted text on the screen and can easily reject any of your changes?

proposal addresses the need for more student housing on and around campus. Who has the power to implement this solution—an off-campus housing complex—that you propose? Probably not fellow students. Your proposal might be a letter to administrators at the school or perhaps the president of the university or the dean of student services. In that case, the students in your peer group should know that they need to transform their identities to fully appreciate what you're trying to say. They have to imagine themselves a dean or president. How might such a person respond to your proposal?

Begin your peer review session clarifying your audience. Then the group might discuss the following questions about your sketch.

- After reading the sketch, can you say back the problem you believe that the sketch is addressing and why this solution(s) is the best one?

- Is the solution(s) offered sufficiently justified?

- Can you imagine other solutions the writer might consider?
- What part of the proposal did you find most interesting?
- Given the purpose and audience of the proposal is there another form it might take?

Reflecting on What You Learned. *While* your proposal sketch is being peer reviewed, record the comments. Draw a line down the middle of a journal page, and on the left side jot down every suggestion or comment about the sketch that you hear—everything, even if you don't agree with it. Following the workshop, fastwrite on the right side about the suggestions that make the most sense to you. Explore how you might follow those suggestions and how they might change your approach to the next draft.

Research and Other Strategies: Gathering More Information

Unless you're an expert on the problem you're writing about, you're going to need to do more research. While the quick and dirty research you did earlier might have given you enough information to draft the sketch, at the very least you'll likely need to fill gaps in your explanation of the problem or more fully justify or explore alternatives to the solutions you propose. Where should you look?

- *Exploit local publications.* Since the assignment asks you to choose a topic of local interest, then sources such as the local daily newspaper, government reports, university policies, and so on may be important sources for your proposal. Some of these, like local newspapers and government documents, may be available in your campus library. For example, my school has microfilm copies of the Boise paper, the *Idaho Statesman,* indexed on electronic database. Many school policies and reports are also offered on university Web pages.
- *Interview experts.* In Chapter 5, you practiced interview skills. Here's a chance to put them to use again. One of the most efficient ways to collect information for your revision is to talk to people who have knowledge about the problem. These may be experts who have researched the problem or people affected by it. A proposal on dealing with binge drinking on campus, for example, would benefit enormously from information gleaned from an interview with a professor who studies student behavior or someone at the local hospital who has dealt with alcohol poisoning. Interviews with students who indulge in binge drinking might also be useful. What do they think of the solutions you propose?

- *Search for experience with similar solutions elsewhere.* If your proposal is calling for an education program on binge drinking, what other universities might have tried it? What was their experience? Some of this information is on the Web. Search for information using the keywords that describe the problem you're writing about ("binge drinking"), and try adding a phrase that describes the solution ("binge drinking education programs"). Also check library databases that might lead you to articles in newspapers, magazines, and journals on the problem and its solutions. A quick search on one database at my own library, *InfoTrack,* produced 154 documents on binge drinking on campus.

Composing the Draft

All of the proposals you read earlier in the chapter begin by dramatizing or explaining a problem. The essay on eliminating the senior year of high school begins with an anecdote about Jess Rojas, a kid who's has a classic case of "senioritis." The authors of the "End of Tall Buildings" begin even more dramatically, with the image of the flaming World Trade Center towers minutes before their destruction. The implication is clear: Tall buildings like these are, among other things, easy targets.

Establishing the problem your proposal addresses and possibly even dramatizing the problem is a very common way to begin the form. As you begin your draft, consider how much you need to say in the beginning about the problem. If your readers aren't aware of the problem, should you dramatize it in some way, perhaps telling a story of someone who is a victim of the problem, or forcefully describing its effects?

Alternatively, you might want to begin the next draft by establishing your solution, a particularly strong beginning if your motive is advocacy and your audience already recognizes the problem. For example, here's the opening of a proposal to lower the drinking age as a way to battle binge drinking:

> As UVM and other universities work to address student alcohol abuse, one of the greatest hindrances they face is the fact that the legal drinking age is set at twenty-one, an age most college students won't reach until their junior or senior years.

> This perspective is built upon more than two decades studying college student drinking patterns and the history of alcohol use in this country and other cultures. My research has led me to believe strongly that perhaps the simplest and most dramatic action we could take to create more responsible alcohol consumption among college students would be to lower the legal drinking age to eighteen or nineteen. Young adults should be allowed to

drink in controlled environments such as restaurants, taverns, pubs and official school and university functions. In these situations—where mature and sensible drinking behavior would be expected—responsible alcohol consumption could be taught through role modeling and educational programs.[1]

Here are some possible approaches to beginning the next draft:

1. Like the opening of "End of Tall Buildings," consider an anecdote, image, description, or profile that dramatizes the problem you're writing about.

2. Lead with an explicit explanation of your proposal, simply stating the problem and advocating your solution.

3. Sometimes the form will influence your method of beginning. For example, if you're writing a brochure, the front panel—the first part readers will see—might include very little text and perhaps a graphic. A Web page might have similar constraints. A grant proposal might begin with an abstract. Choose a beginning that is appropriate to the form or genre of your proposal.

4. Frame the question or pose the problem. What is the question that you're trying to answer, or what part of the problem most needs a solution?

Methods of Development. What are some ways you might organize your proposal?

Problem to Solution. This is the most straightforward way to structure the draft, one that you'll commonly find in proposals of all kinds. In its simplest form, the proposal that works from problem to solution will devote varying emphasis to each, depending on how aware the intended audience is of the problem the proposal addresses. Obviously, more emphasis will be placed on establishing the problem or helping readers understand it if they lack awareness. In fact, some proposals, particularly those that are intended to be more exploratory than persuasive, might place considerable emphasis on problem posing. Other topics, such as binge drinking among college students or messy boyfriends, are well known. What the audience most wants to know is, *What are we going to do about it?* In those cases, the proposal might spend very little time discussing the problem and a great deal offering solutions.

The problem–solution structure need not be a simple two-step performance—first problem then solution—but rather a two-part harmony in which the writer moves back and forth between discussion of an aspect of

---

[1]Engs, Ruch C. "Should the drinking age be lowered to 18 or 19." Adapted from and in "Drinking on Campus," *CQ Researcher* 8 (March 20,1998):257.

the problem and a solution that addresses it. For example, Caroline Hsu begins "Is it Time to Ditch Senior Year?" by dramatizing the problem of senioritis by telling the story of senior Jess Rojas, then presents one solution—eliminating the final year of high school. However, the article then examines different views of both the problem and other solutions. This structure is particularly well suited to a problem that has a number of dimensions and multiple solutions.

Cause and Effect. The essay on procrastination earlier in the chapter is also a great example of how integral a discussion of causes and effects can be to effectively writing about a problem. It's only natural when presented with a problem to ask, *What causes it?* This can be an essential part of explaining the problem, and also a way to introduce solutions; after all, most proposals address in some way the causes of the problem. If one of the causes of procrastination is perfectionism, then a solution will be to have more realistic expectations, perhaps by lowering your standards.

Conventions of the Form. Because this assignment encourages you to consider writing a proposal that might depart from the usual essay form, the method of development might be determined, in part, by the conventions that govern that genre. For example, a proposal for a new course, say, on Chicano literature, written for the English department's curriculum committee, might have to follow a certain format, beginning with the course description followed by a justification. Sometimes these conventions might be more subtle or flexible. Web pages have no strict format, but Web designers do work from some general principles that you'd do well to learn before you design one. This can be one aspect of your research for this assignment. Sometimes merely looking closely at examples of a genre helps you infer some of the basic techniques of writing in that form.

Combining Approaches. As always, the methods of development often involve combining these and other approaches to structuring your draft. The sample proposals in this chapter are a mix of problem to solution, cause and effect, and genre-specific ways of organizing the material.

Using Evidence. What kind of evidence and how much of it you provide to justify the solutions you propose depends, as it often does, on your audience. *How much* evidence you need to provide depends on whether your intended audience is likely to be predisposed to agree or disagree with the solutions you propose. Obviously, if readers need convincing, you need to offer more justification. "Inquiring into Details: Evidence—A Case Study," illustrates how the *type* of evidence you provide is a function of audience, too. As you compose your draft, consider who your readers will be and the kinds of evidence they will find most persuasive.

🔍 INQUIRING INTO THE DETAILS

EVIDENCE—A CASE STUDY

Suppose a proposal argues that the university needs an alternative or independent film series. The proposal, in the form of a memo, is written to the Student Activities Board, a group of students who decide how to spend student fee money collected at registration. Which of the following types of evidence used to justify such a film series would be *most* persuasive to that audience?

1. The writer's personal enjoyment of foreign films.
2. A petition signed by 100 people, that supports the idea.
3. A quotation from Woody Allen about the educational and cultural virtues of independent films.
4. Information about the success of the independent film theater in town.
5. A quote from an English professor supporting the idea.
6. Estimate that shows that the cost of renting five independent films is half the cost of renting the same number of Hollywood films.
7. A survey of 200 students that indicates that 60 percent support the idea.
8. Data on good attendance at a similar series at another, larger university.

Choosing the strongest evidence in a proposal is an exercise in audience analysis. Is your audience likely to favor your idea, oppose it, or have no opinion? If they're neutral or opposed then you better be sure you not only have *appropriate* evidence but a lot of it. What makes evidence appropriate for a particular audience? *It is evidence they are most likely to believe.*

Workshopping the Draft

If your draft is subject to peer review, see Chapter 15 for details on how to organize workshop groups and decide on how your group can help you. The following journal activities and questions should help you make the most of your opportunity to get peer feedback on your work in progress.

Reflecting on the Draft. After you've finished the draft, make an entry in your journal that follows these prompts:

- If I was going to write this over again, the one thing I think I'd do would be. . .

- The most important thing I learned about writing a proposal so far is...

- The most difficult part of the process for me was...

- The biggest question I have about the draft is...

Your instructor may ask you to hand in your responses to these prompts with your draft.

Following the workshop session, repeat the method of reflection you used following peer review of your sketch, drawing a line down the middle of a notebook page and recording your group's comments and suggestions on the left side and later, your reactions on the right.

Questions for Readers. Again remind your workshop group about the particular audience you had in mind for your proposal. The group might then consider the following questions as they discuss the draft.

1. On a scale from 1 to 5, with 5 being "extremely serious" and 1 being "not serious at all," how would you describe your feelings about the severity of the problem addressed in this draft? Discuss the reasons for your ranking. Remember to imagine that you're the audience for whom the proposal was intended.

2. On the same scale, rank how convinced you were that the solutions proposed in the draft were the best ones. A 5 would indicate that you were totally convinced and a 1 would indicate that you weren't convinced at all. Discuss what was convincing and/or how the solutions offered could be more convincing. Be specific.

3. What questions did you have that weren't adequately answered in the draft?

Revising the Draft

You've been revising all along, of course, beginning with the work you did to find a topic and then narrowing it down to something interesting and manageable in a sketch. You were revising when you shared you sketch with peers and used what you learned to compose the next draft. You even were revising when you talked about the essay with your roommate or best friend. Revision involves "re-seeing" your subject, and there are many ways to do that as you go along. (See Chapter 14, "Revision Strategies," for more on new ways to think about revision.)

Proposals also have some fairly typical problems at this stage in the process, most of which can be addressed by repeating some of the steps in this chapter or selecting appropriate revision strategies in Chapter 14. Here are some questions to consider as you decide which of these strategies might be most helpful.

- Have you done enough to dramatize the problem if you're writing for an audience that may not recognize the problem? Should you do more to establish how your readers have a stake in solving the problem?

- How well have you justified your solution? Is there enough evidence? Is it appropriate evidence for your audience?

- Have you overemphasized one solution at the expense of others? Would your proposal be more balanced and persuasive if you considered alternatives, even if you ultimately reject them?

When you refer to Chapter 14, "Revision Strategies," for ideas on how to revise your draft following your workshop use the following table as a guide. Remember that a draft may present problems in more than one category.

Polishing the Draft

After you've dealt with the big issues in your draft—is it sufficiently focused, does it answer the *So what?* question, is it well organized, and so on—you must deal with the smaller problems. You've carved the stone into an appealing figure but now you need to polish it. Are your paragraphs coherent? How do you manage transitions? Are your sentences fluent and concise? Are there any errors in spelling or syntax? Section 5 of Chapter 14 can help you focus on these issues.

Before you finish your draft, make certain that you've worked through the following checklist:

- ❑ Every paragraph is about one thing.
- ❑ The transitions between paragraphs aren't abrupt or awkward.
- ❑ The length of sentences varies in each paragraph.

GUIDE TO REVISION STRATEGIES		
PROBLEMS IN THE DRAFT (CHAPTER 14)	**PART**	**PAGE NUMBER**
Unclear purpose ▪ Not sure what the essay is about? Fails to answer the *So what?* question.	1	633
Unclear thesis, theme, or main idea ▪ Not sure what you're trying to say? Proposal isn't clear?	2	639
Lack of information or development ▪ Needs more information to justify proposed solution. ▪ Evidence offered isn't persuasive enough?	3	646
Disorganized ▪ Doesn't move logically or smoothly from paragraph to paragraph?	4	650
Unclear or awkward at the level of sentences and paragraphs ▪ Does draft seem choppy or hard to follow at the level of sentences or paragraphs?	5	656

❑ Each sentence is concise. There are no unnecessary words or phrases.

❑ You've checked grammar, particularly verb agreement, run-on sentences, unclear pronouns, and misused words (*there / their, where / were,* and so on). (See the handbook at the end of the book for help on all of these grammar issues.)

❑ You've run your spell checker and proofed your paper for misspelled words.

STUDENT ESSAY

Earlier in this chapter, you were treated to Amy Garrett's proposal for a vegetarian fast food restaurant. Garrett revised her sketch by doing some research and expanding on her idea for "The Happy Cow," a place where soy substitutes can fool nearly any chicken nuggets lover, or so she hopes. Are you convinced?

Notice how Garrett organizes her essay to thoroughly integrate her discussion of the problem—American obesity—with the solution—her proposal for a vegetarian fast food restaurant, rather than using the simpler structure of first describing the problem and then explaining the solution. This makes for much more interesting reading. Quickly reread her sketch of this piece and you'll notice other changes she made. Is it a better essay? In what ways might it still be improved in another draft?

THE HAPPY COW

A Deceptively Vegetarian Restaurant

Amy Garrett

Not long ago, I decided to leave the herd of Americans—nearly one in two, according to the Institute of National Health—who are overweight. I lost around 40 pounds by cutting back on my portion sizes, eliminating high fat and fried foods and watching what I put on my food in the way of sauces, spreads and the like. I increased the amount of fresh fruit and vegetables that I eat and eventually I began an exercise routine. I feel great. Sure, I reward myself occasionally with ice cream or biscuits and gravy and cheesy eggs, but only occasionally.

As I've developed a routine, I've come to realize that I am making a lifestyle change, for the rest of my life, not just going on a diet. This brings me to my problem. It is really hard to find good places to eat out. There are a few here in Boise, but one is a natural foods place with really slow service and the others are pretty expensive. I have noticed that even conventional restaurants are getting better. In fact, I was at a local pancake house just today and noticed they devoted a whole page to healthy choices. They offered low fat cheese, garden burgers, nice salads and eggbeaters with veggie sausage, to name a few. I was thoroughly impressed. The trend is catching on, but I think it's time to make healthy habits a norm rather than a hassle.

3   It's hard to argue with the convenience of fast food, so why not a healthy vegetarian fast food restaurant? I'd call it "The Happy Cow." I would love to pull up to a drive thru and get a veggie burger with low fat cheese, lots of fresh toppings and know that the bun isn't slathered with grease and mayo. I'd like to be able to order a large side of carrot and celery sticks instead of fries. Why not give people the opportunity to drive through at The Happy Cow and spend $3.99 on a combo meal that wouldn't make us feel guilty? The "guilt-free" food I'd serve would never be fried, would be healthy (i.e., low fat), fresh and organic (when possible), and it would be deceptively vegetarian; in addition, all of our waste would be recycled and the food would be cheap. These four tenets would be the foundation of the restaurant: 1. body-friendly 2. animal-friendly 3. earth-friendly 4. budget-friendly. Every-one is happy and healthy!

4   Well, not yet. America is actually fat and sassy. The statistics are frightening. Nearly 109 million American adults, or about 55 percent, are overweight and 22 percent are obese ("Statistics"). Obesity can cause all kinds of health complications, which may explain the increase in heart problems. For example, two Canadian researches write that "one hundred years ago, 10 to 15 percent of Americans died from coronary heart disease and strokes. Today it's almost 50 per cent. Back then, less than 6 per cent died of cancer. Today the figure is 24 per cent" (Diehl and Luddington 1).

5   Since World War I, the American diet has changed. It has become high in saturated fats and animal products. People eat more meat than ever and meat today is raised in factory farms. According to John Robbins in *A Diet for a New America,* "factory farmed animals have as much as 30 times more saturated fat than yesterday's pasture-raised creatures" (Robbins 309).

6   The fast food industry is one of the major proponents of this way of life. Many combo meals rack up over 1,600 calories. For example, a Big Mac meal at McDonald's with Supersized Fries and Coke comes to 1,610 calories, which translates to 80% of the Recommended Daily Allowance (2,200 calories daily) ("Fast Food Guide"). Eating processed, greasy, fast food causes weight problems, as well as heart and blood pressure complications. People are beginning to become aware of the risks but there is a gap in the market. Where can health-conscious consumers enjoy the virtues of fast food—low-cost and convenience—but not its vices—high fat and calories? The Happy Cow, of course.

I like the name, Happy Cow, because every fast food restaurant needs a   7
good mascot. Ronald McDonald has ruled the playground for too long. Bessie
with her big eyes and long lashes will appeal to kids and the adults can feel
good about helping save the earth as well as keeping their weight and blood
pressure down.

Yes. Saving the Earth. Cattle and factory farming is detrimental to the   8
planet and humanity's well being. Among the ways that corporate farming directly affects the earth is through the loss of grains as livestock feed, which
could be used to feed the world population. Lester Brown of the Overseas
Development Council has estimated that if American were to reduce their
meat consumption by only 10 percent, it would free over 12 million tons of
grain annually for human consumption. That, all by itself, would be enough to
adequately feed every one of the millions of human beings who will starve to
death on the planet this year (Robbins 352).

This seems impossible, but when you look at how inefficient cattle are as a   9
food source, the numbers add up. According to Robbins, "for every sixteen
pounds of grain and soybeans fed to beef cattle, we get back only one pound as
meat on our plates. We feed these animals over 80% of the corn we grow and
over 95% of the oats" (Robbins 351). This seems ridiculous.

But that's not all.

> It takes nature 500 years to build an inch of topsoil. The U.S. Soil Conservation
> Service reports that over 4 million acres of cropland are being lost to erosion in
> this country every year . . . 7,000,000,000 tons. That's 60,000 for each member
> of the population. Of this staggering topsoil loss, 85 percent is directly associated
> with livestock raising. (Robbins 357, 358)

It's time to quit paying so dearly for beef and try soy instead.

Over the years many conscientious companies have developed meat sub-   10
stitutes which are delicious; some can even fool the hardiest meat eater with
or without the blindfold. There are ground beef substitutes which make the
spitting image of taco meat and stuff a bell pepper beautifully. Breakfast
sausages made from soy and vegetable proteins taste and feel like the real deal.
There is a breaded chicken patty made out of soy and vegetable proteins that
makes a mean sandwich and is not only low fat, but it would fool a Chicken
McNugget fan. I could go on forever. The Happy Cow would be a veritable
Taco Bell, McDonalds and KFC, minus the fat, the grease and the fear waiting
to happen. Breakfast menu included.

Another recent break-through in alternative foods has been the new deli-   11
cious low fat and fat free products available. The Happy Cow would proudly
serve fat free sour cream on their burritos without concern for taste because it
tastes great. Most dairy products that have been lightened are quite good.

Eggbeaters are wonderful and make nice omelets. Low fat cheese is great tasting and fresh veggies and fruit are always good. Imagine a fast food restaurant where you can get a fresh fruit cup with your chicken sandwich! The possibilities are endless.

12   The Happy Cow would take action to ensure our natural resources are endless as well by being conscientious about the products we use and what we do with our waste. We will support organic farmers when possible and use only recycled paper products. We won't even have trash cans, just recycling bins. But we aren't aiming for a politically charged atmosphere where our clientele would be pretentious, condescending and non-existent. We want the average Joe to try our food and realize that it tastes great and is great for him. I am not concerned with advocating vegetarianism, just good health in a healthy environment.

13   Ambience is important. We would make the restaurant look "normal," not boring or generic, but also not full of goddess paintings and nag champa smoke with a stoned server who forgets everything and takes his or her sweet time. We want every health conscious consumer to feel comfortable, even if they are new to the whole "healthy food" thing.

14   At The Happy Cow we want everyone to be able to afford our food. It is silly that soy products cost more than beef. The numbers don't add up; it is simply a matter of supply and demand. As the Happy Cow expands it will require the quantity of product that other fast food restaurants demand, making a new market for soy and vegetable products, thus reducing the price incrementally.

15   We will have value meals and 99-cent menus and Happy Cow toys and the Happy Cow mascot will make an appearance occasionally, waving a hoof at passing traffic. We will have birthday parties and progressive parents will love us, instead of feeling guilty about letting their kids eat at McDonald's. Kids won't know the difference and will grow up eating right and everyone will feel better for it. The brightly colored recycle bins will read "Have A Nice Day" and our customers probably will since they will have more energy, better vitamin intake and they won't be stuck on the toilet wondering why they ate that greasy double bacon cheeseburger and all of those fries.

16   American obesity is our biggest health problem. A Happy Cow or two, or perhaps a thousand in small hamlets to large cities could be one of the best ways to help more overweight Americans break away from the herd.

Works Cited

Diehl, Hans, and Aileen Ludington. "Lifestyle Capsules: Western Diet From Kernel to Colonel." <u>Alive: Canadian Journal of Health & Nutrition.</u> Apr. 1992: 1–23.

Robbins, John. <u>Diet For a New America.</u> Portsmouth, NH: Stillpoint Publishing, 1987.

"Statistics Related to Overweight and Obesity." <u>NDDK: Weight Control Information Group.</u> 12 Feb. 1998. 26 May 2003 <http://www.nikkd.nih.gov/health/nutrit/pubs/statobes.htm>.

"Fast Food Guide." <u>The Fast Food Nutrition Fact Explorer.</u> 26 May 2003 <www.fatcalories.com>.

EVALUATING THE ESSAY

1. Would you buy a soy burger at the Happy Cow? Why or why not?

2. Proposals often use visual elements to make them more persuasive. What pictures, graphics, tables, and so on would you suggest to be used for the next draft of the this essay?

3. Garrett uses two main arguments two justify her solution: A fast food restaurant with healthy food is needed because Americans are obese and too much land and too many resources are devoted to support industrial beef farms. Which of the two arguments works best in support of her proposed solution? How could she improve the weaker of the two arguments?

USING WHAT YOU HAVE LEARNED

1. Think about the proposal draft you've written, and all those that you've read, both in this chapter and in your workshop group. Spend one minute answering, in writing, the following question: *What do you need to know to write an effective proposal?*

2. Draw a line down the middle of the page of your journal. Compare the proposal with another genre of writing you've tried in this book, looking specifically at the following:

   • Degree of difficulty (which was harder, and why?)

   • Audience awareness (when and how much did you consider who you were writing for?)

   • Level of discovery (how much did you learn about your subject, or about yourself?)

   • Application to other situations (how much and what might you use from this form of writing and apply in other writing situations?)

3. What approaches or ideas will you borrow from proposal writing that you can apply to other forms of writing and other writing situations? Can you imagine revising an essay you've already written in another genre using what you've learned here?

Editorial cartoons like the one above by Ben Sargent often appear in newspapers on the op-ed page (opposite the editorial page). While such cartoons are intended to be funny, at their heart they also represent an effort to persuade people through argument. SARGENT © 2004 Austin American-Statesman. Reprinted with permission of UNIVERSAL PRESS SYNDICATE. All rights reserved.

Writing an Argument

8

WRITING TO PERSUADE PEOPLE

About one in four people regularly read newspapers, and among the pages they most often turn to are the editorial pages. These are two facing pages, often at the back of the front or local section that include newspaper editorials, letters to the editor, and editorial cartoons such as the one opening this chapter. The editorial pages of daily newspapers also typically include something called op-ed pieces—short persuasive essays that are literally on the opposite page from editorials, hence the phrase op-ed. Many fine writers have made their mark writing such essays, including Ellen Goodman, William Safire, George Will, Anna Quindlen, and Molly Ivins, to name a few.

At one time or another, you've probably read an op-ed piece although you probably didn't know to call it that. These argument essays are often concise treatments—500 to 1,000 words—of topics meant for a general audience. And they aren't just in newspapers. Magazines and online publications frequently publish comparable pieces, usually written by the publications' editors but sometimes submitted by their readers. At their best, argument essays of this sort are written with style and voice, much like this lead paragraph from the following piece by *Newsweek*'s Anna Quindlen on the impact of recent federal tax cuts:

> Public libraries have become the new poster children for governmental impecunity. Pick a town, any town, and the library, that great nexus of egalitarian self-improvement, is currently in trouble. Oakland, Calif. Swanson, Neb. York, Maine. Richland, Pa. Closing. Layoffs. Shortened

What You'll Learn in This Chapter

- New ways to understand the purpose of argument.

- Some differences between formal and informal arguments.

- The basic argument strategies most writers use.

- How to map an argument.

- How to avoid ten of the most common logical fallacies.

- Revision strategies to fine tune your argument.

hours. Cancelled programs. Matters have gotten so bad in the outposts of borrowed books that the reference librarian in Franklin, Mass., which a sign identifies as HOME OF THE FIRST PUBLIC LIBRARY, asked a reporter, perhaps only half kidding, how much the sign might fetch on eBay.[1]

While we often think of persuasive writing as stiff and formal, Quindlen's opening isn't like that at all (although the word "impecunity" might have driven you to the dictionary). She begins her argument about the impact of federal tax cuts by establishing an effect of that action that most readers can relate to—the risks tax cuts pose to neighborhood public libraries. While such essays are often informal, they are still persuasive forms, and as you'll see later, they often employ the same methods of more formal arguments. However, unlike formal arguments—the kind you might write in a logic or philosophy course—persuasive essays of this kind have a much larger audience. These essays are a great way to participate in public debates that affect your campus and community, and even your nation.

Getting into Arguments

In 1990, the book *You Just Don't Understand* became a runaway best-seller. Written by Deborah Tannen, a linguistics professor, the book analyzed the range of ways in which men and women struggle to communicate with each other. *You Just Don't Understand* made its author famous, and before long she was on the talk show circuit and the subject of newspaper profiles. Despite the many benefits of this exposure, Tannen became increasingly disturbed by how some of the TV shows were orchestrated. Some producers "insisted on setting up a television show as a fight," pitting Tannen against the host or another guest. Newspaper reporters aggressively pursued Tannen's colleagues trying to get them to criticize the book, and some in her discipline obliged, often misrepresenting her work. This experience inspired her 1997 book, *The Argument Culture,* in which she claims that the pervasive "adversarial spirit" in American culture subverts cooperation and community, and reduces complex issues to opposing sides. "Approaching situations like warriors in battle," Tannen writes, "leads to the assumption that intellectual inquiry, too, is a game of attack, counterattack, and self-defense."

Tannen doesn't believe that arguments are things to be avoided, but maintains that there are other ways of approaching subjects that deserve more attention. While this seems like a reasonable position, it's hard to avoid the feeling that being a good debater is what counts most in academia. Yet is argument really "war"?

It sometimes seems that way. It certainly *felt* that way to me at the dinner table those many years ago when I'd walk away from an argument with my dad and feel angry and defeated. Yet my mom's side of the family

[1]Quindlen, Anna. "The Bottom Line: Bogus." *Newsweek* June 30, 2003: 64.

is Italian American, and my best friends growing up came from predominantly Jewish households. In many of my relatives' and friends' homes, arguments were commonplace, raised voices the norm. At times I would find this upsetting, and wonder, "Why can't these people just get along?" But they often *were* getting along because argument and conflict in some cultures is an expression of commitment and caring. For example, Deborah Tannen notes that in many western European countries "agreement is deemed boring." I've often admired, for example, the French and Italian passion for national politics and their eagerness to share political views with each other, particularly disagreements. On the other hand, what Tannen calls "cultures of harmony," such as those of Japan and China, view open conflict and disagreement as a threat to the group. That does not mean that people always agree, but arguing is indirect, and sometimes undetectable to Western ears.

Obviously, culture influences our response to argument. In the United States, by and large, we argue a lot and in the open. We are a litigious society, and even children in the school yard threaten to "sue" each other. Combat metaphors are among the most common ways of talking about conflict—we attempt to "win" an argument, "find more ammunition" to support our position, "leap into the fray," or "attack" our opponent's position. It's hard for the gun-shy among us to feel comfortable participating in such verbal combat, one reason why some of my students retreat into silence when class discussion becomes the least bit combative.

For many of us, then, argument in civic and private discourse is bound by our *feelings* about argument—how comfortable we are with conflict, how confident we are in our ability to say what we think, and how strongly we feel about our opinions. These feelings are complicated by our beliefs about the purpose of argument. Sorting through these beliefs can help us discover new, perhaps more productive ways of approaching argument.

EXERCISE 8.1

What Does It Mean to Argue?

Which of the following statements best reflect your own ideas or beliefs about arguments? Check two.

- ❑ The main purpose of engaging in an argument is to win.
- ❑ Careful logic and reasoning always makes an argument effective.
- ❑ It's essential to think carefully about your audience and how they feel or think about the issue.
- ❑ Ignore your audience and just say what you believe to be true.
- ❑ Discussing views contrary to your own weakens your argument.

- ❑ It's important to avoid the appearance of uncertainty by never changing your main point.

- ❑ Arguing is a process of discovery.

- ❑ Arguments are most effective when the writer or speaker is passionate about her position.

- ❑ Everything's an argument: advertisements, short stories, research papers, reviews, personal essays, and so on.

- ❑ The process of making an argument basically involves picking a side and finding support for your position.

Poll the class on their responses to these beliefs about argument.

- • Which are most widely shared? Which are least widely shared?

- • Discuss why you believe certain of these beliefs are true. Are they true in all situations or just some?

- • Where do these beliefs about argument come from? Which seem most or least helpful as you consider writing an argument?

Making Claims

Arguments make claims, or assertions about which reasonable people might disagree. Argument expert Richard Fulkerson suggests that a claim (or *proposition,* to use his term) is a statement in which the response "I disagree" or "I agree" is a sensible reply. For example, "I have a headache" is a statement but not a claim because it would be goofy to agree or disagree with it. We'll talk more about this later, but on inspection it should be evident that any of the statements listed in Exercise 8.1 would seem to qualify as claims.

Obviously, we make claims all the time: "Robert is a narcissist." "That textbook is boring." "Osama bin Laden misread the Koran." It is human nature to make judgments, interpretations, and assertions about the people, things, and events that swirl around us. Since the beginning of this book, you have been encouraged to use evaluation as a way of inquiring as you responded to readings, images, your own work, and the work of others, asking questions such as: *What's my take on this? What do I find convincing? Do I see things any differently?* We usually describe this as the process of forming opinions.

But we rarely examine the *assumptions* that lurk behind these opinions or claims, those often-shadowy ideas that provide the platform from which we make our assertions about the way things are. For example, if Robert is a narcissist, what does the speaker assume are the behaviors that qualify for such a label? In other words, what *definition* of narcissism seems to provide the basis for the claim about poor Robert? If bin Laden "misreads" the Koran, what does that assume about the "proper" reading of that holy text?

One way to discover these assumptions is to use the word "because" preceding or following the claim. For example, "That textbook is boring *because* it spends too much time explaining things and not enough time inviting students to participate in the learning."

Evaluation is a way of inquiring that is fundamental to all kinds of persuasive writing. In this chapter, however, you'll learn to use evaluation along with other techniques for analyzing how to best present what you think. You'll learn to *build* an argument. And that doesn't necessarily mean picking a side and then developing your case, as you'll discover in the next section.

Two Sides to Every Argument?

TV talk shows stage "discussions" between proponents of diametrically opposed positions. Academic debating teams pit those for and those against. We are nurtured on language like "win" or "lose," "right" and "wrong," and "either/or." It's tempting to see the world this way, as neatly divided into truth and falsehood, light and dark. Reducing issues to two sides simplifies the choices. But one of the things that literature—and all art—teaches us is the delightful and nagging complexity of things. By inclination and upbringing, Huck Finn is a racist, and there's plenty of evidence in *Huckleberry Finn* that his treatment of Jim confirms it. Yet there are moments in the novel when we see a transcendent humanity in Huck, and we can see that he may be a racist, *but* . . . It is this qualification—this modest word "but"—that trips us up in the steady march toward certainty. Rather than either/or can it be both/and? Instead of two sides to every issue might there be thirteen?

Here's an example:

One side: General education requirements are a waste of time because they are often irrelevant to students' major goal in getting a college education—getting a good job.

The other side: General education requirements are invaluable because they prepare students to be enlightened citizens, more fully prepared to participate in democratic culture.

It's easy to imagine a debate between people who hold these positions, and it wouldn't be uninteresting. But it *would* be misleading to think that these are the only two possible positions on general education requirements in American universities. One of the reasons that people are drawn to arguing is it can be a method of discovery, and one of the most useful discoveries is some side to the story that doesn't fall neatly into the usual opposed positions. The route to these discoveries is twofold: *initially withholding judgment and asking questions.*

For instance, what might be goals of a university education other than helping students get a good job and making them enlightened citizens? Is it possible that a university can do both? Are general education courses the only route to enlightenment? Are there certain situations when the vocational motives of students are inappropriate? Are there certain contexts— say, certain students at particular schools at a particular point in their education—when general education requirements might be waived or modified?

All of these questions, and more, tend to unravel the two sides of the argument and expose them for what they often are: *starting points* for an inquiry into the question, *What good are general education requirements?*

To argue well is an act of imagination, not a picking of sides.

In presenting their arguments, then, the best argument essays make a clear claim, but they do it by bowing respectfully to the complexity of the subject, examining it from a variety of perspectives, not just two opposing poles. And you will come to appreciate that wonderful complexity by keeping an open mind.

MOTIVES FOR WRITING AN ARGUMENT

People often have quite strong feelings about arguing. Some of these feelings may originate, like mine, in negative experiences with a parent or other adult who seemed condescending when we expressed naïve or poorly developed opinions. Some scholars maintain that *agonistic* forms of argument, or those that seem to emphasize the contest between ideas and those who hold them, are particularly masculine approaches because they focus on power rather than cooperation, and proclaiming rather than listening. Yet there are people who have always loved arguing. My father did, and not just because he was confident in the game; my father genuinely enjoyed matching wits and logic, looking for faulty reasoning or indefensible claims.

Arguing is a civic duty. In fact, it is an essential activity in any democratic culture, and it's certainly a major element of academic discourse; academic argument is one of the key means of making new knowledge. Argument is also commonplace in relationships. Who hasn't argued with a spouse, a partner, a friend? In fact, one Web site on the Internet sponsored by the magazine *Psychology Today,* http://psychologytoday.psychtests.com/tests/arguing_style_r_access.html offers an arguing style test that analyzes how constructive you are in dealing with relationship conflicts. Therapists and counselors share the conviction that arguing is a natural part of intimate relationships and that much more harm can come from *avoiding* conflict rather than facing it. It's all in *how* you do it, they say.

Knowing how to argue well has practical value, even if you don't become a lawyer. It might help you make the best case to a local legislator to support the bill providing tuition relief to students, or even bargaining with the used car dealer for a better price on that black convertible Mazda Miata. Understanding argument helps you find the flaws in *other people's* arguments as well. Here in Boise, the local paper's editorial page routinely includes letters to the editor that are great case studies in logical fallacies and more rarely excellent examples of strong persuasive writing. I've learned to read these letters—as well as editorials and op-ed essays—with more care and thoughtfulness as I learned about the techniques of argument. This makes me feel better about the opinions I finally do come to hold because I know that I've listened carefully and thought critically.

Argument is an essential activity in any democratic culture, and it's certainly a major element in academic discourse; academic argument is one of the key means of making new knowledge.

Finally, the most important motive behind writing and studying argument is that you care about something. Throughout this book, it's been suggested that the personal motive for writing is the most powerful one of all; in this case, you're passionate about a question or an issue, and building a written argument channels that passion into prose that can make a difference.

THE ARGUMENT AND ACADEMIC WRITING

Argumentative writing is one of the most common of all academic forms. One reason for this is that the ability to argue well requires some command of subject matter. But there is another motive for mastering argument in academic settings, however, and it has less to do with proving that you know your stuff. Argument is really about trying to get at the truth.

This is an open-ended as well as a closed process; it involves suspending judgment *and* coming to conclusions, hearing what has already been said *and* discovering what you think. Dialectical thinking—a process you've applied to all kinds of writing in *The Curious Writer,* from the personal essay to the proposal—is just as useful in crafting an argument. It will help you discover what you think, consider other points of view, and shape your work so it's convincing to others. The dialectical process, along with those habits of mind central to academic inquiry—particularly suspending judgment and tolerating ambiguity—will help you as a writer get to the truth of things as you see it.

In college, the audiences for your arguments are often your instructors. As experts in a particular discipline, professors argue all the time. They're not simply trying to be contrary but trying to get at the truth. Arguing is the main way that the academic community makes knowledge.

Notice I used the word "make." While it often seems that the facts we take for granted are immutable truths—as enduring as the granite peaks I can see through my office window—things aren't often that way at all. Our knowledge of things—how the planet was formed, the best ways to save endangered species, the meaning of a classic novel, how to avoid athletic injuries—are all ideas that are *contested.* They are less mountains than the glaciers that carved them, and in some cases the sudden earthquakes that bring them down. The primary tool for shaping and even changing what we know is argument.

Richard Fulkerson writes that he "wants students to see argument in a larger, less militant, and more comprehensive context—one in which the goal is not victory, but a good decision, one in which all arguers are at risk of needing to alter their views, one in which a participant takes seriously and fairly the views different from his or her own." This is how I'd like you to approach argument within the persuasive essay. This form will challenge you to make arguments that might be convincing to a range of readers, including those who might not agree with your claims. The argument essay is also an invitation to consider how you feel about local issues and controversies as well as national or even international debates that might have some affect on how you live.

FEATURES OF THE FORM

Generally speaking, persuasive writing can take many forms. Indeed, reviews and proposals, two essays addressed earlier in this book, both represent different types of persuasive writing. The argument essay we are covering in this chapter, however, more obviously embodies persuasive writing than either of these two other forms. This essay typically makes explicit claims and backs them up with hard evidence. It also employs the well-established rhetorical devices and the reasoning of formal argumentation in the effort to sway readers to its point of view. However, unlike more formal academic papers, the argument you'll be writing in this chapter is intended for a more general audience. It's the kind of piece you might see in your local newspaper, or in a magazine. *Newsweek*'s "My Turn" column is an excellent example. (See Figure 8.1 for a comparison of argument essays.)

Here are some the features of the informal argument essay:

- *Argument essays are often relatively brief treatments of a topic.* Readers of newspapers and many magazines read fast. They want to quickly get the gist of an essay or article and move on to the next story. In addition, space is often limited, particularly in newspapers. As a result, the op-ed or opinion piece rarely exceeds 1,000 words, or about four double-spaced manuscript pages. Longer arguments may be harder to write because you have to provide deeper analysis of your key claims and more evidence, but don't underestimate the difficulty of writing persuasive essays like the op-ed. They must be concise, direct, and well-crafted.

- *Subject matter often focuses on issues of public concern.* The magazines and newspapers that publish argument essays typically report on news, or events, or issues that might affect a lot of people. Not surprisingly, then, writers of these essays are keen observers of public debates and controversies. While a nationally syndicated essayist such as George Will may write about the federal budget deficit or the need for more troops in Iraq, a locally grounded writer may focus on an issue af-

Rhetorical Context	Academic Argument Essay	Informal Argument Essay
Audience	Academic discourse community	Publication's readers
Speaker	You as a member of above	You as an authority on subject
Purpose	To demonstrate your authority	To make something happen
Subject	Of academic interest	Of community interest
Voice	Conventional, academic	Personal, informed
Research	Always	Usually
Citations	Yes	No
Length	Varies, usually 8–25 pages	Varies, usually 500–1000 words
How to read	Slowly, thoughtfully	Rapidly, mining for meaning

FIGURE 8.1 **A comparison of academic and informal argument.** (from Devan Cook, Boise State University)

fecting a university campus, city hall, or state government, although sometimes writers will find a local angle on a national controversy.

- *An argument essay has a central claim or proposition.* Sometimes we also call this a "thesis," a term that's a holdover from the scientific terminology that dominated American scholarship from the end of the nineteenth century. Classical arguments, the kind many of us wrote in high school, usually state this central claim or thesis in the introduction. But many arguments, particularly op-ed essays that rely on narrative structure or explore the answer to a question or problem, may feature the thesis in the middle or end of the essay.

- *The central claim is based on one or more premises or assumptions.* You already know something about this from the discussion earlier in the chapter. Basically, a premise suggests that something is true *because* of something else; it expresses the relationship between *what* you claim and *why* you believe that claim to be true. This is discussed at greater length later in the chapter.

- *The argument essay relies on evidence that a general audience will believe.* All arguments should make use of evidence appropriate for a particular audience. Academic writers in marine biology, for example, rely on data collected in the field and analyzed statistically because this kind of evidence is most persuasive to other marine biologists. Anecdotes or personal observation alone simply won't cut it in the *Journal of Marine Biology*. But the persuasive essay's more general audience finds a greater range of evidence convincing, including personal experience and observation. The writers of persuasive essays are likely to do the kind of research you use to write research papers—digging up statistics, facts, and quotations on a topic.

- *Argument essays usually invite or encourage a response.* This feature is most obvious in the advertisement, which is a visual argument that asks viewers to *do* something—buy a Jeep, or change toilet bowl cleaners. But op-ed essays often ask for or imply a course of action readers should take. An op-ed might attempt to change the views and behaviors of political leaders, or influence how people vote for them. It might urge support for a school bond issue, or encourage fellow students to protest against the elimination of an academic program. But even academic articles invite reader response in several ways: They encourage other scholars to examine some part of the question that wasn't addressed by the present research, or they offer claims that can be contested in other articles. Put simply, most argumentative forms are out to change people's behavior and attitudes.

- *Readers won't respond unless they know what's at stake.* An essential element of argument is establishing why a certain action, policy, or idea *matters*. How will opposition to the administration's strip mining policies in West Virginia and Kentucky make a difference in the quality of life in those states, but even more important, why should someone in Boise, Idaho, care? The best arguments are built to carefully establish, sometimes in quite practical terms, how a certain action, belief, or idea might make a difference in the lives of those who are the argument's audience.

ARGUMENT

One of the marvels of the online world is the sensation of witnessing an ever-changing landscape, filled with color, images, sound, and motion; it's a bit like gazing out a porthole at a kind of alternative universe, one that looks familiar and unfamiliar at the same time. It's easy to get confused about what's real and what's not in cyberspace, and to assume that the usual rules—the ones that govern our behavior in the "real" world—simply don't apply.

To some extent this is inescapable. Because we travel online in relative anonymity, we can essentially reinvent ourselves, breaking free in some respects of who we are offline. Yet we still do some of the same things online and off. We shop. We hold conversations. We get legal advice. We rent videos. In "Law and Order in the Wild, Wild Web," writer Amitai Etzioni argues that the growth of the Web, and the tendency to assume that the usual rules don't apply, has led to online lawlessness that has gotten out of hand. He proposes a "passport" that users might use as they travel on the Web that verifies their age and identity, among other things.

Etzioni's proposal is controversial. Even if you don't agree with the passport idea, do you agree that lawlessness on the Web is a problem? Can we ensure ethical conduct online without some kind of laws to regulate behavior? After all, isn't the rule of law necessary offline?

LAW AND ORDER AND THE WILD, WILD WEB
Amitai Etzioni

The spam that I have to plow through to find vital e-mail messages is but the latest sign that we must bring the rule of law to the online world. When my grandchildren are visiting, I fear leaving the room; they may misspell the bookseller Amazon or cue in the wrong White House website address and end up on some porn site displaying bestiality. 1

One of my law-school colleagues just joined a whole slew of others who believe that Americans have a God-given right to steal "intellectual property" - copy CDs and DVDs - without paying a penny, as long as they do it online. If they did the same at Blockbuster or Tower Records, they would be fined or jailed or both. 2

Meanwhile, my elderly mother is ordering medications on the Internet, circumventing her physician. 3

And I fully agree with shopkeepers who bitterly complain that their customers have to pay sales tax while those who purchase the same items online are exempt. It's high time to apply to cyberspace the same national and international laws by which we all abide. 4

Once upon a time, cyberspace was a small, exotic territory in which we could tolerate libertarians and cyberanarchists pursuing their fantasy of a world that governs itself. In those faraway days of 1996, John Perry Barlow, the Thomas Jefferson of the online world, authored "A Declaration of the Independence of Cyberspace," in which he stated: "You do not know our culture, our ethics, or the unwritten codes that already provide our society more order than could be obtained by any of your impositions." 5

In those days, it was possible to dream of a cybervillage, in which everybody behaved because they were good citizens. But now we live in a cybermetropolis that has turned into an online jungle, in which all that is socially taboo and illegal is found in abundance and vigorously pushed. 6

7   One can argue whether or not the German parliament was right in banning the sale of Adolf Hitler's "Mein Kampf" ("My Struggle"), or the French government in banning the trade in Nazi paraphernalia. But it is beyond argument that once a democracy has established a law, it is unacceptable for some shadowy creature to preempt national laws and make "Mein Kampf" available or trade Nazi paraphernalia (and everything else) online under the radar.

8   Once upon a time, the volume of transactions on the Internet was so small that the fact that it was tax exempt did not seriously damage bricks-and-mortar shops, although even then it was screamingly unfair. The volume of transactions in cyberspace, however, has swelled exponentially, such that Internet and phone sales are now responsible for 10 percent of the retail market.

9   And then there are small matters such as terrorists, drug lords, and pedophiles. They use cyberspace to meet and coordinate their activities, threatening all that is dear to us.

10   Law enforcement has made some inroads - true. Public authorities can, sometimes, trace the sources of e-mail messages, albeit only with great difficulty, and often they must navigate in a space in which the laws that allow them to proceed are murky, if not altogether antagonistic. Indeed, even when fully armed with a court order, law-enforcement officers find it very difficult to crack encrypted messages, now commonplace online.

11   What we need, first and foremost, is what Lawrence Lessig, author of "Code and Other Laws of Cyberspace," has called a cyberspace passport, an authenticated identity, a unique ID number, for all those who seek to travel in it.

12   They would not be required to present it when they engage in most activities, from sending messages to visiting most Web pages. All those who sell items that are banned for minors, however, would be required to check the age of buyers, as given in their passport. Those who send criminal messages would know that, following a court order, they could be readily identified. Those who ship medications would have to abide by the laws of the jurisdiction to which the drugs are sent, often requiring a prescription. And all those who open shop in cyberspace would be required to collect the appropriate tax and deliver it to the proper state.

13   The argument that abiding by "all these laws," which differ from state to state, would be very complicated, has merit. But if we can make do in the offline world, then those equipped with computers should be at least as capable of adjusting.

14   At the foundation of the law of free societies is the notion that all comers will be treated in the same manner. There is no reason my grandchildren, my aging mother, and all others should not be treated the same way in the online and offline worlds.

INQUIRING INTO THE ESSAY

Explore, explain, evaluate, and reflect about "Law and Order and the Wild, Wild Web."

1. In your journal, explore the idea that the offline and online worlds are different somehow. Fastwrite for five minutes in your journal, and follow your writing as you explore both the similarities and differences between these worlds. Are you a different person online? Do you behave differently? Do you think people operate under a different code of ethics? Should they?

2. Analyze Amitari's argument and explain two things: his claims and the premises or assumptions behind each one. To refresh your memory about these terms and what they mean, consult "Features of the Form" earlier in the chapter. What basic argument strategies does Amitari seem to use. (See "Inquiring into the Details: Some Basic Argument Strategies".)

3. How would you evaluate these claims and premises? Which have merit? Which don't? What might be your own claim about "lawlessness" on the Internet?

4. Do at least one more full reading of the essay, from beginning to end. While you do, pay attention to what you notice in the essay while rereading it that you didn't really notice in earlier readings. How does your own opinion about an author's argument influence the way you reread it? Do you read more selectively? Does the rereading reinforce what you already think or challenge it in some way?

INQUIRING INTO THE DETAILS

SOME BASIC ARGUMENT STRATEGIES

Argument from Generalization: What I've seen or observed of a particular group is true of the group as a whole. *Risk: Are you sure that what you've observed is typical of the larger population?*

Argument from Analogy: If it is true in one situation it's likely true in another similar situation. *Risk: Are the situations really similar?*

Argument from Cause: If one thing always seems present with something else, then one probably causes the other. *Risk: Is cause and effect really the relationship between the two things?*

Argument from Authority: If an expert said it, it's true. *Risk: Is the expertise of the authority really relevant to the question at issue?*

> **Argument from Principle:** This general principle (which most of us agree with) applies in this case. *Risk: Is there really agreement on the rightness of the principle, and does it actually apply in this specific context?*
>
> Adapted from Fulkerson, Richard. *Teaching the Argument in Writing.* Urbana, IL: NCTE, 1996.

ARGUMENT

With grace and intelligence, conservative columnist George F. Will writes about a range of topics from the federal budget to baseball. In this essay, Will strikes close to home for me—and possibly for you, too—when he sharply criticizes writing instruction in the United States, an approach he calls the "growth model," one that Will argues offers no "defensible standards" for good writing and emphasizes the "undirected flowering of the student's personality." He bemoans the absence of instruction in grammar and style.

You are the students Will is talking about in this op-ed essay. Does he accurately describe your experience in this and other writing classes? For example, do you also sense that process matters more than content in composition? Do you agree with Will's basic premise that students graduating from high school are "functionally illiterate?"

THE "GROWTH MODEL" AND THE GROWTH OF ILLITERACY
George F. Will

1   Summertime, and the living is easy. Schools are empty, so the damage has stopped. During this seasonal respite from the education system's subtraction from national literacy, consider why America may be graduating from its high schools its first generation worse educated than the generation that came before. Particularly, why is it common for high school graduates to be functionally illiterate, uncertain when reading, and incapable of writing even a moderately complicated paragraph?

2   Heather Mac Donald knows one reason: More and more schools refuse, on the basis of various political and ethical and intellectual theories, to teach writing. Her essay, "Why Johnny Can't Write," in the summer 1995 issue of

The Public Interest quarterly, is a hair-raising peek into what she calls "one over-looked corner of the academic madhouse."

Mac Donald, a contributing editor of the Manhattan Institute's *City Journal,* explains how the teaching of writing has been shaped by "an indi-gestible stew of 1960s liberationist zeal, 1970s deconstructionist nihilism, and 1980s multicultural proselytizing." Indeed many teachers now consider the traditional idea of teaching to be intellectually suspect and morally of-fensive because it is tainted by the authoritarian idea that there are defensi-ble standards and by the inegalitarian idea that some people do things better than others.

At a 1966 conference organized by the Modern Language Association and the National Conference of Teachers of English, the "transmission model" of teaching composition was rejected in favor of the "growth model." The idea of transmitting skills and standards was inherently threatening to the values of that decade—spontaneity, authenticity, sincerity, equality, and self-esteem. Education in the new era of enlightenment was to be not a matter of putting things into students—least of all putting in anything that suggested a hierarchy of achievement—but of letting things out. Nothing must interfere with the natural, undirected flowering of the student's personality. One interference would be a teacher cast as an authority figure rather than in the role of sup-portive, nurturing friend.

The "growth model" was, Mac Donald notes, impeccably liberationist: Who was to judge anyone else's "growth"? And that model "celebrated inartic-ulateness and error as proof of authenticity." This was convenient for evolving racial policies. In 1966 the City University of New York began the first acade-mic affirmative action program. Open admissions would soon follow, as would the idea that it is cultural imperialism to deny full legitimacy to anything called "Black English." Simultaneously came the idea that demands for literacy oppress the masses and condition them to accept the coercion of capitalism.

"Process" became more important than content in composition. Students would "build community" as they taught each other. A reactionary emphasis on the individual was replaced by a progressive emphasis on the collectivity. But, says Mac Donald, there have been difficulties: "Students who have been told in their writing class to let their deepest selves loose on the page and not worry about syntax, logic, or form have trouble adjusting to other classes." Thus a student at St. Anselm's College complains that in her humanities class, "I have to remember a certain format and I have to back up every general statement with specific examples."

Academic fads have followed hard upon one another, all supplying reasons why it is unnecessary—no, antisocial—to teach grammar and style. The de-constructionists preached that language is of incurably indeterminate meaning.

The multiculturalists, who preach the centrality of identity politics in every endeavor, argue that the rules of language are permeated by the values of the dominant class that makes society's rules and also makes victims. Mac Donald says, "The multicultural writing classroom is a workshop on racial and sexual oppression. Rather than studying possessive pronouns, students are learning how language silences women and blacks."

8   As student writing grows worse, Mac Donald notes, the academic jargon used to rationalize the decline grows more pompous. For example, a professor explains that "postprocess, postcognitive theory . . . represents literacy as an ideological arena and composing as a cultural activity by which writers position and reposition themselves in relation to their own and others' subjectivities, discourses, practices, and institutions."

9   Nowadays the mere mention of "remedial" courses is coming to be considered insensitive about "diversity," and especially insulting and unfair to students from American "cultures" where "orality" is dominant. So at some colleges remedial courses are now called ESD courses—English as a Second Dialect.

10   The smugly self-absorbed professoriate that perpetrates all this academic malpractice is often tenured and always comfortable. The students on the receiving end are always cheated and often unemployable. It is summertime, and the nation is rightly uneasy about autumn.

Inquiring into the Essay

Use the four methods of inquiry to think about Will's essay.

1. For five minutes, fastwrite about your own experience with writing instruction by telling the story of the teachers or teachers that had the most impact on how you think about yourself as a writer and reader.

2. Describe the argument that Will makes in this essay. Begin with a summary of one of his basic claims, then a reason behind the claim, and then list the evidence he offers to support them both. Compare these with other students in the class and analyze the effectiveness of Will's argument. What are the strongest elements of his argument? The weakest?

3. Compose a 250-word letter to the editor that responds in some way to Will's article.

4. Reflect on your own experiences in this composition course. Would Will be scornful of this course—and perhaps this text—and its approach to teaching writing? What have been the most and least effective approaches to teaching reading and writing that you've experienced in high school, or perhaps even in this class?

ARGUMENT

The essay that follows is one of a collection by foreign writers who were asked by the editors of the journal *Granta* to write about what they think of the United States. It's a fascinating collection for many reasons. Americans are a fairly insular people, less likely than many citizens of others nations to be multilingual and to engage in international travel. We are justifiably proud of our American heritage and to others this pride can seem like indifference to other cultures. More often than not, we are surprised by how we are perceived around the world. Therefore, it's instructive to hear voices such as that of Doris Lessing, a British novelist, who comments on her perception of America, especially since the events of September 11, 2001, a tragedy that turned the world's gaze on the United States and our own outward. In this essay, Lessing argues that in America "everything is taken to extremes," and at one point in the essay she suggests that that might also be said of our reaction to the events of September 11. Do you find her argument convincing? Why or why not?

WHAT WE THINK OF AMERICA
Doris Lessing

Busily promoting my book *African Laughter* I flitted about (as authors do) on the East Coast, doing phone-ins and interviews, and had to conclude that Americans see Africa as something like Long Island, with a single government, situated vaguely south ('The Indian Ocean? What's that?'). In New York I had the heaviest, most ignorant audience of my life, very discouraging, but the day after in Washington 300 of the brightest best-informed people I can remember. To talk about 'America' as if it were a homogenous unity isn't useful, but I hazard the following generalizations.

America, it seems to me, has as little resistance to an idea or a mass emotion as isolated communities have to measles and whooping cough. From outside, it is as if you are watching one violent storm after another sweep across a landscape of extremes. Their Cold War was colder than anywhere else in the West, with the intemperate execution of the Rosenbergs, and grotesqueries of the McCarthy trials. In the Seventies, Black Power, militant feminism, the Weathermen—all flourished. On one of my visits, people could talk of nothing else. Two years later they probably still flourished, but no one mentioned them. 'You know us,' said a friend. 'We have short memories.'

Everything is taken to extremes. We all know this, but the fact is seldom taken into account when we try to understand what is going on. The famous Political Correctness, which began as a sensible examination of language for hidden bias, became hysterical and soon afflicted whole areas of education. Universities have been ruined by it. I was visiting a university town not far from New York when two male academics took me out into the garden, for fear of being overheard, and said they hated what they had to teach, but they had families, and would not get tenure if they didn't toe the line. A few years earlier, in Los Angeles, I found that my novel *The Good Terrorist* was being 'taught.' The teaching consisted of the students scrutinizing it for political incorrectness. This was thought to be a good approach to literature. Unfortunately, strong and inflexible ideas attract the stupid . . . what am I saying! Britain shows milder symptoms of the same disease, so it is instructive to see where such hysteria may lead if not checked.

4   The reaction to the events of 11 September—terrible as they were—seems excessive to outsiders, and we have to say this to our American friends, although they have become so touchy, and ready to break off relations with accusations of hard-heartedness. The United States is in the grip of a patriotic fever which reminds me of the Second World War. They seem to themselves as unique, alone, misunderstood, beleaguered, and they see any criticism as treachery.

5   The judgement 'they had it coming', so angrily resented, is perhaps misunderstood. What people felt was that Americans had at last learned that they are like everyone else, vulnerable to the snakes of Envy and Revenge, to bombs exploding on a street corner (as in Belfast), or in a hotel housing a government (as in Brighton). They say themselves that they have been expelled from their Eden. How strange they should ever have thought they had a right to one.

Inquiring into the Essay

Explore, explain, evaluate and reflect on Lessing's essay.

1. Explore your reaction to the essay by playing the believing game and the doubting game. In your notebook, fastwrite for five minutes about the possible merits of Lessing's argument. How can you understand her thesis that Americans "take things to extremes?" What connections does this have to your own experiences and observations? Then fastwrite for five minutes and play the doubting game. What is she ignoring? Where do you take issue with her claims or her evidence? How might things be seen another way?

2. Presenting an outsider's perspective, such as the one in Doris Lessing's commentary on America, is a tough rhetorical position to be in, particularly if you're writing for an audience of insiders, in

this case American readers. Explain why this is a difficult position from which to argue and also offer your analysis of how well she manages to overcome the challenge.

3. Reread the last paragraph of the essay. Is it true that an American reaction to the events of September 11, 2001, was to feel as if we had been "expelled from [our] Eden?" Evaluate that idea using evidence from your own experiences and observations in response to that event.

4. How difficult was it to play the doubting game and believing game in Question 1? Why might it be important to set aside your own support or opposition to an argument and either try on doubting or believing, a stance you wouldn't be inclined to take unless forced to?

 SEEING THE FORM

GUESS.COM AD

If you didn't happen to know that Guess is a clothing retailer, you might think that the Web ad that follows is selling something else. Maybe good luck? It's selling both, of course—clothes and a certain kind of good fortune that wearing the clothes seems to promise. This ad has very little

text, relying mostly on the image and what it implies. We rarely stop to analyze the persuasive power of advertisements like this one, but they are extremely well-crafted and can teach us a lot about how to motivate people to do something.

While rhetoric experts turn to Aristotle for the classical foundations of argument, modern advertisers have been researching persuasion for more than seventy years, ever since the rise of the mass media as a means for reaching potential consumers. These studies on behalf of advertisers have produced a wealth of research on what appeals work and when.

Persuasion theory may have begun with Aristotle's *Rhetoric,* but modern researchers have made it a science. Still, Aristotle and other classical rhetors laid the foundation for the study of persuasion. One of Aristotle's most important contributions to our understanding of argument is shown in Figure 8.2, a variation of the rhetorical triangle you learned about in the beginning of the book.

Each of these terms—ethos, logos, and pathos—represents different kinds of persuasive appeals. *Ethos* refers to the character of the speaker (or writer), and how he or she comes across to the audience. *Logos* is the logic and methods of reason used to make an argument. Pathos is an appeal to the audience's (or reader's) emotion. All three appeals may be at work in any argument, but certain kinds of persuasive appeals, like advertising, emphasize one over the other.

Examine the Guess.com ad. Which of the three appeals—logos, pathos, or ethos—does this visual argument seem to emphasize? In what ways does it seem to incorporate the other features of form? For example, is it making some sort of claim? What implicit assumption is the ad making that might motivate you to click your mouse and place something in an electronic shopping cart? If traditional arguments offer evidence to support a claim, what's the visual evidence here?

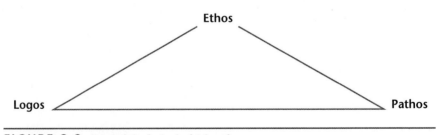

FIGURE 8.2 Aristotle's rhetorical triangle.

▦ THE WRITING PROCESS ▦

INQUIRY PROJECT: Writing an Argument

Now that you've explored various approaches to persuasion and argument, try your hand at writing an argument essay. Remember that these are brief (700- to 1,000-word) essays meant for a general audience. Imagine, for example, that you're writing an op-ed piece for the campus newspaper, the local daily, or *The New York Times.* Your essay should be lively and logical, with a strong personal voice, and also have the following features:

- It focuses implicitly or explicitly on a question. This is always the starting point for inquiry in any genre. In an argumentative essay, you are providing evidence to support a particular answer to this question.

- The essay makes clear premises and claims, including one central claim around which the draft is organized. In other words, *the essay should be clear about what it is asking its readers to do or to believe.*

- It provides specific and appropriate evidence in support of the claims, including research when relevant.

- The essay should address one or more of the counterarguments offered by those who take a different position from yours.

Thinking About Subjects

If you haven't yet figured out a way to make your composition instructor's eyes roll, announce that you want to write an argument essay on gun control. Gun control, abortion rights, and other hot-button public controversies often make the list of banned topics for student essays. This is not because they aren't important public debates. Instead, the problem is much more that the writer has likely already made up her mind and sees the chance to ascend to a soapbox. In addition, polarized debates produce such a mass of information that it's difficult for a writer to locate some territory in the topic that isn't already filled with voices repeating the same things to each other. There is so much background noise that it's almost impossible to hear yourself think.

Now, I have my own favorite soapboxes; people with strong convictions do. But as you think about subjects for your essay consider that the soapbox may not be the best vantage point for practicing dialectical thinking. If you've already made up your mind, will you be open to discovery? If you just want to line up ducks—assembling evidence to support an unwavering belief—will you be encouraged to think deeply or differently? Will you be inclined to filter the voices you hear rather than consider a range of points of view?

The best argument essays make a clear claim, but they do it by bowing respectfully to the complexity of the subject, examining it from a variety of perspectives, not just two opposing poles.

The best persuasive essays often emerge from the kind of open-ended inquiry that you might have used writing the personal essay. What do you want to understand better? What issue or question makes you wonder? Be alert to possible subjects that you might write about *not* because you already know what you think, but because you want to find out. Or consider a subject that you might have feelings about but feel uninformed, lacking the knowledge to know exactly what you think.

Generating Ideas

Begin exploring possible subjects for an argument essay by generating material in your notebook. This should be an open-ended process, a chance to use your creative side by jumping into the sea and swimming around without worrying too much about making sense or trying to prejudge the value of the writing or the subjects you generate. In a sense, this is an invitation to play around. Later, you can judge the material you've generated and choose a topic that interests you.

Listing Prompts. Lists can be rich sources of triggering topics. Let them grow freely, and when you're ready, use an item as the focus of another list or an episode of fastwriting. The following prompts should get you started.

1. In your journal, make a quick list of issues that have provoked disagreements between groups of people in your hometown or local community.

2. Make a quick list of issues that have provoked disagreements on your college's campus.

3. Make another list of issues that have created controversy between groups of people in your state.

4. Think about issues—local, statewide, regional, national, or even international—that have touched your life, or could affect you in some way in the following areas: environmental, health care, civil rights, business, education, crime, or sports. Make quick list of questions within these areas you wonder about. For example, *Will there be enough drinking water in my well if the valley continues to develop at this rate? Or Will I be able to afford to send my children to the state college in twelve years? Or Do new domestic antiterrorism rules threaten my privacy when I'm online? Or Will I benefit from affirmative action laws when I apply to law school?*

5. Jot down a list of the classes you're taking this semester. Then make a quick list of topics that prompt disagreements among people in the field that you're studying. For example, in your political science class did you learn that there are debates about the usefulness of the electoral college? In your biology class, have you discussed global warming? Or in your women studies class did you read about Title 9 and how it affects women athletes?

Fastwriting Prompts. Remember, fastwriting is a great way to stimulate creative thinking. Turn off your critical side and let yourself write "badly." Don't worry too much about what you're going to say before you say it. Write fast, letting language lead for a change.

1. Write for five minutes beginning with one of the questions you raised in Question 4 of the Listing Prompts. Think through writing about when you first began to be concerned about the question, how you think it might affect you, what you currently understand are the key questions this issue raises. Do you have tentative feelings or beliefs about it?

2. In a seven-minute fastwrite, explore the differences between your beliefs and the beliefs of your parents. Tell yourself the story of how your own beliefs about some question evolved, perhaps moving away from your parent's position. Can you imagine the argument you might make to help them understand your point of view?

3. Choose an item from any of the lists you generated in the "Listing Prompts" as a starting place for a fastwrite. Explore what you understand about the issue, what are the key questions, and how you feel about it at the moment.

ONE STUDENT'S RESPONSE

BEN'S JOURNAL

FASTWRITE

Why do students seem so apathetic about politics?

We're in the midst of presidential elections and I can't seem to get anyone interested in talking about it. I wonder why that is? Are college students more cynical about politics and politicians than other groups? It seems like it to me. I can think of a few reasons right off the bat. First, college students are mostly young (though certainly not all at this school) so they don't have the habit of going to the polls.

> Whenever a generation loses the habit of voting, I'll bet the next generation is even more likely to be apathetic. I also think my generation has seen so few effective politicians. My dad talks about being inspired by the likes of JFK but I can't think of too many national politicians that have inspired me as much as JFK inspired him. I also wonder if there is that basic sense of powerlessness. We just don't feel like much of anything makes a difference. I wonder if that is also reflected in volunteerism. Do students volunteer less than they used to? Have to check on that. I guess I just find politics kind of interesting. I wonder why? Hmmm. . . I think it had something to do with my Dad. But I guess I also have this basic belief in voting as an important part of being a citizen. Seems like one of the best ways to be patriotic. . .

Visual Prompts. Sometimes the best way to generate material is to see what we think represented in something other than sentences. Boxes, lines, webs, clusters, arrows, charts, or even pictures and sketches can help us to see more of the landscape of a subject, especially connections between fragments of information that aren't as obvious in prose.

Find an advertisement, poster, or other image with a persuasive purpose and create an argument map (see Figure 8.3, which maps the Guess.com ad on page 301). Choose an image that bothers you for some reason. By visually graphing its implicit argument, you might discover ways to offer a critique or a counterargument in your own essay. Use the first box of the argument map to summarize the main claim of the image you've selected. In the next box, list the (often implicit) reasons or premises behind the claim. Use the word "because" to tease this out. In the next box put the two together, creating a premise and a claim, and then follow this up by listing the evidence the image provides to support the premises and claim. Now use your map to generate a list of quick responses to some of the following questions: *Do you agree with the claim? Do you agree with the premises? Which seems most suspect? Why? What might be a more truthful claim? What might be more accurate premises? Is this an argument you've seen elsewhere? Do the claims and premises represent a way of seeing the world typical of a particular social group? How would you redesign the ad to make it more truthful? What is your argument against this argument?* Use the lists and fastwrites generated from analyzing your argument map to develop an argument of your own.

Research Prompts. By definition, argument essays deal with subjects in which people beyond the writer have a stake. And one of the best ways to collect ideas about such issues is to do a little quick and dirty research. Try some of the following research prompts:

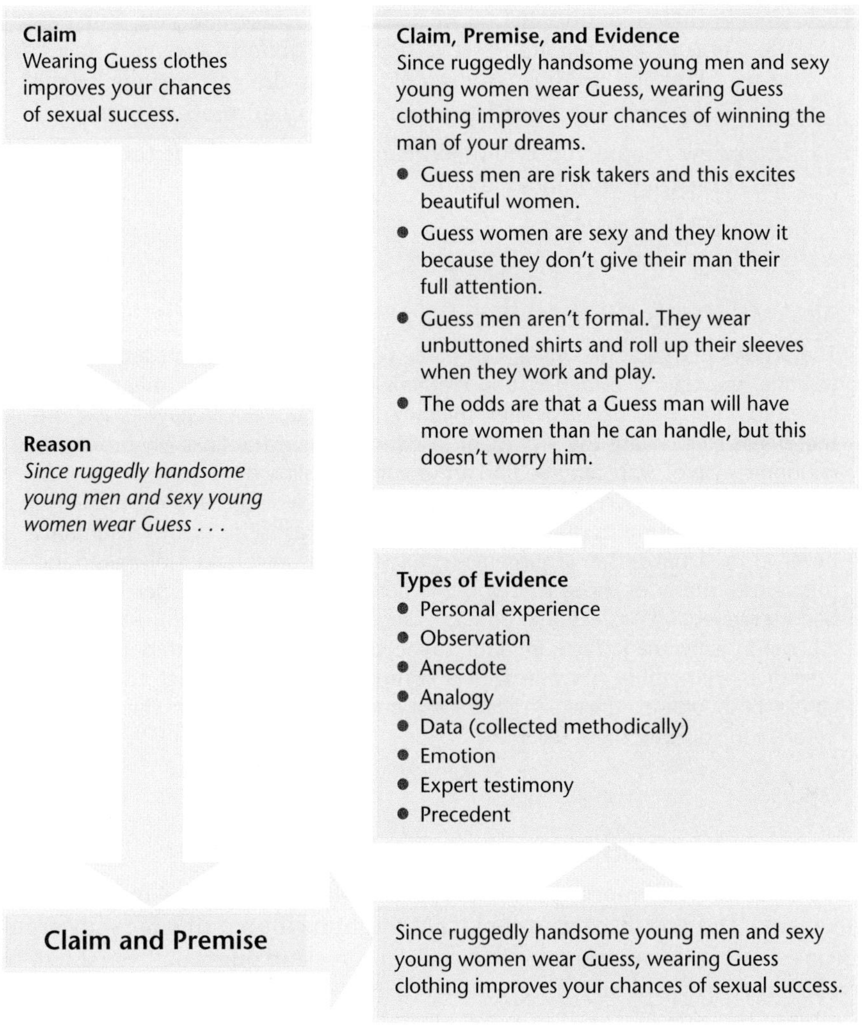

Claim
Wearing Guess clothes improves your chances of sexual success.

Reason
Since ruggedly handsome young men and sexy young women wear Guess . . .

Claim and Premise

Claim, Premise, and Evidence
Since ruggedly handsome young men and sexy young women wear Guess, wearing Guess clothing improves your chances of winning the man of your dreams.

- Guess men are risk takers and this excites beautiful women.
- Guess women are sexy and they know it because they don't give their man their full attention.
- Guess men aren't formal. They wear unbuttoned shirts and roll up their sleeves when they work and play.
- The odds are that a Guess man will have more women than he can handle, but this doesn't worry him.

Types of Evidence
- Personal experience
- Observation
- Anecdote
- Analogy
- Data (collected methodically)
- Emotion
- Expert testimony
- Precedent

Since ruggedly handsome young men and sexy young women wear Guess, wearing Guess clothing improves your chances of sexual success.

FIGURE 8.3 An Argument Map.

1. Spend a few days reading the letters to the editor in your local paper. What issue has people riled up locally? Is there one that you find particularly interesting?

2. Do a Web search to find op-ed essays written by one or more of the following national columnists: Ellen Goodman, Cal Thomas, George Will, David Broder, Nat Hentoff, Mary McGrory, Molly Ivins, Bob Herbert, or Clarence Page. Read their work with an eye toward topics that interest you.

3. Google terms or phrases on an issue that interests you. For example, *"online gaming adolescent boys"* or *"federal tax cuts local library."* Did you produce any results that make you curious, or make you feel something about the issue, one way or another?

4. Interview people you know—on campus or off—about the public issues that they care most about.

WRITING WITH COMPUTERS

ARGUMENTS ON THE INTERNET

The arguments you find online can differ significantly from print arguments. For one, the claims, evidence, and credits within an online argument can be linked to other Web pages or sites, meaning that you will also have to explore these links to evaluate the argument (a difficult task if the links are broken or no longer active). You can also find arguments in online discussion groups and Web logs (blogs). Here, multiple participants, not a single author, influence the way that arguments take shape and arrive at conclusions (some arguments never do!). Unlike the arguments you will find in books, journals, and magazines, many of those that you will encounter on the Internet have not been screened by professional editors. The claims of these arguments, then, are more likely than those in print to be based on unsupported beliefs or prejudice—remember, anyone with a computer and an Internet connection can publish online. Carefully evaluate arguments you find on the Internet before you consider them reliable.

Judging What You Have

Shift back to your more critical mind and sift through the material you generated. Did you discover a topic that might be interesting for your argument essay? Did you stumble over some interesting questions you'd like to explore further? Did anything you wrote or read make you *feel* something? Evaluate the raw material in your journal and keep the following things in mind as you zero in on a topic for your argument essay.

What's Promising Material and What Isn't? Let's take a critical look at the subjects you've generated so far; what promising topics might be lurking there for an argumentative essay? Consider some of the following as you make your choice.

- *Interest.* This almost goes without saying. But you were warned earlier about seizing on a topic if you already have strong convictions about it. Do you already know what you think? If so, why not choose a topic that initially invites more open-ended inquiry? On the other hand, it matters a lot whether you *care*. What topic might touch your life in some way? Do you have some kind of stake in how the questions are answered?

- *Brevity.* One of the most common flaws of student drafts in all genres is that they attempt to cover too much territory. A more *limited* look at a larger landscape is always best. Since these argument essays are brief, consider topics that you can do justice to in less than a thousand words. As you review potential topics for your essay, can you see how some aspect of a larger question can be addressed by asking a smaller question? For example, the topic of spending on athletic programs at American universities relative to spending on academic programs raises this obvious question: *Is too much spent on sports?* It's not very difficult to see how this large question can be focused for an effective argument. For example, *Does Boise State University spend too much on its athletic programs and too little on its academic ones?* You can't write a short piece about the negative impact of affirmative action policies on the nation's colleges and universities, but you can write a brief op-ed about the specific impacts on your school.

- *Disagreement.* A topic lends itself to argumentative writing if it is one that leads to disagreement among reasonable people. *Is smoking bad for your health?* was once a question that was debatable, but now pretty much everyone concedes that this question has been answered. *Did the Holocaust really happen?* is a question that only blockheads debate. But the question, *What are the motives of people who deny the Holocaust?* is a question that would generate a range of views.

- *Information.* Is there sufficient information available on the topic for you to make a reasonable judgment about what is true? Is it accessible? One great advantage of choosing a local question as the focus for an argumentative essay is that often the people are close by and the relevant information can easily be had. It's also essential that you can obtain information from more than just a single viewpoint on the question.

- *Question.* What makes a topic arguable is that it raises questions to which there are multiple answers. Which of them makes the most sense is at issue. But some questions are merely informational. For example, *How do greenhouse gases contribute to global warming?* is a question that will likely lead to explanations rather than argument. On the other hand, *Is the U.S. rejection of the Kyoto accords on global warming a responsible policy?* is an arguable, rather than informational, question.

Questions About Audience and Purpose.   Persuasive writing is a very audience-oriented form. *To whom* you make your case in an argument matters a lot in *how* you make it, but audience also matters in *whether* one topic is a better choice for an essay than another topic. The argument essay is written for a more general audience. Your readers are unlikely to be experts on your topic, and they are likely to read your essay quickly rather than slowly and thoughtfully. What does this imply about the best subjects?

- *Do your readers have a stake in the question you're answering?* The word "stake" can be broadly considered. For example, it's possible that a topic directly affects the readers of your essay; say you're writing for fellow college students on your campus, all of whom pay tuition, and your topic addresses whether a 12 percent hike in fees is justified. Sometimes, however, you choose a topic because readers need to know that they *do* have a stake in how a question is answered. For instance, the argument that new antiterrorist rules threaten online privacy is something you believe your readers, most of whom surf the Web, should consider.

- *Can you identify what your readers might already believe?* One of the key strategies of persuasion is to find ways to link the values and attitudes of your audience with the position you're encouraging them to believe. Is your potential topic one that lends itself to this kind of analysis?

- *Is your purpose not only to inform readers but also to encourage them to believe or do something?* As you know by now, one of the things that distinguishes argument essays such as the op-ed from other forms of writing is the writer's intention to change his or her audience. Frequently this purpose is quite explicit and even behavioral: vote a certain way, support a certain policy, or *don't* do something like buy a gas-guzzling SUV. Other times, persuasive writing attempts to persuade readers to believe something that may lead to some kind of behavior.

Research Considerations.   So you want to look into the controversy over oil drilling in the Alaskan National Wildlife Refuge? Your gut reaction is against proposals that would allow oil companies to drill test wells. It seems to be a real can of worms—if you allow testing and then there's momentum for full-scale development, you wonder if the environmental risks will be worth the gain in oil. But you really don't know very much. What are the risks? Is there a significant promise of oil production? How might it affect your region, your state, or the prices at your local Chevron? This is a big subject, of course, and there is lots of information out there. Where do you begin?

Maybe you believe you already know a lot about your topic—you've had enough experience and observations, or perhaps read enough to feel pretty well informed. But if you took my advice to choose a topic about which you might *feel* something but not really know what you *think,* then once you have selected your topic your next step in the process is to collect information.

While writing this argument essay does involve some research, it isn't exactly a research paper. A research paper is a much more extended treatment of a topic that relies on more detailed and scholarly information than is usually needed for an argument essay. In Chapter 12, you'll find information on research strategies that will help you with this project, especially how to conduct effective Internet searches and how to evaluate the sources you find. The section on library research, particularly key references, may also be valuable.

But for the purpose of this essay, you can have a more modest research agenda, and that's when the Web can be especially useful. Because many of the topics ripe for a good argument essay are current, a major source of information will be publications such as newspapers and magazines. As more of these print sources have gone online, the Web has become a central source for topical information. It's a great place to start learning about your topic, but there are hazards. First, the Web can be a trap. Searching and surfing can suck up an enormous amount of time; it can easily become obsessive—"I need just a few more sources and then I'll quit"—or even worse, digressive—"Gee, I just stumbled on a game site . . . it's got Super Mahjong!" Either of these can become an excuse not to write. The other hazard is the reliability of information on the Web, which is uneven (see "Evaluating Web Sources" in Chapter 12).

Address these pitfalls by making your Web research efficient. Magazines and newspapers are key sources for op-ed essays, and it's likely they're the best place to begin looking for background information. National issues such as oil drilling in the Artic National Wildlife Refuge are addressed by national newspapers, which are usually reliable sources of information. Search sites such as *The New York Times* or *The Washington Post* for information on your topic if you think that it might have garnered national attention. In addition, a useful site at http://www. refdesk.com/paper.html lists the links for newspapers by state and around the world.

Magazines online are good sources as well, but access to their archives may be limited to subscribers. The university library is useful here because it not only subscribes to many magazines but allows you to search them; you may be able retrieve full articles electronically or read them on microfilm. Access to your college's database of magazines is likely online, too, so check the library Web site for more information.

A general search engine such as www.google.com will help you find newspapers, magazines, Web sites, and other online publications for background on your topic. Be ready for an avalanche, however. For example, a Google search on the Artic National Wildlife Refuge turned up nearly 3,000 links.

If you're writing about a campus or community issue, the Web can still be useful, particularly if your campus or local newspapers have sites. State and local governments also post information on the Web (for information on sites visit "State and Local Governments on the Net" at http://www. statelocalgov.net/index.cfm). But campus and local issues often call for a different kind of research: basic footwork. The best way to become knowledgeable is to talk to people who are affected by the topic, perhaps people you've identified with particular points of view about it or even other students in your class who may have some knowledge. The local public library, as well as the campus library, can be a valuable source of information on local issues as well.

🔍 INQUIRING INTO THE DETAILS

THINKING GLOBALLY, ACTING LOCALLY

Your concerns may be broad; for instance, how can we improve race relations? In a short essay, the key is to anchor big questions to something smaller, more concrete. For example:

• Is there a local angle on a larger issue?

• Is there a smaller question under a bigger one?

• Is there a case study or other specific example that could anchor the essay?

Narrowing the Question.   I've been vaguely aware of the crisis in Medicaid funding—federal health care support for the poor—but the issue really came home when officials told Dorothy Misner, a 92-year-old woman in nearby Nampa, that she would have to gum her food because the state refused to pay for dentures. Probably the best way to make a larger controversy a manageable writing topic is to find a local angle. In this case, for example, the larger question—*Should the national Medicaid program do more to support the poor without health insurance?*—becomes a much narrower question—*Is the state's Medicaid program failing people like Dorothy Misner?* Whenever possible, make big issues smaller by finding some connection to the local.

That isn't always possible, however. Unless you live in Alaska, for instance, the debate over development of the Artic Wildlife Refuge is hard to cut as a local issue. Then it becomes important to find a narrower question, something that may not be possible until after you've done a little research. For example, the question, *Should the Artic Wildlife Refuge be open to oil development?* could be narrowed by asking, *Are oil company claims about the potential of recoverable oil in the refuge reasonable?*

Finally, another way to narrow the focus of an argument is to find a useful case study, anecdote, or example that somehow typifies some aspect of the issue you want to examine. Suppose you want to write about the impact of oil development on native subsistence hunting in the wildlife refuge. The story of one family, or one local native community's reliance on the nearby caribou population can provide an anchor for an extended discussion of the risks oil development poses to people like them. George Will's approach to many of his op-ed essays is to use a newly released study, report, academic article, or interview with an expert as the anchor for his piece. He then takes off on his own from there.

Writing the Sketch

Now draft a sketch of roughly 500 to 600 words with the following elements:

- It has a tentative title.
- It makes at least one claim and offers several reasons that support the claim.
- It presents and analyzes at least one contrasting point of view.
- The sketch includes specific evidence to support (or possibly complicate) the reasons offered in support of the claim, including *at least* several of the following: an anecdote or story, a personal observation, data, an analogy, a case study, expert testimony, other relevant quotations from people involved, or a precedent.

STUDENT SKETCH

Inspiring young voters isn't easy. In my own classes, I almost never hear younger students talk casually about elections. On the rare occasions that I actually see a button on a backpack for one candidate or another, I'm always a little surprised. Are young voters apathetic? And if they are what should be done about it? Those were Ben Bloom's questions, both of which arose from a fastwrite. Here is his sketch on the topic. Where should he go from here? What should he research before the next draft? What should he consider that he doesn't consider here?

How to Really Rock the Vote
Ben Bloom

MTV sponsors "Rock the Vote." Presidential candidates swing through college campuses wearing blue jeans and going tieless. There's even an organization called "Kid's Vote" that tries to get high school students involved in the political process. It's pretty clear that student vote matters but are these efforts paying off? 1

It doesn't seem so. On my own campus, fewer than a few hundred students vote in the annual elections for the Student Senate. I can't even get my roommate to talk about the Presidential election, much less who's running for student body president. 2

3   What seems typical is the following comment from a college-age columnist: "On the issue of voter apathy, I look at myself first. I'm not even registered to vote, which is as apathetic as it gets. I do, however, educate myself about presidential candidates and their proposed policies—I just never have thought my one, lonesome vote could matter. I've neglected registering because it has never seemed logical to inconvenience myself, through the registration process, only to give another drop of water to an ocean (to add one vote to millions)."

4   "Never seemed logical to inconvenience" yourself to participate in the most basic part of the democratic process? Has it gotten this bad?

5   The student journalist above was responding to a survey that came out two years ago from a group called Project Vote Smart. It found what I suspected from my own experiences: young voters are staying away from the polls.

6   According to the study, there has been a decline in the numbers of 18 to 25 year olds voting by 13% over the last twenty five years. Actually, I think the situation is worse than that. The main reason they cite is that young people don't think their votes make a difference.

7   What should be done about this? How can we convince young voters to believe in the power of their vote? Are organizations like "Rock the Vote" or "Project Vote Smart" going to convince students like the guy who finds voting "inconvenient" that it's worth the effort?

8   In my opinion, celebrities and rock stars won't make a difference. The key is for political candidates to find a way to talk about issues so that young voters overcome their apathy and actually *feel* something. In the sixties, it was the draft. I'm not sure what the issues with emotional impact are these days. But the people who want students to vote have got to find them.

Moving from Sketch to Draft

A sketch is often sketchy. It's generally underdeveloped, sometimes giving the writer just the barest outline of his subject. But as an early draft, a sketch can be invaluable. It might hint at what the real subject is, or what questions seem to be behind your inquiry into the subject. A sketch might suggest a focus for the next draft, or simply a better lead. Here are some tips for finding clues in your sketch about directions you might go in the next draft.

Evaluating Your Own Sketch. You've read and written about an issue you care about. Now for the really hard part: getting out of your own head and into the heads of your potential readers who may not care as much as you do. At least not yet. Successful persuasion fundamentally depends on giving an audience the right reasons to agree with you, and these are likely both logical and emotional, involving both *logos* and *pathos*.

We've already talked about another element of argument—the writer's *ethos*—or the way he comes across to readers. What's the ethos of your sketch? Imagine that you don't know you. How might you be perceived by a stranger reading the sketch? Is your tone appealing, or might it be slightly off-putting? Do you successfully establish your authority to speak on this issue, or do you sense that the persona you project in the sketch is unconvincing, perhaps too emotional or not appearing fair?

As we develop convictions about an issue, one of the hardest things to manage in early argument drafts is creating a persuasive persona. Another is finding ways to establish connections with our audience; this connection is not just between writers and readers but creating some common ground between readers and *the topic*. There are many ways to do this, including,

1. Connecting your readers' prior beliefs or values with your position on the topic.

2. Establishing that readers have a *stake,* perhaps even a personal one, in how the question you've raised is answered. This may be self-interest, but it may also be emotional (remember the advertiser's strategy).

3. Highlighting the common experiences readers may have had with the topic and offering your claim as a useful way of understanding that experience.

As you look over your sketch, evaluate how well you create this common ground between your topic and your intended audience. Might you revise it by exploiting one or more of the strategies listed above?

Finally, is there enough evidence to support the reasons you've provided in support of your claims? It's pretty common for initial drafts to lack enough specifics. Do you see places in the sketch that could be developed with specific information in the next draft?

Questions for Peer Review. Because the argument essay is such an audience-oriented form, these initial peer reviews of your sketch are invaluable in helping you get your bearings. Much of what you might have felt about how you managed the ethos and connections with readers can be confirmed or challenged by this first public reading. Ask your workshop group some of the following questions:

- How is the *ethos* of the sketch? Do I come across in the sketch as an advocate for my position? For example, am I *passionate, preachy, reasonable, one-sided, sympathetic, overbearing, intimate, detached, objective, subjective, uncaring, empathetic, humorous, serious, angry, mellow, contemptuous, approachable, patronizing, respectful, thoughtful, presumptuous, fair, or judgmental?*

- In your own words, what do you think was my central claim?

- Which reasons did you find most convincing? Which were least convincing?
- What do you think was the best evidence I offered in support of my reasons? Where exactly did you feel that you needed more evidence?

Reflecting on What You've Learned. Spend a few minutes following your peer review workshop to generate a list of everything you heard, and then begin a five minute fastwrite that explores your reaction to these suggestions and your tentative plan for revision. In particular, what will you change? What will you add, and what will you cut in the next draft? What problems were raised that you don't yet know how to solve? What problems *weren't* raised that you expected might be? Do you still need to worry about them? End your fastwrite by writing about what you understand now about your topic, and your initial beliefs about it, that you didn't fully understand when you began writing about it.

Research and Other Strategies: Gathering More Information

Here's a mortifying thought: You've completely changed your mind about what you think about your topic and what you want to say in your argument. That's unsettling, but it's also a sign that you're willing to allow things to get a bit messy before they get sorted out. This is good because it's much more likely to result in an essay that gets at the truth of what you feel than if you doggedly stick to a particular point of view, come what may. If you *have* changed your mind, you have a lot of collecting to do. Return to the Web sites of current publications and search for information that might be relevant to your emerging idea.

There's another research strategy that can be helpful whether you change your mind or not: the interview. People who are somehow involved in your topic are among the best sources of new information and lively material. An interview can provide ideas about what else you should read or who else you might talk to, and it can be a source of quotations, anecdotes, and even case studies that will make the next draft of your argument essay much more interesting. After all, what makes an issue matter is how it affects people. Have you sufficiently dramatized those effects?

For more information on face to face interviewing, see Chapter 5, "Writing a Profile," as well as Chapter 12, "Research Techniques." The Internet can also be a source for interview material. Look for e-mail links to the authors of useful documents you found on the Web and write them with a few questions. Interest groups, newsgroups, or listservs on the Web can also provide the voices and perspectives of people with something to say on your topic. Remember to ask permission to quote them if you decide to use something in your draft. For leads on finding Web discussion groups on your topic, visit the following sites:

Listz, the mailing list directory, www.liszt.com. Organized by subject, Listz includes a database of more than 50,000 discussion groups on countless subjects.

Catalist, the official catalog of listserv lists, www.lsoft.com/lists/listref.html. This site has a database of about 15,000 discussion groups.

One of the most useful things you can do to prepare for the draft is to spend forty-five minutes at the campus library searching for new information on your topic. Consider expanding your search from current newspapers and periodicals to books or government publications (see Chapter 12 for more information about searching for government documents). In addition, almanacs such as the *InfoPlease Almanac* (www.infoplease.com), the *CIA Factbook* (www.odci.gov/cia/publications/factbook/), or statistical information available from sources such as the U.S. Census Bureau's *Statistical Abstracts of the United States* (www.census.gov/statab/www/) can be valuable sources of specific information relevant to your argument. For example, it wouldn't be difficult using an almanac to find out what the Medicaid budget was last year.

Composing the Draft

As always, it's best to work from abundance rather than scarcity. If you don't have enough evidence to support your argument, find more. But if you're feeling reasonably well prepared to develop your argument essay from a sketch (or proposal) to a longer draft, then begin by crafting a strong lead. There are so many ways to begin an essay like this one, which is best? As always, think of a beginning that not only might interest your readers in your topic but that hints at or states your purpose in writing about it. Through tone, your beginning also establishes your relationship with your readers. Here's instructor Andrew Merton's lead in "The Guys are Dumbing Down," a piece that argues that students' baseball caps in class indicate something other than studiousness.

> Here is the big social note from the campus of the University of New Hampshire, where I teach: Dumbing down is in. For guys.

Merton's tone is a strong element of this lead. He begins casually— "Here is the big social note . . . "—suggesting some friendly, almost chatty relationship with his readers. This lead also does what many argument essay beginnings do: it states the writer's main claim. You may assume it is always the case to state your thesis in your introduction, but this isn't true at all. Some argument essays, especially op-ed pieces, may have a delayed thesis, in which the writer works methodically toward her point. Which approach should you use in your draft? In part, that depends on your method of development.

Methods of Development. What are some of the ways you might organize the next draft?

Narrative. Telling a story is an underrated way of developing an argument. One of my favorite persuasive essays is George Orwell's "A Hanging," a piece most don't consider a persuasive essay at all. I've included it in the personal essay chapter of *The Curious Writer* because it is a personal narrative, but like much of Orwell's work, it has a persuasive purpose. "A Hanging" argues against capital punishment by focusing on about eight minutes of the event—the most dramatic eight minutes obviously—and it's only in the middle that Orwell breaks with his story to state his position on the issue. The story is so compelling it's hard to even notice that Orwell is trying to persuade the reader to believe something. Can you imagine a way to turn your topic into an extended story, perhaps by focusing on the experience of a particular person or group of people, in a particular place, at a particular time? Somehow the story must, like Orwell's, be logically linked to your claim; obviously, just any old story won't do.

There are other ways to use narrative, too. Anecdotes, or brief stories used to illustrate an idea or a problem, are frequently used in argument essays. One effective way to begin your essay might be to tell a story that highlights the problem you're writing about or the question you're posing.

Question to Answer. Almost all writing is an attempt to answer a question. In the personal essay and other open forms of inquiry, the writer may never arrive at a definite answer, but an argument essay usually offers an answer. An obvious method of development, therefore, is to begin your essay by raising the question and end it by offering your answer. This can work in a number of ways. For example, an Ellen Goodman essay on recent proposals to bring back publicly funded single-sex schools is organized around what she thinks are some of the key questions this raises. She asks those questions throughout her essay, and answers each before moving on to the next. Following a beginning that provides some background on the proposal, Goodman asks, *How did we get here?* She then explains the "odd coalition" that supports the proposal, describes their arguments and methodically rebuts them. By the middle of her essay, Goodman asks a second question, *Can you have separate but equal schools?* The remainder of her piece examines the answer to this question, and by the end she arrives at her main claim: The solution to poor schools is not an end to coeducation but innovation in teaching.

Are there several key questions around which you might organize your draft, leading, as Goodman does, to your central claim at the end?

Problem to Solution. This is a variation on the question-to-answer structure. But it might be a particularly useful organization strategy if you're writing about a topic readers may know very little about. In that case, you might need to spend as much time establishing what exactly the problem is—explaining what makes it a problem and why the reader should care about it—as you do offering your particular solution. That's what George Will did earlier in the chapter in his argument on the failure of writing instruction. He spent a fair amount of time explaining what he believed were the indefensible current theories of teaching students to write, ideas most of his readers would know little about.

Effect to Cause or Cause to Effect. At the heart of some arguments is the *relationship* between two things, and often what is at issue is pinpointing the real causes for certain undesirable effects. Once these causes are identified, then the best solutions can be offered. Sadly, we know the effects of terrorism, but what are its causes? If you argue, as some do, that Islamic radicalism arose in response to U.S. policies towards Israel and the Palestinians, then the solution offered might be a shift in foreign policy. The international debate over global warming, for some participants, is really an argument about causes and effects. If you don't believe, for example, that U.S. contributions to atmospheric carbon dioxide in the next ten years will match contributions from the developing world, then the U.S. refusal to sign the Kyoto treaty—one proposed solution—may not matter that much. Some arguments like these can be organized simply around an examination of causes and effects.

Combining Approaches. As you think about how you might organize your first draft, you don't necessarily have to choose between narrative, problem-to-solution, or cause-to-effect structures. In fact, most often they are used together. We can easily see that in Doris Lessing's essay earlier in the chapter on how she views America. The piece begins with a narrative account of a recent visit, and then shifts to an exploration of an effect (American extremism) and speculation about its cause (Americans' faith in the sanctity of their "Eden").

INQUIRING INTO THE DETAILS

WHAT EVIDENCE CAN DO

Usually we think of using evidence only to support an idea or claim we're making. But evidence can be used in other ways, too. For example, it can:

- *Support* an idea, observation, or assertion.
- *Refute* or challenge a claim with which you disagree.
- *Show* that a seemingly simple assertion, problem, or idea is really more complex.
- *Complicate* or even contradict an earlier point you've made.
- *Contrast* two or more ways of seeing the same thing.
- *Test* an idea, hypothesis, or theory.

Using Evidence. All writing relies on evidence, usually some specific information in relationships with general ideas (see the box "Inquiring into the Details: What Evidence Can Do"). Evidence in an argumentative essay often has a *particular* relationship to ideas; most often it is offered to support ideas the writer wants the reader to believe. What *kind* of evidence to include is a rhetorical question. To whom are you writing, and what kind of evidence will they be more likely to believe? Generally speaking, the narrower and more specialized the audience, the more particular they will be about the types of evidence they'll find convincing.

For example, as you write more academic papers in your chosen major the types of evidence that will help you make a persuasive argument will be more and more prescribed by the field. In the natural sciences, the results of quantitative studies count more than case studies; in the humanities, primary texts count more than secondary ones. The important thing for this argument essay, which you're writing for a more general audience, is that you attempt to *vary* your evidence. Rather than relying exclusively on anecdotes, include some quotes from an expert as well.

Workshopping the Draft

If your draft is subject to peer review, see Chapter 15 for details on how to organize workshop groups and decide on how your group can help you. The following journal activities and questions should help you make the most of your opportunity to get peer feedback on your work in progress.

Reflecting on the Draft. After you've finished the draft, prepare for peer review by making a journal entry that explores your experience writing the essay.

- What proved hardest?
- What most surprised you about the process?
- What did you find particularly gratifying? What was especially frustrating?
- How did your process for writing this type of essay differ from writing the personal essay or some other form?
- If you were going to start all over again, what would you do differently?

Discuss the insights that might have emerged from this open-ended writing in class or in your workshop group. After your draft was discussed, make some notes in your journal in response to the following questions:

- What most surprised you about your group's response to your essay?
- What did you hear that most made you want to write again?
- What specifically do you think you need to do in the next draft?

Questions for Readers. Here are some questions that might prompt members of your workshop group to offer helpful advice on your argument draft.

1. What was the most interesting part of the draft? What was the least interesting?

2. What did you believe about my topic before you read the draft? What did you believe after you read it?

3. What reason most strongly supported my main point? What reason seemed the weakest?

4. What was the most convincing evidence I offered? What was the least convincing?

INQUIRING INTO THE DETAILS

TEN COMMON LOGICAL FALLACIES

An important way to evaluate the soundness of an argument is to examine its logic and, in particular, look for so-called logical fallacies that may lead writers' reasoning astray. Aristotle was one of the first to point out many of these, and a quick search on the Web using the term "logical fallacies" will reveal dozens and dozens of them that plague public argument. Many of them have indecipherable Latin names, testifying to their ancient origins.

Here are ten of the most common logical fallacies. I think they cover about 90 percent of the ways in which writers stumble when making an argument.

1. **Hasty generalization:** We're naturally judgmental creatures. For example, we frequently make a judgment about someone after just meeting them. Or we conclude that a class is useless after attending a single session. All of these are generalizations based on insufficient evidence. Hasty generalizations might be true—the class *might* turn out to be useless—but you should always be wary of them.

2. **Ad hominem:** When arguments turn into shouting matches, they almost inevitably get personal. Shifting away from the substance of an argument to attack the person making it, either subtly or explicitly, is another common logical fallacy. It's also, at times, hard to resist.

3. **Appeal to authority:** We all know that finding support for a claim from an expert is a smart move in many arguments. But sometimes it's a faulty move because the authority we cite isn't really an expert on the subject. A more common fallacy, however, is

when we cite an expert to support a claim without acknowledging that many experts disagree on the point.

4. **Straw man:** One of the sneakiest ways to sidetrack reason in an argument is to misrepresent or ignore the actual position of an opponent. For example, one way I might criticize George Will's earlier essay on writing instruction is to point out that he conveniently misrepresents the actual goals and practices of what he calls the "growth model" of teaching writing. Therefore he creates a "straw man" that is easy to knock down. When writing critically about the ideas of another, we must always be careful to represent those ideas as accurately as we can.

5. **False analogy.** Analogies can be powerful comparisons in argument. But they can also lead us astray when the analogy simply doesn't hold. Are A and B *really* similar situations? For example, when a critic of higher education argues that a public university is like a business and should be run like one, are the two really analogous? Fundamentally, one is nonprofit and the other is designed to make money. Is this a really useful comparison?

6. **Post hoc or false cause:** Just because one thing follows another doesn't necessarily mean one *causes* the other. It might be coincidence, or the cause might be something else entirely. For example, if you're really keen on arguing that losing the football coach was the cause of the team's losing record, you might link the two. And it's possible that you're right, but it's also just as possible that the injury to the quarterback was one of the real reasons.

7. **Appeal to popularity:** In a country obsessed by polls and rankings, it's not hard to understand the appeal of reasoning that argues that since it's popular it must be good or true. Advertisers are particularly fond of this fallacy, arguing that because their brand is most popular it must be best. In fact, this might not be the case at all. The majority can be wrong.

8. **Slippery slope:** I love the name of this one because it so aptly describes what can happen when reasoning loses its footing. You might start out reasonably enough, arguing, for example, that a gun control law restricts the rights of some citizens to have access to certain weapons, but pretty soon you start sliding toward conclusions that simply don't follow, such as a gun control law is the beginning of the end of gun ownership in the country. Now you might really believe this, but logic isn't the route to get there.

9. **Either/or fallacy:** In a black and white world, something is right or wrong, true or false, good or bad. But ours is a colorful world

with many shades. For instance, while it might be emotionally satisfying to say that opponents of the war in Iraq must not support the troops there, it is also possible that the war's opponents are against the war *because* they're concerned about the lives of American service people. Rather than *either/or* it might be *both/and*. We see this fallacy often in arguments that suggest that there are only two choices and each are opposites.

10. **Begging the question:** This one is also called circular reasoning because it assumes the truth of the arguer's conclusion without bothering to prove it. An obvious example of this would be to say that a law protecting people from Internet spam is good because it's a law, and laws should be obeyed. But *why* is it a good law?

Revising the Draft

You've been revising all along, of course, beginning with the work you did to find a topic and then narrowing it down to something interesting and manageable in a sketch. You were revising when you shared your sketch with peers and used what you learned to compose the next draft. You even were revising when you talked about the essay to your roommate or best friend. Revision involves "re-seeing" your subject, and there are many ways to do that as you go along. For more on new ways to think about revision, read Chapter 14, "Revision Strategies."

Draft argument essays have some typical problems at this stage in the process. Do any of these apply to yours?

- Is your central claim or thesis stated clearly?
- Do you employ any logical fallacies? See the earlier box "Inquiring into the Details: Ten Common Logical Fallacies."
- Do you have sufficient evidence or information to make your assertions convincing? Do you need to gather more facts?
- Have you considered any counterarguments in your essay? This is especially important if you think the audience for your essay might not be inclined to initially agree with your position.
- Have you clearly established what stake your readers have in the issue you're writing about?
- Does the draft use *pathos, logos,* and *ethos* effectively?

Chapter 14, "Revision Strategies," can help you address most of these problems. Refer to the table below to find specific strategies for ideas on how to revise your draft following your workshop. Remember that a draft may present problems in more than one category.

GUIDE TO REVISION STRATEGIES		
PROBLEMS IN THE DRAFT (CHAPTER 14)	**PART**	**PAGE NUMBER**
Unclear purpose ▪ Not sure what the paper is about?	1	633
Unclear thesis, theme, or main idea ▪ Not sure what you're trying to say?	2	639
Lack of information or development ▪ Need more convincing evidence? Need to check for logical fallacies?	3	646
Disorganized ▪ Doesn't move logically or smoothly from paragraph to paragraph?	4	650
Unclear or awkward at the level of sentences and paragraphs ▪ Does draft seem choppy or hard to follow at the level of sentences or paragraphs?	5	656

Polishing the Draft

After you've dealt with the big issues in your draft—is it sufficiently focused, does it answer the *So what?* question, is it well organized, and so on—you must deal with the smaller problems. You've carved the stone into an appealing figure but now you need to polish it. Are your paragraphs coherent? How do you manage transitions? Are your sentences fluent and concise? Are there any errors in spelling or syntax? Section 5 of Chapter 14 can help you focus on these issues.

Before you finish your draft, make certain that you've worked through the following checklist:

- ❑ Every paragraph is about one thing.
- ❑ The transitions between paragraphs aren't abrupt or awkward.
- ❑ The length of sentences varies in each paragraph.
- ❑ Each sentence is concise. There are no unnecessary words or phrases.
- ❑ You've checked grammar, particularly verb agreement, run-on sentences, unclear pronouns, and misused words (*there/their, where/were,* and so on). (See of the handbook at the back of the book for help on all of these grammar issues).
- ❑ You've run your spell checker and proofed your paper for misspelled words.

STUDENT ESSAY

Many Americans are fond of talking about our country's native people in the past tense. We admire the tribal cultures as they existed a century or two ago, and borrow freely from them, engaging in "vision quests" and drumming circles. We feel the tug of nostalgia for these lost tribes, and yes, guilt for the sad history of relations between the mostly white immigrants who dispossessed the tribes and the Indian people who were confined to reservations. It's convenient to assume that the problems were in the past because contemporary Native Americans are largely invisible to us—except if you happen to drive through a reservation as Kelly Sundberg would on her way to visit friends at a nearby university.

Confronting Native Americans in the present tense forced Kelly to examine her own prejudices, and in the essay that follows she argues that the route to understanding begins at school.

I Am Not a Savage
Kelly Sundberg

Salmon, Idaho, is named after the river that runs through it, a river that is filled with turbulent whitewater punctuated by deep and calm pools and shallow riffles. In the spring, I have looked into these riffles and seen waves of silver and red moving gently just underneath the surface of the water.   1

We call them "reds"—spawning salmon. Nowadays, they are diminished in numbers, but at one time the river was full of them, and full of abundance as well for the Lemhi Indians who once lived on the banks. For the Lemhi, the salmon was not solely for sustenance, but also an integral part of their culture and spirituality.   2

Today there are few "reds" and almost no Lemhi left in the valley.   3

The initial influx of Mormon settlers followed by migrations of Californians and Midwesterners forced Native Americans out of the valley. Still, upon entering the Salmon city limits from Highway 28, a large sign proclaims, "Welcome to Salmon, Idaho. Birthplace of Sacagewea!" In a time when anything related to Lewis and Clark means profit, the city of Salmon, my hometown, has now chosen to capitalize on this marketable heritage, even though they once ignored it or treated it derisively.   4

My high school mascot is the "Salmon Savage." The marquee in front of the school has a picture with an Indian warrior on it, and when the football team scores a touchdown a white girl wearing war paint and a "made in China" headdress will ride a horse around the track in celebration.   5

6   I never questioned the integrity or intent of these symbols until I was a sophomore at the school. For Civil Rights Day, the school invited Rosa Abrahamson, a Lemhi Indian, to speak to the students. She cried as she spoke about the injustice of the name "savage." "My people are not savages," she said. "We are peaceful and do not take pride in that name." When she finished speaking the applause was polite but subdued.

7   The next speaker was a rancher named Bud, who lit into a tirade about the government subsidizing "lazy Indians." As he finished with fists raised into the air, he was greeted by a standing ovation. For the first time in my life, I felt ashamed to be a part of the community.

8   It wasn't that those of us in the gym had consciously made the decision to be racist. It was simply ignorance. Despite the history of the Lemhi in the valley, our ideas of their culture are shaped from drives through the reservation on the way to campus visits at the University of Idaho. Our perceptions were safely gleaned from inside of an automobile and never involved real interaction with Native Americans.

9   Once, when asked to write our opinions about reservations in a U.S. government class, I wrote that I thought the government was making it "too easy on the Native Americans and they had become apathetic and unmotivated because of subsidies."

10   I got a better glimpse at my Lemhi neighbors recently reading Sherman Alexie's novel *The Lone Ranger and Tonto Fistfight in Heaven*. Alexie, a member of the Spokane/Coeur d'Alene tribes, conveys the opposition between contemporary and traditional Native American culture. His characters are torn and struggle to reconcile the two: "At the halfway point of any drunken night, there is a moment when an Indian realizes he cannot turn back toward tradition and that he has no map to guide him toward the future."

11   My own community struggles to reconcile two conflicting ideas as well— we embrace the symbols of savagery to inspire the football team, yet in order to make a profit we proudly claim Sacagewea as one of our own. Still, when the Lemhi wanted to build a school near Sacagewea's birthplace, the county refused to sell them the land, claiming it would become a "mini-reservation."

12   Ironically, Salmon shares more than it cares to admit with its neighbors on the reservation. Poverty, alcoholism, and depression are a way of life for many Salmon residents. Yet the perception in the community is that an alcoholic white man is somehow superior to a "drunk Indian."

13   In Salmon, all students are required to take an Idaho history class, yet this class makes almost no mention of Native American history in the valley. None of the readings in Advanced Placement English classes are by Native American authors, and government classes don't address Native American issues at all.

14   Is it any wonder that racism persists?

The local school system needs to lead. English teachers should require   15
readings by authors like Alexie, they should provide field trips to local and national archeological sites, and they should bring in Native American interpreters to speak about local history. By letting go of negative and outdated
ideas, the city of Salmon and the Lemhi can take the first step toward healing.

EVALUATING THE ESSAY

Discuss or write about your responses to Kelly Sundberg's essay using
some or all of the following questions:

1. What is the thesis of the essay? Where in the piece is it most clearly
   stated?

2. Refer to the box that lists ten common logical fallacies and reread
   Sundberg's essay. Do you suspect there are any logical fallacies in "I
   Am Not a Savage?"

3. Consider the *ethos* of this essay. How does the writer come across?
   Is her persona effective?

4. What do you think is the most effective paragraph in the essay?
   Why? What is the least effective?

USING WHAT YOU HAVE LEARNED

You've read published op-ed essays and a student draft. You've also
worked on your own argument essay, a genre that may be new to you.
Take a moment to consider how you might use what you've learned.

1. Reflect on how your thinking about argument and argumentative
   writing may have changed because of the reading and writing in
   this chapter by finishing the following sentence in your journal at
   least four times: *Before I began this chapter I thought _____, but now
   I think _____.*

2. The personal essay (discussed in Chapter 4) and the argument essay might seem at first to be fundamentally different kinds of writing. Do you see any connections between the two genres now?

3. Examine the letters to the editor or the editorial in your local newspaper. How do you read these pages differently after studying and
   writing an argument? Clip a letter or editorial that might best
   demonstrate what you've learned.

The poet, Grace Butcher, pictured here at a reading in Ohio, sometimes writes about crows, which are quite ordinary birds, unless they fly through the imagination of a writer like Butcher. The best literature often finds the extraordinary significance in familiar things.

Writing a Critical Essay

9

WRITING ABOUT LITERATURE

A voice mail message on my machine from Katie, who works the English department office, said that she had received a message meant for me. "Stay on and you can listen to it," she said. "Hello," said a stranger's voice. "This is Grace Butcher. And I'm looking for the Bruce Ballenger or Michelle Payne who edited a collection called *The Curious Reader.* There's an essay about me in it."

My heart sank. Oh God, I thought, maybe we made some mistake and she's angry. But I didn't sense that from the sound of her voice; it sounded velvety, warm. "I'm calling because I wanted to tell the student who wrote the essay how delighted and moved I was by her piece. I'd like to know how to get in touch with the student, Peggy Jordan."

I suddenly remembered. Peggy Jordan, a former student of my colleague Michelle, had written an autobiographical/critical essay about the poet Grace Butcher in *The Curious Reader,* a book I recently co-authored with Michelle. Jordan wrote about attending a reading by Butcher when she was sixteen, and now, twenty-eight years later, finds herself returning to those poems as she struggles with middle age. It's a brutally honest essay—Jordan says there's little to like about growing older, that even if you have a good attitude about it, the body is a nagging reminder of new limitations. But Butcher's poetry, particularly one poem, "What the Crow Does Is Not Singing," helped Peggy Jordan find a new voice, and new wings, which will carry her more gracefully into old age.

I reread the Jordan essay and thought—this is what literature can do. Reading essays, stories, and poems can help us slowly unroll

What You'll Learn in This Chapter

- How literary texts differ from other kinds of writing.

- Methods for finding the questions that drive a critical essay.

- Common literary devices.

- How to analyze literary nonfiction.

- Useful sources for writing about literature.

the tightly bound threads of feeling—our fears, joys, desires, or sorrows—and help us follow them back to the heart and out into the world. Literature helps us to understand ourselves, and in attending to the experiences of others as they are represented in strings of words, we can see how we're delicately tethered to others. Peggy Jordan can see in Butcher's poems that there is a way to grow older that she hadn't yet imagined. But would she have seen this as clearly if she hadn't written about it? I don't think so.

MOTIVES FOR WRITING A CRITICAL ESSAY

By now you understand that writing is a means of thinking and learning, so when your writing comes in contact with the writing of others, the conversation illuminates them both. Sometimes, this dialogue has very personal dimensions. It did for Peggy Jordan because she reread Grace Butcher's poem with an open heart and mind, and because Jordan chose a form of the critical essay—autobiographical criticism—that actively encourages such personal connections. But even more formal critical essays, those that don't involve self-disclosure or first-person writing, can offer personal revelation. After all, what draws you to a certain author, essay, story, or poem is often a feeling, a response that is initially closer to the heart than the head. From there you sustain an intimate encounter with the material, reading closely and reflecting on what it might mean.

It isn't necessary that the story you're writing about be an experience you can relate to, or even about a person anything like you. Reading about different lives, strangely, can help us understand ourselves in unexpected ways. Like a carnival mirror, stories, essays, and poems about others can cause us to reflect on ourselves in ways that make us seem strange, sometimes almost unrecognizable, to ourselves. We see ourselves as others see us. We might read James Baldwin's "Notes of a Native Son" and understand how an African American might have felt in the 1950s or 1960s when seeing an approaching white face; a sense, Baldwin writes, that "one was never looked at but was simply at the mercy of the reflexes the color of one's skin caused in other people." Of course, if we're white we learn a little something about being black in America, but we also learn something about how our own faces might appear to someone who is black. Suddenly, the familiar seems strange.

These are personal reasons for writing about literature, but there are other motives as well. One is that the writing can, simply, help us to *understand* what we read, and appreciate it much more. You've already practiced methods such as the double-entry journal, in which you create conversations with all kinds of texts—essays, excerpts, and even photographs. When it works, this process helps you to figure out what you think and what you might want to say about the thing you're looking at. This is also true when that thing is a literary text, and it becomes even more important to structure these written conversations because what makes texts literary is their complexity.

Most of us are pretty literal, which is why one response to reading, say, a short story is to simply declare, "It's *just a story!* Why do we have to squeeze some deep meaning out of it?" It's a pretty common view that English teachers have created an industry out of squeezing water from stones, of demanding that readers look more deeply at the things they read and consider what might be implied rather than what is explicit. It's true that this can be annoying at times, but the intentions are good. To fully appreciate what authors are saying or what effects they're trying to create in an essay, poem, or story, you often need to look closely, and in doing so, you see beyond the obvious. When you make this reading an act of imagination you will consider possible meanings that weren't necessarily immediately apparent. It is in the conversation between what a text says and what it *might* be saying that you discover fresh understandings of what you read. You share these discoveries by writing about them.

> *To fully appreciate what authors are saying or what effects they're trying to create in an essay, poem or story, you often need to look closely, and in doing so, you see beyond the obvious.*

This is not really impersonal, even if you never mention yourself in your essay, because to do this well you need to bring yourself to the encounter. Whatever interpretations or ideas you discover about a poem, story, or essay is shaped by who you are—the personal experiences, the feelings, the dreams, and the ideas—that lead you to notice some things but not others in a text. You imagine in your own particular ways. How productive this is, however, depends on *how* you read and how you use writing to help you understand and interpret texts. The *process* of reading and writing about literary texts, the subject of this chapter, involves a range of choices, something that you can individualize, too.

THE CRITICAL ESSAY AND ACADEMIC WRITING

Summarizing a work, something that made *Cliff Notes* an industry, is a useful activity, and often is a step in the process, but rarely is it the purpose of a critical essay. (One exception to this is the annotated bibliography; see Appendix C for more information about this form.) Most forms of critical essays are organized around *the writer's ideas* about a text.

In that sense, a critical essay is like most of the other inquiry projects we've discussed so far, with one important difference: the main source of information for the writing is a text, usually a work of literature. Yet the process of thinking and writing is much the same with critical essays as it is in a personal essay, an argument, and a review: You begin with questions, explore possible answers, make judgments and interpretations, and offer evidence that supports, qualifies, or complicates your judgments. In that sense, writing critical essays prepares you for many other kinds of academic writing, especially if it involves working with published texts.

You will encounter various forms of the critical essay mostly in English classes. They might include the following:

- *Short response papers.* As an initial response to reading, you may be asked to write fairly brief analytical, exploratory, or personal responses. These, by our definition, are essentially sketches that may or may not lead to longer essays. Sometimes a response paper focuses on explication of a certain aspect of the essay, poem, or story, like explaining or analyzing use of metaphor or character.

- *Autobiographical criticism.* Personal and sometimes fairly open-ended responses to literary works, such as Peggy Jordan's essay mentioned at the beginning of the chapter, are sometimes encouraged by English instructors. This type of personal criticism makes the critic's emotional relationship to texts explicit, but seeks to illuminate both the writer and the text.

- *Formal critical analysis.* Among the most common forms is the critical essay that makes an argument about the text. Like all other forms, these essays begin with questions: Does Ken Kesey's *One Flew Over the Cuckoo's Nest* use Big Nurse as a misogynistic symbol? Does E. B. White's essay, "Once More to the Lake," comment on mortality and identity? These critical essays generally offer a central claim or thesis, and then, using the literary text as evidence, try to make that claim or thesis convincing. John Greusser's brief critical essay, "Animal Imagery in 'Everyday Use,'" that follows later in the chapter is a good example of this.

FEATURES OF THE FORM

While the critical essay can exhibit considerable variation, certain conventions hold true for the form. These include:

- *The text is the most important source of information.* In a personal response, you might write about how a particular experience helps you understand some aspect of an essay, story, or poem, but even then, everything must be anchored firmly to the text you're writing about or things (letters, interviews, and so on) the writer has said about it. While so-called secondary sources—books or articles written by other critics—may be useful in supporting your interpretation, the best evidence in a critical essay is nearly always material (quotes of passages, summaries, and so on) drawn directly from text or author you're writing about.

- *Most critical essays make an argument.* Most critical essays are built around a main idea, claim, or interpretation you are making about a text. It's like interpreting a painting, however, instead of looking at things such as line, hierarchy, and color, you'll be using literary devices such as theme, character, symbol, scene, and other literary concepts to support and develop your ideas. Response essays may be more exploratory and open-ended rather than argumentative.

- *What has already been said often forms the context for the writer's question.* Typically, a critical essay initially establishes what other critics have claimed about the aspect of the essay, poem, or story on which the writer is focusing. How, for example, have other critics interpreted the haunting song that ends "Lullaby," Leslie Silko's short story? These other sources provide the context for putting forward your own take on the question, and establish the on-going conversation (if any) about the writer or the work.

- *Most critical essays assume readers* are not *familiar with the text.* Unless the literary work is extremely well known, critics generally assume an audience needs to have its memory refreshed. That means that there may be some background information on the essay, story, or poem, and possibly on the author and her other similar works. Frequently this means adding a summary of the story or background on the poem or novel. However, in certain circumstances, such as those involving response essays about a text your entire class has read, this assumption about audience will not apply.

SHORT STORY

Leslie Marmon Silko was raised on the Laguna Pueblo reservation in New Mexico, a place she came to know through stories that were told to her by her father, her aunt, and her grandmother. The storytelling tradition, much of it oral rather than written, is often a powerful element in Native American tribes, preserving certain ways of knowing and helping members recognize their connection to the tribe. But these stories are often living things, adapting and changing to reflect tribal members' struggles to adapt to an often hostile world. They can even be a source of healing, as in the short story "Lullaby" you're about to read here.

Silko is widely recognized as one of the finest living Native American writers, and her novel *Ceremony,* published in 1977, received critical acclaim. She's also a talented poet and essayist. Above all, Leslie Marmon Silko is a storyteller in the Laguna tradition, using a kind of narrative that in many ways will be familiar to nonnative readers. There are characters and scenes and a significant event, but also notice how landscape figures into the telling of this story, and in particular what the narrator's relationship is with the natural world. One of the motives for telling a story like this is to deal with loss by seeking recovery through balance or harmony. This may not be at all obvious when you read this story, which on the surface is an unrelentingly sad tale. Do you see redemption or perhaps resistance here?

LULLABY
Leslie Marmon Silko

1   The sun had gone down but the snow in the wind gave off its own light. It came in thick tufts like new wool—washed before the weaver spins it. Ayah reached out for it like her own babies had, and she smiled when she remembered how she had laughed at them. She was an old woman now, and her life had become memories. She sat down with her back against the wide cottonwood tree, feeling the rough bark on her back bones; she faced east and listened to the wind and snow sing a high-pitched Yeibechei song. Out of the wind she felt warmer, and she could watch the wide fluffy snow fill in her tracks, steadily, until the direction she had come from was gone. By the light of the snow she could see the dark outline of the big arroyo a few feet away. She was sitting on the edge of Cebolleta Creek, where in the springtime the thin cows would graze on a grass already chewed flat to the ground. In the wide deep creek bed where only a trickle of water flowed in the summer, the skinny cows would wander, looking for new grass along winding paths splashed with manure.

2   Ayah pulled the old Army blanket over her head like a shawl. Jimmie's blanket—the one he had sent to her. That was long time ago and the green wool was faded, and it was unraveling on the edges. She did not want to think about Jimmie. So she thought about the weaving and the way her mother had done it. On the tall wooden loom set into the sand under a tamarack tree for shade. She could see it clearly. She had been only a little girl when her grandma gave her the wooden combs to pull the twigs and burrs from the raw, freshly washed wool. And while she combed the wool, her grandma sat beside her, spinning a silvery strand of yarn around the smooth cedar spindle. Her mother worked at the loom with yarns dyed bright yellow and red and gold. She watched them dye the yarn in boiling black pots full of beeweed petals, juniper berries, and sage. The blankets her mother made were soft and woven so tight that rain rolled off them like birds' feathers. Ayah remembered sleeping warm on cold windy nights, wrapped in her mother's blankets on the hogan's sandy floor.

3   The snow drifted now, with the northwest wind hurling it in gusts. It drifted up around her black overshoes—old ones with little metal buckles. She smiled at the snow which was trying to cover her little by little. She could

remember when they had no black rubber overshoes; only the high buckskin leggings that they wrapped over their elkhide moccasins. If the snow was dry or frozen, a person could walk all day and not get wet; and in the evenings the beams of the ceiling would hang with lengths of pale buckskin leggings, drying out slowly.

She felt peaceful remembering. She didn't feel cold any more. Jimmie's blanket seemed warmer than it had ever been. And she could remember the morning he was born. She could remember whispering to her mother, who was sleeping on the other side of the hogan, to tell her it was time now. She did not want to wake the others. The second time she called to her, her mother stood up and pulled on her shoes; she knew. They walked to the old stone hogan together, Ayah walking a step behind her mother. She waited alone, learning the rhythms of the pains while her mother went to call the old woman to help them. The morning was already warm even before dawn and Ayah smelled the bee flowers blooming and the young willow growing at the springs. She could remember that so clearly, but his birth merged into the births of the other children and to her it became all the same birth. They named him for the summer morning and in English they called him Jimmie.

It wasn't like Jimmie died. He just never came back, and one day a dark blue sedan with white writing on its doors pulled up in front of the boxcar shack where the rancher let the Indians live. A man in a khaki uniform trimmed in gold gave them a yellow piece of paper and told them that Jimmie was dead. He said the Army would try to get the body back and then it would be shipped to them; but it wasn't likely because the helicopter had burned after it crashed. All of this was told to Chato because he could understand English. She stood inside the doorway holding the baby while Chato listened. Chato spoke English like a white man and he spoke Spanish too. He was taller than the white man and he stood straighter too. Chato didn't explain why; he just told the military man they could keep the body if they found it. The white man looked bewildered; he nodded his head and he left. Then Chato looked at her and shook his head, and then he told her, "Jimmie isn't coming home any-more," and when he spoke, he used the words to speak of the dead. She didn't cry then, but she hurt inside with anger. And she mourned him as the years passed, when a horse fell with Chato and broke his leg, and the white rancher told them he wouldn't pay Chato until he could work again. She mourned Jimmie because he would have worked for his father then; he would have sad-dled the big bay horse and ridden the fence lines each day, with wire cutters and heavy gloves, fixing the breaks in the barbed wire and putting the stray cattle back inside again.

She mourned him after the white doctors came to take Danny and Ella away. She was at the shack alone that day they came. It was back in the days be-

4

5

6

fore they hired Navajo women to go with them as interpreters. She recognized one of the doctors. She had seen him at the children's clinic at Cañoncito about a month ago. They were wearing khaki uniforms and they waved papers at her and a black ball-point pen, trying to make her understand their English words. She was frightened by the way they looked at the children, like the lizard watches the fly. Danny was swinging on the tire swing on the elm tree behind the rancher's house, and Ella was toddling around the front door, dragging the broomstick horse Chato made for her. Ayah could see they wanted her to sign the papers, and Chato had taught her to sign her name. It was something she was proud of. She only wanted them to go, and to take their eyes away from her children.

7   She took the pen from the man without looking at his face and she signed the papers in three different places he pointed to. She stared at the ground by their feet and waited for them to leave. But they stood there and began to point and gesture at the children. Danny stopped swinging. Ayah could see his fear. She moved suddenly and grabbed Ella into her arms; the child squirmed, trying to get back to her toys. Ayah ran with the baby toward Danny; she screamed for him to run and then she grabbed him around his chest and carried him too. She ran south into the foothills of juniper trees and black lava rock. Behind her she heard the doctors running, but they had been taken by surprise, and as the hills became stepper and the cholla cactus were thicker, they stopped. When she reached the top of the hill, she stopped to listen in case they were circling around her. But in a few minutes she heard a car engine start and they drove away. The children had been too surprised to cry while she ran with them. Danny was shaking and Ella's little fingers were gripping Ayah's blouse.

8   She stayed up in the hills for the rest of the day, sitting on a black lava boulder in the sunshine where she could see for miles all around her. The sky was light blue and cloudless, and it was warm for late April. The sun warmth relaxed her and took the fear and anger away. She lay back on the rock and watched the sky. It seemed to her that she could walk into the sky, stepping through clouds endlessly. Danny played with little pebbles and stones, pretending they were birds eggs and then little rabbits. Ella sat at her feet and dropped fistfuls of dirt into the breeze, watching the dust and particles of sand intently. Ayah watched a hawk soar high above them, dark wings gliding; hunting or only watching, she did not know. The hawk was patient and he circled all afternoon before he disappeared around the high volcanic peak the Mexicans called Guadalupe.

9   Late in the afternoon, Ayah looked down at the gray boxcar shack with the paint all peeled from the wood; the stove pipe on the roof was rusted and crooked. The fire she had built that morning in the oil drum stove had burned

out. Ella was asleep in her lap now and Danny sat close to her, complaining that he was hungry; he asked when they would go to the house. "We will stay up here until your father comes," she told him, "because those white men were chasing us." The boy remembered then and he nodded at her silently.

If Jimmie had been there he could have read those papers and explained to her what they said. Ayah would have known then, never to sign them. The doctors came back the next day and they brought a BIA policeman with them. They told Chato they had her signature and that was all they needed. Except for the kids. She listened to Chato sullenly; she hated him when he told her it was the old woman who died in the winter, spitting blood; it was her old grandma who had given the children this disease. "They don't spit blood," she said coldly. "The whites lie." She held Ella and Danny close to her, ready to run to the hills again. "I want a medicine man first," she said to Chato, not looking at him. He shook his head. "It's too late now. The policeman is with them. You signed the paper." His voice was gentle.   10

It was worse than if they had died: to lose the children and to know that somewhere, in a place called Colorado, in a place full of sick and dying strangers, her children were without her. There had been babies that died soon after they were born, and one that died before he could walk. She had carried them herself, up to the boulders and great pieces of the cliff that long ago crashed down from Long Mesa; she laid them in the crevices of sandstone and buried them in fine brown sand with round quartz pebbles that washed down the hills in the rain. She had endured it because they had been with her. But she could not bear this pain. She did not sleep for a long time after they took her children. She stayed on the hill where they had fled the first time, and she slept rolled up in the blanket Jimmie had sent her. She carried the pain in her belly and it was fed by everything she saw: the blue sky of their last day together and the dust and pebbles they played with; the swing in the elm tree and broom stick horse choked life from her. The pain filled her stomach and there was no room for food or for her lungs to fill with air. The air and the food would have been theirs.   11

She hated Chato, not because he let the policeman and doctors put the screaming children in the government car, but because he had taught her to sign her name. Because it was like the old ones always told her about learning their language or any of their ways: it endangered you. She slept alone on the hill until the middle of November when the first snows came. Then she made a bed for herself where the children had slept. She did not lie down beside Chato again until many years later, when he was sick and shivering and only her body could keep him warm. The illness came after the white rancher told Chato he was too old to work for him anymore, and Chato and his old woman should be out of the shack by the next afternoon because the rancher had hired   12 new people to work there. That had satisfied her. To see how the white man re-paid Chato's years of loyalty and work. All of Chato's fine-sounding English talk didn't change things.

13   It snowed steadily and the luminous light from the snow gradually dimin-ished into the darkness. Somewhere in Cebolleta a dog barked and other vil-lage dogs joined with it. Ayah looked in the direction she had come, from the bar where Chato was buying the wine. Sometimes he told her to go on ahead and wait; and then he never came. And when she finally went back looking for him, she would find him passed out at the bottom of the wooden steps at Azzie's Bar. All the wine would be gone and most of the money too, from the pale blue check that came to them once a month in a government envelope. It was then that she would look at his face and his hands, scarred by ropes and the barbed wire of all those years, and she would think, this man is a stranger; for forty years she had smiled at him and cooked his food, but he remained a stranger. She stood up again, with the snow almost to her knees, and she walked back to find Chato.

14   It was hard to walk in the deep snow and she felt the air burn in her lungs. She stopped a short distance from the bar to rest and readjust the blanket. But this time he wasn't waiting for her on the bottom step with his old Stetson hat pulled down and his shoulders hunched up in his long wool overcoat.

15   She was careful not to slip on the wooden steps. When she pushed the door open, warm air and cigarette smoke hit her face. She looked around slowly and deliberately, in every corner, in every dark place that the old man might find to sleep. The bar owner didn't like Indians in there, especially Navajos, but he let Chato come in because he could talk Spanish like he was one of them. The men at the bar stared at her, and the bartender saw that she left the door open wide. Snowflakes were flying inside like moths and melting into a puddle on the oiled wood floor. He motioned to her to close the door, but she did not see him. She held herself straight and walked across the room slowly, searching the room with every step. The snow in her hair melted and she could feel it on her forehead. At the far corner of the room, she saw red flames at the mica window of the old stove door; she looked behind the stove just to make sure. The bar got quiet except for the Spanish polka music playing on the jukebox. She stood by the stove and shook the snow from her blanket and held it near the stove to dry. The wet wool smell reminded her of new-born goats in early March, brought inside to warm near the fire. She felt calm.

16   In past years they would have told her to get out. But her hair was white now and her faced was wrinkled. They looked at her like she was a spider crawling slowly across the room. They were afraid; she could feel the fear. She looked at their faces steadily. They reminded her of the first time the white people brought her children back to her that winter. Danny had been shy and

hid behind the thin white woman who brought them. And the baby had not known her until Ayah took her into her arms, and then Ella had nuzzled close to her as she had when she was nursing. The blonde woman was nervous and kept looking at a dainty gold watch on her wrist. She sat on the bench near the small window and watched the dark snow clouds gather around the mountains; she was worrying about the unpaved road. She was frightened by what she saw inside too: the strips of venison drying on a rope across the ceiling and the children jabbering excitedly in a language she did not know. So they stayed for only a few hours. Ayah watched the government car disappear down the road and she knew they were already being weaned from these lava hills and from this sky. The last time they came was in early June, and Ella stared at her the way the men in the bar were now staring. Ayah did not try to pick her up; she smiled at her instead and spoke cheerfully to Danny. When he tried to answer her, he could not seem to remember and he spoke English words with the Navajo. But he gave her a scrap of paper that he had found somewhere and carried in his pocket; it was folded in half, and he shyly looked up at her and said it was a bird. She asked Chato if they were home for good this time. He spoke to the white woman and she shook her head. "How much longer?" he asked, and she said she didn't know; but Chato saw how she stared at the boxcar shack. Ayah turned away then. She did not say good-bye.

She felt satisfied that the men in the bar feared her. Maybe it was her face and the way she held her mouth with teeth clenched tight, like there was nothing anyone could do to her now. She walked north down the road, searching for the old man. She did this because she had the blanket, and there would be no place for him except with her and the blanket in the old abode barn near the arroyo. They always slept there when they came to Cebolleta. If the money and the wine were gone, she would be relieved because then they could go home again; back to the old hogan with a dirt roof and rock walls where she herself had been born. And the next day the old man could go back to the few sheep they still had, to follow along behind them, guiding them, into dry sandy arroyos where sparse grass grew. She knew he did not like walking behind old ewes when for so many years he rode big quarter horses and worked with cattle. But she wasn't sorry for him; he should have known all along what would happen. 17

There had not been enough rain for their garden in five years; and that was when Chato finally hitched a ride into the town and brought back brown boxes of rice and sugar and big tin cans of welfare peaches. After that, at the first of the month they went to Cebolleta to ask the postmaster for the check; and then Chato would go to the bar and cash it. They did this as they planted the garden every May, not because anything would survive the summer dust, but because it was time to do this. The journey passed the days that smelled silent and dry like the caves above the canyon with yellow painted buffaloes on their walls. 18

19   He was walking along the pavement when she found him. He did not stop or turn around when he heard her behind him. She walked beside him and she noticed how slowly he moved now. He smelled strong of woodsmoke and urine. Lately he had been forgetting. Sometimes he called her by his sister's name and she had been gone for a long time. Once she had found him wandering on the road to the white man's ranch, and she asked him why he was going that way; he laughed at her and said, "You know they can't run that ranch without me," and he walked on determined, limping on the leg that had been crushed many years before. Now he looked at her curiously, as if for the first time, but he kept shuffling along, moving slowly along the side of the highway. His gray hair had grown long and spread out on the shoulders of the long overcoat. He wore the old felt hat pulled down over his ears. His boots were worn out at the toes and he had stuffed pieces of an old red shirt in the holes. The rags made his feet look like little animals up to their ears in snow. She laughed at his feet; the snow muffled the sound of her laugh. He stopped and looked at her again. The wind had quit blowing and the snow was falling straight down; the southeast sky was beginning to clear and Ayah could see a star.

20   "Let's rest awhile," she said to him. They walked away from the road and up the slope to the giant boulders that had tumbled down from the red sand-rock mesa throughout the centuries of rainstorms and earth tremors. In a place where the boulders shut out the wind, they sat down with their backs against the rock. She offered half of the blanket to him and they sat wrapped together.

21   The storm passed swiftly. The clouds moved east. They were massive and full, crowding together across the sky. She watched them with the feeling of horses—steely blue-gray horses startled across the sky. The powerful haunches pushed into the distances and the tail hairs streamed white mist behind them. The sky cleared. Ayah saw that there was nothing between her and the stars. The light was crystalline. There was no shimmer, no distortion through earth haze. She breathed the clarity of the night sky; she smelled the purity of the half moon and the stars. He was lying on his side with his knees pulled up near his belly for warmth. His eyes were closed now, and in the light from the stars and the moon, he looked young again.

22   She could see it descend out of the night sky: an icy stillness from the edge of the thin moon. She recognized the freezing. It came gradually, sinking snowflake by snowflake until the crust was heavy and deep. It had the strength of the stars in Orion, and its journey was endless. Ayah knew that with the wine he would sleep. He would not feel it. She tucked the blanket around him, remembering how it was when Ella had been with her; and she felt the rush so big inside her heart for the babies. And she sang the only song she knew to sing for babies. She could not remember if she had ever sung it to her children, but she knew that her grandmother had sung it and her mother had sung it:

The earth is your mother,

    she holds you.

The sky is your father,

    he protects you.

Sleep,

sleep.

Rainbow is your sister,

    she loves you.

The winds are your brothers,

    they sing to you.

Sleep,

sleep.

We are together always

We are together always

There never was a time

when this

was not so.

INQUIRING INTO THE STORY

Use the methods of inquiry—exploring, explaining, evaluating, and reflecting—to discover what you think about Silko's short story, and move toward your own interpretations. The questions below might serve as journal prompts and triggers for class discussion.

1. On the left page of your notebook, jot down at least five lines or passages that you believe were key to your understanding of the story. These may include details that seem important, moments that signify turning points, or feelings or ideas suggested by the narrator or another character. On the opposing right page, openly fastwrite about the passages you collected. What do they seem to suggest about possible themes for the story? What do you notice about Ayah, the main character and narrator? What do you consider the significant events that affect all the characters and how do they change them?

2. Explain the significance of the poem that ends "Lullaby."

3. A recurring detail in the story is the blanket that Ayah received from her son, Jimmie. Trace every mention of the blanket in the story. What accumulated meaning does this detail acquire in the story?

4. Some critics have argued that "Lullaby" is a story of healing and re-covery. Do you agree or disagree? What evidence in the story would you point to that either supports or contradicts that contention?

5. One of the most common responses we have to stories we enjoy is to say that we "could relate to it." Did you feel that way about "Lullaby" even though you might not be Native American? Certainly the story helps those of us who are not Native American to under-stand an aspect of the Indian experience in America, but does it also help us understand ourselves?

ONE STUDENT'S RESPONSE

NOEL'S JOURNAL

DOUBLE-ENTRY JOURNAL RESPONSE TO "LULLABY"

"It was worse than if they had died; to lose the children and to know that somehwhere, in a place called Colorado, in a place full of sick and dying strangers, her children were without her."	I think this sets the tone of the whole story. She loses one son to the war and the other two were taken from her. Knowing that one son had died and wouldn't ever come home again. The other two were alive and well but they would not grow up with their mother and were kept from their own culture by the government.
"She stayed on the hill where they had fled the first time, and she slept rolled up in the blanket Jimmie had sent her."	After she lost all her children she finds comfort in the blanket her older son had sent her. She sleeps in the place where she spent the last mo-ments with her other two children.
	She carries the blanket with her wherever she goes. This is how she spent her time mourning her loss and memories. . .

SHORT STORY

Alice Walker is most famous for her novel, *The Color Purple,* which was later turned into a movie starring Oprah Winfrey. But Walker is also a talented essayist and short story writer. "Everyday Use," first published in 1973, is probably Walker's best-known work of short fiction. One way to read literature is to con-sider its historical context, so keep in mind that this story was written at a time in which the black power and women's movements were fundamentally challenging the ways Americans traditionally looked at African Americans and women.

Another way to read a literary work is to explore the choices the writer made about *how* to tell the story and to think about how those choices influence your experience reading it. For instance, one of the most important considerations for fiction writers is point of view (see "Inquiring into the Details: Literary Devices" later in the chapter). There are a range of choices writers can make. For instance, they can tell the story as if the narrator is God, hovering over the narrative and describing everything that is happening. Sometimes such omniscient storytellers use their power to enter the thoughts of one or more characters. Other times, writers narrate a story from a single character's point of view, as Walker does here. As you read "Everyday Use," consider how this choice of point of view shapes your experience of the story. What if Walker had chosen to tell the story through another character or simply described what happened as an omniscient narrator? What might be Walker's motive in choosing Mama as the voice that dominates this tale?

Finally, short stories usually are built around a significant event that causes characters to change in some way. Imagine that a story is like a placid pond, with each character floating like a motionless twig on the surface. Then the writer heaves a stone into the water, and this creates ripples outward that eventually move the twigs—and the characters—this way and that. Some characters are more affected than others, and those that are most moved by the significant event in the story are often important. How did they change? Why? A significant event can be dramatic—someone dies—or more ordinary—a surprise birthday cake was delivered to a couple's table—but it's important enough to move the characters in some way. What is the significant event in "Everyday Use?" Who is changed by it? What is the significance of that change?

Everyday Use

Alice Walker

I will wait for her in the yard that Maggie and I made so clean and wavy yesterday afternoon. A yard like this is more comfortable than most people know. It is not just a yard. It is like an extended living room. When the hard clay is swept clean as a floor and the fine sand around the edges lined with tiny, irregular grooves, anyone can come and sit and look up into the elm tree and wait for the breezes that never come inside the house.

Maggie will be nervous until after her sister goes: she will stand hopelessly in corners, homely and ashamed of the burn scars down her arms and legs, eyeing her sister with a mixture of envy and awe. She thinks her sister has held life always in the palm of one hand, that "no" is a word the world never learned to say to her.

3   You've no doubt seen those TV shows where the child who has "made it" is confronted, as a surprise, by her own mother and father, tottering in weakly from backstage. (A pleasant surprise, of course. What would they do if parent and child came on the show only to curse out and insult each other?) On TV mother and child embrace and smile into each other's faces. Sometimes the mother and father weep, the child wraps them in her arms and leans across the table to tell how she would not have made it without their help. I have seen these programs.

4   Sometimes I dream a dream in which Dee and I are suddenly brought together on a TV program of this sort. Out of a dark and soft-seated limousine I am ushered into a bright room filled with many people. There I meet a smiling, gray, sporty man like Johnny Carson who shakes my hand and tells me what a fine girl I have. Then we are on the stage and Dee is embracing me with tears in her eyes. She pins on my dress a large orchid, even though she has told me once that she thinks orchids are tacky flowers.

5   In real life I am a large, big-boned woman with rough, man-working hands. In the winter I wear flannel nightgowns to bed and overalls during the day. I can kill and clean a hog as mercilessly as a man. My fat keeps me hot in zero weather. I can work outside all day, breaking ice to get water for washing: I can eat pork liver cooked over the open fire minutes after it comes steaming from the hog. One winter I knocked a bull calf straight in the brain between the eyes with a sledge hammer and had the meat hung up to chill before nightfall. But of course all this does not show on television. I am the way my daughter would want me to be: a hundred pounds lighter, my skin like an uncooked barley pancake. My hair glistens in the hot bright lights. Johnny Carson has much to do to keep up with my quick and witty tongue.

6   But that is a mistake. I know even before I wake up. Who ever knew a Johnson with a quick tongue? Who can even imagine me looking a strange white man in the eye? It seems to me I have talked to them always with one foot raised in flight, with my head turned in whichever way is farthest from them. Dee, though. She would always look anyone in the eye. Hesitation was no part of her nature.

7   "How do I look, Mama?" Maggie says, showing just enough of her thin body enveloped in pink skirt and red blouse for me to know she's there, almost hidden by the door.

8   "Come out into the yard," I say.

9   Have you ever seen a lame animal, perhaps a dog run over by some careless person rich enough to own a car, sidle up to someone who is ignorant enough to be kind to him? That is the way my Maggie walks. She has been like this, chin on chest, eyes on ground, feet in shuffle, ever since the fire that burned the other house to the ground.

Dee is lighter than Maggie, with nicer hair and a fuller figure. She's a   10
woman now, though sometimes I forget. How long ago was it that the other
house burned? Ten, twelve years? Sometimes I can still hear the flames and feel
Maggie's arms sticking to me, her hair smoking and her dress falling off her in
little black papery flakes. Her eyes seemed stretched open, blazed open by the
flames reflected in them. And Dee. I see her standing off under the sweet gum
tree she used to dig gum out of; a look of concentration on her face as she
watched the last dingy gray board of the house fall in toward the red-hot brick
chimney. Why don't you do a dance around the ashes? I'd wanted to ask her.
She had hated the house that much.

I used to think she hated Maggie, too. But that was before we raised the   11
money, the church and me, to send her to Augusta to school. She used to
read to us without pity; forcing words, lies, other folks' habits, whole lives
upon us two, sitting trapped and ignorant underneath her voice. She
washed us in a river of make-believe, burned us with a lot of knowledge we
didn't necessarily need to know. Pressed us to her with the serious way she
read, to shove us away at just the moment, like dimwits, we seemed about
to understand.

Dee wanted nice things. A yellow organdy dress to wear to her graduation   12
from high school; black pumps to match a green suit she'd made from an old
suit somebody gave me. She was determined to stare down any disaster in her
efforts. Her eyelids would not flicker for minutes at a time. Often I fought off
the temptation to shake her. At sixteen she had a style of her own: and knew
what style was.

I never had an education myself. After second grade the school was closed   13
down. Don't ask me why: in 1927 colored asked fewer questions than they do
now. Sometimes Maggie reads to me. She stumbles along good-naturedly but
can't see well. She knows she is not bright. Like good looks and money, quick-
ness passed her by. She will marry John Thomas (who has mossy teeth in an
earnest face) and then I'll be free to sit here and I guess just sing church songs
to myself. Although I never was a good singer. Never could carry a tune. I was
always better at a man's job. I used to love to milk till I was hooked in the side
in '49. Cows are soothing and slow and don't bother you, unless you try to
milk them the wrong way.

I have deliberately turned my back on the house. It is three rooms, just   14
like the one that burned, except the roof is tin; they don't make shingle roofs
any more. There are no real windows, just some holes cut in the sides, like the
portholes in a ship, but not round and not square, with rawhide holding the
shutters up on the outside. This house is in a pasture, too, like the other one.
No doubt when Dee sees it she will want to tear it down. She wrote me once
that no matter where we "choose" to live, she will manage to come see us. But

she will never bring her friends. Maggie and I thought about this and Maggie asked me, "Mama, when did Dee ever *have* any friends?"

15   She had a few. Furtive boys in pink shirts hanging about on wash-day after school. Nervous girls who never laughed. Impressed with her they worshiped the well-turned phrase, the cute shape, the scalding humor that erupted like bubbles in lye. She read to them.

16   When she was courting Jimmy T she didn't have much time to pay to us, but turned all her faultfinding power on him. He *flew* to marry a cheap city girl from a family of ignorant flashy people. She hardly had time to recompose herself.

17   When she comes I will meet—but there they are!

18   Maggie attempts to make a dash for the house, in her shuffling way, but I stay her with my hand. "Come back here," I say. And she stops and tries to dig a well in the sand with her toe.

19   It is hard to see them clearly through the strong sun. But even the first glimpse of leg out of the car tells me it is Dee. Her feet were always neat-looking, as if God himself had shaped them with a certain style. From the other side of the car comes a short, stocky man. Hair is all over his head a foot long and hanging from his chin like a kinky mule tail. I hear Maggie suck in her breath. "Uhnnnh," is what it sounds like. Like when you see the wriggling end of a snake just in front of your foot on the road. "Uhnnnh."

20   Dee next. A dress down to the ground, in this hot weather. A dress so loud it hurts my eyes. There are yellows and oranges enough to throw back the light of the sun. I feel my whole face warming from the heat waves it throws out. Earrings gold, too, and hanging down to her shoulders. Bracelets dangling and making noises when she moves her arm up to shake the folds of the dress out of her armpits. The dress is loose and flows, and as she walks closer, I like it. I hear Maggie go "Uhnnnh" again. It is her sister's hair. It stands straight up like the wool on a sheep. It is black as night and around the edges are two long pigtails that rope about like small lizards disappearing behind her ears.

21   "Wa-su-zo-Tean-o," she says, coming on in that gliding way the dress makes her move. The short stocky fellow with the hair to his navel is all grinning and he follows up with "Asalamalakim, my mother and sister!" He moves to hug Maggie but she falls back, right up against the back of my chair. I feel her trembling there and when I look up I see the perspiration falling off her chin.

22   "Don't get up," says Dee. Since I am stout it takes something of a push. You can see me trying to move a second or two before I make it. She turns, showing white heels through her sandals, and goes back to the car. Out she peeks next with a Polaroid. She stoops down quickly and lines up picture after picture of me sitting there in front of the house with Maggie cowering behind

me. She never takes a shot without making sure the house is included. When a cow comes nibbling around the edge of the yard she snaps it and me and Maggie *and* the house. Then she puts the Polaroid in the back seat of the car, and comes up and kisses me on the forehead.

Meanwhile Asalamalakim is going through motions with Maggie's hand. Maggie's hand is as limp as a fish, and probably as cold, despite the sweat, and she keeps trying to pull it back. It looks like Asalamalakim wants to shake hands but wants to do it fancy. Or maybe he don't know how people shake hands. Anyhow, he soon gives up on Maggie.   23

"Well," I say. "Dee."   24

"No, Mama," she says. "Not 'Dee.' Wangero Leewanika Kemanjo!"   25

"What happened to 'Dee'?" I wanted to know.   26

"She's dead," Wangero said. "I couldn't bear it any longer, being named after the people who oppress me."   27

"You know as well as me you was named after your aunt Dicie," I said. Dicie is my sister. She named Dee. We called her "Big Dee" after Dee was born.   28

"But who was *she* named after?" asked Wangero.   29

"I guess after Grandma Dee," I said.   30

"And who was she named after?" asked Wangero.   31

"Her mother," I said, and saw Wangero was getting tired. "That's about as far back as *I* can trace it," I said. Though, in fact, I probably could have carried it back beyond the Civil War through the branches.   32

"Well," said Asalamalakim, "there you are."   33

"Uhnnnh," I heard Maggie say.   34

"There I was not," I said, "before 'Dicie' cropped up in our family, so why should I try to trace it that far back?"   35

He just stood there grinning, looking down on me like somebody inspecting a Model A car. Every once in a while he and Wangero sent eye signals over my head.   36

"How do you pronounce this name?" I asked.   37

"You don't have to call me by it if you don't want to," said Wangero.   38

"Why shouldn't I?" I asked. "If that's what you want us to call you, we'll call you."   39

"I know it might sound awkward at first," said Wangero.   40

"I'll get used to it," I said. "Ream it out again."   41

Well, soon we got the name out of the way. Asalamalakim had a name twice as long and three times as hard. After I tripped over it two or three times he told me to just call him Hakim-a-barber. I wanted to ask him was he a barber, but I didn't really think he was, so I didn't ask.   42

43   "You must belong to those beef-cattle peoples down the road," I said. They said "Asalamalakim" when they met you, too, but they didn't shake hands. Always too busy: feeding the cattle, fixing the fences, putting up salt-lick shelters, throwing down hay. When the white folks poisoned some of the herd the men stayed up all night with rifles in their hands. I walked a mile and a half just to see the sight.

44   Hakim-a-barber said, "I accept some of their doctrines, but farming and raising cattle is not my style." (They didn't tell me, and I didn't ask, whether Wangero [Dee] had really gone and married him.)

45   We sat down to eat and right away he said he didn't eat collards and pork was unclean. Wangero, though, went on through the chitlins and corn bread, the greens and everything else. She talked a blue streak over the sweet potatoes. Everything delighted her. Even the fact that we still used the benches her daddy made for the table when we couldn't afford to buy chairs.

46   "Oh, Mama!" she cried. Then turned to Hakim-a-barber. "I never knew how lovely these benches are. You can feel the rump prints," she said, running her hands underneath her and along the bench. Then she gave a sigh and her hand closed over Grandma Dee's butter dish. "That's it!" she said. "I knew there was something I wanted to ask you if I could have." She jumped up from the table and went over in the corner where the churn stood, the milk in it clabber by now. She looked at the churn and looked at it.

47   "This churn top is what I need," she said. "Didn't Uncle Buddy whittle it out of a tree you all used to have?"

48   "Yes," I said.

49   "Uh huh," she said happily. "And I want the dasher, too."

50   "Uncle Buddy whittle that, too?" asked the barber.

51   Dee (Wangero) looked up at me.

52   "Aunt Dee's first husband whittled the dash," said Maggie so low you almost couldn't hear her. "His name was Henry, but they called him Stash."

53   "Maggie's brain is like an elephant's," Wangero said, laughing. "I can use the churn top as a centerpiece for the alcove table," she said, sliding a plate over the churn, "and I'll think of something artistic to do with the dasher."

54   When she finished wrapping the dasher the handle stuck out. I took it for a moment in my hands. You didn't even have to look close to see where hands pushing the dasher up and down to make butter had left a kind of sink in the wood. In fact, there were a lot of small sinks: you could see where thumbs and fingers had sunk into the wood. It was beautiful light yellow wood, from a tree that grew in the yard where Big Dee and Stash had lived.

55   After dinner Dee (Wangero) went to the trunk at the foot of my bed and started rifling through it. Maggie hung back in the kitchen over the dishpan.

Out came Wangero with two quilts. They had been pieced by Grandma Dee and then Big Dee and me had hung them on the quilt frames on the front porch and quilted them. One was in the Lone Star pattern. The other was Walk Around the Mountain. In both of them were scraps of dresses Grandma Dee had worn fifty and more years ago. Bits and pieces of Grandpa Jarrell's Paisley shirts. And one teeny faded blue piece, about the size of a penny matchbox, that was from Great Grandpa Ezra's uniform that he wore in the Civil War.

"Mama," Wangero said sweet as a bird. "Can I have these old quilts?" 56

I heard something fall in the kitchen, and a minute later the kitchen door 57
slammed.

"Why don't you take one or two of the others?" I asked. "These old things 58
was just done by me and Big Dee from some tops your grandma pieced before
she died."

"No," said Wangero. "I don't want those. They are stitched around the bor- 59
ders by machine."

"That'll make them last better," I said. 60

"That's not the point," said Wangero. "These are all pieces of dresses 61
Grandma used to wear. She did all this stitching by hand. Imagine!" She held
the quilts securely in her arms, stroking them.

"Some of the pieces, like those lavender ones, come from old clothes her 62
mother handed down to her," I said, moving up to touch the quilts. Dee
(Wangero) moved back just enough so that I couldn't reach the quilts. They already belonged to her.

"Imagine!" she breathed again, clutching them closely to her bosom. 63

"The truth is," I said, "I promised to give them quilts to Maggie, for when 64
she marries John Thomas."

She gasped like a bee had stung her. 65

"Maggie can't appreciate these quilts!" she said. "She'd probably be back- 66
ward enough to put them to everyday use."

"I reckon she would," I said. "God knows I been saving 'em for long 67
enough with nobody using 'em. I hope she will!" I didn't want to bring up how
I had offered Dee (Wangero) a quilt when she went away to college. Then she
had told me they were old-fashioned, out of style.

"But they're *priceless!*" she was saying now, furiously; for she had a temper. 68
"Maggie would put them on the bed and in five years they'd be in rags. Less
than that!"

"She can always make some more," I said. "Maggie knows how to quilt." 69

Dee (Wangero) looked at me with hatred. "You will not understand. The 70
point is these quilts, *these* quilts!"

71   "Well," I said, stumped. "What would *you* do with them?"

72   "Hang them," she said. As if that was the only thing you *could* do with quilts.

73   Maggie by now was standing in the door. I could almost hear the sound her feet made as they scraped over each other.

74   "She can have them, Mama," she said, like somebody used to never winning anything, or having anything reserved for her. "I can 'member Grandma Dee without the quilts."

75   I looked at her hard. She had filled her bottom lip with checkerberry snuff and it gave her face a kind of dopey, hangdog look. It was Grandma Dee and Big Dee who taught her how to quilt herself. She stood there with her scarred hands hidden in the folds of her skirt. She looked at her sister with something like fear but she wasn't mad at her. This was Maggie's portion. This was the way she knew God to work.

76   When I looked at her like that something hit me in the top of my head and ran down to the soles of my feet. Just like when I'm in church and the spirit of God touches me and I get happy and shout. I did something I never had done before: hugged Maggie to me, then dragged her on into the room, snatched the quilts out of Miss Wangero's hands and dumped them into Maggie's lap.

77   Maggie just sat there on my bed with her mouth open.

78   "Take one or two of the others," I said to Dee.

79   But she turned without a word and went out to Hakim-a-barber.

80   "You just don't understand," she said, as Maggie and I came out to the car.

81   "What don't I understand?" I wanted to know.

"Your heritage," she said. And then she turned to Maggie, kissed her, and said, "You ought to try to make something of yourself, too, Maggie. It's really a new day for us. But from the way you and Mama still live you'd never know it."

82   She put on some sunglasses that hid everything above the tip of her nose and her chin.

83   Maggie smiled; maybe at the sunglasses. But a real smile, not scared.

84   After we watched the car dust settle I asked Maggie to bring me a dip of snuff. And then the two of us sat there just enjoying, until it was time to go in the house and go to bed.

INQUIRING INTO THE STORY

Explore, explain, evaluate, and reflect on Walker's story "Everyday Use."

   1. A child returns home as an adult and everything is somehow changed. Things that didn't have much meaning before suddenly seem meaningful. Most of us have had this experience. But "Everyday Use" forces us to see this from a mother's point of view.

Explore this in your own life. Think of a time when you returned home after leaving for awhile—perhaps returning after a year at school, serving in the military, or taking a job in another city. In your journal, begin with a moment during a return home in which you were in the presence of one or both of your parents. Now describe yourself through your mother's or your father's eyes. What do they notice about you? What do they think? What pleases and displeases them? How does this exercise affect your understanding of Walker's story?

2. Identify the *significant event* in this story (see "Inquiring into the Details: Literary Devices") and explain how it changes a character. What do you make of these changes? What do they suggest about some of the larger themes of "Everyday Use?"

3. Evaluate the following assertion about the narrator, Mama, in the story: *While Dee seems to be the character who is least sympathetic in the story, Mama is blind to her own role in nurturing both daughters' faults. If there is a villain in this story, it's the narrator.* Do you agree or disagree? What evidence would you point to in the story to support your thinking?

4. One of the most common reasons I hear for liking a story or an essay is that the reader "can relate to it." Reflect for a moment on what this means to you. Does such a principle apply to your experience of reading Walker's story? Does it apply to other stories that open doors to worlds you may not know because of your race and background?

CRITICAL ESSAY

Writing about literature is like rock climbing—you're always looking for a handhold or the right place to sink your bolt. Fortunately, good stories offer writers plenty of places to grasp. You can focus on a particular character, the significance of a scene, a particular motif, or the overall themes of the story. The only essential is that your critical essay be firmly anchored to the story itself—what characters say or do, specific details, particular scenes or passages.

In the essay that follows, critic John Gruesser seizes on the images of animals in Alice Walker's "Everday Use." This is a pretty narrowly focused essay but it works well because Gruesser finds plenty of evidence in the story to support his thesis that animal images "and references to animal husbandry pervade" the story. This brief piece, which recently appeared in the literary journal *Explicator*, nicely models important features of the critical essay you're assigned to write: it's well focused, it never strays far from specific evidence from the story, and is composed around the writer's own idea about one way to understand the story.

ANIMAL IMAGERY IN "EVERYDAY USE"

John Gruesser

1   Images of animals and references to animal husbandry pervade Alice Walker's justly famous 1973 short story "Everyday Use." Not only is each of the three characters, Mama, Maggie, and Dee, explicitly or implicitly associated with animals, but the story takes place in a "pasture," down the road from which several "beef-cattle peoples" live and work. Some of the comparisons between the women and fauna are highly conventional or purely descriptive: Maggie's memory is linked to that of an elephant; the voice of a pleading Dee sounds as "sweet as a bird"; Dee's hair stands erect "like the wool on a sheep"; and her pigtails are compared to "small lizards disappearing behind her ears". Image patterns involving cows and dogs, however, foreshadow the story's climactic scene, in which Mama decides to give the quilts to Maggie rather than Dee, and they play an integral role in the scene itself and its aftermath.

2   Mama frequently describes Maggie as a docile, somewhat frightened animal, one that accepts the hand that fate has dealt her and attempts to flee any situation posing a potential threat. When Dee arrives, Mama tells us that "Maggie attempts to make a dash for the house, in her shuffling way, but I stay her with my hand. 'Come back here,' I say. And she stops and tries to dig a well in the sand with her toe". Maggie's characteristic stance in such situations is aptly summed up by Mama in the word "cowering". Although the etymologies of the words "cow" and "cower" differ, it seems likely that Walker is hinting at the former by employing the latter. Yet Maggie is not the only person described in bovine terms. Mama refers to herself as "a large, big boned woman" and informs us that her own body language, at least in her encounters with white men, resembles Maggie's: "It seems to me I have talked to them with one foot raised in flight, with my head turned in whichever way is furthest from them". Mama and Maggie's connection to cows is reinforced when Dee lines up a Polaroid shot of her mother, her sister, the house, and a real cow that has wandered into the yard. More important, in a key passage that adumbrates the ending of the story, Mama tells us that she used to enjoy milking cows until she was "hooked in the side" in 1949, adding, "Cows are soothing and slow and don't bother you, unless you try to milk them the wrong way". This is precisely the kind of mistake Dee will make later when she demands the quilts that Mama has already promised to Maggie.

3   Mama's comparisons between animals and Maggie, who bears the scars from a fire that destroyed the family's previous home (and who was perhaps burned trying to save the very quilts Dee covets), often seem insensitive. Without a doubt, the most shocking example of this occurs early in "Everyday

Use": "Have you ever seen a lame animal, perhaps a dog run over by some careless person rich enough to own a car, sidle up to someone ignorant enough to be kind him? That is the way my Maggie walks". Near the end of the story, after Maggie tells her mother that Dee can have the quilts because she can "'member Grandma Dee without" them, Mama describes Maggie in similar terms: "I looked at her hard. She had filled up her bottom lip with checkerberry snuff and it gave her face a kind of dopey, hangdog look". It is at this moment in the story that Mama has her epiphany, realizing that her thin, scarred, pathetic daughter, who knows how to quilt and serves as her family's oral historian, deserves the quilts more than her shapely, favored, educated daughter Dee, who only wants the quilts because they are now fashionable. Acting on this flash of insight, Mama does two things that she has never, amazingly enough, done before: she hugs Maggie and she says "no" to Dee. Afterward, in the final paragraph, Maggie's face lights up with a smile that is "real [. . .] not scared". Moreover, Mama asks her for "a dip of snuff", and together the enlightened mother and the faithful daughter sit, enjoying their snuff and each other's company, oblivious to the "dopey, hangdog look" they presumably present to the world. Significantly, in seeing the value in Maggie, Mama has been able to look beneath the surface of things and see the value in herself as well.

It is perfectly appropriate that animal imagery should figure in "Everyday Use," a story with a rural setting, whose matriarch and narrator supports herself by raising livestock. Walker goes a step further, however, by using hooking cows and hangdog looks to reinforce the major themes of her story.

4

Work Cited

Walker, Alice. "Everyday Use." *Everyday Use.* Ed. Barbara Christian. New Brunswick: Rutgers, UP, 1994. 23–35.

INQUIRING INTO THE ESSAY

Use the four ways of inquiring—exploring, explaining, evaluating, and reflecting—to think about your response to Gruesser's essay.

1. Explore your reaction to the essay twice. After reading the piece all the way through the first time, open your journal and fastwrite for three minutes, beginning with the following phrase: *The first thing that strikes me about this essay is . . .* When the writing stalls, use the phrase again: *Another thing that strikes me about this essay is . . .* As you write, try to remember all that you can from the essay without looking at it. After three minutes of writing, reread the essay. Repeat the fastwriting exercise in your journal, except begin with the following phrase: *The second time I read the essay, I thought . . .*

And then I thought ... And then ... Stop and look at the essay again if you want to. Write for five minutes this time.

2. What was your most significant reaction to Gruesser's essay that emerged from your two episodes of fastwriting in the previous question?

3. Using the list in the earlier "Features of the Form" section, explain how this essay exemplifies some of the features.

4. At the end of the essay, Gruesser argues that Walker uses animal imagery, including "hooking cows" and "handog looks" to reinforce "the major themes of the story." How would you evaluate that claim? What is the strongest evidence he offers in its support? What is the weakest?

5. My students often complain that English teachers dig deeply for meaning in stories when it isn't really there. What do you think of this? Do you agree? Would Gruesser's story be an example of this?

ESSAY

In the garage I have a wooden toolbox my father made for himself forty years ago, and in it are some of his old tools—some wrenches, a file or two, a hammerhead missing a handle. I can tell these are his tools because of the faint red nail polish I can still see on each of them. It was his mark. In the essay that follows, Scott Sanders writes about a similar inheritance, but he could just as easily be writing about a sewing machine, an old wooden boat, hand-made clothes, or an old quilt—things that may have been passed down from our mothers and fathers, grandmothers and grandfathers. In the earlier story, "Everday Use," Alice Walker writes about two old quilts that have very different meanings to the daughters who hope to inherit them. What are these meanings?

That's the question behind Sanders' essay, "The Inheritance of Tools." What does he suggest the answers might be by the end of the piece?

Unlike "Lullaby" or "Everyday Use," this is a work of *nonfiction.* In other words, the story Sanders tells actually happened; it was not invented. Nonfiction is not a category of writing that is usually considered literary, but literary nonfiction such as the personal essay predated and, some argue, helped give birth to the short story and novel. "The Inheritance of Tools" has many of the literary qualities you'd expect in a short story, including the backbone of narrative, telling details, characters, scenes, and, most importantly, implicit themes. But we read nonfiction somewhat differently than we read fiction because our expectations are different. (See "Inquiring into the Details: How to Read Nonfiction" immediately following the essay for suggestions about this.) What are these differences?

THE INHERITANCE OF TOOLS
Scott Russell Sanders

At just about the hour when my father died, soon after dawn one February   1
morning when ice coated the windows like cataracts, I banged my thumb with a
hammer. Naturally I swore at the hammer, the reckless thing, and in the moment of swearing I thought of what my father would say: "If you'd try hitting the
nail it would go in a whole lot faster. Don't you know your thumb's not as hard
as that hammer?" We both were doing carpentry that day, but far apart. He was
building cupboards at my brother's place in Oklahoma; I was at home in Indiana
putting up a wall in the basement to make a bedroom for my daughter. By the
time my mother called with news of his death—the long distance wires whit-
tling her voice until it seemed too thin to bear the weight of what she had to
say—my thumb was swollen. A week or so later a white scar in the shape of a
crescent moon began to show above the cuticle, and month by month it rose
across the pink sky of my thumbnail. It took the better part of a year for the
scar to disappear, and every time I noticed it I thought of my father.

The hammer had belonged to him, and to his father before him. The three   2
of us have used it to build houses and barns and chicken coops, to upholster
chairs and crack walnuts, to make doll furniture and bookshelves and jewelry
boxes. The head is scratched and pockmarked, like an old plowshare that has
been working rocky fields, and it gives off the sort of dull sheen you see on fast
creek water in the shade. It is a finishing hammer, about the weight of a bread
loaf, too light really for framing walls, too heavy for cabinetwork, with a
curved claw for pulling nails, a rounded head for pounding, a fluted neck for
looks, and a hickory handle for strength.

The present handle is my third one, bought from a lumberyard in   3
Tennessee down the road from where my brother and I were helping my father
build his retirement house. I broke the previous one by trying to pull sixteen-
penny nails out of floor joists—a foolish thing to do with a finishing hammer,
as my father pointed out. "You ever hear of a crowbar?" he said. No telling how
many handles he and my grandfather had gone through before me. My grandfather used to cut down hickory trees on his farm, saw them into slabs, cure
the planks in his hayloft, and carve handles with a drawknife. The grain in hickory is crooked and knotty, and therefore tough, hard to split, like the grain in
the two men who owned this hammer before me.

After proposing marriage to a neighbor girl, my grandfather used this   4
hammer to build a house for his bride on a stretch of river bottom in northern
Mississippi. The lumber for the place, like the hickory for the handle, was cut
on his own land. By the day of the wedding he had not quite finished the

house, and so right after the ceremony he took his wife home and put her to work. My grandmother had worn her Sunday dress for the wedding, with a fringe of lace tacked on around the hem in honor of the occasion. She removed this lace and folded it away before going out to help my grandfather nail siding on the house. "There she was in her good dress," he told me some fifty-odd years after that wedding day, "holding up them long pieces of clapboard while I hammered, and together we got the place covered up before dark." As the family grew to four, six, eight, and eventually thirteen, my grandfather used this hammer to enlarge his house room by room, like a chambered nautilus expanding his shell.

5   By and by the hammer was passed along to my father. One day he was up on the roof of our pony barn nailing shingles with it, when I stepped out the kitchen door to call him for supper. Before I could yell, something about the sight of him straddling the spine of the roof and swinging the hammer caught my eye and made me hold my tongue. I was five or six years old, and the world's commonplaces were still news to me. He would pull a nail from the pouch at his waist, bring the hammer down, and a moment later the *thunk* of the blow would reach my ears. And that is what had stopped me in my tracks and stilled my tongue, that momentary gap between seeing and hearing the blow. Instead of yelling from the kitchen door, I ran to the barn and climbed two rungs up the ladder—as far as I was allowed to go—and spoke quietly to my father. On our walk to the house he explained that sound takes time to make its way through air. Suddenly the world seemed larger, the air more dense, if sound could be held back like any ordinary traveler.

6   By the time I started using this hammer, at about the age when I discovered the speed of sound, it already contained houses and mysteries for me. The smooth handle was one my grandfather had made. In those days I needed both hands to swing it. My father would start a nail in a scrap of wood, and I would pound away until I bent it over.

7   "Looks like you got ahold of some of those rubber nails," he would tell me. "Here, let me see if I can find you some stiff ones." And he would rummage in a drawer until he came up with a fistful of more cooperative nails. "Look at the head," he would tell me. "Don't look at your hands, don't look at the hammer. Just look at the head of that nail and pretty soon you'll learn to hit it square."

8   Pretty soon I did learn. While he worked in the garage cutting dovetail joints for a drawer or skinning a deer or tuning an engine, I would hammer nails. I made innocent blocks of wood look like porcupines. He did not talk much in the midst of his tools, but he kept up a nearly ceaseless humming, slipping in and out of a dozen tunes in an afternoon, often running back over the same stretch of melody again and again, as if searching for a way out. When

the humming did cease, I knew he was faced with a task requiring great delicacy or concentration, and I took care not to distract him.

He kept scraps of wood in a cardboard box—the ends of two-by-fours, slabs of shelving and plywood, odd pieces of molding—and everything in it was fair game. I nailed scraps together to fashion what I called boats or houses, but the results usually bore only faint resemblance to the visions I carried in my head. I would hold up these constructions to show my father, and he would turn them over in his hands admiringly, speculating about what they might be. My cobbled-together guitars might have been alien spaceships, my barns might have been models of Aztec temples, each wooden contraption might have been anything but what I had set out to make.

Now and again I would feel the need to have a chunk of wood shaped or shortened before I riddled it with nails, and I would clamp it in a vice and scrape at it with a handsaw. My father would let me lacerate the board until my arm gave out, and then he would wrap his hand around mine and help me finish the cut, showing me how to use my thumb to guide the blade, how to pull back on the saw to keep it from binding, how to let my shoulder do the work.

"Don't force it," he would say, "just drag it easy and give the teeth a chance to bite."

As the saw teeth bit down the wood released its smell, each kind with its own fragrance, oak or walnut or cherry or pine—usually pine, because it was the softest and easiest for a child to work. No matter how weathered and gray the board, no matter how warped and cracked, inside there was this smell waiting, as of something freshly baked. I gathered every smidgen of sawdust and stored it away in coffee cans, which I kept in a drawer of the workbench. When I did not feel like hammering nails I would dump my sawdust on the concrete floor of the garage and landscape it into highways and farms and towns, running miniature cars and trucks along miniature roads. Looming as huge as a colossus, my father worked over and around me, now and again bending down to inspect my work, careful not to trample my creations. It was a landscape that smelled dizzyingly of wood. Even after a bath my skin would carry the smell, and so would my father's hair, when he lifted me for a bedtime hug.

I tell these things not only from memory but also from recent observation, because my own son now turns blocks of wood into nailed porcupines, dumps cans full of sawdust at my feet and sculpts highways on the floor. He learns how to swing a hammer from the elbow instead of the wrist, how to lay his thumb beside the blade to guide a saw, how to tap a chisel with a wooden mallet, how to mark a hole with an awl before starting a drill bit. My daughter did the same before him, and even now, on the brink of teenage aloofness, she will occasionally drag out my box of wood scraps and carpenter something. So I have seen my apprenticeship to wood and tools reenacted in each of my children, as my father saw his own apprenticeship renewed in me.

14   The saw I use belonged to him, as did my level and both of my squares, and all four tools had belonged to his father. The blade of the saw is the bluish color of gun barrels, and the maple handle, dark from the sweat of hands, is inscribed with curving leaf designs. The level is a shaft of walnut two feet long, edged with brass and pierced by three round windows in which air bubbles float in oil-filled tubes of glass. The middle window serves for testing whether a surface is horizontal, the others for testing whether it is plumb or vertical. My grandfather used to carry this level on the gun rack behind the seat in his pickup, and when I rode with him I would turn around to watch the bubbles dance. The larger of the two squares is called a framing square, a flat steel elbow so beat up and tarnished you can barely make out the rows of numbers that show how to figure the cuts on rafters. The smaller one is called a try square, for marking right angles, with a blued steel blade for the shank and a brass-faced block of cherry for the head.

15   I was taught early on that a saw is not to be used apart from a square: "If you're going to cut a piece of wood," my father insisted, "you owe it to the tree to cut it straight."

16   Long before studying geometry, I learned there is a mystical virtue in right angles. There is an unspoken morality in seeking the level and the plumb. A house will stand, a table will bear weight, the sides of a box will hold together only if the joints are square and the members upright. When the bubble is lined up between two marks etched in the glass tube of a level, you have aligned yourself with the forces that hold the universe together. When you miter the corners of a picture frame, each angle must be exactly forty-five degrees, as they are in the perfect triangles of Pythagoras, not a degree more or less. Otherwise the frame will hang crookedly, as if ashamed of itself and of its maker. No matter if the joints you are cutting do not show. Even if you are butting two pieces of wood together inside a cabinet, where no one except a wrecking crew will ever see them, you must take pains to insure that the ends are square and the studs are plumb.

17   I took pains over the wall I was building on the day my father died. Not long after that wall was finished—paneled with tongue-and-groove boards of yellow pine, the nail holes filled with putty and the wood all stained and sealed—I came close to wrecking it one afternoon when my daughter ran howling up the stairs to announce that her gerbils had escaped from their cage and were hiding in my brand-new wall. She could hear them scratching and squeaking behind her bed. Impossible! I said. How on earth could they get inside my drum-tight wall? Through the heating vent, she answered. I went

downstairs, pressed my ear to the honey-colored wood, and heard the scritch scritch of tiny feet.

"What can we do?" my daughter wailed. "They'll starve to death, they'll die of thirst, they'll suffocate."   18

"Hold on," I soothed. "I'll think of something."   19

While I thought and she fretted, the radio on her bedside table delivered   20 us the headlines. Several thousand people had died in a city in India from a poisonous cloud that had leaked overnight from a chemical plant. A nuclear-powered submarine had been launched. Rioting continued in South Africa. An airplane had been hijacked in the Mediterranean. Authorities calculated that several thousand homeless people slept on the streets within sight of the Washington Monument. I felt my usual helplessness in face of all these calamities. But here was my daughter weeping because her gerbils were holed up in a wall. This calamity I could handle.

"Don't worry," I told her. "We'll set food and water by the heating vent   21 and lure them out. And if that doesn't do the trick, I'll tear the wall apart until we find them."

She stopped crying and gazed at me. "You'd really tear it apart? Just for my   22 gerbils? The *wall?*" Astonishment slowed her down only for a second, however, before she ran to the workbench and began tugging at drawers, saying, "Let's see, what'll we need? Crowbar. Hammer. Chisels. I hope we don't have to use them—but just in case."

We didn't need the wrecking tools. I never had to assault my handsome   23 wall, because the gerbils eventually came out to nibble at a dish of popcorn. But for several hours I studied the tongue-and-groove skin I had nailed up on the day of my father's death, considering where to begin prying. There were no gaps in that wall, no crooked joints.

I had botched a great many pieces of wood before I mastered the right an-   24 gle with a saw, botched even more before I learned to miter a joint. The knowledge of these things resides in my hands and eyes and the webwork of muscles, not in the tools. There are machines for sale—powered miter boxes and radial arm saws, for instance—that will enable any casual soul to cut proper angles in boards. The skill is invested in the gadget instead of the person who uses it, and this is what distinguishes a machine from a tool. If I had to earn my keep by making furniture or building houses, I suppose I would buy powered saws and pneumatic nailers; the need for speed would drive me to it. But since I carpenter only for my own pleasure or to help neighbors or to remake the house around the ears of my family, I stick with hand tools. Most of the ones I own were given to me by my father, who also taught me how to wield them. The tools in my workbench are a double inheritance, for each hammer and level and saw is wrapped in a cloud of knowing.

25   All of these tools are a pleasure to look at and to hold. Merchants would never paste NEW NEW NEW! signs on them in stores. Their designs are old because they work, because they serve their purpose well. Like folk-songs and aphorisms and the grainy bits of language, these tools have been pared down to essentials. I look at my claw hammer, the distillation of a hundred generations of carpenters, and consider that it holds up well beside those other classics— Greek vases, Gregorian chants, *Don Quixote,* barbed fishhooks, candles, spoons. Knowledge of hammering stretches back to the earliest humans who squatted beside fires chipping flints. Anthropologists have a lovely name for those unworked rocks that served as the earliest hammers. "Dawn stones" they are called. Their only qualification for the work, aside from hardness, is that they fit the hand. Our ancestors used them for grinding corn, tapping awls, smashing bones. From dawn stones to this claw hammer is a great leap in time, but no great distance in design or imagination.

26   On that iced-over February morning when I smashed my thumb with the hammer, I was down in the basement framing the wall that my daughter's ger-bils would later hide in. I was thinking of my father, as I always did whenever I built anything, thinking how he would have gone about the work, hearing in memory what he would have said about the wisdom of hitting the nail instead of my thumb. I had the studs and plates nailed together all square and trim, and was lifting the wall into place when the phone rang upstairs. My wife an-swered, and in a moment she came to the basement door and called down softly to me. The stillness in her voice made me drop the framed wall and hurry upstairs. She told me my father was dead. Then I heard the details over the phone from my mother. Building a set of cupboards for my brother in Oklahoma, he had knocked off work early the previous afternoon because of cramps in his stomach. Early this morning, on his way into the kitchen of my brother's trailer, maybe going for a glass of water, so early that no one else was awake, he slumped down on the linoleum and his heart quit.

27   For several hours I paced around inside my house, upstairs and down, in and out of every room, looking for the right door to open and knowing there was no such door. My wife and children followed me and wrapped me in arms and backed away again, circling and staring as if I were on fire. Where was the door, the door, the door? I kept wondering. My smashed thumb turned purple and throbbed, making me furious. I wanted to cut it off and rush outside and scrape away the snow and hack a hole in the frozen earth and bury the shameful thing.

28   I went down into the basement, opened a drawer in my workbench, and stared at the ranks of chisels and knives. Oiled and sharp, as my father would have kept them, they gleamed at me like teeth. I took up a clasp knife, pried out the longest blade, and tested the edge on the hair of my forearm. A tuft came away cleanly, and I saw my father testing the sharpness of tools on his

own skin, the blades of axes and knives and gouges and hoes, saw the red hair shaved off in patches from his arms and the backs of his hands. "That will cut bear," he would say. He never cut a bear with his blades, now my blades, but he cut deer, dirt, wood. I closed the knife and put it away. Then I took up the hammer and went back to work on my daughter's wall, snugging the bottom plate against a chalkline on the floor, shimming the top plate against the joists overhead, plumbing the studs with my level, making sure before I drove the first nail that every line was square and true.

INQUIRING INTO THE DETAILS

HOW TO READ NONFICTION

While nonfiction essays often seem a lot like short stories, there are some significant differences. For one, we assume that the stories they tell *actually happened*. We also assume that the narrator and author are the same person. This means we read essays a little differently than fiction. Here are some additional frameworks for reading nonfiction essays.

- **Truthfulness.** In nonfiction, there's an implicit contract between reader and writer. We expect everything in an essay to be true, to have actually happened. What happens if you suspect this isn't the case?

- **Ethos.** How do authors of essays come across? Do we believe what they are saying? Do we trust their authority to speak on the subject they're writing about?

- **Questions.** The essay is an exploratory form, and sometimes we can understand writers' purposes best by identifying the question they're trying to answer. This may also mean that it isn't always easy to reduce a literary essay to a thesis or theme. Insights are often "earned"—arrived at through much thought and questioning—and tentative. Essay writers are less concerned with proving a point.

- **The "reflective turn."** Because essays both show *and* tell, it's important that you're alert for moments when essayists say what they mean. To use an earlier metaphor, these are lines or passages when writers are on the mountain of reflection. Cumulatively, these moments of reflection help establish the themes of essays.

INQUIRING INTO THE ESSAY

Use the methods of inquiry—exploring, explaining, evaluating, and reflecting—to discover what you think about Scott Sanders's essay.

1. What have you inherited or hope to inherit that has special meaning for you? Fastwrite for seven minutes about one or more of these things. Describe them as fully as you can and tell yourself the stories that surround them. Focus on the people associated with these particular inheritances, describing who they are and how you see them. After seven minutes, stop and skip a line. Compose an answer to the question that Sanders explores in his essay: *As you look back on one (or more) of these things you've inherited, or hope to inherit, why do they have such meaning for you?*

2. Using excerpts from Sanders's essay, explain your understanding of what kinds of meanings he finds in inheriting his father's tools.

3. One could argue that our desire to inherit things is simple materialism, or at worst, greed. Do you agree or disagree with that assertion? Does Sanders's essay provide some evidence for your position on this?

4. "The Inheritance of Tools" is the only literary work in this chapter that is nonfiction. Does it matter knowing that Sanders's story is true rather than invented? Reflect on how you read a work of nonfiction *differently* than a short story.

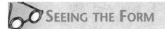 SEEING THE FORM

CHRISTINA'S WORLD BY ANDREW WYETH

If a photograph can be thought of as a form of nonfiction, then a painting compares well with fiction or poetry. The painting certainly has a strong relationship to the real; after all, the painter sees the world we all live in and expresses that vision in the work. That expression may be realistic, impressionistic, or abstract, but it is firmly rooted in things that can be seen, smelled, heard, and touched. Yet unlike photographers who work with the visual materials presented to them through the viewfinder, the painter can transform these materials through invention. If it works better that the woman's dress is pink rather than blue, then pink it shall be. Similarly, fiction writers' primary obligation is to the story, not reality, and they invent characters and make them do things that contribute tension and meaning to the narrative.

Interpreting a painting, then, like Andrew Wyeth's famous work *Christina's World,* is much like interpreting fiction. The painting acts as a text that, like a short story, is a complete invention and whose meaning is implicit rather than explicit. Therefore "reading" Wyeth's painting should involve the kind of interpretive moves you might employ in reading any literature.

Andrew Wyeth, *Christina's World,* 1948. Tempera on gessoed panel, 32 1/4 X 47 3/4". The Museum of Modern Art, New York. Purchase. (16.1949), © Andrew Wyeth.

Andrew Wyeth painted *Christina's World* in 1948, and Christina Olson, who died in 1969, was a frequent subject for the painter. At the invitation of her family, Wyeth spent many years using an upstairs bedroom of the Olson house as a studio. The home and the setting haunted his work for many years that followed. You can still find the old house in this painting in Cushing, Maine.

EXERCISE 9.1

Painting as Literature

In this exercise you will attempt to interpret Andrew Wyeth's *Christina's World* in the same way you might interpret a piece of literature.

STEP ONE: A first reading: Simply experience the power of *Christina's World.* (It's really a pretty powerful image.) Look closely. Pay attention to your own feelings about the painting and your tentative ideas about its meaning. Your first instinct may be to tell a story about the woman in the painting, but for now focus on your ideas about what the painting says or the feelings it evokes. Make a four-minute fastwrite entry in your notebook. Begin this way: *The main feeling or idea I get from this painting is* . . . . When the writing stalls, use this prompt to get you going again for a few minutes: *Among the things I notice in the painting are* . . .

STEP TWO: A second reading: In small groups, spend time focusing on how the Wyeth painting was made, or how it was composed. To do this, it might be helpful to understand a little bit about the composition of paintings. You don't need to be an expert, but the following basic terms and concepts should give you a helpful analytical framework for looking at Wyeth's painting.

- *Line*. In artistic composition, the line is the direction the viewer's gaze travels when looking at the painting, something that is managed by the placement of forms and their relative size. In a good painting, the viewer's eye is directed to the main focal point of the picture, and away from unimportant elements. Some questions to ask about line include whether the painting succeeds in encouraging your gaze to move smoothly to the main objects of interest, or whether the line is confusing, making you feel as if you're not quite sure where to look. Do things flow visually?

- *Hierarchy*. Do you sense that some visual elements are more important than others? In a well-composed painting you should. Artists can manage this in a number of ways, including the size and location of various objects in the painting, and in doing so they are communicating something important about the overall theme of the work. What, for example, might the emphasis on certain objects in the painting imply about its meaning? What is the relationship among these things, and what does that imply?

- *Color*. The arrangement of color in a painting will influence its mood. Certain colors are cool—blues, greens, purples and their many combinations—and these tend to recede in a painting. Other colors—yellows, oranges and reds—are warm and can be perceived as coming forward. Color is obviously enormously expressive when handled well. How do the colors the artist chose affect the mood of the work? How might that mood contribute to its overall theme or idea?

- *Value*. To create the sense of dimension, artists use light and dark tones. In a black and white drawing, these tones are white to black, and all the shades of gray in between. In a color painting, value is often managed by using various shades of a color. Without value, a painting looks flat, one-dimensional. With it, the subjects look more realistic. How much emphasis is there on value in the painting? How realistic is the image?

- *Composition.* All of these qualities—line, color, value, hierarchy—and more contribute to a painting's composition. One of the key qualities of composition is balance, and this can be achieved in a number of ways, including arranging visual elements symmetrically, asymmetrically, or using something called the "golden mean," an ancient mathematical concept that has historically influenced art and architecture, and which represents proportions often seen in nature, including the spiral of a sea shell, and the proportions of the human body (see Figure 9.1). What do you notice about the composition of the painting? How is it arranged to influence your feelings, and how does it seem to contribute to the overall theme or idea?

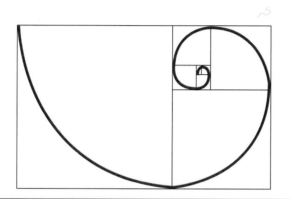

FIGURE 9.1 The golden mean is a mathematical formula that when applied to a rectangle creates spatial relationships that are particularly pleasing to the eye. This is the so-called golden rectangle. For centuries, artists have exploited this principle, creating proportions in paintings and buildings based on these calculations. Can you see how Wyeth's painting is visually organized to adhere to the golden rectangle?

Using these concepts about visual texts, discuss in your small group possible interpretations of Wyeth's painting. What would you say about how he uses line, color, value, hierarchy and composition to create certain feelings or effects in the painting? Do any of these elements account for your own feelings about what the painting expresses?

STEP THREE: As a group, complete the following sentence about the painting: *We believe that the main idea or feeling in the painting 'Christina's World' is* . . . Put this at the top of a piece of newsprint and post in on the wall next to your group. Then make a list of evidence from the painting itself that supports the idea or feeling your group proposed. Put this on the newsprint as well. Share your work with the rest of the class.

Questions for Discussion

1. Which group's interpretation of the painting seems most convincing? Which seemed most original or surprising?

2. Which terms from Step Two of the exercise seemed most helpful in explaining each interpretation?

3. How is this process like interpreting a short story or a poem? How is it different?

■ THE WRITING PROCESS ■

INQUIRY PROJECT: Writing a Critical Essay

Look at a story, essay, or poem, possibly one of the works in this chapter. Interpret it as you did Wyeth's painting, looking closely at what the literary work says and how it says it, and, using some of the elements of literary analysis, offer readers a way of understanding the work that they would find convincing. The full draft should be about 1,000 to 1,500 words. You should do the following:

■ Organize the essay around a question you're trying to answer about the text and its possible meanings. (For example: *Is Silko's "Lullaby" a story that highlights the power of women in Navajo culture?*)

■ Use your question as a guide for reading the story selectively.

■ As you shape your answer to the question, rely mostly on passages and other information from the primary work—the story or essay—as a source of evidence.

■ If possible, use research with secondary sources (articles about the author, published criticism about the work, and so on) to help you revise your paper.

Thinking About Subjects

It's likely that your instructor will ask you to write a critical essay on one or more of the readings in this chapter, or perhaps an assigned reading from another book. If you can choose among the three readings here, consider which work you found most moving. Although analysis often demands a level of detachment and cool logic, literary works are usually intended to make us *feel*. This is a wonderful starting place for a closer look at the story because it's sensible to wonder what it was that made you feel something. The answer will be found in the text, of course, by looking at how the author tells the story and what he says. But it will also be found in what you bring to the text—your own experiences, associations, and values.

The writer Joan Didion once wrote that writing is an "act of aggression," an implicit demand that readers see things the way the writer sees them. We react to stories sometimes because they are asking us to believe something we don't believe, or don't want to believe, or they are imagining us as readers we don't want to be. A good starting point, then, for choosing to write about a work is to choose it because you find yourself resisting it in some way, rather than "relating to it."

On the other hand, it is also true that we are drawn to stories that seem to confirm our sense of how the world works. One of the reasons "The Inheritance of Tools" is so successful is that some of us immediately recognize those feelings of loss and longing for the people we loved and the things we associate with them. It feels good to think after reading something like "Inheritance of Tools" that "Yes, that's exactly how I see it." Choosing a literary text because you can relate to it is fine. But the challenge is to do more than simply express agreement. Write about such a story because you want to more fully understand what it is you're agreeing to. In "Inheritance of Tools," for example, how does the essay suggest that what we inherit has meaning that goes beyond simply reminding of us of the people we love? Are there other ways to define an inheritance that go beyond the sentimental value of things?

> *It is in the coversation between what a text says and what it might be saying that you discover fresh understandings of what you read.*

Generating Ideas

Spend some time in your notebook generating material for possible essays. The following prompts will invite you to first play around, and even write "badly." Approach this material initially in an open-ended way. When you can, let the writing lead thought. The prompts below will be general enough to apply to any text, even if it isn't one of the three in this chapter.

Listing Prompts.   Lists can be rich sources of triggering topics. Let them grow freely, and when you're ready, use an item as the focus of another list or an episode of fastwriting. The following prompts should get you started.

1. Brainstorm a list of questions about the work that you find puzzling.

2. List the names of every important character or person in the story or essay. Choose one or two that seem most important. Under each name, make two new headings: Dreams and Problems. Under

Dreams make a list of the thing that character seems to desire most, even if he or she isn't fully aware of it. Under Problems make a list of everything that seems to be an obstacle to that character achieving those desires.

3. Make a list of details or particulars from the story that seem to say more than they say. In other words, do any details recur? Do any objects have particular significance to one or more characters? Do any descriptions suggest the feelings, dispositions, or values of a particular character?

Fastwriting Prompts.   Remember, fastwriting is a great way stimulate creative thinking. Turn off your critical side and let yourself write "badly."

1. Write a narrative of thought. Begin with *When I first read this story or essay I thought ... And then I thought ... And then ... And then ....*

2. Choose three lines or passages that are key to your current understanding of the themes or ideas behind the story or essay. Write these down on the left page of your notebook. On the opposing right page, fastwrite about each, beginning with *The first thing I notice about this passage is ... And then ... And then ... And then ....* When the writing stalls, write about the next line or passage until you've written about all three.

Visual Prompts.   Sometimes the best way to generate material is to see what we think represented in something other than sentences. Boxes, lines, webs, clusters, arrows, charts, or even sketches can help us to see more of the landscape of a subject, especially connections between fragments of information that aren't as obvious in prose.

1. Create a cluster using the name of the main character as the core word. Reread the story and then build as many associations as you can from that character. Think about feelings and ideas you associate with that person as well as any particulars you remember from the story.

2. Make a visual map of the story. Begin by placing a brief description of what you believe is the most significant moment in the story at the center of a blank page. This might be a turning point, or the point of highest tension, or perhaps that moment when the main character achieves his desires and dreams. Consider that moment the destination of the story. Now map out events or details in the narrative that threaten to lead the protagonist away from that destination, and those that appear to lead the protagonist toward it.

Research Prompts. When writing a critical essay, the most important research you do is carefully reading and rereading the primary text, or the poem, story or essay you're writing about. But secondary sources can be a great help, too. A background article on the writer might help you understand her motives in writing the piece. A little historical research can give you a deeper understanding of the setting.

1. Put the story or essay in a biographical context. First, search the Web for anything you can find about the author. Begin by using the search term "authors" with Google. You'll find a listing of a range of Web pages with biographical information about authors; one or more might feature yours. Several library databases are also useful, including *The Literary Index.*

2. Put the story or essay in a historical context. Search the Web for background information about the period, place, or events relevant to the story. For example, if you were writing about "Lullaby," search for information about life among the Navajo in the late 1940s.

⌕ INQUIRING INTO THE DETAILS

COMMON LITERARY DEVICES

There are many key concepts that provide useful frameworks for analyzing literature. The key is to see the following ideas as an angle for seeing an essay, story, or poem, much like you might move around a subject with a camera. Each provides a different way of seeing the same thing. In addition, each becomes a platform from which to pose a question about a text.

- **Plot and significant event.** This is what happens in a story that moves it forward. One way of thinking about plot is to consider this: What are the key moments that propel the story forward? Why do you consider them key? How do they add tension to the story? In an essay, these moments often give rise to the question the writer is exploring. In short stories, there is often a significant event that may happen in or outside of the story, but the entire narrative and its characters act or think in response to that event. This significant event may be dramatic—a baby has died, perhaps—or not seem so at all—a surprise birthday cake is brought to a quiet couple's table in a crowded restaurant. Naming that significant event becomes a way of seeing how everything in the story revolves around it, exposing the logic (and sometimes lack of logic) in why characters behave the way they do.

- **Characters.** Imagine a still pond upon which small paper boats float. Someone throws a rock in the pond—big or small—and the ripples extend outward, moving the boats this way and that. Depending on the size of the ripples, some of the boats may list or capsize, sinking slowly. Characters in a short story are like those boats, responding in some way to something that happened, some significant event that is revealed or implied. They move almost imperceptibly, or quite noticeably, or even violently. Is there logic to their response? How exactly are they changed? How do they relate to each other? In essays, characters live both inside and outside the text. In nonfiction, they are (or were) real people, which imposes an additional burden on them: Are nonfiction characters believable? Are they accurate?

- **Setting.** Where a story takes place can matter a lot or a little, but it always matters. Why? Because where a story takes place signals things about characters and who they are. A story set in rural Wyoming suggests a certain austere, ranching culture in which the characters operate. Even if they're not ranchers, they must somehow deal with that culture. Similarly, a story set in Chicago's predominantly black south side will introduce another set of constraints within which characters must operate. In some cases, setting even might become a kind of character.

- **Point of view.** In nonfiction essays, point of view is usually straightforward—we assume the narrator is the author. But in fiction, it's much more complicated; in fact, *how* a story is told—from what perspective—is a crucial aesthetic decision. For instance, stories told from the first-person point of view in the present tense give the story a sense of immediacy—this feels like it's happening *now*—but at the same time limit our understanding of other characters because we can't get into their heads. We can only know what the first person narrator knows.

  So-called omniscient narrators can introduce a feeling of distance from the action, but they are also gratifyingly Godlike because they can see everything, hovering above all the action and even entering characters' minds at will. Omniscient narrators can also choose to limit their access to characters and events as well. Why might an author have chosen a particular point of view? Is the narrator trustworthy? What might be his biases and how might they affect the telling?

- **Theme.** One way of understanding a story or essay is to consider that everything—character, point of view, and setting—all contribute to a central meaning. In a good story, everything is there for a purpose—to say something to the reader about what it means to be human. In essays, this theme may be explicit since essays both show *and* tell. Short stories and especially poems are often short on explanation of theme, operating with more ambiguity.

The writer hopes the reader can *infer* certain ideas or feelings by paying close attention to what he *shows* the reader. To get at the theme, begin with the simple question: *So what?* Why is the author telling this story or sharing this experience? What significance are we supposed to attach to it?

- **Image.** Stories and poems ask us to see. When I read them, I imagine that writers take my face in their hands and gently—or sometimes brutally—direct my gaze. What are they insisting that I look at and how do they want me to see it? The critic John Gruesser suggests that in "Everday Use" Alice Walker wants us to see Maggie as a kind of helpless animal. Images that recur may also be significant.

Judging What You Have

Now it's time to look more critically at what you've generated. Do you see some possible directions you could follow in a sketch? Are there tentative ideas and interpretations you might develop? Are there potential beginnings you could follow? The following suggestions use material generated by the prompts in the preceding section.

What's Promising Material and What Isn't? If your assignment is to write about one of the stories in this chapter, by now you should have a sense of which one interests you most. That initial sense usually starts with a gut reaction—the story makes you *feel* something. That's a good starting point, but the generating prompts should give you a fuller sense of *why* you feel something. As you examine the material you generated, consider the following:

- *What's your question?* Remember that your aim in the assignment is to build your essay around a question you want to answer about the story or essay. You may have found one already. A good opening question is specific enough to guide your rereading of the work, encouraging you to look at certain parts rather than the whole thing.

- *What surprised you?* In your fastwrites, do you find that the writing led you from an initial impression or interpretation of the story but then took you toward ideas you didn't expect? For example, perhaps you began fastwriting that "Inheritance of Tools" seemed to be about a sentimental affection for an inherited hammer but then you realized that the hammer stands in for what the author calls a "cloud of knowing." Did you find a lot to say about the significance of certain passages?

- *Does a character in the story seem to emerge as a focus?* A helpful way to write about a story is to focus on the actions and motivations of a particular character. This might have become obvious when you generated lists or clusters about characters, and especially when you generated ideas about a character's dreams and problems. *How* the character attempts to overcome obstacles in the way of his desires can say a lot about the meaning of the story.

- *Is there a recognizable significant event in the story and how do the important characters respond to it?* When you mapped out the story, did you find a scene or moment that seemed to alter the course of the narrative or its characters? How did this change the characters and how did it change their relationships with others in the story? What does this say about what the author seems to be saying about the human condition?

- *Does the story's context help explain the author's purpose?* Literature isn't created in a vacuum. Like all art, it is often a response to things that are going on with and around the artist. It makes an enormous difference that Leslie Marmon Silko is a member of the Laguna Pueblo and has a keen interest in tribal culture and survival. It also helps to know what concerns her and any related historical events to which the writer may be responding. Do these contexts help you to read the story differently? What questions do they raise about its meanings?

- *Do you feel ready to answer the* So what? *question.* Stories aren't merely entertainment. Authors always have certain purposes—ideas they're exploring, comments they want to make, or questions they're trying to answer. In fiction and poems, these intentions are often implicit; that is, stories and poems are often ambiguous and leave us wondering what they're really about. Essays are often much more explicit because authors frequently say what they mean. Answering the *So what?* question—speculating on what authors seem to be saying or implying about being human—is a key move in interpretation. After generating material, you may be ready to finish this sentence, *What I think this story or essay is* really *saying is . . .* If you like what you come up with, turn it into a question that will help organize your rereading of the story.

Questions About Audience and Purpose. Why analyze a work of literature? For the same reason that some of us want to talk about anything complicated, whether it's a relationship gone south or a wrenching movie about war: We simply want to understand. It's fundamentally human to try to make sense of things, and reassuring when we can. Of course, we are drawn to some literature for sheer enjoyment and pleasure, and there's nothing wrong with that, but the best literary works offer readers so much more than that if they're willing to look closely. The best stories offer a glimpse at the human spirit—at what makes people tick, at their longings and fears and possibilities. Ultimately, we learn about ourselves and our own humanity.

Critical analysis of literature is simply a method of discovering these things. In the same way you used some tools of art criticism to interpret Wyeth's painting *Christina's World,* using literary elements of stories such as character, significant event, setting, and especially theme help you to think about what a story is trying to do. You can use these tools for several purposes. The most basic is to simply write a summary of what happens to whom in a story. Often called a plot summary, this is useful as a way of initially understanding the work, but it isn't often a college assignment. In general, however, critical essays work to offer some *interpretation* of what the story or essay seems to be saying, a move that often begins with a question.

In the broadest sense the opening question is simple: *What might this story mean?* But to be really useful, the question needs to be more specific. For example, a slightly more specific question might be, *What are the racial themes in Silko's story "Lullaby?"* Will such a question allow you to read Silko's story selectively? Probably not. What about this: *What is the significance of the recurring image of the blanket in "Lullaby?"* Is this too specific? Possibly. But it's not a bad starting point for your inquiry into the story because the question gives you direction about where to look to find the answers.

Critical essays don't simply ask questions; they attempt to answer them. There are a range of methods for doing that, including,

1. You can focus on a particular element such as character, setting, or plot development, analyzing how it contributes to one or more of the story's themes.

2. You can put the story in relevant contexts—perhaps the biography of the author, background about the story's time and place, or certain kinds of theories or ideas about literature—and exploit these as a way of unraveling the story's themes and ambiguities.

3. You can argue for an interpretation of a story's meaning, and use *both* particular elements such as character and setting, as well as relevant contexts to help you make your interpretation convincing to others.

Each approach implies a different emphasis on certain kinds of information in the essay. *But no matter what angle you use, the text of the story—the words, phrases, passages, and ideas that make up the story—will always be the most important source of evidence.* I want to emphasize this because one of the most common weaknesses of writing about a reading is that it fails to mine material from the text itself.

The audience for a critical essay, as for any form of writing, will make a big difference in what you say and how you say it. Scholarly criticism, which is not what you're attempting here, is written for an audience of fellow critics, most of whom are familiar with the work as well as some of its contexts. For the assignment that follows, assume you're writing for an audience of peers. Ask your instructor whether you should assume that your audience is familiar with the work you're writing about (which might be the case if you're all writing about the same story or essay), or assume that your readers are unfamiliar with the work. If the latter is the case, then you'll obviously have to do some summarizing about the plot and characters that wouldn't be necessary if your readers knew your story or essay.

Writing a Sketch

We'll begin again with an early draft, a sketch that represents an initial attempt to discover what you want to focus on and what you might have to say about the literary work you've chosen.

Develop your sketch with the following things in mind:

- It should have a tentative title. This time, the title should be the question about the work you're trying to answer. (For example, *What is the significance of Ayah's relationship to nature in Silko's "Lullaby?"*)
- It should be at least 500 to 600 words.
- Write it with the appropriate audience in mind. Are you writing for readers who are familiar with the text?
- Explore your question by paying close attention to what the story you're writing about says.

STUDENT SKETCH

When Julie Bird read Leslie Marmon Silko's short story "Lullaby" for the first time, she found it deeply moving. "It almost made me cry," she said. In class, we talked a little about some of the traditions in Native American literature, and you can see in her sketch how she tries out several of the ideas we talked about: the importance of the storytelling tradition, the ways in which identity is tied to going home, and the healing power of the natural world. There are all kinds of literary traditions that are lenses through which you can read a story. Some, like this one, have to do with the race, ethnicity, or culture of the writer. Others have more to do with larger literary movements tied to historical events and histories of thought—for example, realism, modernism, or postmodernism.

But the most important thing is to pay close attention to the text itself. What *exactly* does the story say, and what might it mean? Julie Bird doesn't incorporate many passages from "Lullaby" in her sketch; she's thinking through some ideas about key themes in the story. She underlines several ideas that emerged in this first look. Now she has to return to the story and test the ideas against what the text actually says.

WHAT IS THE ROLE OF NATURE IN 'LULLABY'?
Julie Bird

"Lullaby" written by Leslie Marmon Silko is an intriguing story about the life of a Navajo woman by the name of Ayah and her life . Ayah bared her soul to tell this story, an act of special meaning in a culture that passes on history by oral means. The Navajo's often connect their identity to family, home, and nature. When the white man came to take away her children, Ayah, not fully understanding why, grabbed them and ran up the long slope of the mesa, to wait for her husband to come home. While she was waiting, she allowed the sun to relax her and felt as if "she could walk into the sky, stepping through clouds endlessly." <u>The connection of peace to the natural world is key to the essay's theme</u>.

Ayah, using the wool blanket as an instrument, created strong parallels between her mother (the past) and her son Jimmie (her present). This generational timeline establishes her identity by correlating the comfort of the past with the warmth of the present. The wool blanket is the object of that unbroken line. At the end of the story, Ayah is searching for her husband and she is thinking, "she did this because she had the blanket, and there would be no place for him except with her and the blanket in the old abode barn near the arroyo." The blanket is significant to the characters in revealing the importance of family ties to the Navajos.

<u>The overall theme of the essay relates to the sorrow and loss Ayah feels at the hands of the white man, and her inability to do anything about it.</u> First, a government man comes to tell her that her son Jimmie was killed at war. Next, more government officials dupe her into signing her name in order to take away her children. To this she states "Because it was like the old ones always told her about learning their language, or any of their ways: it endangered you." When Chato was too old to work the rancher made them move out of their home, and they had to go to the barn.

Through all of the sorrow put upon her, Ayah was able to turn to her identity and connection with her heritage, nature, and roots to find peace and strength to continue on.

Moving from Sketch to Draft

Prepare for revision of your sketch by first evaluating it yourself and then sharing it in a small group workshop.

Evaluating Your Own Sketch. Among the key concerns in evaluating this early draft of your critical essay is whether you've discovered a workable focus and if you're beginning to get some clear idea of what it is you're trying to say. In your journal or on a separate sheet you can provide to your instructor when you hand in the sketch, try to answer the following questions:

1. Did the question you were asking about the text help you focus on certain parts of the story? What were they? Was the question too broad or too specific? What might be a more refined question as a focus for the next draft, or are you happy with the original question you posed?

2. Can you summarize in a sentence or two how you might now answer the question you pose in your sketch? Can you summarize an answer to another question that emerged that interests you more?

3. Based on what you tentatively seem to be saying in the sketch about the text you're writing about, what do you think you might do in the rewrite?

Questions for Peer Review. Workshop groups that are discussing the sketches should consider the following questions:

• If you're unfamiliar with the text the writer is analyzing, do you have enough information about the story or essay to understand what the writer is saying about it? What else would you like to know?

• Does the sketch seem to answer the question it's asking? In your own words, what do you think the writer seems to be saying?

• Where is the sketch most convincing? Where is it least convincing?

• Are there any questions or approaches that seem like good alternatives to the one the writer chose?

Reflecting on What You've Learned. To make the best use of the workshop, try to listen without commenting to the discussion of your sketch. Use the double-entry journal approach of taking notes during the discussion. On the left page of your notebook, record all the comments and suggestions you hear, whether you agree with them or not. Later, on the right page, fastwrite your reactions and thoughts about the comments you recorded on the opposing page.

Research and Other Strategies: Gathering More Information

Before you wrote your sketch, you did some initial research that may have helped provide a *context* for the work you're writing about. You may have learned a little biographical information about the author, or perhaps some things about the period, time, or place she was writing about. Now it's time to dig a little deeper. How deep you dig depends on the scope of your project and the details of the assignment.

This time, your campus library, rather than the Web, will be the focus of your investigations, although many of the following sources and databases are probably accessible through your library's Web pages.

- *Researching the author.* Check the online book index to find biographies of your author. You can also gather biographical information on the author you're writing about by consulting the following references at your university library:
  - *Author's Biographies Index.* A key source to 300,000 writers of every period.
  - *Biography Index: A Cumulative Index to Biographical Material in Books and Magazines.* Remarkably extensive coverage, which includes biographies, as well as autobiographies, articles, letters, and obituaries.
  - *Contemporary Authors.* Up-to-date information on authors from around the world.

- *Researching the critics.* What do other people say about your author or the work you're writing about? Check these references or databases:
  - *MLA International Bibliography.* This is the most important database to find articles by others on the work or author you're writing about.
  - *Literary Index.* A database of author biographies.
  - *Contemporary Literary Criticism.* Excerpts of criticism and reviews published in the last twenty-five years.
  - *Magill's Bibliography of Literary Criticism.* Citations, not excerpts, of criticism on more than 2,500 works.
  - *Book Review Index.* Citations for tens of thousands of book reviews on even fairly obscure works.

- *Researching the genre or tradition.* The type of writing—short story, novel, personal essay—that you're analyzing is another useful context for thinking about the work. For example, Leslie Marmon Silko is among the most famous of contemporary Native American writers. Native American writing is an identifiable "tradition" of literary works, and much has been written about certain patterns in these stories and certain ways of understanding them. There are reference resources in your library that will help you research these traditions. For example, *American Indian: Language and Literature* is a reference that lists books and articles on the topic. Similarly, *Afro-American Literature* is a reference exploring the place of black writers and works in American literature. These references can be enormously helpful. Ask your reference librarian about useful books or electronic databases on the tradition you're writing about.

WRITING WITH COMPUTERS

LITERATURE ON THE WEB

There are a host of useful literature resources you can access over the Internet. A small sampling of what is available includes:

- **Bartleby.com** (http://bartleby.com): Offers a range of poetry, fiction, and nonfiction and access to the Columbia Encyclopedia, the American Heritage Dictionary, Roget's Thesaurus, Bartlett's Familiar Quotations, and many resources for writers, all for free.

- **Bibliomania** (http://www.bibliomania.com): Offers 2,000 classic texts for free over the Internet, author biographies, book summaries, bibliographies, and more.

- **The Electronic Text Center** (http://etext.lib.virginia.edu/): Contains 70,000 texts in thirteen languages, many of them available over the Internet for free.

- **Literary Resources on the Web** (http://andromeda.rutgers.edu/~jlynch/Lit/): Broken into a range of categories, including British and American, periods, and traditions.

- **Literature Webliography** (http://www.lib.lsu.edu/hum/lit/lit.html): A rich harvest of links to references, guides, authors, and bibliographies.

- **The Online Books Page** (http://digital.library.upenn.edu/books/archives .html): This online archive contains lists to countless Web sites devoted to literature in English and in foreign languages.

- **The Oxford English Dictionary** (http://dictionary.oed.com/entrance.dtl): The online version of the world's most definitive English dictionary details the shifting meaning and usage of words from their first use in writing to present. Access only available on a subscription basis.

- **Voice of the Shuttle** (http://vos.ucsb.edu/): A general humanities research site with great links to literary sites.

Composing the Draft

Before you begin writing the draft, make sure that you have a workable focusing question that will drive the draft. A workable question needs to be specific enough to allow you to reread the story or essay you're writing about selectively, focusing on certain parts rather than the whole thing. But it also needs to be general enough to allow you to develop the answer in 1,000 to 1,500 words. For example, here's a question that is too general: *What are the main themes in Walker's story "Everyday Use?"* You can certainly answer that question in four or five pages, but the essay will be so general, leaping from one part of the story to the next, that it will be vague and uninteresting. Consider this question: *What's the significance of Wangero Leewanika Kemanjo, the new name Dee adopted in "Everyday Use?"*

This type of question—one that focuses on a particular detail or aspect of plot development—can work extremely well as a focus for a short critical essay. But unless that detail or development seems attached to other details, developments, and themes in the story, it probably won't do.

Here's a good focusing question for a literary analysis, one that strikes a nice balance between specificity and generality: *Why does Silko end with the poem at the end of "Lullaby," and how does it figure in Ayah's efforts to confront her losses?* It seems as if there might be a lot to say about this without resorting to generalities. The question focuses on a particular part of the Silko story, yet also expands outward into other aspects of the work, particularly those relevant to the theme of recovery.

Methods of Development. What are some of the ways you might organize your critical essay?

Narrative. An entirely different approach is to use your question as the starting point for a story you tell about how you arrived at an answer. This approach is more essayistic in the sense that it provides the story of *how* you came to know rather than reporting *what* you think. A narrative essay might also involve relevant autobiographical details that influenced your reading of the literary work, explaining your interest in certain aspects of the story or the question you're asking about it. As always, however, it's critical to read the work closely and discuss your evolving understandings of certain details, passages, or ideas from it.

Question to Answer. Because the assignment is designed around a question you're trying to answer about a literary work, the question-to-answer design is an obvious choice. Consider spending the first part of your essay highlighting the question you're interested in. You can do this in several ways. You can put it in context by demonstrating how your question is relevant to the on-going conversation that other critics have posed about the story, author, or tradition you're writing about. You can also put it in the context of the research you've done about that tradition, or perhaps what you know about the life and interests of the author. Alternatively, establish the importance of the question by highlighting your understanding of the story's meaning or the author's intentions, or perhaps even how the question arises out of your own personal experiences with the events or subjects in the work. The key is to convince readers that yours is a question worth asking, and that the answer might be interesting to discover.

Compare and Contrast. Critical essays often benefit from this method of development. The approach might be to compare and contrast certain elements within the story or essay—perhaps several characters, symbols or metaphors, plot developments, and so on—or you might compare the work to others by the same or even different authors. For example, it might be interesting to explore the significance of the nature imagery in Leslie Marmon Silko's "Lullaby" by examining other essays by the author. Do similar references appear in some of her other stories? These comparisons have to be relevant to the question you're asking.

Combining Approaches. Frequently, a critical essay will use several or even all of the methods of development mentioned here—question to answer, comparison and contrast, and narrative. Consider how you might put them all to work, especially in certain sections of your draft.

Using Evidence. There are two main kinds of evidence that you need to consider in a critical essay: evidence that comes from so-called *primary* sources, especially the work itself, but also letters or memoirs by the author; and evidence that comes from *secondary* sources, or books, articles, and essays by critics who are also writing about the work or author. Primary sources are generally most important. In more personal literary responses, however, your personal associations, anecdotes, stories, or feelings may be used as evidence, if they're relevant to the question you're posing.

Workshopping the Draft

When you finish revising your sketch you should have a more developed draft with a clearer purpose and focus. After all this work, you may feel pretty good about it. But don't worry if you're not satisfied yet; you still have the opportunity to make further changes to your draft. Before you submit your draft for further peer review, explore your own feelings and tentative ideas about what you need to do in the next, and probably final revision.

Reflecting on the Draft. Take a look at the draft before you and circle the passage you think is the best in the essay so far. Now circle the passage that you think is weakest.

In your notebook, fastwrite for five minutes about both passages. What seems to be working in the better passage? What problems to do you notice about the weaker one? Does either one address the question you're writing about? If so, how? If not, how might it? When you compare the two passages, what do you notice about the differences? How might you make the weaker passage more like the stronger one? How might you make the rest of the essay stronger?

Questions for Readers. Share your essay in small groups before you begin the final revision. Group members might consider the following questions about each draft they discuss:

1. If you're unfamiliar with the story or essay the writer is writing about, do you have enough background information about it to understand the draft?
2. Does the draft stay focused, from beginning to end, on the focusing question? If not, where exactly does it seem to stray?
3. Do you find the interpretation of the literary work convincing? Where is the draft most convincing? Where is it least convincing?
4. Where exactly could the writer use more evidence?
5. What part of the draft was most interesting? What part was least interesting?

Revising the Draft

"Rewriting is the essence of writing," the old saying goes. But too often rewriting is limited to changing a word here and there, maybe adding or cutting a sentence or two, or checking for run-on sentences. These activities are certainly an element of revision—and an important one—but as the word implies, it's important to "re-see" both what you are trying to say as well as how you try to say it. Chapter 14, "Revision Strategies" is a useful introduction to the revision process for any essay, including the critical essay. It emphasizes ways writers can break the bonds that limit their ability to find new ways of seeing the draft.

Critical essays typically have some of the following problems to solve. Do any of these apply to your draft?

- When you make an assertion about the significance or importance of something in the work is it supported by specific evidence from the work itself?

- Are you clear about your audience? Do you assume that readers are familiar or unfamiliar with the story, and have you written the draft with that assumption in mind?

- Is your thesis clear? By the end of your essay, could a reader state without much confusion the main thing you're trying to say about the poem, story, or essay?

For help addressing some of these questions and others refer to Chapter 14, "Revision Strategies." Use the following table as a guide to the appropriate revision strategies. Remember that a draft may present problems in more than one category.

Polishing the Draft

After you've dealt with the big issues in your draft—is it sufficiently focused, does it answer the *So what?* question, is it well organized, and so on—you must deal with the smaller problems. You've carved the stone into an appealing figure, but now you need to polish it. Are your paragraphs coherent? How do you manage transitions? Are your sentences fluent and concise? Are there any errors in spelling or syntax? Section 5, "Problems in Clarity and Style" in Chapter 14 can help you focus on these issues.

Before you finish your draft, make certain that you've worked through the following checklist:

- ❑ Every paragraph is about one thing.
- ❑ The transitions between paragraphs aren't abrupt or awkward.
- ❑ The length of sentences varies in each paragraph.
- ❑ Each sentence is concise. There are no unnecessary words or phrases.
- ❑ You've checked grammar, particularly verb agreement, run-on sen-

		PART
PROBLEMS IN THE DRAFT (CHAPTER 14)	**PAGE**	**NUMBER**
Unclear purpose ■ Not sure what the paper is about? ■ Not focused enough?	1	633
Unclear thesis, theme, or main idea ■ Not sure what you're trying to say?	2	639
Lack of information or development ■ Need more convincing evidence?	3	646
Disorganized ■ Doesn't move logically or smoothly from paragraph to paragraph?	4	650
Unclear or awkward at the level of sentences and paragraphs ■ Does draft seem choppy or hard to follow at the level of sentences or paragraphs?	5	656

GUIDE TO REVISION STRATEGIES

tences, unclear pronouns, and misused words (*there/their, where/were,* and so on). (See the handbook at the back of this book for help on all of these grammar issues.)

❑ You've run your spell checker and proofed your paper for misspelled words.

STUDENT ESSAY

Julie Bird's sketch earlier in this chapter about Leslie Marmon Silko's short story "Lullaby" showed traces of the ideas behind this draft. Bird touches on the question behind her inquiry into the story—how does the character Ayah recover from her many losses?—and finds a tentative answer: Ayah finds peace in nature. Sketches are just that—roughly drawn glimpses into our own thinking about something. When they're most helpful, this "bad" writing can help us discover what we want to say, as it did here for Bird.

But notice how Julie takes the idea that nature is a powerful force in the story and extends and deepens it in the draft. The result is that her thesis is richer and more interesting. How did she do this? By returning to the dialectical process—that motion between creative thinking and critical thinking—and immersing in herself the story itself. Bird also did some research on Silko and Native American literature, testing her assertions. She not only found evidence to support them, but new ways of thinking about what she wants to say.

NATURE AS BEING: LANDSCAPE IN SILKO'S "LULLABY"

Julie Bird

Leslie Marmon Silko, the author of "Lullaby," is a Native American writer   1
from the Laguna Pueblo culture in New Mexico. Silko's story is about a Navajo woman, Ayah, and how she copes with the loss of her children—one dies in war, several others die in infancy, and two more are taken by the "white doctors" who suspect the children may have been exposed to tuberculosis. How is Ayah, condemned to poverty and surrounded by white indifference or hatred, able to recover from these losses?

Reflecting the "interrelatedness of man and nature that permeates Native   2
American literature" (Schweniger 49), it is in the landscape that Ayah finds peace in old age. Arizona's natural environment, such as snow and the slope of the mesa, is an integral character in "Lullaby" that shows the intricate relationship between humans and the natural world.

Even the structure of the story echoes these themes. Silko writes her story   3
from the end, to the beginning, to the end in the same cyclical fashion as life in the natural world and on the reservation. The writer portrays this cyclical structure of storytelling beautifully when describing Ayah as an old woman, as she reflects on the birth of her children through to the death of her husband.

Trying to find peace in the harmony of the natural world, Ayah turned   4
herself to the memories of a happier past, and the rituals and rhythms of the earth's cycle. When saddened by thoughts of her dead son Jimmie, lost in some faraway war, Ayah wraps herself in a wool blanket that he had sent to her. This unconscious gesture invariably brings the memory of sitting with her grandma and mother and combing twigs from the freshly washed wool while they weaved it into blankets. Ayah fondly remembers that "the blankets were so soft and woven so tight that rain rolled off them like birds' feathers" (Silko 44). Through Ayah's reference to the feathers, Silko is making the connection to her own beliefs in the natural world. In a sense, Ayah becomes a bird.

When Ayah runs into the foothills of the "juniper trees and black lava" (45)   5
in order to get her children away from the white doctors, she is seeking the place of refuge that is a constant source of comfort. It is her ritual to return to

this spot. Ayah comes to the mesa when her son Jimmie dies, when she buries her children who died too soon, when the doctors take her children; in other words, when she is looking for balance. To Ayah, "the sun's warmth relaxed her and took the fear and anger away. It seemed to her that she could walk into the sky, stepping through clouds endlessly" (46).

6   This harmony that Ayah shares with the natural world is what makes her who she is; it is her identity as a Navajo woman. This is especially obvious at the end of the story when she is sitting with her dying husband, a man crushed by hopelessness and alcoholism. Silko writes that "The light was crystalline. She breathed the clarity of the night sky; she smelled the purity of the half moon and the stars" (51). Silko was making a point that upon the death of her husband, Ayah at last felt a clear ("crystalline") understanding. With the passing of the storm, "steely blue-gray horses startled across the sky" (51), and with the passing away of the last of her family, Ayah was finally free to find her own peace. In old age, Ayah finally achieved her balance with the harmony of nature and was ready for it.

7   Just hearing the word snow evokes images of "freezing" and "icy", but Silko uses snow to project Ayah's feelings of warmth and comfort. Music, like nature, is a very integral part of some Native American cultures, and Silko expresses the correlation between music and the natural world throughout the story. For example, when Ayah is waiting for her husband to return home from a bar, she "sat down with her back against the wide cottonwood tree . . . and listened to the wind and snow sing a high-pitched Yeibechei song" (43).

8   We learn from Silko that the Yeibechei song is the Navajo Night Chant and is a ceremony of healing. The fact that the snow sings such a song further reinforces the idea that nature is a healing force in the story. When Ayah is watching as the "snow drifted . . . with the northwest wind hurling it in gusts," and "she smiled at the snow which was trying to cover her little by little" (44), Silko suggests that the snow, like the blanket, is a source of comfort to Ayah. And when Ayah is sitting next to her dying husband, the snow storm clears up and the night is still and clear. This is significant in that it parallels the clearing of Ayah's troubles, the passing of the figurative storm within herself.

9   At the end, Ayah sings her lullaby: "The earth is your mother, the sky your father, rainbow is your sister, the winds are your brothers" (51). It is hard to miss the balance of nature with humanity that is a part of the Navajo heritage. But Ayah's lullaby also points to Silko's particular vision of the role of nature. Landscapes aren't something to be looked at as separate from people. As the critic Karen E. Waldron notes, "Silko's poems, essays, and novels manifest the relationship between the human being and his or her surroundings as one of *being* rather than viewing" (178) [emphasis added].

The most interesting, but subtle way in which the story is written deals   10
with Silko's use of color, scent, and smell to make the story come alive and to
further reinforce the images of nature as a benign and loving force. When describing the birth of one of Ayah's children, Silko writes "The morning was already warm even before dawn and Ayah smelled the bee flowers blooming and
the young willow growing at the springs" (44). This passage correlates birth
with the smell of spring flowers, very much in tradition of human harmony
with the natural world.

Silko, in trying to show Ayah's relationship to the natural world uses every   11
sense at her disposal to paint a vivid picture to the reader. When reading
"Lullaby" you can feel the snow landing gently about you, hear the screech of
the hawk as it patiently circles above, and smell the pungent odor of the juniper trees. Silko is also able to make the reader feel the intense pain of loneliness associated with the loss of Ayah's family and culture at the hands of the
white man. In the story, Silko weaves the natural world into every nook and
cranny of the narrative so the reader is unaware of its existence but can feel its
essence as its own entity; in this case it's an entity that is not separate from
Ayah but merges with her. Both are "beings"; both share consciousness. And in
the end, she finds comfort in that.

Works Cited

Silko, Leslie Marmon. "Lullaby." Storyteller. New York: Arcade Publshing,
   1981. 43–51.

Schweninger, Lee. "Writing Nature: Silko and Native Americans as Nature
   Writers." Mellis 18 (1993): 47–60.

Waldron, Karen E. "The Land as Consciousness." Such News of the Land: U.S.
   Women Nature Writers. Ed. Thomas S. Edwards and Elizabeth A. De
   Wolfe. Hanover, NH: U P of New England, 2001: 179–190.

EVALUATING THE ESSAY

1. Compare Bird's earlier sketch and her draft. What do you notice
   about her revisions? In particular, do you think the draft is more insightful than the sketch? Why?

2. One of the temptations in writing about Native American literature
   (or any literature by someone from another or unfamiliar culture) is
   to make assumptions about what "they" believe or how "they" think.
   Many of these are based on certain cultural commonplaces that we
   pick up without thinking much about them. One of these is that
   Indians have strong ties to nature. Does Bird find support for her
   assumptions about that? How do you avoid simply accepting such
   assumptions?

3. When you write about literature, the most important source of information is the text you're writing about—the story, poem, essay, or novel. How well does Bird use evidence from "Lullaby" to convince you that what she says about the story is a reasonable interpretation?

USING WHAT YOU HAVE LEARNED

Although literary texts are quite different from the kinds of texts you usually read in school for other classes, practice with writing the critical essay can be useful even if you're not an English major. But how?

1. Think about your experience with this assignment. Can you point to something about *the process* that you could apply to another writing situation? What did you do here that you've done for other assignments in *The Curious Writer?*

2. Compare one of the short stories in this chapter with one of the research essays in Chapter 11. What are the differences between these two kinds of texts—literary fiction and expository writing, a short story and a research essay? What are the similarities? Do you read them differently? Do you read them in similar ways?

3. In sixty seconds, generate a focused list that describes the most important things you've learned about writing a critical essay. How many of these things apply to writing other kinds of papers?

Like captive flies on a spider web, we all are enmeshed in the invisible webs of culture. Shared traditions, rituals, languages, and attitudes help determine how we behave, what we think, and who we want to be. Ethnography makes these invisible webs visible, much like dew on a spider web.

Writing an Ethnographic Essay

10

WRITING ABOUT CULTURE

What You'll Learn in This Chapter

- How to sharpen your observation skills.

- The many ways that culture disciplines our behavior.

- Techniques for field research.

- Awareness of more subjective methods of research.

My daughter hates spiders. In fact, she's so repulsed by spiders she refuses to utter the word, calling them "s-words" whenever she spots one of the bugs. In sadistic moments, I want to explain to her that there are invisible webs everywhere and that we walk into them all the time. In fact, we may spin a few threads ourselves occasionally. Like the spiders in our basement, subcultures abound right under our very noses. We just have to learn to see the webs they weave.

The "web of culture" is a good metaphor because, like spider webs, the many cultures and subcultures we encounter in our everyday lives are often difficult to detect. These webs are also something in which we are all enmeshed, whether we know it or not. To some extent they limit our movements, shape our beliefs, and determine our traditions.

In recent weeks I've been a participant-observer in one of these cultural webs through a recently discovered online game called Think Tanks. Perhaps it's because I'm a complete novice at online gaming, but I find Think Tanks an amazing virtual world. Gamers remotely control tanks with purple brains on a 3-D landscape where the tanks engage in combat. Armor clanks with every well-placed shot, and after you've taken a number of hits your tank begins to smoke ominously. In Scrum Lush, my favorite game, competitors play a variation of Capture the Flag, attempting to score points before your brain pops and your tank succumbs to the armor-clanking firepower of your opponents.

It's possible to communicate in the game, too, sending brief and coded messages to other players, each of whom enters the world with screen names like "TankDork" or "Dungbeetle." Often the messages are complimentary. For example, "n1" is the language for "nice one," and "gg" is the code for "good game." Just as often, the players deride and taunt each other, and the language can get downright nasty.

What began to interest me much more than the game was the realization that the players were largely boys, most probably no older than fourteen. Their youth and gender became particularly striking when a player with a feminine screen name would join the game. "Are you a hottie, Tank Girl?" wrote one player. And soon there were comments that constituted sexual harassment as well as comments that were downright gentlemanly, complimenting the supposed girl's play. (Was "Tank Girl" really a girl? Who knows.)

Other times, two male players would face off against each other, hurling abusive comments along with cannon shots in a way that reminded me of a schoolyard at recess. There were also clear codes of behavior. For example, in Scrum Lush indiscriminate shooting at any tank that wasn't carrying the flag was considered bad form, and camping—simply hanging out near the goal until a player brought the flag to attempt a score—was highly scorned.

The more I played, the more I understood about how the world of Think Tanks operated. I'm not talking about the rules of the game, which were easy enough to understand, but the less-visible threads of behavior, ritual, attitudes, and language that governed how the players operate in this particular online world. Those threads determined how they viewed female players, how they behaved toward better players, how they disciplined each other, and how they accepted outsiders. Think Tanks, in short, is a distinct subculture, and as I logged more hours playing the game and observing how players behaved and talked, I became on online ethnographer.

Ethnography is a method of inquiry into culture that exposes the web in which members of a group are enmeshed, much the way morning dew exposes the intricacies of a spider web in your backyard.

Ethnography is a method of inquiry into culture that exposes the web in which members of a group are enmeshed, much the way the morning dew exposes the intricacies of a spider web in your backyard. In this chapter, you'll practice this approach to research and learn some ways that you can apply ethnographic techniques to all kinds of research projects. The real value of trying ethnography isn't that you'll be writing lots of ethnographies in other classes—you probably won't. Instead, writing an ethnographic essay will test your research skills by bringing them out of academia and into the field. That might be to the park where skateboarders gather, a hall where World War II veterans meet, a mall where fifteen-year-olds congregate, or the fields where migrant workers toil. You might even wander online, as I did. You'll learn to be a more careful observer. And ethnography will also raise interesting questions about whether all research can be objective.

MOTIVES FOR WRITING ETHNOGRAPHY

Ethnography may be new to you, but you've almost certainly enjoyed its nonacademic versions. Magazine articles on other cultures in *National Geographic* or *Discover* have some elements of ethnography, and arguably so do some of the reality TV shows such as *COPS*. These popular versions of ethnography invite readers and viewers to briefly enter unfamiliar worlds and learn a little about other peoples' ways of seeing and knowing. Essentially, the goal of such articles and programs is to show how things work in particular social contexts—a Los Angeles police department, a poor village in South Africa, or the neighborhood bowling alley. While the study of a culture can take the researcher overseas, it can just as easily take him down the street or across town.

There are several motives for using this form. First, ethnography involves inquiry into people, and particularly groups. This is a useful form if the questions you're asking have a social context. Second, it's a great method for questions whose answers are most likely to be found *in situ,* or in the places where the people you're interested in researching are doing what they usually do. You might be interested, for example, in how young male skateboarders view girls, particularly those who take up the sport. You probably could read about this, but it would be far better to actually interview some skateboarders and watch them interact with girls at the local park.

Finally, since the writer/researcher's observations are the source of data in ethnography (after all, you're the one taking the field notes and conducting the interviews), it's an openly subjective form of research. In that way, it's much like the research essay. Some researchers are drawn to this because they believe that foregrounding where they stand with respect to their subjects is essential if the research is to be credible. In the world of so-called qualitative research, methods often preferred in disciplines that study human subjects, researchers believe that their own predispositions, status as an outsider to the culture they're studying, and even emotional responses to what they're seeing are elements that readers should consider when evaluating a study's conclusions.

ETHNOGRAPHY AND ACADEMIC WRITING

Interest in academic ethnography has boomed in recent years, something you'll probably discover if you take an anthropology course. But you may also encounter ethnographic ways of seeing—or interest in the ways social groups behave and believe—in sociology, English, and even the visual arts, where something called "visual ethnography" might be practiced in formal or informal ways. Some researchers are using both film and still photography to capture a subculture in action, something you might consider as you work on your own ethnographic project.

But even if you never are asked to write a formal ethnography for a college class, the skills and habits of mind you practice writing one here will help you in several ways. Writing ethnographically requires that you expand your repertoire of research to include interview and fieldwork, two methods of collecting that can help you with all kinds of research projects.

In addition, the ethnographic essay is closely related to the case study, a method of research frequently used in the social sciences and especially in business. Finally, the project you're about to tackle calls on something you've practiced already—the willingness to suspend judgment while you collect information and then interpret the possible significance of what you've found. Once again, you enact the dialectical thinking that's been a part of every inquiry project in *The Curious Writer:* your observations of and your ideas about something, your record of what happened, and your sense of what *happens.*

FEATURES OF THE FORM

Like other inquiry projects in this book, ethnography is a form with many variations. There are, however, some features that most ethnographic essays share:

- *They focus on groups of people who identify themselves as group members.* It's undoubtedly true that we all belong to subcultures that we don't recognize we belong to—or perhaps refuse to acknowledge. But ethnography tends to focus on people who, at least when pressed, freely identify with a specific group. Sometimes this group identity is particularly strong—local gang members or members of the Church of Latter-Day Saints—and sometimes it might be weaker. Certain groups, like young skateboarders, for example, may have individualistic beliefs that would make them reluctant to admit group membership at first. But they do behave and speak as if they are members, and do express—even indirectly—a sense of identification with the group.

- *Ethnography depends on close observation over time.* More than other forms of inquiry, ethnographers must spend time in the field simply watching and taking notes. Particularly if you're an outsider to the culture you're studying, you can't possibly discover its artifacts, rituals, and insider language unless you hang out long enough with group members. You may not have the time to spend. After all, you have other classes and other demands on your time. Library and Web research on the group you choose to study can help make up for limited field work, but the success of this project absolutely depends on repeated visits to the places the subculture frequents.

- *The bulk of the research takes place in the natural settings where group members gather.* You want to research interstate truck drivers? Go to a truck stop on I-84. You're interested in the culture of college women's basketball? Go to the locker room and spend time at practice. The goal of ethnography is to observe a culture as it behaves normally in typical situations. The hard part, sometimes, is inserting yourself into these situations without disrupting the way things usually are, which is another reason that spending enough time in the field is important; it helps your study subjects get used to you.

- *Ethnography looks closely at the few to get hints of the big picture.* Some researchers gather as much data as they can about a social group or population they're studying in an effort to glimpse the big picture. Typically, this is done through surveys and questionnaires, but ethnographers choose another approach. By carefully describing a very small subset of the larger group—a group of five teenage skateboarders, or one women's basketball team—they hope to be able to infer something about the big picture.

- *Ethnography is often openly subjective.* As a qualitative method of research, ethnography makes the writer/researcher an instrument for collecting data as well as interpreting its significance. We are not objective instruments, of course, and so the subjectivity of the method is inescapable. Consequently, ethnographers frequently have a strong presence in their studies, acknowledging their particular angles of vision. But the aim of the ethnographer, ultimately, is to try to overcome the potential screen of subjectivity and *see the world the way their study subjects see it.*

ETHNOGRAPHIC ESSAY

Our house recently was toilet-papered by a trio of girls—not a big deal particularly, except for the word "Bitch" written in chocolate syrup on the sidewalk and the soiled tampons and sanitary napkins scattered on the lawn. The so-called prank apparently was directed at our daughter, and took us all by surprise. But then it occurred to us that our experience was entirely consistent with the stories described in Rachel Simmons's book *Odd Girl Out,* a recent release about "relational aggression" in girls. Simmons and others argue that since our culture demands that girls be "nice," and that feminine anger is bad form, young girls have little outlet for their aggression. They express their anger in indirect ways: by giving other girls the silent treatment, by using contemptuous facial expressions, or by bonding with girls who share contempt for someone else.

According to Simmons, "the lifeblood of relational aggression is relationship ... [and] where relationships are weapons, friendship itself can be a tool of anger." While boys are often seen as the main perpetrators of physical aggression, the more indirect, subtle forms of aggression by girls may be just as hurtful, if not more so, Simmons argues.

"Intimate Enemies" is an excerpt from *Odd Girl Out.* It offers Simmons's account of her investigation of relational aggression in a small-town middle school in Mississippi that she calls Ridgewood. Her method, while not a formal ethnography, is much like one. She decided to study the problem by spending a length of time getting to know girls in several different communities across the country, earning the girls' trust and confidence by essentially living among them for a few months. In this excerpt, Simmons talks to a group of Ridgewood sixth-grade girls, reporting their answers to her questions but also letting them tell their own stories. Periodically, Simmons also explains theories of relational aggression and how they seem to apply to the experiences of the girls she interviews.

Simmons' research is informed by a fairly elaborate theory that helps explain what she's hearing and observing from her girl subjects. Does this blind her to other interpretations, other ways of seeing?

from ODD GIRL OUT

INTIMATE ENEMIES

Rachel Simmons

1   Ridgewood is a blink-and-you-miss-it working-class town of 2,000 in northern Mississippi. Big enough to have its own Wal-Mart but too small for more than a few traffic lights, Ridgewood is bordered by dusty state roads dotted with service stations and fast-food chains. It is the largest town in a dry county where the mostly Baptist churches outnumber the restaurants. The majority of the town is white, although growing numbers of African American families, mostly poor, are beginning to gather around its edges. Families have long made comfortable livings at local factories here, but threats of an imminent recession have given way to layoffs and a thickening layer of anxiety.

2   Ridgewood is a fiercely tight-knit community that prides itself in its family-centered values and spirit of care for neighbors. When a tornado cuts a fatal mile-wide swath through town, everyone heads over to rebuild homes and comfort the displaced. Ridgewood is the kind of place where grown children make homes next to their parents and where teenagers safely scatter onto Main Street without looking both ways, drifting in and out of the ice-cream parlor and game room after school. Year-round, going "rolling," toilet papering an unsuspecting peer or teacher's home, is a favorite pastime, sometimes supervised by parents.

3   By ten o'clock one October morning in Ridgewood, it was already eighty-two degrees. The Mississippi sun was blindingly bright, and the earth was dry, cracked, and dusty. We were having a drought. I was late getting to school, although the truth is in Ridgewood it doesn't take longer than a song on the radio to drive anywhere.

4   I raced through the front door of the elementary school, sunglass frames in my mouth, spiral notebook in hand. Cassie Smith was waiting. Tall and big-boned, prepubescently round, she had blond hair that waved gently in strings

toward her shoulders, kind green eyes, glossed pink lips, braces, and a soft, egg-shaped freckled face. She was missing sixth-grade band class to be with me. Cassie met my eyes squarely as I nodded to her—I'd been laying low here, trying not to expose the girls who volunteered to talk to me—and we headed silently down the long, blue-gray corridor, down the ramp, underneath a still, rusty red fan, and toward the plain, cluttered room I had been using for interviews. Children were mostly oblivious to us as they slammed lockers and whirled toward class in single motions, their teachers standing stiff as flagpoles in the doorways. We passed class projects in a blur: elaborate trees decorated with sunset-colored tissue paper to welcome the autumn, which had actually been more of a summer than anything.

I motioned for Cassie to sit. We made a little small talk. She was whisper-ing so softly I could barely hear her.   5

"So," I said gently, leaning back in my chipped metal folding chair. "Why did you want to come talk with me today?"   6

Cassie inhaled deeply. "This is happening *right now,* okay?" she said, as though to admonish me that I was not just some archaeologist come here to sift through dirt and bones. "My best friend Becca," she began, staring fiercely at her fingers, which were playing an absentminded game of itsy-bitsy spider against the lead-smeared tabletop, "I trusted her and everything. She called me and asked if I liked Kelly, who is our good friend. Becca said that Kelly talks bad about me and everything." Cassie sounded nervous. "I really didn't want to say anything back about Kelly because I didn't want to go down to her level." On the phone, Cassie tried to change the subject.   7

But when Becca called, Kelly had been over at her house. When Becca hung up, she told Kelly that Cassie had called her names. Kelly called back and told Cassie off.   8

Now, at school, Kelly was teasing Cassie relentlessly—about what she was wearing (she wore that outfit last week) or not (she needs tennis shoes); about how stupid and poor she was. Cassie didn't know what to do.   9

Cassie and Becca had been best friends since first grade. Last summer, Kelly moved to Ridgewood from Texas, and this fall she'd started hanging around Becca. At first they were all three quite close, with some tension be-tween Cassie and Kelly. And then, Cassie said quietly, over the last few weeks, "Kelly kind of forgot me. They started to get really close and they just forgot me. And then they started ganging up on me and stuff like that."   10

"How?" I asked.   11

"They ignored me. They just didn't want to talk with me or anything . . ." Her voice caught and her eyes filled with tears. I squeezed past some desks to the teacher's table and leaned over to grab a box of tissues.   12

13   "Did you try and talk with them about it?" I pulled out a tissue and handed it to her.

14   "No," she said. "Like, after lunch we have a place where we meet and stuff. We have to line up and go to class. That's when everybody starts talking. We get in a circle and just talk. And they'd put their shoulders together and they wouldn't let me, you know, in the circle or whatever. They would never talk to me, and they would never listen to what I had to say. Stuff like that." She was whispering again.

15   "I don't think I've ever done anything to them." Her voice shook. "I've always been nice to them."

16   Lately, it had only gotten worse. Kelly, by now no stranger in the school, had been warning other girls to stay away from Cassie. Becca was saying that Cassie was insulting Kelly behind her back, and Kelly was passing notes that said Cassie lived in a shack and was too poor to buy Sunday clothes.

17   "So how are you feeling?" I asked.

18   "Like I don't want to go to school," she whispered, sinking into her red fleece vest.

19   "Why not?"

20   "Because I don't know what they'll do every day."

21   "What have they done so far?" I asked.

22   "They'll be like, 'Cassie, get back, we're going to talk about you now.'"

23   "They'll say that?"

24   "No, they'll just"—she was getting frustrated with me—"*I can tell*. They don't have to say anything. They'll whisper and look at me, and I know they're talking about me."

25   "Have you talked to your mom?" I asked.

26   "I talk to my mom but it just . . . I don't really want to worry her a lot." She began to cry again.

27   "Does it worry her?"

28   "It kind of makes her mad because—she says I should ignore them. But I *can't*. They just keep on."

29   "Why is it hard to ignore them?"

30   "Because they're like, running over you, you know? And I can't concentrate. They're like—they look at me and stuff like that. They stare at me. I can hear them saying stuff and whispering and they look right at me."

31   Cassie struggled with the absence of a language to articulate her victimization. As the silent meanness of her friends attracted no teacher's attention, Cassie was filled with a helplessness that was slowly turning into self-blame. Without rules or a public consciousness of this behavior, Cassie's only sense that what was happening was real (or wrong) was her own perspective. For a ten-year-old, that would not be enough.

Relational aggression starts in preschool, and so do the first signs of sex 32
differences. The behavior is thought to begin as soon as children become capable of meaningful relationships. By age three, more girls than boys are rela-
tionally aggressive, a schism that only widens as children mature. In a series of
studies, children cited relational aggression as the "most common angry, hurtful . . . behavior enacted in girls' peer groups," regardless of the target's sex.
By middle childhood, the leading researchers in the field report that "physical
aggressors are mostly boys, relational aggressors mostly girls."

Relational aggression harms others "through damage (or the threat of 33
damage) to relationships or feelings of acceptance, friendships, or group inclusion." It includes any act in which relationship is used as a weapon, including
manipulation. First identified in 1992, it is the heart of the alternative aggres-
sions, and for many girls an emotionally wrenching experience.

Relational aggression can include indirect aggression, in which the target 34
is not directly confronted (such as the silent treatment), and some social aggression, which targets the victim's self-esteem or social status (such as rumor
spreading). Among the most common forms of relational aggression are "do
this or I won't be your friend anymore," ganging up against a girl, the silent
treatment, and nonverbal gesturing, or body language.

The lifeblood of relational aggression is relationship. As a result, most re- 35
lational aggression occurs within intimate social or friendship networks. The
closer the target to the perpetrator, the more cutting the loss. As one Linden
freshman put it, "Your friends know you and how to hurt you. They know
what your real weaknesses are. They know exactly what to do to destroy
someone's self-worth. They try to destroy you from the inside." Such pointed
meanness, an eighth grader explained to me, "can stay with you for your entire
life. It can define who you are."

Where relationships are weapons, friendship itself can become a tool of 36
anger. You can, one Ridgewood sixth grader explained, "have a friend, and then
go over there and become friends with somebody else, just to make them jealous." Nor must the relationship be withdrawn or even directly threatened: the
mere suggestion of loss may be enough. One girl may stand among a group,
turn to two friends and sigh, "Wow, I can't *wait* for this weekend!" One girl
may pull another away from a group "and tell them secrets, right in front of
us," a Mississippi sixth grader said. "When she comes back, people ask her
what she said, [and] she's always like, 'Oh, nothing. It's none of your business.'"
No rule has been broken here, yet it takes little more than this for a girl to in-
flict pain on her peers.

A combination of nonphysical, often furtive aggression is extremely dan- 37
gerous, in large part because it is impossible to detect. Relational aggression
has remained invisible because the behavior resists the typical displays that we

normally associate with bullying. Two girls playing quietly together in the corner might be two girls playing quietly in the corner—or they might be one girl slowly wearing down the other.

38   Teachers and parents may not be looking or listening for signs of a problem behind the facade of friendship and play. Who can blame them? Nothing *looks* wrong. It is tempting to interpret signs of trouble as the passing "issues" that afflict all normal childhood relationships, but in some cases, turning the other way can be a terrible mistake.

39   "Nonverbal gesturing," a fancy word for body language, is a hallmark of relational aggression. Denied the use of their voices by rules against female anger, girls like Becca and Kelly have instead learned to use their bodies. Nonverbal gesturing includes mean looks, certain forms of exclusion, and the silent treatment. It also drives girls to distraction. For one thing, body language is at once infuriatingly empty of detail and bluntly clear. It cuts deep precisely because a girl will know someone is angry at her, but she doesn't get to find out why and sometimes with whom it's happening. In girls' worlds, the worst aggression is the most opaque, creating a sort of emotional poison ivy which makes it hard to concentrate on anything else. Teachers become characters in "Peanuts" cartoons, their lecturing unintelligible. Words swim on the page. The victim of this silent campaign looks around the room and everything—a look exchanged, someone writing a note—has crooked, wildly irrational new significance, like reflections in a funhouse mirror.

INQUIRING INTO THE ESSAY

Use the four methods of inquiry to think about your response to the essay.

1. Explore how you experienced aggression when you were young. In your journal, write about a time you felt like a victim of either physical or more indirect violence or aggression. Begin with a scene or moment that stands out in your memory and write about it for seven full minutes with as much detail as you can. Then skip a line, and think critically about the experience. Answer the following question: *As you look back on this now, what do you understand or realize about the experience that you didn't fully understand back then?*

2. One of the things that characterizes a culture is insider language, or ways of communicating that mark membership in the group. Sometimes this language even seems like a code to an outsider. While the talk of these girls is quite comprehensible, what do you notice about the language they use to talk about themselves and others? Is there anything characteristic about it?

3. It's hard to be sympathetic to the perpetrators of relational aggression. After all, it's not nice to be mean. But could you make an argument that these girls are not entirely to blame for their behavior?

4. Reading ethnography is a little voyeuristic. Through the researcher/writer, we get to peek through the window at other lives. Reflect a bit on the ethical responsibilities that you as an ethnographer have toward the people you're studying. Do you have any obligations to your subjects?

ETHNOGRAPHIC ESSAY

In a multicultural nation like the United States, ethnic differences are among the most obvious webs in which we are enmeshed. I grew up in an Italian American family, and as a boy that meant that meals were social events and the quantity of food consumed a measure of gratitude to the cook. Still, I was two generations away from the Italian immigrants in my family, and these rituals were fairly self-conscious expressions of my heritage. Most of the time, I didn't really feel that Italian.

Many among us, however, are recent immigrants, and ethnic ties bind these Americans more tightly to another place and culture. Among the challenges this group faces is how much to retain the rituals and traditions of the place from which they came, and how much to adopt and adapt to traditionally American ways. This dilemma is particularly hard for the children of immigrants. For those of us several generations away from this, it's hard to imagine how profound this dilemma can be.

For California teenage girls who are Muslim, one way these cultural tensions can be explored is by looking at a rite of passage that for many Americans symbolizes adolescence—the prom. How do the Muslim daughters of Pakistani-American parents celebrate the prom—one of high school's most important coming-of-age rituals—when their faith does not permit them to dress in a manner perceived as immodest around boys or allow boys to touch girls? The article that follows, "For the Muslim Prom Queen, There Are No Kings Allowed," is a fascinating look at the cultural adaptation of a new generation of sons and daughters of immigrants. Their solution to the dilemma of negotiating old and new cultures is to reshape the new culture to fit the old, rather than the other way around. Muslim teenagers can have a prom, but it won't look much like the one I attended.

Like all of the essays in this chapter, the piece that follows isn't a formal ethnography. But notice how much you can learn about culture by focusing on how people participate in a single ritual. In this case, it's the high school prom, but it could just as easily be an initiation rite of a fraternity, a funeral, or a birthday. Consider such an approach when you write your own ethnographic essay. Is there a ritual event that could be the focus of your essay?

FOR THE MUSLIM PROM QUEEN, THERE ARE NO KINGS ALLOWED
Patricia Leigh Brown

1   The trappings of a typical high school prom were all there: the strobe lights, the garlands, the crepe pineapple centerpieces and even a tiara for the queen. In fact, Fatima Haque's prom tonight had practically everything one might expect on one of a teenage girl's most important nights. Except boys.

2   Ms. Haque and her friends may have helped initiate a new American ritual: the all-girl Muslim prom. It is a spirited response to religious and cultural beliefs that forbid dating, dancing with or touching boys or appearing without a hijab, the Islamic head scarf. While Ms. Haque and her Muslim friends do most things other teenagers do—shopping for shoes at Macy's, watching "The Matrix Reloaded" at the mall or ordering Jumbo Jack burgers and curly fries at Jack in the Box—an essential ingredient of the American prom, boys, is off limits. So they decided to do something about it.

3   "A lot of Muslim girls don't go to prom," said Ms. Haque, 18, who removed her hijab and shawl at the prom to reveal an ethereal silvery gown. "So while the other girls are getting ready for their prom, the Muslim girls are getting ready for our prom, so we won't feel left out."

4   The rented room at a community center here was filled with the sounds of the rapper 50 Cent, Arabic pop music, Britney Spears and about two dozen girls, including some non-Muslim friends. But when the sun went down, the music stopped temporarily, the silken gowns disappeared beneath full-length robes, and the Muslims in the room faced toward Mecca to pray. Then it was time for spaghetti and lasagna.

5   It is perhaps a new version of having it all: embracing the American prom culture of high heels, mascara and adrenaline while being true to a Muslim identity.

6   "These young women are being very creative, finding a way to continue being Muslim in the American context," said Jane I. Smith, a professor of Islamic studies at the Hartford Seminary in Connecticut. "Before, young Muslims may have stuck with the traditions of their parents or rejected them totally to become completely Americanized. Now, they're blending them."

Non-Muslim students at San Jose High Academy, where Ms. Haque is   7
president of the student body, went to the school's coed prom last month—
renting cars or limousines, dining at the Sheraton, going to breakfast at
Denny's and, for some, drinking. Ms. Haque, meanwhile, was on her turquoise
cellphone with the smiley faces organizing the prom. She posted an announcement on Bay Area Muslim Youth, a Yahoo news group scanned by young people
throughout the San Francisco Bay area, home to one of the country's largest
and most active Muslim communities.

"We got so close, we wanted to hang," said Fatin Alhadi, 17, a friend, ex-   8
plaining the farewell-to-high-school celebration, which involved cooking,
shopping and decorating the room, rented with a loan from Ms. Haque's parents. "It's an excuse to dress and put makeup on. Everyone has so much fun at
the prom."

The sense of anticipation was palpable at Ms. Haque's house this after-   9
noon, including an occasional "Relax, mom!" For Ms. Haque and her friends,
the Muslim prom—like any prom—meant getting your eyebrows shaped at
the last minute and ransacking mother's jewelry box. It was a time to forget
about the clock, to look in the mirror and see a glamorous woman instead of a
teenager. To be radiant.

Ms. Haque and her Muslim girlfriends dwell in a world of exquisite sub-   10
tlety in which modesty is the underlying principle. Though she wears a hijab,
Ms. Alhadi recently dyed her black hair auburn. "Everyone asks me why, because nobody sees it," she said. "But I like to look at myself."

Ms. Haque, who will attend the University of California at Berkeley in the   11
fall, is one of a growing number of young Muslim women who have adopted
the covering their mothers rejected. Islamic dress, worn after puberty, often
accompanies a commitment not to date or to engage in activities where gen-
ders intermingle.

Her parents immigrated from Pakistan, and her mother, Shazia, who has a   12
master's degree in economics, does not wear the hijab.

Ms. Haque's decision to cover herself, which she made in her freshman   13
year, was nuanced and thoughtful.

"I noticed a big difference in the way guys talked," she said. "They were   14
afraid. I guess they had more respect. You walked down the street and you did-
n't feel guys staring at you. You felt a lot more confident." Her parents were
surprised but said it was her decision.

Ms. Haque faced some taunting after the terror attacks on Sept. 11, 2001.   15
"They call you terrorist, or raghead because high school students are imma-
ture," she said.

But she and her friends say Muslim boys, who are not distinguished by   16
their dress, may have a tougher time in American society.

17 "The scarf draws the line," said Ms. Alhadi, the daughter of a Singaporean mother and Indonesian father. "It's already a shield. Without it everything comes to you and you have to fight it yourself."

18 Ms. Haque is enrolled in the academically elite International Baccalaureate program at San Jose High Academy, a public school where, as her friend Morgan Parker, 17, put it, "the jocks are the nerds."

19 But the social pressures on Muslims, especially in less-cloistered settings, can be intense.

20 "I felt left out, big time," said Saira Lara, 17, a senior at Gunn High School in Palo Alto, of her school's prom. But she gets a vicarious taste of dating by talking with her non-Muslim friends.

21 "The drama that goes on!" Ms. Lara said, looking dazzling at the Muslim prom in a flowing maroon gown. "The Valentine's Day without a phone call or a box of chocolates!"

22 Imran Khan, 17, a senior at Los Altos High School, admitted that his school's prom was not easy.

23 "When I told my friends I wasn't going, they all said, 'Are you crazy?'" he said in a telephone interview. "Prom is a you-have-to-go kind of thing. Obviously if all your friends are going and you're not, you're going to feel something. That day I was, 'Oh man, my friends are having fun and I'm not.' But I don't regret not going."

24 Most of Mr. Khan's school friends are not Muslim, and his Muslim friends are scattered across the Bay area.

25 "A lot of times it's difficult," he said. "We guys blend in so you can't tell we're Muslim. We're not supposed to touch the opposite gender. My friends who are girls understand, but when other girls want to hug you or shake your hand, it's hard. I don't want them to think I'm a jerk or something."

26 Adeel Iqbal, 18, a senior at Bellarmine College Preparatory, a boys' Catholic school in San Jose, went stag to his coed senior prom. Mr. Iqbal decided to go in his official capacity as student body president as well as a representative of his Muslim beliefs.

27 "Every day we're bombarded with images of sex and partying and getting drunk, in music and on TV, so of course there's a curiosity," he said. "When you see your own peers engaging in these activities, it's kind of weird. It takes a lot of strength to not participate. But that's how I've been raised. When your peers see you're different in a positive way, they respect it."

28 Nearly all parents of adolescents worry about the pressures of sex, drugs and alcohol, but the anxiety is especially acute in Muslim families who strictly adhere to traditional Islamic dress and gender separation. Many Muslim parents disapprove of what they see as an excessively secularized and liberalized

American culture, and are deeply concerned that young Muslims, especially girls, not be put in compromising situations.

Ms. Haque's father, Faisal, a design engineer at Cisco Systems, said that the pressure to conform was "very significant." It is the subject of frequent family discussions.   29

"It's difficult at best," Mr. Haque said. "It takes a lot of self-control. I have a lot of respect for these kids."   30

The Haques supported their daughter's decision to organize the Muslim prom. "You have to live in this country," Mr. Haque said. "In order to function, the children have to adapt. Prom is a rite of passage. You don't want them to feel like they don't belong."   31

Ms. Haque would like the Muslim prom to become an annual event. "My goal is an elegant ballroom with a three-course dinner—no paper plates—women waiters and a hundred girls," she said.   32

Tonight, the prom room was filled with promise as the young women whirled around the dance floor, strobe lights blinking. "Show off whatever you've got!" Ms. Lara exhorted the throng, sounding like a D.J. "Come on, guys. This is the most magical night of your life!"   33

INQUIRING INTO THE ESSAY

Use the four ways of inquiring to think about your response to Patricia Leigh Brown's article.

1. If you went to an American high school, then you had to decide whether to attend the prom. Was this much of a decision for you? Fastwrite for five minutes in your journal about your social status then. Were you an insider or outsider? How was the prom at your school symbolic of the ways in which social status was expressed at your high school? In what ways was this reflected in how people dressed, what they did, who they hung out with, and how they behaved? Write about your own observations of this and your feelings about it back then.

2. Based on what you may have written in your journal in response to the first question, explain the markers of social status in your high school. How could you tell an insider from an outsider, the popular from the less popular, the socially mainstream from the less so? Be as specific as you can.

3. How would the students of your school respond to Fatima Haque, the girl who organized the Muslim Prom that was described in the article, if she came to the prom in her hijab (head covering) and shawl? What does this suggest about the culture of your high school?

4. Critics of multiculturalism might read this article and argue that recent immigrants should work harder to assimilate and adopt conventional American traditions and rituals. In other words, perhaps what these girls needed to do was to find a way to bend their own beliefs to accommodate the typical prom, rather than appropriate the prom to conform to their own beliefs. How would you evaluate that claim?

5. Empathy is essential if we're going to understand the lives of people with different cultural, racial, or social backgrounds. When you read and write about people who are fundamentally different from you, how do you attempt to get outside of your own biases and the limitations of your own experience?

ETHNOGRAPHIC ESSAY

A "G," writes journalist Nik Cohn, "was the highest condition any hustla could aspire to." In the New Orleans's projects, these were the young men who remembered where they came from no matter how rich they became selling drugs or how long they were put away when they were caught. Ironically, to live as a "G" is to believe in tradition as firmly as the conservative, church-going man in any middle-class suburb in America. The "G-Code" dictates how you dress, how you walk, your basic values, and the respect you expect from subordinates.

In the essay that follows, we get a glimpse at an inner city subculture that emerges in the midst of poverty, drugs, and crime, and the strange dignity and pride that arises from such seemingly poisoned ground. Like any living thing, culture grows in context. People gravitate to others who share their responses to the very local blessings and nightmares that shape everyday life; from this comes order and meaning, and irony, too. Among the many things that cultures provide all of us is a sense of who we are, and perhaps even pride in that, even for a drug dealer and a murderer.

from SOLJAS
Nik Cohn

1   Soljas lived and died by the G-Code. To be recognized as a G was the highest condition any hustla could aspire to. The G was a big-time gangsta, a godfatha, a don. He had all the cars and hoes and bling bling any man could dream of, yet he stayed true to his roots. He was a mighty warlord, but he had a project soul.

It was a matter of honour. 'As far as what I mean by G-code,' said Juvenile,   2
'is the way we dress, the way we talk, the way we was raised. Traditions. When
I say G-code, I'm talkin' about what you went through where you from.'

Terrance 'Gangsta' Williams, half-brother of Slim and Baby, was a G.   3
Around the Magnolia he was a great hero, though he did not live there any
more. He was serving life plus twenty years in a federal pen, for Continuing
Criminal Enterprise, solicitation to commit murder, and conspiracy to sell six
ounces of heroin.

From jail, he gave an interview to *F.E.D.S,* the magazine of 'convicted hus-   4
tlers/street thugs/fashion/sports/music/film/etc'. Questioned by the mag's
ace reporter, Cold Crushin' Kenny Rankin, Gangsta didn't deny the charges,
though he tried to put them in context. When he was still on the streets, New
Orleans had been known as Click Click, murder capital of the world, but he
felt its status was deceptive. 'That's only because New Orleans is a very small
city,' Gangsta argued. 'Everybody's trying to build a reputation and get their
hustle on—the city's not big enough for but so many gangsters. So, somebody
had to go.'

'How many people do they say you've killed?' Rankin asked.   5
'. . . According to the streets they say I've murdered over forty people.'   6
'How old were you when they started calling you a heartstopper?'   7
'I was about fifteen.'   8
'What does "heartstopper" mean?'   9
'When you penetrate someone with some iron.'   10

All in all, he sounded upbeat. 'I do thank God and I will admit that me   11
having this life plus twenty was one of the best things that could've happened
to me. It's all love in the federal system,' he said. He was writing a book and
planning a movie, warning the young not to follow his path. Meanwhile, he
was grateful to be alive, and to have his brothers' support, and most of all to
be who he was. 'To Mister Terrance Gangsta Ooh-Gee Magnolia Williams,' he
concluded, 'all I can say is, "I'm jealous of myself".'

The source of the G's strength was pride. Pride in his family, in his click,   12
in his own legend. But if he came from a project, as most Gs did, pride in that
project came first and last. It was what he represented.

Outsiders found this hard to understand. To them, the projects were   13
dumping grounds. Driving through them, it seemed inconceivable that these
tortured labyrinths of dung-coloured buildings, with their scorched walls and
boarded-up windows and stench of human rot, could be a source of pride to
anyone. Yet they'd started out as model housing. When they were built, mostly
in the 1940s, they were seen as a blessed escape. Ten of them ringed the inner
city, each a small city to itself, each conceived in hope.

14   The G-Code was born of the 1980s, when crack first flooded the streets and raised up a new breed of drug lord, more murderous than any before. The projects turned into fiefdoms, ruled by guns and celebrated by rappers like Juvenile: 'Welcome to the section where it's hotter than a bitch/Niggas breakin' up bricks, niggas tryin' to be rich/All day hustle, boocoo scuffle/Niggas huddle, AK-47s muffled/Blood in puddles, people scatter/Flying pieces of human matter . . . '

15   The G's gift was to harness the slaughter and ride it. But he needed soljas to protect his turf and run his games. Many of these were children; the younger they were, the less hang-ups they had about shooting people: 'I ain't terrified from nuthin'/I'm young, wild, crazy and disgustin . . . '.

16   Your project was who you were. It gave you a tribe, and a cause. Soljas called that love.

17   The enemy was everyone outside. New Orleans was an endless maze of rivalries and ancient feuds. Apart from the projects, there were also eighteen wards. Gerrymandered political districts, drawn up in the nineteenth century, their boundaries defied logic, but soljas held them sacred.

18   Some wards were allied, others at perpetual war. A story is told of a boy called Lawrence from the Sixth Ward, who went to a club in the Fourth Ward. The Fourth and Sixth Wards are friendly, the Fourth and Seventh are not. So when Lawrence got in the club, some niggas asked him his ward. Lawrence held both hands up, one with four fingers extended, the other with two. But he was dancing, and it was dark, and the niggas couldn't see that his thumb was down on the hand with the four fingers out. They thought he was saying seven. So they shot him once in the head, once in the chest and once in the stomach.

19   To soljas, the incident was regrettable, not tragic. Few of them conceived a long-term future; their life was minute by minute. They slung rocks (dealt crack), robbed gas stations and convenience stores, and served their time in the Orleans Parish Prison. Sooner or later, most likely, they were shot.

20   Even that was not all bad. When a solja died in battle, he was memorialized on a T-shirt. His image appeared in four-colour glory, usually in combat gear, with the dates of his sunrise and sunset and a line of tribute from his click. In death, he achieved what life had denied him. He was someone; and he had the T-shirt to prove it.

INQUIRING INTO THE ESSAY

Explore, explain, evaluate, and reflect to discover what you think about the excerpt from *Soljas*.

1. This is a fairly short excerpt. Read it through twice, set it aside, and then begin a fastwrite in your journal that explores, in an open-

ended way, your reaction to the essay. What do you make of these "warlords" who have a "project soul?" Do you see any parallels to this in your own experience? As an outsider to this culture, what has this essay helped you to understand? What questions does it raise for you? Write for seven minutes.

2. On a blank journal page, or in a table you create on your computer, make four headings: Artifacts, Inside Languages, Marks of Status, and Shared Beliefs. Artifacts often are ordinary objects that hold particular meaning or significance for group members. Inside Languages are the particular words and phrases, often in code, that distinguish insiders from outsiders. Marks of status help tell the difference between a leader and a follower; what specifically do members believe establishes these differences? Shared Beliefs summarize basic attitudes toward authority, outsiders, relationships among members, and status. Collect information from the essay about all four of these categories as a means of defining the "soljas" as a distinct urban culture.

ARTIFACTS	INSIDE LANGUAGES	MARKS OF STATUS	SHARED BELIEFS

3. Evaluate Cohn's implied claim that inner city warlords can have honor. What kind of honor is this?

4. Terrence 'Gangsta' Williams, whose admirers claim is responsible for the deaths of forty people, is a "G" serving time in a federal prison. He's a proud man. "I'm jealous of myself," he says without irony. On what basis do we judge such a man? And more generally, reflect on how as outsiders to a culture such judgments are problematic.

SEEING THE FORM

MRS. SMITH'S KITCHEN TABLE AND VANITY THE DAY AFTER SHE DIED

My brother Buzz's neighbor, Mrs. Smith, lived in her small bungalow in Santa Cruz, California, for nearly all of her life. The day after she died, Buzz, a professional photographer, was in Mrs. Smith's house and took the pictures on page 408. One of the many reasons I love these shots is how much can be revealed about a life by the things we choose to surround ourselves with. In these two pictures, I get a sense of a life that was

suddenly interrupted; we are confronted with the frozen image of a coffee cup and saucer, an open phone book, a crumpled tissue, bottles of medicine, and a picture of a fair-haired boy. An ethnographic "reading" of these pictures would place particular emphasis on what these things imply about Mrs. Smith's social status or as markers and artifacts of a culture to which she belonged.

Reading pictures like these, simply to speculate about the kind of person Mrs. Smith was, is a great exercise in ethnographic seeing. Spend a few minutes looking very closely at the pictures. Inventory as many details in the images as you can, perhaps cataloging them in your journal. As you consider these particulars, speculate about Mrs. Smith. What kind of person do you imagine she was? What kinds of things did she seem to care about? What does this brief moment in time suggest about the kind of life she was leading the day she died?

■ THE WRITING PROCESS ■

INQUIRY PROJECT: Writing an Ethnographic Essay

This assignment will take you into the field to observe a subculture in the community. You'll write a 2,500 to 3,000-word essay that uses field research and reading as the basis for an interpretation of how the subculture sees things. This necessarily will be a limited picture, so it should focus on some aspect of the culture that emerges from your observations.

The essay should also have the following qualities:

- Have a limited focus.

- Be organized around some thesis or interpretation of how this culture sees things. For example, how does the culture view authority figures, or what constitutes a leader in the group? (See "Inquiring into the Details: Questions Ethnographers Ask" later in this chapter.)

- Offer a rationale for why this group constitutes a distinct culture.

- Provide enough evidence from your field observations to make your interpretations and commentary convincing.

Thinking About Subjects

Like any of the inquiry projects described in *The Curious Writer,* success depends on what motivates you. What might make you curious about studying a certain local culture? Do you have a family member you've always wanted to know better who just happens to be a truck driver, a farmer, an emergency room nurse, a migrant worker? Maybe your best friend is a member of a social group you'd like to study—a Baptist youth group, rock climbers, or Dead Heads—and can offer access. If you're an older student, perhaps you have a niece or a nephew or possibly one of your own children who is a member of the local girl's tennis team, the youth ballet company, or the bow-hunters club.

Might your professional interests be relevant to this project? Say you want to be a police officer; might it be enlightening to hang out with a few officers to find out what the life is like? If you have an interest in writing, then the ethnography assignment promises to be a great learning experience, no matter what culture you choose to study. You'll get practice in observation, note taking, interviewing, and profiling—skills that are invaluable for writers of any kind.

◩ WRITING WITH COMPUTERS

DIGITAL IMAGES

There may be times when you find it appropriate to incorporate digital images, either photographs or artwork, into your writing (the ethnographic essay and the profile are two forms that are particularly well suited for the inclusion of subject photographs). Computers, scanners, digital cameras, and the Internet can all facilitate this. If you own a digital camera and have access to the subject you want to photograph, you can shoot your own images and transfer them to your computer. Another option is to use a scanner to convert traditional print photographs into digital images; generally, it is easier to work with files saved in *jpeg* or *tiff* formats. Once you have the images on your computer, you can use photo-editing software such as *Photoshop* to crop or otherwise adjust the images. You can then use your word processor to insert (import) the images directly into your draft. You can also copy images directly from the Internet, where you can find numerous photo archives and image banks. Often there are no restrictions on the use of online images in personal writing or in writing shared exclusively within a single class setting. Many online images, however, are protected by copyright and cannot be reproduced for wide distribution without the copyright holder's permission, usually granted only after the payment of a fee. Copyright laws also restrict the digital reproduction of traditional print photographs.

Possible subjects for your ethnography are all around you. We are all enmeshed within intricate webs of cultures. But what should you choose to write about? If you're a student at an urban campus, then the possibilities are nearly limitless, but even if you attend a rural university you can still find a culture to study on your own campus.

Generating Ideas

Begin exploring possible subjects for a review by generating material in your notebook. This should be an open-ended process, a chance to use your creative side without worrying too much about making sense or trying to prejudge the value of the writing or the subjects you generate. In a sense, this is an invitation to play around.

Listing Prompts. Lists can be rich sources of triggering topics. Let them grow freely, and when you're ready, use an item as the focus of another list or an episode of fastwriting. The following prompts should get you started.

1. In class or in your journal, create a four-column table, labeling the first column Trends, the second Hobbies, the third Community

Groups, and the fourth Campus Groups (see the example below). Brainstorm a list of *cultural trends* that are a visible part of American culture in the new millennium. For example, snowboarding is a sport that has boomed in recent years, nearly eclipsing skiing. Write the name of each trend under the first column in the table. Create a similar list for popular hobbies (note that trends and hobbies often overlap—snowboarding can also be a hobby) and write the name of each hobby in the second column. Finally, brainstorm a list of identifiable social groups in the community and on campus. For example, fraternities, truck drivers, goths, and so on. Write these, respectively, in the third and fourth columns of your table.

TRENDS	HOBBIES	COMMUNITY GROUPS	CAMPUS GROUPS
Snowboarding	Fly fishing	Kiwanis	Fraternities
Blogging (participating in Web logs)	Ballroom dancing	Pentecostal Church	Black student alliance
Atkins/South Beach/low-carb diet craze	Computer games	Gospel singers Truck drivers	Graduate students
Reality TV programming	Autograph collecting		

2. Create a new three-column table, labeling the first column Artifacts, the second Language, and the third Rituals. Now choose one of the trends, hobbies, community groups, or campus groups from your first table and under the first column of the new table list all of the artifacts—tools, equipment, devices, clothing—that you can think of that people typically use when they participate in the activity/group you have selected. In the second column, list the language—special terms, jargon, and other words or phrases—that group members regularly use. In the third column, list the rituals—habits, patterns of behavior, or traditions—that are typical of the activity/group. Creating the new table will help you expose some of the threads of a particular activity's or group culture. Objects that group members typically use, their ways of speaking, and the traditions and rituals that govern their behavior are three key elements you need to consider when writing an ethnographic essay. The accompanying table identifies some of the artifacts, language, and rituals of fly fishing.

FLY FISHING		
ARTIFACTS	**LANGUAGE**	**RITUALS**
Fly rod (not "pole")	"Working water"	Keeping physical distance from other flyfishers
Artificial fly	"Skunked"	Catch and release of fish
Vest	"Meat fisherman"	Winter fly tying

Fastwriting Prompts. Choose an item from one of your lists as a fastwrite prompt. Write quickly, exploring each of the following questions:

1. What are your own experiences and observations with this trend, hobby, or group?
2. What are your presuppositions, biases, or assumptions about this trend, hobby, or group? What do you assume about the kind of people who participate in it, for example, and what might their motives be for belonging?
3. Based on what you know now, what things—or artifacts—seem particularly important to participants?
4. What questions do you have about why this trend exists, or why people participate in the group or hobby?

Visual Prompts. Sometimes the best way to generate material is to see what we think represented in something other than sentences. Boxes, lines, webs, clusters, arrows, charts, or even sketches can help us to see more of the landscape of a subject, especially connections between fragments of information that aren't as obvious in prose.

1. If you like to take photographs, go through your collection looking for suggestive pictures of subcultures you've captured on film. Perhaps you took pictures of an on-campus or community event, or you have some shots of people back home that represent certain social groups.
2. Take a word or phrase from the table you created from the first question in "Listing Prompts" and use it as a nucleus word for a cluster on a blank page of your journal. When you cluster a hobby, cultural trend, community or campus group, build associations using the five W's: What, When, Where, Who, and Why. *Where* do participants of this hobby, group, or trend gather, and *when*? *Who* are the kind of people who belong? *What* are their activities and rituals?

Research Prompts. Research can be helpful even this early in the process. New or more detailed information might trigger ideas about possible topics for your paper that you otherwise would never have considered. At this stage, your research will be open-ended and not particularly methodical. Just enjoy poking around.

1. In the United States, there's a magazine for nearly every subculture. Go to a bookstore and survey the hobby and special interest magazines, or visit http://hopcottmagazines.com/magazines/culturaltrends .html, which lists cultural trends magazines. Do any of these interest you?

2. One quick way to gain entry to a culture you don't belong to is to find someone in your class who is a member. Stay alert to what others in the class say about their own identification with certain social groups and interview any who belong to a culture that interests you.

3. Search the Google Web directory under the category "subcultures." The long lists of subcultures you'll see can boggle the mind, but one may inspire you.

Judging What You Have

Generating may produce the messy, incoherent writing that would earn you bad grades in most classes. Its virtue, however, should be obvious by now: "bad" writing gives a writer material to work with. And while it's always better to work from abundance rather than scarcity, this material still must be judged, shaped, and evaluated.

What's Promising Material and What Isn't? In deciding what to write about, keep in mind that you should choose a local culture that meets the following qualifications:

1. The culture is accessible to you.
2. The culture's members gather at places that you can visit.
3. The culture interests you in some way.
4. The culture might lend itself to library or online research.
5. You are not a member of this culture.

The last criterion—that you shouldn't be a member of the group you're studying—isn't a hard and fast rule, especially if you have just a few weeks to complete the assignment, but it is preferred. As an outsider, it takes a bit more time to gain access to the group and earn the members', trust, but this is a particularly useful vantage point for observing the culture because first impressions are enormously valuable. Also, as an outsider you'll be more open to what you see and more likely to see more. Also, keep in mind that it's not enough that people gather in a particular place for the same reasons. Consider, for example, the coffee house trend that has swept the country. At first, the coffee house would seem to be an ideal location for an ethnographic study; after all, caffeine lovers do seem to be a distinct group, and they gather in distinct places with a common sense of purpose. Yet do they really identify with each other as fellow members of a coffee lovers group? In fact, coffee houses attract all kinds of people—from the investment banker to the starving artist. Coffee houses attract a *range* of cultures, each of which may be worthy of study, but there probably isn't a distinct coffee house culture.

How can you know whether a study subject will meet the definition of a culture? If the answer to the following questions is "yes," then your subject probably will qualify:

- Does the group you want to study feel, at least implicitly, a sense of identification with each other as members? (This doesn't necessarily mean that they all like each other or always get along.)
- Do group members share certain behaviors, outlooks, beliefs, or motivations for belonging?
- Do they share a common language? Do they tend to describe things in similar ways, or use words or phrases that have special significance to the group?
- Do they share an interest in certain objects or artifacts? Do they invest these things with similar significance?

This list of questions might seem limiting, but because we are all immersed in social groups that have these kinds of cultural affinities you should find it easy to discover a culture to study from the ideas you generated. Cultures literally are everywhere, including your campus.

Questions About Audience and Purpose. Whatever your personal reasons for writing about a local culture, you need to find a way to make the group as interesting to readers as it is to you. Like any other piece of writing, the ethnography needs to be focused and have something to say about its subject. While you won't be writing for experts—cultural anthropologists or social scientists—your audience of peers is, in a sense, an authority on American culture. After all, we are immersed in it. Your challenge, then, is to help your audience to see what they've probably already seen, but in a new way. For example, most of us have been to a truck stop on the interstate, and we may even be familiar with the women who work there. But we probably know very little about how they see themselves, their jobs, and the people they serve. A good ethnography will illuminate some aspect of what it's like to be a female waiter at an interstate truck stop, making something familiar fresh and new.

Since you'll be writing a brief ethnographic essay, and you won't have as much time to immerse yourself fully in the culture you're studying, finding a focus early on is essential. It may be a bit hard to decide until you've actually started your fieldwork and considered your first impressions, but your study will be far more interesting and useful if you avoid simply inventorying everything you notice about the culture. Instead, build your essay around a question you're trying to answer about the way the group sees things, a move that will lead you to use the data you collect *selectively*. "Inquiring into the Details: Questions Ethnographers Ask" below includes some questions that could guide your own investigation.

Ultimately, what will make your study meaningful for readers will be how well you succeed in helping them see through the eyes of your study subjects. In some ways, this is a literary challenge because it relies on strong use of detail, description, dialogue, and even scene. All of this requires information collected from careful observation and interviews that will be the focus of your sketch.

INQUIRING INTO THE DETAILS

QUESTIONS ETHNOGRAPHERS ASK

When you study a social group, whether it's skateboarders or opera singers, there are certain basic things you want to find out about how that group operates. For example,

- How do group members view outsiders?
- What motivates members to belong?
- What artifacts are present, how are they typically used, and what significance is attached to them?
- What is the nature of gender relations in the group?
- Where does the group gather and why?
- What is the group's social hierarchy, and how is it organized and maintained?
- What's the relationship between this local culture and the larger culture with which it identifies?
- Does this group seem to define itself *in opposition to* other groups, and if so, why?
- What are the culture's most symbolic or significant rituals? Why is meaning assigned to them?
- Is there an initiation of some kind?

Research Considerations. The success of this project, like most of the investigations in this book, depends on working from an abundance of information. Since research usually entails some form of fieldwork, much of that information will come from what you observe. Prepare to do fieldwork by confirming the best places to conduct observations of the culture in which you're interested. Sometimes that's easy to figure out: Snowboarders hang out at the lodge, surfers at the beach, fraternity brothers at the fraternity house, homeless men at the shelter. But there will also be less obvious gathering places, locations you may only learn of through interviews with group members. Are there other locations where group members gather to socialize, to plan activities, celebrate successes, or learn from each other?

Writing ethnographically requires that you expand your repertoire of research to include interview and fieldwork, two methods of collecting that can help you with all kinds of research projects.

If the sites you want to visit aren't public, you may need permission to conduct your observation. In addition, make sure you plan for your own safety. While it's unlikely that you'll study a city gang or a gun-toting right-wing militia or some similar group that can be dangerous to outsiders, make sure that you will be safe wherever you go. Bring a friend with you; tell others where you'll be and for how long.

Taking Notes. The most important source of information for your essay will be the observation notes you take in the field. You've practiced note taking during the profile assignment, but the notes for the ethnography project will involve more observation. In the initial stages, focus on your first impressions of the group you're studying. Jot down everything.

Photographs. Visual ethnography uses photographs, film, or video to document local culture. These can be enormously rich records because pictures extend our perception and preserve information for later study and analysis. In addition, sharing the photographs we take with our study subjects can yield valuable insight about the meanings of the things in the images. A twelve-year-old skateboarder, for example, might look at the picture of someone attempting a trick and offer a commentary about the rider's motives and techniques, and the meanings of his moves. Digital photography has made it possible to instantaneously share this material.

Bring your camera along on your site visits and record what you see. When you print the pictures, attempt to place them in a meaningful order. Try to establish relationships among the pictures. Do they fall into certain categories of activity or significance? In addition, study the photographs for information that you might have missed in your field notes. What do you notice about artifacts, clothing, or the context in which the action is taking place?

Interviews. There is only so much we can see. Simply observing people won't tell us what they think or feel, we have to ask. Your earlier practice with interviews will have prepared you for this method of collecting information; see Chapter 5 and Chapter 12 for more information on interview methods and techniques.

Artifacts. If you can, collect or describe things from the site or that people in this culture routinely make, talk about, or use. For example, if you're studying a truck stop, collect menus, placemats, and so on. If you're studying people in a bowling league, describe the differences among bowling balls or collect score sheets. Photographs can also be helpful in identifying artifacts that you can't haul away. Collecting such things can help you to determine what meaning, if any, is assigned to them by group members. For example, do members of a male bowling league see the weight of a bowling ball as a measure of not only a bowler's strength but also his manhood?

Maps. One way to analyze a group's social relationships and the context in which activities take place is to observe where and how members occupy space. Imagine, for example, your own family dinner table as you were growing up. Did everyone sit in the same chair every night? Was there any logic to that arrangement? Does it say anything about the social roles of each family member? If you were to draw a map of your family's seating arrangement, and then add arrows that follow the movement of each member of your family during a typical meal, what would that suggest about social roles and relationships? If your family was like mine, my mother's chair was always nearest the kitchen, and she moved far more than the rest of us, mostly back and forth, to and from the oven, table, and sink. Consider making similar maps of your study site, noting the arrangement of things and people, as well as their movements.

Research. Because you have weeks rather than months to write your ethnographic essay, you will probably need to rely somewhat on the work of others who have formally or informally studied the culture in which you're interested. Sources may include the hobby or specialty magazines that group members read; visiting Web sites, newsgroups, chat rooms, and listservs that group members frequent online; and searching the library databases for any academic research that scholars may have published on the culture you're studying (see "Inquiring into the Details: Useful Library Databases for Ethnography," later in this chapter). You'd be surprised at how much work has been done on local culture in the United States.

FIELD NOTES

Rita Guerra hasn't bowled often in the past twenty years, but she has fond memories of holding birthday parties at the local bowling alley when she was a girl, and now her own children clamor from time to time to do some ten-pin bowling. Guerra remembers her hometown bowling alley as a social and cultural center for her small town. Wouldn't such a place be a great site to do some fieldwork for her ethnographic essay?

What follows are Guerra's field notes following her first visit to Emerald Lanes—"The Best Alley in the Valley." At this stage, she is focused on collecting data—transcribing conversations she hears, carefully describing what she sees, jotting down text from signs and notices, mapping the space, and simply watching to see what happens when. She uses double-entry field notes. On the left are her observations, and on the right are her impressions or ideas about what she sees, hears, smells, or feels. Notice that she gets a dialogue going between the two columns—speculating, interpreting, and raising questions on the right in response to specific information she collected on the left.

The success of your ethnographic essay depends on the success of your field notes. Always collect more information than you can use—which probably means multiple visits to your field sites—and push yourself to reflect on what you've found as you collect the information. Rita Guerra's field notes are a good model.

FIELD NOTES ON FRIDAY AFTERNOON AT EMERALD LANES
Rita Guerra

Observations of
4/9/04

4:32 Sounds of balls hitting maple lanes, thundering towards pins. There is a constant hum of noise—rolling balls, lane chatter, country music, clanking of pins. Smells like cigarettes and beer. Smoking is allowed throughout the alley.

"That will be a triple," says a woman in shorts and green tank top. She is bowling with two other young couples and they all bowl well, alternating between strikes and spares. Successful frame usually produces a kind of dance, clenched fists, "yessss!" Poor frame—silence, stone faced.

Scores are tallied electronically in monitors above each lane. Large number of families on Friday afternoon, including birthday party in far lanes.

Ideas About

A Friday afternoon at Emerald Lanes appear to be more family oriented, no league play. But I was impressed by how many strong bowlers, mostly young couples played. Emerald Lanes seems a family friendly place though I was surprised that the entire place allowed smoking. This might be indicative of the bowling culture—smoking is still okay.

Need to check for "bowling lingo" on the internet. What is a "triple" Three strikes in a row? I was really interested in watching the preparation and releases of bowlers. Seems like you could tell the experienced bowlers from inexperienced ones by the smoothness of their release and especially the velocity of the ball. But maybe more than anything, I began to interpret their reactions to a good frame and bad frame. Strike produces a "yesss!" and clenched fist but not extended celebration. Bad frame a stony face. No anger,

Observations of	Ideas About
"Got it right where I wanted to," says young player with girlfriend. He cups the ball underneath before his swing and when releasing it give it a spin. Ball breaks from left to right. Wears own bowling shoes, no rentals, and black wrist band. Spends very little time preparing but picks up his ball, sights the pins, and goes into motion within 15 seconds.	no laughter. Seemed to be no difference in this between men and women. Less experienced bowlers would react with more exaggeration.
"The Best Alley in the Valley"	I need to learn more about the theories behind introducing spin in releasing the ball. The ability to do this seems to distinguish the more skilled from the less skilled bowlers. This player consistently produced a left to right break by cupping the ball and obviously spinning it right before he releases it.
"The Bowling Guy's Pro Shop" Ball polisher	
Tropical theme—three plastic palm trees between lanes.	Might be interesting to actually time how long it takes for bowlers to prepare to bowl when it is their turn. My impression is that more experienced bowlers waste very little time; novices diddle and dawdle.
Budweiser sign: Welcome to Emerald Lanes. Good Family Fun?	Like a lot of bowling alleys I've seen this one seems a bit tacky from the outside, and inside seems friendly but with an atmosphere of Budweiser beer and smoke. On a Friday afternoon, though, it seemed Family friendly. Need to plan next visit for a Saturday night during league play. I have a sense that it's an entirely different culture.
Movement	

Writing the Sketch

Begin your ethnography project with a sketch that provides a verbal snapshot of the culture you're studying. Using the ethnographer's questions (posed earlier) as guides for your field observation, go to a place where you can observe your culture in action. Collect observations and interviews that will allow you to create a snapshot of your group in action. For example, if you're interested in gender relations among young skateboarders, go to the skateboard park and carefully observe how the boys and girls interact. If possible, talk to some of them. Take lots of notes, and consider taking photographs as visual records, too.

Try working through the following three steps in your journal in preparation for drafting your sketch.

1. **Narrative of thought.** In your notebook, tell the story of how your thinking has evolved. When you first chose your subject, what did you think about that culture? What assumptions did you make and what did you expect to find? And then? And then? And then? And how about now?

2. **Look at strands in the web.** Which of the following features of a culture apply to the one you're studying?

   - *Shared language* (for instance, are there insider phrases and words that have significance to group members?)

   - *Shared artifacts* (for instance, are there objects that have particular significance to group members?)

   - *Common rituals and traditions* (for instance, are there patterns of behavior that surround certain activities, or are there historical understandings of how something must be done?)

   - *Shared beliefs and attitudes* (for instance, are there common attitudes toward other insiders, towards outsiders, towards new initiates; do group members share beliefs in the significance of the group and its activities?)

   - *Common motivations* (for instance, do members participate for some of the same reasons?)

3. **Examine one strand.** Choose *one* of the features above. In your notebook/journal, generate specific evidence from your research or fieldwork that supports your finding.

After you complete the above steps, write a 500- to 600-word sketch that describes what you saw and heard during one or more of your field experiences. The key is not to simply *explain* what you noticed but to *show* it, too. In addition,

- Choose a title for your sketch.
- Whenever possible, *show* what you observed or heard using description, scene, dialogue, and similar literary devices.
- Offer a tentative theory about a belief or attitude that group members seem to share based on your initial field observations and interviews.

Moving from Sketch to Draft

If it was successful, your sketch provided an initial snapshot of the group you're studying. The draft, of course, will provide a fuller picture. But what should that picture focus on? What kind of information should you try to gather now? Your sketch can provide some useful clues.

Evaluating Your Own Sketch. You have a significant advantage over the people in your workshop group who will read and discuss your sketch: you witnessed what you're writing about. You spent time in the field gathering impressions and information, but quite a bit of that probably didn't end up in your sketch. Use that extra knowledge to guide your revision. But before you workshop your sketch, reread it, and in your notebook fastwrite responses to the following questions:

1. What is my strongest impression of the group so far? What kinds of things did I see, hear, or read that gave me that impression?
2. What is another impression I have?
3. Which one of these two impressions might be a focus for the next draft?
4. What do I most want to know now about the culture I'm observing? What questions do I have?

Questions for Peer Review. Everyone in your workshop group is working on a similar ethnography project, so you can help each other out by identifying the typical problems that these early drafts present: too little information, lack of focus, and insufficient interpretation of the information. Questions for the group to consider about each ethnography sketch include the following:

- What information or observations in the sketch seemed most striking?
- Which of the questions listed in "Inquiring into the Details: Questions Ethnographers Ask," seem to be addressed in the sketch? If the next draft focused on one or two of these, what might they be?
- Based on what you've read so far about this group, what theory would you propose about how its members see things?

Reflecting on What You've Learned. Follow up your workshop by making a schedule that describes your plan for additional research and field observations over the next few weeks. For example:

SUNDAY	MONDAY	TUESDAY	WEDNESDAY	THURSDAY	FRIDAY	SATURDAY
2-4 Field observations at the park		3 PM Pick up photos		7 PM Library research		10-12 Field observations, interview w/Karen

Research and Other Strategies: Gathering More Information

The most important thing you can do to improve the next draft of your ethnography is return to the field for more observations and interviews. This project doesn't permit the kind of immersion in a culture that most ethnographic researchers enjoy, so it's essential that you focus on gathering as much data as you can in the time you have. This will take careful planning and scheduling and your schedule will help. (In fact, your instructor may ask you to hand in your schedule.)

If photography is part of your data gathering, spend some time analyzing the pictures you've taken. Begin by arranging them in some kind of logical order, and note that chronology isn't the only arrangement that makes sense. Do you see the pictures grouping around certain typical activities? Do they seem relevant to any of your particular research questions? Does a sequence suggest something about how group members interact with each other or occupy space? Do certain arrangements of photographs tell a story that seems significant?

Study individual photographs as well. Because the camera's eye misses little, a single picture can be rich source of detailed information about the context or setting in which important group activities take place. A picture can also capture data about artifacts and even the relationships among group members. All of this information can help you write a more informative, interesting draft and make your interpretations of what you've seen more convincing.

Finally, don't forget to continue library and Internet research. Consult specialized indexes and databases you might have skipped earlier (see "Inquiring into the Details: Useful Library Databases for Ethnography"). What can you learn from what others have observed and said about the culture you're studying?

INQUIRING INTO THE DETAILS

USEFUL LIBRARY DATABASES FOR ETHNOGRAPHY

Don't forget to research existing ethnographies that may be published on the culture you're studying. If your library has them, the following specialized databases are worth checking:

- Anthropological Index Online
- EHRAF Collection of Ethnography
- Sociological Abstracts
- Ethnographic Bibliography of North America
- Abstracts in Anthropology
- Abstracts of Folklore Studies
- International Bibliography of the Social Sciences

Composing the Draft

One way to know when you're ready to begin the draft is if you have more, possibly much more, information than you need. But until you have a focus for your ethnography—a pretty clear idea of what *aspect* of the culture you're most interested in presenting or the question you're trying to answer—it will be pretty hard to know whether you have an abundance of information. For example, Tammy was writing an ethnography about Mary Kay cosmetics saleswomen. There was quite a lot to say about this group—including the amazingly sophisticated corporate culture these women belong to, one that not only offers material rewards, but also striking emotional boosts that help maintain the commitment and enthusiasm of the female sales force. From her research, Tammy had information about much of this, but she decided to focus on the initiation rituals of the group. This was an obvious choice for a focus because Tammy decided to experience some parts of this initiation.

The choices you've already made about what and where to observe may help determine your focus, or you may see a focus emerging in the material you collected. However you do it, you must try to limit your look at the culture you're studying. This focus will help you in the field—you can narrow your observations and interviews to certain things—and it will certainly help you write your draft.

Methods of Development. As an extended form of inquiry, the ethnographic essay will probably combine some of the methods of development described below.

Narrative. Because ethnography often involves scene or setting (context), character, dialogue, and action, it's a form that quite naturally accommodates storytelling. One form this might take is to offer a detailed look at a "typical day" of one or more group members. This approach provides a convenient focus for your essay because you're grounding the draft in a particular time and place. You also might focus on specific group members because they're relevant to a particular question in which you're interested. For example, if you're interested in gender relations among preadolescent skateboarders, then you might choose a girl and a boy, focusing on their stories.

Another way to exploit narrative is to create a collage of revealing scenes or situations that are relevant to your research interest. These might be kind of ministories; they might even have their own subtitles, cuing the reader to the significance of each. For example, an ethnography of eighth grade cheerleaders might feature a collage of scenes with titles such as "Making the Team," and "The Squad's Social Hierarchy." The key is to also include theories about the group and interpretations of these scenes— in other words, both show *and* tell.

Question to Answer. Because inquiry projects are frequently organized around a question in which the researcher is interested, an obvious structure is to begin the draft by establishing the focusing question, and to use the remainder of the draft to explore possible answers to it. The earlier list of ethnographer's questions might help you find your focus question. If you're observing, say, the culture of dog handlers at local dog shows, you might ask, *What is the social hierarchy of dog handlers and how is it maintained?* The beginning of an essay that focuses on a question will probably do several things, including some or all of the following:

- Provide some background from research about other studies (if any) that have directly or indirectly addressed the question.
- Explain the writer's interest in the question. What observations, interviews, or readings suggest that the social hierarchy of dog handlers might be interesting or significant to look at?
- Explain the methods the writer used to focus on the question.
- Offer a theory, a possible answer to the question. For example, *"Based on my initial impressions, handlers and trainers who have established reputations as successful breeders tend to get the most respect."*

Compare and Contrast. When I teach graduate workshops in creative nonfiction, I often wonder how gender shapes my students' responses to each other and the work being discussed. If I conducted a study that focused on such a question, I probably would find a range of ways in which men and women interact with each other. One useful way of exploring these would be to look for similarities and differences, to compare and contrast. In fact, it's hard to imagine any ethnography not exploiting this method of development in at least a small way, and it's easy to imagine that comparisons might form the backbone of some essays.

Using Evidence. Ethnographic research is distinctive because it studies social groups in their own environments. It follows, then, that the most important evidence in this kind of essay will be the investigator's detailed field observations. In addition, since the purpose of an ethnography is to attempt to see the world the way your study subjects see it, interviews that bring the voices of group members into the essay provide valuable evidence. After all, who can better articulate a group's beliefs and perspectives than its members? Ethnography mostly relies on *primary* research like this, but secondary sources—articles and essays about the group you're studying—can be useful, too, particularly if they come from academic sources. But it's time in the field that is the most important element in the success or failure of this kind of writing.

Workshopping the Draft

If your draft is subject to peer review, see Chapter 15 for details on how to organize workshop groups and decide on how your group can help you. The following journal activities and questions should help you make the most of your opportunity to get peer feedback on your work in progress. But first, are you happy with the way the first draft turned out? Here is a check to determine the strengths and weaknesses of your draft:

- Is your purpose clear? Do you think readers will understand the question that interests you or what your particular motives were when writing about this culture?
- Have you taken a landscape picture when you needed a close-up? Does the draft try to cover too much territory, include too much information, or say too much?
- Is there enough specific information—observations, scenes, facts, dialogue, and so on? Do you show as well as tell in the draft?
- Is it clear what you're trying to say about this group? Do you propose a certain theory about how it operates or sees things? Do you make a central claim or have a main point? Are you working toward a dominant impression or interpretation of the group?

Reflecting on the Draft. Review the list above, and fastwrite for seven minutes in your journal exploring your answers to some of the questions. End the fastwrite by generating a quick list of ideas in response to this question: *What things might I do to improve this draft when I revise it?*

Questions for Readers. Make the most of your peer review session by asking readers of your draft to answer one or more of the following questions:

1. If you had to summarize in a sentence or two your main impression of the group I studied, what would it be?

2. If you were to imagine the draft as a kind of documentary film that allows you to get a good look at a culture, where in the draft were the camera shots most vivid? Where in the draft did you wish there were close-ups, or long shots?

3. What questions did the draft seem to try to answer about the culture? Which of these seem most important or interesting?

Revising the Draft

You've been revising all along, of course, beginning with the work you did to find a topic and then narrowing it down in a sketch to something interesting and manageable. You were revising when you shared your sketch with peers and used what you learned to compose the next draft. You even were revising when you talked about the essay with your roommate or best friend. Revision involves "re-seeing" your subject, and there are many ways to do that as you go along. For more on new ways to think about revision, read Chapter 14, "Revision Strategies"

Ethnographic essays typically have some of the following problems that should be addressed in revision:

- Does your draft fail to give clear enough pictures to readers about the group you studied? The problem is usually that there simply isn't enough information from field observations of the group. The solution? Get back out into the field.

- Does the draft try to say things about the group rather than focus on a single main thesis, interpretation, or question?

- If your time for fieldwork was limited, did you make up for it by finding some useful research about the culture you studied in the library or on the Web?

Refer to Chapter 14, "Revision Strategies," for ideas about how to address these and many other problems. Use the following table to find other appropriate revision strategies. Remember that a draft may present problems in more than one category.

GUIDE TO REVISION STRATEGIES		
PROBLEMS IN THE DRAFT (CHAPTER 14)	PART	PAGE NUMBER
Unclear purpose ■ Not sure what the paper is about?	1	633
Unclear thesis, theme, or main idea ■ Not sure what you're trying to say?	2	639
Lack of information or development ■ Need more convincing evidence?	3	646
Disorganized ■ Doesn't move logically or smoothly from paragraph to paragraph?	4	650
Unclear or awkward at the level of sentences and paragraphs ■ Does draft seem choppy or hard to follow at the level of sentences or paragraphs?	5	656

Polishing the Draft

After you've dealt with the big issues in your draft—is it sufficiently focused, does it answer the *So what?* question, is it well organized, and so on—you must deal with the smaller problems. You've carved the stone into an appealing figure but now you need to polish it. Are your paragraphs coherent? How do you manage transitions? Are your sentences fluent and concise? Are there any errors in spelling or syntax? Section 5 of Chapter 14 can help you focus on these issues.

Before you finish your draft, make certain that you've worked through the following checklist:

- ❏ Every paragraph is about one thing.
- ❏ The transitions between paragraphs aren't abrupt or awkward.
- ❏ The length of sentences varies in each paragraph.
- ❏ Each sentence is concise. There are no unnecessary words or phrases.
- ❏ You've checked grammar, particularly verb agreement, run-on sentences, unclear pronouns, and misused words (*there/their, where/ were,* and so on). (See the handbook at the back of the book for help on all of these grammar issues.)
- ❏ You've run your spell checker and proofed your paper for misspelled words.

STUDENT ESSAY

Middle school is the best of times, the worst of times. Early adolescence is a time of turbulent change—both socially and physiologically—and therefore a fascinating time to watch . . . from a distance. That's what Jeremy Johnson decided to do. He remembered his own adolescence as a time that "set the mold for the rest of my life," and so Johnson wanted to reenter that world for a short time to see what it was like from the vantage point of his college years.

Johnson's ethnographic essay of his fieldwork at West Junior High follows. It's fun to read, and best of all, closely observed. He listens in on conversations, inventories the artifacts in student lockers, and watches the social hierarchies develop on the basketball court from his position high in the bleachers. Much of what Johnson struggles with in this essay concerns how his position as an outsider to this culture influences how his subjects behave when he's there. More subtly, however, you might detect assumptions and judgments that grow from Johnson's own assumptions about what it means to be a teenager. How does this influence his observations and conclusions? The essay is written in the APA style.

I SEE ME AS YOU SEE ME

An Ethnography of West Junior High

Jeremy Johnson

1   American adolescents stand out as a culture by themselves. They are torn between the Tonka Trucks and Barbie Doll life they have been used to and the dating and driving age they are facing. This is a time when they face a range of anxieties—they must form a concept of self and above all deal with social acceptance.

2   According to psychologist Phillip G. Zimbardo (1997, p. 141), "The essential crisis of adolescence is discovering one's true identity amid the confusion of playing many different roles for different audiences in an expanding social world. Resolving this crisis helps the individual develop a sense of coherent self. Failure to resolve the crisis adequately may result in a self image that lacks a stable core."

3   So what, or who, defines the criteria for social acceptance? According to Rich Webb, principal of Boise's West Junior High School, "Parents play a significant role in their children's lives. More often than not, the confidence (or lack of confidence) learned at home, often determines where their social niche is among their peers."

When asked what other influences shape teen culture, he answered with-   4
out hesitation that "The music they listen to, and what certain high profile people are wearing set the standards for what is and what is not acceptable."

Webb, an eighteen-year veteran of the education system, also noted that   5
"adolescence is a self-defining era in a teen's life." He added that once teens define themselves in response to cultural pressures "those definitions often carry
them throughout their lives . . . . Self-concept is not inherited, it is learned
through a process called reflected appraisal." According to Marks, Settles,
Cooke, Morgan, and Sellers (2004), "The concept of reflective appraisal argued that individuals develop a sense of themselves based in large part from
the way that others view them." This became very evident to me as I sat on the
top row of the bleachers observing the social interactions of the 7th and 8h
graders at West Junior High School, my field site for this study.

West Junior High is located on the Boise bench, a neighborhood west of   6
the city. Built in 1953, West has about 845 students, and its eighth graders perform academically at the district average in reading, math, and language. In
some ways, West could be considered a "typical" junior high in Boise, Idaho.

My goal was to perform what is referred to as a "naturalistic observation,"   7
which is, according to my psychology professor, "A method of observing a
subject, or group of subjects and their actions by placing yourself unnoticed
into their environment and recording data based on uncontrollable stimulus."
However, I wonder if there has ever been a situation where an observer has
been able to observe natural behavior without contaminating the data by being
there. I will discuss later in this paper how I noticed my presence distinctly influenced my subjects' behavior.

7:05 AM

I pull up, and park in front of the school, gather my pens, highlighter and pad   8
of paper and start walking towards the front entrance of the school. A white
Mercedes with gold trim pulled up to the school entrance. The driver was a
middle-aged man in a well-kept suit. The passenger (obviously the driver's
son) stepped out with his bag over one shoulder. He wore baggy khaki shorts
down to just below his knees. A tee-shirt of some kind hid itself underneath a
fleece yellow jacket with a black stripe down the outside of the sleeves and a
thin line of reflection tape in the center of the black stripe. His hair was crew
cut short and gelled into place. He was about 5'10" and had the build of an
athlete. When he walked, his head was held confidently back, and his chest was
out. He was impressive. He acknowledged me with a courteous nod, and continued on into the school, and into the gym. By the way he conducted himself,

and by observing my natural responses to him, I could tell that he was a very confident individual. He was a trendsetter, a leader of the pack.

9   I reported in to the office, received my "Hello, I'm a Visitor" badge, and set out for the gym. The principal had said there would be a lot of students in the gym before classes began.

7:20 AM

10   I've positioned myself on the bleachers in the gym. Kids continue to gather in the center. There are greetings of nods and "whatz up's" and hugs among the girls. I am a bit surprised to see the majority of the guys congregating the middle of the floor, while the girls tend to congregate near the main entrance. No sooner would they (the girls) walk through the door, than they would see one of their girlfriends and receive a hug like they hadn't seen each other for ages. Then engage in a soul bearing, heart to heart conversation. As more and more girls came through the door, the doorway became more and more congested.

11   As the guys would filter through the door, and sift through the cluster of girls, I noticed a lot of flexing of pecks and clenched jaws in an attempt to make themselves look tougher. They don't tarry long, however, for they were determined to mingle with the bro's under the basket. As my attention shifts to the boys under the basket, I notice something very peculiar. There was a fairly moderate-sized cluster of guys. Three guys stand in the middle, including Mr. Yellow Jacket. They conversed for a long time.

12   They discussed a football game they had been involved in. Not once did the conversation leave the boundaries of those three, yet the remaining 15 boys who stood on the outside of the group seemed absolutely riveted on the content of the conversation. Every so often one of them would nod his head and appear that he was part of the discussion. I was reminded of the Discovery Channel. The big bucks were the dominating center of attention. Around the perimeter ran the young bucks, slyly awaiting their moment to step in and be recognized with the big boys.

13   They seemed very aware of the need to be associated with this particular group of young men in order to fit in to their desired niche: "As the need for close friendships and peer acceptance becomes greater, anxiety about the possibility of rejection increases" (Zimbardo, 1997, p. 141). This fear of rejection—as the equally powerful desire to belong—appeared to motivate the boys on the perimeter. There they would stand, anxiously awaiting their moment in the sun.

7:45 AM

14   Suddenly out of nowhere a bell rang. Everyone automatically began moving towards the doorways. This was the five-minute warning. Into the hall, the mob

became a torrid wave of motion. I found myself caught in the frantic river of destination bound students. I followed with the flow, holding my pen and notebook, hoping to fit in. Up ahead was a tall slender girl who obviously seemed to demand the respect of the other students. I will call her Gertrude. Gertrude was on her way to her locker to retrieve her English book. She wore dark denim pants and sandals, and a form-fitting sweater. She had long dark brown hair that flipped with every step, and dark chocolate eyes. As she reached her locker, I noticed her locker partner barely closing the locker on her way to class. She was an equally impressive beauty with stark white hair and blue eyes. Her lipstick was vivid pink, and her shirt was less than modest. She sported faded bell-bottom pants, and Barbie-style plastic sandals. I was a bit surprised to see what happened next. When they spotted each other, each let out a high pitched scream, and made a theatrical show of hugging each other, topped off by a kiss on the check. I watched as they held hands facing each other and talked about a boy that one of them liked. The conversation went something like this:

"Oh-my gosh!" Penelope screamed. "Did you hear what Tony told Samantha?"   15

"No, what did he say?" Gertrude inquired.   16

"He said he might breakup with Kim, because he likes someone else!"   17

"No way! Who do you think he likes?"   18

"Well, he has gone out of his way to talk to me . . . can you believe it?! I   19
mean he is the hottest guy on the planet!!! What I wouldn't give to KISS him!"

It was not very hard to determine one of the main motivations of these   20
two. Boys! And not just boys, it was an issue of whether or not the boys they
liked noticed them. Their main concerns involved what was taking place in
their social surroundings. I have heard the term "gossip" associated with this
behavior. But it became more than this—to these two girls, it was life, extremely unstable and very unpredictable.

As they stood there continuing their conversation, I looked inside of their   21
locker. It had a full array of decor ranging from photos and glamour shots of
themselves, paper hearts with "best friends" notes penned across the face, dried
flowers, pictures of boys and in the middle, a paper that said "Penelope loves
Tony, TLA." (Which I was informed later meant "True Love Always".) In the
bottom of the locker there was an impressive stack of "YM" magazines. "YM"
stands for "young and modern." Across the front of one of the magazines in bold
print was the caption . . . "Win his Heart!" another caption read "Quiz: Are
You Made for Each Other?" also "Moves that Get You on His Romance Radar"
and "Passion Pointers from Crazy in Love Couples." That was all I saw, for in the
same instant, it was closed as the girls prepared to head to class.

As I made my way down the hall, I happened to notice a guy with his   22
locker open. He was a thick-chested guy wearing shorts and a football jersey.

Inside his locker there were no pictures on the wall except a picture of the Nike swoosh and the words "Just Do It" at the bottom. It was apparent that this was (or used to be) a page in a magazine. It was also evident that it had been crudely ripped out, for the tear marks were still noticeable, and you could see wrinkle marks where the page had been pulled from. It hung cock-eyed at a 45-degree angle with a single piece of tape. The top corner hung down to the point that you could barely see what was on the paper. The rest of his locker looked like a bomb had gone off in there. There were wrinkled up papers scattered among broken pencils, bent notebooks, and "Sports Illustrated" magazines. At the top, hung a Yankee's baseball cap.

23   Up ahead some commotion caught my eyes, as I was surprised to see a girl sobbing uncontrollably. She had on a green and white cheerleading outfit, and her hair was flipped up and over a ponytail in the back. Glitter graced her cheeks and a little green silhouette of a mustang ornamented her cheek. Her eyes puffy and red, her voice shaky, she found her way into loving and caring arms of Gertrude and Penelope. All that I could make out of her sobs was something about how Tony had just dumped her.

24   "Oh Kim, you poor thing!" Penelope said, "how did it happen? What did he say?"

25   Kim did the best to reply between her sobs. "(sob) . . . He . . . (sob) . . . said he (sob) liked someone (sob) (sob) else! (lots a sobs)."

26   "What a Jerk!" Gertrude piped in. "You deserve better than him Kim! He is such a jerk! I can't believe he did that!"

27   "No kidding," Penelope agreed, "I mean really . . . . Who could he like more than you?! He is such a jerk!"

28   I wasn't sure how many Kims and how many Tonys there were in this school but how could it be so coincidental that there was another couple named Tony and Kim in the school where the Tony was planning to dump the Kim? They ducked into their math class, and I headed back to the auditorium.

7:55 AM

29   Physical education class was beginning by the time I once again established my perch. It was now that I realized how my presence might be contaminating my data. It was a class evenly split between guys and girls. When they broke up into groups of four, I was very intrigued by the segregation. At one end of the gym went the obvious jocks and cheerleaders, and to the other end went a group that (it appeared) had not developed much athleticism, or social skills for that matter. The cheerleaders seemed more content to go out of their way to make fools of themselves in the attempts to flirt with the boys, and portray a general aura of "cuteness." The jocks seemed content to just play ball.

Now for the contamination: The jocks noticing me would crank up 3 point-   30
ers left and right, glancing over at me to make sure I noticed when they went
in. I got the feeling that they thought I was a college scout or something, looking to recruit a new starting point guard for my college! The cheerleaders on
the other hand seemed to be abnormally klutzy and loud when they knew I was
watching. There seemed to be a lot of hair flipping, and attempted eye contacts.

At the other end of the gym, the un-athletes stood glued to the floor be-   31
neath the basket, praying that the horrid ball would just stay away from them.
I wondered why would any one be afraid of shooting the basketball? Charlene
Gimlin had the answer I was looking for. Mrs. Gimlin is the 7th grade P.E.
teacher. "There are students who lack the social self esteem to excel in sports,"
she said. "Because basketball is so performance oriented, some students feel as
if everyone can see them when they get the ball. They hate being the center of
attention, because they are afraid they might prove to the others that they are
incapable and therefore socially unacceptable."

I watched again as they had begun a game. Jill as I will call her seemed so   32
focused on not standing out that she alone was noticeable to me. It was as if
she could not find a rhythm to save her life. She always seemed to be at the
wrong spot at the wrong time. The ball became like a hot potato to her. The
moment it forced itself into her hands she would throw it to someone else regardless of what team they were on. "She is actually a very bright child," Mrs.
Gimlin said, "It is too bad she lacks the self confidence to express it."

Near the end of Mrs. Gimlin's P.E. class, I heard some students buzzing   33
about something obviously very important. As I tuned my ear into what they
were saying, it became evident to me that one of them, a short girl with her
blonde hair up in a ponytail, was extremely excited because a young man
named Tony had just asked her out. She was obviously thrilled at the prospect,
but I heard her ask one of her girl friends, "Do you think Kim will hate me? I
mean he only broke up with her two hours ago." Another of the girls urged,
"Who cares Tessa! He obviously broke up with her so he could ask you out any
way . . . besides, you never got along with her anyways."

Interpretation of Findings

My fieldwork at West Junior High confirmed that social interactions among   34
teenagers are both turbulent and charged with meaning related to self-esteem.
As Neville (2000) put it, "Peer relations are the major influence on adolescent
identity. While searching for a personal identity, adolescents turn to their
peers for approval and respond most significantly to their reactions, both positive and negative. Identity is intrinsically connected to sameness" (p. 61). The
students I watched were busy watching the so-called "popular" kids, the trend-
setters, for clues about how to behave and how to look, but also for some

sense of how the "in-group" reacted to them. This is the "reflective appraisal" that Principal Webb referred to earlier.

35   The social hierarchies weren't hard to figure out. Students like "Yellow Jacket" both dress and behave like they know they're top dogs. Athletically gifted students are also favored, and athletic ability seems to be an arena that gives teenagers status at West. The scene in the gym during P.E. class was the most dramatic evidence of this.

36   I also noticed how easily alliances within these groups shift. The conversations between the girls about Tony were a good example of this, and the artifacts in the two girls lockers I saw seemed to indicate that as well.

37   "Acceptance is almost a vital necessity for their future," Mr. Webb stated as I discussed my observations with him. "At West Junior High, we as a faculty are aware of this, and our teachers are well trained in positive reinforcement, and teaching general acceptance. The problem will never be eliminated however. It comes as natural as breathing."

References

Marks, B. T., Settles, I. H., Cooke, D. Y., Morgan, L. M., & Sellers, R. M. African-American identity: A review of contemporary models and measures (2004). Retrieved April 9, 2004, from <http://tigger.uic.edu/ ~bryantm/docs/AARI.pdf>.

Neville, K. (2000). *Mature beyond their years.* New York: Oxford UP.

Zimbardo, P., & Weber, A. (1997). *Psychology* (2nd ed.). New York: Longman.

EVALUATING THE ESSAY

1. Review the information—the data—that Johnson collected one morning at West Junior High. What other interpretations would you add to what Jeremy saw that day that he might have neglected to mention in the explanation of his own interpretations?

2. Jeremy's essay is not, strictly speaking, an ethnography. Yours won't be either. An ethnography requires repeated observations and field work over a long period of time, something that is impossible to do in a writing class with many other assignments. If Johnson were going to extend this study, however, can you imagine other sites, situations, or events that he might observe and describe that would help him explore his thesis about "reflective appraisal?"

3. Based on your own experiences in junior high, how well do you think Johnson captures the adolescent culture? What does he miss that you think might be interesting to examine?

USING WHAT YOU HAVE LEARNED

Will you be asked to write an ethnographic essay in another class? Probably not. But the experience of writing an essay like this one will help you be a better researcher and writer in a range of situations. It also raises some interesting questions about the very nature of research.

1. We often think that research requires "objectivity." In the sciences, the experimental method attempts to reduce the influence of the experimenter on the results. That's not possible, of course, with an ethnography. Does that make the information and the conclusions less reliable? Less useful? Can any researcher, even a scientific one, be purely objective?

2. Recall the inquiry model used throughout *The Curious Writer,* the process of moving back and forth from creative thinking to critical thinking. Is that a process that you used to write this essay? Can you imagine how you could apply it to nearly *any* essay?

3. In one minute, write a response to the following question: *Based on your experience with this assignment, how would you define culture?*

Part Three
INQUIRING DEEPER

The research essay is not usually a student favorite. The name conjures thoughts of hours spent reading and taking notes in the library followed by more hours spent figuring out how to use and correctly document source material. And all of this work is for what? In the words of one student, an essay that "is supposed to be boring." But it doesn't have to be this way.

Writing a Research Essay

11

WRITING WITH RESEARCH

About a month into the composition course, Jayne produced "The Sterile Cage," a moving personal essay in which she told of living with a bone disorder as a child. Jayne spent weeks in the hospital living inside a stainless steel cage, her legs suspended in air, while her mother sat silently in a chair next to the hospital bed knitting. Every day, Jayne wrote, she fell asleep to the steady sound of clicking needles.

Jayne continued to write eloquent and insightful essays, until it was time for the research essay. During the conference to talk about her topic—something related to child psychology—I could tell she had little enthusiasm for the project. This lack of enthusiasm was shared by most of the class, a phenomenon I usually see when it is time to write the research essay. I could understand the response to some extent; after all, the details of the research essay—library research, note cards, citations—are time-consuming and can seem tedious. But I had always believed that the students' writing had improved significantly by the time of the research assignment, and I expected that improvement would be evident in their research essays.

When the stack of draft papers came in that semester, I immediately looked for Jayne's essay, thinking I might as well start with a strong one. But it wasn't strong. It was dull and uninspired, completely unlike anything Jayne had written before. As for the other research papers, a few were better, but for the most part I was disappointed. What had happened?

I had a conference with Jayne the following week. Did she like her research paper draft?

What You'll Learn in This Chapter

- How to apply what you've learned about writing shorter inquiry-based papers to an extended research project.

- Which beliefs about research that you may want to "unlearn."

- Techniques for reading academic articles.

- How to discover a "researchable" question.

- How to focus your essay.

"It's okay," she said.

"Where you interested in the topic?" I asked.

"Sort of," she said.

"Do you think this essay is as strong as the ones you wrote earlier in the semester?"

"I know I don't like it as much."

We were both getting a little frustrated with the conversation so I decided to get right to the point. "You know what strikes me about this paper? It seems to have none of the qualities that have been present in everything you've written up until now."

"What do you mean by that?" she asked.

"Well, it doesn't have a clear purpose and focus, and the writing seems lifeless. You had such a strong voice in all your earlier essays, but I don't hear it here," I said.

Jayne had finally had enough. "What do you want from me?" she said. "This is a research paper. It's supposed to be boring!"

That conversation was a turning point in my understanding of how to teach research writing. Jayne taught me two things: first, when it comes to the research paper assignment, students assume a lot of things their teachers may not recognize, and second, I had failed to help students like Jayne to see the connections among all of the types of writing they do in the composition class.

With that lesson in mind, there are a few things I should clarify now about the research essay. The most important is this: *The research essay shares qualities with all of the inquiry projects you've written to this point, whether it's a profile, a proposal, or a personal essay. In fact, the research essay is a natural extension of all of these other essays.* Research is something writers naturally do whenever they have questions they can't answer on their own. This was made clear in earlier chapters of *The Curious Writer*. Indeed, every inquiry project in this book emphasizes the importance of research throughout the writing process.

Research is something writers do whenever they have questions they can't answer on their own.

However, the research essay does present a few differences: First, the research essay may be the most thoroughly documented of the essays you've written so far, and it may be the one that is most likely to require scholarly sources such as journal articles and academic books. It's also likely to be a project that takes more time to do, and may be the longest essay you're assigned, ranging from eight to twenty pages. A writing project with such an extended process of inquiry is more complicated to manage—it has more steps, you have more information to organize, and it's often harder to figure out what you want to say. For all of these reasons, the research essay is a form of inquiry that deserves special attention.

Still, research is hardly something alien to you. You've written research essays before, and although you probably don't consider yourself a researcher, for most of us research is daily affair.

MOTIVES FOR WRITING A RESEARCH ESSAY

I was in the market for a new classical guitar when I drafted this chapter, and for several weeks I'd been studying back issues of an acoustic guitar magazine, searching the Web for guitar makers, and talking to people who play. My process was driven by particular questions I had: *What are the best tone woods for a classical guitar? What are the various models and how much do they cost? What are the sound qualities to consider when selecting an instrument?* While I probably would never write an essay using my research, the stakes were rather high. I was likely to spend a lot of money on a guitar and I didn't want to make a mistake.

Although everyday research may not be as methodical as academic research, both approaches employ many of the same skills and share the same motive: curiosity. Sometimes this curiosity is intellectual interest—Why is the sky blue?—and sometimes it's in response to a need for information—What is the best-quality classical guitar? Either way, the process begins as all inquiry projects do, with a question.

EXERCISE 11.1

An Atheist Goes to Church

When you think of the academic research paper assignment what immediately comes to mind? I often ask my students to think about this initially through metaphor. For example, a student once told me that writing a research paper is "like an atheist going to church." What do you think that metaphor implies about his beliefs and attitudes toward research writing?

STEP ONE: Build a few metaphors of your own. In your journal or notebook, finish one or more of the following sentences:

Writing a research paper is like _____.
Doing research is like _____.
Reading for a research paper is like _____.

STEP TWO: In small groups—or your full class—share the metaphors you came up with by putting them on the board or sheets of newsprint. Just make sure everybody can see them.

STEP THREE: Examine the gallery of research-writing metaphors. Now build on the board or on newsprint a list of the beliefs, assumptions, or attitudes these metaphors imply. For example, that wonderful metaphor comparing research writing to an atheist going to church suggests several things, including this: Writers of research papers don't have to believe in what they say, and, in fact, may say what they don't believe.

Discussion Questions

1. Where do these beliefs and attitudes come from?
2. How helpful are they?
3. Which beliefs do you suspect might be mistaken, and which do you believe are true?

THE RESEARCH ESSAY AND ACADEMIC WRITING

The research paper is a fixture in high school courses, usually lodged in the junior or senior English class and advertised as preparation for The College Research Paper. (Even my nine-year-old daughter is writing research papers.) It is true that research-based writing assignments are probably among the most common in college, across the curriculum. In fact, at my own university almost three-quarters of the faculty surveyed said they assign an "academic paper that requires research." That's one reason you're writing a research essay in your composition class—to help prepare you to write papers in other courses.

These writing assignments can take a number of forms including term papers, proposals, literature reviews, abstracts, reports, and so on. But they all demand facility with finding information in the library, on the Web, or in the field; the skills to evaluate the information you have uncovered; and the ability to *use* that information appropriately and purposefully. Because research writing involves dealing with all of these things—something like a novice juggler trying to keep five balls in the air—even talented writers can see their prose fall apart. Additionally, the writers' beliefs and assumptions may make it harder to get the work done, and their beliefs and assumptions may even be misleading, if not downright wrong.

Some years ago, I surveyed about 250 first-year writing students about the research paper assignment, and the following beliefs were shared by at least 60 percent of them.

- "I have to be objective."
- "I have to know my thesis before I start."
- "I need to follow a formal structure."
- "I can't use 'I'."

There is an element of truth to each of these, but each of these beliefs *works against* a genuine understanding of what it means to do academic research. Then what *is* the nature of academic research and the research essay?

FEATURES OF THE FORM

There's quite a range of research-based writing. Nearly every assignment you've done so far in *The Curious Writer* might be considered research based; reading, interview, and observation could be an element of any of the inquiry projects you've attempted using this book. But the research essay does have a few distinctive features:

- *Academic research is driven by questions, not answers.* Most scholarship begins with a question about something: What is the impact of congressional redistricting on representation of minorities? What are the various ways the river might be understood symbolically in *Huckleberry Finn?* What is the distribution of bracken fern in a mature upland forest? Researchers begin with a question, not an answer, and although they may hypothesize, researchers are always prepared to be proved wrong. Framing the question is a crucial and often difficult part of the process.

- *The question is put in the context of what has already been said.* You're interested in whether so-called relational aggression between girls might be present in your niece's second-grade classroom. That's a great research question. What have others already said about it? How might the answers to your question contribute to the on-going conversation about how young girls treat each other? This often means that you will need to become familiar with the published conversation about your topic, a step in the research process called a literature review (see Appendix B for details about literature reviews).

- *Source material is used in the service of what writers are trying to say about their topics.* Research essays are not like encyclopedia entries or the research reports you may have written in high school. They do not merely present information gathered from source material. Instead, they actively *use* the information to explore or answer questions or to test the truth of an idea or thesis. In this sense, the research essay is very much like the other kinds of essays you have written so far.

- *Sources that contributed to a writer's thinking are formally given credit.* The larger purpose of academic inquiry is to make new knowledge, to contribute in some way to what people understand about how the world works. This always involves standing on the shoulders of others who have already said something about your topic, and this is something that you acknowledge explicitly through citation. While citation has all sorts of conventions, and yes, it can be a pain, the acknowledgment of who helped you to see is both a gracious gesture and a source of authority for you—it indicates that you're party to the on-going conversation about your topic. Accurately acknowledging your sources is also an ethical obligation that all good researchers take seriously.

- *Most research essays have a clearly stated thesis.* Like a long train, research essays carry a lot of freight and they must stay on track. One way to do this is to clearly organize the information you gather around an explicit focusing question. This question should lead readers to some answers, particularly one main idea, claim, or thesis that seems most persuasive to the writer. While some formal papers state this thesis in the introduction, research essays typically have a "delayed" thesis that may be stated somewhere near the end.

- *Research essays typically use four sources of information.* Nonfiction writing draws on four sources of information: memory or experience, observation, interviews, and reading. It's not unusual to read a personal essay that relies solely on the writer's memory of an experience as a source of information. A profile might use two or three sources, including observation and interview. But a research essay may draw information from *all* four sources. Writers cast as wide net as possible to discover the answers to their questions.

RESEARCH ESSAY

The following essay is excerpted from Clifford Bishop's *Sex and Spirit,* a fascinating text that looks at the wide range of sexual attitudes throughout human history. Bishop is a journalist and editor. He has quite a bit of information to report about marriage rituals. But as you read his essay, notice how often he also makes the information his own, using it for the following purposes:

- *To argue* for a central thesis about the purpose of marriage ceremonies around the world.
- *To interpret* the meaning of certain rituals and customs.
- *To connect* the range of marriage traditions to highlight similarities and differences.
- *To generalize* from the information he's gathered, offering ideas about the historical trends in marriage.

As the verbs starting each of the four phrases above suggest, writing a research essay is about action—you're actively *doing* something all the time: arguing, interpreting, analyzing, summarizing, generalizing, and connecting. This can be taxing work because it involves holding at least two things in your mind at once: (1) *What the source material says* and (2) *how the information relates to the research question you're asking.* As you read Bishop's essay, pay attention to how and where Bishop uses the information he's gathered.

MARRIAGE CUSTOMS AND CEREMONIES
Clifford Bishop

Throughout the world, a wedding is a form of treaty between families and   1
a declaration of common interest more often than it is a declaration of mutual
love. The family is the basis of most societies, and marriage is the covenant designed to guarantee the stability of the family. A wedding therefore becomes a
public demonstration of this stability: symbolically, socially and economically.
Even in materially poor areas, weddings are relatively extravagant affairs, because they must, at least partly, be displays of wealth—affirmations that the
new family will be able to survive and prosper, reminders of the material ties
to previous generations, and catalogues of any gifts or money that have been
exchanged in order to cement the marriage.

The marriage feast fulfils both magical and practical roles. If there is no   2
formal, written record of a wedding having taken place, the guests serve as
witnesses to the reality of the union. The feast is also a type of fertility rite. In
ancient Rome, a cake was broken over the head of the bride while she held
three ears of wheat in her left hand, and a similar custom survived into medieval Britain. Now the cake is simply eaten. The Western custom of throwing
rice or confetti is also a fertility charm—the favoured projectiles used to be
ears of wheat or barley. This sort of sympathetic magic is not restricted to the
feast or the post-wedding celebrations: in many religions, fertility spells are a
traditional part of the ceremony, as when a Hindu bride and groom sprinkle
rice or water over each other's head.

Other forms of magic or belief may play a part in wedding preparations.   3
For example, most cultures exercise great care over the choice of wedding
day, and Taoist, Buddhist and Hindu weddings are invariably planned after consultation with an astrologer to find an auspicious date. Another widespread
custom, reported in rural Morocco, as well as among many sub-Saharan
African peoples, and dating at least as far back as the ancient Spartans, is for
the groom to dress in female clothing for the wedding ceremony, apparently
to confuse any mischief-making evil spirits.

The religious status of a wedding varies from culture to culture, but even   4
where the practical elements of the union are emphasized, and any spiritual dimension played down—as in much of traditional Africa—it is still customary
for the couple to ask for blessings from the gods or ancestors. In a number of
religions, such as Islam and some branches of Christianity, marriage may be
conducted only in the sight of God, although in Christianity this was not always the case. Despite the efforts of the early Church to regulate the sex lives
of its worshippers, marriage itself did not actually become a sacrament—re-

quiring ecclesiastical participation—until the 13th century. Prior to this, all that was needed was for the couple to announce their intention of living together, and then to consummate the relationship.

5   The union of husband and wife is symbolized in various ways. In Theravada Buddhism, a silk scarf is wrapped around the couple's hands and they eat from a silver bowl. A cord placed over a Hindu couple's shoulders has the same meaning, while in a Sikh wedding (and elsewhere, such as in parts of Meso-America), scarves worn by the bride and the groom are knotted together. In Judaism and Christianity, the union is represented by a ring, an archaic symbol of completeness. The earliest-known wedding rings, dating back to ancient Egypt, were made of iron. The Israelites, as far back as Moses and Aaron, used gold. In parts of Ireland until the 19th century, people who could not afford to buy a gold ring would borrow one, believing that otherwise the ceremony would not be valid. Because of the wedding ring's pagan origins, it has at times been banned from the wedding ceremonies of Quakers, Puritans and Mormons.

6   Apparently identical symbols can have radically different meanings worldwide. The white dress of the Western, Christian bride is a mark of purity. In some other cultures, notably China, white is the colour of mourning; in Japan, a bride's white dress signifies the ancient belief that, from the moment of her marriage, she is dead to her family. In the 18th century, this was emphasized by making a bonfire of the bride's childhood possessions immediately after the couple was named man and wife. In Taoist weddings, a bride is expected to cry in order to express her sadness at being taken from her family, and in many cultures the man must at least make a show of wresting the woman from her parents by force. The Western practice of carrying the bride across the threshold, which was known in ancient Rome, has been described as a symbolic form of abduction. However, it has also been claimed as an attempt to prevent the bride from striking her foot on the threshold, which would start the marriage with an evil omen.

7   Monogamy is the most common form of marriage, although it is actually insisted upon by less than a fifth of the world's peoples. Some societies arrange marriages between the living and the dead, among them the Mormons, who believe that only the married can be redeemed, and that dead unbelievers can be saved if a Mormon spouse is posthumously found for them. The ancient Persians had a similar custom. Marriage to trees, or to the spirit inside them, has also been common, and can still occasionally be found. Among such symbolic marriages, one of the strangest is the old North American Kwakiutl custom that a man could marry the arm or leg of the chief.

8   While marriage in one form or another may be the backbone of a society, most peoples recognize that an unstable, unhappy marriage is not worth pre-

serving, and make some sort of provision for divorce. Of the great world religions, only traditional Christianity and Hinduism take the view that marriage is indissoluble.

INQUIRING INTO THE ESSAY

Explore, explain, evaluate, and reflect on "Marriage Customs and Ceremonies."

1. Identify the one thing that most surprised you about marriage rituals as explained by Bishop. For five minutes, fastwrite about this fact. Why did it surprise you? What does it say about your own beliefs toward marriage? Toward the practices of other cultures? Alternatively, fastwrite for seven minutes about the role of rituals and traditions in your own life. Begin by describing one of them.

2. What were the results of your investigation into the ways Bishop *actively used* the information he collected? Choose several paragraphs from the essay that best demonstrate this and explain what you found. Also identify any words or phrases that Bishop used to signal to the reader that he was using the information for particular purposes.

3. What was Bishop's main thesis about marriage customs and ceremonies? Do you agree with it?

4. "Marriage Customs and Ceremonies" seems, in many ways, like a traditional research paper. Reflect on the features in this essay that seem conventional, based on your experience with research writing. What seems less so?

RESEARCH ESSAY

Some of the most compelling research writing begins with a question gleaned from ordinary experience, particularly if it's a question that others have wondered about, too. Ann Braley-Smith, like a lot of mothers of boys, wondered about her sons' daily gun battles. She worried that their many imaginary weapons and toy guns, and their passion for staging shootouts everywhere, including Home Depot, might encourage the boys to see violence as a logical solution to problems or kindle a later interest in real weapons that, when extreme, might endanger them and others. Braley-Smith's concern about the effects of gunplay on boys is shared by many parents and others, particularly after dramatic shootings by gun-obsessed teenagers at a several American high schools.

Braley-Smith begins with a simple question: Should I worry about my boys' passion for playing with imaginary guns? Her essay, "Killing Bad Guys," is the story of what she learned about some answers to that question. She evaluates her own experiences and observations, considers the advice of local therapists, and searches the Internet, sharing the insights she gained about boys and guns along the way.

Not all research essays tell the story of the writer's investigation, but many do, reflecting the "essayistic" impulse to find out rather than to prove. Other research essays, such as the preceding Clifford Bishop article, present a central claim or thesis and then a range of evidence that makes the idea as convincing to you as it seemed to the writer. An argumentative research essay can involve just as much exploration as an essayistic one.

Braley-Smith is currently finishing her MFA in poetry at Boise State University.

KILLING BAD GUYS
Ann Braley-Smith

1 Every day, my sons kill bad guys.

2 Despite every intention I held before I had children, my sons are rip-roaring, gun-toting, thing-killing machines who are infinitely more interested in shooting anything that moves than they are in coloring pictures or engaging in sing-along songs or doing anything else suggested by the "How To Encourage Non-Violent Play" Web sites.

3 I know this much is true: little boys like guns. They like swords, they like tanks, and they like light sabers, too—but nothing compares to guns. Every day, three-year-old Matthew and two-year-old William pump imaginary lead into their pets and close family members, as well as each other, before retiring their firearms in favor of a "Bob the Builder" video or a game of tackle football on the kitchen floor. Andrew, my 10-year-old, has, for the most part, grown out of toy guns. These days, all of his shooting takes place upstairs on the Nintendo.

> "I've never seen a game I hate so much in which all the children involved are so happy." Educator Jane Katch, author of *Discovering the Meaning of Children's Violent Play*
> —Salon.com

4 There are two things I did not fully understand before I had children. The first is vulnerability. The second is possibility.

> Michael Gurian: "Most males, who must also contend with an aggressive nature fueled by testosterone, cannot deny their attraction to weapons. And this fascination for weapons exists in all cultures—guns are simply modern weapons."
> —*San Diego Union-Tribune*

Once, when we first started dating, Larry asked me to swing by   5
McDonald's to pick up Happy Meals for his kids. I ordered them in the drive-
thru: chicken nuggets with a Barbie figurine for Kim, who was 6; and a plain
cheeseburger and a Hot Wheels race car for Andrew, who was just 4. I brought
the food home and sat the kids at the breakfast bar, plopped the cartooned
bags in front of them. Andrew pulled a bent french fry from the heap, pointed
it at me, and said the word:

Bang.   6

When we married, we agreed there would be no real guns in our home.   7
We don't hunt, and neither of us has any desire for a handgun. I didn't think
the toy counterparts were such a good idea, either, since Andrew always
seemed to be picking up food or tape measures or a twig in the yard and
shooting at things. And while I knew the notion of Andrew coming across a
real gun while playing at a friend's house was a remote—but very real—possibility, I found myself thinking less about his personal safety—and more about
what drove him to play that way in the first place. I thought it had to be
stopped.

At the time, we were meeting regularly with a child psychologist for Kim,   8
who was still struggling with her parents' divorce. During one session, out of
the blue, I asked the counselor what she thought about toy guns. With
Birkenstocks on her tiny feet, stick-straight hair, no makeup, and a strict vegetarian diet, her answer surprised me.

"You *have* to let little boys play with guns," she said.   9

The counselor explained to me that when little boys are troubled, as they   10
often are when they come to see her, they use guns or swords or knives for
protection in a world where they don't feel safe. She told me how toy guns are
smuggled into her office all of the time, hidden in socks or tucked in the waist-
band of sweatpants. On the rare occasion when a parent is adamant about banning gunplay, she'll tell them she can't help their son, and refers them to
someone else.

But what about Andrew, I asked, because he wasn't unhappy. The coun-   11
selor told me that when little boys are fine, they play with guns for a completely different reason. The slaying of dragons, the ridding the world of monsters, the killing of bad guys—gives boys a sense of purpose, and it makes
them heroes or saviors.

"If a little boy wants to save the world, who are we to stop him?" she says,   12
reaching for her notepad.

> Kristen Kinkel, sister of Kip Kinkel: "Yes, (my parents) were worried about him.
> He was doing things that they didn't approve of. He was doing things and inter-
> ested in things that could potentially be really damaging . . . . They were giving
> him tough love, they were giving him unconditional love, they were having him

see a psychologist, they were setting rules. They were doing absolutely everything a parent is able to do. And they were hoping and praying that it would help."

—PBS *Frontline*

Rohan Malvo, a 33-year-old cabinet maker and son of Leslie Malvo, remembered changing the diapers of his half-brother Lee in Waltham Park, where they lived as children. "It was all right growing up in that part of Kingston. It's a rough neighborhood, but our father raised us right. He tried his best to put the food on the table. He was there for us," he said.

—Associated Press

13   It's hard to come to grips with it—because kids will kill, and we demand a reason. We want something to blame. Kip Kinkel, the Oregon high school sophomore who murdered his parents one night and, on the next morning, opened fire in a cafeteria, killing two students and injuring 25 others, had a close, intact family. He was not allowed to play with guns, play with toy soldiers or even watch Bugs Bunny cartoons. Family and friends remember him as a lonely child who struggled with learning disabilities and severe depression—a child who, despite his parents' best intentions, was obsessed with bombs and guns and their potential to kill.

14   And just the other day, the aunt of Washington DC sniper suspect John Allen Mohammad was the featured guest on a cable news talk show. Her gray hair was messed, and she looked sad. She said her nephew, whom she raised, wasn't allowed to play with guns, either. That the source of his rage was a lack of a father, not the accessibility of weapons, real or imagined. Parenting expert Michael Gurian would agree—he writes that it is not society that separates moms from boys; boys naturally start to move away from their mothers by about age 5 or 6, then strongly around ages 10 to 12. Their brains are "hardwired" to move them to the world of men. Mohammed's accomplice, 17-year-old John Lee Malvo, most likely pulled the trigger that killed ten victims. He lacked a mother during his formative years, and despite a loving, involved uncle, ultimately looked to Mohammad as a father figure, even calling him "Dad."

15   Search the Internet and you will find an infinite number of Web sites touting the dangers of real guns and real children. The statistics are alarming—that 3,000 kids will be injured from accidental firearm discharge this year, and 400 more will die. That 80 percent of children doing the shooting will be boys. That 29 percent of high school-aged boys own a gun. That more children and teens died as a result of gunfire in 2001 than from cancer, pneumonia, influenza, asthma, and AIDS combined.

16   The experts cited on these sites blame the accessibility of weapons in the United States and parents who don't use gun safes or trigger locks—and in some cases, they also point to aggressive video games and graphic movies. But very lit-

tle information exists on the impact of little boys playing with toy guns in relation to violent behavior later in childhood, and later in life. And as far as I can tell, there is little if no evidence that shows boys who play with guns become more violent, or keeping toy guns from little boys keeps them from one day using guns as weapons. In other words, the real danger seems to be putting guns within reach of children at play, rather than letting children play with toy guns.

> "Kids want their families and their community to be speaking to them in primal language and primal stories—the great stories, the stories of heroism and fairness, justice—those are the stories kids really want." This according to Michael Gurian, parenting expert and author of *The Wonder of Boys.*
>
> —*Christian Science Monitor*

Will says: "Put your hands up!" while I stir a pot on the stove. I put my spoon down, reach upwards and he shoots me anyhow, "No, no, no . . . if they put their hands up, you can't shoot them, you take them to jail," I explain for the millionth time. Then they get the dog, and then their sister. I chide them again. Lucy's not a dog, she's a lion, they reason, and Kim, who's on the sofa reading a book and, cloaked in a fleece blanket, is not a sister, she's a bad guy.   17

This is why I let my sons play with guns.   18

For Matt and Will, bad guys that deserve death include, but are not limited to: the kids from Timberline High who swear and push each other into the street while they walk to McDonalds over noon hour, Darth Maul, Darth Vader, Ja-Rule, the Albertsons bag boy on his smoke break, the entire Knights of Columbus chapter at Sacred Heart Church in their full regalia and fake swords, Jared from the Subway commercials, the neighbor kid, the neighbor kid's dog, Boise mayor H. Brent Coles—all bad guys.   19

I won't buy them a gun that looks real—they have plastic squirt guns in hot pink and purple and neon green. They have some corny western-looking pistols with bright orange tips that fit neatly into plastic holsters—holsters they wear to bed sometimes.   20

This is not to say I don't question my decision. Last summer, after Matt and Will took stir sticks and gunned Larry down at Home Depot, I decided it was time to censor their gun play. I went to the Parenting Preschoolers Web site, and looked at the advice offered to pacifist parents. The site offered up this suggestion: 21

"Provide props for fire-fighting and capturing wild animals to doctor up and make well. These alternatives give children power over fearful situations without violence. Also, the evil is not a person."   22

I bought the boys the Rescue Heroes toys—Fisher-Price's wildly popular non-violent action figures featuring police officers, firefighters, lifeguards and other positive role models. Matt put Billy Blazes atop the NYFD Special   23

Edition Fire Engine and used the plastic water missiles to blow up the adjacent Hot Wheels town. Will, in turn, took construction worker Jack Hammer's jack hammer and turned it into what appeared to be an assault rifle. There are monsters in his closet he says, and it's the only one way to get rid of them.

> Michael Gurian: "Males have a hunting template in the brain. Males are naturally fascinated by objects moving through space—rocks and spears and animals, not to mention balls and pucks. Tracking movement was critical to capturing prey for early man; it was critical to survival."
>
> —*San Diego Union-Tribune*

24   Mukta, my babysitter, tells me she's banning toy guns at the preschool where she works. I assume it's because she's Hindu, and gunplay offends her pacifist sensibilities. As it turns out, it's not all the killing that's the problem— it's just that the boys get entirely too wound up and she can't quiet them down. For that reason, she's also banned footballs, football jerseys and any- thing related to Star Wars. So any killing of bad guys, she says, will have to take place on the floor, with dolls and action figures. I watch Matt and Will and three other boys from the preschool, lying on their stomachs, playing to- gether. They come up with elaborate stories, and death scenes are usually long and dramatic, complete with sound effects and last words like: "You can have my Froot Loops! I won't need them where I am going!" Sometimes they cover the deceased action figure with a Kleenex, sometimes they pretend to burn him like Qui-Gon Jinn in Episode One of Star Wars. Sometimes they take a Barbie doll or stuffed animal to be a monster, immune from gunfire, so the others have to come up with another weapon, like a sword or poisoned gas. The thing is, when I watch my kids play this way, they have no trouble knowing what's real and what's not. And they might fight over who's supposed to be dead and who gets to be alive and who gets the next shot—but they get over it, in a second. Then they're on to the next thing, like fake play-by-play of a soccer game or somersaulting across the carpet or having a sword duel where good always overcomes evil. Always.

25   I wonder when we lose this sense of honor. This unabashed confidence.

> Lauren Grandcolas, on Flight 93, shortly before it crashed near Shanksville, Pennsylvania: "We are being hijacked. They are being kind."
>
> —*Time*

26   On September 11, my kids worry me most.

27   Kim, who's 12, seems oddly excited by it all. To her, this is a thrilling di- version from the regular school day. I've tried to distract Matt, who's two, with books, but he's glued to images on the televisions—he loves the planes and the fire and the endless scrolling text. Will, the baby, just sleeps.

He's unaffected by it, the images no more or less real than his Teletubbies   28
and Lion King videos, and it's strange to think he will always feel detached
from a moment that could define the rest of his life.

We are most concerned about 9-year-old Andrew. He's come home from   29
school, acting agitated, and he won't eat, nor will he sit down. He stands just
inches from the television, remote in hand, watching every single station playing the same fiery crashes, the same towers tumbling down over and over
again. "Turn the television off," the experts say. But this is happening right in
front of us, and how in the world are we supposed to just turn it off?

I am both numb and panicked.   30

I felt this way when Will was two weeks old, just a ball, asleep on my shoul-   31
der, breathing in short newborn fits. Once I could be certain he wouldn't wake
up, I pulled him from my neck, and I saw a line of bright red blood trickling
from his ear. My sweatshirt was covered in his blood. I called Larry, in near hys-
terics. He was speeding down ParkCenter Boulevard, trying to get home while
I called the doctor's office, sobbing. The nurse calmly told me the baby's
eardrum had burst, that he simply an ear infection we didn't know about, and it
happens all of the time, and he probably felt a lot better. Two days later, an examination would reveal the eardrum was completely healed, just that fast.

A person can worry—or not worry—about her own safety or well-being.   32
But when children enter into the picture, that perception changes forever.
These brief episodes of peril are like snapshots—over and done with in a moment—but forever captured. Every fall that might warrant a trip to the emergency room; every network news report of a snatched kid; every coffee can
next to a cash register with the scotch-taped photo of a terminally ill child;
every single time I succumb to a sense of dread that simply did not exist before
they were part of my life. Will's broken eardrum. The Sept. 11 attacks. Just
two of so many indelible moments when I fully realized how fragile they are,
how delicate everything really is.

Andrew asks if I'll look at a picture he's drawn on the backside of his math   33
homework. It's some sort of dragon-robot hybrid with long fangs and curled-
back claws and dozens of guns pointed in every direction. He talks in staccato
speech and stutters: "It's my invention," he says, "to get the bad guys before
they get us."

"Before *who* gets us—*how?*"   34

"It's my invention. To shoot down the bad guys in the planes before the   35
planes can get to more buildings!" Andrew replies. He's shifting his weight
from one foot to the next, talking fast, unable to sit down, hands fumbling. I
take a deep breath. I have to think. My gut reaction is to sit him down, and tell
him that violence is no answer to violence.

36   But then, it really isn't about violence at all.

37   "Well, it's really good. But I think you'll need more guns," I say matter-of-factly, "like right here, and right here." And he smiles. A genuine smile. His shoulders relax. His hands stop shaking. Andrew grabs a red pen from the counter and adds more ammunition. Larry comes home, and they start figuring out how they'll clear the garage out and start building the thing. I hang the picture on the refrigerator, next to the grocery list and Kim's orthodontist appointment reminder.

38   I do this because tomorrow, in spite of it all, I will send him out the door.

39   I will send him out the door, and he's still so small. So utterly unstoppable.

INQUIRING INTO THE ESSAY

Use the ways of inquiring—exploring, explaining, evaluating, and reflecting—to discover what you think about "Killing Bad Guys," a piece that may seem unlike typical research papers. The questions below might serve as journal prompts and triggers for class discussion.

1. In a fastwrite, explore your own experience with guns as a child. Begin by imagining a scene that you remember in which you died dramatically, waged a war, shot imaginary enemies, battled aliens, and so on. You might also write about how you were an outsider, a spectator to such things. Perhaps you witnessed your brothers' play. Put yourself back into the scene and fully describe what is happening. Write fast without stopping for five minutes. Then stop, skip a line, and try to finish this sentence: *The main thing I notice about my own childhood fascination with (or dislike of) guns, war, or violence is . . .*

2. "Killing Bad Guys" has a very unconventional structure, particularly for a research essay. Explain what you notice about the essay's structure, and the strengths and weaknesses of this design. Compare it with Bishop's essay "Marriage Customs and Ceremonies."

3. Using the "Methods of Development" section later in this chapter, explain which methods Braley-Smith used to develop her research essay.

4. Braley-Smith finally decided to let her kids play with toy guns, although she confesses to some doubts. Which claim in this essay—either one made by one of the experts she quotes or one that she makes herself—might you contest? How might that claim be qualified, seen another way, or disputed?

5. Reflect on how Braley-Smith approached her research essay and how you've approached writing research essays in the past. Make

a list of similarities and differences between her approach and yours to research writing. Discuss the advantages and disadvantages of each.

RESEARCH ESSAY

For years I've been telling my students that no topic is boring if you ask the right questions about it. This advice has led to fascinating research essays on ticks, Murphy's Law, and floppy disks. What I didn't know was that such research into the ordinary has a scholarly name: "mundane studies." Now studying dust and paper clips is legitimate academic inquiry.

The following research essay tells the story of Cullen Murphy's discovery of this avenue of research; by the end of the piece his enthusiasm for it almost matches mine. There is a method to this madness. Researchers who tackle ordinary subjects like pencils or tooth pulling see in the particular a way to focus their examination of larger themes—history, politics, philosophy, and so on.

What's different about this reading is that the subject of this research essay is research itself. I hope it might inspire you to consider mundane subjects for your own writing (might it be time for an analysis of the contents of garbage cans of male dormitory students?) But I also hope you notice how Murphy *uses* his investigation of this new branch of inquiry to say some things about the power of the ordinary to explain the ironies of American culture.

OUT OF THE ORDINARY
from THE *ATLANTIC MONTHLY*
Cullen Murphy

NOT LONG AGO a friend called my attention to an article by the British historian Colin Jones titled "Pulling Teeth in Eighteenth-Century Paris." I was glad she did. It would be wrong to say that I am captivated by teeth, but they do leave a lasting impression. I recall seeing as a child, in a display case at a museum, a hollow false tooth used by a spy to carry secret messages during the Revolutionary War (not successfully, it would seem). The Centers for Disease Control a few years back released a state-by-state study of tooth loss, the central finding of which I retain: in West Virginia, the most severely afflicted state, almost 50 percent of those over the age of sixty-five have no teeth at all. I can still summon the image, from a book of photographs, of a collection of teeth extracted by Czar Peter the Great, "who fancied himself a dentist," each from a different person, and each carefully labeled. I remember looking twice at an obituary headline that identified its subject as a "DENTIST AND HUMANITARIAN."

2   The ostensible subject of Colin Jones's article is a man known as le Grand Thomas, a freelance tooth puller of formidable girth who plied his trade from a cart on the Pont-Neuf for half a century, until the 1750s. He styled himself the "pearl of charlatans" and the "massive Aesculapius" and displayed a banner bearing the legend DENTEM SINON MAXILLAM ("The tooth, and if not, the jaw"). Tooth-pulling at the time was, like executions, a form of public entertainment. Jones situates Thomas at the beginning of a process that would lead not only to the emergence of modern dentistry but also, as a consequence, to much of the oral iconography of modern advertising.

3   "The mouth," Jones writes, "was becoming the imaginary site around which revolved both a nascent academic industry and a new and broader commercialism." Toothbrushes, toothpowder, and false teeth came into vogue in the eighteenth century among an expanding bourgeoisie. As teeth improved, a new phenomenon took hold in the realm of art. Ever since antiquity the convention had been to depict respectable people with their mouths closed and their teeth hidden; the open-mouthed, gap-toothed look was reserved for the depraved, the demented, and the vulgar. Now, in the 1780s, for the first time, the smile was flashed in formal portraiture, celebrating full sets of even white teeth.

4   Colin Jones's progression from the Pont-Neuf to the Pepsodent smile exemplifies a rapidly expanding genre. Its practitioners are drawn from many fields, and their interests range from the most pedestrian aspects of popular culture to the most rarefied precincts of serious history. The genre doesn't have a single name, but its manifestations could be lumped together under the rubric "mundane studies."

5   Consider two paths to enlightenment. One is to take subject matter that is vast and grand (the Middle Ages, say) and slice it into thin sections for analysis ("Glazed Pottery and Social Class in Ninth-Century Thuringia"). The other path leads from the particular to the general—it takes something seemingly unremarkable (a kind of food, an article of dress, a body part) and from it derives a larger world of meaning. In the mid-1970s the historian and John Adams biographer Page Smith and the biologist Charles Daniel published *The Chicken Book,* a conceptual vivisection of *Gallus domesticus,* and a tour de force. A decade and a half later the engineer Henry Petroski devoted an entire volume to the pencil. Last year the architect Witold Rybczynski produced *One Good Turn,* a history of the screwdriver and the screw. This approach—the mundane-studies approach—continues to gather momentum. The impetus comes partly from the rise of social history, with its focus on ordinary life. The challenge of extracting significance from some unlikely object provides the further incentive of a post-modernist daredevil thrill.

No subject is too small. A few years ago I received a letter from a man   6
named Jay W. Stein, who, as a government archivist working with original
Nazi and Soviet documents, had managed to assemble a museum-quality collection of the binders, fasteners, clamps, and clips that held the bureaucracies'
papers together. Now a librarian, Stein had continued to pursue his passion,
and he enclosed an article of his from the *Law Library Journal*—"Something
Little and Shiny on the Judicial Stage: The Paper Clip." "What I discovered,"
Stein wrote in the article, "was that the paper clip is more taken for granted
than almost anything in the judicial process"—despite the fact that case after
case has hinged on this simple device. Paper clips have figured in deciding
whether pages were part of wills. The fact that a document's edge was marked
by paper clips has been accepted as evidence that the document was in fact
read. Paper clips sometimes turn up as weapons. Stein observed:

> Like the horseshoe nail that crippled the horse and thwarted its rider in battle, the
> paper clip is small compared to most things involved in litigation. Yet, how often it
> is mentioned suggests pausing to remind oneself how much the little things count.

The common potato seems like a little thing—ordinariness in tuber form.   7
But I began to see potatoes differently after reading a recent essay, "The Potato
in the Materialist Imagination," by Catherine Gallagher and Stephen
Greenblatt. As the potato became a European staple, two hundred years ago, it
also became the focus of a fierce intellectual debate. The pro-potato forces celebrated the potato's astonishing utility: it grew with little effort, and fed people and swine alike. The anti-potato forces found this repugnant—and they
worried about an insidious social consequence. Bread, the traditional staple,
caught people up in a complex web of interactions—growing, harvesting,
threshing, milling, baking, selling. The potato required none of that. A vast
rural proletariat in a state of utter isolation could feed on roots from the
ground, breed, and degrade into dust.

Dust itself is the subject of a magisterial book by the historian Joseph   8
Amato. *Dust* surveys many topics—medieval philosophy, Victorian technology,
the cleanliness movement—but the central narrative concerns how dust came
to lose its special status in the poetic and the scientific imagination. Only a few
centuries ago, Amato writes, dust was regarded as "the finest thing the human
eye could see . . . a barrier between the visible and the invisible." Those motes
dancing in shafts of sunlight represented an elemental condition to which all
things would return. Then along came the microscope, revealing an "infinity of
the infinitesimal." Dust was consigned to the dustbin (or the allergist).

I learned about *Dust* by way of an excerpt in the *Journal of Mundane*   9
Behavior (www.mundanebehavior.org), a new peer-reviewed publication
devoted to "research, theory and method regarding the very obvious fea-

tures of our existence." The first few issues offered articles about the morning shave, elevator conversation, shopping at Wal-Mart, on-field prayer by athletes, and the use of the television remote control. One essay, "When Nothing Happened," made the point that days of yore consisted mostly of circumstances that rarely get attention—stability, boredom, daydreaming, business as usual. A personal Web-cam version of ancient Babylon might look very familiar.

10   The journal is off to a promising start, but the task ahead is enormous. If I could give out Guggenheims for mundane studies, I'd channel young scholars toward certain potentially fruitful topics. For instance, a detailed study of the interstitial conversation in wiretap transcripts is long overdue. These documents have obvious short-term utility for what they reveal about criminal mayhem, but the long-term value lies in everything else. Here's Vincent Romano talking to John "Sideburns" Cerrella about his health: "Yeah, all right, the leg feels much better, much better, much, much better. I took a couple of glasses of tomato juice, you know, for potassium." Here's a disquisition on yogurt from Frank "Frankie California" Condo: "Brown Cow with the thick crust on top and you mix the crust, that's the, the bacteria. You mix that all in there . . . Brown Cow. That's what all the health fiends eat. Brown Cow." Eating habits, folk remedies, amorous insights, movie reviews—this is a mundane-studies mother lode.

11   The inane use of quotation marks on menus, advertisements, and public signage—STEAKS AND BURGERS "FROM THE GRILL"; WHEN LEAVING THE BATHROOM "PLEASE TURN OFF THE LIGHT"—would be another prime focus of investigation. The development may not seem like an urgent public issue, but we would do well to assess its subtly corrosive effects. Even the cocktail napkins on *Air Force One* now bear a legend in quotation marks: "Aboard the Presidential Aircraft." What is the semiotic essence of this form of display? If nothing is being quoted, then what is "quotation" coming to mean?

12   Finally, there is the matter of the disappearing object. This linguistic tropism takes form in sentences like "The Yankees amaze" and "The movie fails to excite"—sentences in which a transitive verb, which takes a direct object, has been casually stripped of one. The *Wall Street Journal* recently published the following headline: "STOCK NIGHTMARES? HISTORY MAY COMFORT." Does the potential activity embodied in verbs like "amaze," "excite," and "comfort" exist as an independent force, swirling atmospherically, regardless of whether actual people or things are affected? Is the detachment of verb and object one more step toward a depersonalized world?

13   Sherlock Holmes boasted that he could infer Niagara Falls from a drop of water. William Blake wrote of seeing the world in a grain of sand, and

heaven in a wild flower. Colin Jones chose teeth. Other pioneers of mundane studies have chosen the tulip, the cod, the color mauve, longitude, phosphorus, the F word, the handshake, and the contents of garbage cans. The world is a mundane place if it is anything at all, and the possibilities ahead cannot fail to excite.

INQUIRING INTO THE ESSAY

Use all four ways of inquiring to think about your reaction to this essay.

1. Seize the opportunity to use "Out of the Ordinary" to make a fast list of the ordinary things that might be worthy of study. Look around your room, your desk, and perhaps even under the bed. Make a list of everything you see in your notebook. Choose several objects that seem promising and then generate a list of why, what, where, who, when questions. For example, who is invented the Post-it note, and when? Share these in class.

2. What might be the usefulness of research that focuses on ordinary life? What are its limitations?

3. Murphy suggests "two paths to enlightenment": the first is to study "vast and grand subject matter (the Middle Ages)" and then "slice it into thin sections for analysis (Glazed Pottery and Social Class in Ninth-Century Thuringia)," and the other path is to "derive a larger world of meaning" by looking at the specific and abstracting from it. This does seem like sound advice about research methods. But what other ways of knowing do these two approaches leave out?

4. Reflect on how you felt as you read Murphy's essay. Did you feel as if you were the type of reader for which it was intended? And, speaking of inducting the general from the specific, what are the clues in the essay about its audience?

ACADEMIC RESEARCH ESSAY

Who hasn't wondered whether that move to another city or another state will doom a friendship? It's a popular misconception that much academic research is arcane and irrelevant, but the following article from the journal *Communication Quarterly* tackles that same question about long-distance friendships. In fact, scholars have been interested for some time in how friendships are maintained, and like most academic research, this article by Amy Janan Johnson extends that on-going conversation when she realizes that very little work has been done on "how individuals maintain such relationships over distance."

This published research essay is unlike the other three in this chapter. This is a much more formal study, written for a major journal in the communication field and for an audience of fellow experts. This is the kind of paper you may not write in other college classes but you will certainly need to know how to read for papers of your own. I've also included "Examining the Maintenance of Friendships" because I hope you'll see the differences *but especially the similarities* between formal academic writing and the research essay you'll write. What isn't necessarily evident in this journal article is the process that brought it into being: the struggle to find a good research question, the wrestling with ambiguity and uncertainty, and the difficulty of coming to a conclusion. The research *essay* might make those processes a part of the piece itself. But even in formal academic articles, you can certainly detect some things about the writer's motives, and the ways she subtly establishes her presence even if she doesn't ever mention herself. You might also notice something about how she uses evidence and frames her research question, all things that you'll wrestle with in your own essay.

INQUIRING INTO THE DETAILS

READING ACADEMIC RESEARCH ESSAYS

Just as reading a poem demands some different reading strategies than reading an essay, making sense of academic writing presents its own peculiar challenges. Here are some tips for picking your way through an academic journal article.

- Pay particular attention to the *justification* for why this research question is worthy of study. Do you understand how it extends existing scholarship?

- You don't have to understand all the jargon, just enough that you understand the research question and the conclusions.

- You're probably not in a position to evaluate the methods used, but make an effort to identify and understand them.

- When doing your own research, pay attention to names of people who are cited often. These are often people who have said the most in the on-going conversation about the topic.

- Carefully consider how the author qualifies his or her conclusions. This often mutes the significance of the findings and helps you to understand how seriously to take them.

EXAMINING THE MAINTENANCE OF FRIENDSHIPS

Are There Differences Between Geographically Close and Long-Distance Friends?*

Amy Janan Johnson

With the greater number of communication channels available to individuals every day, the impact of geographic distance is growing smaller, allowing us to form and maintain relationships with individuals who live too far away for us to interact face-to-face with them frequently (Blieszner & Adams, 1992; Wood, 1995). However, little is known about how individuals maintain such relationships over distance (Rohlfing, 1995) even though these relationship are common: Rohlfing found that 90% of individuals she surveyed reported having at least one close long-distance friend. Long-distance friendships have been ignored by communication researchers, but they should be examined because of their implications for traditional views of relational maintenance (Guldner & Swensen, 1995; Rohlfing, 1995). Previous research has focused on the quantity of maintenance behaviors and has suggested that more maintenance behaviors lead to better relationships. For example, Canary and Stafford (1994) claim that "relational properties erode without the benefit of maintenance behaviors" (p. 5). Such a view of maintenance disadvantages the long-distance relationship. How do individuals seek to maintain relationships differently when the relationships are long-distance versus geographically close? What do such possible differences illustrate about the current methods of conceptualizing relational maintenance?

By definition, an increase in distance decreases the opportunity for face-to-face contact between individuals. Davis (1973) claims that face-to-face contact is the easiest method for exchanging rewards in a relationship. An increase in distance between friends should constrain the frequency and type of maintenance behaviors that friends can utilize. Costs are increased (such as long-distance bills and expenses for visits, Rohlfing, 1995) and certain rewards become more difficult to exchange. Some researchers have even cast doubt concerning whether relationships can survive an increase in distance (Allan, 1979; Davis, 1973). For example, Berscheid, Snyder, and Omoto (1989) claim that "people who do not see each other frequently—for whatever reason, even involuntary 'good' reasons—simply cannot be as close, other things being equal, as people who *do* spend a lot of time together" (p. 794).

*From *Communication Quarterly,* Vol. 49, No 4, Fall 2001, Pages 424–435.

3   Therefore, current conceptualization of relational maintenance and closeness would suggest that long-distance friendships should be characterized by
fewer maintenance activities which should lead to these relationships being
less close and satisfying. However, previous research on long-distance *romantic
relationships* does not support this view. Guldner and Swensen (1995) found
few differences between romantic couples who are geographically close (GC)
and those who are long-distance (LD). They found no significant difference in
relational satisfaction. They claim that this finding illustrates that frequency of
visits (face-to-face contact) is not essential for relational maintenance.

4   How long-distance *friends* differ from their geographically close counterparts and cope with the factor of increased distance is unclear. They differ
from long-distance romantic partners on many factors, such as the importance
of the possibility of a decrease in distance (Rohlfing, 1995) and exclusivity of
the relationship. Some previous research appears to predict that long-distance
friendships should be less close and satisfactory (Berscheid, Snyder, & Omoto,
1989), while research concerning long-distance romantic relationships portrays no significant difference in satisfaction. This study seeks to explore this
disparity by examining how long-distance friendships maintain their relationships when they no longer can depend on face-to-face contact. The next section will discuss previous research related to the maintenance of friendships.

Previous Research Concerning Friendship Maintenance

5   Previous relational maintenance research has focused on how maintenance differs by type of relationship but has not taken distance into account. Results
from one study by Canary, Stafford, Hause, and Wallace (1993) support the
contention that different relationships call for varied maintenance actions.
More use of maintenance behaviors was reported for family and romantic
partners than friends, and they claimed that "people are probably less concerned about maintaining their friendships than their romantic and family relationships" (p. 12). However, a rival explanation might suggest that individuals perceive friendships as needing fewer maintenance behaviors than romantic
or family relationships.

6   Canary and his colleagues created a typology of maintenance behaviors,
which has been utilized in many maintenance studies (e.g., Stafford & Canary,
1991, Canary, et al. 1993; Messman, Canary, & Hause, 2000). Canary and
Stafford (1994) delineate this typology. The overarching maintenance strategies fall into ten categories including *positivity,* "attempts to make interactions
pleasant" (p. 15); *openness,* "direct discussions, offering and listening to one another" (p. 15); *assurances,* "covertly and overtly assuring each other" (p. 15);
social networks, "relying on friends and family" (p. 15); *sharing tasks,* "performing
routine tasks and chores in a relationship" (p. 15); *joint activities,* "how interac-

tants choose to spend time with one another to maintain their relationship" (p. 16); *cards, letters, and calls,* "use of various channels to keep contact in relationships" (p. 16); *avoidance,* "evasion of partner or issues" (p. 16); *antisocial,* "behaviors which seem unfriendly" (p. 16); and *humor* "jokes and sarcasm" (p. 16).

Canary et al. (1993) found that friends utilized assurances of the importance of the relationship, attempts at rendering interactions pleasant, and open discussions and listening less often than expected, while romantic partners used these strategies more than expected. Friends were less likely to utilize sharing tasks and less likely to use mediated communication, such as sending cards, letters and phone calls, while relatives utilized these strategies more than expected.

Although these studies illustrate how maintenance activities differ across relationship type, former research on maintenance has not compared geographically close to long-distance relationships. For example, Canary, et al. (1993) noted that 42% of the friends, romantic partners, and family members in their study were long-distance (not in the same town), but they did not examine whether differences existed in maintenance strategies for geographically close versus long-distance relationships. Next, one of the only studies examining long-distance friendships will be discussed.

Long-Distance Friendships

Rohlfing (1995) represents one of the only studies that has examined how individuals maintain their friendships over distance. She interviewed four female long-distance friendship pairs who had been friends for many years (for example one pair of friends had known each other for 33 years, and all the women were over 25). She found that one characteristic which defined these relationships was an acceptance of change in the relationship. Both individuals knew that they were not the same people as they were when the friendship began. However, these friends provided each other with a sense of history and served as part of each other's self-definition.

Rohlfing (1995) explored the channels through which these long-distance friends communicated. She found that these friendship pairs communicated mostly by phone, but the frequency of phone calls ranged from once a month to once a year. These individuals expressed frustration in the telephone as a channel of communication. They tended to have a history of shared intimacy and disclosures. Although they continued this practice over the phone, they believed they could not understand the feelings of the other as well as compared to face-to-face. One topic that the friends often discussed was the importance of their friendship, and they reported that discussion of this topic was more frequent and easier than when friends were geographically close. This study begins to delineate possible behaviors that individuals enact to maintain these friendships over distance. Next, the above information will be synthesized to form two hypotheses and a research question for this study.

Hypotheses and Research Question

11 Therefore, how do geographically close and long-distance friendships differ in how they maintain their relationships? What does such a difference mean for current ways of viewing relational maintenance? As stated previously, lack of face-to-face contact should cause a shift in the types of maintenance behaviors that individuals utilize. Previous research has emphasized spending time together and joint activities as important aspects of relational maintenance (Canary, et al. 1993; Reissman, Aron, & Bergen, 1993). These two factors would appear more of a luxury rather than a common occurrence for long-distance friends.

12 Consider the typology of maintenance activities formed by Canary and his colleagues (e.g., Stafford & Canary, 1991, Canary, et al. 1993) and discussed earlier. Some of the maintenance strategies listed appear to be ones that either geographically close or long-distance friends could utilize such as *positivity,* "attempts to make interactions pleasant" (p. 15) (although the frequency of interaction is probably lower for long-distance friends); *openness,* "direct discussions, offering and listening to one another" (p. 15); and *assurances,* "covertly and overtly assuring each other" (p. 15). However, others may be maintenance activities that geographically close friends can utilize more, such as *social networks,* "relying on friends and family" (p. 15); *sharing tasks;* and *joint activities.* One category, *cards, letters, and calls* might be utilized more by long-distance friends rather than geographically close friends. Various channels such as the phone or e-mail may replace less frequent face-to-face contact.

13 In summary, geographically close friends should be able to enact more maintenance activities than long-distance friends. According to current conceptualizations of relational maintenance, the greater number of maintenance activities should lead to geographically close friends being more satisfied and closer than the long-distance friends. Therefore, current conceptualizations of relational maintenance devalue the long-distance friendship. On the other hand, if no significant differences are found between long-distance and geographically close friendships in closeness and satisfaction, this will suggest that current beliefs that more maintenance behaviors lead to more satisfaction may be incorrect or at least too simplistic. Rather than quantity of maintenance behaviors being the most important criteria, perhaps quality of maintenance behaviors is more important to relationship satisfaction and closeness. Finding different maintenance activities in each type of friendship could suggest that some categories of maintenance activities are more important to the perception of relational satisfaction and closeness. In other words, perhaps for a close, satisfying friendship, it is important to receive support from your

friend, but it is not as important to participate often in joint activities. These musings illustrate the importance of examining maintenance in long-distance friendships and lead to the following hypotheses and research question:

H1: When reporting on geographically close friends, individuals will report a higher number of maintenance activities than when reporting on long-distance friends.

H2: Individuals will report a higher satisfaction and closeness level in their geographically close friendship than in their long-distance friendship.

RQ1: Are certain maintenance activities reported more commonly for one type of friend (geographically close or long-distance)?

Method

Participants

Thirty-six undergraduate students (21 females, 14 males, 1 failed to report his or her sex) in the basic communication course at a large Midwestern university kept a diary about their friendship maintenance behaviors with both a friend who was geographically close and one who was long distance, for a total of 71 friends (38 females, 31 males, one person failed to report the sex of his or her two friends). Undergraduates were considered an ideal population for this study, as they often have left home to attend college, increasingly the likelihood that they would have both a close long-distance friend from home and a close geographically close friend from school. Rawlins (1992) claims that young adulthood is often a time when individuals lose friends because of an increase in distance between friends.

Procedures

Students in an undergraduate communication course at a large Midwestern university were asked to select two friends that they considered to be a "close friend," one who was geographically close (defined as an individual who lives close enough that the friends could interact face-to-face every day and someone one normally sees on a daily basis) and one who was long-distance (defined as an individual who lives far enough away that the person cannot interact face-to-face with the friend every day). A very similar definition of long-distance and geographically close relationships was utilized by Guldner and Swensen (1995) in their work concerning long-distance romantic relationships. Individuals were allowed to self-define a "close friendship." If the student did not possess one type of friend, he or she was asked to pick two close friends of the other type. Four individuals reported on two geographically close friends. Thirty-two participants reported on one geographically close friend and one long-distance friend (only those reporting each type of friend were utilized in the data analysis to allow a repeated measures design). At the beginning of each class period, five minutes were devoted to the participants' recording of their activities and communication (if any) with their friends since the last class session. This continued for six weeks, with the class meeting three days a week for a total of 15 possible diary entries for each individual. Diary entries were not coded if the individual did not follow directions, or reported no contact with the friend since the last diary entry. Because of these stipulations and missing diary entries, a total of 584 diary entries were coded.

16   At the end of the diary collection period, subjects filled out a questionnaire for each friend (long-distance and geographically close) which reported the closeness of the friendship, friendship satisfaction, and perceptions concerning whether the subject believed the friendship was likely to continue into the future. Also, one-item measures indicated the reported friend's age, distance from respondent, and length of friendship.

Measurement

17   Directions for the diaries are presented in Appendix A. Items were developed for the questionnaire to measure satisfaction and closeness of the friendship and expectations concerning whether the relationship would continue.[1] Examples of each type of question include "This friendship is one of the closest I have ever had" for closeness; "There is little I would change about this friendship to make me more satisfied" for satisfaction; and "I doubt that this friendship will last much longer" (reverse coded) for expectations of whether the friendship would continue. Previous scales for closeness and satisfaction were not utilized as some of the items appeared to favor geographically close friendships over long-distance friendships. (For example, in the Relationship Closeness Inventory developed by Berscheid, et al., 1989, factors which measured closeness included frequency of interaction and number and activities with which one has engaged with his or her friend, such as "preparing a meal" or "watching TV." Geographically close friends would be expected to have an advantage for both of these factors.) Reliabilities for the created scales were high: closeness, $=.94$; satisfaction, $=.89$; expectation that friendship would continue, $=.95$.

Analysis

18   The author and another coder unitized 25% of the diaries (9 out of 36). The unit of analysis was one activity reported by the subject in the diary. Agreement on unitizing the nine diaries was 92% and Guetzkow's U was .04 (Guetzkow, 1950). The closer Guetzkow's U is to zero, the higher the agreement between coders. Then, the author unitized the rest of the diaries. Five hundred and eighty-four diary entries were coded into a total of 1957 units. Two undergraduate research assistants were trained to use Canary and

Stafford's (1994) maintenance behavior coding scheme. The two coders achieved 81% agreement in placing the units of 25% of the diaries into this coding scheme. Cohen's Kappa was calculated at .72 (Cohen, 1960). After disagreements were discussed and resolved, the remainder of the diaries were divided between the coders.

Confirmatory factor analysis was performed on the questionnaire using   19
Hamilton and Hunter's CFA program (1988). Individual items were assessed for content, internal consistency, and parallelism. All items met these criteria, for a total of 17 items with three scales: closeness (M=19.36; SD=3.90; a=.94), satisfaction (M=5.74; SD=1.38; =.89), and expectation for friendship continuance (M=6.09; SD=1.26; a=.95).

Results

Tests of Hypotheses and Research Questions

Hypothesis one tested the prediction that when reporting on geographically   20
close friends, individuals would report a higher number of maintenance activities than when reporting on long-distance friends. A paired sample t-test illustrated that when reporting on geographically close friends individuals listed significantly more total activities than when reporting on long-distance friends, with the diary as the unit of analysis ($t(31)$=4.66; p<.21 M_{GC}=38.53; SD_{GC}=18.86; M_{LD}=22.41; SD_{LD}=15.18; ^{2}=.39).

Hypothesis two claimed that individuals would report a higher satisfaction   21
and closeness level for their geographically close friendship than their long-distance friendship. This was to test the assumption that more maintenance activities lead to better relationships. However, this hypothesis was not supported as there was no significant difference in the satisfaction and closeness levels of long-distance and geographically close friends. No hypothesis was advanced regarding whether individuals expected their friendship to continue into the future, but this measure also did not significantly differ between long-distance and geographically close friends. Although these tests might lack power due to the small sample size, these results replicate previous research by the author, a questionnaire answered by 207 people (Johnson, 1999) and a questionnaire answered by 210 people (Johnson, 2000), neither of which found a significant difference between long-distance and geographically close friends in satisfaction, closeness, or whether they expected their friendship to continue. Results were analyzed using paired sample t-tests:

Closeness: $t(24)$=2.01; p=.99; M_{LD}=17.83; SD_{LD}=3.86; M_{GC}=17.84; SD_{GC}=2.70; ^{2}=.00 Satisfaction: $t(25)$=2.50; p=.62; M_{LD}=3.59; SD_{LD}=.42; M_{GC}=3.64; SD_{GC}=.46; ^{2}=.00 Expectation of Friendship Continuance: $t(25)$=1.51; p=.15; M_{LD}=5.02; SD_{LD}=.52; M_{GC}=4.82; SD_{GC}=.57; ^{2}=.04

22   Research question one asked whether certain maintenance activities were reported more commonly for one type of friend. The two types of reported friends were compared to ascertain whether they differed on the Canary and Stafford (1994) maintenance activities of positivity, openness, assurances, social network, joint activities, and cards, letters, calls. The categories of sharing tasks, avoidance, anti-social, and humor were not included because on average fewer than one percent of the units from each diary were coded into each of these categories (See Table One).

Table One
Average Percentage of Each Category in Each Diary

	Geographically Close	Long-Distance
Positivity	.047	.037
Openness	.248	.267
Assurances	.020	.025
Social Network	.055	.030
Sharing Tasks	.003	.006
Joint Activities	.508	.334
Cards, Letters, Calls	.095	.265
Avoidance	.009	.006
Antisocial	.009	.006
Humor	.001	.000
Miscellaneous	.006	.004

23   For these tests, the percentage of units in each individual's diary coded into a category for each type of friend was utilized rather than the total number in each category. This decision was made because of the greater number of overall maintenance activities reported by geographically close friends (see Hypothesis One). Paired sample t-tests were utilized.

24   The two types of friends were found to significantly differ on the following categories. Geographically close friends reported *social networks* a large percentage of the time than long-distance friends ($t(31)=2.42$; $p=.02$; $M_{GC}=.06$; $SD_{GC}=.06$; $M_{LD}=.03$; $SD_{LD}=.05$; $^2=.13$). Geographically close friends also reported *joint activities* a greater percentage of the time than long-distance friends ($t(31)=4.23$; $p<.001$; $M_{GC}=.51$; $SD_{GC}=.18$; $M_{LD}=.33$; $SD_{LD}=.24$; $^2=.34$). Long-distance friends reported *cards, letters, calls* a higher percentage of time than geographically close friends ($t(31)=25.57$; $p<.001$;

25    $M_{GC}=.10$; $SD_{GC}=.10$; $M_{LD}=.27$; $SD_{LD}=.16$; $^2=.48$).

The two types of friends were not found to significantly differ on the following categories: *openness* ($t(29)=20.60$; $p=.55$; $M_{GC}=.25$; $SD_{GC}=.13$;

$M_{LD}=.27$; $SD_{LD}=.15$; $^2=.00$), *assurances* ($t(29)=20.40$; $p=.69$; $M_{GC}=.02$; $SD_{GC}=.04$; $M_{LD}=.03$; $SD_{LD}=.06$; $^2=.00$), and *positivity* ($t(31)=0.58$; $p=.57$; $M_{GC}=.05$; $SD_{GC}=.05$; $M_{LD}=.04$; $SD_{LD}=.09$; $^2=.00$). Concerns about type two error could be considered due to the small sample size. Therefore, effect sizes were calculated, which take into consideration sample size (Cohen, 1977, offers the following rule of thumb for effect sizes: $^2=.01$ is a small effect, $^2=.06$ is a medium effect, $^2=.15$ is a large effect).

Discussion

This study sought to examine an important relationship in many individuals' lives that has been virtually ignored by communication researchers: the long-distance friendship. Some previous research has suggested that long-distance relationships should suffer from lack of face-to-face contact (Allan, 1979; Kelley, et al. 1983), while other research suggests that few differences exist between long-distance and geographically close relationships (Guldner & Swensen, 1995). How people maintain these friendships over distance not only helps individuals to understand friendship and closeness better, but also questions some of the assumptions that exist concerning how individuals maintain relationships. 26

As mentioned, some researchers appear to doubt that close, long-distance friendships can be maintained (Allan, 1979; Kelley, et al. 1983). However, researchers who examine these relationships find that many individuals report having such friends (Rohlfing, 1995). That these relationships exist leads one to question certain assumptions concerning how individuals maintain their interpersonal relationships. For example, Guldner and Swenson (1995) claim that a lack of difference between long-distance and geographically close romantic relationships in satisfaction illustrates that frequency of face-to-face interaction is not necessary for relational maintenance. 27

Canary and Stafford (1994) claim that "relational properties erode without the benefits of maintenance behaviors" (p.5). Almost all prior research on maintenance appears to be based on the assumption that more maintenance activities lead to better relationships. This belief about maintenance immediately disadvantages the long-distance relationship. This study illustrates that geographically close friends reported significantly more maintenance behaviors than long-distance friends; however, this difference was not followed by significant differences in closeness or satisfaction. 28

Rather than the frequency or quantity of maintenance behaviors determining the quality or closeness of the relationship, another possibility is that certain types of maintenance behaviors are more important for a relationship to be close and satisfying. Therefore, a long-distance friendship may lack some of the 29 ongoing every day behaviors common in geographically close friendships, but these maintenance behaviors may not be essential to having a close, satisfying friendship. This possibility is explored by examining the results of this study concerning the proportion of time that each type of friend reported the different maintenance behavior categories. For certain categories, such as *joint activities* and *social networks,* geographically close friends reported these activities a greater proportion of time than long-distance friends. The greater utilization of these categories did not coincide with higher friendship satisfaction among geographically close friends. However, factors such as *openness* and *assurances,* which were not found to significantly differ in the proportion of time that they were reported by geographically close or long-distance friends, may be more essential to maintaining a close, satisfactory relationship. Individuals may thus maintain relationships over a distance by giving up those maintenance behaviors that an increase of geographic distance renders difficult, such as *joint activities* and *social networks,* while continuing factors which might be more important to perceive a relationship as close, such as *openness* and *assurances.* These findings support a conclusion advanced by Guldner and Swensen (1995) concerning their study of long-distance romantic relationships: "It is not the amount of time per se that supports the relationship, but rather some factor associated with even small amounts of time spent together" (p. 319). In the same manner, it is not the number of maintenance activities itself that predicts whether a relationship is satisfactory, but the types or quality of behaviors that are enacted.

30   Another potential explanation is the expectations that individuals have concerning each relationship. Dainton (2000) found that for married couples the degree to which the frequency of maintenance behaviors exceeded expectations predicted marital satisfaction. Perhaps the differing expectations individuals have for geographically close and long-distance friends render both relationships satisfactory even with varied frequency of maintenance activity.

Limitations

31   One potential limitation is the small sample size in this study. This small sample size was selected in order to enable a large amount of data to be gathered from each individual. A small sample size might result in a lack of power in a significance test. Repeated measures design was utilized to increase the power of the study by controlling for individual differences. Also, effect size measures (in this case ω^2) were calculated. Most of the significant findings in this study had very large effect sizes, showing that the differences between geographically close and long-distance friends were so large that only a small sample size was needed to observe them. In any case, the effect size measures indicate that if there is a difference between the two groups on those variables that were not significantly different in this study the difference is *very* small. Only the ef-

fect size measure for whether individuals expected the relationship to continue suggested a potential small effect ($\omega^2 = .04$), where long-distance friends reported a nonsignificantly higher mean than geographically close friends. Future research should replicate this finding and should include more males. As this study only had 14 males, sex differences were not examined but represent an interesting area for future research.

Future Directions

As Parlee (1979) and Rose (1984) state, distance is one of the main reasons   32
cited for a friendship ending. Research is currently being conducted comparing those friendships that continue to be maintained in an active state once the individuals in the dyad are separated geographically compared to those which become dormant or end once geographic distance between the pair increases. This research examines whether there are factors that were apparent when the dyad was geographically close that could predict which friendships continue over distance and which "fade away."

Other future research directions include a closer look at how social sci-   33
ence scholars have defined "relational closeness." Parks and Floyd (1996) state that few studies have sought to specifically define this ubiquitous interpersonal concept. Berscheid, et al. (1989) developed a closeness scale that used frequency of enacting joint behaviors as one criteria for determining friendship closeness. The current study illustrates that this discounts and disadvantages long-distance friendships that are perceived as close by many individuals. Parks and Floyd (1996) examined the way individuals defined closeness and found that the most common were "self-disclosure, support, shared interests and explicit expression of the value of the relationship" (p. 85). Several of these meanings are likely more relevant to long-distance friendships than others. Questions remain to be explored, such as "What factors are essential for having a 'close' relationship? Do long-distance and geographically close friends differ in how they define friendship closeness?"

In conclusion, to fully understand the complete spectrum of interpersonal   34
relationships, the long-distance friendship should not be ignored. It appears to play an important part in the lives of many individuals, especially as people are becoming increasingly mobile (Blieszner & Adams, 1992; Wood, 1995). Not only are these relationships thus interesting in their own right, but they also call into question some of the ways that we examine how relationships are maintained in a satisfactory and close state.

Notes

[1]All of the following questions except the first closeness question were rated on a 7-point Likert-type scale from strongly agree to strongly disagree. Items with an asterisk (*) were reverse coded.

Closeness—"Rate your friend based on how close you think the friendship is on a scale from 0 to 100 (0 would mean 'not close at all,' while 100 would mean 'the closest friend I currently have' _____." "This friendship is one of the closest I have ever had." "I do *not* feel particularly close to this person."* "I would describe myself as close to this person." "This individual and I share a great amount of emotional closeness." "I do *not* consider that person a particularly close friend."*

Satisfaction—"I am generally satisfied with this friendship." "I am *not* satisfied with the relationship with this friend."* "There is little I would change about this friendship to make me more satisfied." "This friendship does *not* bring me much satisfaction."*

Likelihood of Friendship Continuance—"I definitely would like to continue this relationship in the future." "I definitely see this friendship continuing for the rest of my life." "I doubt that this friendship will last much longer."* "I think that this friend and I will probably lose contact with one another."* "I would put much effort into continuing this friendship." "This friendship will certainly last for a long time." "This friend and I will maintain contact throughout our lives."

References

Allan, G. (1979). *A sociology of friendship and kinship.* London: Allen & Unwin.

Berscheid, E., Snyder, M., & Omoto, A.M. (1989). The Relationship Closeness Inventory: Assessing the closeness of interpersonal relationships. *Journal of Personality and Social Psychology, 57*(5), 792–807.

Blieszner, R., & Adams, R.G. (1992). *Adult friendship.* Newbury Park, CA: Sage.

Canary, D.J., & Stafford, L. (1994). Maintaining relationships through strategic and routine interaction. In D.J. Canary & L. Stafford (Eds.), *Communication and relational maintenance* (pp. 3–22). San Diego: Academic Press.

Canary, D.J., Stafford, L., Hause, K.S., & Wallace, L.A. (1993). An inductive analysis of relational maintenance strategies: Comparisons among lovers, relatives, friends, and others. *Communication Research Reports, 10*(1), 5–14.

Cohen, J. (1960). A coefficient of agreement for nominal scales. *Educational and Psychological Measurement, 20,* 37–46.

Cohen, J. (1977). *Statistical power analysis for the behavioral sciences* (Rev. Ed.). New York: Academic Press.

Dainton, M. (2000). Maintenance behaviors, expectations for maintenance and satisfaction: Linking comparison levels to relational maintenance strategies. *Journal of Social and Personal Relationships, 17*(6), 827–842.

Davis, M. (1973). *Intimate relations.* New York: The Free Press.

Guetzkow, J. (1950). Unitizing and categorizing problems in coding qualitative data. *Journal of Clinical Psychology, 6,* 47–58.

Guldner, G.T., & Swensen, C.H. (1995). Time spent together and relationship quality: Long-distance relationships as a test case. *Journal of Social and Personal Relationships, 12,* 313–320.

Hamilton, M., & Hunter, J. (1988). CONFIRMATORY FACTOR ANALYSIS. A computer program to perform confirmatory factor analysis.

Johnson, A.J. *If I Do Not See You Every Day, Are You Still My Friend? Characteristics of Long-Distance Friendships.* Paper presented to the Interpersonal Communication Division of the Western States Communication Association for their annual meeting at Vancouver, British Columbia, February, 1999.

Johnson, A.J. *A Role Theory Approach to Examining the Maintenance of Geographically Close and Long-Distance Friendships.* Paper presented to the Interpersonal Interest Group of the Western States Communication Association for their annual meeting in Sacramento, California, February, 2000.

Kelley, H.H., Berscheid, E., Christensen, A., Harvey, J.H., Huston, T.L., Levinger, G., McClintock, E., Peplau, L.A., & Perterson, D.R. (1983). *Close relationships.* New York: Freeman.

Messman, S.J., Canary, D.J., & Hause, K.S. (2000). Motives to remain platonic, equity, and the use of maintenance strategies in opposite-sex friendships. *Journal of Social and Personal Relationships; 17,* 67–94.

Parks, M.R., & Floyd, K. (1996). Meanings for closeness and intimacy in friendship. *Journal of Social and Personal Relationships, 13*(1), 85–107.

Parlee, M.B. (1979, October). The friendship bond. *Psychology Today,* 43–54, 113.

Rawlins, W.K. (1992). *Friendship matters: Communication, dialectics, and the life course.* New York: Aldine De Gruyter.

Reissman, C., Aron, A., & Bergen, M.R. (1993). Shared activities and marital satisfaction: Causal direction and self-expansion versus boredom. *Journal of Social and Personal Relationships, 10,* 243–254.

Rohlfing, M.E. (1995). "Doesn't anybody stay in one place anymore?" An exploration of the under-studied phenomenon of long-distance relationships. In J.T. Wood & S. Duck's (Eds.), *Under-studied relationships: Off the beaten track* (pp. 173–196). Thousand Oaks: Sage Publications.

Rose, S.M. (1984). How friendships end: Patterns among young adults. *Journal of Social and Personal Relationships, 1,* 267–277.

Stafford, L., & Canary, D.J. (1991). Maintenance strategies and romantic relationship type, gender, and relational characteristics. *Journal of Social and Personal Relationships, 8,* 217–242.

Wood, J.T. (1995). *Relational communication: Continuity and change in personal relationships.* Detroit: Wadsworth Publishing Co.

INQUIRING INTO THE ESSAY

Explore, explain, evaluate, and reflect on Johnson's academic article.

1. Tell the story of one of your long-distance friendships. Fastwrite in your journal about what happened, but don't begin at the beginning. First describe a moment that was "typical" of the things you did together before geographical distance disrupted things. Then describe a moment—perhaps the same situation as before—after the move. Do you sense differences? Alternatively, speculate about why you think the relationship will either be altered or unchanged by the distance between you. If you can, incorporate some of the ideas from the article in this speculation.

2. One of the key features of academic writing is establishing the question you're posing against what has already been said. Explain how and where Johnson does this in her article.

3. Any communication between people who share some of the same knowledge is shaped by conventions. Imagine, for example, a conversation between snowboarders at a competition. They'll use insider language, be aware of the arguments for or against certain kinds of waxes or bindings, and so on. Examine this article and make a list of features in it you might consider conventions of research writing among communication theorists.

4. A key element of argument is evidence, and particularly how it's used and what *kind* of evidence is most convincing. What do you infer about what counts as evidence for readers of an article like this one?

5. Academic research often looks at a very narrow part of the territory illuminated by the research question. As a result, sometimes our own experiences might seem at odds with certain findings. What argument would *you* make about the impact of geographical distance on maintaining close friendships? Where might you agree or differ with Johnson? What does she fail to take into consideration?

6. Reflect on your process of reading this academic article. In your journal, make an entry that attempts to answer some of the following questions: How did I read this article differently than the essays before it? What do I do when I encounter words or language I don't understand? How do I overcome my resistance (if you feel any) to reading academic prose like this? What parts of reading are most difficult or challenging? What problems does reading writing like this raise and how do I attempt to solve them?

SEEING THE FORM

IDAHO STATE PENITENTIARY, WOMEN'S PRISON

I took the accompanying picture on a ridge overlooking the valley where I live. It includes a lot of visual information: long shots of the city of Boise, the university, the state penitentiary, and in the far distance, the Owyhee range, which is currently being considered for wilderness designation. But do you really get a good look at any of these subjects? I don't think so, which is why I don't think much of the photograph. My brother, a professional photographer, would probably consider this shot a throwaway—a kind of photographic "prewriting" activity that might help him discover the visual subject he *really* wants to work with.

At the bottom middle of the photograph is a small building surrounded by high stone walls. This was the women's prison, which was built in the 1920s. It's a fascinating place both visually and historically, and so I "revised" my photographic project to focus on the women's prison rather than attempting to capture the valley. I took a slew of shots of the women's prison, including the two pictures shown here—one of a small cell with the

light streaming through the tiny window and another of a rusting iron door. They are hardly masterpieces, but I do like them a lot better than the landscape shot. Do you agree? If so, why?

If the process of taking these pictures is a good analogy for the process of writing research essays, what do the comparisons between the landscape shot and the women's prison photographs suggest to you about the qualities of a good paper? What do they imply about the research process?

▪ THE WRITING PROCESS ▪

INQUIRY PROJECT: Write a Research Essay

Develop a 2,000- to 3,000-word research essay on a topic of your choice. (Your instructor may present some broad subjects or other limitations on topic choice.) The most important quality of this research essay is that it be organized around your own questions or ideas about the topic; it should be an *essay* not a *report*. The research question should also have a sufficiently narrow focus. Don't look at the entire landscape of a topic but focus instead on a specific feature in that landscape. Your essay should also:

- Be based on a "researchable" question.
- Have a central thesis or claim that represents your answer to the question you pose, even if it's tentative.
- Use appropriate and relevant sources based on your own experiences, observations, interviews, and reading, or all four sources of information.
- Be cited using the conventions recommended by your instructor.
- Be written for an audience of peers rather than experts on the topic.

Thinking About Subjects

"The death of curiosity," writes one educator, "may begin sometime in the second grade." After that the "system takes over" and it's "time to get efficient and serious," preparing for the careers. Whatever the reason for it, the diminished sense of wonder seems most poignant whenever I talk to my students about research writing. In a way, it's no big surprise. Too often, research papers have been exercises in drudgery. But even when students choose their own topics for their investigations, they are initially quite sure that the whole enterprise is *not* about surprise and discovery. A few even sigh and suggest that I should just tell them what to write about. "That would be easier," they say.

Imagine what inspired Clifford Bishop's inquiry into the marriage customs around the world or Ann Braley-Smith's inquiry into boys' penchant for waging imaginary wars—a genuine curiosity that began with an itchy question that motivated them to read things and talk to people and consider what they learned. Even an academic research essay like Amy Johnson's study of the impact of geographical distance on friendship began with a question she really wondered about, possibly one that pestered her after a difficult conversation with a far-away friend.

Begin thinking about subjects for your research essay by remembering that the best reason to investigate something is because you genuinely wonder about it. Let curiosity lead you through the library's heavy glass doors, or into the far reaches of cyberspace, or perhaps to the office of an expert on your topic in a nearby campus building. In many cases, the best subjects grow from your own experiences and observations. Ask yourself this: *What have I seen or experienced or heard about that raises questions that research might help answer?*

Approaching your research project this way is exactly the impulse that might have motivated you to write a personal essay on growing up with an autistic sibling or a persuasive essay on the downside of recruiting NCAA athletes at your school. It's the same motive that inspires all genuine inquiry: How do I feel about this? What do I think about this? What do I want to know?

Generating Ideas

Use your notebook to generate some material. As in previous inquiry projects, at this stage don't prejudge anything you come up with. Let yourself play around with possibilities.

Listing Prompts. Lists can be rich sources of triggering topics. Let them grow freely, and when you're ready, use an item as the focus of another list or an episode of fastwriting. The following prompts should get you started.

1. Inventory your interests by creating five separate lists on a page of your notebook. Choose among the following words as a general category for each of the five lists you will create: Places, Trends, Things, Technologies, People, Controversies, History, Jobs, Habits, Hobbies. In each of the five categories you chose, brainstorm a list of words or phrases that come to mind when you think about *what you know and what you might want to know.* For example, under Places I would put "Florence pigeons" because I want to know more about their impact on Renaissance buildings. Under Hobbies, I would put fly fishing because that's something I know about. Spend about fifteen minutes buildings these lists.

2. Look over your lists and ask yourself, *Are there research topics implied by a few of the items on these lists?* In other words, what here raises questions that more research might answer? What is it about this item that I wonder about?

3. Finally, choose a promising item from one of the lists and generate questions about it that you'd love to have answered. Perhaps you already know something about the topic but would like to learn more. Don't worry yet whether all the questions are great.

Fastwriting Prompts. Remember, fastwriting is a great way stimulate creative thinking. Turn off your critical side and let yourself write "badly."

1. Choose an item from your lists and use it as a prompt for a seven-minute fastwrite. Begin by telling yourself the story of when, where, and why you first got interested in the subject. When the writing stalls, write the following phrase, and follow it for as long as you can: *Among the things I most want to learn about this are . . .*

✎ ONE STUDENT'S RESPONSE

JULIAN'S JOURNAL

TOPIC: JAZZ

My dad was into jazz. Would listen to it all night long after working all day long. He listened to all kinds of jazz—Bird, Miles Davis, Billy Holiday, Monk. It took me years to really appreciate the music but now it's my favorite kind. **Among the things I most want to learn about** jazz is its connection to African music and slave songs. It makes me wonder whether the uniqueness of jazz, its spontaneity especially, has something to do with the hymns and spirituals of the slaves. **Among the other things I want to learn** is whether jazz was accepted in the early days. I seem to remember my Dad saying that the . . .

2. Get a copy of the daily newspaper. Read it quickly and then clip any articles that make you think or feel something, even if you can't quite say much more about your reaction. Choose one article and glue it into your notebook. Just below, use the article as a prompt for a "narrative of thought" response. Begin this way: *When I first read this article, I thought (or felt) . . . And then I thought . . . And then . . .* If the writing takes off in another direction, let it. End by finishing the following sentence: *When I first started thinking about this, I thought _____, but now I think _____.*

Visual Prompts. Sometimes the best way to generate material is to see what we think represented in something other than sentences. Boxes, lines, webs, clusters, arrows, charts, or even sketches can help us to see more of the landscape of a subject, especially connections among fragments of information that aren't as obvious in prose.

1. Cluster the phrase, *"I'm really curious about . . ."* Put the phrase in the center of a blank page and build a web of associations, each of which might begin with the word "why." Explore your curiosity about things in your personal life, in the community, in the region, the state, the country, the world.

2. Do an image search using Google on some person, place, thing, or event that interests you (see the accompanying photo). Might one of the pictures you find be the focus of an investigation? Who *was* that guy? What was going on when this happened? Why did it happen?

Research Prompts. Do some research before you begin your research? Absolutely. By exploring what others have said or done or wondered about, you might discover an interest in something you wouldn't have otherwise considered.

A Google image search on the "Harlem Renaissance" produced this 1936 painting *Aspiration* by Aaron Douglas. The image depicts one reason for the African American artistic renaissance in many American cities back then—the migration of blacks from the South to places such as New York and Chicago. The image suggests a great focus for an investigation of the Harlem Renaissance: Why did this migration occur?

1. Surf the Net, perhaps beginning with a subject directory such as *The Virtual Library* (http://vlib.org). Start by clicking on a subject area that interests you. Keep following the links as you branch more deeply into the subcategories and subdisciplines of that area of knowledge. Look for specific subject areas that intrigue you. For example, you might have begun in the broad subject of history, clicked the link for medieval history (maybe you've always wondered what was dark about the Dark Ages), and ended up reading some fascinating articles on the home life of medieval women. Does it raise some questions you'd like to explore?

2. Study the local newspaper. Devote some time to reading the local paper to discover a local controversy that intrigues you. Say there

was an article on the impact of Title IX on the university's athletic department, and you wonder, "Is the elimination of the men's wrestling team really the result of shifts in funding to women's sports?" Or perhaps there's a letter to the editor about the condition of housing for migrant workers in the valley. Are things really that bad?

Judging What You Have

The great thing about simply generating material is that you can turn off your critical mind and simply muck about all sorts of possible topics for your essay. But as always, the process depends on taking a more analytical look at whether you've discovered anything genuinely useful. Remember your goal at this stage: You want to identify a possible topic—and maybe, if you're lucky, a research question—that will move your investigation forward in the next few days. The following suggestions should help.

What's Promising Material and What Isn't? Deciding what a good research topic is mostly depends on one simple thing: Do you have a researchable *question?* The topic itself may not be the problem at all. Wondering whether Elvis is really dead isn't really a very good research question because the answer is pretty simple—yep. But wondering why certain people keep asking the question in the first place—why there's a need to maintain the fiction that the King is still around—is an excellent opening question for a research project. I've read riveting books on the most common subjects—salt, for example—and what made them succeed is that the writer found interesting questions to ask about them. This, by the way, is the key to writing strong research papers about assigned topics. Virtually any topic can be interesting to you if you find the question that makes you wonder.

Is It a Researchable Question? What is a researchable question? I've already mentioned the most important characteristic: *the question interests you.* But there some other things to consider as well:

- *Is it the right size?* As illustrated in the earlier "Seeing the Form," the quickest way to make any research project unmanageable is to ask a really, really big question: What were the causes of the Gulf War? Why is there racism in America? At the other extreme is the question that is so limited, so small in scope, that it isn't enough to carry the weight of your investigation, but this is rarely a problem. The key is to find an opening question that isn't too broad and isn't too narrow, one that allows you *to exclude* aspects of the topic because they aren't relevant.

- *Has something already been said about it?* In other words, is there information out there that *is* relevant to the question you're asking?

Have experts and others addressed the question in some way, perhaps indirectly or in other contexts? This may be hard to know until you look.

- *Does it raise more questions?* Some questions have pretty simple answers. For example, wondering why the sky is blue might be an interesting question but it probably won't sustain any kind of extended inquiry because the reasons for blue skies are well known. A better research question raises more questions the more you think about it, or seems to lead to controversies, debates, or disagreements among knowledgeable people.

- *Does it matter?* It might matter to you, and it needs to. But the best research questions should be potentially interesting and relevant to other people, too. Doing research on how to deal with your messy boyfriend, for example, may not matter really to anyone but you. But it really depends on how you frame the research question. Do men and women in this culture see domestic spaces differently, use them for different reasons, and talk about them in different ways? That's probably too big a research question, but it certainly transcends your personal problem to address questions many of us find interesting and relevant to our lives.

Questions About Audience and Purpose. The best motive for writing a research essay about a particular topic is the same reason you might want to write about anything—it makes you curious. It could interest you for any number of reasons. Perhaps you want to research an illness because your mother has it; maybe you're an engineering major and you're interested in the early history of the computer; maybe you're a hunter and want to know the impact of gray wolf reintroduction on the elk herd; or maybe you're a single parent interested in the impact of divorce on very young children.

Your personal interests will help you choose a topic, but the question behind your investigation—what I call the tentative focusing question—will also be influenced by some of the conventions of academic research, things I already mentioned as qualities of a researchable question and the interests of your audience. In many cases, we write research papers for an audience of one—the instructor—someone who is likely to know more about the subject you're writing about than you will, even after you've done your research. For this assignment, however, you'll be writing for a larger, less specialized audience—your peers and your instructor in this class. Learning to write about complex or technical subjects for a more general audience is enormously valuable, not only because you have to write papers in future classes. Much of the research-based writing you'll do after college will demand the ability to write clearly for readers who are less knowledgeable than you about a subject.

Practically speaking, then, this means choosing a topic that might interest other nonexperts. It also means choosing a good question to guide your investigation, one that people other than you might want to know the answer to. You can get some direction on this in class; also see "Inquiring Into the Details: Finding the Focusing Question."

INQUIRING INTO THE DETAILS

FINDING THE FOCUSING QUESTION

Once you tentatively settle on a topic, you're ready to do this in-class exercise. It should help you to find questions that will help you focus your project.

1. Each student will take a piece a paper or a large piece of newsprint and post it on the wall. (In computer labs, students can use a word processing program and move from station to station in the steps that follow.)

2. Write your topic at the very top of the paper (for instance, hybrid cars).

3. Take a few minutes to briefly describe why you chose the topic.

4. Spend five minutes to briefly list what you know about your topic already, (for instance, any surprising facts or statistics, the extent of the problem, important people or institutions involved, key schools of thought, common misconceptions, important trends, controversies, and so on).

5. Now spend fifteen or twenty minutes brainstorming a list of questions about your topic that you'd love to learn the answers to. Make the list as long as you can.

6. Look around the room. You'll see a gallery of topics and questions on the walls. Now you can help each other. Move around the room, reviewing the topics and questions other students have generated. For each topic posted on the wall, do two things: Check the *one* question on the list you find most interesting, and add a question *you* would like answered about that topic.

7. Now you have long lists of questions about your topic. Is there one that you think might be researchable, using the criteria for such questions? Which questions seem to generate the most interest in the class? Do any of those interest you, too?

8. Pick one question from the list that could be your initial focusing question. Remember, you can change it later.

ONE STUDENT'S RESPONSE

JULIAN'S JOURNAL

FINDING THE FOCUSING QUESTION

1. The Blues
2. Chose this topic because I've listened to jazz and blues since I was a kid, but never really understood its origins.
3. Some famous blues singers: Robert Johnson, Blind Lemon . . . Some qualities of blues: appeals more to the heart than the head, has a characteristic "bluesy" sound, early music in the south . . .
4. Questions:

   What's the relationship between blues and Jazz?

   Who was the most influential blues musician in the early days?

   How is African music part of the blues?

   Did only blacks listen to blues in the beginning?

   How does the blues vary by region?

Writing the Sketch

The sketch for your research essay will be a little different from those you've written earlier. Rather than writing a "sketchy" draft of a possible essay, you'll develop a project narrative, one that summarizes your working knowledge of the topic and how your thinking about it has evolved so far. A working knowledge of your topic is achieved when you have enough information to be able to talk about it for five minutes without repeating yourself.[1] You develop a working knowledge by conducting basic research on the Web and at the university library. (See Chapter 12 for details on how to develop working knowledge of a topic.)

Once you are ready, your sketch should have the following features:

- The title should be the tentative focusing question you've chosen on your topic.

- The sketch itself should tell the story of your thinking about that question and topic from the beginning until now.

---

[1]Badke, William. *Research Strategies: Finding Your Way Through the Information Fog,* substantial revision of *The Survivor's Guide to Library Research.* Lincoln, NE.: iUniverse.com/Writers Club Press, 2000.

- This narrative of thought should discuss the ways in which your working knowledge of the topic has changed the way you think about it.
- The sketch should be about 500 words.
- Information, ideas, or quotations you borrow from outside sources should be cited. (See the sections "How to Cite Using MLA" or "How to Cite Using APA" in Chapter 13.)

STUDENT SKETCH

It was spring and Amy Garrett began to imagine shorts and bathing suits, but then she took a look at her skin in the mirror. She looked pale and pasty. Wouldn't a nice tan be good about now? But would she be compromising her health for vanity, she wondered? Suddenly, Garrett had a research topic and an opening question. Here's her sketch on the topic.

WHY DO PEOPLE TAN?
Amy Garrett

This started as a simple question spurred by one of my occasional, "people are so stupid" rants. I wondered who was to blame for this, who made it cool for white people to be tan? It seems completely asinine on the surface to waste money and time on a pre-paid tan that will only result in prematurely leathered and wrinkled skin and a much higher risk of developing melanoma or other skin cancers. And then I looked down at my arms and noticed that I've managed to build up a decent tan this summer myself, not via light bulb technology, but the old fashioned way, by playing in the sun. Hmmm . . . am I a hypocrite?

I wondered about that. As I researched sunbathing and the like I came across an interesting article in *The Atlanta Journal-Constitution* titled, "The Rural South These Days Has More Tanning Salons Than John Deeres" by Rheta Grimsley Johnson. Johnson summarizes her point with a quote from E. B. White, "I am fascinated by the anatomy of decline . . . by the spectacle of people passively accepting a degenerating process which is against their own interests." She then explains, "He was writing about the redesign of the automobile—longer and lower with bigger fenders. He also objected to replacing the car window crank with a lazy push-button. If he could see us now, jumping into our foreign cars and speeding down to the tanning bed and nail art salon. Lost, buffed souls" (M 1).

3   It struck me as I read the last lines of this sardonic critique of society that I don't necessarily wonder why people tan, but why they completely gyp themselves of the pleasures of the sun to be rewarded with a battle with cancer at worst and saggy skin at best. It seems like everyone wants to feel active, even if they aren't.

4   In a survey conducted by *Seventeen* magazine, "2/3 of the teens say they look better with a tan and feel healthier, more sophisticated and 50% say they looked more athletic" (qtd. in "Sun Tanning"). Somehow it seems that society has missed the forest for the trees. A nice tan once meant you spent your days on the beach playing volleyball and swimming, hiking in the mountains or riding a horse, riding a bike around town or jogging in the afternoons, it was usually accompanied by fit and trim bodies and healthy smiles. Now, it means you spent $45 a month building a base tan.

5   But, somehow the message isn't translating. People still feel healthy with a bastardized tan? So, there must be something more to it all. Is the fashion industry that powerful? In her fashion column Patricia McLaughlin puts the fascination with a tan into perspective.

> White people have it tough. At least the pale ones, whose skin is really a mottled, unappetizing grayish-yellowish-pinkish off-white threaded with blue veins. Once, amazing as it may seem, it was actually cool to have skin this color. Then Coco Chanel came home with a tan from a cruise on the Duke of Westminster's yacht, and ever since, white people have preferred to be a biscuity golden color. (02)

6   So, maybe that's it, people just like the way it looks to be tan. I know I feel better about putting on a bathing suit if I'm not so starkly white that I worry about blinding young children. I also know that it just feels good to be in the sun. The warm rays beating down on my back and shoulders as I work outdoors or go for a hike seem therapeutic and natural.

7   But the health industry sure doesn't like to condone it. In an article by Alexanra Greely titled, "No Tan is a Safe Tan" she presents her case against spending time in the sun and especially tanning with facts and statistics, but I couldn't help but wonder if she ever has any fun after reading the closing lines to her article. "In the end, there really is nothing new under the sun, except that perhaps more people are staying out of it, heeding medical warnings such as Bergstresser's: 'Less sun is better. No sun is best of all' " (15).

8   I disagree. But, I'm no expert, so I sought proof of my hunch that the sun is really our friend and found it. Of course, I'm not condoning the 1976 "Savage Tan" or complete ignorance of the dangers of a depleted ozone and proof that severe sunburns lead to cancers, but I think there must be some middle ground.

Works Cited

Greeley, Alexandra. "No Tan is a Safe Tan." Nutrition *Health Review: the Consumer's Medical Journal* 59 (Summer 1991): 14–15.

Johnson, Rheta Grimsley. "The Rural South These Days Has More Tanning Salons Than John Deeres." *The Atlanta Journal-Constitution* 23 Apr 2000, home ed.: M1.

McLaughlin, Patricia. "Dying For a Tan This Summer?" *St. Louis Post-Dispatch* 15 Jun 1995: 02.

"Sun Tanning." *Cool Nurse* 2000–2003. 18 Jun 2003 <http://www.coolnurse.com/tanning.htm>.

Moving from Sketch to Draft

Your sketch may not really be an early draft of the essay you'll write later. It's probably more of a record of your thinking about your topic, perhaps leading you to a clearer idea about the best focusing question and perhaps a stronger sense of what you might want to say in the draft. Your sketch also gives you a chance to share what you've discovered so far with others in your class, but not in the usual way. Rather than workshopping your sketch you'll use it to develop a brief presentation.

Evaluating Your Own Sketch. Follow the roadmap of thinking present in your sketch to get a clearer sense of where you want to go in the draft.

1. What seemed to be the turning point in your own thinking about the topic? What caused it?

2. Is the focusing question you wrote at the beginning of the sketch still the right title? Does that question need to be revised or do you need to write a new one?

3. Based on what you know now, how would you answer the question you're asking?

Questions for Peer Review. Rather than workshopping your sketch, it will be the basis for a brief class presentation. Following a press conference format, you will speak for about five to ten minutes, highlighting some or all the following:

- What focusing question did you start with? What question do you want to ask now?

- What is the most surprising thing you've learned so far?

- What do experts on the topic debate about?

- What are the most common misconceptions about the topic?

- What story can you tell about the topic—a case study, a telling event, profile of person involved?

Try to make this presentation lively and interesting. Your purpose, in part, is to get a sense of potential reader interest in your topic and the question you're pursuing. Students listening to the presentations should be encouraged to ask questions about what you've said—or haven't said. They also might have some suggestions of questions about your topic you hadn't considered, or tips on where to search for more information. Allow another five to ten minutes for this question and answer session.

Reflecting on What You've Learned. Spend a few minutes following your presentation generating a list of everything you heard, and then begin a five-minute fastwrite that explores your reaction to these questions and suggestions and your tentative plan for revision. Did the class have a lot of questions about your topic following the presentation? What seems to have most piqued their interest? What questions or controversies seem to ignite the most discussion? What did the discussion suggest might be new avenues for research? End your fastwrite by writing about what you understand now about your topic and your initial beliefs about it, that you didn't fully understand when you began writing about it.

Research and Other Strategies: Gathering More Information

Writing a draft will require more than a working knowledge of your topic. Now you'll need to develop a deep knowledge, one that will give you enough of a grasp of the subject to know some or all of the following things about it:

- Which other writers and researchers have addressed the question you're interested in, and what have they already said about it?
- Which sources did you find particularly persuasive?
- How did those sources influence the way you think about your topic?

Acquiring such an understanding of your topic will require that you cast a wider net for information by using more advanced references, and moving beyond a few general sources to many varied and specialized sources. See Chapter 12 to learn how to systematically find additional sources on the Internet and in the campus library that will help you develop deep knowledge of your subject.

One technique that was introduced to you earlier in *The Curious Writer*—the double-entry journal—will be more crucial now. (Check out alternatives to the double-entry journal in Chapter 12.) You must do some writing *as you research* because not only will it help you figure out what you think about the things you find, it will actually get you started on writing your draft. I know this is a tough sell. What you really want to do is simply to print out copies of Web pages, collect books and articles, and put the library photocopier to work. To imagine spending time writing about a promising article at this stage in the process, rather than simply collecting as many sources as you can, might seem like a waste of time. But consider this: By writing about important sources *as you encounter them* you're essentially beginning to write your paper. You'll be able to use some of what you write in the draft, but more important, you'll be able to use some of what *you thought,* the most important part of any research essay.

Composing the Draft

Sara was a compulsive collector of information. She researched and researched, collecting more books and articles and Web sources until the desk in her apartment looked like a miniature version of downtown Chicago—towering piles of paper and books everywhere. She never felt as if she knew enough to begin writing her essay, and would only begin drafting when forced to—the paper was due tomorrow. Neal figured he could find most of what he needed pretty quickly on the Internet. He printed out a few articles and Web pages and felt confident he could write his paper using those. He didn't feel pressured to begin writing until the due date loomed. When Neal started writing and realized that he probably wouldn't be able to get the required page length, he widened the margins.

Sara and Neal obviously use different strategies for getting to the draft. Sara relies on accumulating great quantities of information, trusting that aggressively collecting sources will make the writing easier—the main source of anxiety for her—although she probably doesn't really believe that. On the other hand, Neal suffers from overconfidence. He figures he can make do with a few sources and doesn't look around much. Both Neal and Sara do what research paper writers have done forever: wait until the last minute. Neither of these writers will be happy with the result.

It's not hard to avoid this situation if you begin the draft after you've accomplished the following:

- *You've done some writing before you start writing.* In other words, have you exploited the double-entry journal or an alternative note-taking method to both collect useful information and to explore what your reaction to what it says?

- *You are working from abundance (but not overabundance).* Neal is much more typical than Sara. He is trying to compose his draft by drawing from a nearly empty well. Almost any writing—and particularly research writing—depends on working from abundance. You need to collect more information than you can use. But not too much. Don't let endless collecting become an avoidance tactic.

- *Your focusing question has helped you* exclude *information.* A good focusing question is a guide. It will help you to see the relevance of certain portions of the sources you've collected and give you reason to ignore the rest. If you sense that this is happening consistently as you review your sources, you're probably ready to write.

- *You have a tentative idea about what you think.* By now, you know enough about your topic to have some feelings or ideas about a possible answer to the question behind your investigation. Remember the draft may make you change your mind—that's fine—but begin composing with at least a tentative point of view.

Methods of Development. The research essay is more likely than the previous essays to combine a range of methods of development. You can see that already from the professional essays earlier in this chapter. However, here are some more typical designs for research essays:

Narrative. We don't usually associate narrative structure with research papers, but, in fact, research-based writing tells stories all the time. Perhaps one of the most common techniques is use of the case study, which can be an excellent way to begin your paper. Case studies or anecdotes about people involved or affected by a topic often bring that topic to life by moving it closer to the everyday *lives* of people. But narrative is also used as the backbone of a research essay. Sometimes an essay tells the story of what the writer wanted to know and what she found out, a kind of narrative of thought. For example, Ann Braley-Smith's research essay on her toy gun-toting boys tells two stories: what she found when she researched the her topic and how that influenced her thinking about it.

Question to Answer. Since much of the research process is devoted to developing a good question to drive the inquiry, it makes sense to consider organizing your essay around what that question is, where it came from, what has already been said about it, and then reporting what you've discovered about possible answers to the question that triggered the investigation. A lot of formal academic research is organized this way, although there might be an added section about the methods the investigator chose to try to seek the answers.

Known to Unknown. This is a variation on the question-to-answer structure that might be particularly useful if you're writing about a complex topic about which much remains unknown. Your research might have led to the discovery that the question you're interested in is a question that has very speculative or limited answers. For example, Andy was writing about the use of psychiatric medicine such as antidepressants and anti-psychotics on children since his family physician had recommended them for one of his own kids. Andy quickly discovered that this was a relatively new use for such drugs and that much mystery surrounded both the diagnosis and treatment of children with emotional problems. It became clear that the purpose of his essay was not to offer a definitive answer to his question, but to suggest areas that still needed further study.

Using Evidence. While every discipline has its own ideas about what counts as good research evidence, the research essay is a less specialized form with a more general audience. Therefore, the rules of evidence for a research essay aren't nearly as strict as they might be, say, in an academic article in psychology or biology. But that's not to say that anything goes. Research writing obviously depends mainly on sources outside the writer—published materials, interviews with people involved in the topic, and observations in the field—but the writer's personal experience can count if it's relevant. In some cases, you may want to cite your own experience as evidence that either supports or contradicts a claim made by someone else, but your experience alone probably isn't sufficient evidence. Find other voices that confirm it.

Not all outside sources are equally convincing either. Figure 11.1 on page 492 suggests a hierarchy that is one way of evaluating how "authoritative" a source might be. Notice that, generally speaking, the more specialized a publication's audience, the more likely the information in it will be valued. For example, an article on dream interpretation in the *Journal of American Psychology* is considered more authoritative than an article on the same subject in *The Ladies' Home Journal*. The reasons for this are pretty obvious: When you write for experts in the field you better know what you're talking about.

Accurately acknowledging your sources is an ethical obligation that all good researchers take seriously.

Finally, an important way to write authoritatively using outside sources is not only to use the right sources but to cite them carefully. It's crucial that you acknowledge those whose ideas have helped you to see more deeply into your topic. In your draft, acknowledge your sources in two ways:

1. Mention them in your essay using attribution tags such as, *according to Jones . . .* or *Hill argues that . . .* or *Baraka said . . .*

2. Cite borrowed information, quotations, and ideas using MLA or APA conventions. (See Chapter 14, "How to Cite Using MLA" and "How to Cite Using APA".)

Workshopping the Draft

Share your research essay in a small group workshop before you begin your final revision. Because of the length of these essays you might want to allow more time for these discussions, or encourage group members to read

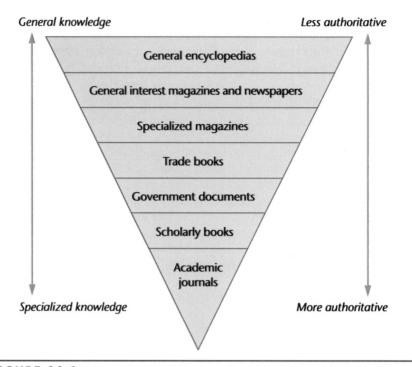

General knowledge   Less authoritative

General encyclopedias

General interest magazines and newspapers

Specialized magazines

Trade books

Government documents

Scholarly books

Academic journals

Specialized knowledge   More authoritative

FIGURE 11.1 A hierarchy of sources places the most credible at the bottom of an inverted pyramid. For academic research, these are usually articles and books that are reviewed by other experts before they're published.

the drafts before the group meets. Your instructor might also put you in smaller groups.

Reflecting on the Draft. A draft is a thing the wind blows through. That might be especially true of the full first draft of your research essay. After all, this project involved juggling a lot more than most other inquiry projects—controlling information and the ideas of a wide variety of sources, the challenge of trying to surround that outside material with your own ideas, worries about following citation conventions, and the struggle not to let the whole project get away from your own purposes and questions. Spend a little time reflecting on how all this went.

In your notebook or on a separate piece of paper you'll attach to the draft when you hand it in, answer the following questions:

- What's the most important thing you learned about your topic after the research and writing you've just completed? Is this important understanding obvious in the draft?

- Choose two paragraphs that incorporate outside sources—one that you think is written pretty well, and another less well. What differences do you notice between the two? Can you identify at least one

WRITING WITH COMPUTERS

FINDING SOURCE INFORMATION ONLINE

You should get in the habit of recording the bibliographic information for your sources as soon as you determine that they are useful and reliable (see Chapters 12 and 13). Finding this information for print sources is generally a simple process, but unfortunately this isn't the case for online sources. The online environment is a fluid one in which standardized publication formats have not yet taken hold. As a result, bibliographic information for online sources does not always appear in the same location from one site to the next. Moreover, sometimes this information appears only in partial form or not at all. The bibliographic information you should record for each online source includes:

1. **Web address or URL** (universal record locator): This information appears in the long horizontal field near the top of your browser window. Be sure you record the complete address otherwise you or others may have difficulty locating it later. For easy access, you may want to bookmark the address or save it to a folder of other online links.
2. **Title of site:** The title should appear at the top of the site's first page, and, if not there, then within the horizontal blue bar at the very top of your browser's window.
3. **Publication information:** This information includes the name of the author and/or sponsoring organization, the author's or sponsoring organization's e-mail address and/or regular mailing address, and the date of publication and/or last revision.

If you cannot find bibliographic information on the Web page where the source appears, try looking for it on the site's home page. Consult the MLA and APA documentation guidelines in Chapter 13 to learn how to accurately cite the bibliographic information.

problem you need to work on in the next draft that will help you improve the way you integrate sources?

• What was your focusing question? How does the draft attempt to answer it?

Questions for Readers. Make sure that you have some specific questions you'd like to ask your workshop group about how the draft is working. Here are some others:

1. In your own words, what do you think is the main thing I'm trying to say in the draft? Where in the draft do you think I say it?

2. What was the most interesting part of the essay? What was the least interesting? Why?

3. After you read the first few paragraphs, did you have a clear sense of what my focusing question was?

4. Did any part of the draft seem to drift away from that focus?

5. Where do I need more information or more evidence?

Revising the Draft

As you prepare to revise this draft, begin by first considering the more global features of the piece: how well you established your purpose, how successfully you limited your focus, and how clearly you made your point. Chapter 14 includes a range of exercises that will help you with each of these. As you plan for revision, do any of the following problems typical of research essay drafts apply to yours?

- Did you collect enough information? Drafts that work from scarcity typically run short, have too broad a focus, or suffer from vagueness. The solution? Go back to the library or the Web and collect more information.

- Is the essay organized around your research question from beginning to end? Are there any paragraphs or passages that strike off in irrelevant directions?

- Does the draft say too much? Remember that a strong research essay not only asks an interesting question about a topic but explicitly states what the writer thinks is the best answer, even if it's speculative. Is this thesis clear?

Refer to Chapter 14, "Revision Strategies," for ideas on how to revise your draft following your workshop. In particular, it would probably be useful to check your draft for logical fallacies, using the table on page 321. Use the following table to find other appropriate revision strategies. Remember that a draft may present problems in more than one category.

Polishing the Draft

After you've addressed the more global problems in your draft, you should focus on more local matters, things such as how effectively you integrate and cite sources, how successfully you've organized your paragraphs, and whether you've written the draft in a clear, lively style. Don't forget to use the handbook at the back of the book to help you with any grammatical and stylistic questions you might have; also use the guide to MLA or APA citations in Chapter 13 to check how well you've followed those conventions.

Before you finish your draft, make certain that you've worked through the following checklist:

❑ Every paragraph is about one thing.

GUIDE TO REVISION STRATEGIES		
PROBLEMS IN THE DRAFT (CHAPTER 14)	**PART**	**PAGE NUMBER**
Unclear purpose ■ Not sure what the paper is about?	1	633
Unclear thesis, theme, or main idea ■ Not sure what you're trying to say?	2	639
Lack of information or development ■ Need more convincing evidence? Need to check for logical fallacies?	3	646
Disorganized ■ Doesn't move logically or smoothly from paragraph to paragraph?	4	650
Unclear or awkward at the level of sentences and paragraphs ■ Does draft seem choppy or hard to follow at the level of sentences or paragraphs?	5	656

❏ The transitions between paragraphs aren't abrupt or awkward.

❏ The length of sentences varies in each paragraph.

❏ Each sentence is concise. There are no unnecessary words or phrases.

❏ You've checked grammar, particularly verb agreement, run-on sentences, unclear pronouns, and misused words (*there/their, where/were,* and so on).

❏ You've run your spell checker and proofed your paper for misspelled words.

❏ You've double-checked your citations and Works Cited or References page to ensure that the formatting is correct.

STUDENT ESSAY

Like several of the published research essays you read earlier in the chapter, Amy Garrett's essay began with a question that arose from her ordinary life. Should she be obsessive about avoiding the sun? How seriously should she take warnings from the sunscreen industry and others that she should never walk outside without slathering on the sunblock?

Through research, Garrett answers these questions in "We Need the Sun," and in the process she argues that the case for avoiding the sun is overstated. It's a controversial conclusion. Do you think the facts that Garrett gathers effectively support the claim? Does her essay raise other questions about sun tanning that she doesn't address? Finally, how well do you think that she weaves in her personal experiences and personal voice along with the factual information? What effect does it have on you as a reader?

Amy Garrett

Professor X

English 101

DATE

We Need the Sun

The other day I was pondering the still popular,
yet seemingly dangerous practice of tanning as I looked
down at my chalky white legs and thought, is the desire
to tan really that mysterious? It seems obvious that
people just like the way it looks to be tan. In fact,
one survey of American teenagers revealed that two
thirds of them feel "healthier" and "more sophisticated" with a tan (qtd. in "Sun Tanning"). I know I
feel better about putting on a bathing suit if I'm not
so starkly white that I worry about blinding young
children. I also know that it just feels good to be in
the sun. The warm rays beating down on my back and
shoulders as I work outdoors or go for a hike seem
therapeutic and natural. I'll admit I've seen the inside of a tanning booth a few times before I took a
spring break trip to California and, yes, that felt
good too. As I searched more deeply into the issue of
why people tan, it became apparent that despite the

Garrett   2

dire warnings there is a deeper, biological reason for
the undying popularity of bronzed skin. We need the
sun.

Actually, the human body is "hard-wired" to need
healthy doses of sunlight. Through our skin we process
vitamin D, which is gained almost solely from the sun's
Ultraviolet B (UVB) rays. We also need the sun to regulate our hormone levels and fend off depression. In an
article about the health benefits of vitamin D, Reinhold
Vieth explains that when "humans evolved at equatorial
latitudes, without modern clothing and shelter, their
vitamin D supply would have been equivalent to at least
100/g day" (275). He goes on to explain that today our
bodies typically harbor only half that amount of vitamin D at best, but that our current genetic make up was
selected at a point in our evolution to demand much
higher amounts (275). This is the most important key to
understanding our longing for the sun—evolutionarily
speaking, we need it.

Almost 100% of our body's necessary vitamin D intake can be gained through sun exposure (Vogel 42). How
does this work? When our skin is exposed to the sun's
UVB rays, a cholesterol compound in the skin is turned
into a catalyst for vitamin D, called vitamin D3. This

compound enters circulation and becomes vitamin D. We depend upon vitamin D for absorption of calcium, for bone strength and maintenance and for immunity to many diseases such as cancer, diabetes and multiple sclerosis (Vogel 42).

But, that's not all of the sun's health benefits. According to Vieth, "studies show that higher serum . . . and/or environmental ultraviolet exposure is associated with lower rates of breast, ovarian, prostate and colorectal cancers, [also] lymphoma, and cancer of the bladder, esophagus, kidney, lung, pancreas, rectum, stomach and corpus uteri" (279).

In a study about the relationship between light and sound, Da Vid explains the necessity of the sun's light on the body's maintenance of hormone levels. Through an almost magical process our body literally turns the sun's light into the chemical components that we need to maintain balance. The sun's light enters the body through the optic nerves and then travels through a complex series of reactions, stimulating the pineal gland, which in turn triggers the hypothalamus. These two functions alone are very important. The pineal gland produces neurohormonal agents which are light sensitive. These agents are connected directly to the

Garrett   4

pineal gland which "mediates from moment to moment all the vital processes of the body" (276). From here the hypothalamus carries the light to the pituitary gland in the form of chromophillic cells. The pituitary gland then turns these cells into hormones which maintain homeostasis (276).

This is one of the major foundations to understanding seasonal depression. We need the sun's light to be happy. Without homeostasis, or balance, we are lost and confused, a mess of delinquent hormones, depressed and unhealthy. No wonder tanning is so popular. Said simply, "Light is a beneficial and vital, biologic resource, affecting everyone medically, psychologically and environmentally" ("Light Touch" 1). Not only is sunlight good for hormone regulation, but it also influences Circadian rhythms and the body's internal clock ("Light Touch" 2).

But, instead of promoting the absorption of healthy levels of vitamin D3 and UVB rays, the health industry frightens us away from the sun. Sales of sun screen, according to Information Resources, topped $416 million in 2002, nearly a 7% increase from the year before ("Just the Facts Stats"); healthy profits apparently means screening consumers from the health benefits

Garrett   5

of exposure to sunlight. We are taught that the sun is bad, when in fact, a good relationship with the sun is very natural and healthy. We are scared. We hide indoors and watch TV or we are too caught up in the grind, we work too much and never see the light of day. When we do get out, we slather ourselves with sunscreen and block vitamin D production.

Other experts contend that we should simply stay out of the sun altogether. In an article by Alexanra Greely titled, "No Tan is a Safe Tan" she presents her case against spending time in the sun, and especially tanning, with potent statistics and facts. But, I couldn't help wonder if she ever has any fun after reading her closing lines: "In the end, there really is nothing new under the sun, except that perhaps more people are staying out of it, heeding medical warning such as Bergstresser's: 'Less sun is better. No sun is best of all'" (15).

All of this sun bashing *is* based on some well-known dangers. Some of the statistics that Greely used were frightening. She mentioned that in 1990, 600,000 people were diagnosed with basal and squamous cell carcinomas, the leading skin cancers. This was an increase of 200,000 victims in ten years (14). But right after that, she concedes that it can't be blamed directly on the sun. The problem is behavioral. "Those people with the highest light exposure appear to have a lower frequency of melanomas than those who get sunlight more episodically . . . [and] those people who have had severe sunburns at an early age are also at higher risk for melanomas" (14).

These hazards would seem to make the case for slathering on the sunblock at the very least. However, progressive health experts are beginning to question our obsessive use of sunblock (Holick 46). According to several reviews in medical journals wearing sunscreen all of the time is not healthy since our bodies need to produce vitamin D. For example, a study of veiled women in Turkey recently exposed that 82% of women in Turkey aren't exposed enough. Their vitamin D levels were severely depleted and another 8% were moderately deficient. These women all complained of poor muscle strength and weakness and their bones were very fragile at young ages, consistent with other vitamin D deficient subjects (Vogel 43).

This is key: it is healthy and beneficial to enjoy the sun on a regular basis, but getting sunburned, especially at a young age is not. Instead of telling us to be wary of sunburns, the suntan lotion industry and

Garrett   7

other experts tell us to stay completely out of the
sun, which isn't healthy either. The repercussions of
vitamin D deficiencies are numerous and very serious.

We must find that middle ground, somewhere between
getting cooked or being completely veiled. Granted,
with the depletion of the ozone and other studies about
the dangers of over-exposure to UVB rays, and the fact
that "a single 15- to 30-minute session with artificial tanning equipment exposes the body to the same
amount of harmful UV rays as a day at the beach" we
should be careful (Hayes 38). We should use good sunscreen and cover up when we are going to be in the sun
all day; we all know that by now. But we shouldn't obsess about it either. We need routine unprotected exposure to the sun; in fact, at least 15 minutes a day
will provide us with the required amount vitamin D
(Holick 47).

So, the most important lesson learned is that we
should enjoy the sun regularly, rather than sporadi-
cally, which is the only behavior that is proven to
lead to skin cancer. We should avoid sunburns and occasional, all-day sun baking and enjoy the sun's rays on
a regular basis instead. We should not fear the sun; we
should relish every minute of our sweat-drenched, sun-
worshipping because, body and soul, we need it.

Garrett   8

Works Cited

Greeley, Alexandra. "No Tan is a Safe Tan." <u>Nutrition
      Health Review: the Consumer's Medical Journal</u> 59
      (Summer 1991): 14–15.

Hayes, Jean L. "Are You Assessing For Melanoma?" <u>RN</u>
      66.2 (February 2003): 36–40.

Holick, Michael F. "Vitamin D—The Underrated
      Essential." <u>Life Extension</u> 9.4 (Apr 2003): 46–48.

Johnson, Rheta Grimsley. "The Rural South These Days Has
      More Tanning Salons Than John Deeres." <u>The Atlanta
      Journal-Constitution</u> 23 Apr 2000, home ed.:M1.

"Just the Facts Stats." <u>36 Expose</u>. 17 September 2003
      <http://www.ecrm-online.com/Expose/V6_1/36.pdf>.

McLaughlin, Patricia. "Dying For a Tan This Summer?"
      <u>St. Louis Post-Dispatch</u> 15 Jun 1995: 02.

"The Light Touch." <u>Total Health</u> 14.3 (June 1992): 43.

Vid, Da. "Sound and Light: Partners in Healing and
      Transformation." <u>Share Guide</u> 5.2 (Winter 1994):
      20–21.

Reinhold, Vieth. "Vitamin D Nutrition and its Potential
      Health Benefits for Bone, Cancer and Other
      Conditions." <u>Journal of Nutritional and
      Environmental Medicine</u> 11 (2001): 275–291.

"Sun Tanning." <u>Cool Nurse</u> 2000–2003. 18 Jun 2003
      <http://www.coolnurse.com/tanning.htm.>.

Vogel, Phillip J. "A New Light on Vitamin D." <u>Life
      Extension</u> 9.4 (Apr 2003): 40–46.

EVALUATING THE ESSAY

1. Choose a page of Garrett's research essay, and using a yellow highlighter, mark every line or passage in which she actually *does* something with information rather than simply explain or report what she found. In other words, where does she interpret, argue, analyze, assert, speculate, or evaluate? How much of the page is covered with color? Do the same thing with your own essay draft. Do you do more than report? Do you control information as well as Garrett did here?

2. Using Garrett's essay as a model, identify at least one question you have about the proper way to cite sources in a research essay.

3. What is Garrett's thesis and where in the essay does she state it? Did you find it persuasive? Why or why not?

4. Compare Garrett's essay "We Need the Sun" with the other published research essays you read in this chapter. What are the strengths and weaknesses of her approach compared to the professional models? If you were to advise Garrett on revising her essay, what would you suggest?

USING WHAT YOU HAVE LEARNED

You've been involved in writing your own research essay and reading published and student essays that use research. What have you learned about the research process and the research essay that you can apply in other writing situations?

1. Explore how your thinking about research writing might have changed by completing the following sentence at least five times in your journal: *Before I worked through this chapter I thought writing research essays involved _____, but now I think _____.*

2. For this chapter, you wrote a research essay that was relatively informal. What have you learned about research writing that you can use in situations when you're asked to write more formal research papers? How can even a formal research paper still incorporate your strong personal presence as a writer?

3. The next time you're given a research assignment in another class, what exactly will you need to know in order to prepare for the assignment? What questions will you expect your instructor to answer to help you understand what you need to do?

Imagine standing at a small threshold looking into a cavernous warehouse the size of Manhattan. Inside, you see sixty-foot shelves towering above you that are filled with disorganized boxes, books, and papers of all shapes and sizes, and extend to the vanishing point several city blocks away. Images flicker and flash; you hear the muffled sounds of a million voices. You feel very, very small. The search pages of applications such as Google are like the doors to the electronic warehouse of information that is the Internet.

Research
Techniques

METHODS OF COLLECTING

One sure sign that research is an integral part of our everyday lives is the fact that Google, the name of an Internet search engine, is now a verb. Someone can say, "I googled it" or "I googled that" and there's a good chance someone else will respond, "Oh really? What did you find?" The Internet makes research easy. It's even fun sometimes. This is a far cry from the experience many of us have had doing academic research at the library, wandering through the stacks trying to find a book that's supposed to be but isn't there, or impatiently waiting in line to commandeer the one photocopy machine on the fifth floor, wondering whether that pocketful of change will be enough to copy Chapter 10 of *The Dreaming Brain*.

But I can also remember moments as a college student—well before the Web—when I hunkered down until midnight in a study carrel in the campus library, reading my way through articles and books that opened doors on the subject I was researching. On rare occasions, I was even blinded by the light that suddenly poured in. Research is a process that, like writing, can be filled with discovery. And it should be, particularly if you've found the questions that really interest you about your subject and you don't have to spend too much time learning the technicalities of how to find what you need.

This chapter should help you know everything you need to know about finding what you need in the university library and on the Web. It is particularly useful for collecting information for research essays, but research is a source of information that can make *any* essay stronger. Every assignment in *The Curious Writer* therefore includes suggestions for research as you're searching for a topic and

What You'll Learn in This Chapter

- How librarians organize knowledge.

- How to use library and Internet sources to develop a working knowledge of your topic.

- How to craft the best search terms for the library and the Internet.

- How to use more advanced research strategies to build on your working knowledge and develop a deep knowledge of your topic.

- How to evaluate sources and make decisions about what you should use in your writing and what you should ignore.

- Methods of note taking that promote a conversation with sources.

- Techniques for developing surveys and conducting interviews.

writing your draft. Research also can be an especially useful revision strategy for any essay.

Use this chapter much as you would a toolbox—it a handy collection of
tips and research tools that you can use for any assignment. Refer to it
whenever you discover a topic that raises questions that research can help
answer, or whenever it would be helpful to hear what other people say
about the things you're thinking about.

RESEARCH IN THE ELECTRONIC AGE

It used to be that the problem was not finding enough information on a research topic. Now, according to some librarians, students are so swamped
with information that they pretty much print out the first few things they
find and rush off to write their papers. "Google has won," lament some librarians. Like any other technological advance, the wide availability of
electronic databases is a mixed blessing. On the one hand, these databases
are really wonderful. They are searchable not only from the library reference room but also from the comfort of students' own computers in their
dorms or apartments. They allow researchers to search twenty years or
more of journals and magazines in seconds, something that would take
hours and hours in the old days when bound indexes were all that was
available.

The downside of the Internet and electronic databases is that student
researchers can quickly produce such long lists of possible sources that
they simply skim off the top, going for the first few that offer full-text
versions and ignoring the rest, many of which might be better. The companies that create and sell databases to your university library are aware
of this fondness for full-text articles, so they keep adding more and
more. This isn't a bad thing, necessarily, except that there is little
thought about which sources would be most valuable to academic researchers. In fact, the more useful sources, often articles from the most
important journals in a discipline, are least likely to be served up as full-
text articles. The buffet of electronic information is heavy on high-calorie,
low-protein offerings, stuff that satisfies your immediate cravings but
leaves you hungry later.

This is especially true of the Web. About 80 percent of the Web is dominated by commercial sites. These are great if you're trying to get the best

Research is easier, faster, and, at times, more pleas-ant in the electronic age, but it does demand new electronic literacies.

price on an answering machine, but commercial sites usually
don't have much value for academic research. Even if you do weed
through the dot-com offerings after a Google search, you should-
n't feel at all confident that your search has been comprehensive.
Although Google and Metacrawler are remarkable search engines, they don't actually search the entire World Wide Web.
What they search is their *own* databases of Web pages, and while
these can be quite substantial, they're only a very small fraction

of what's out there. In fact, some experts believe that the vast majority of the Internet is invisible to conventional search engines. That doesn't mean this information, much of which is quite useful for academic research, is completely inaccessible; you just have to know how to find it.

Despite all of this, the electronic age has made research an even more integral part of our everyday lives. When my daughter Julia wanted to know more about the Lewis and Clark expedition, without prompting she headed to the study, booted up the computer, and searched the Web. As I wrote this book, I paused to find sites that featured visual ethnography, and I discovered not only interesting pictures of a Canadian native culture in the northern reaches of Ontario, but useful definitions and perspectives on photographic research, knowledge that made this book better. When Gracie, a student in my composition class, told me that she searched the PsychINFO database at the university library for her essay on bipolar disorder, I was confident that she had covered a decade of research on the topic in the best psychological journals.

Research is easier, faster, and, at times, more pleasant in the electronic age. But it does demand new *electronic literacies* that include knowledge about how to exploit the technology to find relevant information and new ways of thinking about how to evaluate and analyze what you find.

The Magic Words That Open Doors

One of the key electronic literacies is something that seems so simple you might wonder why I bring it up first: *the words you choose to search for information.* Consider that in 1850 the Harvard library, the first academic library in the nation, had only 84,200 volumes, and many of those were kept behind locked cabinets. To search these stacks, a student would plead with a librarian for a look. Today, my own university's library has more than a half million books and access to millions more through interlibrary loan. In addition, it has tens of thousands of periodicals on microfilm, and access to millions more through electronic databases. Then there's the World Wide Web; it's impossible to know its actual size, but the number of pages is certainly in the billions. All this information can make a researcher giddy, except for this: How do you find your needle in that gargantuan haystack?

In 1850, the Harvard librarian was familiar with the books in the stacks and could lead you to what you wanted. Today, librarians must trust in the language systems and codes they've created to organize knowledge; to find anything, you have to know those language systems. And while information on the Web isn't nearly as organized as it is in the library—for one thing, there isn't any librarian in charge, although there are some Internet directories that librarians maintain—the software that searches the Web also uses a language logic. Using it well means the difference between getting 1 million "hits" on a topic search, which you will never be able to read through, or getting 300 hits, many of which will be relevant to your topic.

How Librarians Organize Books

The Dewey decimal system and the Library of Congress system are the two systems for classifying books. Dewey decimal is what your hometown library uses; Library of Congress is the approach used in the university library. How much do you need to know about a system for shelving books? Not a whole lot, except that there's a logic to it you should be familiar with because it will save you time. The key thing to understand is that the letters on the spines of books actually mean something about the structure of knowledge. In the accompanying Library of Congress System table, you'll note that each letter suggests a division of human knowledge; you'll never memorize this, but it does help you to know, for instance, that when you're browsing books in the "B's" you're in the world of psychological knowledge.

LIBRARY OF CONGRESS SYSTEM

THE ORGANIZATION OF BOOKS BY THE LETTER

A General Works
B Philosophy, Pscyhology, Religion
C Auxiliary Sciences of History
D History: General and Old World
E History: United States
F History: Local United States and America
G Geography, Anthropology, Recreation
H Social Sciences
J Political Sciences
K Law

L Education
M Music
N Fine Arts
P Language and Literature
Q Science
R Medicine
S Agriculture
T Technology
U Military Science
V Naval Science
Z Library Science and Reference

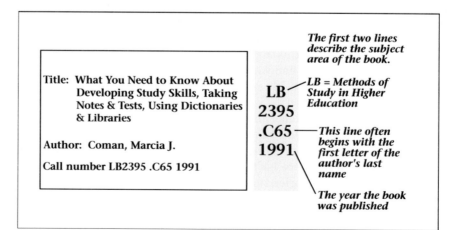

Title: What You Need to Know About Developing Study Skills, Taking Notes & Tests, Using Dictionaries & Libraries

Author: Coman, Marcia J.

Call number LB2395 .C65 1991

LB
2395
.C65
1991

The first two lines describe the subject area of the book.

LB = Methods of Study in Higher Education

This line often begins with the first letter of the author's last name

The year the book was published

Figure 12.1   **The library call card.**

These letters, used in combination with other letters and numbers, make up the call numbers that will help you locate a book in the library. For instance, suppose you're looking for a book about study habits, and your library's book search tool lists a book called *What You Need to Know about Developing Study Skills, Taking Notes and Tests, Using Dictionaries and Libraries* (see Figure 12.1). The call number is LB2395.C65 1991. What may seem like just a bunch of letters and numbers actually gives a lot of information about the book, including the body of knowledge from which it came, when it was published, and the first letter of the author's last name.

But what you want to do is find it. Your library will place books on specific floors or areas of your library according to the first one or two call letters. There should be an index of these locations on the wall. Once you've generally located the book using the letters on the first line (e.g., LB), the second line (e.g., 2395) tells you where it is in relation to the books next to it (see Figures 12.2 and 12.3).

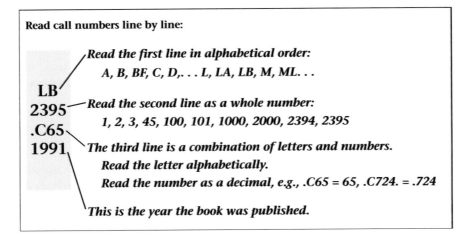

FIGURE 12.2   **How to read call numbers.**

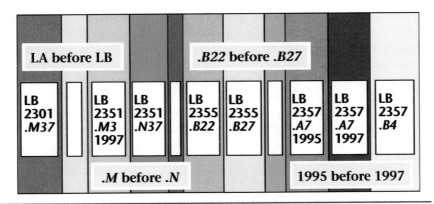

FIGURE 12.3   **How books are arranged on the library shelf.**

Library of Congress Subject Headings

The *Library of Congress Subject Headings* (LCSH) conveniently lists the words that librarians used to index information. This underappreciated and much ignored multivolume book is the key to efficiently finding what you're looking for when using electronic indexes. It holds the magic words to successful searches. For example, if you are writing about the history of arm wrestling you could simply type in *arm wrestling, history* as a subject search in your library's online search form. You might come up with something, but if you turned up nothing, might you give up on the topic? The *LCSH* can help out because it suggests a broader term (BT) for *arm wrestling, history* that might produce some results: *sports records.* Would that have occurred to you on your own? Here's another example: My student Gracie's topic is bipolar disorder. Without checking the *LCHS,* she would quite naturally use *bipolar disorder* to search for books and articles on the subject, and no doubt she'd find some material. But if she checked the *LCSH* under bipolar disorder, Gracie would discover that the term preferred by librarians is *manic-depressive illness.* Searching with that term will open a up many more doors for her.

The *LCHS* will not only help you find books. Many of the companies that develop databases of articles use Library of Congress terms, too. Equally important, however, for searching these periodical databases is something called "Boolean operators."

Google Your Boole

George Boole is the eighteenth-century mathematician who came up with the system for using the words AND, OR, and NOT to help researchers design logical queries. Boole's professional legacy is something every modern college researcher should know. Consider Paul's situation. His grandmother suffers from Alzheimer's disease, and his initial research question was *What are the best therapies for treating Alzheimer's?* When Paul consulted PsychINFO, a popular database of citations from journals relating to psychology, his instinct was simply to enter the word *Alzheimer's* in the online search form. The result was 13,392 citations, and only a portion of these were relevant. But when Paul put the word AND between two key terms from his research question—*Alzheimer's AND therapy*—he managed to reduce his results to 1,955 more relevant citations (see Figure 12.4). As he was looking over his results, Paul became interested specifically in music therapies. His next search was even more focused when he typed in the words *Alzheimer's AND therapy AND music.* That produced seventy-four citations, and nearly all of these seemed promising (see Figure 12.5).

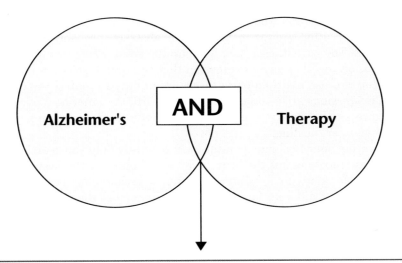

FIGURE 12.4 This query searches all documents that contain *both* words in the abstract or title. PsychINFO returned a list of 1,955 citations for *Alzheimer's AND therapy*.

The Boolean operator AND helped Paul search the PyschINFO database much more efficiently because it asked the computer to look for documents that had all three words in the title or abstract. What would happen if Paul left the AND operators out and simply searched using the three terms *Alzheimer's music therapy?* The result would have been 184,532 documents because the search software would assume that keywords with no operators in between them imply the Boolean operator OR. In other words, *Alzheimer's music therapy* is interpreted as *Alzheimer's OR music OR therapy* (see Figure 12.6). That means it would return citations for documents that had only one of the three words in their titles or abstracts. For a database of psychology publications, that's a lot of documents.

The only other Boolean operator you should know is the word NOT. This simply tells the search software to exclude documents that include a particular keyword. For example, if you were interested in finding information about environmental organizations in Washington State rather than Washington D.C., you might construct a query like this: *environmental AND organizations AND Washington NOT D.C.*

The real art of designing queries using the Boolean system is combining the operators to refine your search. For example, let's take the last search on environmental groups in Washington State. Suppose the previous query didn't produce enough results. Let's broaden it a bit: *(environmental OR conservation) AND organizations AND Washington*

NOT D.C. This search would find documents that use either environmental or conservation groups in the title or abstract, probably returning a longer list. The parentheses simply group the keywords *environmental OR conservation* together as an expression that the search software evaluates first. You can use multiple parentheses in a query to control the order in which expressions are evaluated, beginning with the innermost parenthetical expressions. Librarians call the use of parenthesis to group keywords in this manner "nesting."

Knowing your Boolean operators will certainly help you search library databases since most of the search software relies on the system. Some Web search engines do, too. But more often, search engines such as Google use a somewhat different language that accomplishes the same thing. The accompanying table shows both Boolean and typical Web search engine search terms.

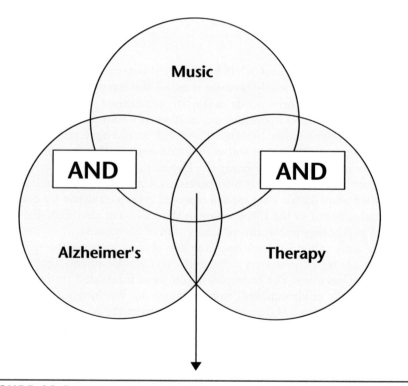

FIGURE 12.5 This focused query finds documents that include all the keywords. It generated a list of 74 citations, many of which were relevant and useful for *Alzheimer's AND therapy AND music.*

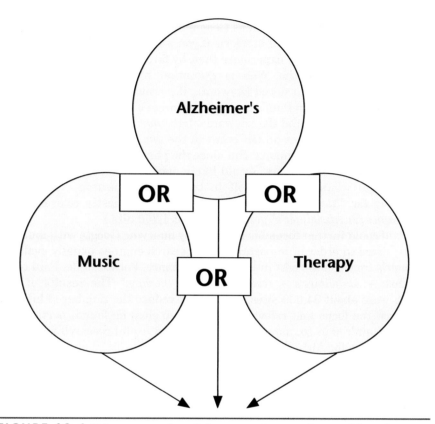

FIGURE 12.6 This query searches all documents that contain *any of* these three words in the abstract or title. PsychINFO returned an overwhelming list of 184,532 citations for *Alzheimer's music therapy.*

	SEARCH TERMS: BOOLEAN AND THEIR EQUIVALENTS IN MOST WEB SEARCH ENGINES		
BOOLEAN	**EXAMPLE**	**WEB SEARCH ENGINES**	**EXAMPLE**
OR	*Romeo OR Juliet*	Omit connectors between keywords	*Hansel Gretel*
AND	*Romeo AND Juliet*	Plus sign in front of keyword	*Hansel + Gretel*
NOT	*Romeo NOT Juliet*	Minus sign in front of keyword	*Hansel − Gretel*
( )	*(Romeo and Juliet)*	No equivalent	
No equivalent		Quotation marks around exact phrase	*"Hansel and Gretel"*

Today, search engines such as Google have an advanced search option that allows you to simply fill in a form if you want to search for certain keywords or phrases. It's my experience that, by far, the most useful syntax to use when searching the Web is quotation marks—an exact phrase search—and carefully ordered keywords, if possible more than three. For example, let's return to Paul's topic of Alzheimer's therapy. If he searched the Web using Google and the keywords *Alzheimer's therapy,* a syntax that you know by now implies an OR between the two words, Google would return about 274,000 documents. But since the phrase "Alzheimer's therapy" or "therapies for Alzheimers" would likely appear in many relevant documents, Paul would be better off to try a phrase search. The result? Searching for *"Alzheimer's therapy"* produced 444 mostly relevant sites (*"Therapies for Alzheimer's"* generated about 1,750 hits.)

Paul could further focus his research by querying Google with multiple terms, listed in order of importance since search engines usually evaluate keywords from left to right in level of importance. For example, Paul could try this: + *Alzheimer's* + *research "music therapy."* The results of this search were about 34,000 sites. Paul didn't reduce the number of hits but increased the focus and relevance of the Web sites he found, particularly the first hundred or so, many of which included useful research studies on music therapy for Alzheimer's patients.

There is much more to know about composing queries, but you now know enough to make a significant difference in the effectiveness of your searches.

DEVELOPING WORKING KNOWLEDGE

Before you actually start researching a topic, it's unlikely that you could talk about it for one minute without stopping or repeating yourself. But when you can, according to librarian William Badke, you have a "working knowledge" of your topic. Depending on the nature of your project, a working knowledge may be quite enough. For example, suppose you're writing a personal essay about being the target of relational aggression, or to put it less technically, being victimized by a group of girls who express their aggression in often subtle ways. Because of the genre—the personal essay—and your purpose in writing about the topic—say, to come to a clearer understanding why a best friend turned against you—you probably don't need to know a great deal about research done in this field. It would probably be enough to understand the basic theory of relational aggression, a few people who have interesting things to say about it, and perhaps something about how other victims handled their feelings.

You might go beyond a working knowledge of your topic and develop a "deep knowledge," the kind often required if you're writing a research essay (deep knowledge is discussed later in this chapter). But if you don't know much about your topic you will always develop a working knowledge first. It's the foundation for further research.

The material that follows will help you develop a working knowledge of a topic using the university library and the Internet. In addition to helping you know enough to talk for a minute without repeating yourself, a working knowledge of a topic helps you to understand:

1. How your topic fits into the *context* of other subjects. Where does it fall relative to larger and smaller categories of relevant knowledge? This is really helpful to know because it can assist you in narrowing your topic.

2. Some of the areas of controversy, debate, questions, or unresolved problems that ripple though the ongoing published conversations about your topic. What, generally, are the people who know something about your topic talking about?

Searching Key Library References

Your first inclination when starting research is probably to boot up your computer and do a Web search on your topic. You should resist this temptation, however; laying some groundwork in the library at the start will save you time later. Begin in the reference room of your university library. As a first step, before you actually begin researching your topic, describe it briefly in a phrase or a sentence, or write out your tentative research question in your journal. It helps enormously to know from the start, if possible, that your topic covers a smaller part of the entire landscape. There's a big difference between wanting to know about *college athletics* versus *college football recruiting practices.*

A good next step is to consult the *Library of Congress Subject Headings.* These several fat volumes are often set out on a table or shelved near the reference desk. Ask a librarian where it is. Since you're probably not familiar with the *LCSH,* you may have to skim the introduction in the

---

Steps for Developing Working Knowledge

1. Frame a research question or identify your topic as narrowly as you can.
2. Find appropriate search terms in the *Library of Congress Subject Headings.*
3. Check general and specialized encyclopedias.
4. Consult the *Guide to Reference Books* for other references.
5. Do a subject search and a keyword search on the World Wide Web.

front of the book. But basically, try to look up your topic in the book's alphabetically arranged index. Under each heading, there are often lists of subheadings. These may suggest broader terms (BT) or narrower terms (NT) (see Figure 12.7 for an example). You might also notice the abbreviations "UF" and "USE." UF means "used for," or less suitable terms for the topic; USE is the standard Library of Congress wording and the one you should use in your library searches. Write down any headings that the *LCSH* suggests for your topic. There may be more than one.

We all grew up with encyclopedias, and while they are pretty useful for that eighth-grade paper on China, general encyclopedias such as *Encyclopaedia Britannica* are less useful as major sources for a college paper. Yet encyclopedias are a good thing to check when developing a working knowledge of your topic. There are, of course, computer-based encyclopedias such as *Encarta,* but these don't hold a candle to the venerable bound version of *Encyclopaedia Britannica,* also in your reference room.

Begin by looking for your topic in a Britannica's Macropaedia, a kind of index and abstract of subjects that may point you to longer treatments in the Micropaedia. Sometimes you will also find information about your topic *within* articles about other subjects.

Alternatively, see if you can find a specialized encyclopedia in your topic's subject area. These are more focused, obviously, and often have a wealth of information on a topic that's lacking in the more general encyclopedia. Ask the reference librarian whether your library has a specialized encyclopedia in your subject area. A list of some of the more common of these can be found in the accompanying table.

SOME COMMON SPECIALIZED ENCYCLOPEDIAS

Humanities
Encyclopedia of World Art
Encyclopedia of Religions
Encyclopedia of Philosophy
Encyclopedia of African-American Culture and History
Encyclopedia of Social History

Social Sciences
Encyclopedia of Marriage and Family
Encyclopedia of Psychology
The Blackwell Encyclopedia of Social Psychology
Encyclopedia of Educational Research
Encyclopedia of Sociology
Encyclopedia of Social Work
Encyclopedia of World Cultures
Encyclopedia of Democracy
Guide to American Law: Everyone's Legal Encyclopedia
Worldmark Encyclopedia of the Nations

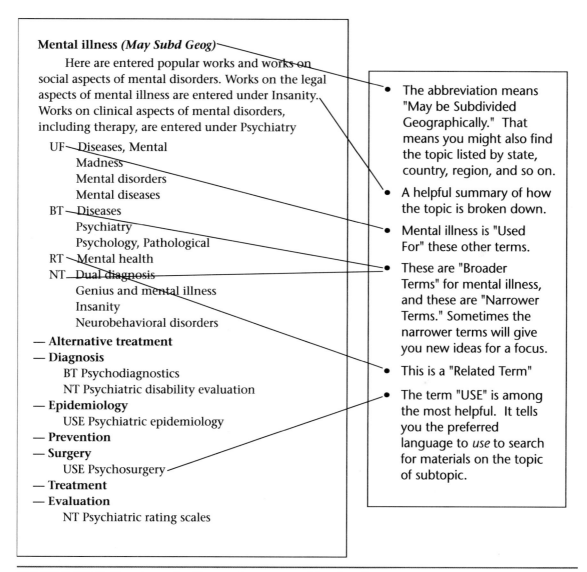

Mental illness *(May Subd Geog)*

Here are entered popular works and works on social aspects of mental disorders. Works on the legal aspects of mental illness are entered under Insanity. Works on clinical aspects of mental disorders, including therapy, are entered under Psychiatry

UF—Diseases, Mental

Madness

Mental disorders

Mental diseases

BT—Diseases

Psychiatry

Psychology, Pathological

RT—Mental health

NT—Dual diagnosis

Genius and mental illness

Insanity

Neurobehavioral disorders

— **Alternative treatment**

— **Diagnosis**

BT Psychodiagnostics

NT Psychiatric disability evaluation

— **Epidemiology**

USE Psychiatric epidemiology

— **Prevention**

— **Surgery**

USE Psychosurgery

— **Treatment**

— **Evaluation**

NT Psychiatric rating scales

- The abbreviation means "May be Subdivided Geographically." That means you might also find the topic listed by state, country, region, and so on.

- A helpful summary of how the topic is broken down.

- Mental illness is "Used For" these other terms.

- These are "Broader Terms" for mental illness, and these are "Narrower Terms." Sometimes the narrower terms will give you new ideas for a focus.

- This is a "Related Term"

- The term "USE" is among the most helpful. It tells you the preferred language to *use* to search for materials on the topic of subtopic.

FIGURE 12.7 How to read a library of congress subject heading entry. At first glance, the *Library of Congress Subject Headings* (*LCSH*) looks like a secret code, one reason that such a valuable research tool initially puts off some student researchers. But using the terms suggested by the *LCSH* can make your research more efficient, particularly when looking for library books or searching databases. Look at the example here. If you are looking for information on bipolar disorder, you might first look in the *LCHS* under "mental disorders," but because the preferred term is "mental illness," the book refers you to this page. What does it tell you? A lot.

Science
Encyclopedia of the Environment
Concise Encyclopedia of Biology
Encyclopedia of Bioethics
Encyclopedia of Science and Technology
Macmillan Encyclopedias of Chemistry and Physics
Food and Nutrition Encyclopedia

Sports
The Baseball Encyclopedia
Encyclopedia of Women and Sports
Encyclopedia of World Sport
Encyclopedia of Sports Medicine and Science

When you find interesting or relevant information in an encyclopedia, jot down the encyclopedia where you found it and record the information by summarizing it, paraphrasing it, or quoting it directly (see "Inquiring into the Details: Methods of Recording Information"). You may find using the double-entry journal method here particularly useful for coming up with ideas and questions you will want to explore in your essay. Summarize, paraphrase, and quote information in the left page of your journal and then fastwrite some of your thoughts in response to that information in the right page. Use questions to direct your fastwriting: *What strikes you most about this information? What do you find interesting? How does the information challenge your initial assumptions about your topic?*

As a final step in the library, consult the *Guide to Reference Books.* This is another one of those incredibly useful and woefully underused reference books that can lead you to a mother lode of sources. The *Guide* includes more than 16,000 indexes, bibliographies, special encyclopedias, almanacs, and other references in several thousand general topic areas. It's organized by field of study (Humanities, Social and Behavioral Sciences, History, Science and Technology, and so forth), but probably the best place to begin is with the index at the back. Try to locate your topic directly, or find some larger subject category that seems relevant. The "General Works" section in each subject category is a great place to begin if the index at the back fails you.

INQUIRING INTO THE DETAILS

METHODS OF RECORDING INFORMATION

The default mode for many student researchers is to simply quote information from a book, article, or Web page, writing down excerpts word for word. Jotting down quotations is fine. But it's often far more useful to summarize and paraphrase a source in your own words. Here's a brief description of each method.

1. **Summary.** One of the more useful ways of taking notes because it challenges you to condense, in your own words, a longer text, capturing key concepts or claims.

2. **Paraphrase.** This also tests your understanding of what you read, prompting you to translate a passage from a source into your own words; your paraphrase will be roughly the same length as the original.

3. **Quotation.** A perennial favorite approach to note taking because it's mere transcription, ranging from a few key words to several paragraphs. Remember to always transcribe the words of the original source exactly.

4. **"Paraquote."** One of the most useful methods of note taking is to cast part of an original passage in your own words, and then integrate a key term or phrase in quotations. For example: *Ballenger claims that the "paraquote," a combination of paraphrase and quotation in a single sentence, is "one of the most useful methods of note taking."*

Write down the name and publication information about any reference sources listed in the *Guide* that seem promising on your topic; find out if your library has it, and if it's an encyclopedia, almanac, or some other general reference source, do some reading on your topic. Again, consider using the double-entry journal method to get the most out of the information.

Conducting Subject Surveys on the Web

One of the genuinely useful qualities of the World Wide Web is how much it offers researchers who want to quickly develop a working knowledge of their topics. The Web is probably where you wanted to start your research rather than in your library's reference room, but if the campus library reflects reference librarians' passion for order and logic in a chaotic universe, the Web is more like the mind of my nine-year-old daughter Julia. She has lots of passions, but one look at her bedroom and it's clear that order isn't one of them. She does try from time to time, as the bins in her closet show: the contents of each bin roughly corresponds to an area of interest, but the stuff is often mixed up and I'm not surprised when she can't find what she's looking for.

Librarians and scholars have tried to bring some order to the similar chaos of the Internet, perhaps with more success. They've introduced plastic bins, too, and these are subject directories such as the "Virtual Library," or the "Internet Public Library." Unfortunately, these sites are often ignored by student researchers who opt instead to begin with a Google search, an effort that will produce some useable results that will be scattered among much less reliable documents. Consulting the subject directories may not generate as much information, but what you find will be better quality for academic research.

A good way to start your research on the Web is to visit one or more of the following subject directories:

- **The Argus Clearinghouse** (www.clearinghouse.net)
- **Infomine** (infomine.ucr.edu)
- **The Librarians Index to the Internet** (lii.org)
- **Best Information on the Net** (library.sau.edu/bestinfo/Default.htm)
- **The Internet Public Library** (www.ipl.org)
- **Virtual Library** (vlib.org)

The way to use the directories is to work from the general to the specific, beginning with broad subject categories relevant to your topic and then mouse-clicking your way down to narrower categories until you find a good match with your topic. If one directory yields little, try another.

Print out copies of any useful documents you find, and consider composing one- or two-paragraph summaries, or *annotations,* for each of the sources you find. *What are the key ideas? What seems most important and relevant to your project?* If your instructor requires you to develop a working bibliography or annotated bibliography on your topic, this might be the beginning of it (see "Inquiring into the Details: The Working Bibliography").

Finish your Web research by using so-called metasearch engines. This is software that deploys multiple search engines in the service of a single search. For example, when you type your keywords into Metacrawler it simultaneously searches using Inktomi, Ask Jeeves, Looksmart, Overture, and several other individual search engines. If this sounds too good to be true, it is; metasearch engines tend to skim off the top of the results for each individual search engine, so you often get a breadth of results but not depth. Still, metasearches are worth doing because they help extend your coverage of the Web.

Use one or more of the following metasearch engines to search on your topic:

- **Metacrawler** (www.metacrawler.com)
- **Dogpile** (www.dogpile.com)
- **Mamma** (www.mamma.com)
- **Search.com** (www.search.com)
- **Profusion** (www.profusion.com)

Remember to play around with the number and order of keywords to get the best results. Several of these sites also provide subject searches. You might try one of those as well.

Add promising sites or documents to your working bibliography, writing summaries or annotations for each individual source. Be sure to list the bibliographic information on each source following the appropriate documentation style (see Chapter 13 for MLA and APA guidelines).

INQUIRING INTO THE DETAILS

THE WORKING BIBLIOGRAPHY

A working bibliography lists sources you've collected that you think will be helpful when you draft your essay. These may include annotations, or brief summaries of what the source says that you find relevant to your research question. Consider the examples below:

Topic: Relational Aggression

Print Sources

Simmons, Rachel. *Odd Girl Out: The Hidden Culture of Aggression in Girls*. New York: Harcourt, 2002.

Simmons argues that the "secret world of girls' aggression"—the backstabbing, the silent treatment, the bartering of friendship for compliance to a group's "rules"—can be just as bad as the less subtle aggression of boys. Her basic thesis is that girls in American culture are supposed to be "nice," and therefore have no outlet for their anger except for exploiting the one thing they do covet: relationships. Because my essay focuses on the popularity phenomenon in high school—How does it affect girls when they are adults?—Simmon's chapter on parents of these girls seems particularly useful since it shows how the parents' responses are often shaped by their own experiences in school.

Web Sources

"What is Relational Aggression?" *The Ophelia Project*. 22 Sept. 2003 <http://www.opheliaproject.org/issues/issues_RA.shtml>.

The page defines relational aggression by contrasting it with physical aggression. It argues that most research, naturally, has focused on the latter because of need to limit physical injury between children. But girls tend to avoid physical aggression and instead indulge in actions that harm others by disrupting their social relationships, like giving someone the silent treatment. The *Ophelia Project* is a nonprofit group created in 1997 by parents who wanted to address the problem.

A working knowledge may be all you need, depending on your project. With a working knowledge, you know enough to search with more efficiency and read with more understanding should you want or need to learn more. If you are writing a research paper you will need to develop deep knowledge about your topic, discussed later in the chapter. But first, consider this: How do you determine which sources you can trust, and which will be most persuasive for your readers? The next sections should help you decide.

EVALUATING LIBRARY SOURCES

One of the huge advantages of finding what you need at the campus library is that nearly everything there was chosen by librarians whose job it is to make good information available to academic researchers. Now that many of the university library's databases are available online, including full-text articles, there really is no excuse for deciding to exclusively use Web pages you downloaded from the Internet for your essays. But even in the campus library, some sources are more authoritative than others. The "Pyramid of Library Sources" (see Figure 12.8) gives you a general idea of the hierarchy of authority for most library sources.

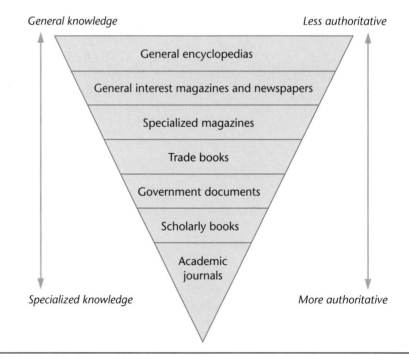

FIGURE 12.8 **Pyramid of library sources.**

In general, the more specialized the audience for a publication, the more authoritatively scholars view the publication's content. Academic journals are at the bottom of this inverted pyramid because they represent the latest thinking and knowledge in a discipline, and most of the articles are reviewed by specialists in the field before they are published. At the top of the inverted pyramid are general encyclopedias and general interest magazines such as *Newsweek* and *Time*. These have broader audiences and feature articles that are written by nonspecialists. They are rarely peer reviewed. As a rule, then, the lower you draw from this inverted pyramid, the more authoritative the sources from an academic point of view. Here are some other guidelines to consider:

- *Choose more recent sources over older ones.* This is particularly good advice, obviously, if your subject is topical; the social and natural sciences also put much more emphasis on the currency of sources than humanities disciplines.

- *Look for often-cited authors.* Once you've developed a working knowledge of your topic, you'll start noticing that certain authors seem to be mentioned or cited fairly frequently. These are likely to be the most listened- to authors, and may be considered the most authoritative on your topic.

- *If possible, use primary sources over secondary sources.* In literary research, primary sources are the original words of writers—their speeches, stories, novels, poems, memoirs, letters, interviews, and eyewitness accounts. Secondary sources would be articles that discuss those works. Primary sources in other fields might be original studies or experiments, firsthand newspaper accounts, marketing information, and so on.

EVALUATING WEB SOURCES

One of the more amusing sites on the Web is titled "Feline Reactions to Bearded Men." At first glance, the site appears to be a serious academic study of the physiological responses of cats—heartbeat, respiration, and pupil dilation—to a series of photographs of men with beards. The researchers are listed with their affiliations with respected universities. The article includes an abstract, methodology, and results section, as well as a lengthy list of works cited.

The conclusions seem genuine and include the following:

1. Cats do not like men with long beards, especially long dark beards.

2. Cats are indifferent to men with shorter beards.

3. Cats are confused and/or disturbed by men with beards that are incomplete and to a lesser degree by men whose beards have missing parts.

A cat reacts to a picture of a bearded man from the study Feline Reactions to Bearded Men.

The study is a hoax, a fact that is pretty obvious to anyone who critically examines it. For one thing, it was "published" in the *Annals of Improbable Research,* but I can usually fool about a third of my class with the site for five to ten minutes as I discuss the conventions of academic research, some of which are accurately reproduced in the "study."

Everyone knows to be skeptical of what's on the Web. But this is even more crucial when using Web sources for college writing. Since it's dominated by commercial sites, much of the World Wide Web has limited usefulness to the academic researcher, and while very few online authors are out to fool researchers with fake scholarship, many have a persuasive purpose. Despite its "educational" mission, for example, the purpose of the Web site *ConsumerFreedom.com* is to promote industry views on laws relating to food and beverages. That doesn't make the information it offers useless, but a careful researcher would be wary of the site's claims and critical of its studies. At the very least, the information on *Consumer-Freedom.com* should be attributed as a pro-industry view.

Imagine as you're researching on the Web that you've been dropped off at night in an unfamiliar neighborhood. You're alert. You're vigilant. And you're careful about who you ask for directions. You can also be systematic about how you approach evaluating online sources. In general, follow these principles:

- *Favor governmental and educational sources over commercial ones.* These are sites that are more likely to have unbiased information. How can you tell which are institutional sites when it's not obvious? Sometimes the domain name—the abbreviation *edu, org,* or *gov* at the end of an Internet address—provides a strong clue, as does the absence of ads on the site.

- *Favor authored documents over those without authors.* There's a simple reason for this: You can check the credentials of authors if you know who they are. Sometimes they provide an e-mail link so you can write authors, or you can do a search on the Internet or in the library for other materials they've published.

- *Favor documents that are also available in print over those only available online.* Material that is published in both forms generally undergoes more scrutiny. An obvious example would be newspaper articles, but also some articles from journals and magazines are available electronically and in print.

- *Favor Web sources that document their claims over those that don't.* This familiar academic convention is strong evidence that the claims an online author is making are supported and verifiable.

- *Favor Web pages that were recently updated over those that haven't changed in a year or more.* Frequently at the bottom of a Web page there is a line indicating when the information was posted to the Internet and/or when it was last updated. Look for it.

For a more systematic approach to evaluating Web sources, follow the steps in Figure 12.9 on page 528. This method begins by dividing Web documents into two broad categories: those with authors and those without authors. Web sites that list authors for documents are generally more trustworthy because you can evaluate who the authors are and whether they have appropriate expertise or a particular bias. But a great many Web documents have no stated authors, forcing you to resort to other ways of evaluating them.

The term "peer reviewed" means that an article was evaluated by other experts in the field and was published because it passed muster. Many of the articles in academic journals are peer reviewed, but very few Web documents undergo that kind of scrutiny; if they were, they usually tell you so.

By far, the most common method of analyzing the value of what you find on the Web is simply considering the source: Is it a commercial or an academic institution? Is it a lone ranger with no affiliations or government group? Are there ads on the page (which suggests a commercial site) or none (which suggests a noncommercial organization)?

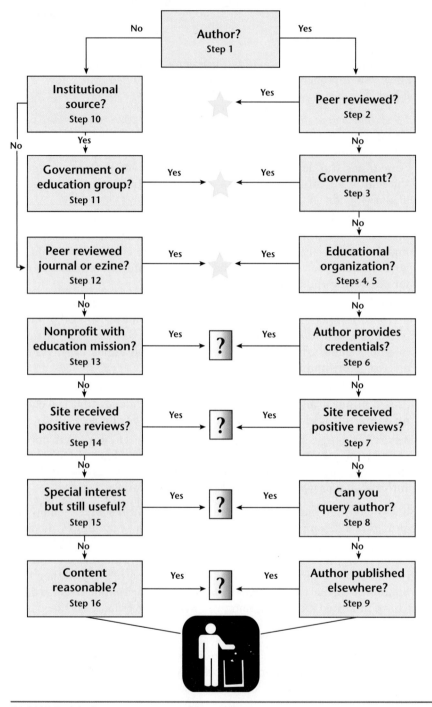

FIGURE 12.9 Steps for evaluating web sources. Begin by trying to find an author of a Web document, and then follow one of the two columns. If subsequent answers to the questions that follow lead you to a star, then you've probably found a credible source. A question mark suggests one that *may* be useful, depending. If you end up at the trash can at the bottom, well, the implication is clear.

DEVELOPING DEEP KNOWLEDGE

If working knowledge equips you to sustain a one-minute monologue on your topic, then deep knowledge is enough for you to make a fifteen- to twenty-minute presentation to your class. You'll probably be able to answer all of your classmates' questions, too.

On acquiring deep knowledge on your topic, you won't become an expert but you should know enough to:

1. Be familiar with some of the *key people* who have participated actively in the professional conversation about your topic.

2. Put your research question in the context of what *has already been said* about your topic.

3. Recognize quickly whether any information you find on your topic is relevant to your project. If it is relevant information, you'll know whether it *supports or develops* a claim you are making or an idea you are exploring, or *challenges or complicates* what you've been thinking about your topic.

Finding Books

The first step in developing deep knowledge in your topic is locating relevant books in your campus library. Here's where your effort to find productive search terms in the *Library of Congress Subject Headings* will really pay off. During your earlier consultation of the *LCSH,* you created a list of suitable subject headings on your topic. Use that list now to search the online book index in your university library. You can probably access this index on any Internet-enabled campus computer or from your home computer. Try several subject headings until you generate promising results.

Next, find two or three books on your subject in your school's library—making note of any other books that look promising—and jot down com-

---

Steps for Developing Deep Knowledge

1. Find relevant books on your topic.
2. Find relevant articles in periodicals on your topic.
3. Find relevant newspaper articles on your topic.
4. Find relevant sources on the Web.
5. Synthesize source information and your own ideas using techniques such as the double-entry journal or research log.

plete bibliographic information, a summary of the book's basic argument or approach, and why it seems relevant to your research question (see "Inquiring into the Details: How to Annotate a Book"). Use this information to start a working bibliography on your topic if you haven't done so already. If you managed to find a particularly good book on your topic, don't forget to check the book's bibliography, if it has one, for more relevant books and articles.

⌕ INQUIRING INTO THE DETAILS

HOW TO ANNOTATE A BOOK

The brevity of an article and most Web pages make them much easier to annotate than a book. You can usually summarize the argument or relevant ideas of such sources fairly easily. But how do you do that with a book that may have hundreds of pages of information and an extended argument? Read strategically.

1. To summarize a book's approach or basic argument, skim the preface and introduction. Sometimes there's a concluding chapter that neatly summarizes things, too. Even the back cover or jacket flap can be helpful for this overview.

2. To explain the relevance of the book to your research question or topic, you may focus on a particular chapter or chapters. Again, at this point you can probably skim the text quickly to discover its relevance. Later, you may do a more careful reading.

3. Evaluate the *part* of the author's treatment of your topic rather than the whole book. Search the table of contents for what you suspect are the most relevant chapters, and focus your reading on those.

Finding Periodicals

Your campus library contains at least three kinds of periodicals: general interest magazines such as *Time, Harper's,* or *People;* special interest magazines such as *PC World, Outside,* and *Sports Illustrated;* and scholarly journals such as *Journal of Mass Communication* or *American Sociologist.* Depending on your topic, you may end up using all three types of periodicals; remember, though, that the scholarly ones are considered more authoritative for college research.

These days, searching for periodicals is easier than ever. Your university library likely has a Web page that includes a long list of databases that index periodicals by discipline (for example, PyschINFO) or that cover periodicals in a range of subjects (for example, Reader's Guide Abstracts or Proquest Direct).

Find your library's Web site that lists databases for periodicals and choose a subject-specific database relevant to your topic or a general subject database. In fact, consider checking both. Again, your knowledge of Boolean logic and your familiarity with search terms suggested by the *Library of Congress Subject Headings* will give you a head start when using the search forms for each database.

As you did before with the books you found, add promising articles to your working bibliography, jotting down the bibliographic information on each article (see Chapter 13 for MLA and APA guidelines) and annotating each entry with a brief paragraph describing the article.

Finding Newspapers

Newspaper databases are also available online at your university library. The most common of these include the National Newspaper Index, Newspaper Source, and Proquest National Newspapers. Most such databases index major newspapers such as *The New York Times, The Wall Street Journal,* and *The Washington Post,* but you might find a database for the local or state paper as well.

Search for newspaper articles on your topic. This will be a particularly important search if you're interested in a current topic, something that has drawn the attention of daily news reporters or columnists. Some of the databases will provide you will full-text articles online, but more often you'll need to find the article on microfilm in the reference room of your university library. As before, add noteworthy newspaper articles to your working bibliography, citing bibliographic information and annotating each article.

Finding Sources on the Web

Build on the working knowledge of your topic that you developed during your preliminary search on the Web. You can maximize your coverage of the Web using various individual search engines. But why bother when a single popular search engine such as Google, has such an enormous database? The extra effort is worthwhile because the overlap between individual search engines actually is quite small, particularly if your topic is uncommon.

Search the Web using at least two or three of the following popular search engines:

- **Google** (www.google.com)

- MSN Search (search.msn.com)
- AltaVista (www.altavista.com)
- Yahoo! (www.yahoo.com)
- Hotbot (www.hotbot.com)
- Search.com (www.search.com)
- AllTheWeb.com (www.alltheweb.com)
- Ask Jeeves (www.askjeeves.com)

Remember that, whenever possible, you should use three or more words in a keyword search, listing the most important term first. Phrases, usually enclosed in quotation marks, can be especially helpful in generating useful results.

The so-called Invisible Web is the vast virtual warehouse of databases and documents that are unreachable by conventional search engines. Since general search engines such as Google or Yahoo! rely on finding Web pages that already have links pointing to them from other sites, "disconnected" pages are largely ignored.[1] These often include PDF files, image and audio files, and databases with their own search forms. How do you gain access to this warehouse of less accessible material? One way is to use specialized search engines that are designed to scour the Invisible Web, including the following:

- Invisible Web Search Engine of Search Engines (www.invisibleweb.com)
- CompletePlanet (www.completeplanet.com)
- Invisible-web.net (invisible-web.net)
- Direct Search (www.freepint.com/gary/direct.htm)
- Librarians Index to the Internet (lii.org)
- Search Adobe PDF (searchpdf.adobe.com/)

Again, whether you find them using standard or specialized search engines, write down citations and brief annotations for any useful sources you discover.

Writing in the Middle: Synthesizing Source Information and Your Own Ideas

It's not news that there is an epidemic of plagiarism and it's not just a problem on the college campus. Recently, several well-known historians admitted to being a bit sloppy about giving their sources proper credit. Naturally, a lot of people assume that the problem of plagiarism has to do

---

[1]Much of my understanding of the Invisible Web comes from Chris Sherman and Gary Price, *The Invisible Web: Discovering Information Sources Search Engines Can't See* (Medford, NJ: Cyberage, 2001).

WRITING WITH COMPUTERS

PLAGIARISM AND THE INTERNET

Plagiarism is the taking of someone else's words, ideas, or information without acknowledging its source. Plagiarism is an academic crime that can have serious consequences for its perpetrators. Unfortunately, the Internet, with the quick and convenient access it provides to source material, has made plagiarizing easier than ever before. Accidental plagiarism generally occurs when students fail to properly manage their electronic sources, often by cutting and pasting source material into their drafts without documenting the source or properly distinguishing the material from their own work. This sort of plagiarism can be avoided by applying more care and diligence to the process of collecting and using online sources. Intentional plagiarism occurs when students knowingly download writing from the Internet and submit it as their own. There are, in fact, numerous Web sites on the Internet that profit from this sort of plagiarism by selling term papers, essays, and even prepackaged research on a wide variety of subjects. Those contemplating buying an essay from such a site should not fool themselves; just because they paid for a paper, doesn't mean they can take credit for writing it. Additionally, prospective plagiarists should know that the Internet has also made detecting plagiarism easier than ever before. Instructors now have access to powerful search tools and software that allow them to compare passages from student drafts with content available online; if the plagiarist can find it on the Internet, so too can the instructor. See Chapter 13 for a detailed discussion of plagiarism.

with ethics. Students cheat. They confuse means and ends. And so on. There's some truth to this, but I contend that the real cause of the problem comes not from what students do, but what they don't do—they don't "write in the middle."

The plagiarism problem usually surfaces when writers are rushed, madly composing drafts at the last minute, and they simply haven't made the time to make the information they've collected their own. As a result, they're controlled *by* the information rather than controlling it for their own purposes. "How can I improve on what this guy says?" The thinking goes, "I guess I should just get it down in my paper." The result is sometimes unintentional plagiarism—some quotation marks were omitted or the paraphrase was too close to the original—but more often the paper suffers from another problem: the absence of an author. The writer doesn't seem to be in charge of where the essay goes and what it says.

There's a solution to this that is really quite simple. Write about what you're reading *as you collect it.*

Note cards aren't what I have in mind unless you use them to do more than simply jot down what a source says. Instead, I strongly recommend that you keep a double-entry journal or a research log that will serve two purposes: collecting information and exploring your reactions to what you've found. This is merely an extension of what I've been suggesting from the beginning of *The Curious Writer*—that you can move dialectically from creative thinking to critical thinking and back again—but this time you'll be creatively exploring information and then reflecting on how it addresses your research question.

The suggestion that you take time to actually do some writing about the information you have collected in the middle of the process may come across as needing a pretty tough sell. *Save the writing for the draft,* you're thinking. But you are essentially *beginning* your draft with thoughtful note taking, which will save you time later.

Double-Entry Journal. You already are familiar with the double-entry journal. This approach uses opposing pages of your notebook to encourage dialectical thinking. On the left page take notes—paraphrases, summaries, and quotations—as you might usually do with conventional note taking, and on the opposing right page *explore* your responses, reactions, and questions about the information you've collected on the left page (for a full description of the double-entry notebook method, see "Using the Double-entry Journal" in Chapter 2).

Research Log. Another method of note taking that also exploits dialectical thinking is the research log. Rather than using opposing pages, you'll layer your notes and responses, one after another. This is a particularly useful method for those who would prefer to work with a keyboard rather than a pencil. Here's how it works:

1. Begin by taking down the full bibliographic information on the source, something you may already have in your working bibliography.

2. Read the article, book chapter, or Web page, marking up your personal copy as you typically do, perhaps underlining key facts or ideas or information relevant to your research question.

3. Your first entry in your notebook or on the computer will be a fastwrite, an open-ended response to the reading under the heading "What Strikes Me Most." As the title implies, you're dealing with first thoughts here. Consider some of the following approaches to this initial response to the source:

   • First play the believing game, exploring how the author's ideas, arguments, or findings seem sensible to you. Then shift to the doubting game, a more critical stance in which you look for gaps, raise questions, or express doubts about what the source says.

   • What strikes you as the most important thing the author was trying to say?

- What do you remember best? What surprised you most after reading the source?
- What seemed most convincing? Least convincing?
- How does the source change your thinking on the topic? What do you understand better now than you did before you read the piece?
- How does it compare to other things you've read?
- What seems most relevant to your research question?
- What other research possibilities does it suggest?

4. Next, take notes on the source, jotting down summaries, paraphrases, quotations, and key facts you glean from it. Title this section "Source Notes."

5. Finally, follow up with another episode of fastwriting. Title this "The Source Reconsidered." This is a *more focused* look at the source; fastwrite about what stands out in the notes you took. Which facts, findings, claims, or arguments shape your thinking now? If the writing stalls, skip a line, take another look at your source notes, and seize on something else to write about.

ONE STUDENT'S RESPONSE

CLAUDE'S RESEARCH LOG

SOURCE
Source Letawsky, Nicole R., et al. "Factors Influencing the College Selection Process of Student Athletes." *College Student Journal* 37.4 (2003): 604–611. *Academic Search Premier.* Ebsco Databases. Albertson's Lib. 5 April 2004 <http://www.epnet.com>.

WHAT STRIKES ME MOST
Really interesting article that studied about 130 student athletes at a large 1-A university. Noted that there have been a lot of research studies on why students choose a particular school but not so much on why student-athletes choose a school. Everyone assumes, of course, that student-athletes go somewhere because they're wined and dined and promised national TV exposure. In other words, it all has to do with the glamour of playing 1-A, particularly the so-called revenue sports like basketball and football. But this study had some surprising findings. They found that the number one reason that student-athletes chose a school was the degree options it offers. In other words, the reasons student-athletes choose a school aren't that much different that the reason regular students choose one. The study also found that the glamour stuff—getting

awards, getting on TV, and future professional possibilities—mattered the least to the student-athletes. This study challenges some of the myths about student recruiting, and should be read by recruiters especially. If you want to get a blue-ribbon player at your school, tell them about the academic opportunities there.

SOURCE NOTES (CUT-AND-PASTE FROM ELECTRONIC VERSION)

"This study found that the most important factor for student-athletes was the degree program options offered by the University. Other important factors were the head coach, academic support services, type of community in which the campus is located, and the school's sports traditions. Two of the top three factors were specifically related to the academic rather than athletic environment. This is a key finding and should be understood as recruiting efforts should be broad based, balancing academics and athletics if they are to be effective."

"A somewhat surprising result of the study concerned relatively low ratings associated with factors considered essential to "Big-Time College Sports." Television exposure, perceived opportunity to play immediately, and perceived future professional sporting opportunities were among the lowest-ranked factors. Furthermore, the participants rated athletic rewards (a 5-item survey scale containing these and other reward items) consistently lower than both the campus and athletic environment. These results may be due to the fact that respondents were from each of the sports offered by the University. Many of the sports (e.g., swimming, track), although funded and supported similar to the other sports, do not receive the national attention, large crowds, and television exposure."

SOURCE RECONSIDERED

This article did more than anything I've read so far to make me question my thesis that big-time college sports recruiting is way out of control. It's pretty convincing on the point that athletes care about the academic programs when they're choosing a school. But then the second quotation has an interesting part that I just noticed. This study surveyed athletes in all sports, not just the big-time sports like football and basketball at the university where the study was conducted. It seems to me that that would really skew the findings because someone participating is a sport like tennis that doesn't get a lot of attention and doesn't necessarily lead to professional opportunities after school *would* be more interested in academics. They're not dreaming of making a name for themselves, but getting a scholarship to pay for school. Seems like a better study would focus on the big-time sports. . .

Whichever note-taking method you choose—the double-entry journal or the research log—what you are doing is taking possession of the information and making it yours by evaluating it for your own purposes. One of the hardest parts of writing with outside sources is doing exactly that—using someone else's ideas or information in the service of your own questions. And that's why taking the time to write in the middle is so important: you're doing the most important intellectual work *as* you encounter the perspectives of others. This will make writing the draft much easier, and will also, I believe, lower the risk of unintentional plagiarism, a mistake that often occurs in the mad rush to begin writing the draft the night before it's due.

INTERVIEWS

Tethered as we are these days to the electronic world of the Web and the increasingly digital university library, it's easy to forget an old-fashioned source for research: a living, breathing human being. People are often the best sources of information because you can have a real conversation rather than the imagined one simulated by the double-entry notebook. Some kinds of writing, such as the profile, fundamentally depend on interviews; with other genres, such as the personal essay or the research paper, interviews are one of several sources of information. But they can be central to bringing writing to life because when we put people on the page, abstract ideas or arguments suddenly have a face and a voice. People on the page make ideas matter.

> *The principal advantage of doing interviews is that you ask the questions that you are most interested in learning the answers to.*

Arranging Interviews

Who do you interview? Basically, there are two kinds of interviews: 1) The interviewee is the main subject of your piece, as in a profile, and 2) The interviewee is *a source of information* about another subject.

The interviewee as a source of information is the far more common type of interview, and it usually involves finding people who either are experts on the topic you're writing about or who have been touched or influenced in some way by it. For example, Tina was writing a research essay on the day care crisis in her community. Among those affected by this issue are the parents of small children, their day care teachers, and even the kids themselves; all were good candidates for interviews about the problem. Experts were a little more difficult to think of immediately. The day care teachers might qualify—after all, they're professionals in the area— but Tina also discovered a faculty member in the College of Health and Social Sciences that specialized in policies related to childcare. Interviewing both types of people—experts and those influenced by the issue—gave Tina a much richer perspective on the problem.

How do you find experts in your topic? Below are a few strategies for locating potential interviewees:

- *Check the faculty directory on your campus.* Many universities publish an annual directory of faculty and their research interests, which may be online. In addition, your university's public information office might have a similar list of faculty and areas of expertise.
- *Ask friends and your instructors.* They might know faculty who have a research interest in your topic, or might know someone in the community who is an expert on it.
- *Check the phone book.* The familiar *Yellow Pages* can be a gold mine. Want to find a biologist who might have something to say about the effort to bring back migrating salmon? Find the number of the regional office of U.S. Fish and Wildlife Service in the phone book and ask for the public information officer. He or she may help you find the right expert.
- *Check your sources.* As you begin to collect books, articles, and Internet documents, note their authors and affiliations. I get calls or e-mails from time to time from writers who came across my book on lobsters, posing questions I love to try to answer since no one in Idaho gives a hoot about lobsters. Google searches of authors who are mentioned in your sources may produce e-mail addresses or Web sites with e-mail links that you might query.
- *Check the Encyclopedia of Associations.* This is another underused book in your university's reference room that lists organizations in the United States with interests ranging from promoting tofu to saving salmon.

Making Contact

The most difficult part of interviewing for some of us is working up the courage to make that phone call to ask for someone's time. Although e-mail queries are also an option these days, a phone call is still the best way to make contact. The important thing to remember is that people generally love talking about themselves and what they know. You may meet initial resistance, but about 90 percent of the time interview subjects *love* being interviewed.

But you must be prepared. Typically, the time to set up an interview is when you already have a working knowledge of your topic and might have specific questions to ask. Even better, if you're aware of an interview subject's work on your topic, use this knowledge in the initial contact. Experts appreciate people who do this kind of prep work before making contact with them.

The ease of e-mail contact is enticing. It saves you the call, and gives your interview subject some control over when he or she answers you. E-mail contact also gives you the chance to electronically interview someone who may live a thousand miles away. But remember e-mail etiquette: Don't pester people with multiple e-mails, and don't write lengthy e-mails with long lists of questions until you've been granted permission to ask them.

Conducting the Interview

The kinds of questions you ask fundamentally depend on what type of interview you're conducting. In a profile, your questions will focus on the interview subject (see Chapter 5). To some extent, this is also true when you interview nonexperts who are *affected* by the topic you're writing about. For example, Tina is certainly interested in what the parents of preschoolers *know* about the day care crisis in her town, but she's also interested in the feelings and *experiences* of these people. Gathering this kind of information leads to some of the questions you may have used in a profile, but with more focused on the subject's experience with your topic:

- What was your first experience with _____? What has most surprised you about it?
- How does _____ make you feel?
- Tell me about a moment that you consider most typical of your experience with _____.

More often, however, your motive in an interview will be to gather information. Obviously, this will prompt you to ask specific questions about your topic as you try to fill in gaps in your knowledge. But there are also some more general, open-ended questions you might find useful to ask. For example:

- What is the most difficult aspect of your work?
- What do you think is the most significant popular misconception about _____?
- What are the significant current trends in _____?
- If you had to summarize the most important thing you've learned about _____, what would that be?
- What is the most important thing other people should know or understand?
- What do you consider the biggest problem?
- Who has the power do to something about it?
- What is your prediction about the future? Ten years from now, what will this problem look like?

Once you have a list of questions in mind, be prepared to ignore them. Good interviews often take turns that you can't predict, and these journeys may lead you to information and understandings you didn't expect. After all, a good interview is like a good conversation; it may meander, speed up or slow down, and reveal things about your topic and your interview subject that you don't expect. But good interviewers also attempt to control an interview when the turns it's taking aren't useful. You do this through questions, of course, but also more subtle tactics. For example, if you stop taking notes most interview subjects notice, and the astute ones quickly understand that what they're saying has less interest to you. A quick glance at your watch can have the same affect.

E-mail interviews produce a ready-made text with both your questions and the subject's answers. This is pretty wonderful. Live interviews, on the other hand, require more skill. It's usually a good idea to use a tape recorder (with your subject's permission), but never rely exclusively on it. *Always take notes*. Your notes, if nothing else, will help you know where on the tape you should concentrate later, transcribing direct quotations or gathering information. Note taking during interviews is an acquired skill; the more you do it, the better you get, inventing all sorts of shorthand for commonly occurring words. Practice taking notes while watching the evening news.

Most of all, try to enjoy your interview. After all, you and your interview subject have something important in common—you have an interest in your topic—and this usually produces an immediate bond that transforms an interview into an enjoyable conversation.

Using the Interview in Your Writing

Putting people on the page is one of the best ways to bring writing to life. This is exactly what information from interviews can do—give otherwise abstract questions or problems a voice and a face. One of the most common ways to use interview material is to integrate it into the lead or first paragraph of your essay. By focusing on someone involved in the research question or problem you're exploring, you immediately capture reader interest. For example, here's the beginning of a *Chronicle of Higher Education* essay, "What Makes Teachers Great?"[2] Quite naturally, the writer chose to begin by profiling someone who happened to be a great teacher, using evidence from the interviews he conducted.

> When Ralph Lynn retired as a professor of history at Baylor University in 1974, dozens of his former students paid him tribute. One student, Ann Richards, who became the governor of Texas in 1991, wrote that Lynn's classes were like "magical tours into the great minds and movements of history." Another student, Hal Wingo, the editor of *People* magazine, concluded that Lynn offered the best argument he knew for human cloning. "Nothing would give me more hope for the future," the editor explained, "than to think that Ralph Lynn, in all his wisdom and wit, will be around educating new generations from here to eternity."

[2]Bain, Ken. "What Makes Teachers Great?" *Chronicle of Higher Education,* 9 April 2004, B7–B9.

This is a strong way to begin an essay because the larger idea—the qualities that make a great teacher—is grounded in a name and a face. But information from interviews can be used anywhere in an essay—not just at the beginning—to make an idea come to life.

Information from interviews can also provide strong evidence for a point you're trying to make, especially if your interview subject has expertise on the topic. But interviews can also be a *source* of ideas about what you might want to say in an essay. The essay on great teaching, for instance, offers seven qualities that great teachers embrace in their classrooms, things such as "create a natural critical learning environment" or "help students learn outside of class." All of these claims grew from interviews with sixty professors in a range of disciplines.

The principal advantage of doing interviews is that *you* ask the questions that you're most interested in learning the answers to. Rather than sifting through other sources that may address your research questions briefly or indirectly, interviews generate information that is often relevant and focused on the information needs of your essay. In other words, interviews are a source of data that can also be a *source* of theories or ideas on your topic. And this is often the best way to use interview material in your essay.

SURVEYS

Mike was writing a persuasive essay whose main claim was that pennies should be abolished. "Everyone I know really hates pennies," he said. "They've become pretty useless currency." I was pretty skeptical—this issue seemed incredibly complicated to me—but then Mike asked, "Would you stoop down to pick up a penny in the parking lot?" Ten years ago, I would, certainly. But I don't think I would today. Wouldn't it be interesting to ask a bunch of people this question as a possible way to go beyond Mike's anecdotal evidence that people hate pennies and think they're worthless? An informal survey was born. In this case, it was remarkably simple. Mike planned to randomly ask fifty people on the quad this simple question: "Would you pick up a penny if you saw it laying on the ground?"

The survey is a fixture in American life. We love surveys. What's the best economical laptop? Should the president be reelected? Who is the sexiest man alive? What movie should win best picture? Some of these are scientific surveys with carefully crafted questions, statistically significant sample sizes, and carefully chosen target audiences. In your writing class, you likely won't be conducting such formal research. More likely it will be like Mike's—fairly simple, and while not necessarily statistically reliable, your informal survey will likely be more convincing than anecdotal evidence or your personal observation, particularly if it's thoughtfully developed.

Defining a Survey's Goals and Audience

A survey is a useful source of information when you're making some kind of claim regarding "what people think" about something. Mike observed that his friends all seem to hate pennies, and he wanted to generalize from this anecdotal evidence to suggest that most people probably share that view. But do they? And which people are we really talking about? As we discussed this in his writing group, Mike pointed out that his grandfather grew up during the Great Depression, and that he has a very different perspective on money than Mike. "So your grandfather would probably pick up a penny in the parking lot, right?" I asked. Probably, Mike said.

Quickly, Mike had not only a survey question but he began to think about qualifying his claim. Maybe younger adults—Mike's generation—in particular share this attitude about the lowly penny. To confirm this, Mike's survey had both a purpose—to collect information about how people view pennies—and an audience—students on his campus. If he had the time or inclination, Mike could conduct a broader survey of older Americans, but for his purposes the quad survey would be enough.

Types of Survey Questions

There are typically two types of questions you can ask on a survey: *open-ended questions* and *direct questions*. Open-ended questions often produce unexpected information, while direct questions are easier to analyze. Open-ended questions are like those on the narrative evaluations students might fill out at the end of the semester, such as, "What did you learn in this course?" or "What were the instructor's strengths and weaknesses?" Direct questions are the kind used on quizzes and tests, the kinds of questions that have a limited number of answers. The simplest, of course, would be a question or statement that people might agree or disagree with: "Would you pick up a penny if you saw it lying on the street?" Yes? No? You don't know?

How do you decide which types of questions to ask? Here are some things to consider:

- *How much time do you have to analyze the results?* Open-ended questions obviously take more time, while direct questions often involve mere tabulation of responses. The size of your sample is a big factor in this.

- *How good are you at crafting questions?* Direct questions need to be more carefully crafted than open-ended ones because you're offering limited responses. Are the responses appropriate to the question? Have you considered all the alternative ways of responding?

- *Do you want statistical or qualitative information?* Qualitative information—anecdotes, stories, opinions, case studies, observations, individual perspectives—are the stuff of open-ended questions. This can be wonderful information because it is often surprising, and it offers an individual's voice rather than the voiceless results of statistical data. On the other hand, statistical information—percentages, averages, and the like—are easily understood and can be dramatic.

Crafting Survey Questions

To begin, you want to ask questions that your target audience can answer. Don't ask a question about a campus alcohol policy that most students in your survey have never heard of. Secondly, keep the questions simple and easy to understand. This is crucial because most respondents resist overly long survey questions and won't answer confusing ones. Third, make sure the questions will produce the information you want. This is a particular hazard of open-ended questions. For example, a broad open-ended questions such as, "What do you think of the use of animals in the testing of cosmetics?" will probably produce verbal shrug rather than an answer of "I don't know." A better question is more focused: "What do you think about the U.S Food and Drug Administration's claim that animal testing by cosmetic companies is 'often necessary to provide product safety?'"

Such a question could be an open-ended or direct question, depending on the kind of responses you're seeking. Focusing the question also makes it more likely to generate information that will help you compose your essay on the adequacy of current regulations governing animal testing. Also note that the question doesn't necessarily betray the writer's position on the issue, which is essential—a good survey question isn't biased or "loaded." Imagine how a less neutral question might skew the results: "What do you think of the federal bureaucrats' position that animal testing for cosmetics is 'often necessary to provide product safety?'" An even more subtle bias might be introduced by inserting the phrase "federal government" rather than "Federal Drug Administration" in the original question. In my part of the world, the Rocky Mountain West, the federal government is generally not viewed favorably, no matter what the issue.

Keep your survey questions to a minimum. It shouldn't take long—no more than a few minutes at most—to complete your survey, unless you're lucky enough to have a captive audience like a class.

Finally, consider beginning your survey with background questions that establish the identity of each respondent. Typical information you might collect include the gender and age, or with student-oriented surveys, the class ranking of the respondent. Depending on your topic, you might be interested in particular demographic facts, for example, whether someone has children or comes from a particular part of the state. All of these questions can help you sort and analyze your results.

Conducting a Survey

How do you reach the audience you've selected for your survey? Professional pollsters have all sorts of methods, including computerized dialing in some regions of the country or purchasing mailing lists. Your project is much more low-tech. Begin by asking yourself whether your target audience tends to conveniently gather in a particular location. For example, if you're surveying sports fans, then surveying people by the main gate at the football stadium on Saturday might work. If your target audience is first-year college students and your university requires English composition, then surveying one or more of those classes would be a convenient way to reach them.

In some situations, you can leave your survey forms in a location that might produce responses from your target audience. For example, a student at my university wanted to survey people about which foothill's hiking trails they liked best, and she left an envelope with the forms and a pencil at several trailheads.

A new possibility for tech-savvy students is the online survey. Software for designing online surveys is available now, but unless the survey is linked to a Web site that is visited by the target audience whose opinions you seek, the response rates can be low. Telephone surveys are always a possibility, but they are often time-consuming and unless you can target your calls to a specific audience—say, people living in the dorms on your campus—it's hard to reach the people you most want to query. The postal mail is usually too slow and expensive, although the intercampus mails can be an excellent option for distributing surveys. Response rates, however, may not meet your expectations.

Using Survey Results in Your Writing

The very best thing about devoting the effort to conducting an informal survey is that you're producing original and interesting information about your topic's local relevance. This can be an impressive element of your essay, and will certainly make it more interesting.

Since analysis of open-ended questions can be time-consuming and complicated, consider the simplest approach: as you go through the surveys, note which responses are worth quoting in your essay because they seem representative. Perhaps the responses are among the most commonly voiced in the entire sample, or they are expressed in significant numbers by a particular group of respondents. You might also chose to quote a response because it is particularly articulate, surprising, or interesting.

In a more detailed analysis, you might try to nail down more specifically the *patterns* of responses. Begin by creating a simple coding system—perhaps numbers or colors—that represent the broadest categories of response. For example, perhaps you initially can divide the survey results into two categories: people who disagree with the university's general education requirements and those who agree with it, Group 1 and Group 2. The next step might be to further analyze each of these groups, looking for particular patterns. Maybe you notice that freshman tend to oppose the requirement in larger numbers than seniors and voice similar criticisms. In particular, pay attention to responses you didn't expect, responses that might enlarge your perspectives about what people think about your topic.

Direct questions that involve choosing limited responses—true/false, yes/no, multiple choice, and so on—often involve tabulation. This is where knowledge of a spreadsheet program such as Microsoft Excel is invaluable.

In the great majority of cases, your analysis of the responses to direct questions will be pretty simple—probably a breakdown of percentages. What percentage of the sample, for example, checked the box that signaled agreement with the statement that their "main goal for a college education was to get a good job?" In a more sophisticated analysis, you might try to break the sample down, if it's large enough, to certain categories of respondents—men and women, class ranking, respondents with high or low test scores, and so on—and then see if there are response patterns correlated to these categories. For example, perhaps you found that a much higher percentage of freshman than seniors sampled agreed that a good job was the most important reason to go to college.

What might this difference mean? Is it important? How does it influence your thinking about your topic or how does it affect your argument? Each of these questions involve interpretation of the results, and sample size is the factor that most influences the credibility of this kind of evidence. If you only surveyed five freshman and three seniors about their attitudes toward your school's general education requirements, then the comparisons you make between what they say are barely better than anecdotal. It's hard to say what the appropriate sample size for your informal survey should be—after all, you aren't conducting a scientific survey and even a small sample might produce some interesting results—but, in general, the more responses you can gather the better.

KNOWING WHEN TO STOP

At this point, having covered various research techniques that you can use to acquire information, the obvious question arises: When is enough enough? How do you know when it's time to stop searching your library's database or surfing the Web and start writing your paper? If you've been *writing in the middle*—doing more than simply taking down facts and quotations from your sources, and actually exploring your thinking about what those sources say—then such questions are moot. You've been writing all along. In fact, if you have already done a great deal of writing on your source information, you may discover that you are closer to completing your essay than you might have imagined.

There is a tendency among many writers, however, to procrastinate. One of the best ways to do this is to declare that you need just one more good source before you start writing your essay, perhaps a final interview, or a quick read of a book that is due back to the library tomorrow. In nearly every writing situation, it pays off to write from abundance rather than scarcity, but don't let the quest for abundance turn into an excuse for not writing much of anything until a deadline forces you into action. Hastily written research-based essays sometimes seem to come together miraculously, but do not let their promise bewitch you. Such essays are almost always not as good as you think, and they can almost always be much, much better if you tend to them over time, encouraging the steady growth of your ideas from the well-tilled soil of thorough—but not endless—research.

USING WHAT YOU HAVE LEARNED

There are countless opportunities, in school and out, to apply your research skills. But have you learned enough about *research techniques* to find good information efficiently? Consider the following situations. What would you suggest to the writer as a good research technique?

1. Casey is revising his essay on the effectiveness and accuracy of Internet voting. His workshop group says he needs more information on the whether hackers might compromise the accuracy of computers used for voting. Casey says he's relied pretty heavily on Internet sources. Where else would you suggest he search for information? What search terms might he use?

2. Alexandra needs to find some facts on divorce rates in the United States. Where might she find them fairly easily?

3. The university is proposing to build a new parking lot on a natural area near the edge of campus. Sherry wants to investigate the proposal to write a paper on whether the parking lot might be built with minimal environmental damage. What are the steps she might take to research the topic? Where should she look for information first? And then?

When researching we often wrestle for control. We gather information from experts, yet as writers we're expected to demonstrate some authority on the topic. Which experts make the most sense? What claims do we find persuasive? Most of all, what do *we* think? The impulse to plagiarize is a form of surrender, a willingness to let the other guy push us around.

Using and Citing Sources

CONTROLLING INFORMATION

The first college paper that really meant something to me was an essay on whaling industry practices and their impacts on populations of humpback and sperm whales. The essay opened with a detailed description of the exploding harpoon, a highly effective and dramatic method of subduing the animals, and was written at a time when the International Whaling Commission exerted little control over the whale harvests of the largest whaling nations. I never forgot that paper because it engaged both my heart and my head; I was intensely curious about the issue and felt strongly that this was a problem that needed to be solved.

Writing from the place of itchy curiosity and strong feelings is a wonderful thing. It will motivate you to read and learn about your topic, and when it comes to writing the draft you might find that you have little trouble enlisting the voices of your sources to make your point. More often, however, you've chosen a topic because you don't know what you think or feel about it—the inquiry-based approach—or you've been assigned a general topic that reflects the content of a course you're taking. In these cases, writing with sources is like crashing a party of strangers that has been going on for a long time. You shyly listen in, trying to figure out what everyone is talking about, and look for an opening to enter the conversation. Mostly you just feel intimidated, so you hang back feeling foolish.

This kind of writing situation is really a matter of control. Will you control the outside sources in your research essay, or will they control you? Will you enter the conversation and make a contribution to it, or will you let others do all the talking? The easiest way to lose

What You'll Learn In This Chapter

- How to control sources so they don't control you.

- How to properly summarize, paraphrase, and quote source material.

- How to avoid plagiarism.

- Methods of citation in the MLA and APA systems.

control is simply to turn long stretches of your paper over to a source, usually with a long quotation. I've seen a quotation from a single source run more than a full page in some drafts. Another way to lose control is to do what one of my colleagues calls a "data dump." Fill the truck with a heavy load of information, back it up to the paper, and dump in as much as you can, without analysis, without carefully selecting what is relevant and what isn't, without much thought at all. The writer in this situation sees his or her essay as a hole that must be filled with information.

USING SOURCES

The appropriate use of sources is really a matter of control. Writers who put research information to work for them see outside sources as serving a clear purpose. There are at least four of these purposes:

1. To use information that provides useful background or a context for understanding the research question.
2. To use information that answers a relevant question.
3. To use information as evidence to support a claim or idea, or in some cases, evidence that seems *not to* support an assertion but might if seen a certain way.
4. To use information to *complicate* a writer's thesis, raising interesting questions.

Let's see how this works in an actual passage. In an essay that asks, "Why Did God Create Flies," writer Richard Conniff argues that the answer might be as a punishment for human arrogance. In the middle of the essay, he draws on research to provide some background for this claim by establishing the long and sometimes unhappy relationship between the housefly and human beings.

> The true housefly, *Musca domestica,* does not bite. (You may think this is something to like about it, until you find out what it does instead.) *M. domestica,* a drab fellow of salt-and-pepper complexion, is the world's most widely distributed insect species and probably the most familiar, a status achieved through its pronounced fondness for breeding in pig, horse, and human excrement. In choosing at some point in the immemorial past to concentrate on the wastes around human habitations, *M. domestica* made a major career move. Bernard Greenberg of the University of Illinois at Chicago has traced human representations of the housefly back to a Mesopotamian cylinder seal from 3000 B.C. But houseflies were probably with us even before we had houses, and they spread with human culture.

Here Conniff demonstrates exquisite control over outside sources, marshalling them in the service of his larger point. But he also does this by not simply quoting extensively or going on and on explaining the relevant information, but by *finding his own way of saying things*. Rather than writing that the housefly's fondness for associating with people had significant ecological implications for the insect, Conniff writes that it was "a major career move."

The sections that follow review the techniques of summarizing, paraphrasing, and quoting. You know these as the three horsemen of note taking. But these should never be thoughtless activities; in fact, they're a great opportunity to exert control over your sources by doing two things:

1. *Taking notes with a particular purpose in mind.* How is the information you're writing about relevant to your purpose in your essay?

2. *Finding your own way of saying things.* By putting other people's words into your own voice, you take possession of the information.

Summarizing

"So basically what you're saying is that we can never win the war on terrorism because it isn't really a war in the conventional sense?"

Imagine that you're in the midst of a conversation with someone about the challenge of defeating terrorism. You've just listened for about a minute to a friend explain in some detail that the battle against terrorism isn't really a battle at all, but a series of surprise attacks which then provoke retaliation, with the two opponents blindly striking out at each other. Your friend adds that the terrorists' tactics are aimed at targets with symbolic rather than military value. Victory for terrorists is not measured in damage inflicted on military forces but in the terror provoked in the civilian population. You listen to all of this and summarize your friend's larger point: This isn't really war as we've historically understood it.

Summary is like making moonshine. You collect some ingredients and distill them into a more concise and powerful concoction, one that accurately captures the main idea of a book, an article, an argument, a chapter, or even a passage. The best summaries involve *thinking*. You're not just searching for a topic sentence somewhere in the source to copy down, but taking it all in as you would information and ideas in a conversation and then trying to find your own way of saying what seems to be at the heart of things.

A summary is usually much shorter than the original. For example, consider the following summary of the earlier extract paragraph about the relationship between houseflies and human beings:

> The common housefly is among the "most familiar" insects because it found its long partnership with human beings, one that goes back thousands of years, extremely beneficial.

Can you see how the summary captures the main idea of the longer paragraph? Also note that when the summary refers to identical language in the original—the phrase "most familiar"—the writer is careful to use quotation marks. Finally, the summary uses original language that breaks with the source, describing the relationship between people and flies as a "long partnership."

Reasons you would want to write a summary rather than quote directly or paraphrase a source include:

- What your essay needs is not a longer explanation of what a source says but a nugget of an idea, one that might have more impact because of its brevity.

- The original source, while useful, doesn't say things in a particularly distinctive way. It isn't quotable, but distilled it does serve a purpose in your essay.

- The source is making an argument, and what matters most is the gist of that argument rather than a discussion of the details.

Paraphrasing

Paraphrasing doesn't get any respect. It's like a difficult cousin that shows up at the family picnic and insists on enlisting everyone in a deep discussion. It's hard work, thinking that hard, particularly when there's beer and potato salad and Grandma's homemade chicken potpies. Of the three forms of note taking, paraphrasing requires the most attention and the greatest care. Your goal is to craft a restatement, in your own words, of what an original source is saying, in roughly the same length as the original.

Obviously, we don't paraphrase books or even entire articles. Paraphrasing usually involves closer work—examining a paragraph or a passage—and then trying to find a way of accurately capturing the original's ideas and information but in a fresh and original way. What this demands is not only a faith in our own way of saying things—that's hard enough—but a pretty thorough understanding of what exactly the source is trying to say. You simply can't paraphrase a source you don't understand.

That's where the brain work comes in, and the payoff is significant. When you successfully paraphrase a source you've written a part of your own essay. You've already done the work of comprehending what the source says, and found your own way of writing about it. This is the essence of using outside sources in your own work.

Here's a paraphrase of the earlier extract paragraph on house flies.

Houseflies, according to Richard Conniff, have had a long partnership with human beings. They are also among "the world's most widely distributed insect species," two factors that explain our familiarity with *Musca domesti-*

cus, the housefly's Latin name. This partnership may have been cultivated for thousands of years, or certainly as long as humans—and their animal companions—produced sufficient excrement in which the flies can breed. Ironically, these pests have benefited enormously from their "fondness" for human and animal wastes, and unwittingly we have contributed to their success at our own expense.

A key element of the translation in a paraphrase is trying not to imitate the structure of the original passage. By deliberately setting out to reorganize the information, you'll find writing a paraphrase much easier. And you'll also find it much less likely that you unintentionally plagiarize the material. Notice as well that whenever the paraphrase borrows wording from the original, quotation marks are included. The very last line of the paraphrase seems to cross over into interpretation, pointing out an irony that the original passage may have only hinted at. This is fine. In fact, it's something that you should try to develop as a habit—don't just translate and transcribe the information, try to make something of it. This move is particularly important when quoting material.

Quoting

Jotting down exactly what a source says—word for word—is relatively mindless work. Beyond selecting *what* you'll write down—a choice that does involve some thought—quoting a source merely involves careful transcription. Is that why it's the most popular form of note taking?

That's not to say that you should never quote a source. Not at all. If you jot down a passage from a source in the left page of your double entry journal, and then use the right page to explore, analyze, question, and interpret what it says, you're doing the kind of work good research writing demands. Well-selected quotes in an essay can also be memorable. But too often writers turn to transcription alone, and this quoted material simply gets dropped into the draft with virtually no analysis or even explanation. Frequently, I notice a quoted sentence appearing in the middle of a paragraph simply because the writer was too lazy to paraphrase. Then there's the long quotation that's thrown in as an obvious ploy to make the paper longer.

When should you turn to quotation in your essay? There are two main reasons:

1. When the source says something in a distinctive way that would be lost by putting it in your own words.

2. When there is a particular passage in the source that you want to analyze or emphasize, and the exact words of the author matter.

I like to tell the story of a moment in the 13-hour documentary *Shoah,* a film about the Holocaust. There is a scene when the filmmakers are riding the train that took hundreds of Jews to their deaths in one of the concentration camps. Amazingly, the engineer who drove that train back then was still on the job, guiding the train on the same tracks past the ruins of the same camps. The filmmakers interviewed this man, and asked him the obvious question: *How does it feel to still be driving the train on which you led so many people to their deaths?* The engineer paused, and said quietly, "If you could lick my heart, it would poison you."

This is the kind of quotation that could never be paraphrased. To do so would be to rob what the man said of all its emotional power and truth. You will rarely find such a memorable quotation in your sources. Much more often, you encounter a voice in your reading that simply sounds interesting and has a nice way of putting things. For instance, the excerpt from "Why Did God Create Flies" is eminently quotable because Richard Conniff, its author, writes with such a lively voice. Consider his sentence:

When you introduce a voice other than your own make it clear what this new voice adds to the conversation you have going about your topic.

> The true housefly is the world's most widely distributed insect species and probably the most familiar, a status achieved through its pronounced fondness for breeding in pig, horse, and human excrement.

What is it about this that seems quotable? Maybe the way it goes along with fairly straightforward exposition until the second half of the sentence, when suddenly the fly seeks status and feels fondness for you know what.

Academic writing also resorts to quotation when it's worthwhile to look more closely at what an author says. This is very common in the critical essay when analyzing literature. But it's also a good move when working with other sources, perhaps excerpts from a transcript or in analyzing an expert's claim or a striking finding. The key is not just using such quotations sparingly—typically a research essay is no more than 20 percent quotation—but *working with them.*

When you bring someone else's voice into your own writing, it's usually a good idea to introduce the source and provide some justification for making such a move. For instance, you might introduce the quote above by saying something like this:

> Richard Conniff, whose popular studies of invertebrate animals have made even leeches lovable, observes that the familiarity of the house fly is no accident. He writes . . .

It's even more important in academic writing to follow up quoted text with your own commentary. What would you like the reader to notice about what the quotation says? What seems most relevant to your own research question or point? How does the quotation extend an important idea you've been discussing or raise an important question? What does it imply? What do you agree with? What do you disagree with? In other words, when you introduce a voice other than your own make it clear what this new voice adds to the conversation you have going about your topic.

CITING SOURCES

Somewhere in the great hall at Mount Olympus, the mist obscuring his or her ankles, there must have been an English teacher. Hardly the right hand of Zeus, this was a minor god. But there were important tasks for this god, for the mortals were careless with their language, running on their sentences and mistaking *their* for *there*. But nothing could make the god's anger flash more brilliantly than a missing citation. There was a special place in Hades reserved for the plagiarist, where the condemned spent eternity composing works-cited pages of endless stacks of books whose title pages were unreadable.

Of all the rules some of my students believe were invented to torture composition students, requirements that they carefully cite their sources in research papers may cause the most anguish. They rarely question these requirements; they seem like divine and universal law. In fact, these aren't rules but conventions, hardly as old as the Greeks, and historically quite new. For many centuries, writers freely borrowed from others, often without attribution, and the appropriation of someone else's words and ideas was considered quite normal. This is still the view in some non-Western cultures; some students, for example, are quite puzzled in their English as a Second Language classes when they have to cite a source in their research essays.

This convention of explicitly acknowledging the source of an idea, quotation, piece of data, or information with a footnote or parenthetical citation and bibliography arose in the past 150 years. It began when mostly German universities began promoting the idea that the purpose of research was not simply to demonstrate an understanding of what already was known but to *make a contribution of new knowledge*. Researchers were to look for gaps in existing scholarship—questions that hadn't yet been asked—or to offer extensions of what had already been posed by someone else. Knowledge-making became the business of the research writer, and like gardeners, scholars saw themselves as tending a living thing, a kind of tree that grew larger as new branches were grafted on existing limbs.

Just as a child clambering up a tree in the park is grateful for the sturdy limbs under his or her feet, research writers acknowledge the limbs they are standing on that have helped them to see a little more of their subjects. That's why they cite their sources. This is an act of gratitude, of course, but is also signals to readers on whose authority the writer's claims, conclusions, or ideas are based. Citation helps readers locate the writer's work on a specific part of the tree of knowledge in a discipline; it gives a useful context of what *has already been said* about a question or a topic.

Student writers cite for exactly the same reasons. Not because it's required in most college research writing but because it makes their research writing more relevant and more convincing to the people who read it.

There are quite a few conventions for citing, and these conventions often vary by discipline. Humanities disciplines such as English often use the Modern Language Association (MLA) conventions, while the social sciences use the American Psychological Association (APA) methods. Both of these documentation styles are detailed later in this chapter. Although there are differences between the two styles, the purpose of each is the same: to acknowledge those from whom you have borrowed ideas and information.

WRITING WITH COMPUTERS

CITATION FORMATTING SOFTWARE

Let's face it: Compiling a correctly formatted "Works Cited" or "References" page for your research essays is tedious work. Those of you who will be writing many research essays may want to invest in citation formatting software, such as Daedalus and BiblioCite. Simply enter the author, title, and publication data for each source into a template and when you are done with your final draft these applications will provide you with a complete MLA-formatted "Works Cited" page or APA-formatted "References" pages. Remember to update your citation formatting software on a yearly basis. Documentation guidelines do change, particularly those for electronically based sources, and if your software is out of date, you may have to edit the citation formats yourself, which defeats the whole purpose of such software.

Avoiding Plagiarism

Modern authors get testy when someone uses their work without giving them credit. This is where the concept of intellectual property comes from, an idea that emerged with the invention of the printing press and the distribution of multiple copies of an author's work. In its most basic form, plagiarism is stealing someone else's words, ideas, or information. Academic plagiarism, the kind that gets a lot of ink these days with the rise of the Internet, usually refers to more specific misdeeds. Your university probably has an academic honesty or plagiarism policy posted on the Web or in a student handbook. You need to look at it. But it probably includes most or all of the following forms of plagiarism:

1. Handing in someone else's work—a downloaded paper from the Internet or borrowed from a friend—and claiming that it's your own.

2. Using information or ideas that are not common knowledge from any source and failing to acknowledge that source.

3. Handing in the same paper for two different classes.

4. Using the exact language or expressions of a source and not indicating through quotations marks and citation that the language is borrowed.

5. Rewriting a passage from a source using minor substitutions of different words but retaining the same syntax and structure of the original.

The great majority of plagiarism cases are unintentional. The writer simply didn't know or pay attention to course or university plagiarism policies. Equally common is simple carelessness. How can you avoid this trap? Check out Tips for Avoiding Plagiarism below.

Intentional plagiarism, of course, is a different matter. There are, of course, plentiful sites on the Web that offer papers on thousands of topics to anyone willing to pay for them. College instructors, however, have more and more tools for identifying these downloaded papers. The consequences of buying and handing in online papers are often severe, including flunking the course and even expulsion, an academic Hades of sorts. Moreover, even if a person is not caught committing this academic crime, intentional plagiarism stems from an intellectual laziness and dishonesty that are bound to catch up with the person doing it sooner or later. Just don't go there.

Intentional plagiarism stems from an intellectual laziness and dishonesty that are bound to catch up with the person doing it sooner or later.

Tips for Avoiding Plagiarism

- **Don't procrastinate.** Many careless mistakes in citation or proper handling of source material occur in the rush to finish the draft in the wee hours of the morning.

- **Be an active note-taker.** Work in the middle of the process to take possession of the material you read, especially exploring your responses to sources *in your own words* and *for your own purposes.*

- **Collect bibliographic information first.** Before you do anything else, take down complete publication information for each source, including the page numbers from which you borrowed material.

- **Mark quoted material clearly.** Whenever you quote a source directly, make sure that's obvious in your notes.

- **Be vigilant whenever you cut and paste.** The great usefulness of cutting and pasting passages in electronic documents is also the downfall of many research writers. Is the copied material directly borrowed, and if so is it properly cited?

EXERCISE 13.1

The Accidental Plagiarist

The vast majority of plagiarism problems are accidental. The writer simply isn't aware that he or she has stumbled into the problem. Here's a low-stakes exercise that can test your understanding of how to avoid the simplest—and most common—types of accidental plagiarism. Get this wrong and the grammar police won't accost you in the middle of the night, throw you against the wall and make you spell difficult words. You'll just learn something.

Using the words and ideas of others in your own writing is essential in most research essays and papers. Doing this without plagiarizing isn't exactly like walking through a minefield, but you do have to step carefully. For example, Beth was exploring the following question, "What might explain the high rate of divorce in the early years of marriage?" She's interested in divorce because she just went through one. In her research, Beth encounters Diane Ackerman's book, *The Natural History of Love,* and Beth finds the following paragraph:

> "Philandering," we call it, "fooling around," "hanky-panky," "skirt chasing," "man chasing," or something equally picturesque. Monogamy and adultery are both hallmarks of being human. Anthropologist Helen Fisher proposes a chemical basis for adultery, what she calls "The Four-Year Itch." Studying the United Nations survey of marriage and divorce around the world, she noticed that divorce usually occurs early in marriage, during the couple's first reproductive and parenting years. Also, that this peak time for divorce coincides with the period in which infatuation normally ends, and a couple has to decide if they're going to call it quits or stay together as companions. Some couples do stay together and have other children, but even more don't. "The human animal," she concludes, "seems built to court, to fall in love, and to marry one person at a time; then, at the height of our reproductive years, often with a single child, we divorce them; then, a few years after, we re-marry once again."

Beth thought this was pretty interesting stuff, and in her draft she summarized the paragraph in the following way:

> According to Diane Ackerman, a hallmark of being human is "monogamy and adultery," and she cites the period right after infatuation subsides—about four years for most couples—as the time when they call it quits.

STEP ONE: In small groups, analyze Beth's summary. Does Beth plagiarize the original passage, and if so, do you have ideas about how she could fix it? Revise the passage on a piece of newsprint and post it on the wall.

STEP TWO: Discuss the proposed revisions. How well do they address any plagiarism problems you see in Beth's summary?

STEP THREE: Now compare the following paraphrases of the same Ackerman passage. Which has plagiarism problems and which seems okay?

PARAPHRASE 1

Divorce may have "chemical basis," something that may kick in after four years of marriage and ironically when partners are reaching their highest potential for having children. Researcher Helen Fisher calls it "The Four-Year Itch," the time that often signals a shift from infatuation into a more sober assessment of the relationship's future: are they going to stay together or "call it quits?" Most end up deciding to end the relationship.

PARAPHRASE 2

When infatuation fades and couples are faced with the future of their relationship, biochemistry may help them decide. According to researcher Helen Fisher, "divorce usually occurs early in a marriage, during the couple's first reproductive and parenting years" (qtd. in Ackerman 165). She suggests that this is often about four years into the relationship, and argues that humans may be designed to behave this way because the pattern seems so entrenched (Ackerman 166).

STEP FOUR: In class, discuss which paraphrase seems acceptable and which does not. Remember the problems are pretty subtle.

STEP FIVE: Now practice your own *summary* of the following passage, applying what you've learned so far in the exercise about ways to avoid plagiarism when using the words and ideas of other people. This is the paragraph in Ackerman's book that follows the passage you worked with above.

> Our chemistry makes it easy to follow that plan, and painful to avoid it. After the seductive fireworks of first attraction, which may last a few weeks or a few years, the body gets bored with easy ecstasy. The nerves no longer quiver with excitement. Nothing new has been happening for ages, why bother to rouse oneself? Love is exhausting. Then the attachment chemicals roll in their thick cozy carpets of marital serenity. Might as well relax and enjoy the calm and security some feel. Separated even for a short while, the partners crave the cradle of the other's embrace. Is it a chemical craving? Possibly so, a hunger for the soothing endomorphins that flow when they're together. It is a deep, sweet river, just right for dangling one's feet in while the world waits.
>
> Other people grow restless and search for novelty.

MLA DOCUMENTATION GUIDELINES

The professional organization in charge of academic writing in literature and languages, the Modern Language Association (MLA), uses one of the two methods of citing sources that you should know. The second, the

American Psychological Association system, is described in the next section. Your English class will most likely use the MLA. When should you cite your sources?

1. Whenever you quote from an original source.

2. Whenever you borrow ideas from an original source, even when you express them in your own words by paraphrasing or summarizing.

3. Whenever you borrow from a source factual information that is not common knowledge (see "Inquiring into the Details: The Common Knowledge Exception").

INQUIRING INTO THE DETAILS

THE COMMON KNOWLEDGE EXCEPTION

The business about *common knowledge* causes much confusion. Just what does this term mean? Basically, *common knowledge* means facts that are widely known and about which there is no controversy.

Sometimes, it's really obvious whether something is common knowledge. The fact that the Super Bowl occurs in late January and pits the winning teams from the American and National Football Conferences is common knowledge. The fact that former president Ronald Reagan was once an actor and starred in a movie with a chimpanzee is common knowledge, too. And the fact that most Americans get most of their news from television is also common knowledge, although this information is getting close to leaving the domain of common knowledge.

But what about a writer's assertion that most dreaming occurs during rapid eye movement (REM) sleep? This is an idea about which all sources seem to agree. Does that make it common knowledge?

It's useful to ask next, How common to whom? Experts in the topic at hand or the rest of us? As a rule, consider the knowledge of your readers. What information will not be familiar to most of your readers or may even surprise them? Which ideas might even raise skepticism? In this case, the fact about REM sleep and dreaming goes slightly beyond the knowledge of most readers, so to be safe, it should be cited. Use common sense, but when in doubt, cite.

Citing Sources

The foundation of the MLA method of citing sources *in your paper* is putting the last name of the author and the page number of the source in parenthesis as closely as possible to the borrowed material. For example,

```
According to Diane Ackerman, researchers believe that there is
an "infatuation chemical" that may account for that almost
desperate attraction we feel when we're near someone special
(Ackerman 164).
```

The parenthetical citation tells a reader two things: the source of the information (for example, the author's name), and where in the work to find the borrowed idea or material. A really interested reader—perhaps an infatuated one—who wanted to follow up on this would then refer to something called the "Works Cited" at the back of the paper. This would list the work by the author's last name and all the pertinent information about the source:

```
Ackerman, Diane. A Natural History of Love. New York: Vintage,
1994.
```

Here's another example of parenthetical author/page citation from another research paper. Note the differences from the previous example:

```
"One thing is clear," writes Thomas Mallon, "plagiarism didn't
become a truly sore point with writers until they thought of
writing as their trade. . . . Suddenly his capital and iden-
tity were at stake" (3-4).
```

The first thing you may have noticed is that the author's last name—Mallon—was omitted from the parenthetical citation. It didn't need to be included, since it had already been mentioned in the text. *If you mention the author's name in the text of your paper, then you only need to parenthetically cite the relevant page number(s).* This citation also tells us that the quoted passage comes from two pages rather than one.

Where to Put Citations.   Place the citation as close as you can to the borrowed material, trying to avoid breaking the flow of the sentences, if possible. To avoid confusion about what's borrowed and what's not—particularly in passages longer than a sentence—mention the name of the original author *in your paper.* Note that in the next example the writer simply cites the source at the end of the paragraph, not naming the source in the text. Doing so makes it hard for the reader to figure out whether Blager is the source of the information in the entire paragraph or just part of it:

```
Though children who have been sexually abused seem to be dis-
advantaged in many areas, including the inability to forge
lasting relationships, low self-esteem, and crippling shame,
they seem advantaged in other areas. Sexually abused children
seem to be more socially mature than other children of their
same age group. It's a distinctly mixed blessing (Blager 994).
```

In the following example, notice how the ambiguity about what's borrowed and what's not is resolved by careful placement of the author's name and parenthetical citation in the text:

> Though children who have been sexually abused seem to be disadvantaged in many areas, including the inability to forge lasting relationships, low self-esteem, and crippling shame, they seem advantaged in other areas. According to Blager, sexually abused children seem to be more socially mature than other children of their same age group (994). It's a distinctly mixed blessing.

In this latter version, it's clear that Blager is the source for one sentence in the paragraph, and the writer is responsible for the rest. Generally, use an authority's last name, rather than a formal title or first name, when mentioning her in your text. Also note that the citation is placed *inside* the period of the sentence (or last sentence) that it documents. That's almost always the case, except at the end of a blocked quotation, where the parenthetical reference is placed after the period of the last sentence. The citation can also be placed near the author's name, rather than at the end of the sentence, if it doesn't unnecessarily break the flow of the sentence. For example:

> Blager (994) observes that sexually abused children tend to be more socially mature than other children of their same age group.

🔍 INQUIRING INTO THE DETAILS

CITATIONS THAT GO WITH THE FLOW

There's no getting around it—parenthetical citations can be like stones on the sidewalk. Readers stride through a sentence in your essay and then have to step around the citation at the end before they resume their walk. Yet citations are important in academic writing because they help readers know who you read or heard that shaped your thinking.

However, you can minimize citations that trip up readers and make your essay more readable by doing the following.

- Avoid lengthy parenthetical citations by mentioning the name of the author in your essay. That way, you usually only have to include a page number in the citation.

- Try to place citations where readers are likely to pause anyway—for example, the end of the sentence, or right before a comma.

- Remember you *don't* need a citation when you're citing common knowledge, or referring to an entire work by an author.

- If you're borrowing from only one source in a paragraph of your essay, and all of the borrowed material comes from a single page of that source, don't bother repeating the citation over and over again with each new bit of information. Just put the citation at the end of the paragraph.

When You Mention the Author's Name. It's generally good practice in research writing to identify who said what. The familiar convention of using attribution tags such as "According to Fletcher . . ." or "Fletcher argues . . ." and so on helps readers attach a name with a voice, or an individual with certain claims or findings. When you do mention the author of a source, then you can drop his or her name for the parenthetical citation and just list the page number. For example,

```
Robert Harris believes that there is "widespread uncertainty"
among students about what constitutes plagiarism (2).
```

You may also list the page number directly after the author's name.

```
Robert Harris (2) believes that there is "widespread uncer-
tainty" among students about what constitutes plagiarism.
```

When There is No Author. Occasionally, you may encounter a source in which the author is anonymous—the article doesn't have a byline, or for some reason the author hasn't been identified. This isn't unusual with pamphlets, editorials, government documents, some newspaper articles, online sources, and short filler articles in magazines. If you can't parenthetically name the author, what do you cite?

Most often, cite the title (or an abbreviated version, if the title is long) and the page number. If you choose to abbreviate the title, begin with the word under which it is alphabetized in the "Works Cited." For example:

```
According to the Undergraduate Catalog, "the athletic program
is an integral part of the university and its total educa-
tional purpose" (7).
```

Here is how the publication cited above would be listed at the back of the paper:

Works Cited

Undergraduate Catalog, Boise State University 2004–2005.
    Boise, ID: BSU, 2004.

For clarity, it's helpful to mention the original source of the borrowed material in the text of your paper. When there is no author's name, refer to the publication (or institution) you're citing or make a more general reference to the source. For example:

```
An article in Cuisine magazine argues that the best way to
kill a lobster is to plunge a knife between its eyes ("How to
Kill" 56).
```

or

```
According to one government report, with the current minimum
size limit, most lobsters end up on dinner plates before they've
had a chance to reproduce ("Size at Sexual Maturity" 3-4).
```

Works by the Same Author. Suppose you end up using several books or articles by the same author. Obviously, a parenthetical citation that merely lists the author's name and page number won't do, since it won't be clear *which* of several works the citation refers to. In this case, include the author's name, an abbreviated title (if the original is too long), and the page number. For example:

```
One essayist who suffers from multiple sclerosis writes that
"there is a subtle taxonomy of crippleness" (Mairs, Carnal
Acts 69).
```

The "Works Cited" list would show multiple works by one author as follows:

Works Cited

```
Mairs, Nancy. Voice Lessons. Boston: Beacon, 1994.
- - - . Carnal Acts. Boston: Beacon, 1996.
```

It's obvious from the parenthetical citation which of the two Mairs books is the source of the information. Note that in the parenthetical reference, no punctuation separates the title and the page number, but a comma follows the author's name. If Mair had been mentioned in the text of the paper, her name could have been dropped from the citation.

Also notice that the three hyphens used in the second entry are meant to signal that the author's name in this source is the same as in the preceding entry.

When One Source Quotes Another. Whenever you can, cite the original source for material you use. For example, if an article on television violence quotes the author of a book and you want to use the quote, try to hunt down the book. That way, you'll be certain of the accuracy of the quote and you may find some more usable information.

Sometimes, however, finding the original source is not possible. In those cases, use the term *qtd. in* to signal that you've quoted or paraphrased a quotation from a book or article that initially appeared elsewhere. In the following example, the citation signals that Bacon's quote was culled from an article by Guibroy, not Bacon's original work:

```
Francis Bacon also weighed in on the dangers of imitation, ob-
serving that "it is hardly possible at once to admire an au-
thor and to go beyond him" (qtd. in Guibroy 113).
```

Personal Interviews. If you mention the name of your interview subject in your text, no parenthetical citation is necessary. On the other hand, if you don't mention the subject's name, cite it in parentheses after the quote:

```
Instead, the recognizable environment gave something to kids
they could relate to. "And it had a lot more real quality to
```

it than, say, <u>Mister Rogers</u> . . .," says one educator. "Kids say the reason they don't like <u>Mister Rogers</u> is that it's un-believable" (Diamonti).

Regardless of whether you mention your subject's name, you should include a reference to the interview in the "Works Cited." In this case, the reference would look like this:

Works Cited

Diamonti, Nancy. Personal interview. 5 Nov. 1999.

Several Sources in a Single Citation. Suppose two sources both contributed the same information in a paragraph of your essay. Or perhaps even more common is when you're summarizing the findings of several authors on a certain topic—a fairly common move when you're trying to establish a context for your own research question. You cite multiple authors in a single citation in the usual fashion, using page name and page number, but separating each with a semicolon. For example,

A whole range of studies have looked closely at the intellectual development of college students, finding that they generally assume "stages" or "perspectives" that differ from subject to subject (Perry 122; Belenky et al. 12).

If you can, however, avoid long citations because they can be cumbersome for readers.

Sample Parenthetical References for Other Sources. MLA format is pretty simple, and we've already covered some of the basic variations. You should also know five additional variations, as follow:

AN ENTIRE WORK

If you mention the author's name in the text, no citation is necessary. The work should, however, be listed in the "Works Cited."

Leon Edel's <u>Henry James</u> is considered by many to be a model biography.

A VOLUME OF A MULTIVOLUME WORK

If you're working with one volume of a multivolume work, it's a good idea to mention which volume in the parenthetical reference. The citation below attributes the passage to the second volume, page 3, of a work by Baym and three or more other authors. The volume number always precedes the colon, which is followed by the page number:

By the turn of the century, three authors dominated American literature: Mark Twain, Henry James, and William Dean Howells (Baym et al. 2: 3).

SEVERAL SOURCES FOR A SINGLE PASSAGE

Occasionally, a number of sources may contribute to a single passage. List them all in one parenthetical reference, separated by semicolons:

> ```
> American soccer may never achieve the popularity it enjoys in
> the rest of the world, an unfortunate fact that is integrally
> related to the nature of the game itself (Gardner 12; "Selling
> Soccer" 30).[1]
> ```

A LITERARY WORK

Because so many literary works, particularly classics, have been reprinted in so many editions, it's useful to give readers more information about where a passage can be found in one of these editions. List the page number and then the chapter number (and any other relevant information, such as the section or volume), separated by a semicolon. Use arabic rather than roman numerals, unless your teacher instructs you otherwise:

> ```
> Izaak Walton warns that "no direction can be given to make a
> man of a dull capacity able to make a Flie well" (130; ch. 5).
> ```

When citing classic poems or plays, instead of page numbers, cite line numbers and other appropriate divisions (book, section, act, scene, part, etc.). Separate the information with periods. For example, (Othello 2.3.286) indicates act 2, scene 3, line 286 of Shakespeare's work.

AN ONLINE SOURCE

Texts on CD-ROM and online sources frequently don't have page numbers. So how can you cite them parenthetically in your essay? You have several options.

Sometimes, the documents include paragraph numbers. In these cases, use the abbreviation *par.* or *pars.,* followed by the paragraph number or numbers you're borrowing material from. For example:

> ```
> In most psychotherapeutic approaches, the personality of the
> therapist can have a big impact on the outcome of the therapy
> ("Psychotherapy," par. 1).
> ```

Sometimes, the material has an internal structure, such as sections, parts, chapters, or volumes. If so, use the abbreviation *sec., pt., ch.,* or *vol.* (respectively), followed by the appropriate number.

In many cases, a parenthetical citation can be avoided entirely by simply naming the source in the text of your essay. A curious reader will then find the full citation to the article on the "Works Cited" page at the back of your paper. For example:

> ```
> According to Charles Petit, the worldwide effort to determine
> whether frogs are disappearing will take somewhere between
> three and five years.
> ```

[1]Jason Pulsifer, University of New Hampshire, 1991. Used with permission.

Finally, if you don't want to mention the source in text, parenthetically cite the author's last name (if any) or article title:

```
The worldwide effort to determine whether frogs are disappear-
ing will take somewhere between three and five years (Petit).
```

Format

The Layout. There is a certain fussiness associated with the look of academic papers. The reason for it is quite simple—academic disciplines generally aim for consistency in format so that readers of scholarship know exactly where to look to find what they want to know. It's a matter of efficiency. How closely you must follow the MLA's requirements for the layout of your essay is up to your instructor, but it's really not that complicated. A lot of what you need to know is featured in Figure 13.1

Printing. Compose your paper on white, 8½" x 11" printer paper. Make sure the printer has sufficient ink or toner.

Margins and Spacing. The old high school trick is to use big margins. That way, you can meet your page length requirements with less material. Don't try that trick with this paper. Leave one-inch margins at the top, bottom, and sides of your pages. Indent the first line of each paragraph

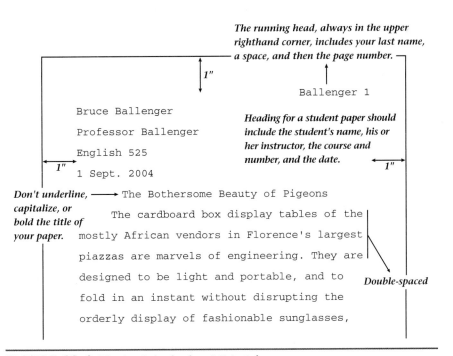

The running head, always in the upper righthand corner, includes your last name, a space, and then the page number.

1"

Ballenger 1

Bruce Ballenger

Professor Ballenger

English 525

1 Sept. 2004

Heading for a student paper should include the student's name, his or her instructor, the course and number, and the date.

1"

1"

Don't underline, capitalize, or bold the title of your paper. → The Bothersome Beauty of Pigeons

    The cardboard box display tables of the mostly African vendors in Florence's largest piazzas are marvels of engineering. They are designed to be light and portable, and to fold in an instant without disrupting the orderly display of fashionable sunglasses,

Double-spaced

FIGURE 13.1 The basic look of an MLA-style paper.

five spaces and blocked quotes ten spaces. Double-space all of the text, including blocked quotes and "Works Cited."

Title Page. Your paper doesn't need a separate title page. Begin with the first page of text. One inch below the top of the page, type your name, your instructor's name, the course number, and the date (see following). Below that, type the title, centered on the page. Begin the text of the paper below the title.

```
Julie Bird
Professor Ballenger
English 102
1 June 2004
        Nature as Being: Landscape in Silko's 'Lullaby'
        Leslie Marmon Silko, the author of "Lullaby," is a Native
American writer from the Laguna Pueblo culture . . .
```

Note that every line is double-spaced. The title is not underlined (unless it includes the name of a book or some other work that should be underlined) or boldfaced.

Pagination. Make sure that every page after the first one is numbered. That's especially important with long papers. Type your last name and the page number in the upper-righthand corner, flush with the right margin: Ballenger 3. Don't use the abbreviation *p.* or a hyphen between your name and the number.

Placement of Tables, Charts, and Illustrations. With MLA format, papers do not have appendixes. Tables, charts, and illustrations are placed in the body of the paper, close to the text that refers to them. Number illustrations consecutively (Table 1 or Figure 3), and indicate sources below them (see Figure 13.2 on the following page). If you use a chart or illustration from another text, give the full citation. Place any table caption above the table, flush left. Captions for illustrations or diagrams are usually placed below them.

Handling Titles. The MLA guidelines about handling titles are, as the most recent *Handbook* observes, "strict." The general rule is that the writer should capitalize the first letters of all principal words in a title, including any that follow hyphens. The exceptions include articles (*a, an,* and *the*), prepositions (*for, of, in, to*), coordinating conjunctions (*and, or, but, for*), and the use of *to* in infinitives. These exceptions apply *only if the words appear in the middle of a title;* capitalize them if they appear at the beginning or end.

The rules for underlining a title or putting it in quotation marks are as follows:

TABLE 1 PERCENTAGE OF STUDENTS WHO SELF-REPORT ACTS OF PLAGIARISM			
ACTS OF PLAGIARISM	NEVER/ RARELY	SOME- TIMES	OFTEN/ VERY FREQ.
Copy text without citation	71	19	10
Copy paper without citation	91	5	3
Request paper to hand in	90	5	2
Purchase paper to hand in	91	6	3

Source: Scanlon, Patrick M., and David R. Neumann. "Internet Plagiarism among College Students." *Journal of College Student Development* 43.3 (2002):379.

FIGURE 13.2 **Example of format for a table.**

1. <u>Underline the Title</u> if it is a book, play, pamphlet, film, magazine, TV program, CD, audiocassette, newspaper, or work of art.
2. "Put the Title in Quotes" if it is an article in a newspaper, magazine, or encyclopedia; a short story; a poem; an episode of a TV program; a song; a lecture; or a chapter or essay in a book.

Here are some examples:

<u>The Curious Researcher</u> (Book)

<u>English Online: The Student's Guide to the Internet</u> (CD-ROM)

"Once More to the Lake" (Essay)

<u>Historic Boise: An Introduction into the Architecture of Boise, Idaho</u> (Book)

"Psychotherapy" (Encyclopedia article)

<u>Idaho Statesman</u> (Newspaper)

"One Percent Initiative Panned" (Newspaper article)

Italics and Underlinings. If you are writing your paper on a computer or word processor, you can probably produce italic type, which is slanted to the right, *like this*. Many magazines and books—including this one—use italic type to distinguish certain words and phrases, such as titles of works that otherwise would be underlined. MLA style recommends the use of underlining, not italics. You should check with your instructor to see what style he or she prefers.

Language and Style.

Names. Though it may seem as if you're on familiar terms with some of the authors you cite by the end of your research project, it's not a good idea to call them by their first names. Typically, initially give the full names of people you cite, and then only their last names if you mention them again in your essay.

Ellipsis. Those are the three (always three) dots that indicate you've left out a word, phrase, or even whole section of a quoted passage. It's often wise to do this since you want to emphasize only certain parts of a quotation rather than burden your reader with unnecessary information, but be careful to preserve the basic intention and idea of the author's original statement. The ellipsis can come at the beginning of a quotation, in the middle, or at the end, depending where it is you've omitted material. The accepted format for using an ellipsis is to enclose them in brackets. For example,

```
"After the publication of a controversial picture that shows,
for example, either dead or grieving victims [. . .], readers
in telephone calls and in letters to the editor, often attack
the photographer for being tasteless [. . .]."
```

Quotations. Quotations that run more than four lines long should be blocked, or indented ten spaces from the left margin. The quotation should be double-spaced and quotation marks should be omitted. In an exception from the usual convention, the parenthetical citation is placed *outside* the period at the end of the quotation. A colon is a customary way to introduce a blocked quotation. For example,

```
Chris Sherman and Gary Price, in The Invisible Web, contend
that much of the Internet, possibly most, is beyond the reach
of researchers who use conventional search engines:

     The problem is that vast expanses of the Web are com-
     pletely invisible to general-purpose search engines
     like AltaVista, HotBot, and Google. Even worse, this
     "Invisible Web" is in all likelihood growing signifi-
     cantly faster than the visible Web that you're familiar
     with. It's not that search engines and Web directories
     are "stupid" or even badly engineered. Rather, they
     simply can't "see" millions of high quality resources
     that are available exclusively on the Invisible Web. So
     what is this Invisible Web and why aren't search en-
     gines doing anything about it to make it visible? (xxi)
```

Preparing the "Works Cited" Page

The "Works Cited" page ends the paper. There are also several other lists of sources that may appear at the end of a research paper. An "Annotated List of Works Cited" not only lists the sources used in the paper but also includes a brief description of each. A "Works Consulted" list includes sources that may or may not have been cited in the paper but shaped your thinking. A "Content Notes" page, keyed to superscript numbers in the text of the paper, lists short commentaries or asides that are significant but not central enough to the discussion to be included in the text of the paper.

The "Works Cited" page is the workhorse of most college papers. The other source lists are used less often. "Works Cited" is essentially an alphabetical listing of all the sources you quoted, paraphrased, or summarized in your paper. If you have used MLA format for citing sources, your paper has numerous parenthetical references to authors and page numbers. The "Works Cited" page provides complete information on each source cited in the text for the reader who wants to know. (In APA format, this page is called "References" and is only slightly different in how items are listed.)

If you've been careful about collecting complete bibliographic information—author, title, editor, edition, volume, place, publisher, date, page numbers—then preparing your "Works Cited" page will be easy. If you've recorded that information on notecards, all you have to do is put them in alphabetical order and then transcribe them into your paper. If you've been careless about collecting that information, you may need to take a hike back to the library.

Format.

Alphabetizing the List. "Works Cited" follows the text of your paper on a separate page. After you've assembled complete information about each source you've cited, put the sources in alphabetical order by the last name of the author. If the work has multiple authors, use the last name of the first listed. If the source has no author, then alphabetize it by the first key word of the title. If you're citing more than one source by a single author, you don't need to repeat the name for each source; simply place three dashes followed by a period (– – –.) for the author's name in subsequent listings.

Indenting and Spacing. Type the first line of each entry flush left, and indent subsequent lines of that entry (if any) five spaces. Double-space between each line and each entry. For example:

Garrett   8

Works Cited

Greeley, Alexandra. "No Tan is a Safe Tan." <u>Nutrition Health Review: The Consumer's Medical Journal</u> 59 (Summer 1991): 14–15.

Hayes, Jean L. "Are You Assessing for Melanoma?" <u>RN</u> 66.2 (Feb. 2003): 36–40.

Holick, Michael F. "Vitamin D—The Underrated Essential." <u>Life Extension</u> 9.4 (Apr. 2003): 46–48.

Johnson, Rheta Grimsley. "The Rural South These Days Has More Tanning Salons Than John Deeres." <u>Atlanta Journal-Constitution</u> 23 Apr. 2000, home ed.: M1.

"Just the Facts Stats." <u>36 Expose</u>. 17 Sept. 2003. <http://www.ecrm-online.com/Expose/V6_1/36.pdf>.

McLaughlin, Patricia. "Dying For a Tan This Summer?" <u>St. Louis Post-Dispatch</u> 15 Jun. 1995: 02.

"The Light Touch." <u>Total Health</u> 14.3 (June 1992): 43.

Vid, Da. "Sound and Light: Partners in Healing and Transformation." <u>Share Guide</u> 5.2 (Winter 1994): 20–21.

Reinhold, Vieth. "Vitamin D Nutrition and Its Potential Health Benefits for Bone, Cancer and Other Conditions." <u>Journal of Nutritional and Environmental Medicine</u> 11 (2001): 275–291.

"Sun Tanning." <u>Cool Nurse 2000-2003</u>. 18 Jun. 2003 <http://www.coolnurse.com/tanning.htm.>.

Vogel, Phillip J. "A New Light on Vitamin D." <u>Life Extension</u> 9.4 Apr. 2003: 40–46.

Citing Books. You usually need three pieces of information to cite a book: the name of the author or authors, the title, and the publication information. Occasionally, other information is required. The *MLA Handbook*[2] lists this additional information in the order it would appear in the citation. Remember, any single entry will include a few of these things, not all of them. Use whichever are relevant to the source you're citing.

1. Name of the author
2. Title of the book (or part of it)
3. Number of edition used
4. Number of volume used
5. Name of the series
6. Where published, by whom, and the date
7. Page numbers used
8. Any annotation you'd like to add

Each piece of information in a citation is followed by a period and one space (not two).

Title. As a rule, the titles of books are underlined, with the first letters of all principal words capitalized, including those in any subtitles. Titles that are not underlined are usually those of pieces found within larger works, such as poems and short stories in anthologies. These titles are set off by quotation marks. Titles of religious works (the Bible, the Koran, etc.) are neither underlined nor enclosed within quotation marks. (See the guidelines in the earlier "Handling Titles.")

[2]Joseph Gibaldi, *MLA Handbook for Writers of Research Papers*, 5th ed. (New York: MLA, 1999).

Edition. If a book doesn't indicate any edition number, then it's probably a first edition, a fact you don't need to cite. Look on the title page. Signal an edition like this: *2nd ed., 3rd ed.,* and so on.

Publication Place, Publisher, and Date. Look on the title page to find out who published the book. Publishers' names are usually shortened in the "Works Cited" list: for example, *St. Martin's Press Inc.,* is shortened to *St. Martin's.*

It's sometimes confusing to know what to cite about the publication place, since several cities are often listed on the title page. Cite the first. For books published outside the United States, add the country name along with the city to avoid confusion.

The date a book is published is usually indicated on the copyright page. If several dates or several printings by the same publisher are listed, cite the original publication date. However, if the book is a revised edition, give the date of that edition. One final variation: If you're citing a book that's a reprint of an original edition give both dates. For example:

```
Stegner, Wallace. Recapitulation. 1979. Lincoln:
     U of Nebraska P, 1986.
```

This book was first published in 1979 and then republished in 1986 by the University of Nebraska Press.

Page Numbers. You don't usually list page numbers of a book. The parenthetical reference in your paper specifies that. But if you use only part of a book—an introduction or an essay—list the appropriate page numbers following the publication date. Use periods to set off the page numbers. If the author or editor of the entire work is also the author of the introduction or essay you're citing, list her by last name only the second time you cite her. For example:

```
Lee, L. L., and Merrill Lewis. Preface. Women,
     Women Writers, and the West. Ed. Lee and
     Lewis. Troy: Whitston, 1980. v-ix.
```

Sample Book Citations
A BOOK BY ONE AUTHOR

```
Keen, Sam. Fire in the Belly. New York: Bantam,
     1991.
```

In-Text Citation: (Keen 101)

A BOOK BY TWO AUTHORS

```
Ballenger, Bruce, and Barry Lane. Discovering the
     Writer Within. Cincinnati: Writer's Digest,
     1996.
```

In-Text Citation: (Ballenger and Lane 14)

A BOOK WITH MORE THAN THREE AUTHORS

If a book has more than three authors, list the first and substitute the term *et al.* for the others.

```
Belenky et al. Women's Ways of Knowing. New York:
     Basic Books, 1973.
```

In-Text Citation: (Belenky et al. 21-30)

SEVERAL BOOKS BY THE SAME AUTHOR

```
Baldwin, James. Tell Me How Long the Train's Been
     Gone. New York: Dell-Doubleday, 1968.
- - -. Going to Meet the Man. New York: Dell-
     Doubleday, 1948.
```

In-Text Citation: (Baldwin, *Going* 34)

A COLLECTION OR ANTHOLOGY

```
Crane, R. S., ed. Critics and Criticism: Ancient
     and Modern. Chicago: U of Chicago P, 1952.
```

In-Text Citation: (Crane xx)

A WORK IN A COLLECTION OR ANTHOLOGY

The title of a work that is part of a collection but was originally published as a book should be underlined. Otherwise, the title of a work in a collection should be enclosed in quotation marks.

```
Bahktin, Mikhail. Marxism and the Philosophy
     of Language. The Rhetorical Tradition.
     Ed. Patricia Bizzell and Bruce Herzberg. New York: St.
     Martin's, 1990. 928-44.
```

In-Text Citation: (Bahktin 929-31)

```
Jones, Robert F. "Welcome to Muskie Country." The
     Ultimate Fishing Book. Ed. Lee Eisenberg and
     DeCourcy Taylor. Boston: Houghton, 1981.
     122-34.
```

In-Text Citation: (Jones 131)

AN INTRODUCTION, PREFACE, FOREWORD, OR PROLOGUE

```
Scott, Jerie Cobb. Foreword. Writing Groups:
     History, Theory, and Implications. By Ann
     Ruggles Gere. Carbondale, IL: Southern
     Illinois UP, 1987. ix-xi.
```

In-Text Citation: (Scott x-xi)

```
Rich, Adrienne. Introduction. On Lies, Secrets,
     and Silence. By Rich. New York: Norton,
     1979. 9-18.
```

In-Text Citation: (Rich 12)

A BOOK WITH NO AUTHOR

```
American Heritage Dictionary. 3rd ed. Boston:
     Houghton, 1994.
```

In-Text Citation: (American Heritage Dictionary 444)

AN ENCYLOPEDIA

```
"City of Chicago." Encyclopaedia Britannica.
     1999 ed.
```

In-Text Citation: ("City of Chicago" 397)

A BOOK WITH AN INSTITUTIONAL AUTHOR

```
Hospital Corporation of America. Employee Benefits
     Handbook. Nashville: HCA, 1990.
```

In-Text Citation: (Hospital Corporation of America 5-7)

A BOOK WITH MULTIPLE VOLUMES

Include the number of volumes in the work between the title and publication information.

```
Baym, Nina, et al., eds. The Norton Anthology of
     American Literature. 5th ed. 2 vols. New
     York: Norton, 1998.
```

In-Text Citation: (Baym et al. 2: 3)

If you use one volume of a multivolume work, indicate which one along with the page numbers, followed by the total number of volumes in the work.

```
Anderson, Sherwood. "Mother." The Norton Anthology
     of American Literature. Ed. Nina Baym et al.
     5th ed. Vol 2. New York: Norton, 1998.
     1115-31. 2 vols.
```

In-Text Citation: (Anderson 1115)

A BOOK THAT IS NOT A FIRST EDITION

Check the title page to determine whether the book is *not* a first edition (2nd, 3rd, 4th, etc.); if no edition number is mentioned, assume it's the first. Put the edition number right after the title.

```
Ballenger, Bruce. The Curious Researcher. 4th ed.
     Boston: Longman, 2003.
```

In-Text Citation: (Ballenger 194)

Citing the edition is only necessary for books that are *not* first editions. This includes revised editions (*Rev. ed.*) and abridged editions (*Abr. ed.*).

A BOOK PUBLISHED BEFORE 1900

For a book this old, it's usually unnecessary to list the publisher.

```
Hitchcock, Edward. Religion of Geology. Glasgow, 1851.
```

In-Text Citation: (Hitchcock 48)

A TRANSLATION

```
Montaigne, Michel de. Essays. Trans. J. M. Cohen.
     Middlesex, England: Penguin, 1958.
```

In-Text Citation: (Montaigne 638)

GOVERNMENT DOCUMENTS

Because of the enormous variety of government documents, citing them properly can be a challenge. Since most government documents do not name authors, begin an entry for such a source with the level of government (U.S. Government, State of Illinois, etc., unless it is obvious from the title), followed by the sponsoring agency, the title of the work, and the publication information. Look on the title page to determine the publisher. If it's a federal document, then the *Government Printing Office* (abbreviated *GPO*) is usually the publisher.

```
United States. Bureau of the Census. Statistical
     Abstract of the United States. Washington:
     GPO, 1990.
```

In-Text Citation: (United States, Bureau of the Census 79–83)

A BOOK THAT WAS REPUBLISHED

A fairly common occurrence, particularly in literary study, is to find a book that was republished, sometimes many years after the original publication date. In addition, some books first appear in hard cover, and then are republished in paperback. To cite, put the original date of publication immediately after the book's title, and then include the more current publication date, as usual, at the end of the citation. Do it like so:

```
Ballenger, Bruce, and Barry Lane. Discovering the
     Writer Within: 40 Days to More Imaginative
     Writing. 1989. Cincinnati, OH: Writer's Digest, 1996.
```

In-Text Citation: (Ballenger and Lane 31)

AN ONLINE-BOOK

Citing a book you found online requires more information than the usual citation for a book you can hold in your hands. As usual, include the author's name (if listed), an underlined title, and publication information. What you include in publication information depends on whether the text was published exclusively online or is also based on a print version. If only a digital book, include the date of electronic publication and the group or organization that sponsored it. If the book also appeared on paper, add the usual information (if provided) about the print version (city of publication, publisher, and date). The citation ends, finally, with the date you accessed the book online and the Internet address (URL). For example,

> Badke, William. <u>Research Strategies: Finding Your</u>
> <u>Way through the Information Fog</u>. Lincoln,
> NE: Writers Club P, 2000. 12 July 2002
> <http://www.acts.twu.ca/lbr/textbook.htm>.

In-Text Citation: (Badke)

Citing Periodicals

Format. Periodicals—magazines, newspapers, journals, and similar publications that appear regularly—are cited similarly to books but sometimes involve different information, such as date, volume, and page numbers. The *MLA Handbook* lists the information to include in a periodical citation in the order in which it should appear:

1. Name of the author
2. Article title
3. Periodical title
4. Series number or name
5. Volume number
6. Date
7. Page numbers

Author's Name. List the author(s) as you would for a book citation.

Article Title. Unlike book titles, article titles are usually enclosed in quotation marks.

Periodical Title. Underline periodical titles, dropping introductory articles (*Aegis,* not *The Aegis*). If you're citing a newspaper your readers may not be familiar with, include in the title—enclosed in brackets but not underlined—the city in which it was published. For example:

> Barber, Rocky. "DEQ Responds to Concerns About Weiser
> Feedlot." <u>Idaho Statesman</u> [Boise, ID] 23 Apr. 2004: B1.

Volume Number. Most academic journals are numbered as volumes (or occasionally feature series numbers); the volume number should be included in the citation. Popular periodicals sometimes have volume numbers, too, but these are not included in the citations. Indicate the volume number immediately after the journal's name. Omit the tag *vol.* before the number.

There is one important variation: Although most journals number their pages continuously, from the first issue every year to the last, a few don't. These journals feature an issue number as well as a volume number. In that case, cite both by listing the volume number, a period, and then the issue number: for example *12.4,* or volume number *12* and issue *4.*

Date. When citing popular periodicals, include the day, month, and year of the issue you're citing—in that order—following the periodical name. Academic journals are a little different. Since the volume number indicates when the journal was published within a given year, just indicate that year. Put it in parentheses following the volume number and before the page numbers (see examples following).

Page Numbers. Include the page numbers of the article at the end of the citation, followed by a period. Just list the pages of the entire article, omitting abbreviations such as *p.* or *pp.* It's common for articles in newspapers and popular magazines *not* to run on consecutive pages. In that case, indicate the page on which the article begins, followed by a "+" *(12+).*

Newspaper pagination can be peculiar. Some papers wed the section (usually a letter) with the page number *(A4)*; other papers simply begin numbering anew in each section. Most, however, paginate continuously. See the sample citations for newspapers that follow for how to deal with these peculiarities.

Online sources, which often have no pagination at all, present special problems. For guidance on how to handle them, see the section "Citing Online Source."

Sample Periodical Citations

A MAGAZINE ARTICLE

> Oppenheimer, Todd. "The Computer Delusion."
> <u>Atlantic Monthly</u> July 1997: 47-60.

In-Text Citation: (Oppenheimer 48)

> Williams, Patricia J. "Unimagined Communities."
> <u>Nation</u> 3 May 2004: 14.

In-Text Citation: (Williams 14)

A JOURNAL ARTICLE

For a journal that is paginated continuously, from the first issue every year to the last, cite as follows:

```
Allen, Rebecca E., and J. M. Oliver. "The
     Effects of Child Maltreatment on Language
     Development." Child Abuse and Neglect 6 (1982): 299-305.
```

In-Text Citation: (Allen and Oliver 299-300)

For an article in a journal that begins pagination with each issue, include the issue number along with the volume number.

```
Goody, Michelle M., and Andrew S. Levine. "Health-
     Care Workers and Occupational Exposure to
     AIDS." Nursing Management 23.1 (1992): 59-60.
```

In-Text Citation: (Goody and Levine 59)

A NEWSPAPER ARTICLE

Some newspapers have several editions (morning edition, late edition, national edition), and each may feature different articles. If an edition is listed on the masthead, include it in the citation.

```
Mendels, Pamela. "Internet Access Spreads to More
     Classrooms." New York Times 1 Dec. 1999,
     morning ed.: C1+.
```

In-Text Citation: (Mendels C1)

Some papers begin numbering pages anew in each section. In that case, include the section number if it's not part of pagination.

```
Brooks, James. "Lobsters on the Brink." Portland
     Press 29 Nov. 1999, sec. 2: 4.
```

In-Text Citation: (Brooks 4)

Increasingly, full-text newspaper articles are available online using library databases such as Newspaper Source or through the newspapers themselves. Citing articles from library databases involves adding information about the specific database you use (e.g., Newspaper Source), the provider of that database (e.g., EBSCOhost), where (which library?) and when (date) you accessed the information online, and the Web address of the provider (e.g., www.epnet.com). You can find the URLS for most database providers in later in this section.

Here's what the citation would look like:

```
"Lobsterman Hunts for Perfect Bait." AP Online
     7 July 2002. Newspaper Source. EBSCOhost.
     Albertson's Lib., ID. 13 July 2002
     <www.epnet.com>.
```

In-Text Citation: ("Lobsterman Hunts")

Here's an example of a citation for an article I found on the newspaper's own Web site:

```
Sterngold, James. "Lessons from '92 Keep Angry
    City Calm." New York Times on the Web 10 July
    2002. 12 July 2002 <http://www.nytimes.com/
    2002/07/11/national/11POLI.html?
    todaysheadlines>.
```

In-Text Citation: (Sterngold)

AN ARTICLE WITH NO AUTHOR

```
"The Understanding." New Yorker 2 Dec. 1991: 34-35.
```

In-Text Citation: ("Understanding" 35)

AN EDITORIAL

```
"Paid Leave for Parents." Editorial. New York
    Times 1 Dec. 1999: 31.
```

In-Text Citation: ("Paid Leave" 31)

A LETTER TO THE EDITOR

```
Levinson, Evan B. Letter. Boston Globe
    29 Jan. 1992: 10.
```

In-Text Citation: (Levinson 10)

A REVIEW

```
Page, Barbara. Rev. of Allegories of Cinema:
    American Film in the Sixties, by David E.
    James. College English 54 (1992): 945-54.
```

In-Text Citation: (Page 945-46)

AN ABSTRACT

It's usually better to have the full text of an article for research purposes, but sometimes all you can come up with is an abstract, or short summary of the article that highlights its findings or summarizes its argument. Online databases frequently offer abstracts when they don't feature full-text versions of an article.

To cite an abstract, begin with information about the full version, and then include the information about the source from which you got the abstract. If the title of the source fails to make it obvious that what you are citing is an abstract (i.e., it's not called something such as "Psychological Abstracts"), include the word "abstract" after the original publication information, but don't underline it or put it in quotation marks. In this example, the source of the abstract is a periodical database called MasterFILE Premier, provided by the company EBSCOhost. Since I accessed the abstract at my library, I include the library name and its location in the citation. In addition, I include the date of access and the Web address of the database's provider is included in the citation. (A list of URLs for these providers appears later in this section.)

```
Edwards, Rob. "Air-raid Warning." New Scientist
        14 Aug. 1999: 48-49. Abstract. MasterFILE
        Premier. EBSCOhost. Albertson's Lib.,
        ID. 1 May 2002 <www.epnet.com>.
```

In-Text Citation: (Edwards)

The following citation is from another useful source of abstracts, the *Dissertation Abstracts International.* In this case, the citation is from the print version of the index.

```
McDonald, James C. "Imitation of Models in the
        History of Rhetoric: Classical, Belletristic,
        and Current-Traditional." U of Texas, Austin.
        DAI 48 (1988): 2613A.
```

In-Text Citation: (McDonald 2613A)

Citing Nonprint and Other Sources

AN INTERVIEW

If you conducted the interview yourself, list your subject's name first, indicate what kind of interview it was (telephone, e-mail, or personal interview), and provide the date.

```
Hall, Lonny. Personal interview. 1 Mar. 1999.
```

In-Text Citation: (Hall)

Or avoid parenthethical reference altogether by mentioning the subject's name in the text: According to Lonny Hall, . . .

If you're citing an interview done by someone else (perhaps from a book or article) and the title does not indicate that it was an interview, you should, after the subject's name. Always begin the citation with the subject's name.

```
Stegner, Wallace. Interview. Conversations with
        Wallace Stegner. By Richard Eutlain and
        Wallace Stegner. Salt Lake: U of Utah P, 1990.
```

In-Text Citation: (Stegner 22)

Or if there are other works by Stegner on the "Works Cited" page:

```
(Stegner, Conversations 22).
```

As radio and TV interview programs are increasingly archived on the Web, these can be a great source of material for a research essay. In the example below, the interview was on a transcript I ordered from the Fresh Air Web site. Note that the national network, National Public Radio, *and* the local affiliate that produced the program, WHYY, are included in the citation along with the air date.

```
Mairs, Nancy. Interview. Fresh Air. Natl. Public Radio. WHYY,
      Philadelphia. 7 June 1993.
```

In-Text Citation: (Mairs)

The following citation is for an interview published on the Web. The second date listed is the date of access.

```
Messner, Tammy Faye Bakker. Interview. The Well
      Rounded Interview. Well Rounded Entertainment.
      Aug. 2000. 14 July 2002 <http://www.
      wellrounded.com/movies/reviews/
      tammyfaye_intv.html>.
```

In-Text Citation: (Messner)

SURVEYS, QUESTIONNAIRES, AND CASE STUDIES

If you conducted the survey or case study, list it under your name and give it an appropriate title.

```
Ball, Helen. "Internet Survey." Boise State
      U, 1999.
```

In-Text Citation: (Ball)

RECORDINGS

Generally, list a recording by the name of the performer and underline the title. Also include the recording company, catalog number, and year. (If you don't know the year, use the abbreviation *n.d.*)

```
Orff, Carl. Carmina Burana. Cond. Seiji Ozawa.
      Boston Symphony. RCA, 6533-2-RG, n.d.
```

In-Text Citation: (Orff)

TELEVISION AND RADIO PROGRAMS

List the title of the program (underlined), the station, and the date. If the episode has a title, list that first in quotation marks. You may also want to include the name of the narrator or producer after the title.

All Things Considered. Interview with Andre Dubus.
    Nat. Public Radio. WBUR, Boston. 12 Dec. 1990.

In-Text Citation: (All Things Considered)

FILMS, VIDEOTAPES, AND DVD

Begin with the title (underlined), followed by the director, the distributor, and the year. You may also include names of writers performers, or producers. End with the date and any other specifics about the characteristics of the film or videotape that may be relevant (length and size).

Saving Private Ryan. Dir. Steven Spielberg. Perf.
    Tom Hanks, Tom Sizemore, and Matt Damon.
    Videocassette. Paramount, 1998.

In-Text Citation: (Saving)

You can also list a video or film by the name of a contributor you'd like to emphasize.

Capra, Frank, dir. It's a Wonderful Life. Perf.
    Jimmy Stewart and Donna Reed. RKO
    Pictures, 1946.

In-Text Citation: (Capra)

ARTWORK

List each work by artist. Then cite the title of the work (underlined) and where it's located (institution and city). If you're reproduced the work from a published source, include that information as well.

Homer, Winslow. Casting for a Rise. Hirschl and
    Adler Galleries, New York. Ultimate Fishing
    Book. Ed. Lee Eisenberg and DeCourcy Taylor.
    Boston: Houghton, 1981.

In-Text Citation: (Homer 113)

LECTURES AND SPEECHES

List each by the name of the speaker, followed by the title of the address (if any) in quotation marks, the name of the sponsoring organization, the location, and the date. Only indicate what kind of address it was (lecture, speech, etc.) when no title is given.

Naynaha, Siskanna. "Emily Dickinson's Last
    Poems." Sigma Tau Delta, Boise, 15 Nov. 1999.

Avoid the need for parenthetical citation by mentioning the speaker's name in your text.

PAMPHLETS

Cite a pamphlet as you would a book.

New Challenges for Wilderness Conservationists. Washington,
      DC: Wilderness Society, 1973.

In-Text Citation: (New Challenges)

Citing "Portable" Databases. Nearly every new computer these days is sold with an encyclopedia on CD-ROM. If you're doing research, I don't think they hold a candle to the more extensive bound versions. Still, a CD-ROM encyclopedia is easy to use and, for quickly checking facts, can be quite helpful. While the encyclopedia is the most familiar *portable* database on CD-ROM, there are many others, including full-text versions of literary classics, journal article abstracts, indexes, and periodicals. The number of such portable databases on CD will continue to multiply along with databases on other media, like diskettes and tapes. Citation of these materials requires much of the usual information and in the usual order. But it will also include these three things: the *publication medium* (for example, CD-ROM, diskette, or tape), the *vendor* or company that distributed it (for example, SilverPlatter or UMI-Proquest), and the *date of electronic publication* (or the release date of the disk or tape).

There are two categories of portable databases: (1) those that are issued periodically, such as magazines and journals, and (2) those that are not routinely updated, such as books. Citing a source in each category requires some slightly different information.

A NONPERIODICAL DATABASE

This is cited much like a book.

- List the author. If no author is given, list the editor or translator, followed by the appropriate abbreviation (*ed., trans.*)
- Publication title (underlined) or title of the portion of the work you're using (if relevant)
- Name of editor, compiler, or translator (if relevant)
- Publication medium (for example, CD-ROM, diskette, magnetic tape)
- Edition or release or version
- City of publication
- Publisher and year of publication

For example:

Shakespeare, William. Romeo and Juliet. Diskette. Vers. 1.5.
      New York: CMI, 1995.

In-Text Citation: (Shakespeare)

```
"Psychotherapy." Microsoft Encarta. CD-ROM.
      2004 ed. Everett, WA: Microsoft, 2003.
```

In-Text Citation: ("Psychotherapy")

A PERIODICAL DATABASE

Frequently a periodical database is a computer version—or an analogue—of a printed publication. For example, the *New York Times* has a disk version, as does *Dissertation Abstracts*. Both databases refer to articles also published in print; therefore, the citation often includes two dates: the original publication date and the electronic publication date. Note the location of each in the citations below.

```
Haden, Catherine Ann. "Talking about the Past with
      Preschool Siblings." DAI 56 (1996). Emory U,
      1995. Dissertation Abstracts Ondisc. CD-ROM.
      UMI-ProQuest. Mar. 1996.

Kolata, Gina. "Research Links Writing Style to
      the Risk of Alzheimer's." New York Times
      21 Feb. 1996: 1A. Newspaper Abstracts.
      CD-ROM. UMI-ProQuest. 1996.
```

In-Text Citation: (Kolata 1A)

Frequently, a periodically issued electronic source doesn't have a printed analogue. In that case, obviously, you can't include publication information about the printed version.

Citing Online Databases. Citing most online sources is much like citing any other sources, with two crucial exceptions:

1. Electronic-source citations usually include at least two dates: the *date of electronic publication* (if available) and the *date of access* (when you visited the site and retrieved the document). There is a good reason for listing both dates: Online documents are changed and updated frequently—when you retrieve the material matters. If the online document you are using originally appeared in print, it might be necessary to include three dates: the print publication date, the online publication date, and your access date (see the McGrory citation that follows in the section "Is It Also in Print?").

2. The MLA now requires that you include the Internet address of the document in angle brackets at the end of your citation (for example, <http:www.cc.emory.edu/citation.formats.html>). The reason is obvious: The Internet address tells your readers where they can find the document.

Other Recent Changes by the MLA. The MLA no longer requires inclusion of a number of items in a citation. For example, it's no longer necessary to include the word *online* in your citations to indicate the publication medium or mention the name of the network or service you used to retrieve the document (for example, *Internet, America Online*). Both are great improvements, I think. Another quirky thing about citing online sources is dealing with page numbers, paragraph numbers, or numbered sections. Many Internet documents simply don't have them. The MLA no longer requires inclusion of the term *no pag.* when a document lacks pagination.

Is It Also in Print? Databases from computer services or networks feature information available in printed form (like a newspaper or magazine) and online, or information available exclusively online. This distinction is important. If the online source has a printed version, include information about it in the citation. For example:

```
McGrory, Brian. "Hillary Clinton's Profile
     Boosted." Boston Globe 26 June 1996: 1.
     Boston Globe Online 27 June 1996. 8 July 1998
     <http://www.boston.com/80/globe/nat/cgi-bin>.
```

In-Text Citation: (McGrory 1)

Note that the first date lists when the print version appeared, the second date when the article was published online, and the third when the researcher accessed the document.

Material that only appeared online is somewhat simpler to cite since you'll only need to include information about the electronic version.

```
Hutchins, Lisa. "The Intelligence of Crows." Pica
     Productions March 1999. 23 April 2004
     <http://home.earthlink.net/~lisamhutchins
     /intelli crows.htm>.
```

In-Text Citation: No page or paragraph numbers were used in this document, so simply list the author's last name: (Hutchins). Or avoid parenthetical citation altogether by mentioning the name of the source in your essay (for example: "According to Lisa Hutchins, the crow is . . .").

You may be missing citation information on some Internet material—such as page numbers and publication dates—that are easy to find in printed texts. Use the information that you have. Keep in mind that the relevant information for a citation varies with the type of electronic source (see citation examples that follow in "Sample Online Citation"). To summarize, the basic format for an online citation includes the following information:

1. Author's name (if given). If there is an editor, translator, or compiler included, list that name followed by the appropriate abbreviation (*ed., trans., comp.*).

2. Publication information:

   - Title of the document, database, or Web site
   - Title of the larger work, database, or Web site (if any) of which it is a part
   - Name of editor (if any) of the project, database, or Web site (usually different from author)
   - Volume, issue, or version number (if any)
   - Date of electronic publication or latest update
   - Page or paragraph numbers (if any)
   - Publication information about print version (if any)
   - Date of access and electronic address

Address Mistakes Are Fatal. When you include Internet addresses in your citations, it is crucial that you take great care in accurately recording them. Make sure you get all your slash marks going in the right direction and the right characters in the right places; also pay attention to whether the characters are upper- or lowercase. These addresses are *case sensitive,* unlike, say, the file names used to retrieve WordPerfect documents. The cut-and-paste function in your word processor is an invaluable tool in accurately transferring Internet addresses into your own documents. One last thing: If an Internet address in your citation must go beyond one line, make sure the break occurs after a slash, not in the middle of a file name, and don't include an end-of-line hyphen to mark the break.

Sample Online Citations

AN ARTICLE

Notice the inclusion of the document length after the publication date in these examples. Sometimes Internet documents number paragraphs instead of pages. Include that information, if available, using the abbreviation *par.* or *pars.* (e.g., "53 pars."). More often, an Internet article has no page or paragraph numbers. Put the title of the article in quotation marks and underline the title of the journal, newsletter, or electronic conference.

```
Haynes, Cynthia, and Jan R. Holmevik. "Enhancing
    Pedagogical Reality with MOOs." Kairos: A
    Journal for Teachers of Writing in a Webbed
    Environment 1.2 (1996): 1 p. 28 June 1996
    <http://english/ttu.edu/kairos/1.2/index.html>.
```

In-Text Citation: (Haynes and Holmevik 1)

```
"Freeman Trial Delayed over Illness."
     USA Today 26 May 1998. 26 May 1998
     <http://www.usatoday.com/news/nds2.htm>.
```

In-Text Citation: ("Freeman")

```
Dvorak, John C. "Worst Case Scenarios." PC
     Magazine Online 26 May 1998: 3 pp. 1 June
     1998 <http://www.zdnet.com/pcmag/insites/
     dvorak/jd.htm>.
```

In-Text Citation: (Dvorak 2)

AN ARTICLE OR ABSTRACT IN A LIBRARY DATABASE

One of the great boons to researchers in recent years is the publication of full-text versions of articles as part of the online databases available on your campus library's Web pages. Quite a few databases, such as MasterFILE or Newspaper Source, offer this service, and more are adding it every year. Some that don't offer full-text versions of articles offer abstracts, and even these can be useful. Citing articles or abstracts from library databases requires some information beyond what is usually required for citing other online articles. Specifically, you need

- The name of the database (e.g., Newspaper Source)
- The name and Web address of the company or organization that provides it to your library (e.g., EBSCOHost)
- The name and location of the library (e.g., Albertson's Library, ID)
- The date you accessed the database to get the article

All of this information is pretty easy to come up with except information about the company that provides the database. You can usually find that name on the search page of the database. The accompanying table lists the Web addresses of some of the most popular of these providers, along with some of the databases each features. You can use the provider's address in your citation. Note in the following example that information on the print version of the article is provided first, and then information about the database and its provider.

```
Winbush, Raymond A. "Back to the Future: Campus
     Racism in the 21st Century." The Black Collegian
     Oct. 2001: 102-3. Expanded Academic ASAP. Gale
     Group Databases. U of New Hampshire Lib. 12 Apr. 2002
     <http://www.infotrac.galegroup.com>.
```

In-Text Citation: (Winbush)

URLS OF POPULAR DATABASE PROVIDERS FOR USE IN CITATIONS

The table lists the Web addresses for most of the major companies that provide databases for libraries. This information is vital if you want to cite an article or abstract you found while searching your campus library's databases online. Usually a database has a specific name, such as Expanded Academic ASAP, as shown in the second column, and then a service that provides it, a name that you can usually find somewhere on the search page of the database. For Expanded Academic ASAP, for example, it's provider is called Gale Group shown in the first column. You need both pieces of information for a citation, as well as the provider's URL.

DATABASE PROVIDER	DATABASES	WEB ADDRESS
Britannica Online	Encyclopaedia Britannica	http://www.britannica.com
EBSCOhost	Academic Search Elite, Academic Search Premier, Business Source Elite, Computer Source, Health Source, MasterFile Elite, MasterFile Premier, Newspaper Source, Nursing and Allied Health Collection, World Magazine Bank	http://www.epnet.com
Gale Group Databases	Contemporary Authors, Biography Index, Expanded Academic ASAP, General Business File ASAP, General Reference Center, Health Reference Center, Info Trac, Literary Index	http://www.infotrac.galegroup.com
LexisNexis	Academic Universe, Government Periodicals Universe, History Universe, Statistical Universe	http://www.lexisnexis.com
OCLC First Search	Art Index, Book Review, Contemporary Women's Issues, EconLit, Essay and General Literature Index, Reader's Guide Abstracts, Social Science Index, WorldCat	http://newfirstsearch.oclc.org
ProQuest	ABI/INFORM, Academic Research Library, Magazine Index, National Newspapers, Wall Street Journal	http://www.bellhowell.infolearning.om/proquest

DATABASE PROVIDER	DATABASES	WEB ADDRESS
SilverPlatter/Web SPIRS	Agricola. Biological Abstracts, CINHAL, EconLit, Essay and General Literature Index, Philosopher's Index, PsychINFO	http://webspirs.silverplatter.com
Wilson Web	Applied Science and Technology Abstracts, Art Index, Bibliographic Index Biography Index, Book Review Digest, Education Index, General Science Index, Reader's Guide, Humanities Index, Social Science Index, World Authors	http://hwwilsonweb.com

When citing an abstract from a library database, include the word "abstract" in the citation. For example,

```
Erskine, Ruth. "Exposing Racism, Exploring Race."
     Journal of Family Therapy 24 (2002): 282-297. Abstract.
     EBSCO Online Citations. EBSCOHost.
     3 Dec. 2002 <www.epnet.com>.
```

In-Text Citation: (Erskine)

AN ONLINE BOOK

I can't imagine why anyone would read *The Adventures of Huckleberry Finn* online, but it's available, along with thousands of other books and historical documents in electronic form. If you use an online book, remember to include publication information (if available) about the original printed version in the citation.

```
Twain, Mark. The Adventures of Huckleberry Finn.
     New York: Harper, 1912. 22 July 1996
     <gopher://wiretap.spies.com/00/Library/
     Classic/huckfinn.html>.
```

In-Text Citation: (Twain)

Or better yet, since there are no page numbers, mention the author in the text rather than citing him parenthetically: In <u>The Adventures of Huckleberry Finn</u>, Twain re-creates southern dialect . . .

When citing part of a larger work, include the title of that smaller part in quotation marks before the title of the work. Also notice that the text cited below is part of an online scholarly project. Include the name of the project, the editor and compiler of the work if listed, and its location.

```
Service, Robert. "The Mourners." Rhymes of a
     Red Cross Man. 1916. Project Gutenberg.
     Ed. A. Light. Aug. 1995. Illinois
     Benedictine College. 1 July 1998
     <ftp://uiarchive.cso.uiuc.edu/pub/etext/
     gutenberg/etext95/redcr10.txt>.
```

In-Text Citation: (Service)

A PERSONAL OR PROFESSIONAL WEB SITE

Begin with the name of the editor or creator of the site, if listed. Include the title of the site, or, if no title is given, use a descriptor such as the term "Home page." Also include the sponsoring organization, if any, the date of access, and the electronic address.

```
Sharev, Alexi. Population Ecology. Virginia Tech
     U. 7 Aug. 1998 <http://www.gypsymoth
     .ento.vt.edu/~sharov/popechome/welcome.html>.
```

In-Text Citation: (Sharev)

```
Battalio, John. Home page. 26 May 1998 <http://
     www.idbsu.edu/english/jbattali>.
```

In-Text Citation: (Battalio)

You may cite a document that is part of a Web site. For example:

```
Cohn, Priscilla. "Wildlife Contraception: An
     Introduction." Animal Rights Law Center
     Web Site. 1998. Rutgers U. 27 May 1998
     <http://www.animal-law.org/hunting/
     contintro.htm>.
```

In-Text Citation: (Cohn)

AN ONLINE POSTING

An online post can be a contribution to an e-mail discussion group such as a listserv, a post to a bulletin board or usenet group, or a WWW forum.

The description *Online posting* is included after the title of the message (usually drawn from the subject line). List the date the material was posted, the access date, and the online address as you would for any other online citation.

```
Alvoeiro, Jorge. "Neurological Effects of Music."
     Online posting. 20 June 1996. 10 Aug. 1996
     <news:sci.psychology.misc>.
```

In-Text Citation: (Alvoeiro)

The following example is from an e-mail discussion group. The address at the end of the citation is from the group's archives, available on the Web. If you don't have an Internet address for the post you want to cite, include the e-mail address of the group's moderator or supervisor.

```
Ledgerberg, Joshua. "Re: You Shall Know Them."
     Online posting. 2 May 1997. Darwin
     Discussion Group. 27 May 1998 <http://
     rjohara.uncg.edu>.
```

In-Text Citation: (Ledgerberg)

AN E-MAIL MESSAGE

```
Tobin, Lad. "Teaching the TA Seminar."
     E-mail to the author. 8 July 1996.
```

In-Text Citation: (Tobin)

A SOUND CLIP

```
Gonzales, Richard. "Asian American Political
     Strength." Natl. Public Radio. 27 May 1998.
     12 July 1998 <http://www.npr.org/ramfiles/
     980527.me.12.ram>.
```

In-Text Citation: (Gonzales)

AN INTERVIEW

```
Boukreev, Anatoli. Interview. Outside Online
     14 Nov. 1997. 27 May 1998 <http://outside.
     starwave.com/news/123097/anatolitrans.html>.
```

In-Text Citation: (Boukreev)

SYNCHRONOUS COMMUNICATION (MOOS, MUDS, IRCS)

```
Fanderclai, Terri. Online interview. 11 Nov. 1996. LinguaMOO.
     11 Nov. 1996 <telnet://purple-crayon.media.mit.edu_8888>.
```

In-Text Citation: (Fanderclai)

A Sample Paper in MLA Style

Most of the student essays in *The Curious Writer* use MLA style. For a fully documented research paper, see Amy Garrett's essay, "We Need the Sun," in Chapter 11.

APA DOCUMENTATION GUIDELINES

The American Psychological Association's (APA) citation conventions are the other dominant approach to acknowledging sources. If you're headed for courses in the social sciences, then this is the system you'll use. It's no harder than the MLA; in fact, the two systems are quite similar. Both use parenthetical citations. Both organize the bibliography (or "References" page) in very similar ways. But there are a few significant differences, some of which are summarized in the accompanying table. Detailed descriptions of the APA system then follow.

MLA VERSUS APA: SOME BASIC DIFFERENCES

MLA APPROACH	APA APPROACH
(Author page #)—Example: According to Ackerman, there is an infatuation chemical (164).	**(Author, year)—Example:** According to Ackerman (1994), there is an infatuation chemical.
Usually no title page.	Usually title page and abstract. An abstract is a short summary of the paper's content, always less than 120 words in APA style.
Pagination uses writer's last name and page number. For example:	Pagination uses running head and page number. A "running head" is the paper's abbreviated title. For example:
Smith 5	Exporting Jobs 5
Figures and tables included within the paper.	Figures and tables included in section at the end of the paper.
Bibliography called "Works Cited" page.	Bibliography called "References" page.

🔍 INQUIRING INTO THE DETAILS

RECENT APA STYLE CHANGES

- Article abstracts should be no longer than 120 words.
- Whenever possible, use italics, rather than underlining.
- When quoting from electronic sources that lack page or paragraph numbers, use subheadings, if available, to pinpoint the location of borrowed material.
- It's okay to use boldface.
- Use the paragraph symbol (¶) or the abbreviation *para* in the citation to identify the location of borrowed material in an electronic source.
- In the references, list up to six authors. For more than six, list the first and use the abbreviation *et al.*
- Expanded list of examples to reflect a wider variety of Internet documents.
- Use serif typeface in text, and san serif in figures, tables, and illustrations.

Source: APA *Publication Manual,* 5th. ed.

How the Essay Should Look

Page Format. Papers should be double-spaced, with at least one-inch margins on all sides. Number all pages consecutively, beginning with the title page; put the page number in the upper-righthand corner. Above or five spaces to the left of the page number, place an abbreviated title of the paper on every page, in case pages get separated. As a rule, the first line of all paragraphs of text should be indented five spaces.

Title Page. Unlike a paper in MLA style, an APA-style paper often has a separate title page, containing the following information: the title of the paper, the author, and the author's affiliation (e.g., what university she is from). See Figure 13.3. At the top of the title page, in uppercase letters, you may also include a *running head,* or an abbreviation of the title (fifty characters or less, including spaces). A page header, which uses the first two or three words of the title followed by the page number, begins on the title page, too. This is different from the running head, which tends to be longer and appears only on the title page. Each line of information should be centered and double-spaced.

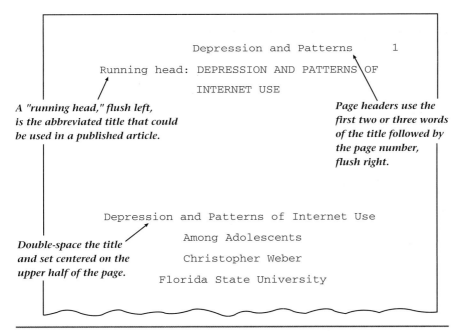

```
                      Depression and Patterns        1
              Running head: DEPRESSION AND PATTERNS OF
                            INTERNET USE




                 Depression and Patterns of Internet Use
                            Among Adolescents
                           Christopher Weber
                        Florida State University
```

A "running head," flush left, is the abbreviated title that could be used in a published article.

Page headers use the first two or three words of the title followed by the page number, flush right.

Double-space the title and set centered on the upper half of the page.

FIGURE 13.3 Title page in APA style.

Abstract. Although it's not always required, many APA-style papers include a short abstract (no longer than 120 words) following the title page. See Figure 13.4. An abstract is essentially a short summary of the paper's contents. This is a key feature, since it's usually the first thing a reader encounters. The abstract should include statements about what problem or question the paper examines and what approach it follows; the abstract should also cite the thesis and significant findings. Type the title "Abstract" at the top of the page. Type the abstract text in a single block, without indenting.

Body of the Paper. The body of the paper begins with the center title, followed by a double space and then the text. A page number (usually an abbreviated title and "3" if the paper has a title page and abstract) should appear in the upper-righthand corner. See Figure 13.5

You may find that you want to use headings within your paper. If your paper is fairly formal, some headings might be prescribed, such as "Introduction," "Method," "Results," and "Discussion." Or create your own heads to clarify the organization of your paper.

An abstract usually follows the title page.
This is a concise (no longer than 120 words)
summary of the article and its thesis,
purpose, or findings.

Depression and Patterns   2

Abstract

With the growth of the Internet as both a

source of information and entertainment,

researchers have turned their attention to

the psychology of Internet use, particularly

focusing on the emotional states of high

Internet users. This project focuses on the

relationship between patterns of Internet

use and depression in adolescent users,

arguing that

Continue the
page header.

FIGURE 13.4 The abstract page.

Depression and Patterns   3

Depression and Patterns of Internet Use

Among Adolescents

Before Johnny Beale's family got a new

computer in August 2002, the sixteen-year-

old high school student estimated that he

spent about twenty minutes a day online,

mostly checking his e-mail. Within months,

however, Beals's time at the computer

tripled, and he admitted that he spent most

of his time playing games. At first, his

family noticed

Center the title
of the paper
and double-space
to begin the body
of the text.

FIGURE 13.5 The body of the paper in APA style.

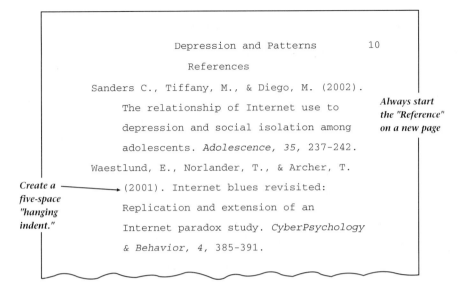

FIGURE 13.6 The references page.

If you use headings, the APA recommends a hierarchy like this:

CENTERED UPPERCASE

Centered Upper- and Lowercase

Centered, Italicized, Upper- and Lowercase

Flush Left, Italicized, Upper- and Lowercase

Indented, Italicized, lowercase; ends with period.

It's rare that a paper will use all five levels of headings. In fact, for the essays you write in your composition class, it's likely that you'll use no more than two levels, a center upper-case title, and a centered lower-case title. For example,

THE INTELLIGENCE OF CROWS

Current Understandings of Crow Intelligence

References Page. All sources cited in the body of the paper are listed alphabetically by author (or title, if anonymous) on the page titled "References." See Figure 13.6. This list should begin a new page. Each entry is double-spaced; begin each first line flush left, and indent subsequent lines five to seven spaces. Explanation of how to cite various sources in the references follows in the "Preparing the 'References' List section."

Appendix. This is a seldom-used feature of an APA-style paper, although you might find it helpful for presenting specific or tangential material that isn't central to the discussion in the body of your paper: a detailed description of a device described in the paper, a copy of a blank survey, or the like. Each item should begin on a separate page and be labeled "Appendix" followed by "A," "B," and so on, consecutively, if there is more than one item.

Notes. Several kinds of notes might be included in a paper. The most common is *content notes,* or brief commentaries by the writer keyed to superscript numbers in the body of the text. These notes are useful for discussion of key points that are relevant but might be distracting if explored in the text of your paper. Present all notes, numbered consecutively, on a page titled "Footnotes." Each note should be double-spaced. Begin each note with the appropriate superscript number, keyed to the text. Indent each first line five to seven spaces; consecutive lines run the full page measure.

Tables and Figures. The final section of an APA-style paper features tables and figures mentioned in the text. Tables should all be double-spaced. Type a table number at the top of the page, flush left. Number tables "Table 1," "Table 2," and so on, corresponding to the order they are mentioned in the text. A table may also include a title. Each table should begin on a separate page.

Figures (illustrations, graphs, charts, photographs, drawings) are handled similarly to tables. Each should be titled "Figure" and numbered consecutively. Captions may be included, but all should be typed on a separate page, clearly labeled "Figure Captions," and listed in order. For example:

```
                        Figure Captions
     Figure 1: A photograph taken in the 1930s by Dorthea Lange.
     Figure 2: Edward Weston took a series of green pepper pho-
     tographs like this. This is titled "No. 35."
```

Language and Style. The APA is comfortable with the italics and bold functions of modern word processors, and underlining is a thing of the past. The guidelines for *italicizing* call for its use when writing the following:

- The title of books, periodicals, and publications that appear on microfilm.

- When using new or specialized terms, but only the first time you use them (e.g., the authors' *paradox study* of Internet users . . .)

- When citing a phrase, letter, or word as an example (e.g., the second *a* in *separate* can be remembered by remembering the word *rat*).

The APA calls for quotation marks around the title of an article or book chapter when mentioned in your essay.

Been nagged all your life by the question of whether to spell out numbers or use numerals in APA style? Here, finally, is the answer: numbers less than 10 that aren't precise measurements should be spelled out, and numbers 10 or more should be numeric.

Citing Sources in Your Essay

When the Author Is Mentioned in the Text. The author/date system is pretty uncomplicated. If you mention the name of the author in text, simply place the year her work was published in parentheses immediately after her name. For example:

```
Herrick (1999) argued that college testing was biased against
minorities.
```

When the Author Isn't Mentioned in the Text. If you don't mention the author's name in the text, then include that information parenthetically. For example:

```
A New Hampshire political scientist (Sundberg, 2004) recently
studied the state's presidential primary.
```

Note that the author's name and the year of her work are separated by a comma.

When to Cite Page Numbers. If the information you're citing came from specific pages, chapters, or sections of a source, that information may also included in the parenthetical citation. Including page numbers is essential when quoting a source. For example:

```
The first stage of language acquisition is called caretaker
speech (Moskowitz, 1985, pp. 50-51), in which children model
their parents' language.
```

The same passage might also be cited this way if the authority's name is mentioned in the text:

```
Moskowitz (1985) observed that the first stage of language ac-
quisition is called caretaker speech (pp. 50-51), in which
children model their parents' language.
```

A Single Work by Two or More Authors. When a work has two authors, always mention them both whenever you cite their work in your paper. For example:

> Allen and Oliver (1998) observed many cases of child abuse and
> concluded that maltreatment inhibited language development.

If a source has more than two authors but less than six, mention them all the first time you refer to their work. However, any subsequent references can include the surname of the first author followed by the abbreviation *et al.* When citing works with six more authors, *always* use the first author's surname and *et al.*

A Work with No Author. When a work has no author, cite an abbreviated title and the year. Place article or chapter titles in quotation marks, and underline book titles. For example:

> The editorial ("Sinking," 1992) concluded that the EPA was
> mired in bureaucratic muck.

Two or More Works by the Same Author. Works by the same author are usually distinguished by the date; works are rarely published the same year. But if they are, distinguish among works by adding an *a* or *b* immediately following the year in the parenthetical citation. The reference list will also have these suffixes. For example:

> Douglas's studies (1986a) on the mating habits of lobsters re-
> vealed that the females are dominant. He also found that the
> female lobsters have the uncanny ability to smell a loser
> (1986b).

This citation alerts readers that the information came from two studies by Douglas, both published in 1986.

An Institutional Author. When citing a corporation or agency as a source, simply list the year of the study in parentheses if you mention the institution in the text:

> The Environmental Protection Agency (2000) issued an alarming
> report on ozone pollution.

If you don't mention the institutional source in the text, spell it out in its entirety, along with the year. In subsequent parenthetical citations, abbreviate the name. For example:

> A study (Environmental Protection Agency [EPA], 2000) pre-
> dicted dire consequences from continued ozone depletion.

And later:

> Continued ozone depletion may result in widespread skin can-
> cers (EPA, 2000).

Multiple Works in the Same Parentheses. Occasionally, you'll want to cite several works at once that speak to a topic you're writing about in your essay. Probably the most common instance is when you refer to the findings of several relevant studies, something that is a good idea as you try to establish a context for what has already been said about your research topic. For example,

> A number of researchers have explored the connection between
> Internet use and depression (Sanders, Field & Diego, 2000;
> Waestlund, Norlander, & Archer, 2001).

When listing multiple authors in the same parenthesis, order them as they appear in the references. Semicolons separate each entry.

Interviews, E-mail, and Letters. Interviews and other personal communications are not listed in the references at the back of the paper, since they are not *recoverable data*, but they are parenthetically cited in the text. Provide the initials and surname of the subject (if not mentioned in the text), the nature of the communication, and the complete date, if possible.

> Nancy Diamonti (personal communication, November 12, 1990)
> disagrees with the critics of Sesame Street.

> In a recent e-mail, Michelle Payne (personal communication,
> January 4, 2000) complained that. . .

New Editions of Old Works. For reprints of older works, include both the year of the original publication and that of the reprint edition (or the translation).

> Pragmatism as a philosophy sought connection between scientific
> study and real people's lives (James, 1906/1978).

A Web Site. When referring to an *entire* Web site (see example below), cite the address parenthetically in your essay. Like e-mail, it isn't necessary to include a citation for an entire Web site in your references list. However, you will cite online documents that contribute information to your paper (see the "Citing Electronic Sources" section).

> One of the best sites for searching the so-called Invisible Web
> is the Librarians Index to the Internet (http://www.lii.org).

Preparing the "References" List

All parenthetical citations in the body of the paper correspond to a complete listing of sources on the "References" page. The format for this section was described earlier (see "References Page").

Order of Sources. List the references alphabetically by author or by the first key word of the title if there is no author. The only complication may be if you have several articles or books by the same author. If the sources weren't published in the same year, list them in chronological order, the earliest first. If the sources were published in the *same* year, include a lowercase letter to distinguish them. For example:

```
Lane, B. (1991a). Verbal medicine . . .

Lane, B. (1991b). Writing . . .
```

While the alphabetical principle—listing authors according to the alphabetical placement of their last names—works in most cases, there are a few variations you should be aware of.

- If you have several entries by the same author, list them by year of publication, beginning with the earliest.
- Since scholars and writers often collaborate, you may have several references in which an author is listed with several *different* collaborators. List these alphabetically using the second author's last name. For example,

  Brown, M., Nelson, A. (2002)

  Brown, M., Payne, M. (1999)
- Sources with the same authors are listed chronologically.

Order of Information. A reference to a periodical or book in APA style includes this information, in order: author, date of publication, article title, periodical title, and publication information.

Author. List all authors—last name, comma, and then initials. Invert all authors' names. Use commas to separate authors' names add an ampersand (&) before the last author's name. When citing an edited book, list the editor(s) in place of the author, and add the abbreviation *Ed.* or *Eds.* in parentheses following the last name. End the list of names with a period.

Date. List the year the work was published, along with the date if it's a magazine or newspaper (see "Sample References," following), in parentheses, immediately after the last author's name. Add a period after the closing parenthesis.

Article or Book Title. APA style departs from MLA, at least with respect to periodicals. In APA style, only the first word of the article title is capitalized, and it is not underlined or quoted. Book titles, on the other hand, are italicized; capitalize only the first word of the title and any subtitle. End all titles with periods.

Periodical Title and Publication Information. Italicize the complete periodical title; type it using both uppercase and lowercase letters. Add the volume number (if any), also italicized. Separate the title and volume number with a comma (e.g., *Journal of Mass Communication, 10,* 138–150). If each issue of the periodical starts with page 1, then also include the issue number in parentheses immediately after the volume number (see examples following). End the entry with the page numbers of the article. Use the abbreviation *p.* or *pp.* if you are citing a newspaper. Other APA-style abbreviations include:

Chap.	p. (pp.)
Ed.	Vol.
Rev. ed.	No.
2nd ed.	Pt.
Trans.	Suppl.

For books, list the city and state or country of publication (use postal abbreviations) and the name of the publisher; separate the city and publisher with a colon. End the citation with a period. Cities that do not require state or country abbreviations include:

Baltimore	Amsterdam
Boston	Jerusalem
Chicago	London
Los Angeles	Milan
New York	Moscow
Philadelphia	Paris
San Francisco	Rome
	Stockholm
	Tokyo
	Vienna

Remember that the first line of each citation should begin flush left and all subsequent lines should be indented five to seven spaces. Double-space all entries.

Sample References

A JOURNAL ARTICLE
Cite a journal article like this:

```
Blager, F. B. (1979). The effect of intervention
    on the speech and language of children. Child
    Abuse and Neglect, 5, 91-96.
```

In-Text Citations: (Blager, 1979)

If the author is mentioned in the text, just parenthetically cite the year: Blager (1979) stated that . . .

If the author is quoted, include the page number(s):

(Blager, 1979, p. 92)

A JOURNAL ARTICLE NOT PAGINATED CONTINUOUSLY

Most journals begin on page 1 with the first issue of the year and continue paginating consecutively for subsequent issues. A few journals, however, start on page 1 with each issue. For these, include the issue number in parentheses following the volume number:

Williams, J., Post, A. T., & Stunk, F. (1991). The
    rhetoric of inequality. *Attwanata, 12* (3),
    54–67.

First In-Text Citation: (Williams, Post, & Stunk, 1991)

Subsequent citations would use *et al.:* (Williams et al., 1991)

If quoting material, include the page number(s):

(Williams et al., 1991, pp. 55–60)

A MAGAZINE ARTICLE

Maya, P. (1981, December). The civilizing of
    Genie. *Psychology Today,* 28–34.

In-Text Citations: (Maya, 1981)

Maya (1981) observed that . . .

If quoting, include the page number(s): (Maya, 1981, p. 28)

A NEWSPAPER ARTICLE

Honan, W. (1991, January 24). The war affects
    Broadway. *New York Times,* pp. C15–16.

In-Text Citations: (Honan, 1991)

Honan (1991) argued that . . .

Honan (1991) said that "Broadway is a battleground" (p. C15).

If there is no author, a common situation with newspaper articles, alphabetize using the first "significant word" in the article title. The parenthetical citation would use an abbreviation of the title in quotation marks, then the year.

A BOOK

Lukas, A. J. (1986). *Common ground: A turbulent decade in the lives of three American families.* New York: Random House.

In-Text Citations: (Lukas, 1986)

According to Lukas (1986), . . .

If quoting, include the page number(s).

A BOOK OR ARTICLE WITH MORE THAN ONE AUTHOR

Rosenbaum, A., & O'Leary, D. (1978). Children: The unintended victims of marital violence. *American Journal of Orthopsychiatry, 4,* 692–699.

In-Text Citations: (Rosenbaum & O'Leary, 1978)

Rosenbaum and O'Leary (1978) believed that . . .

If quoting, include the page number(s).

A BOOK OR ARTICLE WITH AN UNKNOWN AUTHOR

The politics of war. (2004, June 1). *The New York Times,* p. 36.

In-Text Citations: ("Politics," 2004)

Or mention the source in the text:

In an "The politics of war" (2004), an editorialist compared Iraq to . . .

If quoting, provide page number(s) as well.

A manual of style (14th ed.). (1993). Chicago: University of Chicago Press.

In-Text Citations: (*Manual of Style,* 1993)

According to the *Manual of Style* (1993), . . .

If quoting, include the page number(s).

A BOOK WITH AN INSTITUTIONAL AUTHOR

American Red Cross. (1999). *Advanced first aid and emergency care.* New York: Doubleday.

In-Text Citations: (*Advanced First Aid,* 1999)

The book *Advanced First Aid and Emergency Care* (1999) stated that . . .

If quoting, include the page number(s).

A BOOK WITH AN EDITOR

> Crane, R. S. (Ed.). (1952). *Critics and criticism.*
>   Chicago: University of Chicago Press.

In-Text Citations: (Crane, 1952)

In his preface, Crane (1952) observed that . . .

If quoting, include the page number(s).

A SELECTION IN A BOOK WITH AN EDITOR

> McKeon, R. (1952). Rhetoric in the Middle Ages. In
>   R. S. Crane (Ed.), *Critics and criticism*
>   (pp. 260-289). Chicago: University of Chicago
>   Press.

In-Text Citations: (McKeon, 1952)

McKeon (1952) argued that . . .

If quoting, include the page number(s).

A REPUBLISHED WORK

> James, W. (1978). *Pragmatism.* Cambridge, MA:
>   Harvard University Press. (Original work
>   published 1907)

In-Text Citations: (James, 1907/1978)

According to William James (1907/1978), . . .

If quoting, include the page number(s).

AN ABSTRACT

The growth of online databases for articles has increased the availability of full-text versions or abstracts of articles. While the full article is almost always best, sometimes an abstract alone contains some useful information. If the abstract was retrieved from a database or some other secondary source, include information about it. Aside from the name of the source, this information might involve the date, if different from the year of publication of the original article, an abstract number, or a page number. In the following example, the abstract was used from an online database, *Biological Abstracts.*

> Garcia, R. G. (2002). Evolutionary speed of species
>   invasions. *Evolution, 56,* 661-668. Abstract
>   obtained from *Biological Abstracts.*

In-Text Citations: (Garcia, 2002), *or* Garcia (2002) argues that . . .

A SOURCE MENTIONED BY ANOTHER SOURCE

Frequently, you'll read an article that mentions another article you haven't read. Whenever possible, track down that original article and read it in its entirety. But when that's not possible, you need to make it clear that you know of the article and its findings or arguments indirectly. The APA convention for this is to use the expression *as cited in* parenthetically, followed by the author and date of the indirect source. For example, suppose you want to use some information from Eric Weiser's piece that you read about in Charlotte Jones's book. In your essay, you would write something like:

```
Weiser argues (as cited in Jones, 2002) that . . .
```

It isn't necessary to include information about the Weiser article in your references. Just cite the indirect source; in this case, that would be the Jones book.

A BOOK REVIEW

```
Dentan, R. K. (1989). A new look at the brain
     [Review of the book The dreaming brain].
     Psychiatric Journal, 13, 51.
```

In-Text Citations: (Dentan, 1989)

```
Dentan (1989) argued that . . .
```

If quoting, include the page number(s).

A GOVERNMENT DOCUMENT

```
U.S. Bureau of the Census. (1991). Statistical
     abstract of the United States (111th ed.).
     Washington, DC: U.S. Government Printing
     Office.
```

In-Text Citations: (U.S. Bureau, 1991)

```
According to the U.S. Census Bureau (1991), . . .
```

If quoting, include the page number(s).

A LETTER TO THE EDITOR

```
Hill, A. C. (1992, February 19). A flawed history
     of blacks in Boston [Letter to the editor].
     The Boston Globe, p. 22.
```

In-Text Citations: (Hill, 1992)

```
Hill (1992) complained that . . .
```

If quoting, include page number(s).

A PUBLISHED INTERVIEW

Personal interviews are usually not cited in an APA-style paper, unlike published interviews. Here is a citation for a published interview:

```
Cotton, P. (2004, April). [Interview with Jake
     Tule, psychic]. Chronicles Magazine,
     pp. 24-28.
```

In-Text Citations: (Cotton, 2004)

```
Cotton (2004) noted that . . .
```

If quoting, include the page number(s).

A FILM OR VIDEOTAPE

```
Hitchcock, A. (Producer & Director). (1954). Rear
     window [Film]. Los Angeles: MGM.
```

In-Text Citations: (Hitchcock, 1954)

```
In Rear Window, Hitchcock (1954) . . .
```

A TELEVISION PROGRAM

```
Burns, K. (Executive Producer). (1996). The west
     [Television broadcast]. New York and
     Washington, DC: Public Broadcasting Service.
```

In-Text Citations: (Burns, 1996)

```
In Ken Burns's (1996) film, . . .
```

For an episode of a television series, use the scriptwriter as the author, and provide the director's name after the scriptwriter. List the producer's name after the episode.

In-Text Citations: (Duncan, 1996)

```
In the second episode, Duncan (1996) explores . . .
```

A MUSICAL RECORDING

```
Wolf, K. (1986). Muddy roads [Recorded by E.
     Clapton]. On Gold in california [CD].
     Santa Monica, CA: Rhino Records. (1990)
```

In-Text Citations: (Wolf, 1986, track 5)

```
In Wolf's (1986) song, . . .
```

A COMPUTER PROGRAM

```
OmniPage Pro 14 (Version 14) [Computer
    software]. (2003). Peabody, MA:
    Scansoft.
```

In-Text Citation: (OmniPage Pro Version 14, 2003)

```
Scansoft's new software, OmniPage Pro (2003) is reputed . . .
```

Citing Electronic Sources. The ever-changing Internet is forcing continual change on professional organizations such as the APA. The fifth edition of the group's *Publication Manual* significantly expanded instructions on how to cite electronic sources, largely reflecting the growth in the variety of documents on the Web. The APA's Web page, *www.apastyle.org,* includes some excerpted information from the *Publication Manual* and is a good source of news for any new changes in documentation methods. But much of what you need to know can be found here. The key in any citation is to help readers find the original sources if they want to, and for Web-based documents, that means the Internet address, URL, has to be accurate. The copy-and-paste function of your word processing program will be your ally in this.

The essential information when citing an electronic source, in order, includes the following:

- The author(s), if indicated
- The title of the document, Web page, or newsgroup
- A date of publication, update, or retrieval
- The Internet address, or URL

Sample References

AN ELECTRONIC VERSION OF AN ARTICLE ALSO IN PRINT

Because so much scholarly information on the Web is simply an electronic version of an article published in print, some of what you cite will simply list the conventional bibliographic information for any periodical article. But if you only viewed an electronic version, you must indicate that in your citation. For example,

```
Codrescu, A. (March, 2002). Curious? Untouchable
    porcelain meets fluttering pigeons [Electronic
    version]. Smithsonian, 104.
```

In-Text Citation: (Codrescu, 2002), *or* Codrescu (2002) believes that . . .

If you suspect that the electronic version of an article that appeared in print has been changed in any way, then you should include the date you retrieved the article from the Web and the URL of the document. For example,

```
Ballenger, B. (1999). Befriending the Internet.
    The Curious Researcher, 59-76. Retrieved
    July 18, 2002, from http://english. boisestate
    .edu/bballenger
```

In-Text Citation: (Ballenger, 1999) *or* Ballenger (1999) features an exercise . . .

AN ARTICLE ONLY ON THE INTERNET

```
Adler, J. (1996). Save endangered species, not
    the Endangered Species Act. Intellectual
    Ammunition. Retrieved October 12, 1999, from
    http://www.heartland.org/05jnfb96.http
```

In-Text Citations: (Adler, 1996)

According to Adler (1996) . . .

If quoting, include page number(s).

AN ELECTRONIC TEXT

```
Encyclopedia Mythica. (1996). Retrieved December
    1, 1999, from http://www.pantheon.org/myth
```

In-Text Citations: (Encyclopedia Mythica, 1996)

The Encyclopedia Mythica (1996) presents . . .

If the text is an electronic version of a book published in print earlier, include the original publication date in parentheses following the title: (Orig. pub. 1908)

AN ARTICLE OR ABSTRACT FROM A LIBRARY DATABASE

As mentioned earlier, library databases, often accessed online, increasingly offer not just citations of articles, but full-text versions of abstracts, too. This wonderful service can make a trip to the library superfluous. When citing an article or abstract from a database, simply include the name of that database at the end of the citation followed by a period.

```
Ullman, S., & Brecklin, L. (2002). Sexual assault history and
    suicidal behavior in a national sample of women. Suicide
    and Life Threatening Behavior, 32, 117-130. Retrieved
    October 18, 2002, from Electronic Collections Online
    database.
```

In-Text Citations: (Ullman & Brecklin, 2002), *or if you like* Ullman and Brecklin (2002) argue that . . .

An abstract from an electronic database is cited much the same way except to clarify that the source *is* an abstract. For example,

```
Warm, A., & Murray, C. (2002). Who helps? Supporting
     people who self harm. Journal of Mental
     Health, 11, 121-130. Abstract retrieved July
     19, 2002, from PsychINFO database.
```

In-Text Citations: (Warm & Murray, 2002), *or* According to Warm and Murray (2002) . . .

A PART OF A WORK

```
Hunter, J. (n.d.). Achilles. In Encyclopedia
     Mythica. Retrieved January 4, 2000, from http://www.pan-
     theon.org/myth/achill
```

In-Text Citations: (Hunter, n.d.)

According to Hunter (no date), Achilles was . . .

If quoting, include the page or paragraph number(s), if any.

AN ONLINE JOURNAL

```
Schneider, M. (1998). The nowhere man and mother
     nature's son: Collaboration and resentment
     in the lyrical ballads of the Beatles.
     Anthropoetics, 4(2), 1-11. Retrieved
     November 24, 1999, from http://www.humnet
     .ucla.edu/humnet/anthropoetics/ap0402/
     utopia.htm
```

In-Text Citations: (Schneider, 1998)

Schneider (1998) recently observed that . . .

If quoting, include page or paragraph numbers, if any.

A NEWSPAPER ARTICLE

It's not hard anymore to find articles online from all the major American and even international newspapers. Like other nonscholarly periodicals, include more specific information about date of publication in the parenthesis following the author's name, and as usual include the date retrieved and the URL.

```
Broad, J. W. (2002, July 18). Piece by piece a
     Civil War battleship is pulled from the sea.
     New York Times. Retrieved July 18, 2002, from
     http://www.nytimes.com
```

In-Text Citations: (Broad, 2002) *or* Broad (2002) reports that . . .

A WEBSITE

If you're referring to an entire Web site in the text of your essay, include the address parenthetically. However, there is no need to include it in the reference list. For example:

```
One of the best sites for searching the so-called Invisible Web
is the Librarians Index to the Internet (http://www.lii.org).
```

DISCUSSION LISTS

Discussion lists abound on the Internet. They range from groups of flirtatious teenagers to those with a serious academic purpose. Although virtually all of these discussion lists are based on e-mail, they do vary a bit. The most useful lists for academic research tend to be e-mail discussion lists called listservs. Newsgroups, or usenet groups, are extremely popular among more general Internet users. There are various search engines that will help you find these discussion groups on your topic. You can join or monitor the current discussion or, in some cases, search the archives for contributions that interest you. Google is a great search tool for newsgroups and includes an archive for many of them. *If there are no archives, don't include the citation in your references since the information isn't recoverable.* However, you may still cite these in your essay as a personal communication.

The method of citation varies slightly if it's a newsgroup, an online forum, or a listserv. For example,

```
Hord, J. (2002, July 11). Why do pigeons lift one
    wing up in the air? [Msg 5]. Message posted
    to rec://pets.birds.pigeons
```

In-Text Citations: (Hord), *or* Hord asks (2002) . . .

Note that the citation includes the subject line of the message as the title, and the message number of the "thread" (the particular discussion topic). The protocol for this newsgroup is *rec,* which indicates the list is hobby oriented.

Listservs, or electronic mailing lists, would be cited this way:

```
Cook, D. (2002, July 19). Grammar and the teaching
    of writing. Message posted to the CompTalk
    electronic mailing list, archived at
    http://listserv.comptalk.boisestate.edu
```

In-Text Citations: (Cook, 2002), *or* According to Cook (2002) . . .

E-MAIL

E-mail is not cited in the list of references. But you should cite e-mail in the text of your essay. It should look like this:

In-Text Citations: `Michelle Payne (personal communication, January 4,`
`2000) believes that PDAs are silly . . .`

CD-ROM DATABASES AND ENCYCLOPEDIAS

Cite a CD-based database like an online database, including the retrieval date. For example:

`Drugs and Drug Interaction. (1999).` *Encyclopaedia*
`    ` *Britannica.* `Retrieved from Encyclopaedia Britannica.`

In-Text Citation: `("Drugs and Drug Interaction," 1999)`

`Kolata, G. (1996, July 10). Research links writing style to`
`the risk of Alzheimer's.` *New York Times.* `Retrieved from UMI-`
`Proquest/Newspaper Abstracts database`

In-Text Citation: `(Kolata, 1996)`

A Sample Paper in APA Style

To see a documented research paper in APA style, go to Jeremy Johnson's ethnographic essay, "I See Me as You See Me" in Chapter 10 or "Examining the Maintenance of Friendships" by Amy Johnson in Chapter 11.

USING WHAT YOU HAVE LEARNED

The main message you should take from this chapter is that if you don't make the effort to control your sources, your sources will control you, with results ranging from writing that fails to deliver on its promise to accidental plagiarism.

1. List three ways that you can control sources in a research essay so that they don't control you.

2. The concern about plagiarism is growing, and most blame the Internet. Do you agree with both of those premises—that plagiarism is a bigger problem and the Internet is the cause?

3. You won't always be required to cite sources for papers in other classes. In fact, you've probably noticed that some articles in more popular periodicals don't cite information at all, even though it's clearly a product of research. How do you explain this?

Part Four
RE-INQUIRING

Rewriting necessarily involves some time staring off into space. But the work gets done much more quickly when you're *doing* things—exploring different beginnings, fastwriting in your journal about what seems to be working and what needs work, talking to someone about your topic or ideas, doing fresh research, or pruning sentences to make your writing clear. Revision is work. But it's also an opportunity for surprise. The trick is to see what you have written in ways you haven't seen before.

Revision Strategies

RESEEING YOUR TOPIC

"I don't really revise," Amy told me the other day. "I'm usually pretty happy with my first draft."

Always? I wondered.

"Well, certainly not always," she said. "But I know I work better under pressure so I usually write my papers right before they're due. There usually isn't much time for revision, even if I wanted to do it, which I don't, really."

Amy is pretty typical. Her first draft efforts usually aren't too bad, but I often sense tentativeness in her prose, endings that seem much stronger than beginnings, and promises that aren't really kept. Her essay promises to focus on the dangers of genetically engineered foods to teenagers who live on Cheese-Its and Cheetos, but she never quite gets to saying much about that. The writing is competent—pretty clear and without too many awkward passages—but ultimately it's disappointing to read.

You can guess what I'm getting at here—Amy's work could be much stronger if it were rewritten—but the logic of last-minute writing is pretty powerful: "I really think I need to bump up against a deadline."

The writing process has three phases: prewriting, drafting, and rewriting. Prewriting refers to a range of activities writers might engage in before they attempt to compose a first draft, including fastwriting, listing, clustering, rehearsing lines or passages, preliminary research, conversations, or even the kind of deep thought about a topic that for some of us seems to occur best in the shower. The drafting stage is hardly mysterious. It often involves the much slower, much more focused process of putting words to paper, crafting a draft that presumably grows from some of the prewriting activities. Rewriting is a rethinking of that draft. Although this typically in-

What You'll Learn in This Chapter

- How genuine revision involves exactly that: re-vision, or *re-seeing* your topic.

- Basic revision strategies for "divorcing the draft."

- How to become a reader of your own work.

- The five categories of revision.

- Advanced revision strategies.

volves tweaking sentences, it's much more than that. Revision, as the name implies, is a *reseeing* of the paper's topic and the writer's initial approach to it in the draft.

DIVORCING THE DRAFT

In another book, *The Curious Researcher,* I describe my relationship with Jan, a high school girlfriend. At first, I resisted the relationship—in some ways, we seemed mismatched, and at times there were some troubling emotional patterns—but as time went on, Jan and I grew closer, and when we went off to college we remained a committed couple. In fact, I was completely devoted to Jan, so much so that while I was still aware of an undercurrent of problems, I glibly ignored them. Then she met a guy at college named Peter and that was the end of that. Of course, I was devastated.

I think we develop emotional relationships with drafts, too, and one of the factors that most influences this is the amount of time we spend writing them. Like my relationship with Jan, as time goes on the commitment to the draft deepens despite awareness of its problems so that when the time comes for a divorce—and to revise well you must separate from the draft—we feel stuck, unable to see it clearly. Despite all its problems, we're going to embrace the draft and defend it from the ravages of revision.

One of the things you may have noticed in your previous writing experiences is that students who tend to spend a great deal of time drafting (i.e., *going out with Jan*) are people who also tend to have the most difficulty with revision (i.e., *breaking up with Jan*). One solution, of course, is to spend less time cultivating this relationship; for example, such a writer might try composing fast drafts instead, and might then discover that these drafts are much easier to revise. We'll talk about some of these strategies later.

There also is another pattern among resistant revisers. Students who tend to spend a relatively long time on the prewriting stage also struggle with revision. My theory is that some of these writers resist revision as a final stage in the process because *they have already practiced some revision at the beginning of the process.* We often talk about revision as only occurring after you've written a draft, which of course is a quite sensible idea. But the process of revision is an effort to *resee* a subject, to circle it with questions, to view it from fresh angles, and many of the open-ended writing methods we've discussed in *The Curious Writer* certainly involve revision. Fastwriting, clustering, listing, and similar invention techniques all invite the writer to re-see. Armed with these discoveries, some writers may be able to write fairly strong first drafts.

What is essential, however, whether you revise at the beginning of the writing process or, as most writers do, after you craft the draft, is achieving some separation from what you initially thought, what you initially said, and how you said it. To revise well, writers must divorce the draft, even at the risk of heartbreak.

STRATEGIES FOR DIVORCING THE DRAFT

There are some things that you can do to make separation from your work easier, and spending less time on the first draft and more time on the revision process is one of them. But aside from writing fast drafts, what are other strategies for reseeing a draft that already has a hold on you?

1. **Time.** Absolutely the best remedy for revision resistance is setting the draft aside for a week or more. Professional writers, in fact, may set a piece aside for several years and then return to it with a fresh, more critical perspective. Students simply don't have that luxury. But if you can take a week or a month—or even a day—the wait is almost always worth it.

2. **Attack the draft physically.** A cut-and-paste revision that reduces a draft to pieces is often enormously helpful because you're no longer confronted with the familiar full draft, a version that may have cast a spell on you. By dismembering the draft, you can examine the smaller fragments more critically. How does each piece relate the whole? Might there be alternative structures? What about gaps in information? (See Revision Strategy 14.15 later in this chapter for a useful cut-and-paste exercise.)

3. **Put it away.** Years ago, I wrote a magazine article about alcoholism. It was about 25 pages long and it wasn't very good. I read and reread that draft, completely puzzled about how to rewrite it. One morning, I woke up and vowed I would read the draft just once more, then put it away in a drawer and start all over again, trusting that I would remember what was important. The result was much shorter and much better. In fact, I think it's the best essay I've ever written. Getting a troublesome draft out of sight—literally—may be the best way to find new ways to see it.

4. **Readers.** Bringing other people's eyes and minds to your work allows you to see your drafts through perspectives other than your own. Other people have a completely different relationship with your writing than you do. They will see what you don't. They easily achieve the critical distance that you are trying to cultivate when you revise.

5. **Write different leads.** The nonfiction writer John McPhee once talked about beginnings as the hardest thing to write. He described a lead as a "flashlight that shines down into the story," illuminating where the draft is headed. Imagine, then, the value of writing a new

beginning, or even several alternative beginnings; each may point the next draft in a slightly different direction, perhaps one that you didn't consider in your first draft.

6. **Research.** One of the central themes of *The Curious Writer* is that research isn't a separate activity but a source of information that can enrich almost any kind of writing. Particularly in genres such as the personal essay, in which the writer's voice, perspective, and experience dominate the draft, listening to the voices and knowledge of others about a topic can deepen and shift the writer's thinking and perspectives.

7. **Read aloud.** I often ask students in workshop groups to read their drafts aloud to each other. I do this for several reasons, but the most important is the effect *hearing* a draft has on a writer's relationship to it. In a sense, we often hear a draft in our heads as we compose it or reread it, but when we read the words aloud the draft comes alive as something separate from the writer. As the writer listens to herself—or listens to someone else read her prose—she may cringe at an awkward sentence, suddenly notice a leap in logic, or recognize the need for an example. Try reading the work aloud to yourself and the same thing may happen.

8. **Write in your journal.** In the student case study that follows, Jon Butterfield tells the story of revising an essay about loss of innocence. Among the strategies he used to divorce the draft was to return to his notebook, and fastwrite to himself about what he might do to improve the piece. He does this by asking himself questions about the draft and then—through writing—tries to answer them. The method helps him see a new idea that becomes key to the structure of his third draft. Too often we see the journal exclusively as a prewriting tool, but it can be useful throughout the writing process, particularly when you need to think to yourself about ways to solve a problem in revision.

Later in this chapter, we'll build on some of these basic strategies with specific revision methods that may work with particular kinds of writing and with drafts that have particular problems. All of these methods encourage a separation between the writer and his draft or rely on that critical distance to be effective.

PHOTOGRAPHY AS A METAPHOR FOR REVISION

For several years, I taught composition by asking students to bring along a camera. The idea grew out of an experience I had in a graduate seminar with my friend and mentor Donald Murray in which we were asked to apprentice to a creative activity, and then write about how the process seemed to compare to the ways we write. I chose photography. It became clear almost immediately that there were dramatic parallels between the composing processes in each; the most striking was how much taking pictures taught me about revision.

What does it really mean to revise, or put another way, to re*see?* What might be rewarding about such an effort? For many, revision may involve little more than proofreading a first draft. But when most experienced writers imagine revision, they mean something much less superficial (not that proofreading is unimportant!). Rewriting may involve adding or cutting information, reorganizing the draft, or even rebuilding around a new angle or purpose. This kind of revision grows from the conviction that when we first look at a topic there is much we don't notice, and this is a lesson photography teaches as well.

Looking Beyond the First Picture

When I first ask my students to go out and take pictures, the only instructions I provide is that they must shoot an entire roll of film. I don't suggest photographic subjects, and I don't offer tips on technique. "Just go out and take a roll of pictures," I say, "and bring back the slides next week." The results are almost always the same: every student in the class takes one photograph of every subject, a shot that usually captures it in the most familiar angle and light conditions—the school building from across the street, the roommate or friend squinting into the sun, the long shot down the beach at midday. Rarely were these particularly interesting pictures.

The same might be said of first drafts, especially those written in a rush the night before the paper is due. The writer pretty much goes with the first picture of his topic that he sees, and revision is pretty limited to "fixing" things here and there at the last minute. One common characteristic of these one-draft papers is that they often seize on the most obvious point or idea about their topics. A paper on the accuracy of "smart bombs" argues that they aren't always smart. Or a personal essay on fading friendships concludes that "true friends are hard to find." There isn't anything wrong with stating the obvious in a first draft *if* in a revision you plan to dig more deeply, working toward a fresher argument, a better insight, a less familiar way of seeing.

My students' first roll of film makes this point really well. When you take only one picture of a subject you're not likely to see beyond what you've already seen. Our first look at almost anything is likely to reveal only what's most obvious about it. If we *really* want to see, if we really want to learn something we don't already know, we have to look and then look again. Speaking photographically, deep revision requires that we take more than one picture.

The Pepper is More Than a Pepper

The great photographer Edward Weston was famous for his black and white photographs of women, shells, and Western landscapes, but perhaps one of his most well-known projects was a series on vegetables, particularly cabbages and green peppers. His *Pepper No. 30* (see accompanying photograph) is especially famous. In his journal, Weston wrote about the process of trying to get that shot during the summer of 1930. His wife Sonya would bring him fresh peppers from the market and Weston would photograph them in different light conditions and with different backgrounds, one after another, until they were spoiled and he had to throw them away. One day he set a pepper on the porch railing, but just as he was about to take the picture, a fire truck roared by with "half the town following it." The rail shook and the picture was ruined.

"I tried the light from the opposite side in the next morning light—brilliant sun through muslin. Better!" Weston wrote. "But more failures . . . a background of picture backing was placed too close . . . the corrugations . . . spoil the feeling."

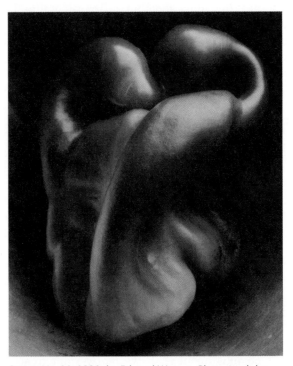

Pepper No. 30, 1930, by Edward Weston. Photograph by Edward Weston.

On July 9, Weston wrote that he "worked with peppers again, surprising myself. Peppers never repeat themselves: shells, bananas, melons, so many forms are not inclined to experiment—not so the pepper . . . ! So I have three new negatives, and two more underway."

Finally, nearly a month later, Weston had a breakthrough. "Sonya keeps tempting me with new peppers! Two more have been added to my collection. While experimenting with one . . . I tried putting it in a tin funnel for background." It was the tin funnel that gave Weston both the background and the diffusion of light that finally led to *Pepper No. 30,* the image he didn't know he was looking for. "I printed my favorite . . . ," Weston wrote in his journal. "Quickly made, but with a week's previous effort." *Pepper No. 30,* Weston concluded gleefully, "is a classic, completely satisfying—a pepper—but more than a pepper."

What's instructive about Edward Weston's account of photographing at least thirty green peppers becomes apparent to my students when I ask them to complete a second assignment with their cameras. This time, I say, choose only two subjects from the first roll and take twelve shots of each one. Make every shot different by varying distance, angle, and light conditions. By composing multiple "drafts" of their subjects, even novice photographers discover new ways of seeing things they've seen before. They see the pattern of three kinds of stone that come together on the corner of Thompson Hall—something they never really noticed before although they walk by the building every day. They see the way the fire escapes cling like black iron insects to the west side of the building, its bricks bloodied by the setting sun. They see the delicate structure of a tulip or their best friend's hand, roughened by a summer of carpentry. Once my students get past the first few pictures of a subject, they really begin to see it freshly. More often than not, the twelfth picture is much more interesting than the fifth or sixth. The principle is simple: *The more you look, the more you see.*

The motive for revision in writing isn't much different from a photographer's inclination to take more than one shot—both writer and photographer know not to trust their first look at something.

Although the Greek origin of the word is "light writing," photography of course is *not* writing. It really isn't hard to look through a camera, take a bunch of pictures, and resee a subject. Doing this in writing is more difficult, because we must "see" through language. Words often get in the way. Yet the motive for revision in writing isn't much different from a photographer's inclination to take more than one shot—both writer and photographer know not to trust their first look at something. They know they won't see it well enough, so both writers and photographers use a process that helps them to see their subjects in new ways. The rewards for doing this are similar, too: the pleasure of surprise and discovery, of learning something new about their subjects and about themselves.

✎ ONE STUDENT'S RESPONSE

AMY'S PHOTOGRAPHIC REVISION

Amy went through multiple "drafts" of the local train station to discover her real subject: the scrawled word "hate" on a rusting beam that seems to be underlined by the railroad tracks. Once she found that subject, she revised by taking multiple pictures of it, working toward what Amy hoped would be a meaningful image.

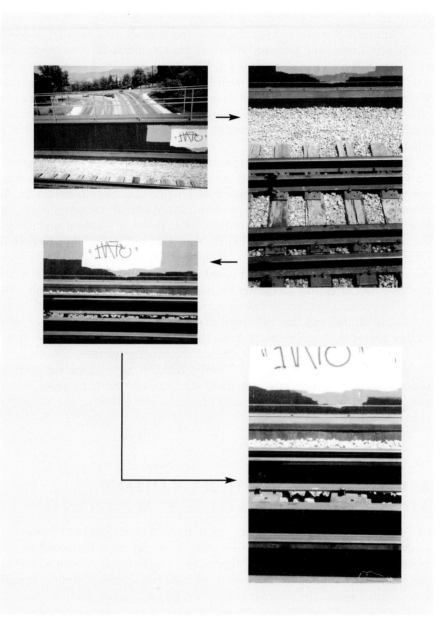

RHETORICAL REVISION

When Jon Butterfield, a student writer, talks about revision, he says it "is just as subjective as the writing process itself." What Jon means is that there isn't a formula, a certain series of steps every writer should take to complete the process correctly. Although the photography metaphor suggests that much revision involves re-seeing a draft or a writing subject, where you direct your gaze and the methods you use to do it vary with the situation. Revision is a rhetorical act. When you write in your private journal, for example, you may very well be engaged in an act of revision but you're not particularly concerned with making your ideas clear to someone else. As a result, you pay little attention to things such as coherence or clarity of language. After all, you're writing for yourself and you know what you're thinking.

Revision is also rhetorical because it is guided by a writer's purposes. Early drafts or sketches typically need attention to global issues, such as purpose and meaning. Writers' motives for revising more polished drafts might focus on smaller things, perhaps the unity of paragraphs or the strength of sentences. In the later stages of revision, writers much more keenly feel an awareness of audience. Sometimes this demands that they attempt to read their own work as if they hadn't written it, with a level of detachment that is often difficult to achieve. We've already discussed some methods for doing this, including letting time pass before attempting a revision or inviting readers to describe what they see.

Revision, like any other element of the writing process is complex, and as Jon observes, it's also individual. But writers' motives for revising do tend to fall into several broad categories: *revising for purpose, meaning, information, structure, or clarity.* Specific revision techniques for each of these categories follow after the case study below; first, however, get a glimpse into the practical challenges of revision by following the story of a student writer.

A CASE STUDY IN REVISION: JON'S HORSE RACE OF MEANING

Like a lot of young college students, Jon Butterfield missed his old friends, so it wasn't at all surprising when Jon found himself writing about that when he was invited to write a personal essay. The process began in his notebook. "When writing a sketch," Jon says, "I often draw from freewriting, a writing journal, even another essay. The material from which I draw is a collection of ideas not unlike a spattering of paint on a palette." In a sense, Jon really *begins* the writing process with revision because his early journal work allows him to take multiple pictures, moving freely from one subject to another or one idea to another. However, this doesn't mean his sketch is very polished, only that he can begin with a clearer sense of possibilities.

Jon's sketch begins as a story of the summer before he moved to Texas with his parents. He describes sitting on the shake roof of a friend's house with seven of his closest companions from high school, hanging out in the easy way of good friends, "simply enjoying each other's company." It was the last time the group shared a moment like that, and although Jon has seen many of these friends since, he writes that he is "still searching for what was lost that summer," wondering to himself if it was "youthful innocence" or perhaps "simplicity."

Jon begins the essay with a scene on that roof, as he smokes a cigar:

Gusts of gray-blue smoke billow from my lips not in their usual slow, controlled style, but they fly out all at once as my diaphragm flexes in laughter. An overpowering smile stretches across my face. The wind is still as the warm sun shines down upon us. The smell of spring wells up around us as we pollute it with pretentious cigars, giving us delusions of grandeur as we gaze over the nearly rural scene. I watch the smoke, intrigued by the way it lingers in perplexed spirals before leaving my sight forever. A melancholic tone strikes me as I watch it flee. It was so enjoyable in my mouth, however, I could never hold it in forever. It had to go, and I would let it sink into memories and escape my presence; it gave me what it could and I had to let it go.

It was a good sketch, not because it was particularly polished or even well-written. It was a good sketch because Jon saw a number of directions it could go. He knew this because he found a lot to underline: "For me, the easiest and most effective means of making sense of a piece is underlining. I look through the piece and underline things that could be important."

Among other things, Jon underlined the final five sentences of his lead paragraph above because it repeats the phrase *let go*. "This must have been an important idea for me to have repeated it this way," Jon notes. Other underlined passages included details he thought were important, and especially "shifts in my train of thought," moments when Jon moves away from the narrative to reflection.

"Looking at the underlinings together," Jon says, "I get a more focused view of the sketch. I see the sketch as a story of a futile search for things left behind in childhood. *I had to let go* becomes a thematic statement. I want to explore further why I can let the spirals go but pursue the things I am missing from childhood. [In the next draft], I will develop the details that I had chosen and rework the piece with the search coming to the forefront."

My friend Barry Lane describes early revision like this as a "horse race of meaning." In the beginning, certain ideas or feelings seem to race to the front only to be outrun from behind by another theme which may later falter when another meaning sprints ahead. This is exactly Jon's experience as he struggles to find direction in his sketch. In the next draft, Jon lets a new idea take the lead: his essay might focus on his search for what was lost that final summer with his childhood friends.

The next draft is longer than the sketch, and it weaves together a series of poignant scenes that Jon remembers with several of his small group of friends—Taryn's backyard and the coffee and cigarettes they shared until dawn, a bar where Jon and Christy pumped quarters in the jukebox and had honest conversations, and the Eagle Grill, a favorite lunch spot where the circle of friends gathered weekly. Jon workshops the draft, and he's once again reminded how "different readers read my draft in different ways." He adds, "It is sometimes hard for us as writers to anticipate how our words are understood by various readers." But the workshop was helpful, and Jon decides to return to his journal again to think through writing about the next draft.

> *This piece has grown into a collection of reminiscent scenes. The smoke spirals seem to set this mood and it continues into the scenes. Maybe the story-telling style I'm using just doesn't fit? Different moods, different styles. What if I were to intentionally separate the scenes? No, there are too many scenes to create a segmented list . . . It wouldn't hurt to try and just see what I came up with? I'd have to have a way to direct the reader through these scenes somehow. The spirals. What if the scenes were spirals?*

What I admire about Jon's approach to revision is his decision to return to his journal to try to work things out. Too often, journal work is limited to prewriting activities. But as Jon demonstrates, the journal can be useful throughout the writing process, and perhaps especially in revision as the writer rehearses new sections, generates additional information, or as Jon shows us, simply talks to himself about a writing problem.

The next draft of the piece, "Blue Spirals," uses that motif throughout. He opens the essay with the image of spiraling cigarette smoke, swirled and dissipated by an "angry" wind. Jon completely rearranges the order of scenes, cuts some and changes others, trying everywhere to emphasize the powerful but ultimately ephemeral quality of adolescent friendships, which, like the smoke, eventually blow away. "To be successful in revision," Jon says, "you have to feel free to take risks. In this case, I chopped up the essay that I had spent a lot of time crafting. I didn't know for sure if it would work or not, but I had to let myself risk failure. If I didn't like it, I would still have something else to look at and I could always scrap this draft and try something new."

While Jon is pleased with this third revision, he acknowledges that he isn't done. "All of the steps I went through for all of the preceding drafts could be revisited for this one," he says, including underlining, journal work, and reordering the information. When is revision done? In practical terms, the process is over when you hand in your paper for a grade. But Jon, like most good writers, recognizes that nearly any essay could be endlessly revised. Writers can continue to make new discoveries and find better ways to say things. "I wrote this essay for a class, submitted it, and received a good grade," Jon says. "However, I have revisited it and other pieces that I've written from time to time, almost always tweaking something."

"You must decide for yourself when it's done," Jon adds. "But always try to be open. The more open you are to change, the more likely it is that you will construct a solid draft."

BLUE SPIRALS
Jon Butterfield

Sitting alone on my hard shake roof with a Montecristo, my mind begins 1
to drift. The wind picks up slightly, forcing a blue-gray gust through my lips.
There's a pause, and it begins to open. A faint lazy spin. Gone.

After another drag and exhale, I am more intrigued. The spirals are 2
thicker this time; they spin in one large spiral, then split and fade. It's a smooth
shift, and I can't catch it—spin, split, spin, fade.

* * *

Dishes clatter through the small window to my left, before being drowned 3
out by Tana's laughter at my sad attempt to sing along with *Brown Eyed Girl.*
"With yoouuewe, my brown eyed girl." I stifle a little laugh and fight forward
"When we used to sing . . ."

Tana's perched on the table with her forearms. Her head's tilted back; 4
smiling as her walnut hair falls down over her long freckled neck. "Bit-by-bit-
by-bit-by-sha-la-la-lah. . . ." I lift a cigarette to my lips, fighting to regain some
lost composure.

Tana and I are the most inseparable of the group. We have probably been 5
together for two days straight, crashing in Reeser's living room, searching for
McDonald's breakfast change in sofas and car consoles.

She looks over at me with her crooked smile, and nods at an old couple walk- 6
ing through the doorway. When they're far enough away, she'll drop an *Aaah.*

An old splintering plastic lawn chair crackles as I sit down. 7

"Can I bum a smoke off you, Taryn?" 8

"Yeah, I guess. They're Marlboros . . ." 9

"Whatever." 10

Taryn smokes disgusting cigarettes, and her coffee is half Vanilla creamer. 11
We agree on nothing, but that's why we click. We are both right, and damn-it-
all we're both going to prove it. She always cheats. Something I think has some
deep psychological roots that we must sidestep to examine or it's just too terrible or horrifying for me to continue admitting that I think that.

I try to avoid psychology all together. My sarcasm is a defense mechanism, 12
and not a sharp sense of humor. I've got issues with this or that affecting the
way I do this. Later, I won't be able to just sit quietly enjoying her company
without her asking "what are you thinking right now?"

I really kind of like it all though. Introspection was something that I had 13
never considered trying before. Besides, being that interesting to somebody is
a pretty cool feeling.

14   The sharp brick pricks my legs, the cold startles me at first, but I quickly relax. I'll sit with Christy talking for hours, about everything. I'm not just young and naïve; after all I generally "hide behind my sarcasm." But on the brick stack I tell Christy stuff I don't even know I think. I'll do that with people later, but now it's genuine, not meaningless tongue in cheek banter.

15   We don't feel the shingles or the breeze. We all sit spread across the roof with our pretentious cigars, laughing out bursts of smoke that we never watched. It wouldn't have ever interested me then. My wet Montecristo slips back in my mouth. The cap is starting to peel, but I don't notice.

16   This was my favorite of our regular spots. From the roof of the hilltop house in Eagle, we could see the edges of Boise, with a small climb to the next level, we saw a hazy blur of downtown, the foothills behind, Tablerock ahead. On the fourth of July, we could clearly see most of the fireworks across the Treasure Valley.

17   "God that's gross!" I say as Tana finishes filling her tea with the repulsive *pink* packets. "I like it! It's good," she says with a smile and the word ends with hard, distinct "d." This is our last main haunt—The Eagle Grill. Most of us used to work here, we know everybody, and occasionally still get an employee discount. We are back on the patio, as usual.

18   Taryn assumes a sophisticated air as she raises the cigarette to her always dry, fat lips. Her eyebrows straighten as she coolly lifts the cigarette to her lips. She opens them slightly, and the smoke rolls in her palate rarely seeping through her lips. Generally this led to some profound commentary on something. But not today. Nothing is going to disturb our last breakfast.

19   As things get more awkward, Christy gets up to go to her car. We talk about something, it doesn't matter; we're not really talking at all, just avoiding silence. They stop talking, and start smiling. When I look up to see why, Christy sets down a metallic blue bag filled with little going-away presents. Nothing spectacular to anyone else—cheap souvenirs: folded notebook paper notes, a blue candy cane, a small cigar. Everything has a story, and we get too carried away in these to notice the red Suburban entering the parking lot.

20   It kept running, and began to honk.

21   "What the hell is your Mom's problem," Christy asks. "Can't she just give just you one minute?"

* * *

I'm back in Boise, sitting on the same rooftop alone. I was back in only a   22
few months, but everything was different. We can't hang out as a group for
more than an hour anymore before somebody pisses somebody else off and
they don't talk for months. I don't really click with anyone anymore; everything's just more complicated now. Everything we had that summer is gone.

I open my lips again and smoke slips out. This never ends. It's not just   23
growing up. Things slip away. What have I fixed sitting here pining for the last
hour? I take the cigar to my lips again, hold it for a moment, then let it go.

EVALUATING THE ESSAY

Spend some time in your journal or in class evaluating the revision strategies Jon used in his essay.

1. If you were in Jon's workshop group, what would you say to him
   about this draft? What do you think works? What needs more work?

2. Revision often involves trying to match your intentions and how the
   draft fulfills those intentions. My students often say, "I just can't
   seem to get down what's in my head." As Jon writes to himself about
   how to revise his sketch, he lands on the idea that he could divide
   the draft into separate scenes that each spiral like cigar smoke.
   How successful is he in making this work in the draft?

3. "Blue Spirals" has some literary qualities, especially its subtlety.
   Jon just doesn't come out and say exactly what he means. What *does*
   he mean? What do you understand Jon is trying to say in this essay
   about what it is he lost? Should the essay be further revised to make
   that meaning more clear?

4. Which of the five categories of revision—purpose, meaning, information, structure, and clarity and style—would you recommend Jon
   emphasize in the next draft of "Blue Spirals?" The next section defines each type of revision.

FIVE CATEGORIES OF REVISION

Below are some characteristics of writers who most need to revise:

- Writers of fast drafts
- Writers who compose short drafts
- Writers who indulge in creative, but not critical, thinking
- Writers who rarely go past their initial way of seeing things

WRITING WITH COMPUTERS

KNOWING WHEN TO STEP AWAY FROM THE COMPUTER

Computers offer writers a number of tools to help them through the process of revision. Using computers, writers can add comments to their drafts; cut or delete text; spell, grammar, and style check their work; track changes to their drafts; and conduct peer review online. Computers clearly can facilitate the practical tasks required of revision, but they can't do the actual work of revision. That job is up to the writer—*you*. With this in mind, make sure you use a computer only when it aids you in your writing. For example, some writers find it challenging to read through and compare multiple drafts on a computer screen. They may find this format hinders their thinking process and may prefer to tackle hard copies of their drafts with a pencil or pen before they sit down at their computers to write another draft. If you are one of these writers, there is no reason to read your drafts on the computer screen. Other writers may find that the comments and tracking functions of their word processor only distract them from the task of revising their work and such writers should avoid using these tools. Remember, writing doesn't necessarily mean sitting at the computer and moving your fingers over the keyboard. There are many other ways to write. Use what works for you.

- Writers who have a hard time imagining a reader other than themselves
- Writers who rely on limited sources of information
- Writers who still aren't sure what they're trying to say
- Writers who haven't found their own way of saying what they want to say
- Writers who haven't delivered on their promises
- Writers who think their draft is "perfect"

These are the usual suspects for revision, but there are many more. In general, if you think there's more to think about, more to learn, more to say, and better ways to say it, then revision is the route to surprise and discovery. Most writers agree that rewriting is a good idea, but where should they start?

Problems in drafts vary enormously. But the diagnosis tends to involve concerns in five general areas: purpose, meaning, information, structure, and clarity and style. Here are some typical reader responses to drafts with each kind of problem:

1. **Problems with Purpose**
   - "I don't know why the writer is writing this paper."
   - "The beginning of the essay seems to be about one thing, and the rest of it is about several others."

- "I think there about three different topics in the draft. Which one do you want to write about?"
- "So what?"

2. **Problems with Meaning**

   - "I can't tell what the writer is trying to say in the draft."
   - "There doesn't seem to be a point behind all of this."
   - "I think there's a main idea, but there isn't much information on it."
   - "I thought the thesis was pretty obvious."

3. **Problems with Information**

   - "Parts of the draft seemed really pretty vague or general."
   - "I couldn't really *see* what you were talking about."
   - "It seemed like you needed some more facts to back up your point."
   - "It needs more detail."

4. **Problems with Structure**

   - "I couldn't quite follow your thinking in the last few pages."
   - "I was confused about when this happened."
   - "I understood your point but I couldn't figure out what this part had to do with it."
   - "The draft doesn't really flow very well."

5. **Problems with Clarity and Style**

   - "This seems a little choppy."
   - "You need to explain this better. I couldn't quite follow what you were saying in this paragraph."
   - "This sentence seems really awkward to me."
   - "This doesn't have a strong voice."

PROBLEMS OF PURPOSE

When you're fulfilling a specific writing assignment for a class—for instance, you are instructed to write on, "What were the initial causes of U.S. intervention in Vietnam?"—then you begin, knowing your purpose. Essay exams are a familiar example of this. But more often, even if you've been assigned a topic, one of the early challenges of the writing process is to discover how you're going to answer the *So what?* question. Why exactly are you writing about this? (And you can't answer, "Because I have to.") Quite simply, readers need a reason to read, and if the writer doesn't supply them with one then they'll be understandably frustrated and bored.

It's a little like riding a tandem bike. The writer sits up front and steers while the reader occupies the seat behind, obligated to peddle but with no control over where the bike goes. As soon as the reader senses that the writer isn't steering anywhere in particular, then the reader will get off the bike. Why do all that pedaling if the bike seems to be going nowhere?

Frequently, when you begin writing about something you don't have any idea where you're headed; that's exactly *why* you're writing about the subject in the first place. When we write such discovery drafts, then revision often begins by looking for clues about your purpose. What you learn then becomes a key organizing principle for the next draft, trying to clarify this purpose to your readers. The first question, therefore, is one writers must answer for themselves: "Why am I writing this?" Of course, if it's an assignment it's hard to get past the easy answer—"Because I have to"—but if the work is going to be any good there must be a better answer than that. Whether your topic is open or assigned, you have to find your own reason to write about it, and what you discover becomes an answer to your bike partner's nagging question, yelled into the wind from the seat behind you: "If I'm going to pedal this hard, you better let me know where we're going."

In general, the motives behind writing reflect the four ways of inquiring, but writing can and often does involve more than one of these following four purposes.

1. **To explore.** One way to handle complicated questions is to approach the answers in an open-ended way; the writer writes to discover what he thinks or how he feels and reports to the reader on these discoveries.

2. **To explain.** Much of the writing we encounter in daily life is meant simply to provide us with information: This is how the coffee maker works or this is the best way to prepare for a trip to New Zealand. Expository writing frequently explains and describes.

3. **To evaluate.** In a sense, all writing is evaluative because it involves making judgments. For instance, when you explain how to plan a New Zealand vacation, you're making judgments about where to go. But when the explicit purpose is to present a judgment about something, the writer encourages readers see the world the way the writer does. He may want the reader to think or behave a certain way: It makes sense to abolish pennies because they're more trouble than they're worth, or you should vote for the bond issue because it's the best way to save the foothills.

4. **To reflect.** Less frequently, we write to stand back from what we're writing about and consider *how* we're thinking about the subject, the methods we're using to write about it, and what we might learn from this writing situation that might apply to others.

Revision Strategy 14.1: What's Your Primary Motive?

It may help to begin revision by attempting to determine your *primary motive* for the next draft. Do you want to explore your topic, explain something to your readers, offer a persuasive judgment, or step back and reflect on what you're saying or how you're saying it? The genre of writing has a great deal to do with this (see the table that follows). If you're writing a personal essay, your purpose is likely to be exploratory. If you're writing a review, a proposal, a critical essay, or an argument essay, it's likely your primary motives are to evaluate. One way, then, to get some basic guidance for the next draft is to carefully craft the second half of the following sentence:

My primary motive in writing this paper is to explore/evaluate/explain/reflect about _____ .

GENRE	PRIMARY MOTIVES
Personal essay	Explore
Profile	Explore or explain
Review	Evaluate
Proposal	Evaluate
Argument	Evaluate
Critical essay	Evaluate
Ethnographic essay	Explore or evaluate
Research essay	Explore or evaluate
Reflective essay	Reflect

Of course, any one essay may involve all four motives, but for the purpose of this exercise, choose your *main* purpose in writing the essay. Composing the second half of the sentence may not be so easy because it challenges you to limit your subject. For instance, the following is far too ambitious for, say, a five-page essay: *My main motive in writing this paper is to evaluate the steps taken to deal with terrorism and judge whether they're adequate.* That's simply too big a subject for a brief persuasive paper. This is more reasonable: *My main motive in writing this paper is to evaluate passenger screening procedures in Europe and decide whether they're better than those in the United States*

Since largely exploratory pieces often are motivated by questions, a writer of a personal essay might compose the following sentence: *My main motive in writing this essay is to explore why I felt relieved when my father died.*

After you craft your motive sentence, put it on a piece of paper or index card and post it where you can see it as you revise the draft. Periodically ask yourself, "What does this paragraph or this section of the draft have to do with my main motive?" The answer will help you decide what to cut and what needs more development in the next draft. Remember, the essay should be organized around this motive from beginning to end.

Revision Strategy 14.2: What Do You Want to Know About What You Learned?

Since inquiry-based writing is usually driven by questions rather than answers, one way to discover your purpose in a sketch or draft is to generate a list of questions it raises for you. Of course, you hope that one of them might be behind your purpose in the next draft. Try the following steps with a draft that needs a stronger sense of purpose.

1. Choose a draft or sketch you'd like to revise, and reread it.

2. On the back of the manuscript, craft an answer to the following question: *What do I understand about this topic now that I didn't understand before I started writing about it?*

3. Next, if you can, build a list of questions—perhaps new ones—that this topic still raises for you. Make this list as long as you can, and don't censor yourself (see "One Student's Response" below).

4. Choose one or more of the questions as a prompt for a fastwrite. Follow your writing to see where it leads and what it might suggest about new directions for the revision.

5. If you can't think of any questions, or find you didn't learn much from writing about the topic (Step 2), you may have several options. One is to abandon the draft altogether. Is it possible that this is simply a topic that doesn't interest you anymore? If abandoning the draft isn't possible, then you need to find a new angle. Try Revision Strategy 14.3.

✎ ONE STUDENT'S RESPONSE

JULIA'S DRAFT

What do I understand about this topic now that I didn't understand before I started writing about it?

After writing this essay, I understand more clearly that there's a relationship between a girl's eating disorders and how her father treats her as a child.

LIST OF QUESTIONS

- Why the father and not the mother?

- What is it about father/daughter relationships that make them so vulnerable to feminine body images?

- Is the father's influence on a girl's body image greater at certain ages or stages in her life?

- How can a father be more informed about his impact on a daughter's body image?

Revision Strategy 14.3: Finding the Focusing Question

The best topics, and the most difficult to write about, are those that raise questions for you. In a sketch or first draft, you may not know what these questions are. But if your subsequent drafts are going to be purposeful and focused, then discovering the main question behind your essay is essential. This is particularly important in essays that are research-based since the drafts are longer and you're often trying to manage a lot of information. This revision strategy works best when it's a class activity.

1. Begin by simply putting your essay topic on the top of a large piece of paper like newsprint or butcher paper. If yours is a research topic— say, Alzheimer's disease—jot that down. Post your paper on the classroom wall.

2. Spend a few minutes writing a few sentences explaining why you chose to write about this topic in the first place.

3. Make a quick list of everything you *already know* (if anything) about your topic. For instance, surprising facts or statistics, the extent of the problem, important people or institutions involved, key schools of thought, common misconceptions, familiar clichés that apply to the topic, observations you've made, important trends, typical perspectives, and so on. Spend about five minutes on this.

4. Now spend fifteen or twenty minutes brainstorming a list of questions about your topic that you'd love to learn the answers to. Make this list as long as possible.

5. As you look around the room, you'll see a gallery of topics and questions on the walls. You can help each other. Circulate around the room and do two things: add a question that you're interested in about a particular topic, and check the question (yours or someone else's) that seems most interesting.

When you return to your newsprint or butcher paper, it should be covered with questions. How will you decide which of them might provide the best focus for the next draft? Consider the following criteria as you try to make this decision:

- **What question do *you* find most intriguing?** After all, it's your essay, and it should be driven by your own interests in the subject.

- **Which question seems most manageable?** This mostly has to do with the level of generality or specificity of the question. You want a focusing question that isn't too general or too specific. For example, a question like, "*What causes international terrorism?*" is a landscape question—it contains so much possible territory that you'll never get a close look at anything. But a question like, "*How effective has the Saudi royal family been in limiting terrorist activities?*" is a much more focused, and therefore manageable, question.

- **What question seems most appropriate for the assignment?**
  For example, if you're assigned a research essay, certain questions
  are more likely than others to send you to the library. If you're writing a persuasive essay, gravitate toward a question that might point
  you toward a claim or thesis.

- **What seems most relevant to the information you've already
  collected?** It would be convenient if information from your research
  or first draft is relevant to the question that's behind the next draft.
  While this might make the revision go more quickly, always be open
  to the possibility that a question that takes you in new directions
  might simply be more interesting to you.

- **What question is likely to yield answers that interest your
  readers?** You already have a sense of this from the questions that
  students in your class added to your newsprint about your topic. The
  challenge in any piece of writing, of course, is to answer the *So what?*
  question. Does your focusing question promise to lead you somewhere
  that readers would care to go?

Revision Strategy 14.4: What's the Relationship?

One of the more common purposes for all kinds of essays is to explore a relationship between two or more things. We see this in research all the
time. What's the relationship between AIDs and IV drug use in China?
What's the relationship between gender and styles of collaboration in the
workplace? What's the social class relationship between Huck and Tom in
The Adventures of Huckleberry Finn?

Exploring the relationships between things isn't just the province of
research, however. For instance, Barbara Kingsolver's personal essay,
"Life Without Go-Go Boots" (in Chapter 4), literally examines her relationship with fashion trends as she grew up. But in a larger sense, Kingsolver
is exploring the relationship between fashion and *style*. How might one distinguish between the two, she wonders, and Kingsolver arrives at a definition that fits with the way she feels about clothes.

One way, then, to clarify your purpose in revision is to try to identity
the relationship that may be at the heart of your inquiry. Relationships between things can be described in several different ways.

- **Cause and effect.** What is the relationship between my father's
  comments about my looks and my eating disorder when I was a
  teenager? What is the relationship between the second Iraqi war and
  destabilization in Saudi Arabia? What is the relationship between
  the decline of the Brazilian rainforest and the extinction of the native
  eagles? What is the relationship between my moving to Idaho and the
  failure of my relationship with Kevin?

- **Compare and contrast.** How is jealousy distinguished from envy? How might writing instruction in high school be distinguished from writing instruction in college? What are the differences and similarities between my experiences at the Rolling Stone's concert last month and my experiences at the Stone's concert fifteen years ago?

Review your sketch or draft to determine if what you're really trying to write about is the relationship between two (or more) things. In your journal, try to state this relationship in sentences similar to those listed above. With this knowledge, return to the draft and revise from beginning to end with this purpose in mind. What do you need to add to the next draft to both clarify and develop the relationship you're focusing on? What should you cut that is irrelevant to that focus?

PROBLEMS WITH MEANING

Fundamentally, most of us write something in an attempt to say something to someone else. The note my wife Karen left for me yesterday said it in a sentence: "Bruce—could you pick up some virgin olive oil and a loaf of bread?" I had no trouble deciphering the meaning of this note. But it isn't always that easy. Certain poems, for example, may be incredibly ambiguous texts, and readers may puzzle over them for hours, coming up with a range of plausible interpretations of meaning.

Implicit or Explicit Meaning

Two broad categories of writing are texts that embody *implicit* or *explicit* meaning. Certain literary forms such as poems or short stories are often implicit—writers may not step forward and say what they mean—while much nonfiction prose (although some of it, like the essay, is also literary) may be much more explicit.

College writing is almost always explicit in meaning, and one of the most common complaints I hear about student writing is that it's not explicit enough. Recently, the theater faculty at my university told me that their Theater 101 students have difficulty producing writing that has a clear thesis. "Some of them have never even heard the word," one professor told me. Thesis, of course, is only one (scientific) term to describe how meaning can be expressed in a piece of writing. Other terms include main point, theme, controlling idea, and central claim or assertion. I've used some of these words interchangeably in *The Curious Writer* because they basically mean pretty much the same thing: *Most well-written essays have a single dominant meaning that should be clear to the reader.*

In certain genres of academic writing, the thesis is stated very early on in a paper. This was true, for example, of the essays the theater faculty asked students to write in their 101 class. This kind of essay is often called

---

Terms to Describe Dominant Meaning

Thesis

Main point

Theme

Controlling idea

Central claim or assertion

---

the "thesis/support" paper, and the basic structure is probably familiar to you: Say what you're going to say, say it with supporting evidence, and say it again to conclude.

Other genres, including the personal and even some persuasive essays, may follow a less formal structure, working their way less directly to an important idea or point. Such essays may have a delayed thesis that appear toward the end of the piece. But make no mistake—*all* essays have some kind of controlling idea or question at their hearts. An essay that fails to make that meaning clear will frustrate the reader because the essay will seem pointless.

Looking Beyond the Obvious

Sketches and first drafts often have problems with meaning. Frequently, they are written because their authors are trying to discover what they want to say. These discovery drafts then provide guidance about what that meaning might be, and the revision then will be more focused and more explicit about meaning. The challenge, of course, is learning how to read your drafts for clues about your thesis or main idea.

However, sometimes the problem isn't so much that you don't know what you're trying to say as that what you're saying seems obvious. Clichés, conventional wisdoms, or broad generalizations are typical examples of this. You're writing about the performance you saw of Tennessee William's *Streetcar Named Desire* and your draft's thesis is something like, "This was a really sad play." Okay, true . . . but that's pretty obvious. Or perhaps you're writing about losing touch with your childhood buddy, and in the last paragraph of your essay you write, "True friends are hard to find." Well, that sounds familiar. Isn't there more to say that might be a little less obvious?

The revision strategies that follow address each of these problems separately. Featured first are techniques that should help you discover what you're trying to say in a sketch or draft when you're not sure. These are followed by techniques that will help you refine a thesis or theme to make it more insightful (and less obvious) or more accurate and truthful.

Methods for Discovering Your Thesis

Use the following strategies if you're not quite sure whether you know what you're trying to say in a sketch or draft. How can you discover in what you're already written clues about your main point or meaning?

Revision Strategy 14.5: Find the "Instructive Line"

It may seem odd to think of reading your own drafts for clues about what you mean. After all, your writing is a product of your own mind. But often a draft can reveal to us what we didn't know we knew—an idea that surfaces unexpectedly, a question that we keep asking, or a moment in a narrative that seems surprisingly significant. Part of the challenge is to recognize these clues to your own meanings, and understand what they suggest about the revision.

This isn't always easy, which is one reason it's often so helpful to share your writing with other readers; they may see the clues that we miss. However, this revision strategy depends on reading your own drafts more systematically for clues about what your point might be. What is it that you say in this draft that might suggest what you really want to say in the next one?

1. **Find the "instructive line."** Every draft is made up of many sentences. But which of these is *the most important sentence or passage?* What do I mean by important? Which line or passage points to a larger idea, theme, or feeling that seems to rise above much of the draft and illuminates the significance or relevance of many other lines and passages? The writer Donald Murray calls this the "instructive line," the sentence that seems to point upwards toward the meaning of what you've set down. Underline the instructive line or passage in your draft. It may be subtle, only hinting at larger ideas or feelings, or quite explicitly stated. In a narrative essay, the instructive line might be a moment of stepping back to reflect—"As I look back on this now, I understand that . . ." In a review or persuasive essay, it might be an assertion of some kind—"American moviegoers are seduced by the 'twist' at the end of a film, and learn to expect it."

2. **Follow the thread of meaning.** If the instructive line is a ball of string, tightly packed with coils of meaning that aren't readily apparent, then to get any guidance for revision you need to try to unravel it. At the top of a journal page, write the line or passage you selected in your draft as most important. Use it as a prompt for five minutes of exploratory writing, perhaps beginning with the following seed sentence: *I think / feel this is true because . . . And also because . . . And also . . . And also . . .*

3. **Compose a thesis.** Reread your fastwriting in the preceding step and, keeping your original passage in mind, craft a single sentence

that best captures the most important idea or feeling you'd like to bring into the next draft. For example, *Because of the expectation, encouraged by Hollywood, that every good movie has a surprise ending, American moviegoers often find even superior foreign films a disappointment.*

4. **Post-it.** Put this thesis on the wall above your computer, or use a Post-it and place the thesis on your computer screen. Revise with the thesis in mind, from beginning to end. Add information that will *illustrate, extend, exemplify, complicate, clarify, support, show, background,* or *prove* the thesis. Cut information from the draft that does none of these things.

Revision Strategy 14.6: Looping Toward a Thesis

I've argued throughout *The Curious Writer* for a dialectical approach to writing, moving back and forth between creative and critical modes of thinking, from your observations of and your ideas about, from generating and judging, from specifics and generalities. This is how writers can make meaning. The approach can also be used as a revision strategy, this time in a technique called "loop writing." When you loop write you move back and forth dialectically between both modes of thought—opening things up and then trying to pin them down. I imagine that this looks like an hourglass.

1. Reread the draft quickly, and then turn it upside down on your desk. You won't look at it again but trust that you'll remember what's important.

2. Begin a three-minute fastwrite on the draft in which you tell yourself the story of your thinking about the essay. When you first started writing it, what did you think you were writing about, and then what, and then . . . Try to focus on your ideas about what you were trying to say and how it evolved.

3. Sum up what you said in your fastwrite by answering the following question in a sentence: *What seems to be the most important thing I've finally come to understand about my topic?*

4. Begin another three-minute fastwrite. Focus on scenes, situations, case studies, moments, people, conversations, observations, and so on that stand out for you as you think about the draft. Think especially of specifics that come to mind that led to the understanding of your topic that you stated in the preceding step. Some of this information may be in the draft, but some may *not* yet be in the draft.

5. Finish by restating the main point you want to make in the next draft. Begin the revision by thinking about a lead or introduction that dramatizes this point. Consider a suggestive scene, case study, finding, profile, description, comparison, anecdote, conversation, situa-

tion, or observation that points the essay toward your main idea. For example, if your point is that your university's program to help second language learners is inadequate you could begin the next draft by telling the story of Maria, an immigrant from Guatemala, who was a victim of poor placement in a composition course that she was virtually guaranteed to fail. Follow this lead into the draft, always keeping your main point or thesis in mind.

Revision Strategy 14.7: Reclaiming Your Topic

When you do a lot of research on your topic you may reach a point when you feel awash in information. It's easy at such moments to feel as if you're losing control of your topic, besieged by the voices of experts, a torrent of statistics and facts, and competing perspectives. Your success in writing the paper depends on making it your own again, gaining control over the information for your own purposes, in the service of your own questions or arguments. This revision strategy, a variation of Revision Strategy 14.6, should help you gain control of the material you collected for a research-based inquiry project.

1. Spend ten or fifteen minutes reviewing all of the notes you've taken and skimming key articles or passages from books. Glance at your most important sources. If you have a rough draft, reread it. Let your head swim with information.

2. Now clear your desk of everything but your journal. Remove all your notes and materials. If you have a rough draft, put it in the drawer.

3. Now fastwrite about your topic for seven full minutes. Tell the story of how your thinking about the topic has evolved. When you began, what did you think? What were your initial assumptions or preconceptions? Then what happened, and what happened after that? Keep your pen moving.

4. Skip a few lines in your notebook, and write "Moments, Stories, People, and Scenes." Now fastwrite for another seven minutes, this time focusing more on specific case studies, situations, people, experiences, observations, facts, and so on that stand out in your mind from the research you've done so far, or perhaps from your own experience with the topic.

5. Skip a few more lines. For another seven minutes, write a dialogue between you and someone else about your topic. Choose someone who you think is typical of the audience you're writing for. If it helps, think of someone specific—an instructor, a fellow student, a friend. Don't plan the dialogue. Just begin with the question most commonly asked about your topic, and take the conversation from there, writing both parts of the dialogue.

6. Finally, skip a few more lines and write these two words in your note-book: *So what?* Now spend a few minutes trying to summarize the most important thing you think your readers should understand about your topic, based on what you've learned so far. Distill this into a sentence or two.

As you work your way to the last step, you're reviewing what you've learned about your topic without being tyrannized by the many voices, perspectives, and facts in the research you've collected. The final step, Step 6, leads you toward a thesis statement. In the revision, keep this in mind as you reopen your notes, reread your sources, and check on facts. Remember in the rewrite to put all of this information in the service of this main idea, as examples or illustrations, necessary background, evidence or support, counterexamples, and ways of qualifying or extending your main point.

Revision Strategy 14.8: Believing and Doubting

In persuasive writing such as the argument, review, proposal, or research paper, we often feel that a thesis involves picking sides—"the play was good" or "the play was bad," "the novel was boring" or "the novel was fun to read." Instead of *either/or*, consider *both/and*. This might bring you to a more truthful, more sophisticated understanding of your subject, which rarely is either all bad or all good. One way to do this is to play the doubting game and the believing game.

1. Draw a line down the middle of a page in your notebook. First, on the right side, make a list of the things in response to the following questions:

THE BELIEVING GAME	THE DOUBTING GAME
Give the author, performer, text, performance the benefit of the doubt. Suspend criticism.	Adopt a critical stance. Look for holes, weaknesses, omissions, problems.
1. What seems true or truthful about what is said, shown, or argued?	6. What seems unbelievable or untrue?
2. How does it confirm your own experiences or observations of the same things?	7. What does it fail to consider or consider inadequately?
3. What did you like or agree with?	8. Where is the evidence missing or insufficient, or where do the elements not work together effectively?
4. Where is it strongest, most compelling, most persuasive?	
5. How does it satisfy your criteria for being good, useful, convincing, or moving?	9. How does it fail to meet your criteria for good in this category of thing?
	10. Where is it the least compelling or persuasive? Why?

2. From this work in your notebook, try to construct a sentence—a the-sis—that is more than a simple statement of the worth or worthless-ness of the thing you're evaluating, but an expression of *both* its strengths and weaknesses: *Although _____ succeeds (or fails) in _____, it mostly _____.* For example: *Although reality television presents viewers with an often interesting glimpse into how ordinary people handle their fifteen minutes of celebrity, it mostly exaggerates life by creating drama where there often is none.*

Methods for Refining Your Thesis

You may emerge from writing a draft with a pretty clear sense of what you want to say in the next one. But does this idea seem a little obvious or per-haps too general? Does it fail to adequately express what you really feel and think? Use one or more of the following revision strategies to refine a thesis, theme, or controlling idea.

Revision Strategy 14.9: Questions as Knives

Imagine that your initial feeling, thesis, or main point is like an onion. Ideas, like onions, have layers and to get closer to their hearts you need to cut through the most obvious outer layers to reveal what is less obvious, probably more specific, and almost certainly more interesting. Questions are to ideas as knives are to onions: They help you slice past your initial impressions. The most important question—the sharpest knife in the drawer—is simply *Why? Why* was the Orwell essay interesting? *Why* do you hate foreign films? *Why* should the university do more for second lan-guage speakers? *Why* did you feel a sense of loss when the old cornfield was paved over for the mall?

Why may be the sharpest knife in the drawer, but there are other "W" questions with keen blades, too, including *What, Where, When,* and *Who?* In Figure 14.1 you can see how these questions can cut a broad thesis down to size. The result is a much more specific, more interesting controlling idea for the next draft.

1. Subject your tentative thesis to the same kind of narrowing. Write your theme, thesis, or main point as a single sentence in your note-book.

2. Slice it with questions and restate each time.

3. Continue this until your point is appropriately sliced; that is, when you feel that you've gone beyond the obvious and stated what you think or feel in a more specific and interesting way.

As before, rewrite the next draft with this new thesis in mind, reorga-nizing the essay around it from beginning to end. Add new information

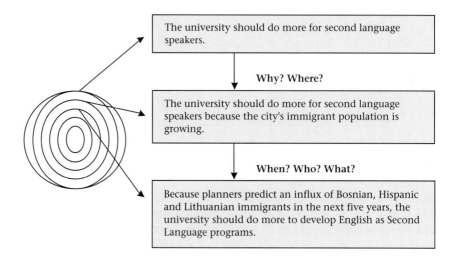

FIGURE 14.1   **Using why? where? when? who? and what?** questions to narrow the focus of a thesis is like using a knife to cut into the heart of an onion.

that supports the idea, provides the necessary background, offers opposing views, or extends it. Cut information that no longer seems relevant to the thesis.

PROBLEMS WITH INFORMATION

Writers who've spent enough time generating or collecting information about their topics can work from abundance rather than scarcity. This is an enormous advantage because the ability to throw stuff away means you can be selective about what you use, and the result is a more focused draft. But as we revise, our purpose and point might shift, and we may find ourselves in the unhappy position of working from scarcity again. Most of our research, observation, or fastwriting was relevant to the triggering subject in the initial sketch or draft, not to the generated subject we decide is the better direction for the next draft. In some cases, this might require that you research the new topic or return to the generating activities of listing, fastwriting, clustering, and so on that will help provide information for the next draft.

More often, however, writers don't have to begin from scratch in revision. Frequently, a shift in the focus or refining a thesis in a first draft just means emphasizing different information or perhaps filling in gaps in later drafts. The strategies that follow will help you solve this problem.

Revision Strategy 14.10: Explode a Moment

The success of personal essays that rely on narratives frequently depends on how well the writer renders an important scene, situation, moment, or description. When you're telling a story from experience, not all parts of the story are equally important. As always, emphasis in a narrative depends on the writer's purpose in the essay. For example, Matt's essay on the irony of the slow poisoning of Butte, Montana, his hometown, by a copper mine that once gave the city life would emphasize those parts of the story that best highlight that irony. Or a description of the agonizing death of the snow geese that unwittingly landed on the acid pond—their white beauty set against the deadly dark water—might be an important scene in Matt's next draft; it nicely portrays life and death, beauty and ugliness in much the same way the town and the mine might be contrasted. Matt should "explode that moment" because it's an important part of the story he's trying to tell about his Montana home town.

If you're trying to revise a draft that relies on narratives, this revision strategy will help you first identify moments, scenes, or descriptions that might be important in the next draft, and help you develop these as more important parts of your story.

1. Choose a draft that involves a story or stories.
2. Make a list in your journal of the moments (for example, scenes, situations, turning points, and so on) that stand out in the narrative.
3. Circle one that you think is most important to your purpose in the essay. It could be the situation that is most telling, a dramatic turning point, the moment of a key discovery that is central to what you're trying to say, or a scene that illustrates the dilemma or raises the question you're exploring in the draft.
4. Name that moment at the top of a blank journal page (for example, *the snow geese on the acid pond, when the ice broke,* or *when I saw grandfather in his coffin*).
5. Now put yourself back into that moment and fastwrite about it for seven full minutes. Make sure that you write with as much detail as possible, *drawing on all your senses*. Write in the present tense if it helps.
6. Use this same method with other moments in the narrative that might deserve more emphasis in the next draft. Remember that real time means little in writing. An experience that took seven seconds can easily take up three pages of writing if it's detailed enough. Rewrite and incorporate the best of the new information in the next draft.

Revision Strategy 14.11: Beyond Examples

When we add information to a draft we normally think of adding examples. If you're writing a research essay on living with a sibling who suffers from Down's Syndrome, you might mention that your brother typically tries to avoid certain cognitive challenges. Members of your workshop group wonder, "Well, what kind of challenges?" In revision, you add an example or two from your own experience to clarify what you mean. This is, of course, a helpful strategy; examples of what you mean by an assertion are a kind of evidence that helps readers more fully understand your work. But also consider other types of information it might be helpful to add to the next draft. Use the following list to review your draft for additions you might not have thought of for revision.

- **Presenting counterarguments.** Typically, persuasive essays include information that represents an opposing view. Say that you're arguing that beyond "avoidance" behaviors, there really aren't personality traits that can be attributed to most people with Down's Syndrome. You include a summary of a study that says otherwise. Why? Because it provides readers with a better understanding of the debate, and enhances the writer's ethos since you appear fair.

- **Providing background.** When you drop in on a conversation between two friends, you initially may be clueless about the subject. Naturally, you ask questions: "Who are you guys talking about? When did this happen? What did she say?" Answers to these questions provide a context that allows you to understand what is being said and to participate in the conversation. Background information like this is often essential in written communication, too. In a personal essay, readers may want to know the time and place the event took place, or the relationship between the narrator and a character. In a critical essay, it might be necessary to provide background on the short story because readers may not have read it. In a research essay, it's often useful to provide background information about what has already been said on the topic and the research question.

- **Establishing significance.** Let's say you're writing about the problem of obesity in America, something that most of us are generally aware of these days. But the significance of the problem really strikes home when you add information from research suggesting that 30 percent of American adults are overweight, up from 23 percent from just six years ago. It is even more important to establish the significance of a problem about which there is little awareness or consensus. For example, most people don't know that America's national park system is crumbling and in disrepair. Your essay on the problem needs to provide readers with information that establishes the significance of the problem. In a profile, readers need to have a reason to be interested in someone—perhaps your profile subject represents a particular group of people of interest or concern.

- **Giving it a face.** One of the best ways to make an otherwise abstract issue or problem come to life is to show what it means to an individual person. We can't fully appreciate the social impact of deforestation in Brazil without being introduced to someone like Chico Mendes, a forest defender who was murdered for his activism. Obesity might be an abstract problem until we meet Carl, a 500-pound 22-year-old who is "suffocating in his own fat." Add case studies, anecdotes, profiles, descriptions that put people on the page to make your essay more interesting and persuasive.

- **Define it.** If you're writing about a subject your readers know little about, then it's likely that you'll use concepts or terms that readers will want you to define. What exactly do you mean, for example, when you say that the Internet is vulnerable to cyberterror? What exactly is cyberterror anyway? In your personal essay on your troubled relationship with your mother, what do you mean when you call her a "narcissist?" Frequently your workshop group will alert you to things in the draft that need defining, but also go through your own draft and ask yourself, "Will my readers know what I mean?"

Revision Strategy 14.12: Research

Too often, research is ignored as a revision strategy. We may do research for the first draft of a paper or essay, but never return to the library or search the Web to fill in gaps, answer new questions, or refine the focus of a rewrite. That's crazy, particularly since well researched information can strengthen a draft of any kind. That has been one of the themes of *The Curious Writer* since the beginning of the book: research is not a separate activity reserved only for the research paper, but a rich source of information for any type of writing. Try some of these strategies:

1. For quick facts, visit http://www.refdesk.com on the Web. This enormously useful site is the fastest way to find out the exact height of the Great Wall of China or the number of young women suffering from eating disorders in America today.

2. Return to the *Library of Congress Subject Headings,* the reference mentioned in Chapter 12 that will help you pinpoint the language you should use to search library databases on your topic. Particularly if the focus of your next draft is shifting, you'll need some fresh information to fill in the gaps. The *LCSH* will help you find more of it, more quickly.

3. To maximize Web coverage, launch a search on at least three single search engines (for example, Google, MSN Search, and Yahoo!), but

this time search using terms or phrases from your draft that will lead you to more specific information that will fill gaps in the draft.

4. Interview someone relevant to your topic. (See Chapter 12.)

5. To ferret out some new sources on your topic, search library databases under author rather than keyword. Focus on authors that you know have something to say on your topic.

6. Return to any of the steps in Chapter 12 that involve developing deep knowledge about your topic.

PROBLEMS WITH STRUCTURE

When it's working, the structure of a piece of writing is nearly invisible. Readers don't notice how the writer is guiding them from one piece of information to the next. When structure is a problem, the writer asks readers to walk out on a shaky bridge and trust that it will help them get to the other side, but the walkers can think of little else but the shakiness of the bridge. Some professional writers, such as John McPhee, obsess about structure, and for good reason—when you're working with a tremendous amount of information, as McPhee often does in his research-based essays, it helps to have a clear idea about how you'll use it.

Formal Academic Structures

In some academic writing, the structure is prescribed. Scientific papers often have sections—introduction, methodology, results, discussion—but within those sections writers must organize their material. Certain writing assignments may also require you to organize your information in a certain way. The most common of these is the thesis-support structure. In such essays you typically establish your thesis in the first paragraph, spend the body of the paper assembling evidence that supports the thesis, and conclude the essay with a summary that restates the thesis in light of what's been said.

Thesis-support is a persuasive form, so it lends itself to arguments, critical essays, reviews, proposals, and similar pieces. In fact, you may have already structured your draft using the approach. If so, the following revision strategy may help you tighten and clarify the draft.

Revision Strategy 14.13: Reorganizing around Thesis and Support

Since the thesis-support structure is fairly common, it's useful to master. Most drafts, even if they weren't initially organized in that form, can be revised into a thesis-support essay. (Personal essays would be an exception.) The order of information in such in an essay generally follows this design:

- **Lead paragraph:** Introduces topic and explicitly states the thesis, usually as the last sentence in the paragraph. For example, a thesis-support paper on the deterioration of America's national parks system might begin this way:

> Yellowstone National Park, which shares territory with
> Idaho, Montana, and Wyoming, is the nation's oldest park,
> and to some, its most revered. Established on March 1,
> 1872, the park features Old Faithful geyser, which spouts
> reliably every 76 minutes on average. What isn't nearly as
> reliable these days is whether school groups will get to
> see it. Last year 60% of them were turned away because the
> park simply didn't have the staff. <u>This essay will argue
> that poor funding of our national park system is a dis-
> grace that threatens to undermine the Park Service's mis-
> sion to preserve the areas "as cumulative expressions of a
> single national heritage" ("Famous Quotes").</u>

  The thesis (underlined) is the final sentence in the paragraph for emphasis.

- **Body:** Each succeeding paragraph until the final one attempts to prove or develop the thesis. Often each paragraph is devoted to a single *reason* the thesis is true, frequently stated as the topic sentence of the paragraph. Specific information then explains, clarifies, and supports the reason. For example, here's a typical paragraph from the body of the national parks essay:

> <u>One aspect of the important national heritage at risk be-
> cause of poor funding for national parks is the pride many
> Americans feel about these national treasures.</u> Newsweek
> writer Arthur Frommer calls the national park system among
> the "crowning glories of our democracy." He adds, "Not to
> have seen them is to have missed something unique and pre-
> cious in American life" (12). To see the crumbling roads
> in Glacier National Park, or the incursion of development
> in Smoky Mountain National Park, or the slow strangulation
> of the Everglades is not just an ecological issue; it's a
> sorry statement about a democratic nation's commitment to
> some of the places that define its identity.

  The underlined sentence is the topic sentence of the paragraph and is an assertion that supports and develops the thesis in the lead of the essay. The rest of the paragraph offers supporting evidence of the assertion, in this case a quotation from a *Newsweek* writer who recently visited several parks.

- **Concluding paragraph:** Reminds the reader of the central argument, not simply by restating the original thesis from the first paragraph but reemphasizing some of the most important points. This may lead to an elaboration or restatement of the thesis. One common technique is to find a way in the end of the essay to return to the beginning. Here's the concluding paragraph from the essay in national park funding:

> We would never risk our national heritage by allowing the White House to deteriorate or the Liberty Bell to rust away. <u>As the National Park Service's own mission states, the parks are also "expressions" of our "single national heritage," one this paper contends is not only about preserving trees, animals, and habitats, but our national identity.</u> Old Faithful Geyser reminds Americans of their constancy and their enduring spirit. What will it say about us if vandals finally end the regular eruptions of the geyser because Americans didn't support a park ranger to guard it? What will we call Old Faithful then? Old Faithless?

Note the underlined sentence returns to the original thesis but doesn't simply repeat it word for word. Instead, it amplifies the original thesis, adding a definition of "national heritage" to include national identity. It returns to the opening paragraph by finding a new way to discuss Old Faithful. Revise your draft to conform to this structure, beginning with a strong opening paragraph that explicitly states your thesis and with an ending that somehow returns to the beginning without simply repeating what you've already said.

Revision Strategy 14.14: Multiple Leads

A single element that may affect a draft more than any other is how we begin it. There are many ways into the material, and of course you want to choose a beginning or lead that a reader might find interesting. You also want to choose a beginning that makes some kind of promise, providing readers with a sense of where you intend to take them. But there are less obvious effects of a lead on both readers and writers. How you begin often establishes the voice of the essay, signals the writer's emotional relationship to the material, the writer's ethos, and might suggest the form the essay will take.

This is, of course, why beginnings are so hard to write. But the critical importance of where and how we begin also suggests that examining alternative leads can give writers more choices and more control over their essays. To borrow John McPhee's metaphor, if a lead is a "flashlight that shines into the story," then pointing that flashlight in four different directions might reveal four different ways of following the same subject. This can be a powerful revision strategy.

1. Choose a draft that has a weak opening, doesn't have a strong sense of purpose, or needs to be reorganized.

2. Compose four *different* openings to the *same* draft. One way to generate ideas for this is to cluster your topic, and write leads from four different branches. Also consider varying the type of lead you write (see "Inquiring into the Details: Types of Leads").

3. Bring a typed copy of these four leads (or five if you want to include the original lead from the first draft) to class and share them with a small group. First simply ask them to choose the beginning they like best.

4. Choose the lead *you* prefer. It may or may not be the one your classmates chose. Find a partner who was not in your small group and ask him or her the following questions after sharing the lead you chose:

- Based on this lead, what do you predict this paper is about?

- Can you guess the question, problem, or idea I'm writing about in the rest of the essay?

- Do you have a sense of what my thesis might be?

- What is the ethos of this beginning? In other words, how do I come across to you as a narrator or author of the essay?

INQUIRING INTO THE DETAILS

TYPES OF LEADS

Writer John McPhee says beginnings—or leads—are "like flashlights that shine down into the story." If you imagine that information about your topic is collected in a darkened room, then where and how you choose to begin an essay will, like a flashlight, illuminate some aspect of that room. Different beginnings point the flashlight in different directions and imply the different directions the essay might develop. Consider a few types of leads:

1. **Announcement.** Typical of a thesis-support essay, among others. Explicitly states the purpose and thesis of the essay.

2. **Anecdote.** A brief story that nicely frames the question, dilemma, problem, or idea behind the essay.

3. **Scene.** Describe a situation, place, or image that highlights the question, problem, or idea behind the essay.

4. **Profile.** Begin with a case study or description of a person who is involved in the question, problem, or idea.

5. **Background.** Provide a context through information that establishes the significance of the question, problem, or idea.

6. **Quotation or Dialogue.** Begin with a voice of someone (or several people) involved or whose words are relevant.

7. **Comparison.** Are there two or more things that, when compared or contrasted, point to the question, problem, or idea?

8. **Question.** Frame the question the essay addresses.

If the predictions were fairly accurate using the lead you preferred, this might be a good alternative opening to the next draft. Follow it in a fastwrite in your notebook to see where it leads you. Go ahead and use the other leads elsewhere in the revision, if you like.

If your reader's predictions were off, the lead may not be the best choice for the revision. However, should you consider this new direction an appealing alternative for the next draft? Or should you choose another lead that better reflects your current intentions rather than strike off in new directions? Either way, follow a new lead to see where it goes.

Revision Strategy 14.15: The Frankenstein Draft

One way to divorce a draft that has you in its clutches is to dismember it; that is, cut it into pieces and play with the parts looking for new arrangements of information or new gaps to fill. Writing teacher Peter Elbow's cut-and-paste revision can be a useful method, particularly for drafts that don't rely on narrative structures (although sometimes playing with alternatives, particularly if the draft is strictly chronological, can be helpful). Research essays and other pieces that attempt to corral lots of information seem to benefit the most from this strategy.

1. Choose a draft that needs help with organization. Make a one-side copy.

2. Cut apart the copy, paragraph by paragraph. (You may cut it into smaller pieces later.) Once the draft has been completely disassembled, shuffle the paragraphs to get them wildly out of order so the original draft is just a memory.

3. Now go through the shuffled stack and find the *core paragraph*. This is the paragraph the essay really couldn't do without because it helps answer the *So what?* question. It might be the paragraph that contains your thesis or establishes your focusing question. It should be the paragraph that explains, implicitly or explicitly, what you're trying to say in the draft. Set this aside.

4. With the core paragraph directly in front of you, work your way through the remaining stack of paragraphs and make two new stacks: one of paragraphs that don't seem relevant to your core (such

as unnecessary digressions or information) and those that do (they support the main idea, explain or define a key concept, illustrate or exemplify something important, provide necessary background).

5. Put your reject pile aside for the moment. You may decide to salvage some of those paragraphs later. But for now focus on your relevant pile, including the core paragraph. Now play with order. Try new leads, ends, middles. Consider trying some new methods of development as a way to organize your next draft (see below, "Methods of Development"). As you spread the paragraphs out before you and consider new arrangements, don't worry about the lack of transitions; you can add those later. Also look for gaps, places where more information might be needed. Consider some of the information in the reject pile as well. Should you splice in *parts* of paragraphs that you initially discarded?

6. As a structure begins to emerge, begin taping together the fragments of paper. Also splice in scraps in appropriate places that note what you might add in the next draft that is currently missing.

Now you've created a Frankenstein draft. But hopefully this ugly mess of paper and tape and scribbled notes holds much more promise than the monster. On the other hand, if you end up with pretty much the original organization perhaps your first approach wasn't so bad after all. You may at least find places where more information is needed.

Revision Strategy 14.16: Make an Outline

While outlines can be a useful tool for planning a formal essay, they can also help writers revise a draft. Begin by identifying the main point or thesis of your essay, and write that at the top of a piece of paper. For example,

---

Methods of Development

Narrative

Problem to solution

Cause to effect or effect to cause

Question to answer

Known to unknown, or unknown to known

Simple to complex

General to specific or specific to general

Comparison and contrast

Combinations of any of these

Thesis: The Endangered Species Act often permits the federal government to trample on the water rights of farmers in Western Oregon.

Now go through your draft and number each paragraph. On the piece of paper, begin a list that summarizes the point or purpose of each paragraph. For instance,

1. Introduces the problem using the Klamath Basin controversy last year.
2. Gives background on passage of the Endangered Species Act.
3. Makes point that ESA hasn't been that effective in preserving species.
4. And so on . . .

As you continue making this draft outline, from the first paragraph to the last, consider how it develops the story you want to tell or the point you want to prove. Does each paragraph contribute to your purpose, and are the paragraphs in a logical order? Can you identify gaps or other ways of arranging the paragraphs?

PROBLEMS OF CLARITY AND STYLE

One thing should be made clear immediately: problems of clarity and style need not have anything to do with grammatical correctness. You can have a sentence that follows all the rules and still lumbers, sputters, and dies like a Volkswagen bug towing a heavy trailer up a steep hill. Take this sentence, for instance:

> Once upon a point in time, a small person named Little Red Riding Hood initiated plans for the preparation, delivery and transportation of foodstuffs to her grandmother, a senior citizen residing at a place of residence in a wooded area of indeterminate dimension.

This beastly sentence opens Russell Baker's essay, "Little Red Riding Hood Revisited," a satire about the gassiness of contemporary writing. It's grammatically correct, of course, but it's also pretentious, unnecessarily wordy, and would be annoying to read if it wasn't pretty amusing. This section of the chapter focuses on revision strategies that improve the clarity of your writing and will help you to consider the effects you want to create through word choice and arrangement. Your questions about grammar and mechanics can be answered in the handbook in the back of this book.

Strong writing at the sentence and paragraph level always begins with clarity.

Maybe because we often think that work with paragraphs, sentences, and words always involve problems of correctness, it may be hard to believe at first that writers can actually manage readers' responses and feelings by using different words or rearranging the parts of a sentence or paragraph. Once you begin to play around with style, however, you will discover it's much more than cosmetic. In fact, style in writing is lot like music in movies. Chris Douridas, a Hollywood music supervisor who picked music for *Shrek* and *American Beauty* said recently that he sees "music as a integral ingredient to the pie. I see it as helping to flavor the pie and not as whip cream on top." Certainly people don't pick a movie for its music, but we know that the music is central to our experience of a film. Similarly, *how* you say it in a piece of writing powerfully shapes the reader's experience of *what* you say.

But style is a secondary concern. Strong writing at the sentence and paragraph levels always begins with clarity. Do you say what you mean as directly and economically as you can? This can be a real problem, particularly with academic writing, where it's easy to get the impression that the longer word is always better than the shorter word, and the absence of anything interesting to say can be remedied by sounding smart. Nothing could be further from the truth.

Solving Problems of Clarity

Begin by revising your draft with one or more revision strategies that will make your writing more direct and clear.

Revision Strategy 14.17: Untangling Paragraphs

One of the things I admire most in my friends David and Margaret is that they both have individual integrity—a deep understanding of who they are and who they want to be—and yet they remain just as profoundly connected to the people close to them. They manage to exude both individuality and connection. I hope my friends will forgive the comparison, but good paragraphs have the same qualities: alone they have their own identities, yet they are also strongly hitched to the paragraphs that precede and that follow them. This connection happens quite naturally when you're telling a story, but in expository writing the relationship between paragraphs is more related to content than time.

The following passage is the first three paragraphs from Paul de Palma's essay on computers, with the clever title "http://www.when _is_enough_enough?.com." Notice the integrity of each paragraph—each is a kind of mini-essay—as well as the way each one is linked to the paragraph that precedes it.

In the misty past, before Bill Gates joined the company of the world's richest men, before the mass-marketed personal computer, before the metaphor of an information superhighway had been worn down to a cliché, I heard Roger Schank interviewed on National Public Radio.

A paragraph should be unified focusing on a single topic, idea or thing. It's like a mini-essay in that sense.

Then a computer science professor at Yale, Schank was already well known in artificial intelligence circles. Because those circles did not include me, a new programmer at Sperry Univac, I hadn't heard of him. Though I've forgotten details of the conversation, I have never forgotten Schank's insistence that most people do not need to own computers.

Note how the first sentence in the new paragraph links with the last sentence in the preceding one.

That view, of course, has not prevailed. Either we own a personal computer and fret about upgrades, or we are scheming to own one and fret about the technical marvel yet to come that will render our purchase obsolete. Well, there are worse ways to spend money, I suppose. For all I know, even Schank owns a personal computer. They're fiendishly clever machines, after all, and they've helped keep the wolf from my door for a long time.

As before, the first sentence links with the last sentence in the previous paragraph.

It is not the personal computer itself that I object to. What reasonable person would voluntarily go back to a typewriter? The mischief is not in the computer itself, but in the ideology that surrounds it. If we hope to employ computers for tasks more interesting than word processing, we must devote some attention to how they are actually being used, and beyond that, to the remarkable grip that the idol of computing continues to exert.

The final sentence is the most important one in a paragraph. Craft it carefully.

Well-crafted paragraphs like these create a fluent progression, all linked together like train cars; they make readers feel confident that this train is going somewhere. This might be information that clarifies, extends, proves, explains, or even contradicts. Do the paragraphs in your draft work well on their own and together?

1. Check the length of every paragraph in your draft. Are any too long, going on and on for a full page or more? Can you create smaller paragraphs by breaking out separate ideas, topics, discussions, claims?

2. Now examine each paragraph in your draft for integrity. Is it relatively focused and unified? Should it be broken down further into two or more paragraphs because it covers too much territory?

3. In Figure 14.2, note the order of the most important information in a typical paragraph. Is each of your paragraphs arranged with that order in mind? In particular, how strong is the final sentence in each paragraph? Does it prepare readers to move into the next paragraph? In general, each paragraph adds some kind of new information to the old information in the paragraphs preceding it. This new material may clarify, explain, prove, elaborate on, contrast, summarize, contradict, or it may alter time. Sometimes you should signal the nature of this addition using transition words and phrases (see "Inquiring into the Details: Transition Flags"). Are there any awkward transitions? Should you smooth them using transition flags?

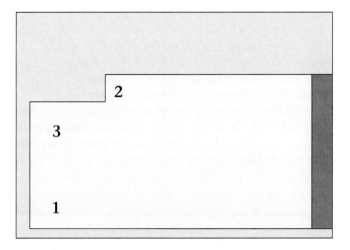

FIGURE 14.2 Order of important sentences in a paragraph. Often the first sentence is the second most important sentence in a paragraph. The third most important sentence follows immediately thereof. The most important sentence usually comes at the end of the paragarph.

⌕ **INQUIRING INTO THE DETAILS**

TRANSITION FLAGS

One way to connect paragraphs is to signal to a reader with words what the relationship is between them.

Clarifying: *For example, furthermore, specifically, also, to illustrate, similarly.*

Proving: *In fact, for example, indeed.*

Time: *First . . . . second . . . , finally, subsequently, following, now, recently.*

Cause or effect: *Therefore, consequently, so, accordingly.*

Contrast or contradiction: *On the other hand, in contrast, however, on the contrary, despite, in comparison.*

Summarizing: *Finally, in the end, in conclusion, summing up, to conclude.*

Revision Strategy 14.18: Cutting Clutter

Russell Baker's overinflated version of "Little Red Riding Hood" suffered from what writer and professor William Zinsser called "clutter." This is a disease that afflicts much writing, particularly in academic settings. Clutter, simply put, is saying in three or four words what you might say in two, or choosing a longer word when a shorter one will do just as well. It grows from the assumption that simplicity means simple-mindedness. This is misguided. Simplicity is a great virtue in writing. It's respectful of the readers, for one thing, who are mostly interested in understanding what you mean without unnecessary detours or obstacles.

In case Russell Baker's tongue-and-cheek example of cluttered writing isn't convincing because it's an invention, here's a brief passage from a memo I received from a fellow faculty member some years ago. I won't make you endure more than a sentence.

> While those of us in the administration are supporting general excellence and consideration of the long-range future of the University, and while the Faculty Senate and Caucus are dealing with more immediate problems, the Executive Committee feels that an ongoing dialogue concerning the particular concerns of faculty is needed to maintain the quality of personal and educational life necessary for continued educational improvement.

That's a 63-word sentence, and while there is nothing inherently wrong with long sentences, I'm pretty sure that at least half of the words are unnecessary. For the fun of it, see if you can cut at least thirty words from the sentence without compromising the writer's intent. Look for ways to say the same things in fewer words, and look for shorter words that might replace longer ones. What kinds of choices did you make to improve the clarity of the sentence?

Now shift your attention to one of your own drafts and see if you can be as ruthless with your own clutter as you were with the memo writer's.

1. One of the most common kinds of clutter is stock phrases, things we mindlessly say because we've simply gotten in the habit of saying them. "Due to the fact that . . ." is the one that drives me most crazy. Why not the simpler word, "Because?" The table below lists some of the most common stock phrases used in student writing. Read your draft from beginning to end and when you see one of these, cut it down to size.

STOCK PHRASE	SIMPLER VERSION
Due to the fact that . . .	Because
At the present time . . .	Now
Until such time as . . .	Until
I am of the opinion that . . .	I think
In the event of . . .	When

STOCK PHRASE	SIMPLER VERSION
This is an appropriate occasion to . . .	It's time
Proceed with the implementation of . . .	Begin
Referred to as . . .	Called
Until such time as . . .	Until
Totally lacked the ability to . . .	Couldn't
A number of . . .	Many
In the event of . . .	If
There is a need for . . .	Must

2. Another thing to consider is choosing a shorter, simpler word rather than a longer, more complicated word. For example, why not say *many* rather than *numerous,* or *ease* rather than *facilitate,* or *do* rather than *implement, found* rather than *identified.* Go through your draft and look for opportunities like these to use simpler, more direct words.

3. In his book, *Style: Ten Lessons in Clarity and Grace,* Joseph Williams cleverly calls the habit of using meaningless words "verbal tics." These are words, he writes, that "we use unconsciously as we clear our throats." My favorite verbal tic is the phrase *in fact* which I park at the front of a sentence when I feel like I'm about to clarify something. Mostly I can do without it. In fact, most of us have verbal tics, and we should learn to recognize them. Williams mentions a few common ones, including *kind of, actually, basically, generally, given, various,* and *certain.* For example: *It's generally assumed that certain students have various reasons for being apolitical these days.* A better version would be, *Students have reasons for being apolitical these days.*

Go through your draft and search for words and phrases that you use out of habit, and cut them if they don't add meaning.

Revision Strategy 14.19: The Actor and the Action Next Door

I live in a relatively urban neighborhood, and so I can hear Kate play her music across the street and Gray powering up his chainsaw to cut wooden palettes next door. I have mixed feelings about this. Kate and I have different taste in music and Gray runs the saw at dusk. But I am never confused about who is doing what. That's less obvious in the following passage:

A conflict that was greeted at first with much ambivalence by the American public, <u>the war in Iraq</u>, which caused a tentativeness that some experts call the "Vietnam syndrome," <u>sparked protests</u> among Vietnam veterans.

The subject or actor of the sentence—*the Iraq war*—and the action—*sparked protests*—are separated by a few city blocks. In addition, the subject is buried behind a long introductory clause. As a result, it's a bit hard to remember who is doing what. Putting actor and action next door to each other makes the writing livelier, and bringing the subject up front helps clarify who is doing what.

The <u>war in Iraq sparked</u> protests among Vietnam veterans even though the conflict was initially greeted with public ambivalence. Some experts call this tentativeness the "Vietnam syndrome."

Review your draft to determine whether the subjects in your sentences are buried or in the same neighborhood as the verbs that modify them. If not, rewrite to bring the actors up front in your sentences and to close the distance between actors and actions.

Improving Style

These revision strategies will improve the style of your writing. In the same way that a John Williams score can make the movies *Indiana Jones* or *Star Wars* more memorable and moving, style in writing can add to readers' experiences of a text. These are often calculated moves. Writers adopt a style because it serves a purpose, perhaps encouraging a certain feeling that makes a story more powerful, enhancing writers' ethos to make an essay more convincing, or simply giving certain information particular emphasis. For example, here's the beginning of an article about Douglas Berry, a Marine drill sergeant.

He is seething, he is rabid, he is wound up tight as a golf ball, with more adrenalin surging through his hypothalamus than a cornered slum rat, he is everything these Marine recruits with their heads shaved to dirty nubs have ever feared or ever hoped a drill sergeant might be.

The style of this opening is calculated to have an obvious effect—the reader is pelted with words, one after another, in a breathless sentence that almost simulates the experience of having Sgt. Douglas Berry in your face. There's no magic to this. It is all about using words that evoke action and feeling, usually verbs or words based on or derived from verbs.

Revision Strategy 14.20: Actors and Actions

My favorite verb yesterday was *shattered.* I often ask my writing students to come to class and share their favorite verb of the day; last spring, my senior seminar consistently selected *graduate* as their favorite.

As you know, verbs make things happen in writing, and how much energy prose possesses depends on verb power. Academic writing sometimes lacks strong verbs, relying instead on old passive standbys such as *the study concluded* or *it is believed.* Not only are the verbs weak, but the actors, the people or things engaged in the action, are often missing completely from the sentence. *Who* or *what* did the study? *Who* believes?

This is called *passive voice,* and while it's not grammatically incorrect, passive voice can suck the air out of a room. While there are reasons for using passive voice (sometimes, for instance, the writer wants the reader to focus on the action not the actor), you should avoid it in your own writing. One of the easiest ways to locate passive voice in your drafts is to conduct a *to be* search. Most forms of the verb *to be* (see table below) usually signal passive voice. For example,

> It is well known that medieval eating habits were unsavory by contemporary health standards. Cups were shared, forks were never used, and the same knifes used to clean under fingernails or to gut a chicken were used to cut and eat meat.

What is missing, of course, are the actors. To revise into active voice you simply need to add the actors, whenever possible:

> Medieval diners had unsavory eating habits by contemporary health standards. Friends shared cups, never used forks, and they used their knives, the same ones they used to clean under their fingernails or gut a chicken, to cut and eat their meat.

1. Conduct a *to be* search of your own draft. Whenever you find passive construction, try to put the actor into the sentence.
2. Eliminating passive voice is only one strategy for giving your writing more energy. Try to use lively verbs as well. Can you replace weak

---

Forms of *To Be*

Is

Are

Was

Were

Has been

Have been

Will be

verbs with stronger ones? How about *discovered* instead of *found,* or *seized* instead of *took, shattered* instead of *broke.* Review every sentence in the draft and when appropriate revise with a stronger verb.

Revision Strategy 14.21: Smoothing the Choppiness

Good writing reads like a Mercedes drives—smoothly, suspended by the rhythms of language. One of the most important factors influencing this rhythm is sentence length, or more precisely, pauses in the prose that vary as the reader travels from sentence to sentence and paragraph to paragraph. We rarely notice either the cause or the effect, but we certainly notice the bumps and lurches. Consider the following sentences, for example:

> When the sun finally rose the next day I felt young again.(14) It was a strange feeling because I wasn't young anymore.(13) I was fifty years old and felt like it.(10) It was the smell of the lake at dawn that thrust me back into adolescence.(18) I remembered the hiss of the waves.(9) They erased my footprints in the sand.(9)

This really isn't awful; it could pass as a bad Hemingway imitation. But do you notice the monotony of the writing, the steady, almost unvarying beat that threatens to dull your mind if it goes on much longer? The cause of the plodding rhythm is the unvarying length of the pauses, something I show by adding syllable counts in parenthesis at the end of every sentence. The last two lines in the passage each have nine syllables, and the first two lines are nearly identical in length as well (14 and 13 syllables respectively).

Now notice how this choppiness disappears by varying the lengths of the pauses through sentence combining, insertion of other punctuation, and dropping a few unnecessary words.

> When the sun finally rose the next day I felt young again,(14) and it was a strange feeling because I wasn't young.(11) I was fifty years old.(6) It was the smell of the lake at dawn that thrust me back into adolescence and remembering the hiss of the waves as they erased my footprints in the sand.(35)

The revision is much more fluent and the reason is simple: The writer varies the pauses and the number of syllables within each of them—14, 11, 6, 35.

1. Choose a draft of your own that doesn't seem to flow or seems choppy in places.
2. Mark the pauses in the problem areas. Put slash marks next to periods, commas, semicolons, dashes, and so on—any punctuation that prompts a reader to pause briefly.

3. If the pauses seem similar in length, revise to vary them, combining sentences, adding punctuation, dropping unnecessary words, or varying long and short words.

Revision Strategy 14.22: Fresh Ways to Say Things

It goes without saying that a tried and true method of getting to the heart of revision problems is to just do or die. Do you know what I mean? Of course you don't, because the opening sentence is laden with clichés and figures of speech that manage to obscure meaning. One of the great challenges of writing well is to find fresh ways to say things rather than relying on hand-me-down phrases that worm their way into our speech and writing. Clichés are familiar examples: *home is where the heart is, hit the nail on the head, the grass is greener,* and all that. But even more common are less figurative expressions: *more than meets the eye, rude awakenings, you only go around once, sigh of relief,* and so on.

Removing clichés and shopworn expressions from your writing will make it sound more as if you are writing from your own voice rather than someone else's. It gives the work a freshness that helps readers believe you have something interesting to say. In addition, clichés especially tend to close off a writer's thoughts rather than open them to new ideas and different ways of seeing. A cliché often leaves the writer with nothing more to say because someone else has already said it.

1. Reread your draft and circle clichés and hand-me-down expressions. If you're not sure whether a phrase qualifies for either category, share your circled items with a partner and discuss it. Are these things you've heard before?

2. Cut clichés and overused expressions and rewrite your sentences finding your own way to say things. In your own words, what do you really mean by "do or die" or "striking while the iron is hot" or becoming a "true believer?"

USING WHAT YOU HAVE LEARNED

Take a few moments to reflect on what you learned in this chapter and how you can apply it.

1. Which revision strategy has proved most helpful to you so far? Does it address one of your most common problems in your drafts?

2. Here's a common situation: You're assigned a paper for another class and the professor doesn't require you to hand in a draft. She's

just interested in your final version. What incentive do you have to work through a draft or two?

3. If revision is rhetorical, then the kinds of revision strategies you need to use depend on the particular situation: to whom you're writing and why, and in what form. The kind of writer you are—and the kinds of problems you have in your drafts—also matters. Consider the following forms: the essay exam, the review, the annotated bibliography, the letter, the formal research paper, and the reading response. Which of the five revision strategies would probably be most important for each form?

Writers rarely experience the impact their writing has on readers. When they do experience this in a writing workshop, the idea of writing for an audience ceases to be an abstraction. Writers actually witness and hear readers' responses. In some ways, though, it doesn't matter what readers say or what advice they give; it's that experience of writing for a real audience that matters most of all.

The Writer's Workshop

MAKING THE MOST OF PEER REVIEW

Sharing your writing with strangers can be among the most frightening and gratifying social experiences. It can be a key to the success of the next draft or a complete waste of time. One thing sharing your writing can't be, however, is avoided, at least in most composition courses, which these days frequently rely on small and large group workshops to help students revise. This is a good thing, I think, for three reasons:

1. It's useful to experience *being* read by others.
2. Workshops can be among the most effective ways for writers to divorce the draft.
3. The talk about writing in workshops can be enormously instructive.

Being Read

Being read is not the same thing as being read to. As we share our writing, sometimes reading our own work aloud to a group, we are sharing ourselves in a very real way. This is most evident with a personal essay, but virtually any piece of writing bears our authorship—our particular ways of seeing and saying things—and included in this are our feelings about ourselves as writers.

Last semester, Matthew told me that he felt he was the worst writer in the class, and that seemed obvious when I watched him share his writing in his workshop group. Matthew was quiet and compliant, readily accepting suggestions with little comment, and he seemed to rush the conversation about his draft as if to make the or-

What You'll Learn in This Chapter

- The purpose of peer review.

- The most common approaches for organizing writing workshops.

- How to plan to make the most of the chance to share your draft.

- What can go wrong and how to deal with it.

- Response formats for guiding how readers evaluate your drafts.

deal end sooner. When Matthew's drafts were discussed, his group always ended in record time, and yet he always claimed that they were "helpful."

Tracy always began presenting her drafts by announcing, "This really sucks. It's the worst thing I've ever written." Of course it wasn't. But this announcement seemed intended to lower the stakes for her, to take some of the pressure off of her performance in front of others, or, quite possibly, it was a hopeful invitation for Tracy's group members to say, "You're too hard on yourself. This is really good."

To *be read* in a workshop group can mean more than a critique of your ideas or sentences; for students like Matthew and Tracy it is an evaluation of *themselves,* particularly their self-worth as writers. Of course, this isn't the purpose of peer review at all, but for those of us with sometimes nagging internal critics, it's pretty hard to avoid feeling that both your writing and your writing self are on trial. This is why it's so helpful to articulate these fears before being read (see Exercise 15.1). It's also helpful to imagine the many positive outcomes that might come from the experience of sharing your writing.

While taking workshop comments about your writing personally is always a risk, consider the really rare and unusual opportunity to *see* readers respond to your work. I often compare my published writing to dropping a very heavy stone down a deep well and waiting to hear the splash. And waiting. And waiting. But in a workshop, you can actually hear the murmurs, the sighs, and the laughter of your readers as you read to them; you can also see the smiles, puzzled expressions, nodding heads, and even the tears. You can experience your readers' experiences of your writing in ways that most published authors never can.

In a workshop you can actually hear the murmurs, the sighs, and the laughter of your readers as you read to them; you can also see the smiles, the puzzled expressions, nodding heads, and even the tears.

What is so valuable about this, I think, is that audience is no longer an abstraction. After your first workshop, it's no stretch to imagine the transaction that most writing involves—a writer's words being received by a reader who thinks and feels something in response. And when you take this back to the many solitary hours of writing, you may feel you have company; that members of your workshop group are interested in what you have to say.

This is a powerful thing. In some ways, it's the most important thing about the workshop experience.

EXERCISE 15.1

Workshopaphobia

STEP ONE: In your journal, fastwrite for three minutes in response to these questions:

1. How do you feel about yourself as a writer? How do you feel about your writing?

2. What are your biggest fears about sharing your writing with others?

3. Imagine, for a moment, the worst thing that could happen.

4. Imagine the best thing.

STEP TWO: Finish this exercise by completing the simile: *Sharing my writing with others is like _____.*

STEP THREE: Discuss these entries in small groups or with the entire class. Then generate a list of qualities of a really good workshop group, one you believe would be the most satisfying for you.

Divorcing the Draft

Our writing relationships include our emotional connection to drafts, and this often has to do with the time we spent writing them. In Chapter 14, I described my relationship with my high school girlfriend, Jan, as analogous—although I wasn't very committed at first, the more time we spent together, the more I became attached to her, so much so that I was blinded to the problems between us. Similarly, when we work hard and long on a first draft it's difficult to get much perspective on it. We are so entangled with what has already been set down that it's often difficult to imagine what we might say instead. Sometimes, we need to divorce a draft, and the best remedy for this is time away from it. But students rarely have that luxury.

Workshops provide an alternative to time and are effective for the same reason some people see therapists—group members offer an "outsider's" perspective on your work that may give it new meanings and raise new possibilities. If nothing else, readers offer a preview of whether your current meanings are clear and whether what you assume is apparent *is* apparent to someone other than yourself. It's rare when a workshop doesn't jerk writers away from at least a few of their assumptions about a draft, and the best of these experiences inspire writers to want to write again. This is the outcome we should always hope to attain.

Instructive Talk

Consider a few comments I overheard during workshops last semester:

- "I don't think the focus is clear in this essay. In fact, I think there are at least two separate essays here, and it's the one on the futility of antiwar protests I'm most interested in."

- "Do you think that there's a better lead buried on the third page, in the paragraph about your sister's decision to go to the hospital? That was a powerful scene, and it seemed to be important to the overall theme."

- "I was wondering about something. What is it about the idea that we sometimes keep silent not only to protect other people but to protect ourselves that surprised you? I mean, does knowing that change anything about how you feel about yourself as a parent?"
- "I loved this line. Simply loved it."

The talk in workshops is not always about writing. The "underlife" of the classroom often surfaces in workshops, a term one educator uses to describe the idle talk about the class itself. Most writing classes ask students to step out of their usual student roles. Rather than quietly listen to lectures or study a textbook, in a writing course you are asked to make your own meanings and find your own ways of making meaning. Whenever we are asked to assume new roles, some resistance can set in, and workshops can become an occasion for talk about the class, often out of earshot of the instructor. This talk isn't always complaining. Often workshops are opportunities to share understandings or approaches to assignments and especially experiences with them. They can also be a chance for students to try out new identities—"I really liked writing this. Maybe I'm an okay writer after all."

While this kind of talk may not be directly about a draft, it can help you negotiate the new roles you're being asked to assume in your writing class. This is part of becoming better writers who are confident that they can manage the writing process in all kinds of situations. However, the main purpose of workshop groups is to help students to revise their drafts. But why seek advice from writers who are clearly less experienced than the instructor? Here are four reasons:

1. By talking with other students about writing you get practice using the language you've learning in the writing classroom, language that helps you describe important features of your own work.
2. Since writing is about making choices among a range of solutions to problems in a draft, workshop groups are likely to surface possibilities that never occurred to you (and perhaps wouldn't occur to the instructor, either).
3. Your peers are also student writers and because they come from similar circumstances—demands of other classes, part-time jobs, and perhaps minimal experience with college writing—they are in a position to offer practical and realistic revision suggestions.
4. Finally, in most writing courses, the students in the class are an important audience for your work. Getting firsthand responses makes the rhetorical situation real rather than imagined.

Will you get bad advice in a peer workshop? Of course. Your group members will vary in their experience and ability to read the problems and possibilities in a draft. But in the best writing workshops, you learn together, and as time goes by the feedback gets better and better. Paradoxically, it pays off in your own writing to be generous in your responses to the work of others.

MODELS FOR WRITING WORKSHOPS

The whole idea of peer review workshops in writing classes has been around for years. Collaboration is hardly a novelty in the professional world, but small group work in academia is a relatively recent alternative to lecture and other teaching methods in which the student listens to a professor, takes notes on what is said, and later takes a test of some kind. You won't learn to write well through lecture, although it may be a perfectly appropriate approach for some subjects. Since collaboration in the writing classroom fits in perfectly with the class's aim of generating knowledge about the many ways to solve writing problems, peer review of drafts in small groups is now fairly commonplace. You'll find workshops in writing classes ranging from first-year composition to advanced nonfiction writing.

What will workshops be like in your course? Your instructor will answer that question, but the workshop groups will likely reflect one or more of the following models.

Full-Class Workshops

Sometimes you may not work in small groups at all. Depending on the size of your class and your instructor's particular purposes for using peer review, you may share your work with everyone in a full-class session. This is the approach that is popular in creative writing classes, and it's typically used in composition classes to introduce students to the process of providing responses to other students' work. It also can work nicely in small classes with ten students or less.

In a full-class workshop, you'll choose a draft to share and you (or your instructor) will provide copies for everyone either a few days before the workshop, or at the beginning of the workshop session. On drafts you receive days ahead of the session, you're often expected to read and bring written comments to class with you. If you receive the draft at the beginning of the workshop session, you might make notes while the draft's author reads the piece aloud, or take some time to write some comments either immediately after the draft is read or following the group discussion.

Reading your draft aloud to your workshop group is a common convention in all kinds of workshop groups, large or small. This might be something you resist at first. It will quickly become apparent, however, how useful it is to read your own work aloud. It's an entirely different reading to literally give voice to your words. You'll stumble over passages in your draft that seemed fine when you read them silently, and you may notice gaps you glossed over. You'll hear what your writing voice sounds like in this particular essay, and whether it works for you and your readers.

Your instructor may lead the discussion in a full-class workshop, or she may sit back and wait while students share their responses. There may be guidelines and ground rules for responses as well (for some examples of these, see, "The Reader's Responsibilities" section that follows later in the chapter). If your draft is being discussed, your instructor may ask you to simply listen. Sometimes it's best to avoid defending certain choices you made in a draft and simply take in the range of responses you receive to what you have done. In other cases, you may be asked to present the large group with questions to consider. It certainly can be scary sharing your work with twenty or twenty-five people, but imagine the range of perspectives you'll get!

Small-Group Workshops

Far more typical is the workshop group of between three and seven members, either chosen randomly, by your instructor or self-selected. These groups may stay together all semester, part of the semester, or you may find yourself working with fresh faces every workshop session. There are advantages and disadvantages to each of these alternatives, all of which your instructor has considered in making a choice.

Ideally, your workshop group will meet in a circle, because when everyone, including the writer presenting a draft, is facing each other you'll have more of a conversation and be able to engage each other directly (see Figure 15.1). Like so many writing group methods, this is a basic principle of teamwork borrowed from the business world.

Some of the methods of distributing drafts apply to the small groups as well as the full-class workshop discussed earlier: writers will distribute copies of their drafts either a few days before their workshops or at the beginning of the sessions. You will provide written comments to each writer either before or after the workshop.

One-on-One Peer Review

Your instructor also may ask you to work with a partner, exchanging drafts and discussing them with each other. While you lose some of the range and quantity of feedback by working with a single reader, this conversation is often richer because each of you is reading the other's work with particular care and attention. It's likely you'll also have more time to talk since you'll be discussing only two rather than four or five drafts.

One variation of this kind of one-on-one peer review is the draft exchange. Your instructor will ask you to make a pile of drafts at the front of the room and ask you to take a draft from the pile, comment on it, return it, and then take another. You may return multiple times to collect, comment, and return a draft, and the result is that each draft may have three or four readers during the class session.

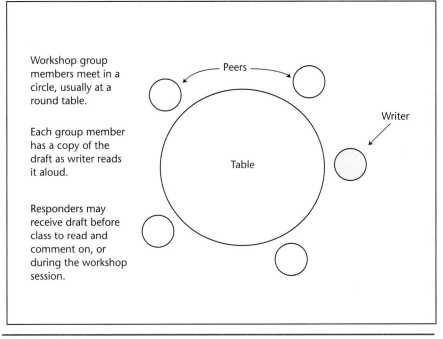

Workshop group members meet in a circle, usually at a round table.

Each group member has a copy of the draft as writer reads it aloud.

Responders may receive draft before class to read and comment on, or during the workshop session.

Peers

Writer

Table

FIGURE 15.1 The small group workshop.

THE WRITER'S RESPONSIBILITIES

No matter what model your instructor chooses, the success of the workshop depends largely on the writers themselves. Sure, it can be harder to get what you need from some groups, but in the end, you can always get *some* help with a draft if you ask the right questions and seek certain kinds of responses.

How should you prepare for a workshop to make the most of it and what are your responsibilities during the workshop? Here's a list you might find helpful:

- Make sure everyone in the group has a copy of the draft in a timely way.
- Reread and reflect on the draft before the workshop session. What kinds of responses would be most helpful from your group? What questions do you have about the draft's possible problems?
- Time the discussion so that your draft gets the allotted time and no more, particularly if there are other drafts to discuss.
- Avoid getting defensive. Listen to comments on your work in an open-minded way. Your obligation is simply to listen, not to take all the advice you're offered.

- Take notes. There are two reasons for this. First, it will help you remember other students' comments, and second, it will signal that you take those comments seriously. This increases everyone's engagement with your work.

THE READER'S RESPONSIBILITIES

Tina poured her heart and soul into her personal essay draft, and she was anxious to get some response to it. When it was her turn to workshop the piece, however, one of the group's members was absent, and two others failed to write her the required response. "It was so lame," she told me. "It was as if no one cared about my essay. It sure makes me feel less inclined to read their stuff carefully." If this workshop group were at Hewlett-Packard or any of the thousands of business that encourage teamwork, the slackers would be in trouble. It's true, however, that teamwork in the writing class depends more on internal motivation—a sense of responsibility to others—than any external reward or punishment. But there is some external motivation: it pays to be generous with your responses to others' work because you'll learn more about your own.

You can increase your own learning in workshop and contribute to a writer's positive experience by taking the following responsibilities seriously:

- Always read and respond to a writer's draft in a timely way. The writer may suggest the type of response that would be most helpful, and if so, always keep that in mind.

- Whenever possible, focus your responses on particular parts or passages of the draft, but except in an editorial workshop, avoid a focus on grammar or mechanics.

- Offer suggestions not directives. The word "could" is usually better than "should." Remember that the purpose of workshop is to help identify the range of choices a writer might make to improve a draft. There is almost always more than one.

- Identify strengths in the draft. This is often a good place to begin because it sets writers at ease, but, more importantly, writers often build on strengths in revision.

- Consider varying the roles you play in conversation with your group (see "Inquiring into the Details: Finding a Role"). It's easy to fall into a rut in group work, pretty much sticking to saying the same kinds of things or developing certain patterns of response. Stay vigilant about this and try deliberating shifting the role you play in the workshop group.

INQUIRING INTO THE DETAILS

FINDING A ROLE

The slacker is a role that's easy to slide into in small group work. It's completely passive, and it's really pretty selfish. Active roles ask more of you, but they pay off big because you learn more about your own writing. There are several active roles you might assume in a workshop group. Try them out.

ROLES THAT HELP GROUPS GET THINGS DONE

Initiators: "Here's how we might proceed with this."
Information seekers: "What do we need to know to help the writer?"
Information givers: "This seems to be an important example."
Opinion seekers: "What do you think, Al?"
Opinion givers: "I think this works."

Clarifiers: "We all seem to be saying that the lead doesn't deliver, right?"
Elaborators: "I agree with Tom, and would add . . . "
Summarizers: "I think we've discussed the thesis problem enough. Should we move on to the evidence?"

ROLES THAT HELP MAINTAIN GROUP HARMONY

Encouragers: "I love that idea, Jen."
Expressivists: "My silence isn't because I'm not moved by the essay, but I'm still trying to figure out why. Is that why you're quiet, Leah?"
Harmonizers: "I think we disagree about this, but that's okay. Let's move on to discussing this next page."
Compromisers: "Maybe both Richard and Joseph are right, particularly if we look at it this way . . . "
Gatekeepers: "Jon, we haven't heard anything from you yet."

WHAT CAN GO WRONG AND WHAT TO DO ABOUT IT

Lana is not a fan of workshops. In an argument essay, she complained that they "lack quality feedback" and sometimes workshop groups encourage "fault finding" that can hurt the writer and the writing. Things can go wrong in workshops, of course, and when they do students like Lana feel burned. Typically, unsuccessful workshop groups suffer from two major problems: lack of commitment by group members and lack of clarity about the process of giving feedback. It's like a cold and a runny nose—when a group is afflicted with one problem it usually suffers from the other.

Lack of commitment is easy to see. The writer whose draft is to be discussed forgets to make copies for the rest of her group. Members who were supposed to provide written responses to a writer's draft before class hastily make notes on his manuscript as its being discussed. The group is supposed to allot fifteen minutes to discuss each draft but finishes it in five. Members are frequently absent and make no effort to provide responses to drafts they missed. Discussion is limited to general, not particularly thoughtful, compliments: "This is really good. I wouldn't change a thing," or "Just add a few details."

This lack of commitment is contagious and soon infects nearly every group meeting. Things rarely improve; they frequently get worse. Part of the problem may be that workshop participants may not be clear about what is expected of them, a problem that should be minimized if you reviewed the checklists about the writer's and reader's responsibilities in workshop discussed in the preceding sections. A solution that is beyond your control is that the instructor evaluates or even grades workshop participation, but a group can evaluate itself, too. Since it's awkward to evaluate a specific student's performance in your workshop group, consider filling out a survey similar to the one shown here following every workshop session. Surveys such as this generate information that the group and its members can consider as they attempt to improve.

GROUP SELF-EVALUATION

Check the box that applies.

1. Overall, how effectively did your group work together today?

   ❑ Poorly
   ❑ Adequately
   ❑ Well
   ❑ Extremely well

2. How would you evaluate the participation of group members?

   ❑ Participation was limited to a few people
   ❑ Participation was adequate, although more people could have been actively participating
   ❑ Participation was good; only a few people were inactive
   ❑ Participation was excellent; everyone was involved

3. How do you feel about your own performance today?

   ❑ Poor
   ❑ Fair
   ❑ Good
   ❑ Excellent

4. If you shared a draft in workshop today, were you satisfied with the responses? Were they helpful?

   ❑ Very unsatisfied
   ❑ Unsatisfied
   ❑ Somewhat satisfied
   ❑ Satisfied
   ❑ Very satisfied
   ❑ Not sure

5. What one thing could your group change—or could you do—that would improve how the group works together? (Answer briefly.)

Groups that work together over a period of time should always monitor how things are going, and the group evaluations can be particularly helpful for this. If problems persist, the instructor may intervene or the group might consider intervention of its own (consider Exercise 15.2 as one option). Remember, the best workshops have a simple but powerful effect on writers who share their work: *it makes them want to write again.*

EXERCISE 15.2

Group Problem Solving

If group self-evaluations reveal persistent problems, devote ten minutes to exploring possible solutions.

STEP ONE: Choose facilitator and recorder. The facilitator times each step, directs questions to each participant, and makes sure everyone participates. The recorder takes notes on newsprint.

1. Your instructor can give you a tally of the responses to the group evaluation survey and discuss the patterns of problems. Do writers seem dissatisfied? Do readers feel like they're performing poorly?
2. What is behind these problems? Brainstorm a list.
3. What might be done to change the way the group operates? You must come up with *at least* one concrete idea that you agree to try.

STEP TWO: After the next workshop session, set aside five minutes at the end to discuss whether the change improved the group's performance. Is there something else you should try?

ONE STUDENT'S RESPONSE

AMY'S PERSPECTIVE ON WORKSHOPS

WHEN THINGS GO RIGHT

In both small and large workshops things are most productive when the conversation delves deep into a couple of issues instead of skimming the surface on a broad range of topics. My best experiences have been in small workshops because the groups were willing to get more deeply involved in a piece. It probably helps that there aren't too many ideas in a small group and the ones that get thrown out for debate are well considered. I always appreciate it when the group writes notes on my paper for future reference and my absolute best workshops have been multiple sessions with the same small group. Assessing each other's progress really helps in the revision stages.

WHEN THINGS GO WRONG

Especially in a small workshop people can take things too personally and ruin the objective atmosphere, letting their own agenda take precedence over progression. In one of the worst workshops I've been a part of, we were assessing an essay by a writer who chose to write about her relationship with God. The essay had many problems, she used very vague metaphorical language and the attempted symbolism didn't really work. It was a bit hard to read because of the overly sentimental tone of the piece. Instead of discussing these points though, the workshop turned into an argument about outside topics and became pretty vicious. The writer was very open to most of the comments I made about some major changes that needed to happen in the piece, but very defensive (understandably) to the personal attacks. The communication simply broke down due to varying personal beliefs when they could have been a strength of the group.

In a large group a fine balance must be achieved. It is important that the conversation runs deep, but also that it covers more than one topic. Because of the multitude of opinions in a large group the entire workshop can get stuck on one topic or section of the piece. Not only is it unproductive when the debate gets stuck, but it's also really hard to sit through.

METHODS OF RESPONDING

One thing I don't need with an early draft is someone to tell me that I misspelled the word "rhythm." It is a word I'll never be able to spell, and that fact makes me eternally grateful for spell checkers. I do like to know whether an early draft delivers on its implied promises to the reader, and especially whether there is another angle or another topic lurking there that I might not have noticed. But I don't want my wife Karen to read my stuff until I have a late draft to show her because I sometimes find her comments on early drafts discouraging.

The kinds of responses we seek to our writing in workshops depend on at least two things: where we are in the writing process and how we feel about the work in progress.

The *kinds* of responses we seek to our writing in workshops depend on at least two things: where we are in the writing process and how we feel about the work in progress. There's nothing particularly surprising about this. After all, certain kinds of problems arise during different stages of the writing process, and sometimes what we really need from readers of our work is more emotional than practical. We want to be motivated, encouraged, validated, or feel any number of things that will help us work well.

Experiential and Directive Responses

It makes sense, then, to invite certain kinds of readings of your work that you'll find timely. In general, these responses range from experiential—

this is how I experienced your draft—to more directive—this is what you could do to make it better. Which of these two forms would make reader comments on your work most helpful? For example, depending on who you are and how you work, it may be most helpful to get less directive responses to your work early on. Some people feel that very specific suggestions undermine their sense of ownership of rough drafts. They don't want to know what readers think they should do in the revision but how readers experienced their draft. What parts were interesting? What parts confusing? On the other hand, other writers feel particularly lost in the early stages of the writing process; they could use all the direction they can get. You decide (or your instructor will make suggestions), choosing from the menu of workshop response methods below. These begin with the most experiential methods of response to those which invite your readers to offer quite specific suggestions about the revision.

Response Formats

The following formats for responding to workshop drafts begin with the least directive, most experiential methods and move to the more directive approaches. While many of these formats feature some particular ways of responding to drafts, remember that the writer's and reader's responsibilities described earlier apply to all of them. Participate thoughfully and ethically (see below, "The Ethics of Responding") and you'll be amazed at what you learn about your own writing from talking with other writers about theirs.

The No-Response Workshop. Sometimes the most useful response to your work comes from simply reading it aloud to your group and asking them to just listen, nothing more. Why? You may not be ready for comments because the work is unformed and you're confident that'll you discover the direction you want to go in the next draft. Comments may confuse or distract you. It's always helpful to read your work aloud to yourself, but it's also valuable to read to an audience even if you don't invite a response. You will read with more attention and awareness. Finally, you may simply feel unprepared for a response because your confidence is low.

The method couldn't be simpler. You read your draft with little or no introduction while your group quietly listens. They will not comment unless they want you to repeat something because it was inaudible. Remember to read slowly and clearly.

The Initial Response Workshop. Robert Brooke, Ruth Mirtz, and Robert Evans[1] suggest a method that is useful for "maintaining your motivation to write while indirectly learning what to improve in your text." It might also be appropriate for an early draft.

---

[1]Robert Brooke, Ruth Mirtz, and Robert Evans, *Small Groups in Writing Workshops.* (Urbana, IL: NCTE, 1994).

The Ethics of Responding

Respect the writer.

Everyone contributes.

Say "could" rather than "should."

Say "I" rather than "you" as in "I couldn't follow this," rather than "you weren't very clear."

They suggest that you invite three kinds of responses to your work: a "relating" response, a "listening" response, and a "positive" response. These three types of response to a draft could be made in writing, in workshop discussion, or both.

- **Relating response.** As the name implies, group members share what personal associations the writer's topic inspires. Perhaps they've had a similar or a contradictory experience. Maybe they've read something or seen something that is relevant to what the writer is trying to do in the draft.

- **Listening response.** This is much like the "say back" method some therapists use with patients. Can you summarize what is it that you hear the writing saying in the draft? Is this something that is helpful to know?

- **Positive response.** What parts of the draft really work well and why? Might these be things the writer might build on in the next draft?

The Narrative of Thought Workshop. A writer who hears the story of readers' thinking *as they experienced the draft* can get great insight about how the piece shapes readers' expectations and how well it delivers on its promises. This method borrows a term from Peter Elbow—"movie of the mind"—to describe the creation of such a narrative response to a piece of writing.

The easiest way to create stories of your readers' experiences is to prepare your draft ahead of time to accommodate them. Before you make copies for your workshop group, create 2- to 3-inch white spaces in the manuscript immediately after the lead or beginning paragraph, and then again in the middle of the essay. Also make sure there is at least that much white space after the end of the piece.

You will read your draft episodically, beginning by just reading the lead or introductory paragraph, then allowing three or four minutes for your group's members to respond in writing in the space you provided for some of the questions below. The writer should time this and ask everyone to stop writing when it's time to read the next section of the draft. Repeat the process, stopping at the second patch of white space after you've read roughly half of the essay. Give your group the same amount of time to respond in writing and then finish the essay to prompt the final episode of writing.

- **After hearing the lead:** What are your feelings about the topic or the writer so far? Can you predict what the essay might be about? What questions does the lead raise for you that you expect might be answered later? What has struck you?
- **After hearing half:** Tell the story of what you've been thinking or feeling about what you've heard so far. Has the draft fulfilled your expectations from the lead? What do you expect will happen next?
- **After hearing it all:** Summarize your understanding of what the draft is about, including what it *seems* to be saying (or not quite saying). How well did it deliver on its promises in the beginning? What part of your experience of the draft was most memorable? What part seemed least clear?

Discuss with your group each of the responses—after the lead, after the middle, and at the end of the draft. This conversation, and the written comments you receive when you collect their copies of your draft, should give you strong clues about how well you've established a clear purpose in your essay and sustained it from beginning to end. The responses also might give you ideas about directions to take the next draft that you hadn't considered.

The Instructive Lines Workshop. Most essays balance on a thesis, theme, question, or idea. Like the point of a spinning top, these claims, ideas, or questions are the things around which everything else revolves. Essay drafts, however, may easily topple over because they lack such balance— there is no clear point, or there are too many, or some of the information is irrelevant. In discovery drafts especially, a writer may be seeking the piece's center of gravity—or *centers* of gravity—and a useful response from a workshop group is to help the writer look for the clues about where that center might be.

This format for a workshop invites the members to try to identify the draft's *most important lines and passages,* by clearly marking them with underlining or highlighter. What makes a line or passage important? *These are places where writers explicitly or implicitly seem to suggest what they're trying to say in a draft* and they may include:

- A line or passage where the writer seems to state his thesis.
- A part of a narrative essay when the writer adopts a critical stance- and seems to be trying to pose a question or speculate about the meaning of an experience or some information.

- A part of the draft in which the writer seems to make an important claim.

- A scene or comparison or observation that hints at the question the writer is exploring (or could explore).

- A comment in a digression that the writer didn't seem to think was important, but you think might be.

These underlinings become the subject of discussion in the workshop session. Questions to consider include: Why did this particular line seem important? What does it imply about what you think is the meaning of the essay? Do the different underlined passages speak to each other—can they be combined or revised into a controlling idea or question for the next draft—or do they imply separate essays or treatments? Would the writer underline something else? How might the different interpretations of the draft be reconciled?

The Purpose Workshop. Sometimes writers know their purpose in a draft: "I'm trying to argue that the Enron collapse represented the failure of current methods of compensating CEOs," or "I'm proposing that having vegetarian fast food restaurants would reduce American obesity," or "This essay explores the question of why I was so relieved when my father died." What these writers may need most from their workshop groups is feedback on how well the draft accomplishes particular purposes.

Before the workshop session, the writer crafts a statement of purpose similar to those in the preceding paragraph—a sentence that clearly states what the writer is trying to do in the draft. This statement of purpose should include a verb that implies what action you're trying to take—for example, *explore, argue, persuade, propose, review, explain, analyze,* and so on. As you probably guessed, these verbs are usually associated with a particular form of inquiry or genre.

The writer should include this sentence *at the end* of the draft. It's important that you make your group members aware of your purpose only after they've read the entire piece and not before. Discussion and written responses should then focus on some of the following questions:

- Were you surprised by the stated purpose, or did the essay prepare you for it?

- If the stated purpose did surprise you, what did you think the writer was trying to do in the draft instead?

- Does the lead explicitly state or hint at the stated purpose?

- What parts or paragraphs of the draft seemed clearly relevant to the stated purpose, and which seemed to point in another direction?

- Did the draft seem to succeed in accomplishing the writer's purpose?

If more directive responses would be helpful to you, consider also asking some questions such as whether there might not be a stronger beginning or lead buried elsewhere in the draft, or soliciting suggestions about which parts or paragraphs should be cut or what additional information might be needed. Which parts of the draft seemed to work best in the context of the writer's stated purpose, and which didn't work so well?

The Graphing Reader Interest Workshop. What commands readers' attention in a draft and what doesn't? This is useful to know, obviously, because our overall aim is to engage readers from beginning to end. This is something that is difficult to do, particularly in longer drafts, and reader attention will often vary from paragraph to paragraph in shorter drafts, too. But if your draft drones on for three or four paragraphs or a couple pages then the piece isn't working well and you need to do something about it in revision.

One way that you can know this is by asking your workshop group to literally graph their response to your essay, paragraph by paragraph, and then discuss what is going on in those sections that drag.

For this workshop, consecutively number all the paragraphs in your draft. You or your instructor will provide each member of your group with a "Reader Interest Chart" (see Figure 15.2), on which the corresponding paragraph numbers are listed. On the vertical axis is a scale that represents reader interest, with "5" being high interest and "1" being low interest in that particular paragraph. As you slowly read your draft aloud to

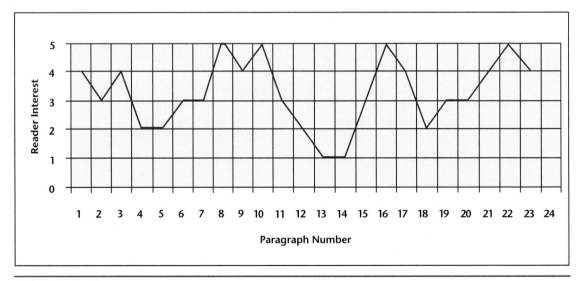

FIGURE 15.2 **Reader interest chart.**

your group's members, they'll be marking the graph after each paragraph to roughly indicate their interest in what the paragraph says and how it says it.

When you're finished, you'll have a visual representation of how the essay worked, paragraph by paragraph, but the important work is ahead. What you need to discuss with your group is *why* a paragraph or section of the draft failed to hold some readers' attention. What is going on in those parts of the draft?

- Are they confusing?
- Do they needlessly digress?
- Is the prose awkward?
- Is there too much or too little explanation?
- Are they too loaded with facts and not enough analysis?
- Does the writer seem to lose his voice?

One way to find out what's going on with the weaker parts of your essay is to look at the stronger ones. What do you notice about those paragraphs that were rated a "4" or a "5" by your group members? What are the particular strengths of these sections? Can you do more of that in other, less lively sections of the draft?

The Sum-of-the-Parts Workshop. Like a watch, a well-written essay moves fluently forward because all of its parts work together. In workshops you can never talk about all those parts; there is too little time, and often it's hard to tease apart all the gears and the springs that make an essay go. But you can try to be as thorough as you can during a workshop, essentially running through a checklist of some of the most important elements, including purpose, theme, structure, information, and style. In this workshop, you attempt to cover as much territory as possible, so the responses you get will have breadth but not depth. You also invite some directive responses from your readers—suggestions for the revision and specific areas of confusion—as well as their interpretation of your purpose and theme.

One of the best ways to solicit this information is to use a worksheet like the one below. Typically, this worksheet would be filled out by your group's members outside of class and before you workshop the draft. It would then be attached to the copies of your draft and returned to you after the group discusses the work. If your peers respond thoughtfully to the worksheet, it can generate a wealth of information for you about your draft.

WORKSHOP WORKSHEET

Purpose: In your own words, what is the writer's motive in the draft? Use one of the following verbs to describe this in a sentence: explore, explain, argue, analyze, review, report, propose, persuade, reflect.

Theme: State in your own words what you think the thesis, main point, or central question is in this draft. What question does this idea or question raise for you?

Information: Name at least two specific places in the draft where you wanted more information to fully appreciate what the writer was trying to say. What kind of information do you suggest (anecdote, story, fact, detail, background, example, interview, dialogue, opposing perspective, description, case study, etc.)?

Design: Identify *at least* one paragraph or passage that seemed out of place. Any suggestions about where it belongs?

Style: Place brackets [ ] around several sentences or passages in the draft that seemed awkward or confusing to read.

The Thesis Workshop. An alternative to the sum-of-all-parts format is to focus on a single element of the draft that you are particularly concerned about, and no part is more important than the thesis. An essay without an implicit theme or an explicit thesis is an essay without meaning. No one is particularly interested in reading a pointless story or research essay, nor are most readers interested in points that seem unrelated to the information in the draft or that are painfully obvious. For example, the idea that the death of your Aunt Trudy was sad for you is a much less compelling theme to build an essay around than the idea that her death—and the deaths of family members generally—upset the family system in ways that helped you to take on new roles, new identities.

A thesis workshop will help you make sure there is a controlling idea or question behind the draft, and help you think more deeply about what you're trying to say. Your workshop members can help with this because they bring a range of perspectives and experiences to a conversation about your theme that might make it richer and more informative for you.

In this workshop, group members receive the drafts ahead of time. Before the workshop session they should underline the thesis, main idea, theme, or question that seems to be behind the draft. This will be the *main thing* the writer seems to be saying or exploring. This isn't particularly difficult in essays with explicit thesis statements, such as arguments or proposals, but in personal essays and other more literary pieces, the theme may not be so explicit. In that type of essay, they should underline the passage that seems central to the meaning of the essay. This may be a reflective passage or it might be a scene or moment.

Second, at the top of a piece of paper, they should write down in a sentence or two—at most—the thesis or theme as they understand it. This may involve simply copying it down from the draft. However, if thesis or theme is not that clear or explicit, each reader should write it down in his own words, trying to capture the main point of the draft.

Then, members should fastwrite for five minutes about their own thoughts and experiences about the writer's thesis or theme, constantly hunting for questions it raises for them. Say the draft's thesis is that the university athletic programs have become too powerful and have undermined the university's more important academic mission. In the fastwrite, explore what you've noticed about the football team's impact on the school. Where does the football program get funds? Does it compete with academic programs? Then fastwrite about what you've heard—for instance, that athletics have strong alumni support, and so on. Keep the fastwrite focused on the thesis; if it helps, stop and reread it for another prompt.

The workshop session that follows will be a conversation that is largely focused on what people thought was the point of the draft, and their own thoughts and feelings about it. The writer should facilitate the conversation without comment and make sure the following two things are discussed in this order:

1. What seems to be the thesis, theme, or question behind the essay? Is it clear? Are there alternative ideas about what it might be?

2. What does each group member think or feel about what the writer seems to be saying? How do the reader's experiences and observations relate to the writer's main point or question? And especially, what questions should the writer consider in the next draft?

Although it may be hard to keep quiet if your draft is being discussed, the conversation will probably surprise you. You may discover that several of your group members either failed to understand what you were trying to say in the draft or give you a completely new idea about what you were up to. At its best, the thesis workshop inspires you to think more deeply about your theme or main idea as you consider the range of experiences and questions that other people have about it. Take lots of notes.

The Editing Workshop. In a late draft, the larger issues—for example, having a clear purpose, focus, and point, as well as appropriate information to support it—may be resolved to your satisfaction, or you may feel that you already have some pretty good ideas about how to deal with them. If so, what you may need most from your workshop group is editorial advice: responses to your work at the sentence and paragraph levels.

In the editing workshop, you invite your group members to focus on style and clarity (and perhaps grammar and mechanics). The questions that direct the reading of the draft might include some or all of the following:

- Did you stumble over any awkward passages that seemed to interrupt the fluency of the writing?
- Were there any sentences or passages that you had to read a few times to understand?
- Could any long paragraphs be broken down into smaller ones? Did any paragraphs seem to be about more than one thing?
- Are the first and last lines of the essay well crafted? Are the last lines of paragraphs strong enough?
- Were there any abrupt transitions between paragraphs?
- Was the voice or tone of the draft consistent?
- (Optional) Did you notice any patterns of grammatical problems, including run-on sentences, unclear pronoun references, lack of subject–verb agreement?

Group members who see any of these problems should bracket [ ] the sentence or passage and refer to it when discussing the editorial issue with the group. The workshop discussion has the following ground rules:

- Be respectful of the writer's feelings. Some of us feel that style is a very personal issue, and that grammar problems are related somehow to our self-worth.
- Don't have arguments about editorial judgments. It isn't necessary for group members to agree. In fact, you probably won't agree about a lot of things. Offer your comments on style as suggestions and then move on, although don't hesitate to offer a differing opinion.
- Make sure to identify places in the draft where the writing is working just fine. Editorial workshops need not focus exclusively on problems. Sentences, paragraphs, or passages that work well stylistically can often help the writer see how to revise the less effective parts.
- If readers have some comments about larger issues in the draft, things such as purpose or theme, ask the writer first if she welcomes that kind of feedback. Otherwise, keep the workshop focused on editorial matters.

An editing workshop may sound a little harrowing. It really isn't, particularly if the group knows the ground rules. My students often tell me that these conversations about style are some of the best workshops they have had. Everybody learns something, not just the writer, a principle that applies to many workshop formats and another reason that peer review is such a useful practice in the writing classroom.

Reflecting on the Workshop

The real work follows the workshop. Then you have the task of mulling over the things you've heard about your draft and deciding how you're going to rewrite it. This calls for a way of inquiring—reflection—that you've already practiced. As soon as possible after your workshop session, reread your notes and your readers' comments, then go to your journal and fast-write for five minutes. Choose one of the following prompts to get—and keep—you going.

- What did I hear that seemed most useful? What did I hear that I'm not sure about?
- What responses to my draft do I remember most? Why?
- What did I think I needed to do to revise the draft before the workshop? Did my peer review experience change my mind? Did it reinforce my initial plans?
- What do I plan to do to revise this draft to make it stronger?

USING WHAT YOU HAVE LEARNED

The writing workshop is just one of many forms of collaboration that you'll likely experience both during and after college. Even unsuccessful workshops are instructive because they'll help you to understand how groups work and what roles you can play to make them function better. Consider your experience so far.

1. What is the best workshop group experience you've had in this class? What made it so good? What was the worst experience? What made it so bad?

2. As you reflect on your own performance in groups, what have you learned about yourself as a collaborator? How would you describe yourself as a group member? How would you *like* to describe yourself?

3. If you're currently involved in a group project in another class, how would you compare your writing workshop with that other group project? Can what you've learned in one provide useful guidance for the other?

APPENDIX A

THE WRITING PORTFOLIO*

WHAT IS A PORTFOLIO?

While you might be used to your writing teachers grading each of your essays individually, some of your writing instructors in college might evaluate your essays a little differently. Instead, your instructor might ask you, at the end of the term, to collect your best writing for the class, essays that have been revised, workshopped, and polished based on what you've learned during the entire course. You might collect them in a folder or notebook. Then, your instructor might grade this collection of essays as a whole, rather than individually assign each a grade. In fact, if you are reading this section, it is probably because your instructor will be using this type of evaluation, something that's called a writing portfolio.

You've probably heard about stock portfolios and artist portfolios, but the term "writing portfolio" may be something new. "Portfolio" in these three examples means a collection of stocks, photographs or paintings, or writing that represent something about the compiler: for example, if you have a stock portfolio where 75 percent of your money is invested in high-risk growth funds and the other 25 percent is in safe bond funds, then you might be showing that you're a risk taker. If you are an artist and you select a range of photographs taken over a long period of time, you might be showing how you've developed and changed as a photographer.

Writing portfolios can reflect similar things about their authors. As a collection of the work you've done for a writing class, a portfolio can demonstrate how you've developed as a writer, it can show specific writing principles you've learned, or it can illustrate the range of genres you have worked with (to name a few). Often it will be a large percentage of your course grade, so the work you submit will have been revised several times and you might be asked to reflect on your assembled work, exploring what you want the portfolio to illustrate. In fact, the whole idea of using a portfolio to evaluate your work emphasizes the principles of inquiry and reflection at the heart of this book.

Instructors use portfolios in different ways: some require certain essays and assignments to be included, some allow *you* to choose what to in-

*Appendixes A, B, C, and D were written by Dr. Michelle Payne, writing director at Boise State University.

clude, others ask that you choose according to particular guidelines (for example, pieces that demonstrate your ability to conduct research, to put a lesson plan together if it's a teaching portfolio, or to revise). It's important that you understand what kind of portfolio your instructor is requiring and why. We'll talk about the why later—let's look first at the different kinds of portfolios you might be asked to assemble.

TYPES OF PORTFOLIOS

It's important here to distinguish between *unevaluated* and *evaluated* portfolios. An unevaluated portfolio would be one where you are collecting all your work for the course, like a journal or working folder, but your instructor will not be evaluating the material. You keep class notes, doodles, drafts of essays, exercises, and anything else that relates to the course. From that folder, you then might be asked to *choose specific assignments,* continue working on them, and turn them in for your final portfolio. A final portfolio is one type of evaluated portfolio. Your instructor either gives you the evaluation criteria for it or helps the class develop those criteria with him or her. You turn in selected pieces from the course, either freely chosen by you or required by your instructor. The work is "final" in that you have stopped revising, done your best to make it as effective an essay as possible, and are ready to have it graded. Unevaluated portfolios, then, are places where you experiment, collect and play around with your ideas and your writing, not worrying about evaluation as much as you would when you assemble an evaluated portfolio. All the activities in this book, for example, would be part of a writing journal or working folder that your instructor might not evaluate. Then, as you develop essays from those exercises, you revise them into final products that your instructor can grade.

Unevaluated Portfolios

The unevaluated portfolios you are most likely to encounter in your college writing are:

- *A journal or working folder.* In this type of unevaluated portfolio, keep all your work for your writing course—everything that you do in and out of class, all your assignments and drafts. It's a place where you can track your progress as a writer because you have everything there. Some instructors ask you to turn this type of portfolio in for a holistic grade (that is, the entire body of work is evaluated, not individual pieces), based on criteria that is different from the criteria used for evaluating a portfolio of final drafts (for example, in evaluating a writing journal, your instructor might consider whether you've completed all the assignments, taken risks in your writing, and experimented).

- A *learning portfolio.* For this type of unevaluated portfolio, you collect materials from your course and possibly other places that reflect something about your learning process. Let's say your writing instructor wants you to keep a record of your learning in another course, such as sociology. You might include class notes that changed the way you understood a concept, restaurant napkins scribbled with conversations you've overheard, a paper you are assigned to write, and some reflections on how the theories you've been learning affect how you perceive your world. You can include both print and non-print materials, like photos or music. Learning portfolios often allow for free choice, so you have to carefully select what you will include and why. This type of portfolio may be helpful as you apply the concepts you learn in this course—about inquiry, essay writing, and reflection—to another course.

Evaluated Portfolios

Evaluated portfolios include the following:

- A *midterm portfolio.* As the name suggests, this portfolio is assembled at midterm. Your instructor might ask you to include particular assignments—such as your two best reading responses and a revised essay—and write a cover letter that explains, for example, what you've learned about writing that is reflected in these pieces. You might also be asked to evaluate the portfolio yourself and discuss your goals for the rest of the course. A midterm portfolio might be evaluated, but it might also be used as a practice run for the final portfolio at the end of the course and not be evaluated.

- A *final portfolio—limited choice.* Your instructor may require you to include specific assignments and essays in the portfolio you turn in at the end of the course. Let's say your university's writing program, for example, requires all students to write a research essay in their first-year writing course and to demonstrate they can use documentation effectively, support their claims with evidence, and do more than simply string information together. Your instructor, then, would ask you to include one or more research essays in the final portfolio so he can assess whether you have learned what is required. That might be the only required essay and you would have some choice about what else to include. Or, you might be required to include a profile, an argument, and an ethnographic essay, as well. In addition, instructors might ask you to include a reflective essay with your final portfolio (explained in more detail below). In general, a final portfolio emphasizes the final products of the course, the revised and polished work that shows what you've learned for the entire term.

- A *final portfolio—open choice.* While all your work will be revised and polished, your instructor may ask you to choose your best writing for the course and not require particular essays. She might ask that you only choose from the essays you've written or that you choose from the informal writing you've done, as well (like the writing exercises in this book). She may require a certain number of pages (say, twenty to twenty-five pages), a certain number of assignments (three out of the five essays required in the course), or leave the length and number of assignments open. Here are a couple of examples: If you feel your research essay is better than your ethnographic essay, then you might include it and not work any further on your ethnographic essay. You might also include your personal essay, argument, and your response to particular writing exercises. You would include these pieces because you believe they are your best work, but you want to be sure you can talk specifically about *why* they are the best and *what* they show your instructor about what you've learned. For instance, do you want to show your growth, your success in using writing as inquiry, or what you've learned about crafting paragraphs?

WHY REQUIRE A PORTFOLIO?

Before we talk more about how to choose the materials to include in your portfolio, we should talk about why you will be expected to assemble one. If you are keeping an unevaluated portfolio, your instructor wants to emphasize your learning process at least as much as your final product. We rarely take the time to reflect on how we learn, but doing so can help you learn better in your other courses. Are you a visual learner? Do you learn best when you have a relationship with your teacher or when the teacher is more removed? If you learn more outside of school, why? Learning portfolios enable you to develop even better learning strategies and understand why you might struggle with certain learning situations. The same is true for a writing journal or working folder. As you collect everything you do in a writing course, you can pause periodically and reflect on which writing strategies seem to sabotage your efforts, which seem to work well, how you might work through writer's block, or what principles about writing you've been learning. Many of the exercises in this book prompt you to reflect on your writing process, your reading strategies, your learning and thinking, so if you've been doing them, you have already seen the benefits of reflecting on your process.

In both kinds of unevaluated portfolios, the *process* of whatever you're doing is being emphasized and valued. You don't have to worry about writing beautifully styled sentences the first time around or having a complicated reading all figured out the first time through. An unevaluated portfolio allows for—in fact encourages—the messiness of writing and thinking instead of focusing only on polished work. These kinds of portfolios emphasize risk, experimentation, and reflection on the process of writing and learning, all of which are central to the ideas in this book. These types of portfolios, then, reflect and reinforce what you've been learning about writing so far.

Evaluated portfolios are important for very similar reasons. In order to get your drafts to the point that they are ready to be evaluated, you are encouraged all term to experiment, rewrite, and critique them. In fact, most of the term you are working in your writing journal, exploring ideas, commenting on peers' drafts in workshop, revising your own drafts, and taking them apart again, all in an effort to learn more about writing and make your essays more effective. Portfolios allow you to do all that over a long period of time and in a relatively "evaluation-free" zone, so you are graded based on your final product at the end, not in the middle, of the process.

Your final product, though, is the result and reflection of all that work you did throughout the semester. In addition, the reflection exercises in this book have had you thinking about your learning all term. You will be more conscious of the writing and reading strategies that work best for you, and so will be better prepared to write the reflective essay that your instructor may require in the portfolio.

Of course, the final product is what is evaluated in a final portfolio, so while this kind of portfolio reinforces the process of inquiry and reflection, it also emphasizes the way a sentence is crafted, the way an essay is organized, and the way a writer explores an idea. A portfolio, then, allows an instructor to evaluate *both* the process of writing and the quality of the final product.

ORGANIZING PORTFOLIOS

Because a writing portfolio emphasizes the *process* of writing and learning as much as the final product, you'll want to keep your course materials organized—that is, the materials that reflect your process. Whether or not your instructor assigns a journal or working folder, it's a good idea to keep one yourself. You can do this on the computer or in a notebook. There are several ways of organizing your writing journal or working folder, including these options:

1. **Organize by chronological order.** Keep everything that you do in the course in the order you complete it.

2. **Organize by assignments.** Within each category, include all the writing you've done (fastwriting, drafts, exercises), peer and teacher responses, notes, research materials, and so on. As an example, your portfolio might be broken out into the following categories:

   - Profile
   - Ethnographic essay
   - Review
   - Argument

- Reflective Exercises
- Reading Responses
- Essay Exam

3. **Organize by subjects.** Here you place your writing into categories defined by the subject or theme of the writing. For example:

   - Racism (Profile, Research Essay)
   - Italy trip (Personal Essay, Review, Argument)

   With this approach, you have a better sense of how you've explored a topic through different genres, comparing what you've learned about the subject as well as about the form.

4. **Organize by stage of process.** Here you place your writing into categories based on what place in the writing process it falls, starting with your fastwriting and journal writing and ending with your final drafts and reflective writing. For example:

   - Fastwriting/journal writing
   - Exercises
   - Sketches
   - Early Drafts
   - Peer Responses
   - Instructor Responses
   - Revisions
   - Final Drafts
   - Reflective Writing

You can also create your own categories to organize your class work. However you choose to organize your writing, be sure to keep everything you write for the course; don't throw anything away. If you are using a computer, *save all of your writing files and keep a separate back-up copy.*

If you are expected to include a reflective letter or essay as a preface to your portfolio, it's a good idea to create a separate section in your journal or folder for all the reflective writing you've done in the class. You can do all the reflective exercises in that separate section, or you can include them for each separate assignment. However you do it, keeping your reflective writing in one place will make it easier to compose your reflective letter or essay.

WHAT TO INCLUDE

Before you can sort through your writing and choose what to put in your portfolio, you need to understand what is expected and how your work will be evaluated. At the same time, you'll want to sort through your writing and think about which essays you like, which you don't want to work on anymore, which might show your instructor how much you've learned about writing, and so on. Your decisions about what to include and how to revise will be guided by your own goals and the goals of the course, so it's important to be sure you know what those goals are.

You might create a separate section in your writing journal or working folder titled "Final Portfolio" and, on the first page, spend some time, with your instructor's help if necessary, answering the questions below. These questions will help you decide what to include.

Portfolio Requirements

- How many pages are you required to include? Or, how many papers?
- What degree of choice do you have? Are you required to include specific essays? Can you add informal writing, such as in-class exercises, fastwriting, and reading responses? Can you include nonprint materials, such as photos or Web pages you've designed? Can you include material from other classes?
- Are you required to write a reflective essay or letter introducing the portfolio? What are you expected to address in that essay or letter?
- What degree of revision is expected of the material you include?
- Are you expected to include previous drafts of each essay so your instructor can see your revisions and evaluate your growth?
- How should the papers be organized? In a notebook? Folder? Bound by the copy center?
- What are the formatting expectations (for instance, font size and style, margins, placement of page numbers)?

Context for Evaluation

- Has your instructor given you her evaluation criteria for the portfolio? Is it listed in your syllabus? Have you developed it as a class? What will she expect you to demonstrate in your portfolio?
- Does your college or university have specific criteria you must meet? Where is that posted—in the syllabus? the writing program Web page? the course catalog?
- Will each paper in the portfolio be graded individually, or will the portfolio be graded holistically?
- Will your instructor or a group of instructors you don't know evaluate it?
- How will your portfolio grade be factored into your overall course grade? What percentage of your final grade will it be?

Personal Goals and Preferences

- As you sort through all your work for the course, which pieces are you bored with? Which seem too frustrating to continue working on? Which do you not want to work on anymore?

- Which pieces do you feel good about? Which are still interesting to you, make you want to continue exploring or developing the ideas you've written about? Which surprised you? Which did you learn the most from?

- If you aren't sure whether you want to continue working on a particular essay, consider what it might demonstrate in your portfolio: growth in your abilities? Development of your overall theme for the portfolio? Variety in the kinds of writing you can do?

Because you will be spending the next few weeks revising your essays for the portfolio, you want to be sure you choose the ones that still interest you and make you want to keep writing. You also, of course, want to choose strong examples of your work. Your next step will involve balancing your own interests and goals with the goals of the course.

Now that you've answered these questions, create another page in your "Final Portfolio" section where you will reflect on whether each of the essays and/or informal writing you *think* you want to work on meet the criteria you've been given. For each piece of writing, answer the following questions:

- Which of the standards for evaluation (in the course or the writing program as a whole) does this piece of writing meet? Here's an example:

Writing Program Minimum Competencies	**Draft of Argument Essay**
a. Essay has a clear focus, purpose, and point	a. Yes
b. Essay is developed with relevant, credible, and substantive details/evidence and each assertion is supported with such details/evidence	b. No—too many assertions not supported with credible evidence
c. Essay is organized clearly, using a form appropriate to the content and purpose	c. No—essay rambles; the most important ideas are buried in the middle; no transitions

- If I'm allowed to choose any essays I want, which do I believe reflect my best writing *and* meet the standards for evaluation?

- Of the essays I'm required to or think I might want to include, what do I need to do when I revise to make them more effective and meet the standards for the course? Create a separate category for each essay and list your revision goals for each one. Refer to your instructor's and peers' comments as well as the standards of evaluation for the course. In addition, consult the chapters in this book that list the qualities of the kind of essay you are writing.

Once you've done this, you will have a clear sense of which essays you might want or need to include, as well as a sense of what you need to revise and how. But evaluation criteria aren't the only factors you need to consider when you assemble your portfolio. You also need to consider your audience, your overall purpose in choosing the entries, and the way you present yourself as a writer, reader, and learner.

Consider Your Audience

When you assemble your portfolio, think of it the way you would any piece of writing. You have a particular purpose or controlling question you are exploring, you are communicating that to a particular audience, and you want to come across as knowledgeable and credible. The audience for your portfolio is fairly clear: your instructor, an instructor from another class, or a group of instructors you do not know. You need to know who will be reading your portfolio and what is expected. If you've answered the questions listed above, you probably have a good sense of who will evaluate your work and what criteria will be used. It's always a good idea to talk with your instructor about his expectations so you understand what he values and will expect to see you demonstrate in your work.

If your audience is not someone you know, ask your instructor to clarify what that person or group might expect. What will be important for you to focus on in the portfolio? What does this person or group value? How can you best prepare to meet this audience's expectations?

Consider Your Purpose

You have a number of purposes in assembling your final portfolio. You want, of course, to receive the best grade you can, to show that you have met the standards for the course, have presented your best writing, and are a reflective learner. You may, however, also have some freedom in choosing what you want to emphasize about your work. So, in addition to thinking about how your entries meet the evaluation criteria, you might be able to do one of the following:

- Do you want to show how you've grown over the term? If so, you'll choose work that you struggled with initially and then work that shows how you dealt with those struggles and learned new skills.
- Do you want to show that you can write well in a range of genres or forms? If so, you'll want to include a range of genres, not simply a series of argument essays or profiles, for example.

- Is your strength actually in only one or two genres or forms (such as the personal essay and ethnographic essay, or the argument and review)? If so, you might include only work in these forms, provided your instructor allows this kind of choice.
- Do you want to show your ability to reflect on your writing and learning? If so, you'll want to choose essays from which you've learned a great deal about writing (which is true in general, but particularly in this case). Was the argument essay especially challenging? Did you learn more about research from the research essay or the ethnographic essay or the profile? Did you learn more about using details from one particular essay? And so on. You would then address these kinds of questions in your reflective letter or essay that prefaces the portfolio.
- Do you want to show your willingness to take risks, to experiment, to direct your own writing projects and make them distinctive? The essays you include would be the ones that best illustrate these qualities.

You may have another quality you want your portfolio to demonstrate that isn't listed here. Whatever you choose to emphasize, be sure it meets your instructor's expectations. You don't want to show how creative and experimental you can be if your writing teacher will be evaluating you on how well you can reflect on your learning.

So, when you are determining your purpose for the portfolio, you need to balance demonstrating that your work meets the stated evaluation criteria and demonstrating what else you believe is important about your work. You are meeting both your audience's expectations and your own

SELF-PRESENTATION

When you're in the middle of revising your work, it's easy to forget that you are presenting an image of yourself on the page by the words you use, the subjects you write about, and the ways you write about them. It's unavoidable, though. And when several of your essays are together, readers can get an even broader sense of who you are as a writer and thinker than if they read only one or two of your essays. So, when you choose the material to include, you'll want to think about the image you present of yourself.

That's part of what you were doing in the previous section as you thought about your purpose in assembling your portfolio. Do you want to present yourself as someone who has grown as a writer? Someone who takes risks and experiments? You might also want to come across as someone who is serious about her work, conscientious, and thorough, qualities you can prove through the material in your portfolio. But what else might your portfolio convey that you want to be aware of?

Let's say your final work has quite a few errors and typos. What will that convey to your instructor? Will he know that you didn't take the time to proofread? Will he perceive you as careless or forgetful or lacking knowledge in sentence style, grammar, punctuation? If you use a lot of words you aren't really familiar with but that "sound good," (that is, you found them in the thesaurus) how will your instructor see you? As you pay attention to the words you choose and the ways you write about your subjects, think about what you are conveying to a reader about yourself. Are you coming across as preachy? Thoughtful? Credible? Reactionary? Honest? Conversational? Formal? Is that what you want to convey? Is it appropriate to your subject and genre?

Because reflection is so important to the process of inquiry you've been learning about in this book, it will also be important for you to present yourself as a reflective learner. How might you do that?

WRITING A REFLECTIVE LETTER OR ESSAY

You may have to preface your final portfolio with a letter or essay that introduces the pieces you've included and reflect on what you've learned about writing, reading, and inquiry. For some instructors, this letter or essay becomes crucial in evaluating the whole portfolio because it gives coherence and purpose to the material as well as articulates what you've learned. In my own classes, the reflective essay can make the difference of half a letter grade in the overall evaluation of the portfolio. As always, clarify with your instructor what is expected in the reflective letter or essay and how it will be weighed in the portfolio grade. While some instructors require a five- to seven-page essay or letter that begins the portfolio, others may require a prefatory letter for *each piece* you include in the portfolio. Some only want a reflection on the writing process for each essay, others may only want a narrative of how your thinking changed about each subject you wrote about. Regardless, you'll want to spend some time going through your writing journal or folder and reflecting on what you notice. Here are some questions that might help:

- **Patterns.** As you flip through the pages of your writing journal or folder, what patterns do you notice? What seems to happen frequently or stand out to you? For example, you might notice that you always begin your essays the same way, or you ended up writing about the same subject the whole semester without realizing it, or you got better at organizing your essays and using significant detail.
- **Reflective writing.** As you look only at the reflective writing you've done throughout the course (the reflective exercises in this book), what do you notice? What five things have you learned about writing, reading, and inquiry based on that early reflective writing?

- **Change over time.** How did you describe your writing process (and/or reading process) at the beginning of the course? How would you describe it now? If it has changed, why and how?
- **Writing principles.** List five to seven principles about writing you have learned in this course, the five to seven most important things you've learned about writing, reading, and inquiry. Or, list five to seven strategies for writing and reading that you will take with you into other writing situations.
- **Revision.** For each of the essays you are including in your portfolio, what would you do differently if you had more time?
- **Writing processes.** For each of the essays in your portfolio, describe the writing and thinking process that led to the final product. Emphasize the most important changes you made and why you made them.
- **Most and least effective writing.** Which essay in the portfolio is your strongest? Your weakest? Why?
- **Effect of peer response.** How have your peers and other readers of your work affected the revisions you've made?
- **Showing what you've learned.** What does your portfolio demonstrate about you as a writer, a student, a reader, a researcher? How? Be as specific as possible.
- **What's missing.** What is *not* reflected in your portfolio that you believe is important for your instructor to know?
- **Expectations.** How does your portfolio meet the expectations for effective writing defined in your class?
- **Applying the textbook.** How have you applied the principles about each essay form that are outlined in this textbook?
- **Personal challenge.** In what ways did you challenge yourself in this course?

Your instructor might ask you to address only three or four of these questions in the letter or essay itself, but it's a good idea to do some fast-writing on all of them. Doing so will help your essay or letter be more specific, thoughtful, and persuasive.

As with any essay, you'll want to take this one through several revisions and get feedback from readers before you include it in the portfolio. Your instructor might even ask you to workshop a draft of this with your group. If you've done some fastwriting on the questions above, you are in good shape to compose a first draft of your reflective letter or essay. Keep in mind who your audience is—your teacher, teachers unknown to you, and/or your peers—and address what that audience expects. Be as specific as possible, citing examples from your work, drawing on the terms and principles you've discussed in class and read about in this book.

Typical Problems in Reflective Essays/Letters

- Use of overly general and vague comments.
- Not enough specific details.
- Giving the teacher only what you think she wants whether it's true or not.
- Critiquing the course (usually this is reserved for end-of-term evaluations that are confidential and anonymous); it's not wise to risk criticizing the person who is evaluating you.
- Comments that suggest you don't take the assignment seriously.

If you've been doing reflective writing all term, you will have plenty of material to draw from to make your reflective essay or letter concrete, substantive, and as honest as it can be (given the circumstances). You'll probably surprise yourself with all that you've learned.

FINAL PREPARATIONS

Before you turn your portfolio in, take time to proofread it carefully, possibly asking one of your peers for help. Check again to be sure you've met all the criteria for the portfolio, including what is required, assembling it appropriately, and formatting it as required. This is work that you are proud of, so the way you present it should reflect that pride. It should meet high standards for presentation and quality.

APPENDIX B

THE LITERATURE REVIEW

WHAT IS A LITERATURE REVIEW?

Have you ever wondered why those academic articles you read for your research projects seem to begin with a list of the other people who've talked about the same ideas? Somewhere in the first few pages you find a section that seems to list everyone who's ever had anything to say about the subject of, say, Charlotte Bronte or quantum physics. This who's who list, though, is actually a common academic convention called the "literature review." In it a writer reviews or summarizes what has already been said about his research question and then offers an analysis of it. This move is very similar to what we do when we're relaying a conversation we had with friends: "You know how Margy and Joan have always disagreed about _____? Well, at lunch the other day we were talking about _____ and Margy said, '_____.' Then Joan said, '_____.' I couldn't believe it—they never agree on anything. But both of them believed Mark when he said, '_____,' and now we've decided to do something about it." We're usually careful to let our audience know who said what so no one is confused, especially if our audience doesn't know much about what our friends believe about a subject.

An explicit example of giving this kind of background is the opening to "Is the Medium the Message?" by Ellen M. Bennet, et al. As you read it, notice the way the writers acknowledge the specific people who are a part of this conversation and try to accurately summarize their contributions (I've italicized some of the phrases these writers use to signal this summary). Imagine this as the writers' way of introducing us to the conversation that we've just walked into. The article begins:

> When Pennsylvania official Budd Dwyer committed suicide during a press conference in January 1987, television coverage of the incident was criticized sharply, although most stations cut the tape before the shot was fired. Somehow, coverage of this even by print reporters and photojournalists did not stir the same scorn from the critics or the public that TV news accounts evoked.
>
> The "bad news" bias of journalism professionals has been of increasing concern generally, and much of the criticism has been leveled specifically at television news. Both _practitioners of the profession and news consumers_ have complained that TV news exploits graphic and grotesque news events for the purpose of increasing ratings in the competitive race for profits. _Two_

common responses to these criticisms are that, first, the morbid event is newsworthy and, second, that this is what the audience wants.

A *common criticism* leveled at television is that it is excessively morbid in its presentation of news. Even *those who have pioneered the field of television news* identify the medium as uniquely able to portray tragedy because it is so visual.

Researchers have also noted the near universal appeal of stories about disturbing, unpleasant, tragic events. *Haskins* has observed that "throughout history humans have been drawn to public spectacles involving bloody death and disfigurement, to helpless victims, to public hangings and crucifixions and decapitation." The purpose of the present study . . .

Although this introduction doesn't cover a wide range of specific experts in the field, it does summarize what most people in the field have said—or what people *outside* have said. It gives us an overview, a brief summary with background on the issue so we all know why it is important and what has been said about it already. After all, how can we determine how significant someone's research is unless they tell us how it compares with the work of other people in the same field?

While this excerpt comes from the beginning of an article, writers also acknowledge the contributions of others later in their texts when they address a specific issue. Darryl Pifer does this in the introductory pages to his play, *Small Town Race: A Performance Text.* After describing how he gathered his information and the methods he used to interpret it, Pifer spends some time explaining the idea of a "performance text." While you won't be reading the entire play, you might be wondering how a "performance text" could also be a research essay. I had never read a research article in the form of a play and I was curious where this idea came from and how it had gained enough credibility to be published. Fortunately, Pifer provided all the information I needed. All we need to do is look up the people he cites (using APA style) in these two paragraphs and we'll learn more about where this idea of a performance text came from:

I constructed the information along with some autobiographical reflections into a performance text, drawing on the writings and works of Barry (1996), Denzin (1997), Donmoyer and Yennie-Donmoyer (1995), Jackson (1993), Mienszakowski (1995, 1997), Richardson (1997), Saldana (1998), and Yordan (1997). This ethnodrama has not been performed yet . . .

My performance text is a compiled script centered on the theme of race in a small town. It is constructed so that the performers and audience can investigate the theme. I consulted literature about and examples of readers theater (Donmoyer and Ynnie-Donmoyer, 1995; Jackson, 1993; Yordan, 1997) in constructing the text. I adhere to Denzin's (1997) explanation that the performance text is the single, most powerful way for ethnography to recover yet interrogate the meanings of "lived experience" (pp. 94–95). I believe that through performance the lives, voices, and events presented will have a life and power not possible through other forms of presentation. It is my hope that this performance text will stimulate discussion and reflection on the issues it attempts to address.

You'll notice in these paragraphs that the names of the same researchers keep coming up. That's a good indication that these writers are probably fairly prominent in this field. Here's another way of thinking about it: If Pifer and other members of this community of social scientists wanted to throw a party, you can bet that Denizen, Donmoyer, Ynnie-Donmoyer, and Jackson would be the first to be invited.

So, in a literature review, a writer gives readers an overview of the conversation that other scholars, writers, or researchers have been having over the years so they will understand why his question is important and where it comes from. But he also gives us this critical overview to signal that he's done his research, he knows who has said what and why it's important, and therefore he has credibility to write about the subject, too. A literature review, then, does at least three things:

1. **Summarizes the established knowledge** on a particular subject and **analyzes it** within the context of the writer's overall thesis or research question.

2. **Establishes why the writer's question is significant,** given what has already been said, and how it emerged as an important subject for further study.

3. **Establishes the writer's ethos or credibility,** signaling membership in a particular community (like the field of biology or engineering) and demonstrating thoroughness in researching.

As you might guess, writing a literature review means you will focus on two ways of inquiring we've discussed in this book: *explanation* and *evaluation.* The thinking and reading you do *before* you write the review, however, will demand that you use all four ways of inquiring, including reflection and exploration.

WHEN TO WRITE THE LITERATURE REVIEW

A literature review could be a separate assignment given in one of your college courses, or it could be required as part of a longer research paper (usually in the introductory section). People who write research and grant proposals often have to write literature reviews, and graduate students who write theses or dissertations often devote an entire chapter to reviewing the literature that is relevant to their project. In addition to showing readers that you know the conversation that's been going on about your subject, a literature review is also a great way to refine your research question and explore your ideas. It's an important thinking tool.

HOW TO WRITE THE LITERATURE REVIEW

The easiest and most efficient way to write a literature review is to approach its composition systematically. This will include gathering materials, reading strategies, organizing, and drafting processes.

Gathering Materials

First, you have to conduct some research: do a thorough search for materials related to your research question and sort out which are most relevant and most important in the field. Often you can discover who the important researchers and scholars are in an area by looking at the bibliographies of the articles and books you have found. Whose name seems to occur frequently? Who seems to be cited quite often? Whose work seems to be central to the ideas you're talking about?

Sorting out what is relevant to your question all depends on your question and the scope of your research.

- If your research question hasn't been explored by others yet, then you need to look at material that helps you discuss *why* it hasn't been researched before.

- If you are using a particular theory or approach to your research—such as feminist literary theory to interpret *Jane Eyre* or an ethnographic approach to understanding reading skills in third graders—you will need to discuss that particular theory or approach. What has been argued about this theory or approach? What are the key principles and arguments that will be relevant to your own work?

- If your research question touches on an area that has been written about a great deal—let's say Shakespeare or World War II—then you need to narrow your overview to the particular issue about that subject you are focusing on—say, gender in Shakespeare's tragedies or military strategies during the invasion of Normandy. Then you have to choose the sources that are most relevant and significant in the conversation that has been going on about the particular subject you're researching.

You cannot cover everything that has been said in the last seventy-five years—nor should you. You have to have criteria for deciding what you will include in your literature review. How many sources you discuss is often dependent on how long your project is (for a thesis or dissertation, a literature review is a chapter of about thirty pages; for a ten- to fifteen-page research paper, the review might be several paragraphs).

Reading Strategies

Like any other assignment, the reading strategies you use for this assignment will have a particular purpose. Your main task will be to understand well the argument each source is making, and then to judge its conclusions, methods of research, evidence, and relevance to your overall question or purpose. Most importantly, when you get ready to write your literature review, you need to have made connections among all the materials you've read, not only evaluating them against each other, but showing how each is related to the other. Below are some questions you should keep in mind as you read individual texts:

- What is the author's overall question and her conclusions? What argument is she making?
- What research methods does she use (for example, empirical, ethnographic, theoretical, case study)? What are the strengths and limitations of this method? Has she addressed them? How reliable are her conclusions?
- How well does she review the literature relevant to her subject?
- How effectively does she argue her case? Are her conclusions logical? Is her evidence relevant, specific, and substantial? Are her emotional appeals effective? Does she include counterarguments?
- What seem to be the gaps or unanswered questions in her research and/or conclusions? In other words, what does she not address or seem to dismiss or ignore that you think is relevant?
- What other approach might she have taken to this issue?
- How does this particular article/review/book/study fit into what has already been said? What is its relationship to other studies? For example, does it build on the work of another scholar, does it refute a long-standing theory, does it critique the research methods used, does it answer a question raised at the end of an earlier study?

After you finish reading individual texts, there are some broader questions you will want to ask:

- As you read all the material you've gathered, what seem to be the overall patterns that emerge? For example, what seems to be common knowledge among the people in this area?
- Do the studies share similar research methods?
- Do they address different perspectives on the same question?
- Do they come to similar conclusions?
- Do they all seem to ignore similar assumptions or limitations?
- In other words, what kind of picture can you get about this conversation?

Finally, before you begin writing your literature review, use this seed sentence to help you summarize the material and articulate how your question is related to what you've read: *When most people think about/study/write about _____, they say/assert/argue _____. However, what they don't address is _____.*

Organizing

Once you have a sense of the conversation going on about your subject and you've carefully read and evaluated your sources, you need to figure out how you will organize your review. What you don't want to do is simply list all the relevant sources like a grocery list or a list of summaries, beginning each paragraph with "According to . . . " While you'll want to introduce the authors using this kind of signal phrase, you don't want to organize your literature review by author. Instead, you need to organize the material around each source's *relationship* to the others and its significance to your project. That's what you've begun to do by answering the questions above about the patterns you see among all the sources you've read.

When you focus on the relationship among sources, you will be comparing, contrasting, and evaluating them based on particular criteria. You might, for example, want to focus on the trends in the research or compare the various conclusions of researchers. You need an organizing strategy. The following strategies are only a few of the possibilities:

- Trends in current research.
- Types of research methods used (quantitative, qualitative).
- Theoretical approaches.
- Specific purposes for the research/arguments.
- Conclusions reached.
- Gaps in the literature, questions not answered, and/or conflicts among theories, conclusions, evidence, or research methods.
- Chronology, or a history of how one idea led to the next.

The organizational strategy you choose will also be related to the question you're pursuing in your own research, especially if your literature review is part of a longer essay. If you are writing an essay about the medical uses of leeches, for example, you probably won't focus on the types of research methods used or the theoretical approaches. You might write a narrative of how leeches have been used in history, you might focus on what is known and what is not, or you might look at conflicting studies on the effectiveness of using leeches in medicine. The literature review should offer the reader context for your own question, reasons why it's important, and your own approach to the subject compared to that of others in the field.

You can use the above organizational strategies to create sections in your literature review or to organize by paragraph. It all depends on the number of sources you plan to study and the length of your essay.

Drafting

Here are a few things to keep in mind while you draft your literature review:

- If the review is an assignment in itself, not connected to a larger project, be sure you understand the purpose of the assignment and the criteria you are to use as you review the literature.
- Tell the reader the criteria you will use to evaluate the material.
- Explain why you have left other material out of the review.
- Don't assume your reader knows the material you will be discussing; summarize each significant source and give as much or as little detail as seems necessary for your purposes. It may be that you want to focus on three majors articles, but you'll be giving an overview of six. You'll spend more time discussing those three than the others.
- Point out what is known and/or accepted knowledge about your subject and discuss what still needs to be studied. A common move writers make in a literature review is, "What most people think about X is _____; however, what they don't realize/haven't studied/need also to consider is _____." With such a move, you summarize what has been said, what you will focus on, and why it's important.

APPENDIX C

THE ANNOTATED BIBLIOGRAPHY

WHAT IS AN ANNOTATED BIBLIOGRAPHY?

You've had experience putting together a "Works Cited" or "References" page for your research essays, but you may not have had experience writing an annotated bibliography, which includes descriptions and comments about each of your sources. It is a list where each citation is followed by a short descriptive and sometimes evaluative paragraph or annotation. Many scholars use published annotated bibliographies during their research to help them narrow down the material that seems most relevant to their work, but you might be asked to write one as part of a larger project for a class, sometimes in preparation for a literature review or a research proposal. Annotated bibliographies, then, can serve a lot of different purposes, so if you are assigned one, you want to be sure you understand your role as a researcher and writer.

We will examine four types of annotated bibliographies in this appendix.[1] Their purposes include indicating content and coverage, describing thesis and argument, evaluating the work and a combination of these three. If you have looked at published annotated bibliographies, you have probably seen one of these types. When you are assigned to write an annotated bibliography, you'll need to decide which of the following four forms is the most appropriate, but you can also consider using these at various stages of your own research process.

Indicative Bibliography. Are you being asked to *indicate* what the source contains or simply identify the topic of the source, but *not evaluate or discuss the argument and evidence?* If so, explain what the source is about ("This article explores gender in Shakespeare's tragedies."). List the main ideas it discusses—this may include chapter titles, a list of authors included if the source is an anthology, or the main ideas included in the subsections if it's an article ("Topics covered include male homosocial desire, women as witches, and conceptions of romantic love."). Usually, in a descriptive annotation, you don't evaluate the source's argument or relevance, nor do you describe its overall thesis.

---

[1]The four forms discussed are found on the Writing Center Web site for the University of Wisconsin–Madison (http://www.wisc.edu/writing/Handbook/AnnBib_content.html).

Why Write an Annotated Bibliography?

- It can help you compile a list of sources on your subject that will need to be sorted through later. It can also help you decide if you want to return to a source later in your process.
- If you have been keeping a dialogue journal for your research project, you can refer to it in composing these annotations. This type of bibliography can help you further think through your own developing thesis or conclusions.
- This type of bibliography will also help as you are developing your own thesis, and it will help if you have to write a literature review, as well.

Informative Bibliography.   Are you being asked *to summarize the argument* for each source? If so, briefly state each work's thesis, the primary assertions and evidence that support the main argument, and any conclusions the author makes. You are not evaluating the effectiveness of the argument, nor are you delineating the content of the source (as you would in an indicative form); instead, you are informing your audience about the works' arguments and conclusions.

Evaluative Bibliography.   Are you being asked *to evaluate the sources* you find? If so, your annotations will include a brief summary of the argument and conclusions and then move on to critically evaluate it: How useful is the source to your particular project? What are the limitations of the study or argument? What are the strengths? How reliable are the conclusions? How effective are the research methods? The criteria you use for evaluating each source depends on the purpose of the bibliography, whether you are compiling one to help focus your research project and sort out the most important articles or writing one to help others decide what is most relevant in the subject area. Be sure you are clear about the evaluation criteria.

Combination of Types.   Are you being asked to be *both informative and evaluative?* Many annotated bibliographies have multiple purposes, so you will be combining the above forms. Because most annotations can be up to 150 words, you need to devote only a sentence or two for each purpose. In other words, a few lines to summarize and describe, a few to evaluate and comment. However, you may be told exactly what to include in the annotations and how many words or sentences to use. Your instructor might, for example, ask that you write one sentence summarizing each work's argument and then another sentence describing how the work relates to your own developing thesis.

WHEN TO WRITE AN ANNOTATED BIBLIOGRAPHY

An instructor might assign an annotated bibliography in a college course because she believes it will help you write a stronger, well-researched paper. She might want you to explore your subject, write an annotated bibliography, and then compose a research proposal based on what you've discovered. In this case, the bibliography helps you narrow down your subject, gives you an overview on what has already been said, and helps you evaluate the sources that are most important to your own work. The bibliography then helps with the prewriting stage for your paper. Or your instructor might want you to compose a literature review as part of a research paper for your class, and he wants you to do an annotated bibliography first. Again, the bibliography becomes part of your prewriting for the paper—or in this case, one section of the paper—and helps you focus on the relevant sources, their quality, and their relationships to one another. In both these cases, you are also demonstrating the kind of research you can do, showing that you know how to find credible, reliable, valid, and substantive material on your subject.

While an annotated bibliography can be a prelude to a research proposal or a literature review, it can also simply examine and present the sources that are available on a subject, offering the reader an introduction to key sources and ideas. These kinds of bibliographies are helpful for researchers because someone else has already sifted through the available material and culled what is significant. At the same time, such a bibliography relies on the compiler's own sense of what is significant and so must be used critically. It's important in an introduction to such an annotated bibliography that you explain the criteria you are using to select and evaluate sources. Sometimes this kind of bibliography can also provide readers with additional materials to explore, beyond what you may have used in your paper or presented in a speech.

HOW TO WRITE AN ANNOTATED BIBLIOGRAPHY

Before you can begin writing an annotated bibliography you must choose a subject on which to focus. From there you will move to gathering materials, applying reading strategies, and finally writing the annotated bibliography.

Gathering Materials

See Chapter 12, "Research Techniques," to help you find material relevant to your subject. Are you supposed to find a wide range of materials, such as reviews, scholarly articles, and books? Are you to focus only on materials from the last five years? What are the parameters for your researching? Be sure to clarify these issues with your instructor.

Reading Strategies

You'll again use the critical reading strategies you've learned as you read the sources you've decided to include in your bibliography. If the materials you've gathered will later become part of a research essay, then you will be taking notes and writing about them as discussed in Chapter 12. But to create your annotated bibliography, you'll have an additional purpose for reading your sources. If you simply need to describe the content of the sources (indicative form), you will do little critical evaluation; instead, you'll focus on explanation. Once you determine the focus for your annotations, use the following questions (which primarily apply to evaluative forms of annotation, but can also help with informative and indicative forms) to guide your reading.

- Who is the intended audience for this article, review, or book?
- What is the central research question or claim that the material addresses? Write it out in one or two sentences.
- What kind of evidence is used to support the conclusions, argument, thesis? How valid is it given what the intended audience values? For example, literary examples wouldn't be taken seriously as evidence in a biology paper, nor would anecdotal evidence about an experiment.
- How effectively has the author(s) addressed the central question or claim?
- Sketch out the main argument in a brief outline. Note the main subjects covered, the authors listed (if it's a collection of articles), and the general organization of the work.
- What is known about the credibility of this author(s)? Have you seen his name appear in other works on this subject? Is he publishing in his area of expertise?
- Note the dates of publication, usually on the copyright page. Is the material current? Does it need to be? Is this a revised edition?
- Compare the source to others on the same subject. Are the ideas similar enough to suggest that this author is working with accepted knowledge? If they aren't, do you find them valid, significant, or well researched? Is one source on this subject better than another, and why or why not? Does the source build on the ideas of others, critique them, add new knowledge?
- How effectively is the source written?
- If you can, try to find reviews of the material or commentaries from other scholars in the area. This will give you a sense of how the work was received, what if any controversy it has generated, and what has been lauded and/or criticized.

Writing the Annotated Bibliography

Because annotations are so brief, it's tempting to think they are easy to write. But like any writing project, you need to have a lot of material to draw from—in this case, substantive notes and reflective writing about each work. It is better to work from a place of abundance than one of scarcity—remember, you need material to work with if you are going to identify what's worth keeping and what should be dropped.

Length.   Depending on the requirements for and purposes of the annotations, they could be one paragraph or only a few sentences, so you have to choose your words carefully and use specific details judiciously. Clarify with your instructor the kind of writing style she expects; that is, does she want brief phrases, almost like a bulleted list of main points, or full sentences and paragraphs?

Content.   Begin with the proper citation form for the source, following the guidelines for the specific documentation style your instructor requires (APA or MLA). Organize this list alphabetically. After each source, compose a paragraph or two that addresses your purpose for the bibliography. That purpose, again, will depend on the requirements your instructor has given you. If you are describing the content of the source, for example, begin with an overview of the work and its thesis, then select the specific points you want to highlight about it (such as chapter titles, subjects covered, authors included). If you are explaining the main argument of the work, begin with the central thesis, then include the main claims, evidence, research methods, and conclusions. Finally, if you are evaluating the source, add comments that summarize your critique.

SAMPLE STUDENT ANNOTATED BIBLIOGRAPHIES

In the two examples that follow, students in a course on feminist literary theory were asked to compose an annotated bibliography of the sources they'd found for their research essay. In the first example, Lauren Tussing wanted to apply what she's learned about feminist theory to the film *Lost in Translation,* and her annotated bibliography helped her focus her research question and decide which of the sources would be most useful in composing her essay. Notice that she has written an annotated bibliography that combines the informative and evaluative forms—she primarily summarizes the main argument of each source and then discusses its relevance to her research project.

In the second example that follows, you'll notice that the student doesn't evaluate her sources; instead, Tracy Schuck provides clear, succinct, and substantive summaries of each source. As you compare the two sample bibliographies, what do you notice about the different purposes they serve for the writer? For readers?

Lauren Tussing

Instructor Michelle Payne

Engl 497

18 April 2004

Annotated Bibliography

Doane, Mary Ann. "Film and the Masquerade: Theorising
the Female Spectator." *Feminism and Film.* Ed. E.
Ann Kaplan. Oxford: Oxford University Press, 2000.
418–436.

This is an article in a collection of articles on
feminist film theory. In the essay, Doane works to create a theory for the female spectator, moving away from
prior focus on the male spectator. Doane does, however,
reintroduce the idea of Laura Mulvey's binary opposition of passive/female and active/male that she introduced in her essay, "Visual Pleasure and Narrative
Cinema." Doane applies the notion of distance to
Muvley's binary opposition.

This essay, written for an academic audience, is
esoteric and sometimes difficult to understand, but it
might be helpful for my paper if I decide to talk about
the female spectator. Despite my difficulty with this
essay, Doane did give me some ideas about how to think

about *Lost in Translation,* the film that I discuss in my essay. A woman directs this film, so I wonder how her direction affects the gaze. Is there a uniquely female gaze for this film? Or does the film conform to the male gaze? How might viewers, both male and female, gaze upon this film?

Gaines, Jane. "White Privilege and Looking Relations: Race and Gender." *Feminism and Film.* Ed. E. Ann Kaplan. Oxford: Oxford University Press, 2000. 336-355.

This essay, also included in the same collection as the above essay, argues that psychoanalysis isn't a good way to critique films, particularly because it overlooks racial and sexuality issues. Even when theorists use psychoanalysis to describe black family interaction, they impose "an erroneous universalisation and inadvertently reaffirm white middle-class norms" (337). When feminist theory uses gender first and foremost in discussing oppressions, it "helps to reinforce white middle-class values" (337). Also, Gaines argues, because feminist theory universalizes white middle-class values, it ideologically hides other forms of oppression from women.

This essay has given me new ideas about how to read *Lost in Translation*. Although I wasn't initially going to talk about issues of race, I might want to. Race actually plays a big role in the movie because it is about white people in an Asian country. Also, I think this essay is helpful in its critique of psychoanalysis. In my research of feminist film theory, I have found that you can't escape psychoanalysis. I don't particularly like psychoanalysis, but I realize that it is an important theory to understand. It is at the basis of many articles on feminist film theory. However, I don't think I will be discussing psychoanalysis in my essay.

Jayamanne, Laleen, ed. *Kiss Me Deadly: Feminism and Cinema for the Moment.* Sydney: Power Institute of Fine Arts, 1995.

This is a collection of articles about feminism and film. The articles in this book focus mostly on directors, such as Kathryn Bigelow, Rainer Werner Fassbinder, Alexander Kluge, and Nicolas Roeg. Before looking at this book, I never heard of any of these directors. I didn't find this book particularly helpful, especially because, as Jayamanne notes in the introduction, some of the directors and films discussed are "foreign to the semi-official canons of feminist film theory" (14).

Johnston, Claire. "Dorothy Arzner: Critical

    Strategies." *Feminism and Film.* Ed. E. Ann Kaplan.

    Oxford: Oxford University Press, 2000. 139-150.

    In this essay, Johnston discusses Dorothy Arzner,

a director from the 1920s to the 1940s who was nearly

the only woman during her time to create a lucid bulk

of work in Hollywood. Because not many studies have

been written about Arzner – especially in male-domi-

nated film studies – Johnston's purpose is to explore

various approaches to Arzner's work and to discuss how

her films are important for contemporary feminists.

    This essay also gave me a new idea about how to

look at the film I will be discussing in my paper. I'd

like to discuss the director of *Lost in Translation.*

Are her films, particularly *Lost in Translation,* impor-

tant for contemporary feminists?

Kaplan, E. Ann, ed. *Women in Film Noir.* London: British

    Film Institute, 1978.

    This book is a collection of articles about film

noir. Because the book is aimed at scholars who are ed-

ucated in feminist film theory, it does not actually

give a definition of film noir, and I didn't know what

film noir was, so I looked it up in the Oxford English
Dictionary. According to the Oxford English Dictionary,
film noir is "a cinematographic film of a gloomy or fa-
talistic character." I don't think the film I will be
discussing falls into this category, so I don't think I
will be using this source for my essay.

——. *Feminism and Film*. Oxford: Oxford University
        Press, 2000.

This is a collection of articles on feminist film
theory. Many of the essays in this book are esoteric
and difficult to understand, but I think this is an invaluable resource to my research essay because of the
range of essays it includes. The book is split into 4
phases: (1) Pioneers and Classics, (2) Critiques of
Phase 1 Theories: New Methods, (3) Race, Sexuality, and
Postmodernism in Feminist Film Theory, and (4)
Spectatorship, Ethnicity, and Melodrama. By employing
these different "phases" of feminist film theory, the
book allows the reader to see the conversations within
feminist film theory and its subsequent evolutions. I
have summarized a few of the articles contained in this
collection above.

Kuhn, Annette. *Women's Pictures: Feminism and Cinema.*

   London: Verso, 1994.

   In this book, Kuhn argues that "feminism and film,
taken together, could provide the basis for new forms
of expression, providing the opportunity for a truly
feminist alternative cinema in terms of film language,
of reading that language and of representing the
world." The book provides a systematic view of film.
First, Kuhn discusses the dominant cinema. Then, she
explores "rereading dominant cinema" from a feminist
stance. Finally, she discusses "replacing dominant cinema" with feminist film.

   I think this book will be helpful when I attempt
to understand where *Lost in Translation* fits into film
culture. Is the film part of dominant cinema? How can it
be read from a feminist viewpoint? How is it a feminist
film? How isn't it a feminist film?

Tracy Schuck

Instructor Michelle Payne

Engl 497

18 April 2004

Annotated Bibliography

Bell, Elizabeth, Lynda Haas, Laura Sells. <u>From Mouse to</u>
    <u>Mermaid</u>. Bloomington: Indiana UP, 1995.

The three editors Bell, Haas, and Sells choose to
include authors that helped pull together the idea that
they had been trying to culminate for three years. They
researched many organizations, a few mentioned include
the International Association for the Fantastic in the
Arts (IAFA), the Southeast Woman's Studies Association
(SEWSA), and the Southern States Communication
Association (SSCA). This book is filled with articles
that question the politics, gender and culture that
Disney movies harbor and represent.

Three sections of the book that will be particularly helpful in studying how women and especially
mothers are portrayed in Disney include: "Eighty-Six
the Mother," that looks at the murder, matricide and
the idea of the "good mother," "Somatexts at the Disney

Shop," looks at how Disney constructs the female animated bodies, and "Where Do the Mermaids Stand?" that
looks at the voice and body in the movie *The Little
Mermaid*.

Craven, Allison. "Beauty and the Belles: Discourse of
    Feminism and Femininity in Disneyland." <u>European
    Journal of Women's Studies</u> 9.2 (2002 May): 123-143.

    This article presents a critical analysis of
Disney's <u>Beauty and Beast</u>. It places specific emphasis
on the character Belle and a historical look at the
original fairy tale. It is also a "response to feminism
that involves compressing feminist ideology into conventions of popular romance."
    This article also looks at the representation of
the female characters in <u>Snow White and the Seven
Dwarfs</u>. It also reviews other feminist women and actors
perspectives on how women are portrayed in Disney
movies.

Flower, Joe. <u>Prince of the Magic Kingdom</u>. New York:
    John Wiley & Sons, Inc., 1996

    Flower's idea for this book began with an inter-
view with Michael Eisner. During his research for this
book he began to see how much a part of life Disney had

become. He saw the good sides of it and also began to uncover the bad. He wrote, "In tracking the story down, I found that part, at least to be true. There was something magical about Disney . . . . But I met something else as well—a corporation intent on the bottom line, a global entertainment conglomerate that could be as grasping, as controlling, as juiceless and impersonal as any company in America." Flower is very clear that his book is not a book about corporate history, it is about the struggle over ideas and value that men and women give up.

Giroux, Henry A. <u>The Mouse that Roared</u>. Maryland:

    Rowman & Littlefield Publishers, Inc., 1999.

This book written by Henry Giroux examines how cultural practices and institutions shape nearly every aspect of our lives. He is one of the leading cultural critics and has written many books and essays that deal with American politics, society and cultural influences. Giroux goes on to say that the Disney Corporation is one of the world's most influential. He explores how the corporation has "become a political force in shaping images of public memory, producing children as consuming subjects, and legitimating ideological positions that constitute a deeply conservative and disturbing view of the roles imparted to children and adults alike." He also looks at how Disney's influence will lead to the end of childhood innocence by corruption.

Griffin, Sean. <u>Tinker Belles and Evil Queens</u>. New York: New York UP, 2000.

Author Sean Griffin received his doctorate in Critical Studies from the School of Cinema-Television at the University of Southern California. He is an openly homosexual instructor who has a great interest in Disney, soap operas, and the media. His book is about the Walt Disney corporation and how it used to be and how it has evolved.

The sections in his book primarily deal with how homosexuality has been represented in the fairy tale stories and how sexuality has been evaded by the company and purposefully built up a "wholesome" image. However Griffin goes on to explain in his book how sexuality has been influential in all aspects of the Disney Corporation and that they have been simply overlooked.

Hastings, Waller A. "Walt Disney and the Roots of Children's Popular Culture." <u>A Critical Journal of Children's Literature</u> 20 (1996 Dec.): 264-271.

Hastings points out in his review that the Disney Corporation has become a critical "hot spot" for public debate and controversy. He argues that the portrayal of the characters and their interaction will influence how children communicate and interact with one another.

Hastings looks at how the interaction and the bodies are represented in the animated cartoons and how they have influenced how we are conditioned to think and interact. He also goes on to discuses how the Disney corporation tried to cover up the fact that there was major turmoil among the employees and that the company tried to keep their "dirt" from the pubic eye.

Henke, Jill, and Diane Umble. "Construction of the
    Female Self: Feminist Readings of the Disney
    Heroine." Woman's Studies in Communication 19
    (1996 Summer): 229-246.

The authors of this essay try to examine the way in which the female self is constructed in five Disney films: Cinderella, Sleeping Beauty, The Little Mermaid, Beauty and Beast, and Pocahontas. They use these films in order to examine the way in which Disney tries to portray the "perfect girl." These authors use feminist theory and feminist scholarship to review the portrait of the Disney heroine.

They review how the ideals of the perfect girl are used to question selfhood, relationships, power, and voice. They also look at how the animated movies reflect the stereotypes of white, middle-class, patriarchal society.

Lee, Christina. "*Mulan:* Woman Warrior as Embodied Ambiguity." Rev. of <u>Mulan</u>, dir. Barry Cook and Tony Bancroft. <u>Intersections</u> 19 May 1999.

This review looks at the way in which the movie <u>Mulan</u> influences they way we view the heroin and our ideas of what a hero is. It also looks at the real story behind <u>Mulan</u> and the way that Disney manipulates the storyline to fit their ideals and stereotypical images of woman.

This film review is written in a unique style that includes numerical ordering and concise arguments. The main point of the review is to look at how the main character in <u>Mulan</u> disguises herself as a man to join the army. It touches upon the idea that the character is neither feminine nor masculine but rather occupies an ambiguous space. In the end she must re-establish her role as a woman in order to maintain our idea of social sexual and identity order.

Maio, Kathy. "Woman, Race and Culture in Disney's
    Movies." NI: Global Issues for Learners of
    English. Online. http://www2.gol.com/users/
    bobkeim/Disney/women.html. 19 June 1999.

This article written by a feminist journalist in
Boston named Kathy Maio covers a wide range of Disney
movies and how they influence and perpetuate the cultural expectations of what the characters are supposed
to represent. The article also outlines for the readers
in the margin the ideas that the movies represent. They
give definitions for the readers to be clear about how
the images are defined.

This essay is a follow up from another briefer
piece that the same author wrote entitled, "Disney's
Dolls." Maio examines how the Disney heroines have been
portrayed as happy house wives and does not think it is
a good message to send to young girls. This article reflects her concern with the way Disney movies represent
women, races, and other cultures.

Reising, Russell. "It's a Dirty World After All."
    American Quarterly 49.4 (1997 Dec.): 851-858.

This piece written by Russell Reising is in response to the book of essays referenced above entitled
From Mouse to Mermaids. This response to the book looks

at how "the Disney version" of reality is portrayed in society and then scrutinized in the essays of the book. It agrees for the most part with arguments that the book represents.

This essay further capitalizes on how the Disney heroines are subject to male power and their submissive nature is applauded and when or if they do evoke power the power is then taken back my the male figures in the end, either by love or by fatherhood. This essay also looks at how the book expands on the ideas that Disney tries to suppress not only women and race but anything problematic no matter how real the ideas or suppression represents.

Wloszczyna, Susan. "Disney Princesses Wear Merchandising Crown." USA Today 17, Sept. 2003: 02d.

This article found in the newspaper <u>USA Today</u> discusses how influential the Disney culture is upon little girls. This negative influence is "corrupting" our little girls. This notion of "my little princess" as mothers say, will "elevate our child's status. The problem evolves when the princess thinks she is above everyone else."

The basic aim of this article is to warn mothers about the ideas represented by Disney movies and that it

might turn our daughters into "royal pains." This article says nothing about how Disney portrays the male
character as heroes. . . should we then be cautious of
what message is being sent to little boys, that they are
heroes, saviors, and above everyone else? This article
infuriated me as I read it. . . . it perpetuated the same
ideals that Disney tries to influence. . . . It couldn't be
healthy for girls to think highly of themselves!

Youngs, Gillian. "The Ghost of <u>Snow White</u>."

<u>International Feminist Journal of Politics</u> 1 (1999

Sept.): 311-314.

This critical article looks at the relationship
between Walt Disney's <u>Mulan</u> and <u>Snow White</u> and the
stereotypical heroine the characters represent. This is
yet another article that points out how characters, in
order to be seen as action packed or heroesque, must
posses male-identified characteristics.

This article also looks at the roles in which not
only the main heroines play but also the roles in which
their mothers have. In the case of <u>Mulan</u>, the mother is
disappointed when the daughter disobeys her culture and
her father. Also the character plays the role of helpless and in need of rescuing as soon as it is discovered she is a woman.

APPENDIX D

THE ESSAY EXAM

If you've written quite a few essay exams in school already, you're well aware of how different that type of writing is from what you've learned in this textbook. The rhetorical context is quite different, you have limited time to come up with ideas and draft your answer, and seemingly no time to revise. Your audience is only your instructor. You have to demonstrate your expertise with the subject matter by drawing on facts and concepts, but without having the sources there to help you. You are writing in a genre that is specific only to educational situations: a written exam. While you may be expected to demonstrate the habits of intellectual inquiry, your main purpose is often to show that you've mastered a certain body of knowledge and a particular way of analyzing it—to explain and to evaluate. So, given what you've learned about writing in this book, what strategies might help you write an effective essay exam in such a constrained writing situation?

The table below explains the differences between essay exams and the essays you write for class assignments. From this we can figure out which writing and reading strategies will be most useful when you're sitting in a classroom with only fifty minutes to craft an argument on one of Shakespeare's plays or apply an economic theory to a specific scenario.

	ESSAY EXAM	ESSAY FOR CLASS ASSIGNMENT
Time	Usually limited to a class period (60–75 minutes), within which time you have to generate ideas, focus, plan, draft, and revise.	Usually several days to several weeks to generate ideas, explore and focus them, draft, workshop, and revise.
Purpose	To show your instructor how well you know class material and how well you can *analyze and apply it.*	Depending on subject, genre, and focus of the class, can vary from demonstrating competency at certain writing strategies to mastering a particular genre to making a persuasive argument.

	ESSAY EXAM	ESSAY FOR CLASS ASSIGNMENT
Choice	While you may have a choice of which essay questions you'll respond to, often your choice of subject is limited by the question. Within the question you might have some choice over texts or materials to which you will refer.	Often students have a wider range of choices for subjects when writing for a class assignment.
Process	Your writing process is truncated into a shorter period, so you might go right to drafting an outline, drafting the response to the question, and then revising; you won't have time to experiment or explore ideas; your goals are to demonstrate your knowledge, not explore it.	More time to explore ideas, experiment, revise, and get feedback from other writers.
Methods of Inquiry	You will have little if any time for reflecting or even exploring ideas; instead, you will have to focus on explaining and evaluating, stating a claim and providing explanation and evidence.	At various times you will use all the methods of inquiry: exploring, reflecting, explaining, and evaluating. The methods used in a particular paper are dependent on the assignment, the audience, the form, and the subject.
Form	Depending on the nature of the exam question, the form expected is something similar to a five-paragraph thesis essay: an introduction that states your thesis; supporting paragraphs that "prove" it using details from class materials; and a conclusion that wraps everything up (this is not true for short-answer essay questions). Essay exams are often expected to be close-ended forms.	Depending on the subject and audience: from narrative to thesis-example structure, open-ended to closed-ended form. Much more flexibility in choosing a form that fits the material than in an essay exam.

	ESSAY EXAM	ESSAY FOR CLASS ASSIGNMENT
Thesis	Many instructors expect a thesis statement in the first paragraph.	Some instructors expect a thesis to be implied (as in the personal essay and the profile); others expect it to be explicit (as in the critical essay). How explicit it is depends on the genre, purpose, audience, and subject.

HOW TO WRITE ESSAY EXAMS

Given the difference between essay exams and the essays you write for class assignments, there are very specific strategies you should employ when writing in this form.

Gathering Materials

Because the purpose of an essay exam is different from that of a regular essay, the sources of information are going to be different. This may seem obvious, but it's crucial to understanding how to prepare for the exam. For a research essay, textbooks are rarely considered good reference sources, and while class lectures can be used in a course paper, they cannot form the basis of the paper. Yet these sources are often the sole basis for essay exams, and you usually can't have these sources open at your side as you write. So how do you figure out what is important to focus on in this rhetorical context?

Let's talk first about the purposes of essay exams. For many instructors, the essay exam offers a forum for students to demonstrate one or more of the following achievements.

- Students *understand* the main course concepts.
- Students can *apply* those concepts to other kinds of information, situations, or problems.
- Students can *evaluate and support* that evaluation with relevant evidence and criteria.
- Students can *analyze* a subject: this includes *synthesizing and summarizing* a range of information, as well as *making connections* among that information by considering cause/effect and using comparison and contrast.

Of the four ways of inquiring, the two most frequently employed in essay exams are *explanation* and *evaluation*. Throughout the course, as you learned the class material, you also used exploration and reflection, but when it comes time to write a timed essay, you need to focus on methods that help you make judgments, test evidence, summarize, and illustrate the relationships among ideas.

But how can you do all that in a short period of time? The challenge is knowing how to read and assemble your course materials so you can demonstrate all those things. What kinds of material will you be using? The course textbook, class lectures, and supplementary materials (readings on reserve, for example, Web materials your instructor has posted, handouts and work sheets). As you begin studying for your exam, gather all these materials together in one place. Then, use the strategies in the next section as you scan them for key concepts and main points.

Reading Strategies

Throughout the course for which you will be writing the essay exams, you've needed to keep up with the reading, attend lectures, participate in workshops and class discussions as well as labs, and take thoughtful notes on most everything. A large part of preparing for an exam is simply keeping up with the course itself.

What you might be struggling with, though, is what kinds of reading and note-taking strategies to use given this very different writing situation. Given the purposes outlined above, what kinds of reading strategies do you think you might need? As with other kinds of reading you do in school, you'll want to use dialectical thinking while reading for the purpose of an essay exam. Most of your focus, however, will be on the *interpreting and judging side of the dialectic* because that's what will help you remember the facts and concepts, and fulfill the demands of that particular writing situation. Consider, also, the following reading strategies:

- **Review course goals.** Refer to the course syllabus to remind yourself what the goals and purposes of the course are, then read with those in mind, marking whatever seems important to those goals.

- **Read for main ideas.** When reading your textbook, look for signals that indicate main ideas: headings and subheadings, text boxes that emphasize particular concepts, highlighted terms and definitions, and chapter summaries.

- **Annotate the text.** In the margins of your textbook (and class notes) briefly highlight the main idea for a paragraph or section—it makes it easier to review later.

- **Engage in dialogue.** Have a conversation with your textbook and your class notes. Write questions in the margins, note your interpretations and arguments with the material, make connections to other course concepts, put the concepts into another context and consider how you understand them differently, and so on. Later, as you are studying for your exam, have these conversations with a small study group. Also, brainstorm a list of other situations you might apply the ideas to—you might be asked to do that on the exam.

- **Create categories for remembering details.** Don't get bogged down in the details: lists of evidence or data can easily seem to be the most important information, but they aren't always. Ask yourself the *purpose* of those details. Do they illustrate a main concept? If so, you may need to know only a few examples for illustration. Or, are they each important to know in some detail? If so, try to group them by common patterns, themes, or categories that help you remember them. Here's an example: In my microbiology course, my instructor had given us a list of the various antibiotics used to fight bacteria and the effects each had on different cell parts. I knew it would be on the test, so I organized the list by the parts of the bacterial cell that were affected (the mitochondria, the nucleus, and so on). This class was, after all, focused on cells, not on antibiotics, so I figured the instructor would want us to know *how* the drugs affected the cells differently. When I took the test, I saw exactly the chart I had constructed on my own, and I was one of the few people who got that question right.

- **Create an outline.** When you take notes on a class lecture or discussion, try to organize them into an outline or series of lists that highlight the main ideas and then a couple of illustrations or explanations. If your instructor gives you lecture notes, pay attention to how he has organized them—the outline form usually indicates which ideas are most and least important.

Anticipating the Exam

If you've been paying attention to the main ideas of the course and the methods of inquiry your instructor seems to value, then you are in good shape to anticipate the questions that might be on the exam. One of the best ways to prepare for an exam is to play the role of your instructor.

- What does she want you to learn and why?
- What kinds of questions has she asked on previous exams?
- What kinds of questions would best show how you've met the course goals?

After you've thought about these questions, generate a good list of possible exam questions and then answer them, either alone or in a small study group. You'll quickly learn what you need to go back and learn in more depth because you will be in a group reflecting on your learning process. And you may just find some version of those questions on the exam.

Since your instructor is your only audience and will be forming the questions, you might ask about the kinds of questions you can anticipate: How long will they be? What kinds of questions will there be? What criteria will be used for evaluating the answers? And, if they are available, look over previous exams from the same course and instructor.

If you've been engaging in symphonic inquiry throughout the course—using all four ways of inquiring at once while you read and write—then you will most likely have a good grasp of the main ideas in the course and your judgments about them. Symphonic inquiry can reduce the amount of time you spend memorizing the course material. You will have already been doing more than simply collecting facts and theories while your instructor lectures; you will have been posing questions, making connections, evaluating, and exploring, then reflecting on what you know and what more you need to know. You will, in short, understand the material. By the time you sit down to commit some key concepts and details to memory, you'll remember them better because you understand their purpose and their relationship to each other.

Analyzing Essay Questions

When you get the exam, read through all of it before you do anything else and consider the following factors before you start writing your answers:

Time.   Make some choices about how much time you will spend on each question based on:

- *Point value.* How many points is each question assigned? Prioritize them based on how much they are worth so you spend more time on those questions that are worth more. If you run out of time, then the questions you haven't responded to won't hurt you quite as much.
- *Priorities.* Based on your priorities, divide the time up for each question. Spend more time on questions worth more points. Try to stick to the time limits you've given yourself.
- *Ability to answer the question.* If you have a choice of questions, consider carefully which one you will answer. To decide, quickly brainstorm in the margins your ideas for each question. That will tell you how much you know about each and whether you can do what the question asks. For example, you might be able to explain a concept, but not compare it to something else, which is what the exam question actually demands that you do.

Key Phrases/Verbs.   Once you've tentatively decided which questions you'll answer and how much time you'll devote to each, analyze the questions as quickly as you can. Your first step is to figure out what a question is asking you to *do.* Circle the key verbs that indicate your purpose when writing your answer. One way to understand what an essay question is asking you to do is to think of it in terms you already know: the ways of inquiring. In general, essay exams ask you to evaluate or explain. The accompanying table lists some of the verbs that imply one or the other way of inquiring:

VERBS OF EVALUATION	REQUIRED ACTION
Prove/Justify/Support	Offer reasons and evidence in support of a position.
Argue	Like "prove" and "justify," this verb demands that you present an argument with reasons and evidence, but often the essay question will give you a position to take or ask you to choose a particular position.
Evaluate/Assess	Make a judgment about the value or importance of a particular idea or subject, being clear about the criteria you're using for evaluation and supporting your claim with reasons and evidence.
Analyze	Usually this means you examine the parts of something—like an argument—breaking it into sections and discussing the relationship among them; sometimes it may mean assessing those parts, or explaining your response. The rest of the question should indicate how much you should describe the parts and how much you should judge them.
Critique	To analyze and evaluate the subject in the essay question (an idea or argument or theory).
Respond	Often this verb will mean you need to evaluate or justify your response to whatever the question asks of you.
Synthesize	Bring together two or more ideas/subject/concepts that haven't been considered together and do more than simply summarize and compare them; explain why you have brought them together and what new understanding emerges from that.

VERBS OF EXPLANATION (INFORMATION)	REQUIRED ACTION
Define	Describe and give the meaning of the idea presented, using authoritative sources, comparing and contrasting it to other ideas that are related.
Enumerate	Present the steps, sequence, events involved in a particular process in some detail.

VERBS OF EXPLANATION (INFORMATION)	REQUIRED ACTION
Trace	Like "enumerate," trace asks you describe a series of events, but to do so in chronological order.
List	Like "enumerate," this verb asks that you name several things that are connected to a main idea presented in the question.
Review	Quickly summarize something.
Summarize	Present the main ideas of an argument or concept in an organized way.
Explain Why/How	Offer reasons and examples of why and/or how something happened or relates to a larger idea.
Illustrate	Describe specific examples of something and their relationship to each other and the larger subject given in the question.
Identify	Like "illustrate," this verb asks you to describe something and show its relationship to a larger idea, but often it implies looking at just one or two things.
Discuss	At length and from different perspectives, describe and analyze the idea presented in the question, using specific examples and evaluating the strengths and weaknesses.
Research	Just as it implies, gather sources and analyze what you've found.

VERBS OF EXPLANATION (RELATIONSHIPS AND CONNECTIONS)	REQUIRED ACTION
Compare	Illustrate the similarities of two or more things.
Contrast	Illustrate the differences of two or more things.
Relate	Show the relationships among various things.
Cause	Illustrate how various events relate to each other and resulted in a particular effect.
Apply	Take a theory or concept and illustrate how it works in another situation.
Construct	Sometimes ask you to create a model or diagram through which to present your ideas.

Noun Phrases. Now that you know you need to contrast two different ideas, you need to be sure you know what to contrast. Some essay questions are rather long and it may be hard to decipher what, exactly, the subject of your answer should be. Usually the clues are in the noun phrases ("parts of the cell," "factors that led to the Civil War," "three influences on Sylvia Plath's poetry"). If the question begins with a quotation, read the question carefully to see whether it's background information for the question, or something you need to address in your answer. Underline all the key noun phrases that indicate the ideas/concepts you are expected to discuss.

Organizational Clues.   Based on the subject and purpose of your answer, how might you best organize it? You may need to use a cause-effect, step-by-step, or thesis-support structure. Sometimes the question itself implies a structure. For example, if you are asked to analyze the cause and effect of the Great Depression, you'll use a cause-effect structure. If you are asked to identify three influences on Sylvia Plath's poetry and argue which is most significant, you'll name those three, then devote a separate paragraph for each one to discuss in more detail, ending with the one you believe is most significant. Before you begin writing, sketch an outline that seems appropriate for the question.

Planning and Drafting

Once you have analyzed the exam question and you have a good sense of what you are being asked to do, you need to draft an answer in a very short period of time. Before you begin writing your response, jot down a rough outline of what you'll say and the supporting details and examples you'll use. Put your points in the order of most to least important in case you run out of time. That way you know you've touched on the most important ideas before time is up. Then, draft an introductory paragraph that summarizes your argument and gets right to your thesis statement at the end. Your lead doesn't need an attention grabber as much as it needs a clear direction for the essay and a clear statement of your answer in one or two sentences.

Focus your writing on the body of the essay, developing your points as fully as you can. Keep in mind what your instructor will value the most, and use the key terms that are used in the exam question to show how you are directly addressing it. Essay exams necessarily demand clear, simple, and direct writing. Then, leave some time at the end to reread your answer, editing it carefully and considering which sections need more information. Sometimes it helps to write on every other line of notebook or blue book paper so you have space to write in when you revise. If you don't finish your answer in time, briefly describe for your instructor what you would do if you had more time. Write as legibly as you can, minimizing scratch-outs and keeping in mind how many exams your instructor will have to read.

When you analyzed the essay question you paid some attention to the kind of structure the question was probably demanding. You may need to use a cause-effect pattern, a step-by-step pattern, or a thesis-support structure. Within the body of that structure, though, keep each paragraph to one main idea, using specific details to illustrate or support your main assertions. Then, try to connect the idea in the paragraph back to your main thesis, explaining why it's important to what you are trying to say ("Another example of this phenomenon is _____," or "An additional factor that complicates this process is _____"). Your conclusion, then, will tie the essay together with a sentence or two restating your main claim and telling your instructor what all this information means.

CREDITS

Text Credits

INDEX

A

Abstract
   in APA style, 595, 596, 606
   in MLA style, 580–581
Academic research essays, 460. *See also* Research; Research essay
Academic writing
   APA documentation style for, 593–613
   argument and, 289–290
   critical essay and, 331–332
   ethnography and, 391–392
   formal structures in, 648
   personal essays and, 97
   profiles and, 149
   proposal writing and, 243
   research essay and, 442
   reviews and, 197
Accessibility, of profile subject, 172–173
Acknowledgments, B2–B3
Action/actor
   clarity and, 661–662
   style and, 662–664
Adaptive response, to reading, 55–57
Ad hominem fallacy, 321
Advertisement
   marketing strategy, 75, 76, 77
   persuasive power of, 301–302
   as proposal, 257–258
   reading of, 59
Afro-American Literature, 377
Agonistic forms of argument, 288
Almanacs, 317
Amelie (movie), 194, 195–196
American Indian: Language and Literature, 377
American Psychological Association (APA) style. *See* APA documentation style
America's Strength, All of Us Pulling Together (Miller), 62
Analogy, argument from, 295
Anecdote

in argumentative writing, 318
in drafting, 136, 137
as lead, 653
"Animal Imagery in 'Everyday Use'" (Gruesser), 352–353
inquiring into the essay, 353–354
Annotated bibliography, C1–C20
   combination of types, C2
   defined, C1–C2
   evaluative, C2
   how to write, C3–C5
   indicative, C1
   informative, C2
   student samples of, C5, C6–C20
   when to write, C3
Annotating books, 530
Announcement, as lead, 653
Anonymous source, 563
Anthology, in MLA style, 574
APA documentation style, 556, 593–613
   electronic sources in, 609–613
   essay appearance in, 594–599
   MLA style compared with, 593
   order of information in, 602–603
   order of sources in, 601–602
   recent changes in, 594
   references page in, 597–598
   in research essay, 491
   sample paper in, 613
   of Web information, 493
Appeal to authority fallacy, 321–322
Appendix, in APA style, 598
Argument
   academic writing and, 289–290
   claims in, 286–287
   classical, 302
   in critical essays, 333
   details in, 295–296, 319
   drafting of, 314–316, 317–320
   evaluation and, 77
   as expression of caring, 285
   features of, 290–292
   "How to Really Rock the Vote" (student sketch), 313–314

informal essay, 290–292
judging what you have, 308–309
"Law and Order and the Wild, Wild Web" (Etzioni), 293–295
map of, 307
meaning of, 285–286
motives for writing, 288–289
narrowing question for, 312–313
nature of, 284–285
persuasion through, 282
"picking sides" in, 644
profile for, 149
in review, 207
sides to, 287–288
strategies for, 295–296
student journal, 305–306
"What We Think of America" (Lessing), 299–300
writing of, 303–309
writing to persuade and, 283–288
Aristotle
   classical argument and, 302
   rhetoric and, 12
Art. *See also* Image(s); Photography; Visual(s)
   digital images and, 410
   MLA style for, 583
Article (online)
   in APA style, 609
   in MLA style, 587
Article or abstract in library database, in MLA style, 588–590
Artifacts, for ethnographic essay, 417
Aspiration (Douglas), 480
Assignment order, portfolio organization by, A5–A6
Assumptions
   in claims, 286–287
   about reading, 41
Audience, 12, 668
   for argumentative writing, 309–310
   for critical essay, 372–374
   for ethnographic essay, 414–415
   evaluation by, 78–79